Nation of Nations

A Narrative History of the American Republic

THIRD EDITION

Volume A

James West Davidson

William E. Gienapp

Christine Leigh Heyrman

Mark H. Lytle

Michael B. Stoff

The McGraw-Hill Companies, Inc.
Primis Custom Publishing

New York   St. Louis   San Francisco   Auckland   Bogotá
Caracas   Lisbon   London   Madrid   Mexico   Milan   Montreal
New Delhi   Paris   San Juan   Singapore   Sydney   Tokyo   Toronto

McGraw·Hill

A Division of The McGraw·Hill Companies

Nation of Nations
A Narrative History of the American Republic, Volume A

1 2 3 4 5 6 7 8 9 0   9 0 9 8

ISBN 0-07-007052-0

Primis Custom Publishing Editor: Beth Kundert
Cover Design: Mary Good
Binder: Dunn and Company, Inc.

CONTENTS

PART 1

THE CREATION OF A NEW AMERICA 2

After the Fact: Historians Reconstruct the Past
White and Black Southerners Worshiping Together 232

PART 4

THE UNITED STATES IN AN INDUSTRIAL AGE   594

LIST OF MAPS AND CHARTS

PREFACE
TO THE THIRD EDITION

The third edition of *Nation of Nations* holds firm to its original premise: that students will be drawn more readily to the study of history if they are presented with an engaging narrative of past events rather than with a mere encyclopedic compendium. Inevitably the creation of such a narrative has entailed difficult choices. The undergrowth of facts, dates, and qualifying clauses must be pruned and shaped so that what remains appears in bolder relief. Fortunately the job was made easier because the authors recently prepared a concise version of *Nation of Nations*. That task suggested to us ways we could profitably sharpen the full edition without losing either our narrative thread or the more detailed context provided by a full-length survey. Consequently, this edition is shorter than the second and, we believe, all the better for it.

Paradoxically, several changes have been inspired by the very success of our narrative approach. Some professors have written suggesting that precisely because the tale flows so smoothly, students may be seduced into thinking that the writing of history is without controversy—that the past must have occurred just as we have sketched it and that any questions of interpretation must be minor matters. To combat this misimpression every chapter now incorporates a discussion labelled "Counterpoint," which explores contrasting ways historians have interpreted one of the chapter's central topics. These discussions are deliberately not separated out as boxed features; instead, they are integrated into the narrative so that students come to understand such debates as an inevitable (and productive) part of writing history. In addition, we have added six longer essays focusing on the process of doing history. Entitled "After the Fact: Historians Reconstruct the Past," the essays introduce students to the methods used by historians to analyze a variety of sources, ranging from typescript drafts of presidential memoirs or handwritten notations in church records to military casualty estimates, public monuments, and even climate data derived from the analysis of tree rings.

Other changes in the new edition reflect history's inevitable expansion, both chronologically and thematically. Late nineteenth-century topics originally covered in Chapters 21 and 22 ("The Failure of Traditional Politics" and "The New Empire") have been incorporated into a single chapter, "The Political System Under Strain." The text's final chapter, "A Nation Still Divisible," brings the narrative up through the Republican resurgence of 1994 and the reelection of President Clinton. Many other changes both large and small have been made throughout. Coverage of environmental history has been expanded, and there is an increased emphasis on the new western history, particularly in Chapter 20. New maps and charts have been added, including some never before seen in a survey text. Finally, in addition to the full bibliographies appearing at the back of the book, each chapter has an expanded annotated bibliography, called "Additional Reading," as well as specific bibliographical references within the "After the Fact" features.

Despite these changes, the text's basic structure remains. Each of the book's six parts begins with an essay setting American events in a global context. We believe it is important to show that the United States did not develop in a geographic or cultural vacuum and that the broad forces shaping it also influenced other nations. Each global essay features a timeline comparing political and social events in the United States with developments elsewhere. Marginal headings throughout the entire text help students focus on key terms and concepts, while each chapter concludes with a succinct summary and a timeline of significant events. Complementing the core narrative are our "Daily Lives" essays, focusing on one of five themes that give insight into the lives of ordinary Americans: clothing and fashion; time and travel; food, drink, and drugs; public space/private space; and popular entertainment.

We are grateful to the many reviewers who were generous enough to offer comments and suggestions at various stages in our development of this manuscript. Our thanks go to Thomas Altherr, Metropolitan State College of Denver; Carol Berkin, Baruch College and the Graduate Center of the City University of New York; Winifred E. A. Bernhard, University of Massachusetts, Amherst; Roger W. Biles, Oklahoma State University; Carol Brown, Houston Community College; Victor Chen, Chabot College; Vincent A. Clark, Johnson County Community College; Mario S. DePillis, University of Massachusetts, Amherst; Leonard Dinnerstein, University of Arizona; Mark Dollinger, Pasadena City College; Alan Downs, Georgia Southern University; Lynn Dumenil, Claremont McKenna College; Robert Elam, Modesto Junior College; Robert G. Fricke, West Valley College; Richard Frucht, Northwest Missouri State University; John Gauger, Lehigh Carbon Community College; James L. Gormly, Washington and Jefferson College; Robert Greenblatt, Mass Bay Community College; Peter Iverson, Arizona State University; Priscilla Jackson-Evans, Longview Community College; George Juergens, Indiana University; Burton I. Kaufman, Virginia Polytechnic Institute and State University; John L. Larson, Purdue University; Mark H. Leff, University of Illinois, Urbana–Champaign; John Little, St. Augustine's College; Norman Love, El Paso Community College; John McCardell, Middlebury College; C. K. McFarland, Arkansas State University; Gerald W. McFarland, University of Massachusetts, Amherst; William E. Mahan, Sacramento City College; John Mauer, Tri County Technical College; Sonya Michel, University of Illinois, Urbana–Champaign; William Howard Moore, University of Wyoming; Christopher Morris, University of Texas, Austin; Betty Owens, Greenville Technical College; Robert Pierce, Foothill College; Charles Pilant, Cumberland College; Leo P. Ribuffo, George Washington University; Randolph Roth, Ohio State University; Dennis C. Rousey, Arkansas State University; Tom Ryan, Broward Community College; Susan Rugh, St. Cloud State University; James C. Schneider, University of Texas, San Antonio; Ronald Schultz, University of Wyoming; Rebecca Shoemaker, Indiana State University; Lewright B. Sikes, Middle Tennessee State University; Nina Silber, Boston University; Gregory Holmes Singleton, Northeastern Illinois University; David Sloan, University of Arkansas, Fayetteville; Daniel B. Smith, University of Kentucky; Donna J. Spindel, Marshall University; Thomas E. Terrill, University of South Carolina; Emory M. Thomas, University of Georgia; Richard H. Thompson, Indiana University—Purdue University, Indianapolis; Stephen G. Weisner, Springfield Technical Community College; Frank J. Wetta, Galveston College; William Bruce Wheeler, University of Tennessee, Knoxville; Gerald Wilson, Duke University; Phillip B. Winkler, Dyersburg State College; and

William Young, Johnson County Community College. In addition, many friends and colleagues contributed their advice and constructive criticism in ways both small and large. These included Michael Bellesiles, Lawrence A. Cardoso, Dinah Chenven, James E. Crisp, R. David Edmunds, George Forgie, Erica Gienapp, Drew McCoy, James McPherson, Stephen E. Maizlish, Jim Sidbury, Harold Silesky, David J. Weber, and Virginia Joyner.

The division of labor for this book was determined by our respective fields of scholarship: Christine Heyrman, the colonial era, in which Europeans, Africans, and Indians participated in the making of both a new America and a new republic; William Gienapp, the 90 years in which the young nation first flourished, then foundered on the issues of section and slavery; Michael Stoff, the post-Civil War era, in which industrialization and urbanization brought the nation more centrally into an international system constantly disrupted by depression and war; and Mark Lytle, the modern era, in which Americans finally faced the reality that even the boldest dreams of national greatness are bounded by the finite nature of power and resources both natural and human. Finally, because the need to specialize inevitably imposes limits on any project as broad as this one, our fifth author, James Davidson, served as a general editor and writer, with the intent of fitting individual parts to the whole, as well as providing a measure of continuity, style, and overarching purpose. In producing this collaborative effort, all of us have shared the conviction that the best history speaks to a larger audience.

JAMES WEST DAVIDSON
WILLIAM E. GIENAPP
CHRISTINE LEIGH HEYRMAN
MARK H. LYTLE
MICHAEL B. STOFF

INTRODUCTION

History is both a discipline of rigor, bound by rules and scholarly methods, and something more: the unique, compelling, even strange way in which we humans define ourselves. We are all the sum of the tales of thousands of people, great and small, whose actions have etched their lines on us. History supplies our very identity—a sense of the social groups to which we belong, whether family, ethnic group, race, class, or gender. It reveals to us the foundations of our deepest religious beliefs and traces the roots of our economic and political systems. It explores how we celebrate and grieve, sing the songs we sing, weather the illnesses to which time and chance subject us. It commands our attention for all these good reasons and for no good reason at all, other than a fascination with the way the myriad tales play out. Strange that we should come to care about a host of men and women so many centuries gone, some with names eminent and familiar, others unknown but for a chance scrap of information left behind in an obscure letter.

Yet we do care. We care about Sir Humphrey Gilbert, "devoured and swallowed up of the Sea" one black Atlantic night in 1583; about George Washington at Kips Bay, red with fury as he takes a riding crop to his retreating soldiers. We care about Octave Johnson, a slave fleeing through Louisiana swamps trying to decide whether to stand and fight the approaching hounds or take his chances with the bayou alligators; about Clara Barton, her nurse's skirts so heavy with blood from the wounded she must wring them out before tending to the next soldier. We are drawn to the fate of Chinese laborers, chipping away at the Sierras' looming granite; a Georgian named Tom Watson seeking to forge a colorblind political alliance; and desperate immigrant mothers, kerosene in hand, storming Brooklyn butcher shops that had again raised prices. We follow, with a mix of awe and amusement, the fortunes of the quirky Henry Ford ("Everybody wants to be somewhere he ain't"), turning out identical automobiles, insisting his factory workers wear identical expressions ("Fordization of the Face"). We trace the career of young Thurgood Marshall, crisscrossing the South in his own "little old beat-up '29 Ford," typing legal briefs in the back seat, trying to get black teachers to sue for equal pay, hoping to get his people somewhere they weren't. The list could go on and on, spilling out as it did in Walt Whitman's *Leaves of Grass*: "A southerner soon as a northerner, a planter nonchalant and hospitable,/A Yankee bound my own way ... a Hoosier, a Badger, a Buckeye, a Louisianian or Georgian. . . ." Whitman embraced and celebrated them all, inseparable strands of what made him an American and what made him human:

> In all people I see myself, none more and not one a barleycorn less,
> And the good or bad I say of myself I say of them.

To encompass so expansive an America Whitman turned to poetry; historians have traditionally chosen *narrative* as their means of giving life to the past. That mode of explanation permits them to interweave the strands of economic, political, and social history in a coherent chronological framework. By choosing narrative, they affirm the multicausal nature of historical explanation—the insistence that events be portrayed in context. By choosing narrative, they are also acknowledging that, while long-term economic and social trends shape societies in significant ways, events often take on a logic (or an illogic) of their own, jostling one another, being deflected by unpredictable personal decisions, sudden deaths, natural catastrophes, and chance. There are literary reasons, too, for preferring a narrative approach, since it supplies a dramatic force usually missing from more structural analyses of the past.

In some ways, surveys like this one are the natural antithesis of narrative history. They strive, by definition, to be comprehensive: to furnish a broad, orderly exposition of their chosen field. Yet to cover so much ground in so limited a space necessarily deprives readers of the context of more detailed accounts. Then, too, the resurgence of social history—with its concern for class and race, patterns of rural and urban life, the spread of market and industrial economies—lends itself to more analytic, less chronological treatments. The challenge facing historians is to incorporate these areas of research without losing the story's narrative drive or the chronological flow that orients readers to the more familiar events of our past.

With the cold war of the past half-century at an end, there has been increased attention to the worldwide breakdown of so many nonmarket economies and, by inference, to the greater success of the market societies of the United States and other capitalist nations. As our own narrative makes clear, American society and politics have indeed come together centrally in the marketplace. What Americans produce, how and where they produce it, and the desire to buy cheap and sell dear have been defining elements in every era. That market orientation has created unparalleled abundance and reinforced striking inequalities, not the least a society in which, for two centuries, human beings themselves were bought and sold. It has made Americans powerfully provincial in protecting local interests and internationally adventurous in seeking to expand wealth and opportunity.

It goes without saying that Americans have not always produced wisely or well. The insistent drive toward material plenty has levied a heavy tax on the global environment. Too often quantity has substituted for quality, whether we talk of cars, education, or culture. When markets flourish, the nation abounds with confidence that any problem, no matter how intractable, can be solved. When markets fail, however, the fault lines of our political and social systems become all too evident.

In the end, then, it is impossible to separate the marketplace of boom and bust and the world of ordinary Americans from the corridors of political maneuvering or the ceremonial pomp of an inauguration. To treat political and social history as distinct spheres is counterproductive. The primary question of this narrative—how the fledgling, often tumultuous confederation of "these United States" managed to transform itself into an enduring republic—is not only political but necessarily social. In order to survive, a republic must resolve conflicts between citizens of different geographic regions and economic classes, of diverse racial and ethnic origins, of competing religions and ideologies. The resolution of these conflicts has produced tragic consequences, perhaps as often as noble ones. But tragic or noble, the destiny of these states cannot be understood without comprehending both the social and the political dimensions of the story.

PART ONE

THE CREATION OF A NEW AMERICA

GLOBAL ESSAY

It is now half a millennium—a full 500 years—since the civilizations of Europe and Africa first made sustained contact with those of North America. The transformations arising out of that event have been astonishing. To gain a rough sense of the scale involved, both in time and in space, we start not at the beginning of our story but somewhere nearer its midpoint: with Meriwether Lewis and William Clark in August 1805, as they stand atop the continental divide on their traverse of the North American continent. The two men, on orders from President Thomas Jefferson, had been sent on the first American exploratory mission to report on the lands west of the Mississippi. From Lewis and Clark's vantage point, high in the Rocky Mountains, what can we see?

At first glance we see pretty much what we expect: a vast, seemingly endless land stretching from sea to sea. But living as we do in the late twentieth century, we tend to take for granted that the country spread before us is united as a continental republic under a single national government. Only hindsight makes this proposition seem natural. In 1800 the sheer size of the land made the notion of political unity difficult to grasp, for the United States themselves remained a group of colonies only recently unified. Even Jefferson, who possessed the vision to send Lewis and Clark on their mission, had long been in the habit of referring to Virginia as "my country." And the lands west of the Mississippi were still controlled primarily by scores of independent Indian nations.

Just how diverse the landscape was can be seen by the methods Lewis and Clark used to communicate. With no common language spanning the territory, speech making became a series of translations that reflected the route over which the party had traveled. In present-day Idaho, Clark addressed the Tushepaw tribe in English. His speech was translated into French by a trapper in the party; then a second trapper translated into Minataree, a language that his Indian wife, Sacajawea, understood. Sacajawea, the only female member of the party, had grown up farther west with the

2

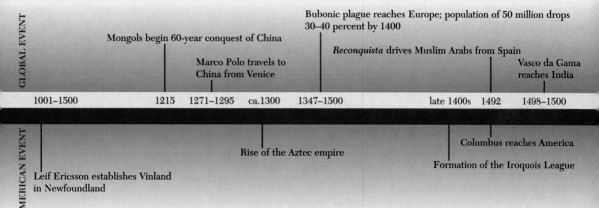

Shoshone, so she in turn translated the Minataree into Shoshone, which a boy from the Tushepaw nation understood. He translated the Shoshone into his own people's tongue.

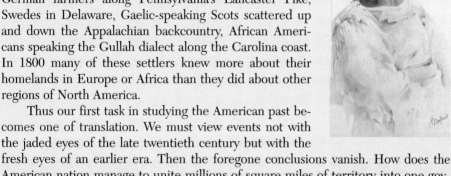

If the Louisiana Territory seemed a patchwork of governments and cultures, the young "United States" appeared nearly as heterogeneous. Dutch-speaking patroons could be found along New York's Hudson River, Welsh and German farmers along Pennsylvania's Lancaster Pike, Swedes in Delaware, Gaelic-speaking Scots scattered up and down the Appalachian backcountry, African Americans speaking the Gullah dialect along the Carolina coast. In 1800 many of these settlers knew more about their homelands in Europe or Africa than they did about other regions of North America.

Thus our first task in studying the American past becomes one of translation. We must view events not with the jaded eyes of the late twentieth century but with the fresh eyes of an earlier era. Then the foregone conclusions vanish. How does the American nation manage to unite millions of square miles of territory into one governable republic? How do New York and San Francisco (a city not even in existence in Lewis and Clark's day) come to be linked in a complex economy as well as in a single political system? Such questions take on even more significance when we recall that Europe—roughly the same size as the United States—is today still divided into over four dozen independent nations speaking some 33 languages, not to mention another 100 or so spoken within the former Soviet Union. A united Europe has not emerged and indeed seems even farther away after the momentous breakup of the Soviet empire.

How, then, did this American republic—this "teeming nation of nations," to use Walt Whitman's phrase—come to be? In barest outline, that is the question that drives our narrative across half a millennium.

The question becomes even more challenging when we move toward the beginning of our story. In 1450, about the time Christopher Columbus was born, only the

3

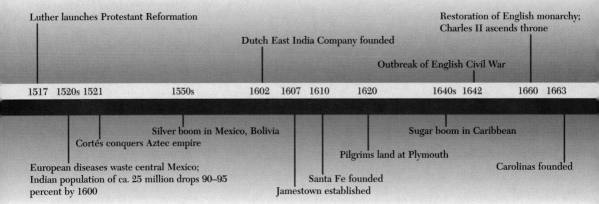

Luther launches Protestant Reformation

Dutch East India Company founded

Restoration of English monarchy; Charles II ascends throne

Outbreak of English Civil War

| 1517 | 1520s | 1521 | 1550s | 1602 | 1607 | 1610 | 1620 | 1640s | 1642 | 1660 | 1663 |

Silver boom in Mexico, Bolivia

Cortés conquers Aztec empire

Sugar boom in Caribbean

Pilgrims land at Plymouth

European diseases waste central Mexico; Indian population of ca. 25 million drops 90–95 percent by 1600

Santa Fe founded

Jamestown established

Carolinas founded

first stirrings of European expansion to the west had begun. To be sure, Scandinavian seafarers led by Leif Ericsson had arrived at the northern reaches of the Americas, planting a settlement in Newfoundland in A.D. 1001. But news of Vinland, as Ericsson called his colony, never reached Europe. The site was soon abandoned and forgotten. In Columbus's day localism still held sway. Italy was divided into five major states and an equal number of smaller territories. The Germanic peoples were united loosely in the Holy Roman Empire, which (as historians have long delighted in pointing out) was neither holy, Roman, nor an empire. French kings ruled over only about half of what is now France. Spain was divided into several kingdoms, with some areas held by Christians and others by Islamic Moors, whose forebears came from Africa. England, a contentious little nation, was beginning a series of bitter civil conflicts among the nobility, known eventually as the Wars of the Roses. The only country pushing beyond the boundaries of the known European world was Portugal, whose sailors were advancing down the coast of Africa in search of gold and slaves.

Localism was also evident in the patterns of European transportation and trade. For the most part, goods moving overland were carried by wheeled carts or pack animals over rutted paths. Rivers and canals provided another option, but lords repeatedly taxed boats that crossed their territories. On the Seine River, greedy tollkeepers lay in wait every six or seven miles. Travel across the Mediterranean Sea and along Europe's northern coastlines was possible, but storms and pirates made the going dangerous and slow. Mapmakers filled the seas with threatening monsters. Under good conditions a ship might reach London from Venice in only 9 days; under bad, it might take 50.

European peoples during this time had some dealings—though not extensive ones—with Africa. What contact there was arose primarily from sharing the Mediterranean Sea. North African culture had been shaped since the seventh century by the religion of Islam, whose influence spread even up through Spain. Farther south in Africa, the kingdom of Songhai prospered along the Niger

4

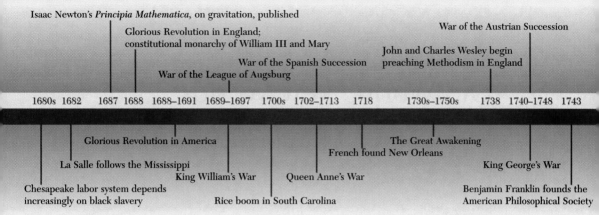

Isaac Newton's *Principia Mathematica*, on gravitation, published
Glorious Revolution in England; constitutional monarchy of William III and Mary
War of the Spanish Succession
War of the League of Augsburg
War of the Austrian Succession
John and Charles Wesley begin preaching Methodism in England

| 1680s | 1682 | 1687 | 1688 | 1688–1691 | 1689–1697 | 1700s | 1702–1713 | 1718 | 1730s–1750s | 1738 | 1740–1748 | 1743 |

Glorious Revolution in America
La Salle follows the Mississippi
King William's War
Queen Anne's War
French found New Orleans
The Great Awakening
King George's War
Chesapeake labor system depends increasingly on black slavery
Rice boom in South Carolina
Benjamin Franklin founds the American Philosophical Society

River. But Africans from the interior regions were linked with Europeans primarily through trading caravans, which made their way across the Sahara Desert with African gold—essential to Europe's economy. The west African coast, which faced the Atlantic, was only beginning to receive the attention of the Portuguese.

If Europe in 1450 was less unified and dynamic than we might have imagined, the civilizations of North and South America were more complex and populous than historians once thought. Earlier estimates suggested that when Europeans first arrived, about 10 million people were living in Central and South America, with another million living north of Mexico. More recently these figures have been raised tenfold, to perhaps as many as 100 million people in Central and South America and 5 to 10 million north of Mexico. In 1492, when Columbus landed on Hispaniola, that island alone may have held some 7 to 8 million people—a number roughly equal to the entire population of Spain. Tenochtitlán, capital of the Aztec empire, may have held as many as 250,000 inhabitants, double the size of the largest European cities of the day. Such dense urban populations were supported by sophisticated agricultural techniques, including canal, irrigation, and drainage systems.

North America was far from being as heavily populated, but neither was it sparsely settled. From one end of the continent to the other, native cultures actively shaped their environments, burning the forests and plains to promote the growth of vegetation as well as animal populations, which they harvested. As we shall see, Amerindian agricultural achievements were so remarkable that they eventually revolutionized eating habits across the rest of the globe.

Here then are three worlds—Europe, Africa, the Americas—poised on the brink of contact. What social and economic forces led so many Europeans—desperate and opportunistic, high-minded and idealistic—to turn westward in pursuit of their dreams? How did the civilizations of North and South America react to the European invaders? And not least, how did the mix of cultures from Africa, Europe, and North America come together to create what was truly a new America, in which some of the most independent-minded individuals prospered in provinces that exhibited some of the harshest examples of human slavery? These are among the questions we seek to answer as our narrative unfolds.

5

1

Old World, New Worlds

ll the world lay before them. Or so it seemed to mariners from England's seafaring coasts, pushing westward toward unknown lands in the far Atlantic.

The scent of the new land came first—not the sight of it, but the sounds and smells, wafted from beyond the horizon, delicious to sailors who had felt nothing but the rolling sea for weeks on end. In northerly latitudes around June, it would be the scent of fir trees or the sight of shore birds wheeling about the masts. Straightaway the captain would call for a lead to be thrown overboard to sound the depths. At its end was a hollowed-out socket with a bit of tallow in it, so some of the sea bottom would stick when the lead was hauled up. Even out of sight of land, a good sailing master could tell where he was by what came up—"oosy sand" or perhaps "soft worms" or "popplestones as big as beans." If the ship was approaching unknown shores, the captain would hope to sight land early in the day, allowing time to work cautiously toward an untried harbor on uncharted tides.

West Country fishing culture Since the time of King Arthur, the English living along the rugged southwestern coasts of Devon and Cornwall had followed the sea. From the wharves of England's West Country seaports like Bristol, ships headed west and north to Ireland, bringing back animal hides as well as timber for houses and barrels. Or they turned south, fetching wines from France and olive oil or figs and raisins from the Spanish and Portuguese coasts. In return, West Country ports offered woven woolen cloth and codfish, caught wherever the best prospects beckoned.

Through much of the fifteenth century the search for cod drew West Country sailors north and west, toward Iceland. In the 1480s and 1490s, however, a few English tried their luck farther west. Old maps, after all, claimed that the bountiful *Hy-Brasil*—Gaelic for "Isle of the Blessed"—lay somewhere west of Ireland. These western ventures returned with little to show for their daring until the coming of an Italian named Giovanni Caboto, called John Cabot by the English. Cabot, who hailed from Venice, obtained the blessing of King Henry VII to hunt for unknown lands. From the port of Bristol his lone ship set out to the west in the spring of 1497.

Cabot discovers Newfoundland This time the return voyage brought news of a "new-found" island where the trees were tall enough to make fine masts and the codfish were plentiful. After returning to Bristol, Cabot marched off to London to inform His Majesty, received 10 pounds as his reward, and with the proceeds dressed himself in dashing silks. The multitudes of London flocked after him, wondering over "the Admiral"; then Cabot

During the sixteenth century, West Country fisherfolk from England sailed from harbors like Plymouth, shown here. Such seaports were small; the fortifications dotting the coastline and a wall around the town itself were used to defend against invaders.

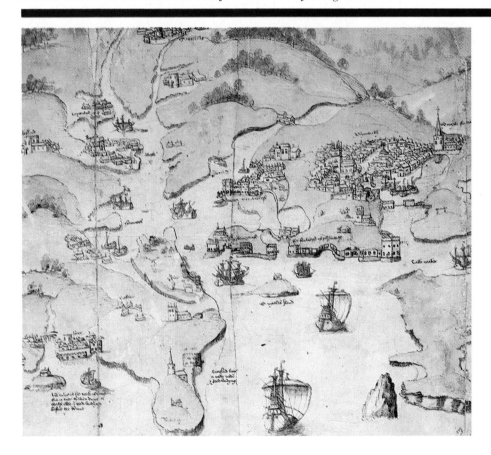

returned triumphantly to Bristol to undertake a more ambitious search for a north-west passage to Asia. He set sail with five ships in 1498 and was never heard from again.

By the 1550s Cabot's island, now known as Newfoundland, attracted 400 vessels annually, fishermen not only from England but also from France, Portugal, and Spain. The trip was not easy. Individual merchants or a few partners outfitted small ships with provisions, fishing boats, and guns to ward off sea-roving pirates. As early in the season as they dared, crews of 10 or 20 would catch the spring easterlies, watching as familiar roofs and primitive lighthouses burning smoky coal sank beneath the horizon.

The fishing season

Weeks after setting sail the sailors sighted Newfoundland's fog-shrouded beaches. Seals and walruses played along the rocks offshore, and the encircling sea teemed with cod and flounder, salmon and herring. Throughout the summer men

EXPLORERS' ROUTES

Columbus (Spanish)
- — — — 1492
- — · — · 1493
- · · · · · 1498
- — — — — 1502
- ———— Other Spanish

Other European
- ———— French
- ———— English

0 ___ 250 ___ 500 Miles
0 ___ 250 ___ 500 Kilometers

NORTH AMERICA

HUDSON BAY

LABRADOR

NEWFOUNDLAND

JOHN CABOT 1497

GILBERT 1583

CARTIER 1534-35

St. Lawrence River

Missouri River

Ohio River

Colorado River

Cibola

Arkansas River

DE SOTO 1539-42

Roanoke

RALEIGH 1585

VERRAZANO 1524

DE VACA 1528-36

CORONADO 1540-42

Mississippi River

Rio Grande

La Paz

DE NARVÁEZ 1528

FLORIDA

PONCE DE LEÓN 1513

ATLANTIC OCEAN

GULF OF MEXICO

Mexico City (Tenochtitlán)

Veracruz

CORTÉS

AZTEC EMPIRE

Chichen Itza

YUCATAN PENINSULA

MAYA EMPIRE

Cuba

Jamaica

Hispaniola

Puerto Rico

PACIFIC OCEAN

DRAKE 1577-80

CARIBBEAN SEA

BALBOA 1513

80°W

ISTHMUS OF PANAMÁ

Panamá

PIZARRO 1531-33

Orinoco River

RALEIGH 1595

0° Equator

SOUTH AMERICA

Quito

INCA EMPIRE

60°N

40°N

20°N

60°W

100°W

PRINCIPAL ROUTES OF EUROPEAN EXPLORATION

8

launched little boats from each harbor and fished offshore all day and into the night. With lines and nets, and baskets weighted with stones, they scooped fish from the sea and then dried and salted the catch on the beach. In odd hours, sailors traded with the native Indians, who shared their summer fishing grounds and the skins of fox and deer.

The harbor of present-day St. John's, Newfoundland, served as the informal hub of the North Atlantic fishery. Portuguese, English, and French vessels all dropped anchor there, either to take on supplies in the spring or to prepare for the homeward voyage in autumn. Besides trading, there was much talking, for these seafarers knew as much as anyone about the new world of wonders that was opening to Europeans. They were acquainted with names like Cristoforo Colombo, the Italian from Genoa whom Cabot might have known as a boy. They listened to Portuguese tales of sailing around the Horn of Africa in pursuit of spices and to stories of Indian empires to the south, rich in gold and silver that Spanish treasure ships were bringing home.

Indeed, Newfoundland was one of the few places in the world where so many ordinary folk of different nations could gather and talk, crammed aboard dank ships moored in St. John's harbor, huddled before blazing fires on its beaches, or crowded into smoky makeshift taverns. When the ships sailed home in autumn, the tales went with them, repeated in the tiniest coastal villages by those pleased to have cheated death and the sea one more time. Eager to fish, talk, trade, and take profits, West Country mariners were almost giddy at the prospect of Europe's expanding horizons.

THE MEETING OF EUROPE AND AMERICA

Most seafarers who fished the waters of Newfoundland's Grand Banks remain unknown today. Yet it is well to begin with these ordinary fisherfolk, for the European discovery of the Americas cannot be looked upon simply as the voyages of a few bold explorers. Adventurers like Christopher Columbus and John Cabot were only the most visible representatives of a much larger expansion of European peoples and culture that began in the 1450s. That expansion arose out of a series of gradual but telling changes in the fabric of European society—changes that were reflected in the lives of ordinary seafarers as much as in the careers of explorers decked out in flaming silks.

Some of these changes were technological, arising out of advances in the arts of navigating and shipbuilding and the use of gunpowder. Some were economic, involving the development of trade networks like those linking Bristol with ports in Iceland and Spain. Some were demographic, bringing about a rise in Europe's population after a devastating century of plague. Other changes were religious, adding a dimension of devout belief to the political rivalries that fueled discoveries in the Americas. Yet others were political, making it possible for kingdoms to centralize and extend their influence across the ocean. Portugal, Spain, France, and England—all possessing coasts along the Atlantic—led the way in exploration, spurred on by Italian "admirals" like Caboto and Colombo, Spanish "conquistadores" like Cortés and Pizarro, and English sea dogs like Humphrey Gilbert and Walter Raleigh. Ordinary folk rode these currents too. The great and the small alike were propelled by forces that were remolding the face of Europe.

Changes in European society

The Portuguese Wave

In 1450 all the world known to western Europeans was Asia and Africa. Most sailors traveled only along the coast of western Europe, following the shores between Norway and the southern tip of Spain, seldom daring to lose sight of land. Beginning in the fifteenth century, bolder seafarers groped down the coast of western Africa, half expecting to be boiled alive in the Atlantic as they approached the equator. Europeans had traded with Asia through the Muslims of the eastern Mediterranean and across an overland route called the "Silk Road." But they had only vague notions about "the Indies"—China and Japan, the Spice Islands, and the lands lying between Thailand and India. What little they knew, they had learned mainly from Marco Polo, whose account of his travels in the East was not published until 1477, more than 150 years after his death.

Revolution in geography   But a revolution in European geography began in the middle decades of the fifteenth century, as widening networks of travel and trade connected Europeans to civilizations beyond western Europe. The Portuguese took the lead, encouraged by Prince Henry, known as the Navigator. The devout Henry, a member of Portugal's royal family, had heard tales of Prester John, a Catholic priest rumored to rule a Christian kingdom somewhere beyond the Muslim kingdoms of Africa and Asia. Henry dreamed of joining forces with Prester John and trapping the Muslims in a vise. To that end, he helped finance a series of expeditions down the coast of west Africa. He founded an informal school of navigation on the Portuguese coast, supplying shipmasters with information about wind and currents, as well as navigational charts.

Portuguese merchants, who may or may not have believed in Prester John, never doubted there was money to be made in Africa. They invested in Prince Henry's voyages in return for trading monopolies of ivory and slaves, grain and gold. A few may have hoped that the voyages down the coast of west Africa would lead to a direct sea route to the Orient. By discovering such a route, Portugal would be able to cut out the Muslim merchants who funneled all the Asian trade in silks, spices, dyes, drugs, and perfumes through Mediterranean ports.

The Portuguese focus on Africa and Asia   While Portugal's merchants were establishing trading posts along the west coast of Africa, its mariners were discovering islands in the Atlantic: the Canaries, Madeira, and the Azores. Settlers planted sugarcane and imported slaves from Africa to work their fields. The Portuguese might have pressed even farther west, but for the daring of Bartholomeu Dias. In 1488 Dias rounded the Cape of Good Hope on the southern tip of Africa, sailing far enough up that continent's eastern coast to claim discovery of a sea route to India. Ten years later Vasco da Gama reached India itself, and Portuguese interests ultimately extended to Indochina and China. With the trade of Africa and Asia to occupy them, they showed less interest in exploring the Atlantic.

By 1500, all of seafaring Europe sought the services of Portuguese pilots, prizing their superior maps and skills with the quadrant. That instrument made it possible to determine latitude fairly accurately, allowing ships to plot their position after months out of the sight of land. The Portuguese had also pioneered the caravel, a lighter, more maneuverable ship that could sail better against contrary winds and in rough seas. More seaworthy than the lumbering galleys of the Middle Ages, caravels combined longer, narrower hulls, a shape built for speed, with triangular lateen sails, which allowed for more flexible steering.

This stately ivory mask made by an African artist in the early sixteenth century for the Court of Benin (present-day Nigeria) is adorned with 10 bearded heads of white men, representing Portuguese explorers and traders who had first arrived in Benin in 1472.

Despite its focus on the Indies, Portugal continued to dominate trade along Africa's west coast. At its way stations set up on islands off the coast, European traders intermarried with Africans who converted to Christianity. This culturally mixed society became a linchpin of the Atlantic trade in African slaves. In the centuries to come, hundreds of thousands of slaves would be shipped to the Portuguese colony of Brazil, whose shores were discovered when a storm blew Pedro Álvares Cabral off course in 1500. But the Atlantic slave trade did not blossom in earnest until after Spain had made a much greater mark on the Americas.

The Spanish and Columbus

From among the international community of seafarers and pilots, it was a sailor from Genoa, Cristoforo Colombo, who led the Spanish to the Americas. Columbus (the Latinized version of his name survives) had knocked about in a number of harbors, picking up valuable navigation skills by sailing Portugal's merchant ships to Madeira, west Africa, and the North Atlantic. In the Irish port of Galway, Columbus saw two boats drift into the harbor, bearing the dead bodies of "a man and a woman of extraordinary appearance." Most likely they were Lapps or Finns, the victims of a shipwreck. But everyone in Galway, including Columbus, assumed that they were Chinese, "blown across" the Atlantic.

His experiences convinced Columbus that the quickest route to the Indies lay west, across the Atlantic—and that his destiny was to prove it. Perhaps a mere 4500 miles, he reckoned, separated Europe from Japan. His wishful estimate raised eyebrows whenever Columbus asked European monarchs for the money to meet his destiny. Most educated Europeans agreed that the world was round, but they also believed that the Atlantic barrier between themselves and Asia was far wider than Columbus allowed and that it was impossible to navigate. The kings of England, France, and Portugal dismissed him as a crackpot.

Almost a decade of rejection had grayed Columbus's red hair when Spain's monarchs, Ferdinand and Isabella, finally agreed to subsidize his expedition in 1492. For the past 20 years they had worked to drive the Muslims out of their last stronghold on the Iberian peninsula, the Moorish kingdom of Granada. In 1492 they completed this *reconquista,* or battle of reconquest, expelling many Jews as well. Yet the Portuguese, by breaking the Muslim stranglehold on trade with Asia, had taken the lead in the competition to smite the Islamic powers. Ferdinand and Isabella were so desperate to even the score with Portugal that jealousy overcame common sense: they agreed to take a risk on Columbus.

The reconquista

Columbus's first voyage across the Atlantic could only have confirmed his conviction that he was destiny's darling. His three ships, no bigger than fishing vessels that sailed to Newfoundland, plied their course over placid seas, south from Seville to the Canary Islands and then due west. A little more than two months after leaving Spain, on October 11, branches, leaves, and flowers floated by their hulls, signals that land lay near. Just after midnight, a sailor spied cliffs shining white in the moonlight. On the morning of October 12, the *Niña,* the *Pinta,* and the *Santa Maria* set anchor in a shallow sapphire bay, and their crews knelt on the white coral beach. Columbus christened the place San Salvador (Holy Savior).

Like many men of destiny, Columbus did not recognize his true destination. At first he confused his actual location, the Bahamas, with an island off the coast of Japan. He coasted along Cuba and Hispaniola (Haiti), expecting at any moment to catch sight of gold-roofed Japanese temples or to happen upon a fleet of Chinese junks. He encountered instead a gentle, generous people who knew nothing of the Great Khan but who showed him their islands. Columbus's journals note that they wore little clothing (see Daily Lives, "Barbaric" Dress, page 32), but they did wear jewelry—tiny pendants of gold suspended from the nose. He dubbed the Arawak people "Indians"—inhabitants of the Indies.

The four voyages of Columbus

Columbus crossed the Atlantic three more times between 1493 and 1504. On his second voyage he established a permanent colony at Hispaniola and explored other Caribbean islands. On his third voyage he reached Venezuela on the continent of South America, and on his last sailing he made landfalls throughout Central America. Everywhere he looked for proof that these lands formed part of Asia.

Columbus died rich in titles, treasure, and tales—everything but recognition. During the last decade of his life, most Spaniards no longer believed that Columbus had discovered the Indies or anyplace else of significance. And shortly after his death in 1506, another Italian stamped his own name on the New World. Amerigo Vespucci, a Florentine banker with a flair for self-promotion, cruised the coast of Brazil in 1501 and again in 1503. His sensational report of his travels misled a German mapmaker into crediting Vespucci with discovering the barrier between Europe and Asia, and so naming it "America."

Christopher Columbus

EARLY NORTH AMERICAN CULTURES

The Americas were a new world only to European latecomers. To the Asian peoples and their native American descendants who had settled the continents tens of thousands of years earlier, Columbus's new world was their own old world. But it is doubtful that the first nomadic hunters who crossed from Siberia over the Bering Strait to Alaska considered themselves discoverers or recognized what they had found—a truly new world, one wholly uninhabited by humans.

The First Inhabitants

The first passage of people from Asia to America probably took place during a prehistoric glacial period—either before 35,000 B.C. or about 10,000 years later—when huge amounts of the world's water froze into sheets of ice. Sea levels dropped so drastically that the Bering Strait became a broad, grassy plain. Across that land bridge between the two continents both humans and animals escaped icebound Siberia for ice-free Alaska. Whenever the first migration took place, the movement of Asians to America continued, even after 8000 B.C. when world temperatures rose again and the water from melting glaciers flooded back into the ocean, submerging the Bering Strait. Over a span of 25,000 years settlement spread down the Alaskan coast, then deeper into the North American mainland, and finally throughout Central and South America.

Native Americans remained nomadic hunters and gatherers for thousands of years, as did many Europeans, Africans, and Asians of those millennia. But American cultures gradually diversified, especially after about 5500 B.C., when the peoples of central Mexico discovered how to cultivate food crops. As this "agricultural revolution" spread slowly northward, native American societies were able to grow larger and develop distinctive forms of economic, social, and political organization. By the end of the fifteenth century, the inhabitants of North America, perhaps 5 to 10 million people, spoke as many as 1000 languages. Although later Europeans, like Columbus, lumped these societies together by calling them Indian, any cultural unity had vanished long before 1492. *Diversity of cultures*

The simplest Indian societies were those that still relied on hunting and gathering, like the Eskimos of the Arctic and the Serrano, Cahuilla, Luiseño, and Diegueño of southern California, Arizona, and the Baja peninsula of Mexico. Stark deserts and frozen tundra defied cultivation and yielded food supplies that could sustain nomadic bands numbering no more than about 50 people. Families occasionally hunted together or wintered in common quarters, but for most of the year they scattered across the landscape, the women gathering plants and seeds, making baskets, and cooking meals while the men hunted for meat and hides. Political authority lay with either the male family head or the "headman" of a small band. "Shamans"—any tribesmen claiming spiritual powers—enlisted the supernatural to assist individuals.

Societies of Increasing Complexity

In the densely forested belt that stretched from Newfoundland to the Bering Strait, resources more generous than those of the tundra to the north made for larger pop-

Hunters and gatherers

ulations and more closely knit societies. Northeastern bands like the Montagnais, the Micmac, and the Penobscot and northwestern tribes like the Yellowknife and the Beaver traveled forests in moccasins and snowshoes, stalking deer, elk, moose, bear, and caribou; they speared fish in icy lakes and streams from birch-bark canoes. Their environment encouraged cooperative economic pursuits. Leading men assigned several families to specific territories that they hunted together, dividing the returns among the whole band. Religious beliefs strengthened the ties of kinship: each family had a "totem," a particular animal from which it claimed descent.

Women in agricultural societies

While men dominated Indian bands based on hunting, women assumed more influence in societies that relied for part of their food on settled agriculture. Among the Pueblo peoples of Arizona and New Mexico, the Hopi and Zuñi tribes, men hunted deer and cultivated corn and beans, but women owned the fields, the crops, and even the tools. They also owned the sun-baked dwellings of adobe and stone, some of which rose to several stories, that housed the families of their daughters. By 1540 some 70 Pueblo villages flourished, as more reliable food supplies swelled the size and number of clans (families sharing a common ancestry). A council of religious

---

An artist traveling with Francis Drake (probably in the 1590s) painted this Indian tending a tropical Caribbean garden. Maize corn flourishes (right) as well as beans on two poles, while a papaya tree can be seen (upper left) as well as a manioc shrub (middle left) and gourds (lower left). Many of these crops—corn and manioc especially—eventually became important staples in diets around the globe.

elders drawn from the different clans governed each village. Pueblo religious ceremonies, in contrast to those of simpler Indian societies, involved elaborate rituals celebrating tribal unity and seeking the gods' blessing for hunts and harvests. Thousands
of miles to the northeast, in a natural setting far different from the semiarid
Southwest, the Iroquois created a remarkably similar culture.

More complex Indian civilizations arose in the bountiful environments of the
Pacific Northwest and the coastal region reaching from Virginia to Texas. The seas
and rivers from eastern Alaska to northern California teemed with fish, humpback
whales, seals, and otters. In the Southeast fertile soil and temperate climate encouraged the cultivation of maize, rice, and a variety of fruits. Settlements became larger
and more complex as tribes harvested these resources and developed techniques to
preserve food supplies. Far less egalitarian than nomadic hunting bands or even the
Pueblo and Iroquois, these tribes developed elaborate systems of status. Among
southeastern tribes like the Natchez, below the chief, or "Great Sun," stood a hereditary nobility of lesser "Suns," who demanded elaborate displays of respect from the
lowly "Stinkards," the common people.

INDIANS OF NORTH AMERICA, CIRCA 1500

Mesoamerican Empires

Even more advanced were the vast agricultural empires of Mesoamerica—south and central Mexico and Guatemala. As the Roman empire was declining in Europe, the civilization of the Mayas was flourishing in the lowland jungles of Central America. They built cities filled with palaces, bridges, aqueducts, baths, astronomical observatories, and temples topped by pyramids. Their priests developed a written language, their mathematicians discovered the zero, and their astronomers devised a calendar more accurate than any then existing.

Rise of the Aztecs

The Aztecs, who invaded central Mexico from the north in the fourteenth century, built on the Mayas' achievements. Within a century Aztec conquest had created an empire of several million people. The capital, Tenochtitlán, was a glittering island metropolis with a population in 1400 of perhaps a quarter of a million—several times the size of London. The Great Temple of the Sun dominated the center of the city, and through the canals leading to Tenochtitlán flowed gold, silver, exotic feathers, cocoa, and millions of pounds of maize—all trade goods and tribute from other Mexican city-states conquered by the Aztecs.

In many ways, the world of the Aztecs paralleled the societies of early modern Europe. Both worlds were predominantly rural, most of their inhabitants living in small villages and engaging in agriculture. In both worlds, merchants and specialized craftworkers clustered in cities, organized themselves into guilds, and clamored for protection from the government. And, as in Europe, Aztec noble and priestly classes took the lead in politics and religion, demanding tribute from the common people.

The question of human sacrifice aside, there was at least one crucial difference between Aztec and European civilizations. Aztec expansion did not take the form of

---

COUNTERPOINT

The role of human sacrifice

Some students of history, however, emphasize that the Aztecs differed from Europeans in one striking way: they practiced ritual human sacrifice. Every year, Aztec priests wielding razor-sharp knives sliced open the chests of thousands of captives and offered up to the sun hearts still beating, the essence of life. Indeed, the primary purpose of Aztec warfare was less to extend their empire than to maintain a steady supply of captives for such rites. Aztecs believed that they were the chosen people—chosen to nourish the earth by sustaining the life of the sun with offerings of human blood. Put simply, the Aztecs slaughtered other human beings in the name of religion. As one recent historian noted, "In numbers, in the elevated sense of ceremony which accompanied the theatrical shows involved, as in its significance in the official religion, human sacrifice in Mexico was unique."

But were the Aztecs really so different in this regard from invading Europeans? The sense of being a "chosen people" that underlay Aztec rituals also inspired Christians in their own crusades. They campaigned ruthlessly against "Muslim infidels," massacred Jews, and executed thousands of witches during the Middle Ages and even into the seventeenth century. Put just as simply, European Christians, too, slaughtered other human beings in the name of religion. But it was a similarity that Europeans found convenient to overlook. They preferred to portray themselves as "civilizers" of a people whose "savagery" was proved by the practice of human sacrifice.

---

colonial settlements that spanned the oceans—indeed, the globe. That difference reflected a host of distinctive changes in European social, economic, and political development during the fourteenth and fifteenth centuries. It was these transformations that made it possible for bold sailors like Columbus and Cabot or anonymous fisherfolk and traders to dream of profit, glory, and empire.

THE EUROPEAN BACKGROUND OF AMERICAN COLONIZATION

Europe in the age of discovery was a world graced by the courage of explorers like Columbus and the genius of artists like Michelangelo. It was also a world riddled with war, disease, and uncertainty. In 1450 the continent was still recovering from the ravages of the Black Death, an epidemic of the bubonic plague. Under such vibrant, often chaotic conditions, a sense of crisis was mixed with a sense of possibility. Indeed, it was this blend of desperation and ambition that made the newly discovered Americas so attractive to Europeans. Here were strange and distant lands like the island paradises spoken of in legends, like that of the fabled kingdom of Atlantis. Here were opportunities and riches for the daring to grasp. Here were salvation and security for those escaping a world full of violence and sin or oppressed by disease and poverty.

Life and Death in Early Modern Europe

During the fourteenth and the fifteenth centuries 90 percent of Europe's people, widely dispersed in small villages, made their living from the land. But warfare, poor transportation, and low grain yields all created food shortages, and undernourishment produced a population prone to disease. Under these circumstances life was nasty, brutish, and usually short. One-quarter of all children died in the first year of life. People who reached the ripe age of 40 counted themselves fortunate.

It was also a world of sharp inequalities, where nobles and aristocrats enjoyed several hundred times the income of peasants or craftworkers. It was a world with no strong, centralized political authority, where kings were weak and warrior lords held sway over small towns and tiny fiefdoms. It was a world of hierarchy and dependence, where the upper classes provided land and protection for the lower orders. It was a world of violence and sudden death, where homicide, robbery, and rape occurred with brutal frequency. It was a world where security and order of any kind seemed so fragile that most people clung to tradition and feared change.

Into that world in 1347 came the Black Death. In only four years that plague swept away one-third of Europe's population, disrupting both agriculture and commerce. For the next century, recurring outbreaks created additional social disruption and economic depression. Yet the sudden drop in population restored the balance between people and resources. Survivors of the Black Death found that the relative scarcity of workers and consumers made for better wages, lower prices, and more land.

Plague and recovery

St. Sebastian Interceding for the Plague-Stricken City captures the desperation of Europeans during an outbreak of the Black Death. While a priest reads prayers over the bodies being buried in a common grave, a man suddenly taken by the plague writhes in agony. In the background, a cart moves through the street to collect more corpses. At the top, St. Sebastian, a Christian martyr, intercedes with God to end the suffering.

But by the time Columbus reached America, nearly 150 years after the outbreak of the Black Death, Europe again confronted its old problem. Too many people were again competing for a limited supply of food and land. Throughout the sixteenth century diets became poorer, land and work less available, crime and beggary more common. Inflation compounded these problems when prices doubled at the end of the fifteenth century and then quadrupled between 1520 and 1590. To keep pace with the "Price Revolution," landlords raised rents, adding to the burden of the peasantry.

To Europe's hopeful and desperate alike, this climate of disorder and uncertainty led to dreams that the New World would provide an opportunity to renew the Old. As Columbus wrote eagerly of Hispaniola: "This island and all others are very fertile to a limitless degree. . . . There are very large tracts of cultivated land. . . . In the interior there are mines and metals." Columbus and many other Europeans expected that the Americas would provide land for the landless, work for the unemployed, and wealth beyond the wildest dreams of the daring.

The Conditions of Colonization

Sixteenth-century Europeans sought to colonize the Americas, not merely to escape from scarcity and disruption at home. They were also propelled across the Atlantic by dynamic changes in their society. Revolutions in technology, economics, and politics made overseas settlement practical and attractive to seekers of profit and power.

The improvements in navigation and sailing also fostered an expansion of trade. By the late fifteenth century Europe's merchants and bankers had devised more efficient ways of transferring money and establishing credit in order to support commerce across longer distances. And although rising prices and rents pinched Europe's peasantry, that same inflation enriched those who had goods to sell, money to lend, and land to rent. Wealth flowed into the coffers of sixteenth-century traders, financiers, and landlords, creating a pool of capital that those investors could plow into colonial development. Both the commercial networks and the private fortunes needed to sustain overseas trade and settlement were in place by the time of Columbus's discovery.

Expansion of trade and capital

The direction of Europe's political development also paved the path for American colonization. After 1450 strong monarchs in Europe steadily enlarged the sphere of royal power at the expense of warrior lords. Henry VII, the founder of England's Tudor dynasty, Francis I of France, and Ferdinand and Isabella of Spain began the trend, forging modern nation-states by extending their political control over more territory, people, and resources. Those larger, more centrally organized states were able to marshal the resources necessary to support colonial outposts and to sustain the professional armies and navies capable of protecting empires abroad.

Political centralization

It was the growing power of monarchs as well as commercial and technological development that allowed early modern Europeans to establish permanent settlements—even empires—in another world lying an ocean away. That accomplishment had eluded the Aztecs, who lacked knowledge of ocean navigation. Equally important, Aztec rulers had not established their sovereign authority over powerful nobles. The absence of a strong, centralized power made it impossible for the Aztecs to launch a more ambitious expansion. Although their armies put down disturbances in conquered territories and protected trade routes, the Aztecs never exported their people or their way of life to other places. Instead, conquered city-states retained their distinctive languages and customs—and bitterly resented Aztec rule. The result was an empire vulnerable to division from within and to attack from abroad.

Limits to Aztec expansion

SPAIN'S EMPIRE IN THE NEW WORLD

By the reckoning of the Aztecs it was the year 12-House—a time, they believed, when the fate of the whole world hung by a thread. According to their calendar, a 52-year cycle had come to an end. Now the gods might extinguish the sun with a flood or a great wind. The end of this particular cycle had been marked with a chilling omen. In one of the canals, fishermen caught a bird "the color of ashes" with a strange mirror in the crown of its head. They brought the creature to their ruler, Moctezuma II, who looked in the mirror and saw ranks of men mounted on animals resembling deer and moving across a plain.

Two years later, the Aztecs' worst fears were fulfilled. Dust rose in whirlwinds on the roads from the hooves of horses and the boots of men in battle array. "It was as if the earth trembled beneath them, or as if the world were spinning . . . as it spins during a fit of vertigo," one Aztec scribe recorded. This was no image in a magic mirror:

Hernando Cortés and his army of Spaniards were marching on Tenochtitlán. By Cortés's calculations, it was A.D. 1519.

Spanish Conquest

Balboa and Magellan

To Cortés and the other Spanish explorers who had followed Columbus across the Atlantic, a new and remarkable world was opening. By 1513 the Spanish had explored and mastered the Caribbean basin. In that year too, Vasco Nuñez de Balboa crossed the Isthmus of Panama and glimpsed the Pacific Ocean. North and South America were revealed as continents of vast size, separated from Asia by another ocean. And Ferdinand Magellan finally did reach the Orient by sailing west across the immense Pacific. After his death in the Philippines in 1521, Magellan's shipmates completed the first circumnavigation of the globe.

From their bases in the islands of the Caribbean, the Spanish pressed outward. To the north they met mostly with disappointment. Juan Ponce de León vainly scoured the shores of the Florida peninsula for the fabled "Fountain of Youth," as well as Indian populations he might enslave to work the gold mines of the Caribbean. Several decades later, Hernando de Soto plundered his way through Florida and into the southeastern interior as far west as the Mississippi River. Between 1540 and 1542 Francisco Vásquez de Coronado moved through Arizona, New Mexico, Texas, Oklahoma, and Kansas. But reports of fantastic cities of gold proved to be merely the stuff of dreams.

Cortés conquers the Aztecs

During these same decades, however, the Spanish found golden opportunities elsewhere. Those who had first rushed to Hispaniola immediately started scouring the island for gold—and enslaving Indians to work the mines. As for Cortés, when Moctezuma's ambassadors met him on the road to Tenochtitlán in 1519 and attempted to appease him with gold ornaments and other gifts, an Indian witness recorded that "the Spaniards . . . picked up the gold and fingered it like monkeys. . . . Their bodies swelled with greed." For nearly half a year Cortés dominated the indecisive Moctezuma by imprisoning him in his own capital. The Aztecs drove the Spanish out after Moctezuma's death, but Cortés returned with reinforcements, set siege to Tenochtitlán, and in 1521 conquered it. The Aztec empire lay in ruins.

Role of the Conquistadors

To the conquistadors—a motley lot of minor nobles, landless gentlemen, and professional soldiers—the newfound land seemed more than a golden opportunity. They resented the Spanish monarchy's growing strength at home and aimed to re-create in the New World a much older world of their own dreaming. Like medieval knights, Cortés and other conquistadors hoped to establish themselves as a powerful nobility that would enjoy virtual independence from the Spanish Crown an ocean away.

For a time the conquistadors succeeded. By the 1540s Cortés and just 1500 men had taken all of Mexico and the southwestern portion of North America. During the 1530s the ruthless Pizarro brothers and an even smaller band of conquistadors sailed along South America's Pacific coast and overthrew the Incas in Peru, an Andean civilization as impressive as that of the Aztecs. They also laid claim to Ecuador, Chile, Argentina, and Bolivia.

SPANISH AMERICA, CIRCA 1600
By 1600, Spain was extracting large amounts of gold and silver from Central and South America, as well as profits from sugar plantations in the Caribbean. Each year Spanish treasure ships ferried bullion from mines like Potosí to the Isthmus of Panama, where it was transported by land to the Caribbean coast, and from there to Spain. An expedition from Acapulco sailed annually to the Philippines as well, returning with Asian spices and other trade goods.

How did a handful of gentlemen heading a rabble of soldiers, seamen, and criminals bring down sophisticated Indian empires in the span of a generation? To begin with, the Spanish enjoyed the edge of surprise and technological superiority. The sight of ships and the explosion of guns at first terrified the Indians, as did men on horseback whom some Indians, at first, took to be single creatures. The only domesticated animals known to the Aztecs were small dogs; the Spanish provided them with their first glimpse of horses and, later, cattle, sheep, oxen, pigs, goats, donkeys, mules, and chickens.

Reasons for Spain's success

What delivered a more lasting shock to Indian civilizations was exposure to European infections. Smallpox, influenza, typhus, and measles, disease strains against which the Indians had developed no biological resistance, ravaged entire villages and tribes. Tenochtitlán surrendered to Cortés after a siege of 85 days, during which many died from starvation but many more died of smallpox contracted from the Spanish. When the Spanish finally entered the conquered city, "the streets, squares, houses, and courts were filled with bodies, so that it was almost impossible to pass. Even Cortés was sick from the stench in his nostrils."

An equally important factor in the swift conquest was the political disunity within Indian empires. The Aztecs and Incas had subdued the native Indian populations of Mexico and Peru only 100 years before the Spanish invasion. Resentment at Aztec and Inca rule brought the conquistadors eager allies among the subject Indian tribes. But by aiding the Spanish overthrow of the Aztecs and the Incas, the native Indians only substituted one set of overlords for another.

Spanish Colonization

Royal control replaces the conquistadors

The conquistadors did not long enjoy their mastery in the Americas. The Spanish monarchs, who had just tamed an aristocracy at home, were not about to allow a colonial nobility to arise across the Atlantic. The Crown bribed the conquistadors into retirement—or was saved the expense when men like the Pizarro brothers were assassinated by their own followers. The task of governing Spain's new colonies passed from the conquistadors to a small army of officials, soldiers, lawyers, and Catholic bishops, all appointed by the Crown, reporting to the Crown, and loyal to the Crown. Headquartered in urban centers like Mexico City (formerly Tenochtitlán), an elaborate, centralized bureaucracy administered the Spanish empire, regulating nearly every aspect of economic and social life.

Few Spaniards besides imperial officials settled in the Americas. By 1600 only about 5 percent of the colonial population was of Spanish descent, the other 95 percent being either Indian or African. Even by 1800 only 300,000 Spanish immigrants had come to Central and South America. Indians remained on the lands that they had farmed under the Aztecs and the Incas, now paying Spanish overlords their taxes and producing livestock for export. The Indians were not enslaved outright, but the Spanish compelled them to provide yearly tributes of food and other goods, a system known as *encomienda*. The Spanish also established sugar plantations in the West Indies; these were worked by black slaves who were being imported from Africa in large numbers by 1520.

Spain's colonies returned even more spectacular profits to the mother country after 1540, when silver deposits were discovered in both Mexico and Peru. Silver mining developed into a large-scale capitalist enterprise requiring substantial investment. European investors and Spanish immigrants who had profited from cattle rais-

The dignity and grace of this Mexican woman drawn in the 1550s, possibly by a Spanish priest, may reflect the sympathetic influence of the missionary Bartolomé de Las Casas—sentiments most Spaniards did not share.

ing and sugar planting poured their capital into equipment that would mine the sil- *Discovery*
ver deposits more efficiently—stamp mills, water-powered crushing equipment, and *of silver*
pumps. To provide workers, the Spanish government introduced another form of
forced labor known as *repartimiento*. Whole villages of Indians were pressed into service in the mines, joining black slaves and free white workers employed there.

In the last decades of the sixteenth century the economies of Mexico and Peru
revolved solely around the mines. By 1570 the town of Potosí, the site of a veritable
mountain of silver, had become larger than any city in either Spain or its American
empire, with a population of 120,000. Local farmers who supplied mining centers
with food and Spanish merchants in Seville who exported European goods to Potosí
profited handsomely. So, too, did the Spanish Crown, which claimed one-fifth of the
silver extracted. All told, between 1500 and 1600 some 16,000 tons were exported
from Spanish America to Europe.

The Effects of Colonial Growth

Its American riches made Spain the dominant power in Europe. But that dominance
was purchased at a fearful human cost. Devastated by warfare, disease, and exploitation, the Indians of the Caribbean were virtually wiped out within a century. In
Mesoamerica, a native population of 20 million was reduced to 2 million.

Only a few of the Spanish spoke out against the exploitation of the natives.
Among them was Bartolomé de Las Casas, a Spanish priest who became a bishop in   *Las Casas*
southern Mexico. His writings, reprinted in many translations and illustrated with
gruesome drawings, circulated throughout Europe, becoming the basis of the "Black
Legend" of Spanish oppression in the Americas.

Most did not share Las Casas's scruples. They justified their conquest by claiming that they had "delivered" the Indians from Aztec and Inca tyranny and replaced
native "barbarism" and "paganism" with European civilization and Christianity. The
sheer size of the Spanish conquest fostered a heady sense of superiority. By the beginning of the seventeenth century Spain's dominions in the Americas spanned 8000
miles, stretching from Baja California to the Straits of Magellan at South America's
southern tip. The prevailing mood was captured by the portrait of a Spanish soldier
that adorns the frontispiece of his book about the West Indies. He stands with one
hand on his sword and the other holding a pair of compasses on top of a globe.
Beneath is inscribed the motto "By compasses and the sword/More and more and
more and more."

THE REFORMATION IN EUROPE

Spain met with little interference in the Americas from rival European nations for
most of the sixteenth century. One reason was religious upheaval in Europe. During
the second decade of the sixteenth century—the same decade in which Cortés laid
siege to Tenochtitlán—religious changes of enormous significance began in Europe.
That revolution in Christianity, known as the Protestant Reformation, would figure as
a crucial force in shaping the later history of the Americas.

Backdrop to Reform

During the Middle Ages, the Roman Catholic church defined what it meant to be a Christian in western Europe. Like other institutions of medieval society the Catholic church was a hierarchy. At the top was the pope in Rome, and under him were the descending ranks of other church officials—cardinals, archbishops, bishops. At the bottom of the Catholic hierarchy were parish priests, each serving his own village, as well as monks and nuns living in monasteries and convents. But medieval popes were weak, and their power was felt little in the lives of most Europeans. Like political units of the era, religious institutions of the Middle Ages were local and decentralized.

Rise of the papacy   Between about 1100 and 1500, as the monarchs of Europe were growing more powerful, so too were the popes. As the papacy grew in wealth and power, a larger bureaucracy of church officials emerged. The Catholic church acquired land throughout Europe and added to its income through tithing (collecting taxes from church members) and by collecting fees from those appointed to church offices. In the thirteenth century, church officials also began to sell "indulgences." For ordinary believers who expected to spend time after death purging their sins in purgatory, the purchase of an indulgence promised to shorten that punishment by supposedly drawing on a "treasury of merit" amassed by the good works of Christ and the saints.

By the fifteenth century the Catholic church and the papacy had become enormously powerful but increasingly indifferent to popular religious concerns. Church officials meddled in secular politics. Popes and bishops flaunted their wealth, while poorly educated parish priests neglected their pastoral duties. At the same time, popular demands for religious assurance grew increasingly intense. The concern for salvation swelled in response to the disorienting changes sweeping the continent during the fifteenth and sixteenth centuries—the widening gulf between rich and poor, the rise in prices, and the discovery of America.

The Teachings of Martin Luther

Into this climate of heightened spirituality stepped Martin Luther, who abandoned studying the law to enter a monastery. Like many of his contemporaries, Luther was consumed by fears over his eternal fate. He was convinced that he was damned, and he could not find any consolation in the Catholic church. Catholic doctrine taught that a person could be saved by faith in God and by his or her own good works—by leading a virtuous life, observing the sacraments (such as baptism, the Mass, and penance), making pilgrimages to holy places, and praying to Christ and the saints. Since Luther believed that human nature was innately evil, he despaired of being able to lead a life that "merited" salvation. If men and women are so bad, he reasoned, how could they ever win their way to heaven with good works?

Justification by faith alone   Luther finally broke through his despair by reading the Bible. It convinced him that God did not require fallen mankind to earn salvation. Salvation, he concluded, came by faith alone, the "free gift" of God to undeserving sinners. The ability to live a good life could not be the *cause* of salvation but its *consequence:* once men and women believed that they had saving faith, moral behavior was possible. That idea, known as "justification by faith alone," Luther elaborated between 1513 and 1517.

Luther was ordained a priest and then assigned to teach at a university in

In early modern Europe, the uncertainties of religious war and economic upheaval created a pervasive social and spiritual unease, reflected in both these engravings. A contemporary of Martin Luther portrayed St. Anthony (left) being tormented by a host of demons. Their bizarre and twisted shapes bear a notable resemblance to the sea monsters (right) menacing the oceans leading to the newly discovered worlds of Asia and the Americas.

Wittenberg, Germany. Still, he became increasingly critical of the Catholic church as an institution. In 1517 he posted on the door of a local church 95 theses attacking the Catholic hierarchy for selling salvation in the form of indulgences.

The novelty of this attack was not Luther's open break with Catholic teaching. Challenges to the church had cropped up throughout the Middle Ages. What was new was the passion and force behind Luther's attacks. Using the blunt, earthy Germanic tongue, he expressed the anxieties of many devout laypeople and their outrage at the church hierarchy's neglect. The "gross, ignorant asses and knaves at Rome," he warned, should keep their distance from Germany, or else "jump into the Rhine or the nearest river, and take . . . a cold bath."

The pope and his representatives in Germany at first tried to silence Martin Luther, then excommunicated him. But opposition only pushed Luther toward more radical positions. He asserted that the church and its officials were not infallible; only the Scriptures were without error. Every person, he said, should read and interpret the Bible for himself or herself. In an even more direct assault on church authority, he advanced an idea known as "the priesthood of all believers." Catholic doctrine held that salvation came only through the church and its clergy, a privileged group

Attacks on church authority

that possessed special access to God. Luther asserted that every person had the power claimed by priests.

Although Luther had not intended to start a schism within Catholicism, independent Lutheran churches were forming in Germany by the 1520s. And during the 1530s, Luther's ideas spread throughout Europe, where they were eagerly taken up by other reformers.

The Contribution of John Calvin

The most influential of Luther's successors was John Calvin, a French lawyer turned theologian. Calvin agreed with Luther that men and women could not merit their salvation. But while Luther's God was a loving deity who extended his mercy to sinful humankind, Calvin conceived of God as an awesome sovereign, all-knowing and all-powerful, the controlling force in human history who would ultimately triumph over Satan. To bring about that final victory, Calvin believed, God had selected certain people as *The elect* his agents for ushering in his heavenly kingdom. These people—"the saints," or "the elect"—had been "predestined" by God for eternal salvation in heaven.

Calvin's emphasis on predestination led him to another distinctively Protestant notion—the doctrine of calling. How could a person learn whether he or she belonged to the elect who were saved? Calvin answered: strive to behave like a saint. God expected his elect to serve the good of society by unrelenting work in a "calling," or occupation, in the world. In place of the Catholic belief in the importance of good works, Calvin emphasized the goodness of work itself. Success in attaining discipline and self-control, in bringing order into one's own life and the entire society, revealed that a person might be among the elect.

Calvin fashioned a religion to change the world. Where Luther believed that *An activist* Christians should accept the existing social order, Calvin called on Christians to be-
theology come activists, reshaping society and government to conform with God's laws laid down in the Bible. He wanted all of Europe to become like Geneva, the Swiss city that he had converted into a holy commonwealth where the elect regulated the behavior and morals of everyone else. And unlike Luther, who wrote primarily for a German audience, Calvin addressed his most important book, *The Institutes of the Christian Religion* (1536), to Christians throughout Europe. Reformers from every country flocked to Geneva to learn more about Calvin's ideas.

The English Reformation

While the Reformation went forward in Europe, King Henry VIII of England was striving for a goal more modest than those of Luther and Calvin. He wanted only to produce a male heir to carry on the Tudor dynasty. When his wife, Catherine of Aragon, gave birth to a daughter, Mary, Henry decided to do something less modest. He set out to get his marriage to Catherine annulled by the pope. This angered

John Calvin

Catherine's nephew, the king of Spain, who persuaded the pope to refuse. Defiantly, Henry went ahead with the divorce and married his mistress, Anne Boleyn.

Henry then widened this breach with Rome by making himself, and not the pope, the head of the Church of England. In 1534 Parliament formalized the relationship with the Act of Supremacy. But Henry, who fancied himself a theologian, had no fondness for Protestant doctrine. Under his leadership the Church of England remained essentially Catholic in its teachings and rituals. *Henry VIII breaks with Rome*

England's Protestants gained ground during the six-year reign of Edward VI but then found themselves persecuted when his Catholic halfsister, Mary, became queen in 1553. Five years later the situation turned again, when Elizabeth (Anne Boleyn's daughter) took the throne, proclaiming herself the defender of Protestantism.

Still, Elizabeth was no radical Calvinist. A vocal minority of her subjects were reformers of that stripe, calling for the English church to purge itself of bishops, elaborate ceremonies, and other Catholic "impurities." Because of the austerity and zeal of such Calvinist radicals, their opponents proclaimed them "Puritans." *English Puritans*

The Protestant Reformation shattered the unity of Christendom in western Europe. Spain, Ireland, and Italy remained firmly Catholic. England, France, Scotland, the Netherlands, and Switzerland developed either dominant or substantial Calvinist constituencies. Much of Germany and Scandinavia opted for Lutheranism. As these religious groups competed for political power and the loyalties of believers, brutal wars racked sixteenth-century Europe. Protestants and Catholics slaughtered each other in the name of Christianity.

ENGLAND'S ENTRY INTO AMERICA

In 1562 Queen Elizabeth gave her blessing to an English army that set sail for France to aid Calvinists there being suppressed by the government. Perhaps the most dashing of the army's captains was a red-faced and robust West Country gentleman, Sir Humphrey Gilbert. "There is not a vallianter man that liveth," the Earl of Warwick assured the queen.

Like so many West Country boys in search of honor and fortune, Gilbert was eager to seize the main chance. In the early 1560s, that seemed to be fighting for the Protestant cause in France. Gilbert's stepfather, the seafarer Walter Raleigh, had done a good deal of his own seizing, mostly from Spanish silver ships along the South American coast. Like the conquistadors, Raleigh wanted more. He merely decided he could get more a bit more easily if he let Spain dig and refine the silver first.

If France had not beckoned, Humphrey Gilbert would surely have been happy to harass the Spanish too, along with his stepbrother, the young Walter Raleigh (named after his plundering father). But as Gilbert and young Raleigh came of age, they began to consider more ambitious schemes than the mere plundering of treasure. They looked to conquer Spain's empire—or, at least, to carve out for England a rival empire of its own. During the late 1570s and 1580s, when Queen Elizabeth felt confident enough to challenge Spain in the Americas, Gilbert and Raleigh were ready to lead the way. *Ambitious West Country gentlemen*

The English Colonization of Ireland

Reasons for England to soothe Spain

During the 1560s, however, England was too deeply distracted by religious and po-litical turmoil to pursue dreams of glory across the Atlantic. For Elizabeth, privateers like the senior Walter Raleigh stirred up more trouble than they were worth. Spain, after all, was England's ally against a common rival, France. And the Netherlands, which was then controlled by Spain, imported a good deal of English cloth. Elizabeth had good reason to pursue a policy that would soothe Spain, not offend it.

The queen also worried about Catholic Ireland to the west. She feared that the French or the Spanish might use the island as a base for invading England. Beginning in 1565 Elizabeth encouraged a number of her subjects, mainly gentlemen and aris-tocrats from the West Country, to sponsor private ventures for subduing the native Irish and settling English families on Irish land. Among the gentlemen eager to win fame and fortune were Humphrey Gilbert and Walter Raleigh.

English repression of the Irish

The English invaders of Ireland, almost all ardent Protestants, regarded the na-tive Catholic inhabitants as superstitious, pagan savages. "They blaspheme, they mur-der, commit whoredome," complained one Englishman, "hold no wedlocke, ravish, steal and commit all abomination without scruple." Thus the English found it easy enough to justify their conquest. They proclaimed it their duty to teach the Irish the discipline of hard work, the rule of law, and the truth of Christianity. And while the Irish were learning civilized ways, they would not be allowed to buy land or hold of-fice or serve on juries or give testimony in courts or learn a trade or bear arms.

When the Irish rebelled at that program of "liberation," the English ruthlessly repressed native resistance, slaughtering not only combatants but civilians as well. Most English in Ireland, like most Spaniards in America, believed that native peoples who resisted civilization and Christianity should be subdued at any cost. No scruples stopped Humphrey Gilbert, in an insurgent country, from planting the path to his camp with the severed heads of Irish rebels.

England's efforts to settle and subdue Ireland would serve as a rough model for later efforts at colonization. The approach was essentially military, like that of the conquistadors. More ominously, it sanctioned the savage repression of any "inferior race." Not only Gilbert but also Raleigh and many other West Country gentry soon turned their attention toward North America. "Neither reputation, or profytt is to be wonne" in Ireland, concluded Gilbert. They wanted more.

Renewed Interest in the Americas

After hard service in France and Ireland, Gilbert and Raleigh returned to England. Elizabeth's court buzzed with gossip of their boasting and pride, "which exceedeth [that] of all men alive." Her cautious bureaucrats who had been enlarging royal power considered the two swaggering gentlemen insufferable if not downright dan-gerous, much as the Spanish officials distrusted their conquistadors. Still, England was becoming more receptive to the schemes of such hotheaded warrior lords for challenging Spain overseas. English Protestantism, English nationalism, and English economic interests all came together to increase support for English exploration and colonization.

The turning point for the English came during the 1570s when Calvinist Dutch in the Netherlands rebelled against their rule by Catholic Spain. The Spanish retaliated savagely by sacking the city of Antwerp, which was England's major European market for cloth. Forced to look elsewhere for markets and investment opportunities, merchants combined in joint stock companies to develop a trade with Africa, Russia, the East Indies, and the Mediterranean. These private corporations, in which many shareholders pooled small amounts of capital, also began to plow money into Atlantic privateering voyages. They pressed Elizabeth to unleash England's sea rovers on Spain's silver ships.

Joint stock companies

Joining English merchants in the new interest in overseas exploration were gentry families. The high birthrate among England's upper classes throughout the sixteenth century had produced a surplus of younger sons, who stood to inherit no share of family estates. The shortage of land for their sons at home stirred up support among the gentry for England to claim territory across the Atlantic.

With the backing of England's leading merchants and gentlemen, Elizabeth now needed little encouragement to adopt a more belligerent stance toward Spain. But she got more encouragement from Spain itself, which made no secret of wanting to restore England to Catholicism, by armed invasion if necessary. Elizabeth was not yet prepared to provoke open warfare with Spain, but she watched with interest the exploits of a new generation of English explorers in North America.

The Failures of Frobisher and Gilbert

The adventurer who first caught the queen's eye was Martin Frobisher, the veteran of slaving voyages to west Africa, privateering raids in the Atlantic, the fighting in Ireland, and other unsavory enterprises. In 1576 he sailed on another search for a Northwest Passage to Asia.

After sailing north of Labrador, Frobisher returned to England with an Eskimo (plucked, kayak and all, from the Atlantic) and a shiny black stone that seemed to be gold ore. With royal backing, Frobisher made two more voyages to his "New Peru" in 1577 and 1578, hauling back nearly 2000 tons of black rock. Closer inspection revealed all the rock to be "fool's gold," and Frobisher's reputation fell under a cloud.

Because Humphrey Gilbert had refused to invest in this fiasco, Frobisher's disgrace became Gilbert's opportunity. In 1578 Elizabeth granted Gilbert a vague patent—the first English colonial charter—to explore, occupy, and govern any territory in America "not actually possessed of any Christian prince or people." That charter, ignoring the Indian possession of North America, made Gilbert lord and proprietor of all the land lying between Florida and Labrador.

Gilbert pictured himself and his heirs as manorial lords of a colony filled with loyal tenant farmers paying rents in return for protection. In a sense his dreams resembled those of Spain's conquistadors: to re-create an older, nearly feudal world that would remain largely free of royal control. Yet Gilbert's vision also looked forward to a utopian society. He planned to encourage England's poor to emigrate by providing them free land and a government "to be chosen by consent of the people."

Gilbert's colonial plans

In the end, the dreams foundered in a stormy present. Gilbert set sail in June 1583, but a late start forced him to turn back before he could scout the North American coast. Then his two ships met with foul weather. Gilbert, with characteristic bravado, sat on the deck of the smaller *Squirrel,* reading a book. "We are as neere to Heaven by sea as by land," he shouted across the heaving swells. The men aboard the *Golden Hind* recognized the words of Thomas More, whose *Utopia*—a dialogue

Martin Frobisher, his face frozen in a glare, a horse pistol fixed in his fist, exemplified the ruthless ambition of England's West Country adventurers.

about an ideal society in the New World—Gilbert held in his hand. Gilbert was nearer to heaven than he hoped. Around midnight, the crew of the *Golden Hind* saw the lights of the *Squirrel* extinguished and the ship "devoured and swallowed up by the sea."

Raleigh's Roanoke Venture

Raleigh had been eager to accompany his stepbrother's ill-fated expedition, but Elizabeth's many favors made it hard for him to leave. He was dining on food from palace kitchens, sleeping in a bed adorned with green velvet and spangled plumes of white feathers. Still, Raleigh was restless—and envious when another West Country adventurer, Sir Francis Drake, returned from circumnavigating the globe in 1580, his ships heavy with Spanish plunder.

Hakluyt publicizes America   Raleigh's ambitions led him to Richard Hakluyt, a clergyman with a passion for spreading knowledge of overseas discoveries. At Raleigh's request, Hakluyt wrote an eloquent plea to Elizabeth for the English settlement of America, titled *A Discourse*

Concerning Westerne Planting. The temperate and fertile lands of North America, Hakluyt argued, would provide a perfect base from which to harry the Spanish, search for a Northwest Passage, and extend the influence of Protestantism. He also stressed the advantages of colonies as sources of new commodities, as markets for English goods, and as havens for the poor and unemployed.

Raleigh's chance to settle American lands finally came in 1584, when Elizabeth granted him a patent nearly identical to that of Gilbert. By the summer Raleigh had sent Philip Amadas and Arthur Barlowe across the Atlantic, their two small ships coasting the Outer Banks of present-day North Carolina. Amadas and Barlowe established cordial relations with the Roanoke tribe, ruled by a "werowance," or chief, named Wingina. The enthusiastic Hakluyt promptly envisioned a colony that would become the Mexico of England, full of plantations producing sugar and silk and mountains yielding gold. Elizabeth knighted Raleigh and allowed him to name the new land "Virginia," after his virgin queen. The following summer a full-scale expedition returned to Roanoke Island.

Raleigh apparently aimed to establish on Roanoke a mining camp and a military garrison modeled on Frobisher's venture of the 1570s. In a stroke of genius, he included in the company of 108 men a scientist, Thomas Hariot, to study the country's natural resources and an artist, John White, to make drawings of the Virginia Indians. *A Briefe and True Reporte of the New Found Land of Virginia* (1588), written by Hariot and illustrated by White, served as one of the principal sources about North America and its Indian inhabitants for more than a century. Far less inspired was Raleigh's choice to lead the expedition—two veterans of the Irish campaigns, Sir Richard Grenville and Ralph Lane. Even his fellow conquistadors in Ireland considered Lane proud and greedy. As for Grenville, he was given to breaking wineglasses between his teeth and then swallowing the shards to show that he could stand the sight of blood, even his own.

The first colony at Roanoke

The bullying ways of both men quickly alienated the natives of Roanoke. After a year, in response to rumors of an imminent Indian attack, Lane and his men attacked Wingina's main village and killed him. All that averted an Indian counterattack was the arrival of Drake and Frobisher, fresh from freebooting up and down the Caribbean. The settlement's 102 survivors piled onto the pirate fleet and put an ocean between themselves and the avenging Roanokes.

A Second Attempt

Undaunted, Raleigh organized a second expedition to plant a colony farther north, in the Chesapeake Bay. He now projected an agricultural community modeled on Humphrey Gilbert's manorial dreams. He recruited 119 men, women, and children, members of the English middle class, granting each person an estate of 500 acres. He also appointed as governor the artist John White, who brought along a suit of armor for ceremonial occasions.

From the moment of first landfall in July 1587, everything went wrong. The expedition's pilot, Simon Ferdinando, insisted on putting off the colonists at Roanoke Island rather than the Chesapeake. Even before Ferdinando weighed anchor, the settlers were skirmishing with the local Indians. Sensing that the situation on Roanoke could quickly become desperate, White sailed back with Ferdinando, hoping to bring reinforcements.

CLOTHING AND FASHION

"Barbaric" Dress—Indian and European

It was remarkable to sixteenth-century Europeans how many things seemed to be missing from Indian culture. Even more remarkable, the Indians themselves did not seem to notice. Michel de Montaigne, a French philosopher who had never been to America but liked to talk with explorers and read their accounts, managed to compile quite a list. According to Montaigne, Indians had "no kind of traffic [trade], no knowledge of letters, no intelligence of numbers, no name of magistrate, nor of politics, no use of service [servants], of riches, or of poverty, no contracts, no successions, no partitions, no occupation but idle, no apparel but natural. . . ." When other Europeans, with and without experience in America, made similar lists, they never failed to mention that last crucial item missing in Indian culture—clothing. Even Europeans who never traveled beyond their villages associated America's inhabitants with nakedness, for woodcuts, engravings, and paintings showed native peoples either entirely nude or clad in skimpy loincloths or grass skirts.

Europeans interpreted the simplicity of Indian dress in two different ways. Some saw the lack of clothing as evidence of "barbarism." André Thevet, a shocked French visitor to Brazil in 1557, voiced this point of view when he attributed nakedness to simple lust. If the Indians could weave hammocks, he sniffed, why not shirts? But other Europeans viewed unashamed nakedness as the Indians' badge of innocence. As remnants of a bygone "golden age," they believed, Indians needed clothing no more than government, laws, regular employment, or other corruptions of civilization.

In fact, Indians were no more "naked" than they were without trade, politics, employment, or religion. While the simplest tribes of the Caribbean and Brazil wore little, the members of more advanced Indian cultures in Central and North America clothed themselves with animal pelts sewn into mantles and robes, breechclouts, leggings, and moccasins. They wrought bird feathers into headdresses and ear decorations and fashioned reptile skins into belts and pouches. Even more formidably clad were the Eskimos of the far North, who dressed head to foot in sealskin suits with waterproofed seams, turning the furry side inward for warmth in the winter and outward in the summer.

By the late sixteenth century, Europeans, and especially the English, were paying more heed to what the Indians wore, hoping to assure prospective colonists that the natives would not affront European standards of modesty. Captain John Smith, for example, left descriptions of the attire of Virginia's tribes, noting in a telling comparison that "the better sort use large mantels of deare skins not much differing in fashion from the Irish mantels." Even more reassuringly, Smith added, "The women are alwaies covered about their midles with a skin and very shamefast [ashamed] to be seen bare."

If natives struck whites as starkly un-

But White returned home in 1588, just as the massive Spanish navy, the Armada, was marshaling for an assault on England. Elizabeth was enlisting every seaworthy ship and able-bodied sailor in her realm to stave off invasion. Blocked by the war with Spain, Raleigh left the Roanoke colonists to shift for themselves. When White finally returned to Roanoke Island in 1590, he found only an empty fort and a few cottages derdressed, Europeans seemed, by the Indians' standards, grotesquely overdressed. Indeed, European fashion was ill suited to the environment between the Chesapeake and the Caribbean. Elizabethan gentlemen strutted in silk stockings attached with garters to padded, puffed knee breeches, topped by long-sleeved shirts and tight quilted jackets called "doublets." Men of lesser status wore coarse woolen hose, canvas breeches, shirts, and fitted vests known as "jerkins"; when at work, they donned aprons of dressed leather. Women wore gowns with long, full skirts, low-cut bodices, aprons, and hosiery held up by garters. Ladies went about in silk and wore hoods and mantles to ward off the sun, while the rest dressed in flannels or canvas and covered their heads with linen caps or coifs. Both sexes favored long hair, and men sported mustaches and beards.

Such fashions complicated life in the American environment, especially since heavy clothing and even shoes rotted rapidly from sweat and humidity. The pungent aroma of Europeans also compounded the discomfort of natives who came in contact with them. For despite sweltering heat, the whites who swaddled themselves in woolens and brocades also disdained regular bathing and regarded Indian devotion to daily washing as another uncivilized oddity.

It would have been natural for Indians to wonder why the barbaric newcomers did not adapt their dress to a new setting. The answer may be that for Europeans—entering an alien environment inhabited by peoples whom they identified as "naked savages"—the psychological risk of shedding familiar apparel was simply too great. However inappropriate or even unhealthy, heavy, elaborate dress afforded the comfort of familiarity and distinguished "civilized" newcomer from "savage" native in America.

Columbus meeting the natives on Hispaniola

in a clearing. The sole clue to the colony's fate was carved on a post: CROATOAN. It was the name of a nearby island off Cape Hatteras.

Had the Roanoke colonists fled to Croatoan for safety? Had they moved to the mainland and joined Indian tribes in the interior? Had they been killed by Wingina's people? The fate of the "lost colony" remains a mystery. White sailed back to

33

1420	1500	1600	1700

1420s Madeira and Azores colonized

1430s and 1440s Exploration of West African coast

1488 Dias rounds the Cape of Good Hope

1498 Da Gama reaches India

PORTUGAL   **1500** Cabral discovers Brazil

1492-1502 Voyages of Columbus

1508-1513 Expansion into the Caribbean

1519-1521 Conquest of the Aztecs

1530s Conquest of the Incas

SPAIN   **1540** Discovery of silver

1480s West Country mariners fish the western Atlantic

1497 John Cabot reaches Newfoundland

1500-1550s Growth of Newfoundland fishery

1565 Conquest of Ireland begins

1577-1583 Frobisher and Gilbert's failed colonies

ENGLAND   **1585-1590** Roanoke expeditions

EUROPEAN EXPLORATION: FIFTEENTH AND SIXTEENTH CENTURIES

England, leaving behind the little cluster of cottages that would soon be overgrown with vines and his suit of armor that was already "almost eaten through with rust."

All the world lay before them. Or so it had seemed to the young men from England's West Country who dreamed of gold and glory, conquest and colonization. Portugal had sent slave and gold traders to Africa, as well as merchants to trade with the rich civilizations of the Indies. Spanish conquerors like Cortés had toppled Indian empires and brought home silver. But England's would-be conquistadors had met only with frustration. In 1600, over a century after Columbus's first crossing, not a single English settlement existed anywhere in the Americas. The Atlantic had swallowed up Gilbert and his hopes for a manorial utopia; Roanoke lay in ruins.

What was left of the freebooting world of West Country adventurers? Raleigh, his ambition unquenchable, sailed to South America in quest of a rich city named El Dorado. In 1603, however, Elizabeth's death brought to the English throne her cousin James I, the founder of the Stuart dynasty. The new king arrested the old queen's favorite for treason and left him to languish 15 years in the Tower of London. Set free in 1618 at the age of 64, Raleigh returned to South America, his lust for El Dorado undiminished. Along the way he plundered some Spanish silver ships, defying James's orders. It was a fatal mistake, for England had made peace with Spain. Raleigh lost his head.

James I did not want to harry the king of Spain; he wanted to imitate him. The Stuarts were even more determined than the Tudors to enlarge the sphere of royal power. There would be no room in America for a warrior nobility of conquistadors, no room for a feudal fiefdom ruled by the likes of Raleigh or Gilbert. Instead, there would be English colonies in America like the new outpost of Jamestown, planted on the Chesapeake Bay in Virginia in 1607. There would be profitable plantations and other bold enterprises, enriching English royalty and managed by loyal, efficient bureaucrats. Settling America would strengthen English monarchs, paving their path to greater power, just as the dominions of Mexico and Peru had enlarged the authority of the Spanish Crown. America would be the making of kings and queens.

Or would it? For some in Europe, weary of freebooting conquistadors and sea rovers, the order and security that Crown rule and centralized states promoted in western Europe would be enough. But others, the desperate and idealistic men and women who sailed to the world that lay before them, would want more.

CHAPTER SUMMARY

During the late fifteenth century, Europeans made their first contact with North and South America. These voyages of discovery were not simply the efforts of a few bold explorers like Columbus, John Cabot, and others. The expansion of European peoples and culture arose out of a series of gradual changes in European society. Technological advances in navigation, shipbuilding, and firearms contributed. So did the development of new trade networks. A rise in population, following a devastating century of plague, increased interest in new lands, while the Reformation added a dimension of devout belief to the era's political rivalries. Finally, increased political centralization made it possible for kingdoms to extend their bureaucratic influence across the ocean.

When Europeans arrived in the Americas, native cultures were numerous and diverse. They ranged from the hunting and gathering societies of the Great Plains to the Aztecs in Mesoamerica, a society similar in many ways to that of sixteenth-century Europe. Aztec expansionism differed from that of Europe in one crucial way, however: it did not take the form of exploration and colonization across the Atlantic. Spain took the lead in exploring and colonizing the Americas, consolidating a vast empire of its own in the place of Aztec and Inca civilizations. Both divisions within Indian empires and the devastating effects of European diseases made Spanish conquest possible. But conquest under the conquistadors quickly gave way to direct rule by the royal bureaucracy. The empire that developed during the sixteenth century proved enormously profitable, especially after the discovery of silver.

England was slower to pursue its interest in the Americas, since Queen Elizabeth wished to avoid conflict with Spain. But as Spain's economic and military power became more of a threat to England, Elizabeth adopted a more aggressive stance toward the Spanish. Adventurers like Gilbert and Raleigh, whose energies for a time went into religious wars in Europe and the conquest of Ireland, turned their attention to North America in the 1570s and 1580s. English merchants and gentlemen, in search of new markets and new land, lent greater support to colonizing expeditions. Early efforts like those at Roanoke failed. But they signaled England's renewed interest in America.

SIGNIFICANT EVENTS

ca. 50,000–25,000 B.P. (before the present)	First Asians arrive in the Americas
ca. A.D. 1300	Rise of the Aztec empire
1271–1295	Marco Polo travels to China from Italy
1347	First outbreak of the Black Death
1420s	Portuguese settlements in the Atlantic islands
1488	Dias rounds the tip of Africa
1492	Columbus discovers America
1497	John Cabot discovers Newfoundland
1498	Da Gama reaches India
1517	Luther posts his 95 theses
1519–1522	Magellan circumnavigates the globe
1521	Tenochtitlán surrenders to Cortés
1540	Discovery of silver in Mexico and Peru
1558	Elizabeth I becomes queen of England
1565	England begins its conquest of Ireland
1576–1578	Frobisher searches for Northwest Passage
1583	Gilbert's quest for a North American colony
1584–1590	Roanoke voyages

ADDITIONAL READING

For a description of the entrepreneurs, mariners, and ordinary folk who participated in the era of exploration and discovery, see Kenneth R. Andrews, *Trade, Plunder, and Settlement: Maritime Enterprise and the Genesis of the British Empire, 1480–1630* (1985) as well as James Lang, *Conquest and Commerce: Spain and England in the Americas* (1975). Alfred Crosby, Jr., provides a fascinating account of the biological and ecological effects of contact between Native Americans and Europeans in *The Columbian Exchange* (1972). M. Leon Portilla's *The Broken Spears* (1962) is a vivid account of Cortés's conquest, seen through Aztec eyes. For a good introduction to the Reformation, see Owen Chadwick, *The Reformation* (1964). For early English attempts at colonization, both in Ireland and in the Americas, consult the works of Nicholas Canny in the main bibliography. David Beers Quinn's *Set Fair for Roanoke* (1985) contains tantalizing speculation about what happened to the lost colony at Roanoke.

There are a number of studies that memorably evoke the cultures coming into contact with each other during the sixteenth and seventeenth centuries. For Native American society, see Alvin M. Josephy, ed., *America in 1492* (1992) and Bruce G. Trigger and Wilcomb E. Washburn, eds., *Cambridge History of the Native Peoples of the New World,* vol. 3: *North America* (1993). For early modern Spain, a lively and polemical account is Kirkpatrick Sale, *The Conquest of Paradise* (1990), and for England, one of the most readable studies remains Wallace Notestein, *The English People on the Eve of Colonization, 1603–1630* (1954). For a fuller list of readings, see the Bibliography.

Tracking the First Americans

Sometimes the most ordinary circumstances end in the most extraordinary discoveries. One of those times was a morning in 1908 when George McJunkin, an African American cowboy scanning the range near Folsom, New Mexico, for stray cattle, dropped his gaze into a dry gully and spotted some large bones poking through the soil. Intrigued, he began digging and found a stone spearpoint lodged in the skeleton. He carried the lot back to his ranch, where they remained for the next seventeen years. Then McJunkin's curiosities somehow came to the attention of archaeologists, who identified the bones as those of a long-extinct form of bison which had ranged throughout the Southwest at least ten thousand years earlier. They realized, too, that only a spear-wielding human could have killed the bison.

That discovery rocked the scientific community, which for the previous century had confidently declared that Indians had first arrived in the Americas only about 4000 years ago. Shortly thereafter, in 1932, another shock wave followed when some amateur collectors digging at Clovis, New Mexico, unearthed more bones and spearheads suspected to be even older. Finally, in 1949, scientists established the great

antiquity of both finds by using "radiocarbon dating," a method for measuring decay rates of the radioactive isotope of carbon, which exists in organic matter like bone and starts to break down immediately after an organism dies. Tests

Arrowheads known as Clovis points found with the skeleton of a mammoth revealed that the Indians whose hunting grounds were now called Folsom and Clovis had been turning bison into bones between 10,800 and 11,500 years ago.

Those conclusions pointedly raised the question of exactly how much earlier the first American ancestors of such hunters had come to the New World. This tantalizing mystery puzzles (and divides) archaeologists and anthropologists, geologists and historians, right down to the present. Such men and women devote their lives to the hard work of digging in remote sites or exploring the ocean's floor, to the harder work of analyzing their finds in laboratories, and to the hardest work of all—trying to make sense of what it all means. Their efforts have yielded much new evidence and increasingly sophisticated techniques for understanding its significance, but many important questions still remain unanswered.

Even so, almost all of them agree on a number of points. First, whoever the first inhabitants of the New World were, they came, originally, from the Old World: scientists have found no fossil remains to support the view that human beings evolved into modern men and women in the Americas. Second, these first Americans were almost certainly fully evolved human beings, known as *Homo sapiens sapiens*—not their less developed forerunners, the Neanderthals, or even earlier ancestors. These *Homo sapiens sapiens* excelled at surviving anywhere, armed as they were with the intellectual ability to plan and project and the technology to sew warm clothing and to store food. About 35,000 years ago, these resourceful adapters came to predominate, edging out the Neanderthals, whose more limited skills had restricted their settlements to the tropical and temperate parts of the world.

The new species multiplied rapidly, and the pressure of its growing population pushed many into settling in less hospitable regions—including the arctic frontier of Siberia in northeastern Asia. Indeed, a third point of general agreement among scholars is that the descendants of these migrants to Siberia continued the wandering

ways of their ancestors and somehow, at some time, wandered into North America by way of Alaska. The research of physical anthropologists documents key biological similarities between Siberians and American Indians. Both groups share not only certain genetic variants that suggest their descent from common ancient ancestors but also distinctive formations of the roots and crowns of their teeth known as Sinodonty.

But how did Asians get to Alaska—a region now separated from Siberia by fifty miles of ocean known as the Bering Strait? It is not impossible that they sailed across, for some *Homo sapiens sapiens* could build boats sturdy enough to navigate short stretches of open ocean. Archaeologists have discovered that Southeast Asians floated across 55 miles of ocean on rafts to reach Australia some 35,000 years ago. Could their contemporaries in northeast Asia, using bark canoes, have made a voyage of similar length over the Bering Strait? Not impossible, scientists conclude, but not likely either, if only because navigating calm, tropical waters of the southern Pacific is far less difficult than mastering the Bering Strait, which, even in summer, is choked with ice floes. Such an undertaking would

way into an exposed, inhabitable lowland plain was the coldest phase of the last Ice Age, which began about 30,000 years earlier when plunging temperatures caused the world's oceans to drop in depth by freezing great expanses of seawater into sheets of ice. Those climatic changes formed "Beringia," a land bridge between Siberia and Alaska that existed from about 25,000 B.P. (before the present) until about 15,000 B.P. During those millennia, most scientists now believe, Siberians gradually settled the length of this link to the Americas. Thereafter, when temperatures began to warm again and the seas rose and closed over Beringia, some of its inhabitants strayed into Alaska.

But even now, there are some scientists who doubt this account. True, no one has yet discovered an archaeological site in Alaska—or anywhere else in the Americas—that can be positively dated to earlier than about 15,000 B.P. Yet a few archaeologists working mainly in South America claim to have found artifacts in rock-shelters dating to 30,000 B.P. Many others argue that such "finds" are not the result of human manufacture but natural processes like erosion. Then, too, those

Strong shoveled incisor
Single root
Double root
SINODONT

Double root
Weak shoveled incisor
Triple root
SUNDADONT

UPPER JAW

have been even more daunting to the earliest Siberians, who, as anthropologists have discovered, were land-based hunters, not seafaring folk.

So most scientists now believe that Siberians did not sail to the New World: instead, they walked. They were able to do that because the Bering Strait is not a timeless feature of arctic geography. On the contrary, geologists have discovered submerged far below the Bering Strait traces of a landmass that once connected Siberia to Alaska. Even in the late nineteenth century, some naturalists suspected that such a land bridge had once existed after noting that the vegetation and wildlife of Siberia was nearly identical to that in Alaska. By the 1930s, scientists had enough information to speculate that what turned a water-

scientists who take the position that the first Americans arrived 30,000 years ago or even earlier—before the existence of the Beringia land bridge—must prove the improbable: that Siberians crossed into Alaska by sailing across the Bering Strait.

A recent discovery in the state of Washington is also prompting scientists to wonder whether the first inhabitants of the Americas might have included peoples other than Asians. In 1996, the sheriff of a small desert town, puzzled by a half-buried human skeleton found along the shores of the Columbia River, showed the bones to an anthropologist, James Chatters. Like McJunkin's find of almost a century earlier, this skeleton encased a stone spearpoint, and radiocarbon dating

Dr. James Chatters, an anthropologist found a skull approximately 9300 years old along the Columbia River in 1996. The skull's Eurasian features suggest that at least some migrants over the Bering Strait may also have been of European stock.

revealed it to be nearly as old (9300 years) as the Folsom bones. But unlike McJunkin's specimen, this is almost certainly—and astonishingly—the skeleton of a Caucasian. Such is the judgment of Chatters and other scientists who have carefully examined and measured its skull, which is far narrower than any Indian skull of similar antiquity. Within the last thirty years, other ancient skull remains with Caucasian features have been found, but none so well preserved as the Columbia River specimen, which even has some teeth intact. To date it is the strongest evidence that some people

of European stock may have migrated across northern Asia and then joined Siberians in crossing to the Americas.

Are today's Native Americans descended from both Asians and Europeans? Other scientists are quick to point out that the evidence of one skeleton can hardly support such sweeping conclusions. For their part, many Indians still living along the Columbia River reject all scientific explanations of their origins in favor of religious accounts—tribal creation myths which proclaim that their people have always lived in the Americas. Angered by the conduct of earlier anthropologists, who freely dug up Indian grave sites, they have demanded the right to rebury the skeleton under the terms of the Native American Graves Protection and Repatriation Act of 1990.

So the debates about America's first colonizers continue, and, if recent history is any guide, so too will the discoveries. This part of the past, like every other, holds in store many surprises for those in the present determined to probe its secrets.

BIBLIOGRAPHY. Keeping up with recent discoveries in this field poses many challenges. New discoveries turn up frequently, and most reports of those findings are written in a highly technical language. Fortunately, a few well-written books provide a guide to both the early Asian migration to and throughout the Americas and the evolution of scholarly debate. Bryan M. Fagan, *The Great Journey* (London, 1987) is lucid, and the same author has more recently written a more detailed textbook on both ancient Native American archaeology and history, *Ancient North America* (1991). A less comprehensive but elegantly written treatment of these topics is William MacLeish's *The Day before America* (1994). Students seeking more advanced and specialized information should consult Stuart J. Fiedel, *Prehistory of the Americas* (2d ed., Cambridge, 1992). Bear in mind, too, that the science section of each Tuesday's *New York Times* regularly features articles on the ongoing research of archaeologists, anthropologists, and geologists. For the report on the Columbia River skeleton, see *The New York Times* for September 30, 1996, A12.

2

The First Century of Settlement in the Colonial South

 n the year 1617, as Europeans counted time, on a bay they called the Chesapeake, in a land they named Virginia, an old Indian chief surveyed his domain. It had all worked according to plan, and Powhatan, leader of the Pamunkeys, had laid his plans carefully. While in his prime, the tall, robust man had drawn some 30 smaller tribes along the Virginia coast into a powerful confederacy. As tribute for his protection and leadership, Powhatan collected food, furs, and skins. He installed his relatives as their new leaders and as his new vassals.

Powhatan's confederacy   By 1607 Powhatan's confederacy numbered nearly 9000, a political alliance that had overcome formidable obstacles. The natives of Virginia, like the peoples who inhabited the length of eastern North America, were seminomadic. They lived for most of the year in small villages and ranged over tribal hunting and fishing grounds, following the game from one season to the next. Rivalries over trade, territorial boundaries, and leadership had often erupted into armed conflict. Some coastal tribes had fiercely resisted Powhatan's efforts to incorporate them; other tribes to the west still threatened the security of his confederacy.

After 1607 Powhatan was forced to take into account yet another tribe. The English, as this new people called themselves, came by sea, crammed into three ships. They were 100 men and 4 boys, all clad in heavy, outlandish clothing, many dressed in gaudy colors. The ships followed a river deep into Powhatan's territory and built a fort on a swampy, mosquito-infested site that they called Jamestown.

Powhatan was not frightened. The English had larger boats and louder, more deadly weapons than he did. But the Indians quickly learned how to use guns, and they vastly outnumbered the English, an inferior race who seemed unlikely to live long and prosper in Powhatan's land. They could not even manage to feed themselves from the rich resources of the Chesapeake. With bows and arrows, spears and nets, Indian men brought in an abundance of meat and fish. The fields tended by Indian women yielded generous crops of corn, beans, squash, and melon, and edible nuts and fruits grew wild. Still the English starved, and not just during the first few months of their settlement but for several years afterward.

Powhatan could understand why the English refused to grow food. Cultivating crops was women's work—like building houses; or making clothing, pottery, and baskets; or caring for children. And the English settlement included no women until two

The early southern gentry idealized their life as one of grace, plenty, and independence —qualities evoked by this painting, The Plantation. *Typically, this plantation fronts a river, ensuring good access to the markets for tobacco and rice across the Atlantic.*

arrived in the fall of 1608. Yet even after more women came, the English still starved, and they expected—no, they demanded—that the Indians supply them with food.

Most incredible to Powhatan was that the inferior English considered themselves a superior people. They boasted constantly about the power of their god—they had only one—and denounced the Indians' "devil-worship" of "false gods." The English also boasted without end about the power of their king, James I, who expected Powhatan to become his vassal. The English had even planned a "coronation" to crown Powhatan as a "subject king." He had not been impressed. "If your king has sent me presents," he responded, "I also am a king, and this is my land. . . . Your father is to come to me, not I to him." In the end the English did come to Powhatan, only to find what "a fowle trouble there was to make him kneele to receave his crowne. . . . [he] indured so many perswasions, examples and instructions as tired them all. At last by leaning hard on his shoulders, he a little stooped, and . . . put the Crowne on his head."

It was inconceivable to Powhatan that he should willingly bow before this King James, the ruler of so savage a race. When the Indians made war, they killed the male warriors of rival tribes but adopted their women and children. But when Powhatan's people withheld food or defended their land from these invaders, the English retali-

No stranger to self-promotion, Captain John Smith included this portrait of himself and verses celebrating his ennobling exploits at the beginning of his *Description of New England* (1616). As the military armor and knightly bearing suggest (note Smith on horseback, lower right), the outspoken captain stood in the tradition of West Country adventurers and Spanish conquistadors.

ated by murdering Indian women and children. To make matters worse, the English could not even keep order within their own tribe. Too many of them wanted to be chiefs, and they squabbled constantly among themselves.

Captain John Smith   Only one man, a brash fellow called Captain John Smith, had briefly been able to bring order to the English settlement. Powhatan granted him a grudging respect, though he boasted so much, even other English seemed modest by comparison. Smith bragged endlessly of his earlier exploits across the ocean, where he had fought as a soldier of fortune. He told wonderful tales of his irresistible appeal to beautiful women who had rescued him from harrowing perils. A rough man, he bullied the Indians for food and would have enslaved them if it had been in his power. Even so, Smith took a genuine interest in Indian ways.

But Smith returned to England in 1609 after being injured when some of the white people's gunpowder blew up by mistake. Thereafter the English returned to squabbling and starving. Small wonder that some English had deserted their settlement to live among Powhatan's people. Anyone could see the superiority of Indian culture to English ways.

The temptation to wipe out the helpless, troublesome, arrogant tribe of English—or simply to let them starve to death—had been almost overwhelming. But *Powhatan's strategy* Powhatan allowed the English to survive because he had decided that even these barbaric people had their uses. English labor, English trading goods, and, most important, English guns would help him quell resistance within his confederacy and subdue his Indian rivals in the west. In 1614 Powhatan cemented his claim on the English and their weapons with the marriage between his favorite child, Pocahontas, and a white settler, John Rolfe.

By 1617 events had vindicated Powhatan's strategy of tolerating the English. His empire flourished, ready to be passed on to his brother, Opechancanough. Powhatan's people still outnumbered the English, who seldom starved outright now but continued to fight among themselves and sicken and die. Only one thing had changed in the Chesapeake by 1617: the English were clearing woodland along the rivers and planting tobacco.

That was the doing of Powhatan's son-in-law, Rolfe, a man as strange as any of his tribe, all of them eager to store up wealth and worldly goods. Rolfe had been obsessed with finding a crop that could be grown in Virginia and then sold for gain across the sea. When he succeeded by growing tobacco, other English followed his lead. Odder still, not women but men tended the tobacco fields. Here was more evidence of English inferiority. Men wasted long hours laboring when they might supply their needs with far less effort.

In 1617 Powhatan, ruler of the Pamunkeys, surveyed his empire, and sometime in that year, he looked no longer. He had lived long enough to see the tobacco fields lining the riverbanks, straddling the charred stumps of felled trees. But he died believing that he had bent the English to his purposes—died before those stinking tobacco weeds spread over the length of his land and sent his hard-won empire up in smoke.

ENGLISH SOCIETY ON THE CHESAPEAKE

While the chief of the Chesapeake was expanding his dominions and consolidating his power, the king of England was doing the same. Just as Spain had begun to profit from the riches of silver mines and sugar plantations, James I of England hoped that the wealth and power of his kingdom would grow as English colonists settled the American coasts north of Spain's empire. The first newcomers clustered along the many bays of the Chesapeake, as well as in a few island outposts of the Caribbean. A generation later, during the 1670s and 1680s, colonists from the Caribbean hopscotched to the mainland to found colonies along the Carolina coast. As the English struggled to put down roots, the ambitions of merchants and planters and kings clashed with the conflicting goals of Indian leaders like Powhatan.

The result was a chaotic and deadly landscape. During much of the seventeenth century, ambitious colonists scrambled to control the land and the labor needed to secure profits from tobacco, sugar, and rice. Only after decades of uncertainty, violence, and high mortality did the colonies along the southern Atlantic crescent begin to prosper. Even then, stability was bought at a high price. In order to supply the workers so desperately sought by plantation owners, English colonists introduced the institution of slavery.

Instability of the southern colonies

The Mercantilist Impulse

As European powers began establishing permanent colonies in America, they were putting into practice a theory about how best to attain national wealth and influence. That idea, which guided Europe's commercial expansion for 200 years, was named "mercantilism" by the eighteenth-century economist Adam Smith. Mercantilists called for the state to regulate and protect industry and commerce. Their primary objective was to enrich the nation by fostering a favorable balance of trade. Once the value of exports exceeded the cost of imports, they theorized, gold and silver would flow into home ports.

Mercantilism

If a nation could make do without any imports from other countries, so much the better, and it was here that the idea of colonies entered the mercantilist scheme. Colonial producers would supply raw materials that the mother country could not produce, while colonial consumers swelled demand for the finished goods and financial services that the mother country could provide. Convinced that colonies would enhance national self-sufficiency, mercantilists urged states to sponsor overseas settlements.

Mercantilist notions appealed to Europe's monarchs. A thriving trade meant that more taxes and customs duties would fill royal coffers, increasing royal power. That logic led James I to lend his approval to the private venture that brought the first white settlers to the Chesapeake.

The Virginia Company

In 1606 the king granted a charter to a number of English merchants, gentlemen, and aristocrats, incorporating them as the Virginia Company of London. The members of the new joint stock company sold stock in their venture to English investors, as well as awarding a share to those willing to settle in Virginia at their own expense. With the proceeds from the sale of stock, the company planned to send to Virginia hun-

In Jamestown's early years its military orientation was clear. The fort's heavy palisades and its strategic location upriver and some distance inland underscore the colonists' concern for defense—as does the imposing figure of Powhatan seated at the right.

dreds of poor and unemployed people as well as scores of skilled craftworkers. These laborers were to serve the company for seven years in return for their passage, pooling their efforts to produce any commodities that would return a profit to stockholders. If gold mines like Spain's could not be found, perhaps North America would yield other valuable commodities—furs, pitch, tar, or lumber. In the spring of 1607 the first expedition dispatched by the Virginia Company, 104 men and boys, founded Jamestown.

Making the first of many mistakes, Jamestown's settlers pitched their fort on an inland peninsula in order to prevent a surprise attack from the Spanish. Unfortunately, the marshy, thickly wooded site served as an ideal breeding ground for malaria. The Virginia Company settlers, weakened by bouts of malaria and then beset by dysentery, typhoid, and yellow fever, died by the scores. *Jamestown's problems*

Even before sickness took its toll, many of Jamestown's first settlers had little taste for labor. The gentlemen of the expedition expected to lead rather than to work, while most other members of the early colonizing parties were gentlemen's servants and craftworkers who knew nothing about growing crops. The settlers resorted to bullying Powhatan's people for food. Many colonists suffered from malnutrition, which heightened their susceptibility to disease. Only 60 of Jamestown's 500 inhabitants lived through the winter of 1609–1610, known as the "starving time." Some desperate colonists unearthed and ate corpses; one settler even butchered his wife.

Reports of starvation and staggering death rates stiffened the Virginia Company's resolve: in 1611 it imposed on the colonists what amounted to martial law. Company officials in Virginia organized the settlers into work gangs and severely punished the lazy and the disorderly. Still the company failed to turn a profit. And after 1617, skirmishes with the Indians became more brutal and frequent as rows of tobacco plants steadily invaded tribal lands.

Reform and a Boom in Tobacco

Desperate to salvage their investment, Virginia Company managers in 1618 set in place sweeping reforms. To attract more capital and colonists, the company established a "headright" system for granting land to individuals. Those already settled in the colony received 100 acres apiece. New settlers each received 50 acres, and anyone who paid the passage of other immigrants to Virginia—either family members or servants—received 50 acres per "head." The company also abolished martial law, allowing the planters to elect a representative assembly. Along with a governor and an advisory council appointed by the company, the House of Burgesses had the authority to make laws for the colony. It met for the first time in 1619, beginning what would become a strong tradition of representative government in the English colonies. *Key reforms*

The new measures met with immediate success. The free and unfree laborers who poured into Virginia during the 1620s made up the first wave of an English migration to the Chesapeake that numbered between 130,000 and 150,000 over the seventeenth century. Drawn from the ranks of ordinary English working people, the immigrants were largely men, outnumbering women by six to one. Most were young, ranging in age from 15 to 24. Because of their youth, most lacked skills or wealth.

Some of those who came to the Chesapeake as free immigrants prospered, lured by the chance to make a fortune in tobacco. During the 1620s Virginia's tobacco economy took off. As demand soared and prices peaked in European markets,

The Smokers, painted by Adriaen Brouwer, a seventeenth-century Dutch artist, suggests that the use of tobacco was both popular and disreputable. Native American peoples like the Costa Rican shown (right) had been cultivating and smoking tobacco long before the arrival of Europeans. He holds a pipe in his right hand.

colonists with an eye for profit planted every inch of their farms in tobacco and reaped windfalls. But for the vast majority of settlers—and, specifically, the three-quarters of all immigrants who arrived in the Chesapeake as indentured servants—the future was far grimmer.

Indentured servants   For most of the new servants, the crossing to Virginia was simply the last of many moves made in the hope of finding work. Although England's population had been rising since the middle of the fifteenth century, the demand for farm laborers was falling because many landowners were converting croplands into pastures for sheep. The search for work pushed young men and women out of their villages, sending them through the countryside and then into the cities. Down and out in London, Bristol, or Liverpool, some decided to make their next move across the Atlantic and signed indentures. Pamphlets promoting immigration promised abundant land and quick riches once servants had finished their terms of four to seven years.

Even the most skeptical immigrants were shocked at what they found. The death rate in Virginia during the 1620s was higher than that of England during times of epidemic disease. The life expectancy for Chesapeake men who reached the age of 20 was a mere 48 years; for women it was lower still. Servants fared worst of all, since malnutrition, overwork, and abuse made them vulnerable to disease. As masters scrambled to make quick profits, they extracted the maximum amount of work before death carried off their laborers. An estimated 40 percent of servants did not survive to the end of their indentured terms.

The expanding cultivation of tobacco also claimed many lives by putting un-   *War with the*
bearable pressure on Indian land. After Powhatan's death in 1617, leadership of the   *confederacy*
confederacy passed to Opechancanough, who watched, year after year, as the tobacco
mania grew. In March 1622 he coordinated a sweeping attack on white settlements
that killed about one-fifth of Virginia's white population. Swift English retaliation
wiped out whole tribes and cut down an entire generation of young Indian men.

News of the Indian war jolted English investors into determining the true state
of their Virginia venture. It came to light that, despite the tobacco boom, the Virginia
Company was plunging toward bankruptcy. Nor was that the worst news.
Stockholders discovered that over 3000 immigrants had not survived the brutal conditions of Chesapeake life. An investigation by James I brought out the grisly truth,
causing the king to dissolve the Virginia Company and take control of the colony himself in 1624. Henceforth Virginia would be governed as a royal colony.

Settling Down in the Chesapeake

During the 1630s and 1640s the fever of the tobacco boom broke, and a more settled
social and political life emerged in Virginia. The settlers who had become wealthy by
exploiting servant labor now began to acquire political power. They established local
bases of influence in Virginia's counties, serving as justices of the peace and sheriffs,
maintaining roads and bridges, collecting taxes, and supervising local elections. They
organized all able-bodied adult males into militias for local defense and sat on
vestries, the governing bodies of local Anglican parishes, hiring the handful of clergy
who came to Virginia and providing for the neighborhood poor.

The biggest tobacco planters of each county also dominated colony politics.
Even though King James had replaced the Virginia Company's government with his
own royal administration, the colony's elected assembly continued making laws for
the colony. Along with the council (the upper house of the legislature), the assembly
resisted interference in Virginia's affairs from the royal governor, the king's representative.

The colony's growing stability was reflected in improved conditions for less powerful Virginians. Although servants still streamed into the colony, the price of tobacco
leveled off. That meant planters were less likely to drive their servants to death in
search of overnight fortunes. As tobacco became less profitable, planters raised more
corn and cattle, and mortality rates declined as food supplies rose. Freed servants   *Decline in*
who survived their indentures usually worked a few more years as hired hands or ten-   *mortality*
ant farmers. In doing so, most managed to save enough money to buy their own land   *rates*
and become independent planters. For women who survived servitude, prospects
were even better. With wives at a premium, single women stood a good chance of improving their status by marriage. Even so, high mortality rates still fractured families:
one out of every four children born in the Chesapeake did not survive to maturity,
and among those children who reached their eighteenth birthday, one-third had lost
both parents to death.

By 1650 Virginia could boast about 15,000 inhabitants, although much of that increase resulted from servants and free immigrants arriving in the colony every year.
But Virginians looking to expand into more northerly bays of the Chesapeake found
their way blocked by a newer English colony.

The Founding of Maryland and the Renewal of Indian Wars

Proprietary colonies

Unlike Virginia, which was first settled by a private corporation and later converted into a royal colony, Maryland was founded by a single aristocratic family, the Calverts. Indeed, it was the first of several such "proprietary" colonies given by English monarchs to loyal followers. Thus in 1632, Maryland became the private preserve of the Calverts. They held absolute authority to dispose of 10 million acres of land, administer justice, and establish a civil government. All these powers they exercised, granting estates, or "manors," to their friends and dividing other holdings into smaller farms for ordinary immigrants. From all these "tenants"—that is, every settler in the colony—the Calverts collected "quitrents" every year, fees for use of the land. The Calverts appointed a governor and a council to oversee their own interests, while allowing the largest landowners to dispense local justice in manorial courts and make laws for the entire colony in a representative assembly.

Virginians liked nothing at all about Maryland. To begin with, the Calvert family was Catholic and had extended complete religious freedom to all Christians, making Maryland a haven for Catholics. Worse than that, the Marylanders were a source of economic competition. Two thousand inhabitants had settled on Calvert holdings by 1640, virtually all of them planting tobacco on land coveted by the Virginians.

Another obstacle to Virginia's expansion was the remnant of the Powhatan confederacy, still determined to repel white invaders. Opechancanough led a new generation of Indians into battle in 1644 against the encroaching Virginia planters. The hostilities inflicted as many casualties on both sides as the fighting did in 1622.

Changes in English Policy in the Chesapeake

Throughout the 1630s and 1640s colonial affairs drew little concern from royal officials. England itself had become engulfed first by a political crisis and then by a civil war.

The English Civil War

The conflict grew out of efforts by both James I and Charles I (who succeeded his father in 1625) to expand their royal power and rule the nation without the nuisance of having to consult Parliament. When Parliament condemned Charles for usurping its power to raise money, he simply dissolved that body in 1629. But when the Scots invaded England in 1639, Charles found he could raise funds to pay for an army only by calling Parliament back into session. By then, many of the merchants and landed gentlemen who were members were beginning to believe that the Stuart kings might be more trouble than they were worth. In 1642 Parliament and its Puritan allies squared off against Charles I and his royalist supporters, defeated them in battle, and, in 1649, beheaded the king. England became a republic ruled by Oliver Cromwell, the man who had led Parliament's army.

In truth, Cromwell's "republic" more accurately resembled a military dictatorship. After his death, most English were happy to see their throne restored in 1660 to Charles II, the son of the beheaded king. And the new king was determined to ensure that not only his subjects at home but also his American colonies abroad con-

Oliver Cromwell

COLONIES OF THE CHESAPEAKE
Settlements in Virginia and Maryland spread out along the many bays of the Chesapeake, where tobacco could easily be loaded from plantation wharves. The "fall line" on rivers, dividing Tidewater and Piedmont regions, determined the extent of commercial agriculture, since ships could not pick up exports beyond that point.

tributed to England's prosperity. His colonial policy was reflected in a series of regulations known as the Navigation Acts.

The first, passed by Parliament in 1660, gave England and English colonial merchants a monopoly on the shipping and marketing of all colonial goods. It also ordered that the colonies could export certain "enumerated commodities" only to

The Navigation Acts

England or other British ports. These goods included sugar, tobacco, cotton, ginger, and indigo (a blue dye). In 1663 Parliament added another regulation, giving British merchants a virtual monopoly on the sale of European manufactured goods to Americans by requiring that most imports going to the colonies had to pass through England. In 1673 a third Navigation Act placed duties on the coastal trade of the American colonies and provided for customs officials to collect tariffs and enforce commercial regulations.

Parliament later made minor modifications in the Navigation Acts, adding other exports such as rice to the category of enumerated commodities, prohibiting the colonies from exporting certain textiles or hats, and offering incentives to encourage colonists to produce indigo and iron. All these regulations were mercantilistic. That is, they were designed to ensure that England—and no foreign nations or their merchants—would profit from colonial production and trade.

CHESAPEAKE SOCIETY IN CRISIS

The regulations of trade put in place by Restoration kings Charles II and James II and their Parliaments had a decisive impact on colonials. Chesapeake planters chafed under the Navigation Acts. They were accustomed to conducting their affairs as they pleased—and they were often pleased to trade with the Dutch. What was worse, the new restrictions came at the same time as a downturn in tobacco prices. In the effort to consolidate its empire, England unintentionally worsened the economic and social difficulties of Chesapeake society.

The Conditions of Unrest

Diminishing opportunities

The Chesapeake colonies were heading for trouble partly because of their success. As inhabitants had started to live longer, more servants survived their terms of service. Once free, they set up as independent tobacco planters. More planters meant more production, and overproduction sent the price of tobacco plummeting, especially between 1660 and 1680. To maintain their advantage, the biggest planters bought up all the prime property along the coast, forcing newly freed servants to become tenants or to settle on unclaimed land in the interior. Either way, poorer men lost. Depending on bigger planters for land and credit made the small farmers vulnerable to debt. Moving to the frontier made them vulnerable to Indian attack.

The slim resources of small planters were stretched even thinner, not only from county taxes but also from export duties on tobacco paid under the Navigation Acts. During the hard times after 1660, many small planters fell deeply into debt, and some were forced back into servitude. By 1676 one-quarter of Virginia's free white men were landless. Many former servants were unable to gain a foothold even as tenants.

Diminishing opportunity in the 1660s and 1670s provided the tinder for unrest in Virginia. As the discontent of poor men mounted, so did the worries of big planters. The assembly of the colony lengthened terms of servitude, hoping to limit the number of servants entering the free population. It curbed the political rights of landless men, hoping to stifle opposition by depriving them of the vote. But these measures only set off a spate of mutinies among servants and protests over rising taxes among small planters.

Bacon's Rebellion and Coode's Rebellion

Those tensions came to a head in 1676 when civil war erupted. The immediate catalyst of the rebellion was renewed skirmishing between whites expanding westward and Indians. Virginia's royal governor, William Berkeley, favored building forts to contain the Indian threat, but frontier farmers opposed his plan as an expensive and ineffective way to defend their scattered plantations. As they clamored for an expedition to punish the Indians, Nathaniel Bacon stepped forward to lead it.

Wealthy and well connected, Bacon had arrived recently from England, expecting to receive every favor from the governor—including permission to trade with the Indians from his frontier plantation. But Berkeley and a few select friends already held a monopoly on the Indian trade. When they declined to include Bacon, he took up the cause of his poorer frontier neighbors against their common enemy, the governor. Other recent, well-to-do immigrants who resented being excluded from Berkeley's circle of power and patronage also joined Bacon. *Nathaniel Bacon*

In the summer of 1676 Bacon marched into Jamestown with a body of armed men and bullied the assembly into approving his expedition to kill Indians. While Bacon carried out that grisly business, slaughtering friendly as well as hostile tribes, Berkeley rallied his supporters and declared Bacon a rebel. Bacon retaliated by turning his forces against those led by the governor. Both sides sought allies by offering freedom to servants and slaves willing to join their ranks. Many were willing: for months the followers of Bacon and Berkeley plundered one another's plantations. In September 1676 Bacon reduced Jamestown itself to a mound of ashes. It was only his death from dysentery a month later that snuffed out the rebellion.

Political upheaval also shook Maryland, where colonists had long resented the sway of the Calvert family. As proprietors, the Calverts and their favorites monopolized political offices, just as Berkeley's circle had in Virginia. Well-to-do planters wanted a share of the Calverts' power. Smaller farmers, like those in Virginia, wanted a less expensive and more representative government. Compounding the tensions were religious differences: the Calverts and their friends were Catholic, but other colonists, including its most successful planters, were Protestant.

The unrest among Maryland's discontented planters peaked in July 1689. A former member of the assembly, John Coode, gathered an army, captured the proprietary governor, and then took grievances to authorities in England. There Coode received a sympathetic hearing. The Calverts' charter was revoked and not restored until 1715, by which time the family had become Protestant.

After 1690 rich planters in both Chesapeake colonies fought among themselves less and cooperated more. In Virginia older leaders and newer arrivals divided the spoils of political office. In Maryland Protestants and Catholics shared power and privilege. Those arrangements ensured that no future Bacon or Coode would mobilize restless gentlemen against the government. By acting together in legislative assemblies, the planter elite managed to curb the power of royal and proprietary governors for decades. *Growing stability*

But the greater unity among the Chesapeake's leading families did little to ease that region's most fundamental problem. That was the sharp inequality of white society. The gulf between rich and poor planters, which had been etched ever more deeply by the troubled tobacco economy, persisted long after the rebellions of Bacon and Coode. All that saved white society in the Chesapeake from renewed crisis and conflict was the growth of black slavery.

From Servitude to Slavery

Like the tobacco plants that spread across Powhatan's land, a labor system based on slavery had not figured in the first plans for the Chesapeake. Both early promoters and planters preferred buying English servants to importing alien African slaves. Black slaves, because they served for life, were more expensive than white workers, who served only for several years. Since neither white nor black emigrants lived long, cheaper servant labor was the logical choice. The black population of the Chesapeake remained small for most of the seventeenth century, comprising just 5 percent of all inhabitants in 1675.

The lives of servants and slaves   The first Africans landed in Virginia in 1619, brought by the Dutch, who dominated the slave trade until the middle of the eighteenth century. The lives of those newcomers resembled the lot of white servants, with whom they shared harsh work routines and living conditions. White and black bound laborers socialized with each other and formed sexual liaisons. They conspired to steal from their masters and ran away together, and if caught, they endured similar punishments. There was more common ground: many of the first black settlers did not arrive directly from Africa but came from the Caribbean, where some had learned English and adopted Christian beliefs. And not all were slaves: some were indentured servants, and a handful were free.

A number of changes after 1680 caused planters to invest more heavily in slaves than in servants. First, declining mortality rates in the Chesapeake made slaves the more profitable investment. Although slaves were more expensive than servants, planters could now expect to get many years of work from their bondspeople. Equally important, masters would have title to the children that slaves would now live long enough to have. At the same time, the influx of white servants was falling off just as the pool of available black labor was expanding. When the Royal African Company lost its monopoly on the English slave trade in 1698, other merchants entered the market. The number of Africans sold by British dealers swelled to 20,000 annually.

During the decades after 1680, more than 80 percent of black people imported as slaves came directly from Africa. Much of the trade was centered on the coast of Africa that Portuguese explorers had first probed, between the Senegal and Niger rivers. Seized by other Africans, captives were yoked together at the neck and marched hundreds of miles through the interior to the Atlantic shores of Senegambia, the Windward Coast, and the Gold Coast. Farther south, slaves were also taken from the agrarian societies of Angola.

Middle Passage   After the trauma of capture and the long trek to the ocean, there followed the horror of the Middle Passage, a journey of 5000 miles across the Atlantic to America. As many as 200 black men, women, and children were crowded onto each slave ship, but perhaps one out of every six did not live through the crossing. Shipmasters crammed their human cargo onto platforms built between the decks of their vessels,

THE AFRICAN TRANSATLANTIC SLAVE TRADE, 1450–1760
Toward the end of the seventeenth century, Chesapeake and Carolina planters began importing increasing numbers of slaves. In Africa, the center of that trade lay along a mountainous stretch of Africa known as the Gold Coast. Between 1450 and 1760 only about 4 percent of the total transatlantic slave trade went to North America. Brazil received the largest proportion of slaves, about 32 percent.

tiers spaced so low that sitting upright was impossible. Among white sailors and slaves alike, the death toll from disease was staggering.

When the numb, exhausted survivors of the Middle Passage reached American ports, they faced more challenges to staying alive. The first year in the colonies was the most deadly for new, unseasoned slaves. The sickle cell genetic trait gave black Africans a greater immunity than white Europeans had to malaria, but slaves were highly susceptible to respiratory infections. One-quarter of all Africans died during their first year in the Chesapeake, and among Carolina and Caribbean slaves, mortality rates were even higher. In addition to the new disease environment, Africans were forced to adapt to lives without freedom in a wholly unfamiliar country and culture.

A Changing Chesapeake Society

Exchanging a labor system based on servitude for one based on slavery transformed the character of Chesapeake society. Most obviously, the number of black Virginians rose sharply. By 1740, 40 percent of all Virginians were black, and most were African-born. Unlike black men and women who had arrived earlier, they had little familiarity with English language and culture. This larger, more distinctively African community was also locked into a slave system that was becoming ever more rigid and demeaning. By the late decades of the seventeenth century, laws were in place making it more difficult for masters to free slaves. Other legislation systematically separated the races by prohibiting free black settlers from owning white servants and outlawing interracial marriages and sexual relationships. The legal code encouraged white contempt for black Virginians in a variety of other ways. While masters were prohibited from whipping their white servants on the bare back, slaves had no such protection. And "any Negro that shall presume to strike any white" was to receive 30 lashes for that rash act.

Racism   The new laws both reflected and encouraged racism among white colonists of all classes. Deepening racial hatred, in turn, made it unlikely that poor white planters, tenants, and servants would ever join with poor black slaves to challenge the privilege of great planters. Instead of identifying with the plight of the slaves, the Chesapeake's poorer white residents considered black Virginians their natural inferiors. They could pride themselves on sharing with wealthy white gentlemen the same skin color and on being their equals in the eyes of the law.

Opportunities   The leaders of the Chesapeake colonies cultivated unity among white inhabi-
for white   tants by improving economic prospects for freed servants and lesser planters. The
settlers   Virginia assembly made provisions for freed servants to get a better start as independent farmers. It lowered taxes, allowing small planters to keep more of their earnings. New laws also gave most white male Virginians a vote in elections, allowing them an outlet to express their grievances. Economic trends toward the end of the seventeenth century contributed to the greater prosperity of small planters, as tobacco prices rose slightly and then stabilized. As a result of Bacon's savage campaign against the Virginia Indians, new land on the frontier became available. Even the domestic lives of ordinary people became more secure as mortality rates declined and the numbers of men and women in the white population evened out. As a result, virtually all men were now able to marry, and families were fragmented less often by the premature deaths of spouses and parents.

After 1700 the Chesapeake evolved into a more stable society. Gone were the bands of wild, landless, young bachelors one step ahead of the law, the small body of struggling lesser planters one step ahead of ruin, and the great mass of exploited servants one step away from rebellion. Virginia and Maryland became colonies of farming families, most of them small planters who owned between 50 and 200 acres. These families held no slaves, or at most two or three. And they accepted, usually without question, the social and political leadership of their acknowledged "superiors," great planters who styled themselves the "gentry."

The Chesapeake Gentry

The new Chesapeake gentry were the sons of well-to-do London merchant families, many of whom had intermarried with England's landed gentry. For both classes Virginia offered new prospects for land and commercial wealth. Enterprising fathers sent their sons to the Chesapeake between 1640 and 1670 to establish family interests in America by creating vast plantations. This new colonial generation of merchant-gentlemen did not plunge into the feverish gambling and exploitation practiced by the first planters along the Chesapeake. Instead, they and their coolly calculating descendants achieved status and power by shrewdly using their capital and influence and by skillfully managing their family estates.

The gentry's fortunes rested in part on the cultivation of tobacco on thousands of acres by hundreds of slaves. But the leading planters made even more money by marketing the tobacco of their humbler neighbors, selling them manufactured goods, supplying them with medical and legal services, lending money, and hiring out slaves. Unlike the rough-hewn barons of the early tobacco boom, the gentry did not owe their wealth to wringing work from poor whites. Instead they amassed great estates by wringing work from black slaves while converting their white "inferiors" into modestly prosperous small planters and paying clients.

The basis of gentry power

But the gentry wanted more than money: they wanted the respect of lesser whites. On election days, when all the voters in the county assembled, each ap-

George Booth, the son of a wealthy planter family in Gloucester County, Virginia, was being raised for mastery. The young man's self-assured stance, the bow and arrows, the dog at his feet clutching the kill, the classical busts of women flanking his figure, and his family estate in the distance all suggest the gentry's concern for controlling the natural and social worlds.

proached in his turn the gentleman candidate he preferred, publicly announced his vote, and sometimes made a brief, flattering speech about his choice. At militia musters, when every able-bodied man in the county over the age of 16 gathered, gentlemen officers led the military drills. On court days, defendants and plaintiffs testified before gentlemen justices of the peace, bedecked in wigs and robes and seated on raised benches. And every Sunday, when many in the county came to worship at the Anglican chapel, families filed soberly into the church in order of their social rank, with the gentlemen vestry heading the procession. The courthouse and church, the tavern and training field—all served as theaters in which the new Chesapeake gentry dramatized their superiority and lesser men deferred.

Stability in the Chesapeake

The plantation societies of Virginia and Maryland remained as unequal after 1700 as they had been a century earlier. Indeed, they were even more unequal because the rise of slavery sharpened economic distinctions within the white population. Those who owned slaves enjoyed a decided economic edge over those who did not. But while extreme economic inequality persisted, social tension between richer and poorer white settlers lessened. As racism unified all classes within white society and economic and political gains eased discontent among small planters, the changing character of the Chesapeake's leaders also reduced social friction. The unscrupulous scoundrels who once dominated society had been replaced by gentlemen-planters who fancied themselves the "fathers" of their plantations and neighborhoods.

FROM THE CARIBBEAN TO THE CAROLINAS

During the same decade that the English invaded Powhatan's land, they began to colonize the Caribbean. A century earlier, Columbus had charted the route: ships picked up the trade winds off Madeira and the Canary Islands and headed west across the Atlantic to paradise. At journey's end the surf broke over shores rimmed with white sand beaches that rose sharply to coral terraces, then to broad plateaus or mountain peaks shrouded in rain forests.

Transformation of the Caribbean

Paradise was lost to the Indians of the Caribbean, or at least to those few remaining alive. European diseases, combined with Spanish exploitation, had eliminated virtually all the natives of Hispaniola by the 1520s. Over the next century those living in Cuba, Puerto Rico, the Bahamas, the Lesser Antilles, and Jamaica would follow. And the "paradise" that remained was filled with plants and animals that would have been strange to natives only a century earlier. Hogs and cattle, now wild, had been imported by Europeans, as had figs, oranges, pomegranates, and African yams. That ecological migration of flora and fauna would continue to transform the Americas in the century to come.

Paradise was lost to the English as well. At first they came to the Caribbean intending not to colonize but to steal from the Spanish. Even after 1604 when some English settled on the islands, few intended to stay. Yet not only did the English establish permanent plantation colonies in the West Indies, their Caribbean settlements became the jumping-off points for a new colony on the North American mainland, South Carolina. Because of the strong West Indian influence, South Carolina

In 1650, when this map of Barbados was drawn, the sugar boom was only beginning. Most of the settlements lie on the leeward side of the island, away from the prevailing winds. The map's drawings indicate that already escaped slaves (upper left) were being hunted down in their mountain hideaways. Hogs (two are shown) ran wild everywhere on the island. They were an import from Europe that in a few short years had multiplied more rapidly than the humans who brought them.

developed a social order in some ways distinct from that of the Chesapeake. Yet in other ways, the development of the Carolinas paralleled Virginia and Maryland's path from violence, high mortality, and uncertainty toward relative stability.

Paradise Lost

The English had traded and battled with the Spanish in the Caribbean since the 1560s. From those island bases English buccaneers conducted an illegal trade with Spanish settlements, sacked the coastal towns, and plundered silver ships bound for Seville. Weakened by decades of warfare, Spain could not hold the West Indies. The Dutch drove a wedge into Caribbean trade routes, and the French and the English began to colonize the islands.

In the 40 years after 1604, some 30,000 immigrants from the British Isles planted crude frontier outposts on St. Kitts, Barbados, Nevis, Montserrat, and Antigua. The settlers—some free, many others indentured servants, and almost all young men—devoted themselves to working as little as possible, drinking as much as

FOOD/DRINK/DRUGS

A Taste for Sugar

It is said that shortly before his death in A.D. 735, the Venerable Bede, an English abbot, bequeathed a precious treasure to his brother monks. It consisted of a cache of spices, including a little stock of sugar. What separated Bede's world, where sugar was counted a costly luxury, from twentieth-century Americans' world of ever-present sweetness was the discovery of America and the establishment of plantation economies in the Caribbean and Brazil.

Europeans first learned of sugar during an earlier surge of expansion—the Arab conquests in the Mediterranean, North Africa, and Spain during the seventh and eighth centuries. From then until the fourteenth century, Europe's merchants imported small quantities of sugar at great expense from Arab plantations, as well as from distant Persia and India, countries that had produced sugar since A.D. 500.

Throughout the Middle Ages and the early modern era, only the royal and the rich of Europe could indulge their desire for sugar, and even those classes partook sparingly. Europeans classified sugar as a spice, like the equally scarce and exotic pepper, nutmeg, ginger, and saffron. Nobility valued sugar as a medicine for sore throats, stomach disorders, and infertility. It was also used as a remedy for the Black Death and tooth decay. The cooks of castle kitchens seasoned food and sauces with a pinch of sugar or sprinkled it on meat, fish, fowl, and fruit to preserve freshness—or to conceal rot. Only on great occasions did the confectioners of noble families splurge, fashioning for courtly feasts great baked sugar sculptures of knights and kings, horses and apes, called "subtleties."

For the rest of Europe, life was not as sweet. While the rich and royal savored sugary treats, the diets of ordinary people ran to monotonous, meager starches. The staff of everyday life consisted of bread, peas, beans, and, in good years, a little milk, butter, and cheese. The occasional pig slaughtered, rabbit trapped, or fish caught supplied stray protein for the poor.

That pattern of consumption started to change as Europeans turned to African slave labor to grow sugar for them. Madeira and the Canary Islands became more than stepping-stones across the Atlantic for Spain and Portugal. The sugar plantations established there were a foretaste of veritable sugar factories created in the Caribbean colonies of England and France.

By the sixteenth and seventeenth centuries, Europe's merchant classes could imitate elite patterns of eating by pouring sugar into pastries and puddings. And by the middle of the eighteenth century, an increasingly large and inexpensive supply from the Caribbean was making sugar essential to the poorest Europeans. Among England's laboring classes, another colonial import—Indian

possible, and returning to England as soon as possible. They cultivated for export a poor quality of tobacco, which returned just enough profit to maintain straggling settlements of small farms.

Caribbean sugar   Then, nearly overnight, sugar cultivation transformed the Caribbean. In the 1640s Barbados planters learned from the Dutch how to process sugarcane. The Dutch also supplied African slaves to work the cane fields and marketed the sugar for

The Sugar Mill.

Once harvested, sugarcane in the West Indies was crushed, as in this sugar mill. The juice was collected and channeled to the sugar works, where it was concentrated through boiling and evaporation. This neat diagrammatic picture belies the harsh conditions of labor and high mortality slaves experienced: sweetness came at a steep price.

tea, laced heavily with sugar—began to accompany an otherwise cold supper of bread. Sweet tea and bread comprised the entire diet of those at the bottom of English society.

Cheaper, warmer, and more stimulating than milk or beer (its prime competitors), sugared tea won the loyalty of England's mass market and ranked as the nonalcoholic beverage of national choice. By the nineteenth century, English working families were also combining sugar and starch by pouring treacle (molasses) over porridge and spreading jams or marmalades on their bread.

Europe and America affected each other in many ways, but diet figured among the more fundamental conditions of life altered by colonization. More than coffee, chocolate, rum, or tobacco—indeed, more than any of the other "drug foods" produced by the colonies except tea—sugar provided a major addition to the diet of the English and other Europeans.

Even though sugar changed gradually from a scarce, coveted luxury to a mass-marketed basic foodstuff, its association with power persisted. But by the eighteenth century, it was no longer the *consumption* of sugar that bestowed status. On the contrary, as sweeteners found their way into the barest cupboards, the rich and royal probably used less sugar than the poor and powerless. Instead, after 1700 it was the *production* of sugar that conferred power. Planters who grew it, merchants who shipped and sold it, industrialists who refined it, and politicians who taxed it discovered in sugar sources of profit and distinction less perishable than the subtleties of noble banquets or the legacy of the Venerable Bede.

high prices in the Netherlands. Sugar plantations and slave labor rapidly spread to other English and French islands as Europeans developed an insatiable sweet tooth for the once scarce commodity. Caribbean sugar made more money for England than the total volume of commodities exported by all the mainland American colonies.

Even though its great planters became the richest people in English America, they could not have confused the West Indies with paradise. Throughout the seventeenth century, disease took a fearful toll, and island populations grew only because of immigration. In the scramble for land, small farmers were pushed onto tiny plots that barely allowed them to survive.

Slavery in the Caribbean

The desperation of bound laborers posed another threat. After the Caribbean's conversion to cultivating sugar, black slaves gradually replaced white indentured servants in the cane fields. By the beginning of the eighteenth century, black inhabitants outnumbered white residents by four to one. Fear of servant mutinies and slave rebellions frayed the nerves of island masters. They tried to contain the danger by imposing harsh slave codes and inflicting brutal punishments on white and black laborers alike. But planters lived under a constant state of siege. One visitor to Barbados observed that whites fortified their homes with parapets from which they could pour scalding water on attacking servants and slaves. During the first century of settlement, seven major slave uprisings shook the English islands.

As more people, both white and black, squeezed onto the islands, some settlers looked for a way out. With all the land in use, the Caribbean no longer offered the opportunity to freed servants or even planters' sons. It was then that the West Indies started to shape the history of the American South.

The Founding of the Carolinas

The colonization of the Carolinas began with the schemes of Virginia's royal governor, William Berkeley, and Sir John Colleton, a supporter of Charles I who had been exiled to the Caribbean at the end of England's civil war. Colleton saw that the Caribbean had a surplus of white settlers, and Berkeley knew that Virginians needed room to expand as well. Together the two men set their sights on the area south of Virginia. Along with a number of other aristocrats, they convinced Charles II to make them joint proprietors in 1663 of a place they called the Carolinas, in honor of the king.

A few hardy souls from Virginia had already squatted around Albemarle Sound in the northern part of the Carolina grant. The proprietors provided them with a gover-

North Carolina

nor and a representative assembly. About 40 years later, in 1701, they set off North Carolina as a separate colony. The desolate region quickly proved a disappointment. Lacking good harbors and navigable rivers, the colony had no convenient way of marketing its produce. North Carolina remained a poor colony, its sparse population engaged in general farming and the production of masts, pitch, tar, and turpentine.

South Carolina

The southern portion of the Carolina grant held far more promise, especially in the eyes of one of its proprietors, Sir Anthony Ashley Cooper, earl of Shaftesbury. In 1669 he sponsored an expedition of a few hundred English and Barbadian immigrants, who planted the first permanent settlement in South Carolina. By 1680 the

---

THE CAROLINAS AND THE CARIBBEAN
The map underscores the geographic link between West Indian and Carolina settlements. Emigrants from Barbados dominated politics in early South Carolina, while Carolinians provided foodstuffs, grain, and cattle to the West Indies. As South Carolinians began growing rice, Caribbean slave ships found it an easy sail north and west to unload their cargoes in Charleston.

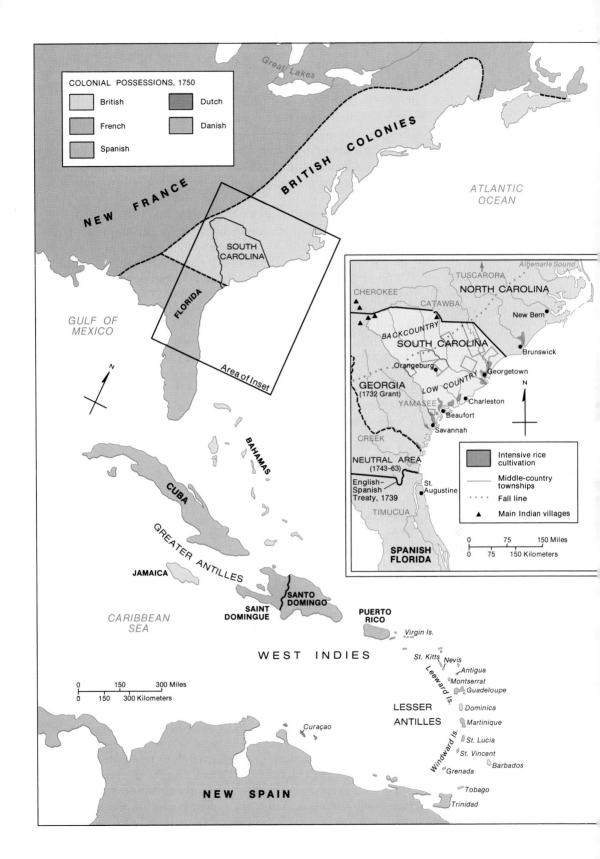

COLONIAL POSSESSIONS, 1750

British

French

Spanish

Dutch

Danish

Great Lakes

NEW FRANCE

BRITISH COLONIES

ATLANTIC
OCEAN

SOUTH
CAROLINA

FLORIDA

GULF OF
MEXICO

N

Area of Inset

Albemarle Sound

TUSCARORA

CHEROKEE

CATAWBA

NORTH CAROLINA

New Bern

BACKCOUNTRY

SOUTH CAROLINA

Brunswick

Orangeburg

Georgetown

GEORGIA
(1732 Grant)

LOW COUNTRY

YAMASEE

Charleston

Beaufort

CREEK

Savannah

NEUTRAL AREA
(1743–63)

English–
Spanish
Treaty, 1739

St.
Augustine

TIMUCUA

SPANISH
FLORIDA

N

Intensive rice
cultivation

Middle-country
townships

Fall line

Main Indian villages

0   75   150 Miles

0   75   150 Kilometers

BAHAMAS

CUBA

GREATER ANTILLES

JAMAICA

SANTO
DOMINGO

SAINT
DOMINGUE

PUERTO
RICO

Virgin Is.

CARIBBEAN
SEA

WEST INDIES

St. Kitts Nevis

Antigua

Montserrat

Guadeloupe

Leeward Is.

LESSER
ANTILLES

Dominica

Martinique

0   150   300 Miles

0   150   300 Kilometers

Curaçao

St. Lucia

St. Vincent

Windward Is.

Grenada

Barbados

Tobago

Trinidad

NEW SPAIN

colonists established the center of economic, social, and political life at the confluence of the Ashley and the Cooper rivers, naming the site Charles Town (later
Charleston) after the king.

Cooper had big plans for his Carolina colony. Charleston stood at the hub of a
network of river routes, allowing for easy development of the region's commercial potential. Since the proprietors were offering liberal land grants and had promised religious toleration and a representative government, settlers would flock to the colony.
These new inhabitants would enrich the proprietors by paying quitrents, a halfpenny
per acre annually.

Such plans were big enough to satisfy most of the Carolina proprietors, who regarded their venture simply as land speculation. But Cooper, like others before him,
hoped to create an ideal society in America. Cooper's utopia was one in which a few
landed aristocrats and gentlemen would rule with the consent of many smaller property holders. With his personal secretary, John Locke, Cooper drew up an intricate
The   scheme of government, the Fundamental Constitutions. The design provided
Fundamental Carolina with a proprietary governor and a hereditary nobility who, as a Council of
Constitutions Lords, would recommend all laws to a Parliament elected by lesser landowners.

The Fundamental Constitutions met the same fate as other lordly dreams for
America. Instead of peacefully observing its provisions, Carolinians plunged into the
political wrangling that had plagued Maryland's proprietary rule. Assemblies resisted
the sweeping powers granted to the proprietary governors. Ordinary settlers protested
against paying quitrents claimed by the proprietors. Political unrest in North Carolina
triggered three rebellions between 1677 and 1711. In South Carolina opposition to
the proprietors gathered strength more slowly but finally exploded with equal force.

Early Instability

Immigrants from Barbados, the most numerous among the early settlers, came
quickly to dominate South Carolina politics. Just as quickly, they objected to proprietary power. To offset the influence of the Barbadians, most of whom were Anglican,
the proprietors encouraged the migration of French Huguenots and English
Presbyterians and Baptists. The stream of newcomers only heightened tensions, split-
ting South Carolinians into two camps with competing political and religious loyalties.

Meanwhile, settlers spread out along the coastal plain. Searching for a profitable
export, the first colonists raised grains and cattle, foodstuffs that they exported to the
West Indies. South Carolinians also developed a large trade in deerskins with coastal
tribes like the Yamasee and the Creeks and Catawbas of the interior. More numerous
than the Indians of the Chesapeake and even more deeply divided, the Carolina
tribes competed to become the favored clients of white traders. Southeastern Indian
economies quickly became dependent on English guns, rum, and clothing. To repay
Indian slavery   their debts to white traders, Indians enslaved and sold to white buyers large numbers
of men, women, and children taken in wars waged against rival tribes.

Provisions, deerskins, and Indian slaves proved less profitable for South
Carolinians than rice, which became the colony's cash crop by the opening of the
eighteenth century. Constant demand for rice in Europe made South Carolina the
richest colony and South Carolina planters the richest people on the mainland of
North America.

Unfortunately, South Carolina's swampy coast, so perfectly suited to growing rice, was less suited for human habitation. Weakened by chronic malaria, settlers died in epic numbers from yellow fever, smallpox, and respiratory infections. The white population grew slowly, through immigration rather than natural increase, and numbered a mere 10,000 by 1730.

Early South Carolinians had little in common but the harsh conditions of frontier existence. Most colonists lived on isolated plantations; early deaths fragmented families and neighborhoods. Immigration after 1700 only intensified the colony's ethnic and religious diversity, adding Swiss and German Lutherans, Scots-Irish Presbyterians, Welsh Baptists, and Spanish Jews. The colony's only courts were in Charleston; churches and clergy of any denomination were scarce. On those rare occasions when early Carolinians came together, they gathered at Charleston to escape the pestilential air of their plantations, to sue each other for debt and to haggle over prices, or to fight over religious differences and proprietary politics.

White, Red, and Black: The Search for Order

By the opening decades of the eighteenth century, South Carolina seemed as strife-torn and unstable as the early Chesapeake colonies. In addition to internal tensions, external dangers threatened the very life of the Carolina settlements. The Spanish were rattling their sabers in Florida, the French filtering into the Gulf region, and pirates lurking along the North Carolina coast.

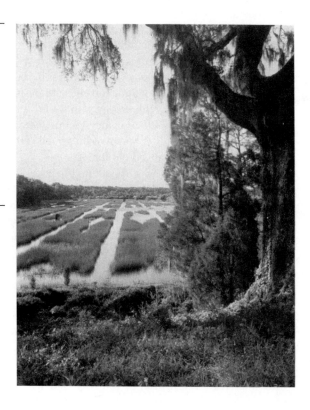

Mulberry Plantation in South Carolina was first carved from coastal swamps in 1714. This photograph from 1935 suggests the way that the landscape may have looked. Stands of live oak hung with Spanish moss ringed the paddy fields, where African slaves skilled in rice cultivation oversaw the difficult and arduous task of properly irrigating the crop.

Yamasee War

Most menacing were the Indians, and in 1715 they struck. The Yamasee of the coast allied themselves with the Creeks farther inland, launching a series of assaults that nearly pushed white Carolinians into the sea. All that saved the colony was an alliance with the Cherokee, another interior tribe who, in return for trading privileges, mounted a counterattack against their Indian rivals.

The end of proprietary rule

As colonists reeled from the Yamasee War, opposition mounted against the proprietors, who had done nothing to protect their vulnerable colony. Military expenses had also forced Carolinians to fall into greater debt, to pay higher taxes, and to struggle with an inflated currency that month by month was worth less. Even Presbyterians, Baptists, and Huguenots, who had once defended the proprietors, shifted their sympathies because they disapproved of more recent attempts to establish the Church of England as South Carolina's official religion. During the 1720s, mass meetings and riots so disrupted government that it all but ground to a halt. Finally, in 1729, the Crown formally established royal government; by 1730 economic recovery had done much to ease the strife. Even more important in bringing greater political stability, the white colonists of South Carolina came to realize that they must unite if they were to counter the Spanish in Florida and the French and their Indian allies to the southwest.

Slavery in South Carolina

The growing black population gave white Carolinians another reason to maintain a united front. During the first decades of settlement, frontier conditions and the scarcity of labor had forced masters to allow enslaved Africans greater freedom within bondage. White and black laborers shared chores on small farms. On stock-raising plantations, called "cowpens," black cowboys ranged freely over the countryside. Black contributions to the defense of the colony also reinforced racial interdependence and muted white domination. Whenever the Spanish, the French, or the Indians threatened, black Carolinians were enlisted in the militia.

White Carolinians depended on black labor even more after turning to rice as their cash crop. In fact, planters began to import slaves in larger numbers because of west African skill in rice cultivation. But whites harbored deepening fears of the black workers whose labor built planter fortunes. As early as 1708 black men and women had become a majority in the colony, and by 1730 they outnumbered white settlers by two to one. Like Caribbean planters, white Carolinians put into effect strict slave codes that converted their colony into an armed camp and snuffed out the freedoms that black settlers had enjoyed earlier.

The ever-present threat of revolt on the part of the black majority gave all white South Carolinians an incentive to cooperate, whatever their religion, politics, or ethnic background. To be sure, the colony's high death rates and cultural differences persisted, while local government and churches remained weak. Yet against all these odds, white South Carolinians prospered and political peace prevailed after 1730. Any course except harmony would have exacted too high a price.

The Founding of Georgia

After 1730 South Carolinians could take comfort not only from their new prosperity and new political harmony but also from the founding of a new colony on their southern border. South Carolinians liked Georgia a great deal more than the Virginians had liked Maryland, for the colony formed a defensive buffer between British North America and Spanish Florida.

The Yuchi were neighbors of one of Georgia's early settlements, and one of the newly emigrated German colonists painted this watercolor of a Yuchi celebration. Judging from the guns hanging at the back of the shelter, these Indians were already trading with white settlers in the area.

Enhancing the military security of South Carolina was only one reason for the founding of Georgia. More important to General James Oglethorpe and other idealistic English gentlemen was the aim of aiding the "worthy poor" by providing them with land, employment, and a new start. They envisioned a colony of hardworking small farmers who would produce silk and wine, sparing England the need to import those commodities. That dream seemed within reach when George II made Oglethorpe and his friends the trustees of the new colony in 1732, granting them a charter for 21 years. At the end of that time Georgia would revert to royal control. *James Oglethorpe*

The trustees did not, as legend has it, empty England's debtors' prisons to populate Georgia. They freed few debtors but recruited from every country in Europe paupers who seemed willing to work hard—and who professed Protestantism. They paid their passage and provided each with 50 acres of land, tools, and a year's worth of supplies. Settlers who could pay their own way were encouraged to come by granting them larger tracts of land. Much to the trustees' dismay, that generous offer was taken up not only by many hoped-for Protestants but also by several hundred Ashkenazim (German Jews) and Sephardim (Spanish and Portuguese Jews), who established a thriving community in early Savannah.

The trustees were determined to ensure that Georgia became a small farmers' utopia. Rather than selling land, the trustees gave it away, but none of the colony's settlers could own more than 500 acres. The trustees also outlawed slavery and hard liquor in order to cultivate habits of industry and sustain equality among whites. This design for a virtuous and egalitarian utopia was greeted with little enthusiasm by *Utopian designs*

Georgians. They pressed for a free market in land and argued that the colony could never prosper until the trustees revoked their ban on slavery. Since the trustees had provided for no elective assembly, settlers could express their discontent only by moving to South Carolina—which many did during the early decades.

As mounting opposition threatened to depopulate the colony, the trustees caved in. They revoked their restrictions on land, slavery, and liquor a few years before the king assumed control of the colony in 1752. Under royal control, Georgia continued to develop an ethnically and religiously diverse society, similar to that of South Carolina. Similarly, its economy was based on rice cultivation and the Indian trade.

Similarities among the plantation colonies

Although South Carolina and the English West Indies were both more opulent and more embattled societies than Virginia and Maryland, the plantation colonies stretching from the Chesapeake to the Caribbean had much in common. Everywhere planters depended on a single staple crop, which brought both wealth and political power to those commanding the most land and the most labor. Everywhere the biggest planters relied for their success on the very people whom they deeply feared—enslaved African Americans. Everywhere, that fear was reflected in the development of repressive slave codes and the spread of racism throughout all classes of white society.

THE SPANISH BORDERLANDS

When the English founded Jamestown, Spanish settlement in the present-day United States consisted of one feeble fort in southeastern Florida and a single outpost in New Mexico. Hoping both to intimidate privateers who preyed on silver ships and to assert their sovereign claim to the Americas, Spain had established St. Augustine on the Florida coast in 1565. But for decades the place remained a squalid garrison town of a few hundred soldiers and settlers beleaguered by hurricanes, pirates, and Indians. Meanwhile, the Spanish planted a straggling settlement under azure skies and spectacular mesas near present-day Santa Fe in 1598. Their fervent desire was to create colonies in the Southwest that would prove more richly profitable than even those in Central and South America.

St. Augustine and Santa Fe

Defending both outposts proved so great a drain on royal resources that the Spanish government considered abandoning its precarious footholds in North America. Only the pleas of Catholic missionaries, who hoped to convert the native peoples, persuaded the Crown to sustain its support. But even by 1700, St. Augustine could boast only about 1500 souls, a motley assortment of Spaniards, black slaves, and Hispanicized Indians. New Mexico's colonial population amounted to fewer than 3000 Spanish ranchers, soldiers, and clergy, scattered among the "haciendas" (cattle and sheep ranches), "presidios" (military garrisons), and Catholic missions along the Rio Grande river. There, the native Pueblo Indians numbered some 30,000.

Mission communities

Still, during these years the Catholic clergy remained active, creating mission communities designed to incorporate native tribes into colonial society. In New Mexico, Franciscan friars supervised Pueblo women (who traditionally built their people's adobe homes) in the construction of over 30 missions. By 1675 in Florida, perhaps 10,000 Indians were living in 35 Indian villages where the friars came to stay. Although the new churches were built with native materials, their rectangular forms

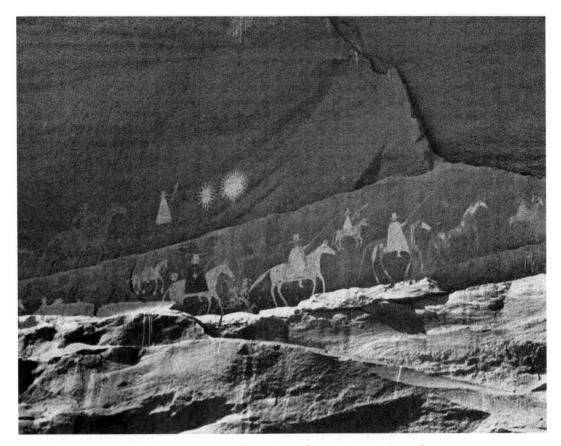

This Native American drawing on a canyon wall in present-day Arizona represents the progress of the Spanish into the Southwest. The prominence of horses underscores their novelty to the Indians, an initial advantage enjoyed by the invaders. "The most essential thing in new lands is horses," one of Coronado's men emphasized. "They instill the greatest fear in the enemy and make the Indians respect the leaders of the army." Many Indian peoples soon put the horse to their own uses, however, and even outshone the Spanish in their riding skills.

contrasted sharply with the circular public halls preferred by the Indians of both New Mexico and Florida. Like the curves of a circle interrupted by the right angles of a square, Spanish and Indian cultures coexisted uneasily.

Unlike the English, the Spanish projected a place in their colonies for the Indians. Homes, workshops, granaries, and stables clustered around the church. The missionaries taught Indians European agricultural techniques and crafts. At mission schools, adults as well as children learned to say prayers, sing Christian hymns, and speak Spanish. In 1675, when the Bishop of Cuba toured Florida's missions, he spoke enthusiastically of converts who embraced "with devotion the mysteries of our holy faith."

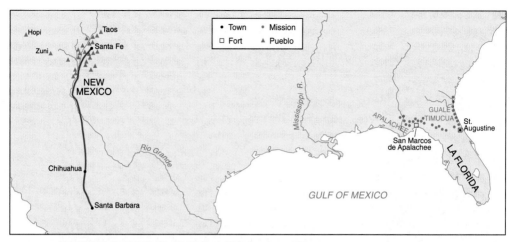

SPANISH MISSIONS IN NORTH AMERICA, CA. 1675
From St. Augustine, Spanish missionaries spread north into Guale Indian villages in present-day Georgia and westward among the Indians of Timacua, Apalachee, and Apalachicola. In New Mexico, missions radiated outward from the Rio Grande, as distant as Hopi Pueblo in the west.

The Indians were selective, however, in the European "mysteries" they chose to adopt. Some natives regarded the friars' presence simply as a means of protecting themselves against the harsher treatment of Spanish soldiers and ranchers. Other Indians used the Spanish presence to give them the upper hand in dealing with rival tribes, just as Powhatan had used white Virginians to further his own designs. And in their religious ceremonies, many natives simply placed Jesus, Mary, and Christian saints beside the other mythological deities they honored. They continued their own religious devotions, much to the frustration of the friars.

Indian and Spanish cultures bumped up against each other in material ways as well. When the Spanish at St. Augustine found the climate unsuitable for growing wheat, olives, and grapes, they turned to Indian maize, beans, and squash. Indians adopted domesticated animals from Europe—horses, cattle, sheep, mules, and donkeys. Watermelons and peach trees, brought to the Atlantic coast by the Spanish, spread quickly along Indian trade routes, often ahead of Europeans themselves.

To their dismay, Indians discovered that in the long run, becoming "civilized" usually meant learning to work for Spanish masters as docile servants. The labor was harsh enough to send many to an early death. European diseases, too, took a gruesome toll among mission Indians. As the population dropped sharply, the demand by Spanish colonists rose for increasingly scarce Indian labor. In theory, Spanish laws protected Indians from ruthless exploitation, but soldiers and settlers illegally forced natives to tend herds, till their fields, and haul heavy loads. In New Mexico, captured Indians were sent south to be sold as slaves in the mines of New Spain.

Indian resistance   As the abuses increased, so did the resentment. Indians regularly fled the mission settlements; others made life miserable for their "benefactors." One padre at

Taos Pueblo was served corn tortillas laced with urine and mouse meat. From beyond Spanish lines, the Apache used the horses introduced from Europe to rustle Spanish cattle. On occasion discontent and anger ignited major insurrections. The most successful was the Pueblo Revolt of 1680, which drove the Spanish out of New Mexico for more than a decade. Popé, an Indian spiritual leader in Taos, coordinated an uprising of several Pueblo tribes that vented the full force of their hatred of Spanish rule. They killed 400 people in outlying haciendas, burned their Spanish-style houses and churches to the ground, and even exterminated the livestock introduced by the Spanish. The attack wiped out one-fifth of the Spanish population of 2500 and sent survivors scurrying for refuge down Dead Man's Road to El Paso, Texas.

Despite native opposition, the Spanish persisted, especially as they saw their European rivals making headway in North America. By the end of the seventeenth century, English settlements in South Carolina were well entrenched. Closer by, the French built forts near the mouth of the Mississippi River, signaling their own designs on the Gulf of Mexico. As a counterweight the Spanish added a second military outpost in Florida, at Pensacola, and founded several missions in present-day Texas. And after 1769, to secure their claims to the Pacific coast from England and Russia, Spanish soldiers and missionaries began colonizing California. Led by the Franciscan friar Junípero Serra, they established 20 communities along the Pacific coastal plain.

COUNTERPOINT

Beyond the Black Legend

For many centuries, the Black Legend shaped the accounts of Spanish colonization written by most English and American chroniclers. This was the conviction that Spaniards were uniquely deplorable colonizers—greedy and corrupt, cruel and treacherous, fanatical and tyrannical—an opinion that had first taken hold during the sixteenth century in an England envious of imperial Spain's new power and wealth. But late in the nineteenth century, American historians rejected this interpretation— indeed, they embraced its opposite—a strongly pro-Spanish view of the New World's Hispanic past that celebrated the valor of explorers, the dedication of missionaries, the achievements of government officials. That challenge to the Black Legend performed the invaluable service of reminding people in the United States that besides the familiar cast of colonizers among the English, French, and Dutch, the Spanish had also made crucial contributions to their heritage. But it was also a perspective that romanticized Spanish colonialism, all too readily overlooking the toll taken on Native Americans by colonization.

This emphasis on Spain's "frontiering genius" dominated histories of the American Southwest until the 1960s. But thereafter, a new generation of scholars, many of them Chicanos, drew attention to the fact that most inhabitants of the Spanish Southwest were "mestizos" or Mexican. In their view, it is important to recover the story of colonization as it was experienced by native peoples as well as Spaniards and to recognize that whatever "triumphs" Spain achieved often came at a terrible cost to the Indians. Telling that more complicated story of how cultures cooperated and contended with one another on the borderlands of Spain's empire does not mean reviving the Black Legend. But it is a call for recounting the history of the early Southwest fully, from both sides, an effort that will yield a richer understanding of what was gained and what was lost on this historic American frontier.

Empire ... utopia ... independence. ... For more than a century after the founding of Jamestown in 1607, those dreams inspired the inhabitants of the Chesapeake, the Carolinas and Georgia, the Caribbean, and the Spanish borderlands. The regions served as staging grounds where kings and commoners, free and unfree, men and women, red, white, and black played out their hopes. Most met only disappointment and many met disaster in the painful decades before the new colonies achieved a measure of stability.

The dream of an expanding empire faltered for the Spanish, who found no new El Dorado in the Southwest. The dream of empire failed, too, when James I and Charles I, England's early Stuart kings, found their power checked by Parliament. And the dream foundered fatally for Powhatan's successors, who were unable to resist both white diseases and land-hungry tobacco planters.

English lords had dreamed of establishing feudal utopias in America. But proprietors like the Calvert family in Maryland and Cooper in the Carolinas found themselves hounded by frontier planters and farmers who sought economic and political power. Georgia's trustees struggled in vain to nurture their dream of a utopia for the poor. The dream of a Spanish Catholic utopia brought by missionaries to the American Southwest dimmed with Indian resistance.

The dream of independence proved the most deceptive of all, especially for the inhabitants of England's colonies. Just a bare majority of the white servant immigrants to the Chesapeake survived to enjoy freedom. The rest were struck down by disease or worn down at the hands of tobacco barons eager for profit. Not only in the Chesapeake but also in the Caribbean and the Carolinas, real independence eluded the English planters. Poorer people were dependent on richer people for land and leadership—deferred to them at church and on election days and depended on them to buy crops or to extend credit. Even the richest planters depended on the English and Scottish merchants who supplied them with credit and marketed their crops, as well as on the English officials who made colonial policy.

And everywhere in the American South and Southwest, white people's lingering dreams were realized only through the labor of the least free members of colonial America. In the Southwest the Spanish made servants of the Indians. Along the southern Atlantic coast and in the Caribbean, English plantation owners (like the Spanish before them) turned for labor to the African slave trade. Only after slavery became firmly established as a social and legal institution did England's southern colonies begin to settle down and grow: during the late seventeenth century for the Chesapeake region and the early eighteenth for the Carolinas. That stubborn reality would haunt Americans of all colors who continued to dream of freedom and independence.

CHAPTER SUMMARY

While the English established their outpost on the Chesapeake with a set of goals in mind, native peoples were also intent upon pursuing their own aims. Although he considered the English a nuisance, the Indian leader Powhatan made use of their numbers and weapons to strengthen his power. But after Powhatan's death and the beginning of the tobacco boom, the Virginia Company transported an increasing number of white settlers into Virginia—some of them free men and women but the vast majority indentured servants. Mounting tensions finally exploded in 1622 into a full-scale war between whites and Indians. When an investigation of the colony after the fighting uncovered high death rates from disease and the abuse of servants, the king dissolved the Virginia Company and converted Virginia into a royal colony.

As the price of tobacco leveled off, a more coherent society took shape in Virginia. Even so, tensions swelled in the 1660s because of rivalries among leading men, diminishing opportunity for freed servants and small planters, religious hatreds, and a renewal of hostilities with the Indians. Civil war erupted—Bacon's Rebellion in Virginia and Coode's Rebellion in Maryland. What finally eased the divisions within white society in the Chesapeake was the conversion from servitude to slavery as the region's dominant labor system. The growing black presence dictated greater unity among whites of all classes and religions, and a racist consensus emerged. Their profits now secured by exploiting black rather than white labor, a new Chesapeake "gentry" encouraged the development of a prosperous small planter class.

As the tobacco economy evolved in the seventeenth-century Chesapeake, a booming sugar economy also transformed the Caribbean into a slave-based plantation society. Land scarcity on the English island of Barbados led to the settlement of South Carolina, another proprietary colony. More prosperous than North Carolina or Virginia, South Carolina still suffered from political factionalism and social instability, the result of ethnic and religious diversity, high mortality rates, and strained relations with local Indian tribes. Reorganized as a royal colony after 1729, South Carolina recovered its former prosperity, based on the export of rice. Greater social and political harmony resulted from whites recognizing the need to unify against the threat posed by their colony's black majority of slaves. Georgia, a colony that developed a similar economy, also brought stability by serving as a buffer between South Carolinians and Spanish Florida. As the English colonies in southern North America took shape, the Spanish extended their empire in both Florida and New Mexico, establishing military garrisons, missions, and cattle ranches. Like the English in the Chesapeake and the Carolinas, the Spanish met with sustained Indian resistance.

ADDITIONAL READING

The best treatment of early Virginia is Edmund S. Morgan, *American Slavery, American Freedom* (1975). A more intimate portrait of an early Virginia community can be found in Darrett and Anita Rutman's study of Middlesex County, *A Place in Time* (1984). Karen Kupperman offers an excellent overview of relations between whites and Indians not only in the early South but throughout North America in *Settling with the Indians* (1980), while James Merrell sensitively explores the impact of white contact on a single southern tribe in *The Indians' New World* (1989). Two other notable treatments of slavery and race relations in Britain's southern colonies are Richard Dunn's study of the Caribbean, *Sugar and Slaves* (1972), and Peter Wood's work on South Carolina, *Black Majority* (1974). And for the Spanish borderlands, see David J. Weber, *The Spanish Frontier in North America* (1992).

The Chesapeake has always drawn more notice from early American historians than South Carolina has, but in recent years some important studies have redressed that neglect. The best overview of that colony's development remains Robert Weir, *Colonial South Carolina* (1982); for fine explorations of more specialized topics, see Daniel C. Littlefield, *Rice and Slaves* (1981), Peter Colclanis, *The Shadow of a Dream* (1989), and Timothy Silver, *A New Face on the Countryside* (1990). For a fuller list of readings, see the Bibliography.

SIGNIFICANT EVENTS

late 1500s	Formation of Powhatan's confederacy
1603	James I becomes king of England; beginning of Stuart dynasty
1604	First English settlements in the Caribbean
1607	English settle Jamestown
1610	Founding of Santa Fe
1619	First Africans arrive in Virginia
1620s	Tobacco boom in Virginia
1622	White–Indian warfare in Virginia
1624	Virginia becomes a royal colony
1625	Charles I becomes king of England
1632	Calvert founds Maryland
1640s	Sugar boom begins in the Caribbean
1660	Parliament passes the first of the Navigation Acts
1669	First permanent settlement in South Carolina
1676	Bacon's Rebellion in Virginia
1680	Pueblo Revolt in New Mexico
1689	Coode's Rebellion in Maryland
ca. 1700	Rice boom begins in South Carolina
1715	Yamasee uprising in South Carolina
1732	Chartering of Georgia

3

The First Century of Settlement in the Colonial North

hey came to her one night while she slept. Into her dreams drifted a small island, and on the island were tall trees and living creatures, one of them wearing the fur of a white rabbit. When she told of her vision, no one took her seriously, not even the wise men among her people, shamans and conjurers whose business it was to interpret dreams. No one, that is, until two days later, when the island appeared to all, floating toward shore. On the island, as she had seen, were tall trees, and on their branches—bears. Or creatures that looked so much like bears that the men grabbed their weapons and raced to the beach, eager for the good hunt sent by the gods. They were disappointed. The island was not an island at all but a strange wooden ship planted with the trunks of trees. And the bears were not bears at all but a strange sort of men whose bodies were covered with hair. Strangest among them, as she had somehow known, was a man dressed all in white. He commanded great respect among the bearlike men as their "shaman," or priest.

In that way, foretold by the dreams of a young woman, the Micmac Indians in 1869 recounted their tribe's first meeting with whites more than two centuries earlier. Uncannily, the traditions of other northern tribes record similar dreams predicting the European arrival: "large canoes with great white wings like those of a giant bird," filled with pale bearded men bearing "long black tubes." Perhaps the dreamers gave shape in their sleep to stories heard from other tribes who had actually seen white strangers and ships. Or perhaps, long before they ever encountered Europeans, these Indians imagined them, just as Europeans fantasized about a new world. The first whites seen by those tribes might have been English or Dutch. But probably, like the party met by the Micmacs, they were French, the most avid early adventurers in the northern reaches of the Americas.

Cartier and Champlain
For the time being, few French had dreams of their own about settling in the Americas. Jacques Cartier looked for a Northwest Passage to Asia in 1535 and instead discovered the St. Lawrence River. But not until 1605 did the French plant a permanent colony, at Port Royal in Acadia (Nova Scotia). Three years later, Samuel de Champlain shifted French interests to the St. Lawrence valley, where he founded Quebec. His plan was to follow the network of rivers and lakes leading from Quebec into the interior, exploring the continent for furs and a passage to the Pacific.

Over the next several decades the handful of soldiers, traders, and missionaries

John Foxe's Actes and Monuments *(1563), a book revered by the Puritan founders of New England, arrayed the forces of righteousness (left side of the page) against a host of devils, priests, and their sheeplike followers within the Church of England at right.*

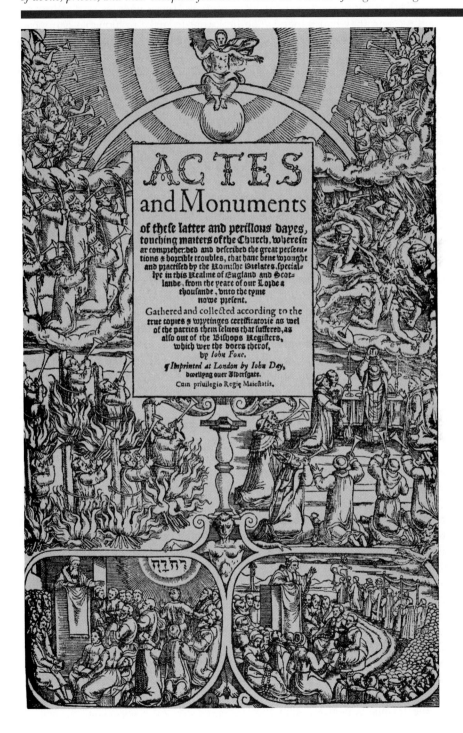

who came to New France established friendly relations with tribes of expert fishers and hunters. There were the Algonquin and Montagnais of the St. Lawrence valley; and in the fertile meadows and rich forests around Georgian Bay there was Huronia, a nation 25,000 strong. In return for French goods, these peoples traded beaver, otter, and raccoon they had trapped. The furs went to make fashionable European hats, while mink and marten were sent to adorn the robes of high-ranking European officials and churchmen. The French had a name for what New France had become by 1630—a *comptoir,* a storehouse for the skins of dead animals, not a proper colony.

That began to change when other French with their own dreams took responsibility for Canada. Louis XIII and his chief minister, Cardinal Richelieu, hoped that American wealth might be the making of France and its monarchs. In the 1630s they granted large tracts of land and a trading monopoly to a group of private investors, the Company of the Hundred Associates. The Associates brought a few thousand French farmers across the Atlantic and scattered them over 200 miles of company lands along the St. Lawrence.

Religious zeal, as much as the hope of profit, spurred France's renewed interest in colonization. Throughout Europe the Catholic church was enjoying a revival of religious piety as a result of the Counterreformation, an effort to correct those abuses that had prompted the Protestant Reformation. To reclaim members lost to Protestantism, the Counterreformation also launched an aggressive campaign of repression in Europe and missionary work abroad. In France the Catholic majority persecuted Protestant Huguenots and targeted Canada as a field for harvesting Indian converts.

The Jesuits   The shock troops of these missions, not only in the Americas but also in India and Japan, were the Jesuits, members of the Society of Jesus. With Richelieu's encouragement Jesuit missionaries streamed into Canada to assist other French settlers in bringing the Indians the "right" kind of Christianity. At first, it seemed unlikely that the Jesuits would shake the Indians' strong belief in the superiority of their own cultures. In Indian eyes these spiritual soldiers were a joke—men encumbered by their effeminate robes, deformed by their "very ugly" beards, and forbidden physical pleasure by their vow of celibacy. The Jesuits were also a nuisance. Not content to preach at French settlements and Indian villages, they undertook "flying" missions to the nomadic tribes, tagging along with Indian trappers. Once in the wilderness the Jesuits were a disaster—tangling in their snowshoes as they tried to surmount wintry drifts, trying for a first and last time to stand in canoes, refusing to carry any weapons, and sponging off the Indians for food and shelter.

Some Indians gradually formed a better opinion of the French and their priests. French traders, known as *coureurs du bois,* and their soldiers often adopted the native way of life and married Indian women. More to the point, the French were still relatively few. Interested primarily in trade, they had no designs on Indian land. The Jesuits, too, won acceptance among some tribes. Their lack of interest in Indian land, furs, and women made them a novelty among white men, while their greater immunity to the diseases that killed many Indians confirmed their claims to superior power. And once the Jesuits got the hang of native tongues, they showed a talent for smooth talk that the Indians, who prized oratory, greatly admired.

Jesuit persistence slowly paid off. Christian factions formed in many tribes, especially those in which shamans or important families embraced the new religion. Part of the Jesuits' appeal was that they accepted and even appreciated much of

Converts of the French Jesuits, these women of the Caughnawaga tribe (right) are kneeling before a statue of the Virgin Mary, taking vows of celibacy. One cuts her hair, a symbol of banishing pride, in imitation of the practice of Catholic nuns like Marguerite Bourgeoys (left), who founded a religious community dedicated to the education of young girls. Women, as well as men, in religious orders dedicated their lives to missionary work in Canada.

Indian culture. The Jesuits never wavered in their zeal to replace Indian religions with Catholicism, but they did not try to transform the Indians into French men and women. If the natives chose to become Catholics in their religion, while retaining the rest of their culture, it was all to the good—a good deal better than their becoming English and Protestant.

Throughout the seventeenth century, the French in North America remained relatively few. Instead, it was English Protestants who established the most populous settlements along the north Atlantic coast, challenging Indian dreams with religious visions of their own. Just as Jesuit crusaders of the Counterreformation shaped the culture of New France, so the zealous followers of John Calvin left their unmistakable imprint on New England.

THE FOUNDING OF NEW ENGLAND

The English regarded the northern part of North America as a place in which only the mad French could see possibility. English fisherfolk who strayed from Newfoundland to the coast of Acadia and New England carried home descriptions of the long, lonely coast, rockbound and rugged. Long winters of numbing cold melted into short summers of steamy heat. There were no minerals to mine, no crops suitable for export, no large native population available for enslaving. The Chesapeake, with its temperate climate and long growing season, seemed a much likelier spot.

But by 1620, worsening conditions at home instilled in some English men and women the mixture of desperation and idealism needed to settle an uninviting, unknown world. Religious differences among English Protestants became a matter of sharper controversy during the seventeenth century. Along with the religious crisis came mounting political tensions and continuing problems of unemployment and recession. Times were bad—so bad that the anticipation of worse times to come swept men and women to the shores of New England.

The Puritan Movement

The settlement of New England started with a king who chose his enemies unwisely. James I, shortly after succeeding Elizabeth I in 1603, vowed to purge England of all radical Protestant reformers. The radicals James had in mind were the Puritans, most

Presbyterians and Congregationalists

of whom were either Presbyterians or Congregationalists. Although both groups of Puritan reformers embraced Calvin's ideas, they differed on the best form of church organization. Individual Presbyterian churches (or congregations) were guided by higher governing bodies of ministers and laypersons. Congregationalists, on the other hand, believed that each congregation should conduct its own affairs independently, answering to no other authority.

King James angered not only the Puritans but also members of Parliament, who objected to his attempts to levy taxes without their consent. The hostility of both Parliament and the Puritans did not bode well for James's reign. In Parliament he faced influential landowners and merchants who were convinced that law was on their side. And in the Puritans he faced determined zealots who were convinced that God was on their side.

Predestination

Like all Christians, Protestant and Catholic, the Puritans believed that God was all-knowing and all-powerful. And like all Calvinists, the Puritans emphasized that idea of divine sovereignty known as predestination. At the center of their thinking was the belief that God had ordained the outcome of history, including the eternal fate of every human being. The Puritans found comfort in their belief in predestination because it provided their lives with meaning and purpose. They felt assured that a sovereign God was directing the fate of individuals, nations, and all of creation. The Puritans strove to play their parts in that divine drama of history and to discover in their performances some signs of personal salvation.

The divine plan, as the Puritans understood it, called for reforming both church and society along the lines laid down by John Calvin. It seemed to the Puritans that England's government hampered rather than promoted religious purity and social order. It tolerated drunkenness, theatergoing, gambling, extravagance, public swearing, and Sabbath breaking. It permitted popular recreations rooted in pagan custom and superstition—sports like bear baiting and maypole dancing and festivals like the celebration of Christmas and saints' days.

Puritan calls for reform

What was worse, the state had not done enough to purify the English church of the "corruptions" of Roman Catholicism. The Church of England counted as its members everyone in the nation, saint and sinner alike. To the Puritans, belonging to a church was no birthright. They wished to limit membership and the privileges of baptism and communion to godly men and women. The Puritans also deplored the hierarchy of bishops and archbishops in the Church of England, as well as its elaborate ceremonies in which priests wore ornate vestments. Too many Anglican clergy were "dumb dogges" in Puritan eyes, too poorly educated to instruct churchgoers in the truths of Scripture or to deliver a decent sermon. In Foxe's vision of good and evil (page 77), Anglican priests on the right side of the drawing are shown in vestments and headdresses worshiping Satan before an altar. Worshipers (bottom right) superstitiously count rosary beads and follow a priestly precession like so many dumb sheep. In contrast, Puritan worshipers (bottom left) conspicuously hold their Bibles and attend only to the word of God.

Because English monarchs had refused to take stronger measures to reform church and society, the Puritans became their outspoken critics. Elizabeth I had tolerated this opposition, but James I would not endure it and intended to rid England of these radicals. With some of the Puritans, known as the Separatists, he seemed to succeed.

The Pilgrim Settlement at Plymouth Colony

The Separatists were Congregationalists who concluded that the Church of England was too corrupt to be reformed. They abandoned Anglican worship and met secretly in small congregations. From their first appearance in England during the 1570s, the Separatists suffered persecution from the government—fines, imprisonment, and in a few cases, execution. Always a tiny minority within the Puritan movement, the Separatists were people from humble backgrounds: craftworkers and farmers without the influence to challenge the state. By 1608 some had become so discouraged that they migrated to Holland, where the Dutch government permitted complete freedom of religion. But when their children began to adopt Dutch customs and other religions, some Separatists decided to move again, this time to Virginia.

It can only be imagined what fate would have befallen the unworldly Separatists if they had actually settled in the Chesapeake during the tobacco boom. But a series of mistakes—including an error in charting the course of their ship, the *Mayflower*—landed the little band in New England instead. In November 1620, some 88 Separatist "Pilgrims" set anchor at a place they called Plymouth on the coast of present-day southeastern Massachusetts. They were sick with scurvy, weak from malnutrition, and shaken by a shipboard mutiny, and neither the site nor the season invited settlement. As one of their leaders, William Bradford, later remembered:

Early difficulties

> For summer being done, all things stand upon them with a weatherbeaten face, and the whole country, full of woods and thickets represented a savage hue. If they looked behind them, there was the mighty ocean which they had passed and was now as a main bar and gulf to separate them from all the civil parts of the world.

For some, the shock was too great. Dorothy Bradford, William's wife, is said to have fallen overboard from the *Mayflower* as it lay anchored off Plymouth. It is more likely that she jumped to her death.

Few Pilgrims could have foreseen founding the first permanent white settlement in New England, and many did not live long enough to enjoy the distinction.

They had arrived too late to plant crops, and the colonists had failed to bring an adequate supply of food. By the spring of 1621, half of the immigrants had died. English merchants who had financed the *Mayflower* voyage failed to send supplies to the struggling colony.

EARLY NEW ENGLAND

Despite some variety among emigrants to New England, the region remained relatively homogeneous and stable, with everyday life centered in small towns like Sudbury (located to the west of Boston). Most families lived close to one another in houses clustered around the meetinghouse, in contrast to the decentralized plantations of the South. The privately held farm lots were mixed together as well, so that neighbors worked and lived in close contact with one another.

Plymouth might have become another doomed colony if the Pilgrims had not received better treatment from native inhabitants than they did from their English backers. Samoset and Squanto, two Indians who had learned to speak English from visiting fishermen, introduced the settlers to native strains of corn. They also arranged a treaty between the Pilgrims and the region's main tribe, the Wampanoags.

The Pilgrims also set up a government for their colony, the framework of which was the Mayflower Compact. That agreement provided for a governor and several assistants to advise him, all to be elected annually by Plymouth's adult males. In the eyes of English law, the Plymouth settlers had no clear basis for their land claims or their government, for they had neither a royal charter nor approval from the Crown. But English authorities, distracted by problems closer to home, left the tiny colony of farmers alone.

The Mayflower Compact

The Puritan Settlement at Massachusetts Bay

Among the Crown's distractions were two groups of Puritans more numerous and influential than the gentle Pilgrims. They included both the Presbyterians and the majority of Congregationalists who, unlike the Pilgrim Separatists, still considered the Church of England capable of being reformed. But the 1620s brought these Puritans only fresh discouragements. In 1625 Charles I inherited his father's throne and all his enemies. When Parliament attempted to limit the king's power, Charles simply dissolved it in 1629 and proceeded to rule without it. When Puritans pressed for reform, he supported a host of measures proposed by his archbishop, William Laud, for purging England's parishes of ministers with Puritan leanings.

Charles I clashes with Puritans

This persecution swelled a second wave of Puritan migration that also drew from the ranks of Congregationalists. Unlike the humble Separatists, these emigrants included merchants, landed gentlemen, and lawyers who organized the Massachusetts Bay Company in 1629. Those able Puritan leaders aimed to build a better society in America, an example to the rest of the world. Unlike the Separatists, they had a strong sense of mission and destiny. They were not abandoning the English church, they insisted, but merely regrouping for another assault on corruption from across the Atlantic. They began organizing a mass migration to Massachusetts Bay that had the efficiency of a military maneuver and the martial spirit of a crusade. One of the immigrants, Edward Johnson, described his fellows as "Soldiers of Jesus Christ," who "for England's sake . . . are going from England to pray without ceasing for England."

Despite the company's Puritan leanings, it somehow obtained a royal charter confirming its title to most of present-day Massachusetts and New Hampshire. Advance parties in 1629 established the town of Salem on the coast well north of Plymouth. In 1630 the company's first governor, John Winthrop, sailed from England with a dozen other company stockholders and a fleet of men and women committed to the Puritan cause. Winthrop, a landed gentleman, was both a tough-minded lawyer and a visionary determined to set an example for the world. "We shall be as a city on a hill," he told his fellow passengers during the crossing on the ship *Arbella*.

Once established in the Bay Colony, Winthrop and the other stockholders trans-

John Winthrop, the first governor of the Massachusetts Bay Colony

Establishing the colony's government

formed the charter for their trading company into the framework of government for a colony. The company's governor became the colony's chief executive; and the company's other officers, the governor's assistants. The charter provided for annual elections of the governor and his assistants by company stockholders, known as the freemen. But to create a broad base of support for the new government, Winthrop and his assistants expanded the freemanship in 1631 to include every adult male church member.

The governor, his assistants, and the freemen together made up the General Court of the colony, which passed all laws, levied taxes, established courts, and made war and peace. In 1634 the whole body of the freemen stopped meeting and instead each town elected representatives or deputies to the General Court. Ten years later, the deputies formed themselves into the lower house of the Bay Colony legislature, and the assistants formed the upper house. By refashioning a company charter into a civil constitution, Massachusetts Bay Puritans gained full control of their future, fulfilling their dream of shaping society, church, and state to their liking.

NEW ENGLAND COMMUNITIES

Contrary to expectations, New England proved more hospitable to the English than the Chesapeake. The character of the migration itself gave New England settlers an advantage, for most arrived in family groups—not as young, single, indentured servants of the sort whose discontents unsettled Virginia society. The heads of New England's first households were typically free men—farmers, artisans, and merchants. Most were skilled and literate. Since husbands usually migrated with their wives and children, the ratio of men to women within the population was fairly evenly balanced.

The "Great Migration"

Most immigrants, some 21,000, came in a cluster between 1630 and 1642. Thereafter new arrivals tapered off because of the outbreak of the English Civil War. This relatively rapid settlement fostered solidarity because immigrants shared a common past of persecution and a strong desire to create an ordered society modeled on Scripture.

Stability and Order in Early New England

Long-lived New Englanders

Puritan emigrants and their descendants thrived in New England. The first generation of colonists lived to an average age of 70, nearly twice as long as Virginians and 10 years longer than English men and women. With 90 percent of all children reaching adulthood, the typical family consisted of seven or eight children who came to maturity. Because of low death rates and high birthrates, the number of New Englanders doubled about every 27 years—while the populations of Europe and the Chesapeake barely reproduced themselves. By 1700, New England and the Chesapeake both had populations of approximately 100,000. But whereas the southern population grew because of continuing immigration, New England's expanded through natural increase.

As immigrants arrived in the Bay Colony after 1630, they carved out an arc of small villages around Massachusetts Bay. Within a decade settlers pressed into

Connecticut, Rhode Island, and New Hampshire. Connecticut and Rhode Island received separate charters from Charles II in the 1660s, guaranteeing their residents the rights to land and government. New Hampshire, to which Massachusetts laid claim in the 1640s, did not become a separate colony until 1679. The handful of hardy souls settled along the coast of present-day Maine had also accepted the Massachusetts Bay Colony's authority.

Early New Englanders planted most of their settlements with an eye to stability *Patterns of* and order. Unlike the Virginians, who scattered across the Chesapeake to isolated *settlement* plantations, most New Englanders established tightly knit communities like those they had left behind in England. In fact, migrating families from the same village or congregation back in England often petitioned the colony government for a tract of land to found their own new town. All prospective adult townsmen initially owned in common this free grant of land, along with the right to set up a local government. Townsmen gradually parceled out among themselves the land granted by the colony. Each family received a lot for a house along with about 150 acres of land in nearby fields. Farmers left many of their acres uncultivated as a legacy for future generations, for most had only the labor of their own families to work their land. While the Chesapeake abounded with servants and tenant farmers, almost every adult male in rural New England owned property.

The economy that supported most of New England's families and towns offered few chances for anyone to get rich. Farmers could coax a yield of food crops sufficient to feed their families, but the stony soil and long winters could not support cash crops like tobacco, rice, or sugar. With no resources for commercial agriculture, New England farmers also had no incentive to import large numbers of servants and slaves or to create large plantations.

Strong family institutions contributed to New England's order and stability. While the early deaths of parents regularly splintered Chesapeake families, two adult generations were often on hand to encourage order within New England households. Husbands and fathers exacted submission from wives and strict obedience from children. Land gave New England's long-lived fathers great authority over even their grown children, for sons and daughters relied on paternal legacies of farms in order to marry and establish their own families.

New Englanders also created, quite deliberately, a distinctive village leadership. *Hierarchy in* Few members of the English upper class migrated to New England, but the Puritan *village* colonists, like most other seventeenth-century English, believed that a stable society *leadership* depended on some degree of inequality. Each town favored certain families in its land distribution, awarding them a little more than the average allotment. The heads of such families were often ministers or other men with university educations or artisans with skills useful to the community. Such men became the "town fathers" and took the lead in directing local affairs. The trust that most New Englanders invested in their leaders contrasts sharply to the attitudes of early Virginians, who constantly challenged the authority of their elites.

Congregational Church Order

Equally important in preserving local order was the church. Most settlers formed churches as quickly as they founded towns, and each congregation ran its own affairs, hiring and dismissing ministers, admitting and disciplining members.

The interior of the Old Ship Meetinghouse, built in Hingham, Massachusetts, in 1681, expresses the importance of hierarchy among New England Puritans. Families with wealth and influence enjoyed the comfort of enclosed wooden pews on the ground floor, while those with slimmer means sat on rows of benches on the second-floor gallery. The raised pulpit at the front of the meetinghouse bespeaks the congregation's respect for the authority and learning of the clergy.

Church membership   Membership in New England's Congregational churches was voluntary, but it was not available for the asking. Those wishing to join had to satisfy the church that they had experienced "conversion." Puritans understood conversion to mean a turning of the heart and soul toward God, a spiritual rebirth that was reflected by a pious and disciplined life. In New England, believers who could credibly relate their conversions to the minister and other church members gained admission to membership. Most early New Englanders sought and received church membership, a status that entitled them to receive communion and to have their children baptized. Widespread membership also enabled the churches to oversee public morality. Although the churches of New England could not inflict corporal punishment or fines on their members, as church courts did in England, Puritan churches could and did censure and expel wayward members for misbehavior.

Separation of church and state   Everywhere in New England except Rhode Island, civil laws obliged everyone to attend worship services on the Sabbath and to pay taxes to support Congregationalist ministers. Although the separation between church and state was incomplete, it had progressed further in New England than in most nations of Europe. New England ministers did not serve as officers in the civil government, and the Congregational churches owned no property. By contrast, Catholic and Anglican church officials wielded real temporal power in European states, and the churches held extensive tracts of land.

Colonial Governments

The last institution fostering order in daily life was the town meeting, the basis of local self-government. In every New England village, all white adult male inhabitants met regularly at the meetinghouse to decide matters of local importance. Nearly all of them could vote for town officials. The town fathers generally set the meeting's agenda and offered advice, but the unanimous consent of townsmen determined all decisions. Reaching consensus was a practical necessity because the town fathers had no means of enforcing unpopular decisions.

Colony governments in early New England also evolved into representative and responsive institutions. Typically the central government of each colony, like the General Court of Massachusetts Bay, consisted of a governor and a bicameral legislature, including an upper house, or council, and a lower house, or assembly. All officials were elected annually by the freemen—white adult men entitled to vote in colony elections. Voting qualifications varied, but the number of men enfranchised made up a much broader segment of society than that in seventeenth-century England.

Communities in Conflict

Not every community in early New England was a small, self-sufficient farming village in which strong families, town fathers, and watchful churches pursued the ideals of Puritanism. Along the edges of settlement, several towns departed dramatically from the usual patterns.

One such outpost was Marblehead, a fishing port on the Massachusetts coast settled by immigrant fisherfolk from every port in the British Isles. Most eked out a bare existence as suppliers and employees of Boston merchants, who managed Marblehead's fishery. Single men dominated the population, and their brawls and drunken cavorting often spilled out of the town's many taverns onto the streets. Local government remained weak for most of the seventeenth century, and inhabitants managed to avoid founding a local church for 50 years. *Commerce and "company towns"*

Similar problems plagued Springfield, Massachusetts, in the fertile Connecticut River valley. A single powerful family, the Pynchons, founded the town as a center of the fur trade and later developed a thriving commercial agriculture. Here, too, profit-minded merchants dominated local life and exploited the labor of most inhabitants—an assortment of Scottish convicts and English indentured servants.

The rest of Massachusetts tolerated chaotic "company towns" like Marblehead and Springfield because their inhabitants produced what few commodities New England could trade to the rest of the world. Marblehead's fish found a ready market in Catholic Spain and Portugal; Springfield's grain and livestock commanded a good price among Caribbean planters. In exchange, New Englanders acquired wine, sugar, molasses, textiles, and iron goods—commodities that they needed but could not produce.

More commonly, conflicts in New England towns were likely to arise over reli-

Conflict over religious differences

gious differences. Although most New Englanders called themselves Puritans and Congregationalists, the very fervency of their convictions often led them to disagree about how best to carry out the teachings of the Bible and the ideas of John Calvin. The Puritans of Plymouth Colony, for example, believed that religious purity required renouncing the Church of England, while those of the Bay Colony clung to the hope of reforming the Anglican church from within.

Even within Massachusetts Bay, Puritans differed among themselves about how to organize their churches. During the first decades of settlement, those differences led to the founding of new colonies in New England. In 1636 Thomas Hooker, the minister of Cambridge, Massachusetts, led part of his congregation to Connecticut, where they established the first English settlement. Somewhat more liberal than other Bay Puritans, Hooker favored more lenient standards for church membership. He also opposed the Bay's policy of limiting voting in colony elections to church members. By contrast, New Haven (a separate colony until it became part of Connecticut in 1662) was begun in 1638 by strict Congregationalists who found Massachusetts too liberal. Massachusetts recognized its southern neighbors, including Separatist Plymouth, as colonies within the Puritan fold, respectable suburbs of Winthrop's city on a hill.

Heretics

The same could not be said of Rhode Island, for that little colony on Narragansett Bay began as a ghetto for heretics. While voluntary migration formed Connecticut and New Haven, enforced exile filled Rhode Island with men and women whose radical ideas unsettled the rest of Massachusetts.

Roger Williams

Roger Williams, Rhode Island's founder, had come to New England in 1631, serving as a respected minister of Salem. But soon Williams announced that he was a Separatist, like the Pilgrims of Plymouth. He encouraged the Bay Colony to break all ties to the corrupt Church of England. He also urged a more complete separation of church and state than most New Englanders were prepared to accept, and later in his career he endorsed full religious toleration. Finally, Williams denounced the Bay's charter—the legal document that justified Massachusetts's existence—on the grounds that the king had no right to grant land that he had not purchased from the Indians. When Williams made bold to suggest that Massachusetts actually inform the king of his mistake, angry authorities prepared to deport him. Instead Williams fled the colony in the dead of winter to live with the Indians. In 1636, he became the founder and first citizen of Providence, later to be part of Rhode Island.

Anne Hutchinson

Another charismatic heretic from Massachusetts arrived soon after. Anne Hutchinson, a skilled midwife and the spouse of a wealthy merchant, came to Boston in 1634. Enthusiasm for her minister, John Cotton, started her on a course of explaining his sermons to gatherings of her neighbors—and then to elaborating ideas of her own in which many of the Bay's leaders detected the dangerous heresy of "Antinomianism."

The Bay Puritans, like all Calvinists, denied that men and women could "earn" salvation simply by obeying God's laws. They held that salvation came through divine grace, not human actions. But many Puritans believed that the ability to lead an upright life was a natural consequence of being saved. A minority in the Puritan movement, including Anne Hutchinson, rejected that notion. Hutchinson contended that outward obedience to God's laws indicated nothing whatsoever about the inward state of the soul. She was certain that those predestined for salvation knew it intuitively and could recognize the same grace in others.

When most of the Bay Colony's ministers rejected her views, Anne Hutchinson denounced them. Her attack on the clergy, along with the popularity of her preaching among many important merchant families, prompted the Bay Colony government to expel Hutchinson and her followers for sedition in 1638. She settled briefly in Rhode Island before moving on to Long Island, where she died in an Indian attack.

Colony leaders were especially critical of Hutchinson because she was a woman, who by their lights should have remained less assertive of her beliefs. In later religious controversies, the devil of dissent assumed the shape of a woman as well. The Quakers, one of the most radical religious groups produced by the Protestant Reformation in England, sent Ann Austin and Mary Fisher as their first missionaries to the Bay. Women were among the most active early converts, and one of them, Mary Dyer, was hanged for her persistence, along with three Quaker men, in 1656. Like the Antinomians, the Quakers attached great significance to an inward state of grace, called the "Light Within." Through that inner light, the Quakers claimed, God revealed his will directly to believers, enabling men and women to attain spiritual perfection. Because they held that everyone had immediate access to God, the Quakers also dispensed with a clergy and the sacraments.

Quakers of New England

The artist who sketched this Quaker meeting called attention to one of that sect's most controversial practices by placing a woman at the center of his composition. Women were allowed to speak in Quaker worship services and to preach and proselytize at public gatherings of non-Quakers. The Puritans roundly condemned this liberty as contrary to the teachings of St. Paul.

Goodwives and Witches

If Anne Hutchinson and Mary Dyer had been men, their ideas would still have been deemed heretical. On the other hand, if these women had been men, they might have found other ways to express their intelligence and magnetism. But life in colonial New England offered women, especially married women, little scope for their talents.

Most adult women were hardworking farm wives who cared for large households of children. Between marriage and middle age, most New England wives were pregnant except when breast-feeding. When they were not nursing or minding children, mothers were producing and preparing much of what was consumed and worn by their families. They planted vegetable gardens and pruned fruit trees, salted beef and pork and pressed cider, milked cows and churned butter, kept bees and tended poultry, cooked and baked, washed and ironed, spun, wove, and sewed. While husbands and sons engaged in farm work that changed with the seasons, took trips to taverns and mills, and went off to hunt or fish, housebound wives and daughters were locked into a humdrum routine with little time for themselves.

Legal barriers for women   Women suffered legal disadvantages as well. English common law and colonial legal codes accorded married women no control over property. Wives could not sue or be sued, they could not make contracts, and they surrendered to their husbands any property that they possessed before marriage. Divorce was almost impossible to obtain until the late eighteenth century. Only widows and a few single women had the same property rights as men, but they could not vote in colony elections.

The one arena in which women could attain something approaching equal standing with men was the churches. Women wielded the greatest influence among the Quakers. They could speak in Quaker meetings, preach as missionaries, and oversee the behavior of other female members in "women's meetings." Puritan women could not become ministers, but after the 1660s they made up the majority of church members. In some churches membership enabled them to vote for ministerial candidates and to voice opinions about admitting and disciplining members. Puritan doctrine itself rejected the medieval Catholic suspicion of women as "a necessary evil," seeing them instead as "a necessary good." Even so, the Puritan ideal of the virtuous woman was a chaste, submissive "helpmeet," a wife and mother who served God by serving men.

Witchcraft   Communities sometimes responded to assertive women with accusations of witchcraft. Like most early modern Europeans, New Englanders believed in wizards and witches, men and women who were said to acquire supernatural powers by signing a compact with Satan. A total of 344 New Englanders were charged with witchcraft during the first century of settlement, with the notorious Salem Village episode of 1692 producing the largest outpouring of accusations and 20 executions. More than three-quarters of all accused witches were women, usually middle-aged and older, and most of those accused were regarded as unduly independent. Before they were charged with witchcraft, many had been suspected of heretical religious beliefs, others of sexual impropriety. Still others had inherited or stood to inherit property.

COUNTERPOINT   Few events in American history have compelled the imagination of historians more than the witchcraft hysteria that wracked one small New England village early in the 1690s. It is true that colonial America witnessed nothing like the recurring mass

Bewitched by Salem Village

panics over witchcraft that swept through early modern Europe for centuries and resulted in the executions of thousands of men and women. The outbreak of accusations that led to the deaths of 20 accused Salem Village "witches" was, as one eminent American historian observed, "a small episode in the history of a great superstition." Even so, many scholars have been lured into closely investigating the Salem tragedy in the hope that it may shed light on that lost world of the past in which it took place and lead to a richer understanding of early New England society and culture.

In recent years, many historians studying the Salem Village tragedy—and, indeed, witchcraft in general—have focused on the preponderance of women accused of that crime. For those scholars, what witchcraft panics illustrate is the deep and widespread hostility to women in all early modern cultures. But other scholars think that women were targeted as witches only because they were the most vulnerable members of these societies and thus fell prey to being scapegoated during periods of uncertainty and instability. In the case of Salem Village, some historians argue that witchcraft hysteria arose in response to communal divisions over commercial development—that subsistence farmers who both resented and coveted the new wealth of their more profit-minded neighbors vented their frustrations in charges of witchcraft. Other historians believe that political upheavals in New England during the early 1690s so disrupted the local judicial system that Salem Villagers seeking redress for their grievances fell back on charging their adversaries with witchcraft, charges that were handled by specially appointed courts. Still other historians see the late seventeenth century as a period when New England Puritans felt deeply threatened by the growth of rival groups like the Quakers and Anglicans, noting that a high percentage of those accused of witchcraft came from families related by blood or marriage to those religious "outsiders." All of these interpretations of what happened in Salem Village enrich our understanding of the role of witchcraft beliefs in early New England and the changing character of that society.

Whites and Indians in Early New England

Most white settlers in New England, like those in the Chesapeake, condemned the "savagery" and "superstition" of the Indians around them. Unlike the French, however, the Puritans made only a few efforts to spread their faith to the Indians.

In truth, the "godly" New Englanders had more in common with the natives in the region than they might have cared to admit. Perhaps 100,000 Algonkian-speaking men and women lived in the area reaching from the Kennebec River in Maine to Cape Cod. Like the Puritans, they relied for food on fishing in spring and summer, hunting in winter, cultivating and harvesting food crops in spring and fall. And, to an even greater degree than among white settlers, Indian political authority was local. Within each village, a single leader known as the "sachem" or "sagamore" directed economic life, administered justice, and negotiated with other tribes and English settlers. Like New England's town fathers, a sachem's power depended on keeping the trust and consent of his people. *Similarities between Puritans and Indians*

The Indians of New England shared one other characteristic with all Europeans: they quarreled frequently with neighboring nations. The antagonism among the English, Spanish, Dutch, and French was matched by the hostilities among the Abenaki, Pawtucket, Massachusett, Narragansett, and Wampanoag tribes of the

POPULAR ENTERTAINMENT

A World of Wonders and Witchcraft

Early in the 1680s the Reverend Increase Mather, a learned and devout Boston minister, was putting the finishing touches on a book. It would be a plump volume when published, its pages packed with remarkable occurrences that had taken place during the first 50 years of New England's settlement. Those occurrences dealt not with politics, nor even with the churches, but rather with "wonders"—interventions of the supernatural in the normal order of things. Ministers throughout New England contributed accounts of such wonders to Mather's book. Reverend John Higginson of Salem told of a "Conjuring Book," which filled readers with "a strange kind of Horror" and caused their hair to stand on end. From Newbury, Massachusetts, Reverend Joshua Moodey reported a house inhabited by evil spirits and a "monstrous birth." From Connecticut came the story of a phantom ship sighted sailing into New Haven harbor that suddenly disappeared. Other ministers related cases of bewitchment, appearances of the devil, and dire events forecast by comets, eclipses, earthquakes, and rainbows.

Mather's book of wonders became one of many available to New England readers—a numerous group, for literacy was almost universal. Accounts of marvellous events poured from presses in England, the Continent, and the colonies. Some were splashed across a single sheet by literary hacks; others, like Mather's book, filled the fat volumes written by learned men. The authors drew their reports of visions and voices, untimely deaths and natural disasters from ancient and early Christian authors, medieval chronicles, the Bible, and local lore collected by contemporaries, like Mather's network of New England ministers.

Most seventeenth-century New Englanders favored religious books: the Bible, psalmbooks, sermons, stories of the sufferings of Protestant martyrs, and accounts of the battles against temptation waged by ordinary people. Even so, authors like Increase Mather recognized that a wider audience might be reached by volumes blending godly messages with sensational topics. Ministers recounted wonders to make the religious argument that the world was shot through with mystery and miracle and that men and women were at the mercy of God's will and the devil's wiles. At the same time they titillated readers with accounts of witches, apparitions, and freaks of nature. Published narratives of New Englanders taken captive by the Indians and the confessions of convicted murderers combined the same mixture of religion and sensationalism. The pious message that God prevailed over Satan and his servants was mixed with lurid depictions of violence and evildoing.

Knowing what early New Englanders

north Atlantic coast. Rivalries kept different tribes from forging an effective defense against white colonials. New England settlers, like those in the Chesapeake, exploited Indian disunity.

War   The first New England natives to put up a strong resistance to Europeans were the Pequots, whom white settlers encountered when they began to push into Connecticut. Had the Pequots allied with their neighbors, the Narragansetts, they could have retarded English expansion. But the Narragansetts, bitter enemies of the

Daily Lives

liked to read offers a glimpse not only of their entertainments but of their inner world. Especially significant was their enduring fascination with wonders, which were believed to be true both by learned men and by humble farmers and their wives. The popularity of wonder lore is powerful proof that all New Englanders inhabited an enchanted universe. Their world brimmed with invisible forces and supernatural beings that could interrupt the order of nature.

Witchcraft trials and executions took place throughout Europe in the sixteenth and seventeenth centuries, occurring far more frequently and claiming many more victims than in colonial America. But, as this engraving of an English hanging of witches indicates, women composed a majority of those charged and executed on both sides of the Atlantic.

That widely shared belief made witchcraft a crime punishable by death and allowed for the unfolding of the notorious witchcraft trials in Salem Village. There, in the early months of 1692, a group of adolescent girls used the white of a raw egg suspended in a glass of water as a kind of crude crystal ball to divine what sorts of men their future husbands might be. Somehow, the seance went sour and the frightened adolescents began behaving in ways that other villagers took to be signs of bewitchment. Crying out in pain and terror, the afflicted women claimed to see taunting specters of witches, whom they recognized as fellow villagers. In the hysteria that ensued, hundreds of accusations of witchcraft led to the trial and execution of 20 innocent men and women. Only when Increase Mather and 14 other Massachusetts ministers publicly warned against the trials' excesses did the hangings stop.

Many historians have tried to explain the deeper causes behind the Salem episode. Some point to the Puritan mistrust of independent women, others to the bitter rivalries among Salem Village families. Still others have noted ties between accused witches and heretical groups like the Quakers. Whatever the source of Salem's particular troubles, the witchcraft charges there and elsewhere in seventeenth-century New England were rooted in the widespread belief in a world of wonders, at once terrible and fascinating.

Pequots, allied with the English instead. Together they virtually destroyed the Pequots in 1637. Then, in 1643, the English turned against their former allies, joined forces with the Narragansetts' rivals, the Mohegans, and intimidated the Narragansetts into ceding much of their territory. Only a few whites objected to those ruthless policies, among them Roger Williams. "God Land," he warned one Connecticut leader, "will be (as it now is) as great a God with us English as God Gold was with the Spanish."

Playing one tribe off against another finally left the Wampanoags of Plymouth the only coastal tribe capable of resisting Puritan expansion. In 1675, their sachem Metacomet, whom the English called King Philip, organized an uprising that devastated white frontier settlements. By the spring of 1676, Metacomet's forces were closing in on the coast, raiding towns that lay within 20 miles of Boston.

Faced with shortages of food and ammunition, Metacomet called for assistance from the Abenaki, a powerful Maine tribe, and from the Iroquois of New York. But those tribes withheld their support, not wishing to jeopardize their trade with the English. In the summer of 1676 Metacomet met his death in battle, and the Indian offensive collapsed. In seventeenth-century New England, as in the Chesapeake, the clash between Indians and white settlers threatened the very survival of both groups. Perhaps 20,000 whites and Indians lost their lives in Metacomet's War.

Even if the natives of New England had been able to unify against whites, they still would have had no defense against another deadly enemy—disease. In 1618, even before whites settled permanently, visiting fishermen introduced an epidemic that ravaged the coastal tribes. As contact with Europeans increased, epidemics recurred with deadly frequency, drastically reducing tribal populations.

THE MIDDLE COLONIES

The inhabitants of the Middle Colonies—New York and New Jersey, Pennsylvania and Delaware—enjoyed more secure lives than most southern colonials. But they lacked the common bonds that lent stability to early New England. Instead, in each of the Middle Colonies a variety of ethnic and religious groups vied for wealth from farming and the fur trade and contended bitterly against governments that commanded little popular support.

The Founding of New Netherlands

New York was settled in 1624 as New Netherlands, an outpost of the Dutch West India Company. Far more impressed with the commercial potential of Africa and South America, the company limited its investment in North America to a few fur-trading posts along the Hudson, Connecticut, and Delaware rivers.

Ethnic and religious diversity

Intent only on trade, the Dutch had little desire to plant permanent colonies abroad because they enjoyed prosperity and religious freedom at home. Most of New Netherlands' few settlers clustered in the village of New Amsterdam on Manhattan Island at the mouth of the Hudson. One hundred and fifty miles upriver lay a fur-trading outpost, Fort Orange (Albany), and by the 1660s a few other farming villages dotted the west end of Long Island, upper Manhattan Island, Staten Island, and the lower Hudson valley. In all, there were fewer than 9000 New Netherlanders—a mixture of Dutch, Belgians, French, English, Portuguese, Swedes, Finns, and Africans. The first blacks had arrived in 1626, imported as slaves; some later became free, intermarried with whites, and even owned white indentured servants.

This ethnic diversity ensured a variety of religions. Although the Dutch Reformed church predominated, other early New Netherlanders included Lutherans, Quakers, and Catholics. There were Jews as well, refugees from Portuguese Brazil, who were required by law to live in a ghetto in New Amsterdam.

New Amsterdam (later New York City) in about 1626. Despite having this outpost in New Netherlands, the Dutch had far more interest in vying with the Portuguese for control of commerce with the Far East than in competing with the English for the fur trade in North America.

Yet another religious group kept to themselves by choice: New England Congregationalists. Drawn by promises of cheap land and self-government, they planted farming communities on eastern Long Island during the 1640s.

New Netherlanders knew that their cultural differences hampered the prospects for a stable social and political life. The Dutch West India Company made matters worse by appointing corrupt, dictatorial governors who ruled without an elective assembly. The company also provided little protection for its outlying settlers; when it did attack neighboring Indian nations, it did so savagely, triggering terrible retaliations. By the time the company went bankrupt in 1654, it had virtually abandoned its American colony.

New Englanders on Long Island, who had insisted on a free hand in governing their own villages, now began to demand a voice in running the colony as well. By the 1660s they were openly challenging Dutch rule and calling for English conquest of the colony.

English Rule in New York

Taking advantage of the disarray in New Netherlands, Charles II ignored Dutch claims in North America and granted his brother James, the Duke of York, a proprietary charter there. It granted James all of New Netherlands to Delaware Bay, as well as Maine, Martha's Vineyard, and Nantucket Island. In 1664 James sent an invading fleet, whose mere arrival caused the Dutch to surrender.

Managing the new colony, renamed New York, did little to ease ethnic tensions or promote political harmony. The Dutch resented English rule, and only after a generation of intermarriage and acculturation did that resentment fade. James also failed to win friends among Long Island's New Englanders. He grudgingly gave in to their demand for an elective assembly in 1683 but rejected its first act, the Charter of Liberties, which would have guaranteed basic political rights. The chronic political strife discouraged prospective settlers. By 1698 the colony numbered only 18,000 inhabitants, and New York City, the former New Amsterdam, was an overgrown village of a few thousand.

The League of the Iroquois

While New York's colonists wrangled, many of its native Indians succumbed to the same pressures that shattered the natives of New England and the Chesapeake. Only one tribe of Indians in New York's interior, the Iroquois nation, actually gained greater strength from its contacts with whites.

The Indian trade   Like the tribes of South Carolina, the Indians of northern New York became important suppliers of furs to white traders. As in the Carolinas, powerful tribes dominated the interior, far outnumbering white settlers. The handful of Dutch and, later, English traders had every reason to keep peace with the Indians. But the fur trade heightened tensions among interior tribes. At first the Mahicans had supplied furs to the Dutch. But by 1625 the game in their territory had been exhausted, and the Dutch had taken their business to the Iroquois. When the Iroquois faced the same extinction of fur-bearing animals in the 1640s, they found a solution. With Dutch en-

Many French colonials showed an abiding interest in and respect for Native American culture. Among them was George Heriot, an eighteenth-century Quebec-based painter, who produced a series of watercolor sketches of Iroquois ceremonies, including this portrayal of a calumet (or peace-pipe) dance.

couragement and Dutch guns, the Iroquois virtually wiped out the neighboring Huron nation and seized their hunting grounds.

The destruction of the Huron made the Iroquois the undisputed power on the northern frontier. More successfully than Powhatan's confederacy in the Chesapeake, the League of the Iroquois welded different tribes into a coherent political unit. This union of the Five Nations (to become six after the Tuscaroras joined them in 1712) included the Mohawk, Oneida, Onondaga, Cayuga, and Seneca tribes and stretched from the lands around the upper Hudson in the east to the Genesee River in the west. Political strength enabled the Iroquois to deal effectively with their Algonkian rivals in New England as well as European newcomers. As the favored clients of the Dutch and, later, the English, they became opponents of the French.

The League's strength rested on an even more remarkable form of political and social organization, one in which men and women shared authority. The most powerful women anywhere in colonial North America were the matriarchs of the Iroquois. Matrilineal kinship formed the basis of Iroquois society, as it did among the Pueblos of the Southwest. When men married, they joined their wives' families, households over which the eldest female member presided. But unlike Pueblo women, Iroquois matriarchs wielded political influence as well. The most senior Iroquois women selected the confederation's council of chiefs, advised them, and "dehorned"—removed from office—those deemed unfit. Throughout the eighteenth century, the League of the Iroquois would continue to figure as a major force in North America. *Iroquois women*

The Founding of New Jersey

New Jersey took shape in the shadow of its stronger neighbors to the north. Its inhabitants were less united and powerful than the Iroquois, less wealthy and influential than New Yorkers, and less like-minded and self-governing than New Englanders.

Confusion attended New Jersey's beginnings. The lands lying west of the Hudson and east of the Delaware River had been part of the Duke of York's proprietary grant. But in 1664 he gave about 5 million of these acres to Lord Berkeley and Sir George Carteret, two of his favorites who were already involved in the proprietary colonies of the Carolinas. New Jersey's new owners guaranteed settlers land, religious freedom, and a representative assembly in exchange for a small quitrent, an annual fee for the use of the land. The proprietors' terms promptly drew Puritan settlers from New Haven, Connecticut. At the same time, unaware that James had already given New Jersey to Berkeley and Carteret, New York's Governor Richard Nicolls granted Long Island Puritans land there.

More complications ensued when Berkeley and Carteret decided to divide New Jersey into east and west and sell both halves to Quaker investors—a prospect that outraged New Jersey's Puritans. Although some English Friends migrated to West Jersey, the Quakers quickly decided that two Jerseys were less desirable than one Pennsylvania and resold both East and West Jersey to speculators. In the end the Jerseys became a patchwork of religious and ethnic groups. Settlers who shared a common religion or national origin formed communities and established small family farms. When the Crown finally reunited east and west as a single royal colony in 1702, New Jersey was overshadowed by settlements not only to the north but now, also, to the south.

Quaker Odysseys

Religious and political idealism similar to that of the Puritans inspired the settlement of Pennsylvania, making it an oddity among the Middle Colonies. The oddity began with an improbable founder, William Penn. Young Penn devoted his early years to disappointing his distinguished father, Sir William Penn, an admiral in the Royal Navy. Several years after being expelled from college, he finally chose a career that may have made the admiral yearn for mere disappointment: young Penn undertook a lifelong commitment to put into practice Quaker teachings. By the 1670s he had emerged as an acknowledged leader of the Society of Friends, as the Quakers formally called themselves.

Quaker beliefs   The Quakers behaved in ways and believed in ideas that most people regarded as odd. They dressed in a deliberately plain and severe manner. They withheld from their social superiors the customary marks of respect, such as bowing, kneeling, and removing their hats. They refused to swear oaths or to make war. They allowed women public roles of religious leadership. That pattern of behavior reflected their egalitarian ideals, the belief that all men and women shared equally in the "Light Within." Some 40,000 English merchants, artisans, and farmers embraced Quakerism by 1660, and many suffered fines, imprisonment, and corporal punishment.

Pennsylvania established   Since the English upper class has always prized eccentricity among its members, it is not surprising that Penn, despite his Quakerism, remained a favorite of Charles II. More surprising is that the king's favor took the extravagant form of presenting Penn in 1681 with all the land between New Jersey and Maryland. Perhaps the king was repaying Penn for the large sum that his father had lent the Stuarts. Or perhaps the king was hoping to export England's Quakers to an American colony governed by his trusted personal friend.

Penn envisioned that his proprietary colony would provide a refuge for Quakers while producing quitrents for himself. To publicize his settlement, he distributed pamphlets praising its attractions throughout the British Isles and Europe. The response was overwhelming: by 1700 its population stood at 21,000. The only early migration of equal magnitude was the Puritan colonization of New England.

Patterns of Settlement

Perhaps half of Pennsylvania's settlers arrived as indentured servants, while the families of free farmers and artisans made up the rest. The majority were Quakers from Britain, Holland, and Germany, but the colonists also included Catholics, Lutherans, Baptists, Anglicans, and Presbyterians. In 1682 when Penn purchased and annexed the Three Lower Counties (later the colony of Delaware), his settlement included the Dutch, Swedes, and Finns living there, about 1000 people.

Quakers from other colonies—West Jersey, Maryland, and New England—also flocked to the new homeland. Those experienced settlers brought skills and connections that contributed to Pennsylvania's rapid economic growth. Farmers sowed their rich lands into a sea of wheat, which merchants exported to the Caribbean. The cen-

William Penn, the founder of Pennsylvania

ter of the colony's trade was Philadelphia, a superb natural harbor situated at the confluence of the Delaware and Schuylkill rivers.

In contrast to New England's landscape of villages, the Pennsylvania countryside beyond Philadelphia was dotted with dispersed farmsteads. Commercial agriculture required larger farms, which kept settlers at greater distances from one another. As a result, the county rather than the town became the basic unit of local government in Pennsylvania.

Another reason that farmers did not need to cluster their homes within a central village was that the coastal Indians, the Lenni Lenapes (also called Delawares by the English), posed no threat. Thanks to two of the odder Quaker beliefs—their commitment to pacifism and their conviction that the Indians rightfully owned their land—peace prevailed between native inhabitants and newcomers. Before Penn sold any land to white settlers, he purchased it from the Indians. He also prohibited the sale of alcohol to the tribe, strictly regulated the fur trade, and learned the language of the Lenni Lenapes. "Not a language spoken in Europe," he remarked, "hath words of more sweetness in Accent and Emphasis than theirs." *Quakers and Indians*

"Our Wildernesse flourishes as a Garden," Penn declared late in 1683, and in fact, his colony lived up to its promises. New arrivals readily acquired good land on liberal terms, while Penn's Frame of Government instituted a representative assembly and guaranteed all inhabitants the basic English civil liberties and complete freedom of worship.

The tidy, productive farmsteads of the Pennsylvania countryside were the basis of that colony's prosperity during the eighteenth century. Their produce fueled the growth of Philadelphia as well as sustained the expansion of sugar plantations on England's Caribbean islands.

Quakers and Politics

Even so, Penn's colony suffered constant political strife. Rich investors whom he had rewarded with large tracts of land and trade monopolies dominated the council, which held the sole power to initiate legislation. That power and Penn's own claims as proprietor set the stage for controversy. Members of the representative assembly battled for the right to initiate legislation. Farmers opposed Penn's efforts to collect quitrents. The Three Lower Counties agitated for separation, their inhabitants feeling no loyalty to Penn or Quakerism.

Penn's compromises   Penn finally bought peace at the price of approving a complete revision of his original Frame of Government. In 1701 the Charter of Privileges, Pennsylvania's new constitution, stripped the council of its legislative power, leaving it only the role of advising the governor. The charter also limited Penn's privileges as proprietor to the ownership of ungranted land and the power to veto legislation. Thereafter an elective unicameral assembly, the only single-house legislature in the colonies, dominated Pennsylvania's government.

As Pennsylvania prospered, Philadelphia became the commercial and cultural center of England's North American empire. Gradually the interior of Pennsylvania filled with immigrants who harbored no "odd" ideas about Indian rights—mainly Germans and Scots-Irish—and the Lenni Lenapes and other tribes were bullied into moving farther west. As for William Penn, he returned to England and spent time in a debtors' prison after being defrauded by his unscrupulous colonial agents. He died in 1718, an ocean away from his American utopia.

ADJUSTMENT TO EMPIRE

In the year 1685, from the city of London, a new English king surveyed his American domains. The former Duke of York, now James II, had hoped that America might contribute to the making of kings and queens. Like earlier Stuart monarchs, James hoped to ride to absolute power on a wave of colonial wealth, just as Spain's monarchs had during the previous century. To encourage colonial settlement, Stuart kings had chartered the private trading companies of Virginia, Plymouth, and Massachusetts Bay. They had rewarded their aristocratic favorites with huge tracts of land— Maryland, the Carolinas, New York, New Jersey, and Pennsylvania.

Yet to what end? Although North America now abounded in places named in honor of English monarchs, the colonies themselves lacked any strong ties to the English state. In only three colonies—New Hampshire, New York, and Virginia— did England exercise direct control through royally appointed governors and councils. Until Parliament passed the first Navigation Acts in 1660, England had not even set in place a coherent policy for regulating colonial trade. Even more disheartening, ungrateful colonists were resisting their duty to enrich the English state and the Stuarts. While Chesapeake planters grumbled over the customs duties levied on tobacco, New Englanders, the worst of the lot, ignored the Navigation Acts altogether and traded openly with the Dutch. New Yorkers were turning out just as badly, as James, the first proprietor of that colony, recalled all too well. Even in recently settled colonies like New Jersey, the Carolinas, and Pennsylvania, the stirrings of opposition to royally appointed proprietors did not bode well.

England, in an effort to regulate colonial trade, required all ships bound from America to pass through British ports and pay customs duties. Places like Plymouth, Liverpool, and Bristol (shown here) thrived as a result. Contrast this large, bustling commercial center with the modest size of Plymouth 200 years earlier (illustration, page 7).

What was needed, in James's view, was an assertion of royal authority over America, starting with Massachusetts. His brother, Charles II, had laid the groundwork in 1673 by persuading Parliament to authorize the placement of customs agents in colonial ports to suppress illegal trade. Charles also formed the Lords of Trade and Plantations, a committee to oversee colonial affairs. When reports of defiance continued to surface, the king delivered the decisive blow: an English court in 1684 revoked Massachusetts' original charter, leaving the Bay Colony without a legal basis for its claim to self-government. *Control over the colonies tightened*

The Dominion of New England

Charles died the following year, leaving James II to finish the job of reorganization. In 1686, at the king's urging, the Lords of Trade consolidated the colonies of Connecticut, Plymouth, Massachusetts Bay, Rhode Island, and New Hampshire into a single entity to be ruled by a royal governor and a royally appointed council. By 1688 he had added New York and New Jersey to that domain, now called the Dominion of New England. Showing the typical Stuart distaste for representative government, James also abolished all northern colonial assemblies. The king's aim to centralize authority over such a large territory made the Dominion not only a royal dream but a radical experiment in English colonial administration.

Sir Edmund Andros, a tough professional soldier sent to Boston as the Dominion's royal governor, quickly came to rival his king for the title of most unpopular man north of Pennsylvania. Andros set in force policies that outraged every seg- *Edmund Andros* ment of New England society. He strictly enforced the Navigation Acts, which slowed down commerce and infuriated merchants and workers in the maritime trades. He commandeered a Boston meetinghouse for Anglican worship and immediately angered devout Congregationalists. He abolished all titles to land granted under the old charter, alarming farmers and speculators. He imposed arbitrary taxes, censored the press, and forbade all town meetings, thereby alienating almost everyone.

The Aftershocks of the Glorious Revolution

About the same time northern colonials were reaching the end of their patience with Andros, the English decided they had taken enough from his royal master. James II had revealed himself to be yet another Stuart who tried to dispense with Parliament and who had embraced Catholicism besides. As they had before with Charles I, Parliament dispensed with the king. In a quick, bloodless coup d'état known as the Glorious Revolution, Parliament forced James into exile in 1688. In his place they elevated to the throne of England his daughter, Mary, and her Dutch husband, William of Orange. Mary was a distinctly better sort of Stuart. A staunch Protestant, she agreed to rule with Parliament.

The Dominion overthrown   The deposing of James II proved so popular among New Englanders that even before Parliament had officially proclaimed William and Mary king and queen, Boston's militia seized Governor Andros and sent him home in April 1689. William and Mary officially dismembered the Dominion and reinstated representative assemblies everywhere in the northern colonies. Connecticut and Rhode Island were restored their old charters, but Massachusetts received a new charter in 1691. Under its terms Massachusetts, Plymouth, and present-day Maine were combined into a single royal colony headed by a governor appointed by the Crown rather than elected by the people. The charter also made property ownership rather than church membership the basis of voting rights and imposed religious toleration.

Leisler's Rebellion

The new charter did not satisfy all New Englanders, but they soon adjusted to the political realities of royal rule. By contrast, the violent political infighting that plagued New York mirrored that colony's instability.

Word of revolution in England and rebellion in Massachusetts roused New Yorkers into armed opposition in May 1689. Declaring their loyalty to William and Mary, the New York City militia forced from office Andros's second-in-command, the Dominion's lieutenant governor. In his place they installed one of their own leaders, Jacob Leisler, a German merchant.

Since James II had won few friends in New York, the rebellion met no opposition. But Leisler could not win commanding support for his authority. While Protestant Dutch farmers, artisans, and small shopkeepers stood by him, the leaders of the colony—an intermarried elite of English and Dutch merchants—considered Leisler an upstart who threatened their own influence. After royal rule was restored to New York in 1691, a jury comprised of Englishmen convicted Leisler and his son-in-law, Jacob Milburne, of treason. Their executions guaranteed a long life to the bitter political rivalries that Leisler's Rebellion had fueled in New York.

Royal Authority in America in 1700

In the wake of upheaval at home and in North America, England focused its imperial policy on reaping maximum profit from the colonial trade. In 1696 Parliament enlarged the number of customs officials stationed in each colony to enforce the Navigation Acts. To help prosecute smugglers, Parliament established colonial vice-admiralty courts, tribunals without juries presided over by royally appointed justices. To keep current on all colonial matters, the king appointed a new Board of Trade to replace the old Lords of Trade. The new enforcement procedures generally succeeded in discouraging smuggling and channeling colonial trade through England. *Closer regulation of trade*

That was enough for England and its monarchs for half a century thereafter. English kings and queens gave up any dreams of imposing the kind of centralized administration of colonial life that James II had attempted in his Dominion of New England. To be sure, royal control had increased over the previous half century. By 1700 royal governments had been established in Virginia, New York, Massachusetts, and New Hampshire. New Jersey, the Carolinas, and Georgia would shortly be added to the list. Royal rule meant that the monarch appointed governors and (everywhere except Massachusetts) also appointed their councils. Royally appointed councils could veto any law passed by a colony's representative assembly, royally appointed governors could veto any law passed by both houses, and the Crown could veto any law passed by both houses and approved by the governor.

Despite the ability to veto, the sway of royal power remained more apparent than real after 1700. The Glorious Revolution asserted once and for all that Parliament's authority—rule by the legislative branch of government—would be supreme in the governing of England. In the colonies members of representative assemblies grew more skilled at dealing with royal governors and more protective of their rights. They guarded most jealously their strongest lever of power—the right of the lower houses to levy taxes. *The limits of royal power*

The political reality of the assemblies' power reflected a social reality as well. No longer mere outposts along the Atlantic, the colonies of 1700 were becoming more firmly rooted societies. Their laws and traditions were based not only on what they had brought from England but on the conditions of life in America. That social reality had already blocked Stuart ambitions to shape the future of North America, just as it had thwarted the designs of lordly proprietors and the dreams of religious reformers.

Still, the dream of empire would revive among England's rulers in the middle of the eighteenth century—in part because the same dream had never died among the rulers of France. By 1663, Louis XIV had decided that kings could succeed where the enterprise of private French traders had failed: he placed New France under royal rule. Thereafter France's fortunes in America steadily improved. Soldiers strengthened Canada's defenses, colonists and traders expanded the scope of French influence, and the Jesuits made more converts among the tribes of the interior. Under the Sun King, as Louis was known to admiring courtiers, royal rule became absolute, and the hopes for empire grew absolutely. Louis and his heirs would continue their plans for the making of France by contending for empire with the English, both in the Old World and in the New.

CHAPTER SUMMARY

While the Catholic Counterreformation encouraged the French colonization of Canada, the Protestant Reformation in England spurred the settlement of New England and Pennsylvania. As the French slowly established a fur trade, agricultural communities, and religious institutions in Canada, radical English Puritans planted more populous settlements between Maine and Long Island. The migration of family groups and a rough equality of wealth lent stability to early New England society. So did the shared commitment to Puritanism, the rapid organization of churches, and a strong tradition of self-government at both the town and colony levels. In all of those respects New England's early development contrasted strikingly with that of the southern colonies. Even so, early New England's history was not without conflict. Religious differences could cause bitter divisions among English settlers, and contests between whites and Indians erupted into violent confrontations—the Pequot War and Metacomet's War.

The Middle Colonies shared New England's rapid population growth and quickly established an even more profitable economy. Unlike New England, however, all of the Middle Colonies were founded as proprietary governments, like Maryland and South Carolina. Representative government was therefore weaker, and ethnic and religious diversity contributed to political strife. Relations between whites and Indians in the Middle Colonies also developed in ways different from New England's pattern. While the Puritans tried to subdue native peoples, New Yorkers wooed the powerful league of the Iroquois in order to maintain a competitive edge over the French for the fur trade. Because of their religious convictions, Quaker Pennsylvanians coexisted peaceably with the Lenni Lenapes for many decades.

The efforts of the later Stuart kings, Charles II and James II, to centralize England's empire aroused controversy in every northern colony except newly established Pennsylvania. That experiment in centralization, the Dominion of New England, ended with the Glorious Revolution in 1688. James II went into exile and was replaced on the throne by William and Mary. While New England weathered these years of political instability without severe internal division, Leisler's Rebellion plunged New York into turmoil. The dismantling of the Dominion, however, greatly reduced the tensions between England and its colonies. For more than half a century, English monarchs took no further steps to impose a centralized administration on America, and all of the colonies continued to enjoy relative independence under an imperial policy of "benign neglect."

ADDITIONAL READING

James Axtell's *The Invasion Within* (1985) offers a readable and fascinating account of relations between northern Indian tribes and French and English colonials. The best introductions to Puritanism are still Francis Bremer, *The Puritan Experiment* (1976) and Edmund S. Morgan, *The Puritan Dilemma* (1958), but David Hall's *Worlds of Wonder, Days of Judgment* (1989) provides the best coverage of the religious experiences and supernatural beliefs of ordinary New Englanders. There are many studies of individual New England communities, but the classic account of local political and social life remains Kenneth Lockridge, *A New England Town* (1970). Family life and women's experience in the early northern colonies are ably described by Laurel Ulrich's *Good Wives* (1982) and Barry Levy's provocative study of Pennsylvania, *Quakers and the American Family* (1988). David Lovejoy's *The Glorious Revolution in America* (1972) provides a useful overview of that event, but the most thoughtful assessment of British imperial policy in the late seventeenth century is Richard R. Johnson's *Adjustment to Empire* (1981).

The ethnic and religious diversity of the Middle Colonies offers an intriguing and instructive contrast to the relative homogeneity of early New England. Among the recent studies that render memorable portraits of those complex societies in early New York are Donna Merwick, *Possessing Albany, 1630–1710* (1990) and Joyce Goodfriend, *Before the Melting Pot* (1991). For Pennsylvania, see the fine overview of Joseph Illick, *Colonial Pennsylvania* (1976) and the topical essays in Richard Dunn and Mary Maples Dunn, eds., *The World of William Penn* (1986). For a fuller list of readings, see the Bibliography.

SIGNIFICANT EVENTS

late 1500s	Formation of the League of the Iroquois
1535	Cartier discovers the St. Lawrence
1608	Champlain founds Quebec on the St. Lawrence; Separatists flee to Holland
1620	Pilgrims land at Plymouth
1624	Dutch found New Netherlands
1630	Winthrop fleet arrives at Massachusetts Bay
1637	Pequot War
1642–1648	English Civil War
1649	Charles I executed
1660	English monarchy restored: Charles II becomes king
1664	New Netherlands becomes English New York; founding of New Jersey
1675–1676	Metacomet's War
1681	Founding of Pennsylvania
1685	James II becomes king of England
1686	Dominion of New England established
1688	Glorious Revolution; William and Mary become monarchs of England
1689	Massachusetts Bay overthrows Andros; Leisler's Rebellion in New York
1692	Witchcraft trials in Salem
1696	Creation of the Board of Trade and Plantations

4

The Mosaic of Eighteenth-Century America

bout 150 Iroquois sat facing the colonial commissioners in Albany, New York, on the morning of June 29, 1754. In front of the governor's house, servants had set up rows of long wooden planks, upon which the delegates from the Six Nations of the Iroquois now sat. The commissioners themselves, 25 in all, were not about to make do with planks; each had his own chair. They represented seven colonies, from Massachusetts Bay on the north to Maryland on the south.

Governor James DeLancey of New York stood and read a proclamation of welcome, pledging to "brighten the Chain of Friendship" between the Iroquois and the English. As each paragraph of the governor's speech was translated, the Iroquois were presented with a decorative belt, to which they responded with a ceremonial "Yo-heigh-eigh," shouted in unison. The noise unsettled those colonials attuned to the subtleties of Iroquois diplomacy. Normally, each nation voiced its agreement individually: six Yo-heigh-eighs coming one after another. By mixing them together, noted one observer, the delegates "had a mind to disguise that all the Nations did not universally give their hearty assent" to uniting with the English.

Unity—and not merely the unity of the Iroquois—was much on the mind of one commissioner from Philadelphia. Several chairs to the left of Governor DeLancey sat the most influential member of the Pennsylvania delegation, Benjamin Franklin. He knew that the question of whether the Iroquois would unite in an alliance with British America was only half the issue for this gathering at Albany. Equally important was whether the British colonies themselves could unite to deal effectively with France's threat throughout North America. Franklin had a plan for bringing the colonies together, but whether they would pay any notice remained an open question.

Rivalry between France and England

In a sense that plan grew out of a lifetime of experience, for the imperial rivalry between England and France had begun well before Franklin's birth and had flared, on and off, throughout his adult years. In 1689 England had joined the Netherlands and the League of Augsburg (several German-speaking states) in a war against France. While the main struggle raged on the continent of Europe, French and English colonials, joined by their Indian allies, skirmished in what was known as King William's War. Peace returned in 1697, but only until 1702, when the Anglo-French

In the mid-eighteenth century, Philadelphia became the largest city in the colonies and the second largest in all the British empire. Its busy harbor served not only as a commercial hub but also as the disembarkation point for thousands of immigrants. (The Library Company of Philadelphia)

struggle resumed again, four years before Franklin was born. It continued throughout his boyhood, until 1713.

For a quarter of a century thereafter, the two nations waged a kind of cold war, competing for position and influence. At stake was not so much control over people or even territory as control over trade. In North America, France and England vied for access to the sugar islands of the Caribbean, a monopoly on supplying manufactured goods to New Spain, and title to the fur trade. The British had the advantage of numbers: nearly 400,000 subjects in the colonies in 1720, compared with only about 25,000 French spread along a thin line of fishing stations and fur-trading posts. Yet the French steadily strengthened their chain of forts, stretching from the mouth of the Mississippi north through the Illinois country and into Canada. The forts helped channel the flow of furs from the Great Lakes and the Mississippi River valley into Canada, thus keeping them out of the clutches of English traders. And the forts neatly encircled England's colonies, confining their settlement to the eastern seaboard.

When fighting again engulfed Europe and the colonies in 1744, the results were inconclusive. King George's War, as the colonials dubbed it, ended four years later, but peace did nothing to diminish the old rivalry. As English traders and settlers filtered steadily into the Ohio River valley, the French built a new line of forts in 1752, from south of Lake Erie to the Ohio River. Two years later they erected Fort

Settlements like this one anchored the French position along the lower St. Lawrence River. Fields of wheat and peas as well as kitchen gardens supplied food; so did the eel traps, seen extending into the river beyond the salt marshes. (National Gallery of Canada)

Duquesne at the strategic forks of the Ohio, flush against the border of Franklin's Pennsylvania. That startled Pennsylvania and other colonies into sending commissioners to Albany in 1754 to coordinate efforts to deal with the worsening crisis. Franklin put the message plainly in his newspaper, the *Pennsylvania Gazette*, in a cartoon of a snake cut into segments. It was inscribed "Join, or Die."

Throughout those years of imperial maneuvering, the Iroquois League maintained a cool neutrality. They had become uneasy at the prospect of a North America without the French. Without French competition for Indian furs, what would spur British colonials to offer fair prices and trade goods of high quality? Without the arc of French settlement encircling the British American colonies, what would halt the westward spread of white settlement? Increasingly, too, the Iroquois were impressed by the show of French military might.

For the time being, the commissioners at Albany could do little to satisfy Iroquois doubts, except lavish as much hospitality as their budgets would allow. In the end the Iroquois made vague promises of loyalty and then hauled away 30 wagons full of presents.

The Albany Plan of Union

But would the colonies themselves unite? On the way to the Albany Congress Franklin had sketched out a framework for colonial cooperation. He proposed establishing "one general government" for British North America—a federal council composed of representatives from each colony, presided over by a president-general appointed by the Crown. The council would assume all responsibility for colonial defense and Indian policy, building forts and patrolling harbors with taxes levied on all Americans. The commissioners were bold enough to accept the plan, alarmed by the wavering Iroquois and the looming French threat.

JOIN, or DIE.

But the union born at Albany was smothered by the jealous colonies, who were unwilling to sing "yo-heigh-eigh" either in unison or separately. Not a single assembly approved the Albany Plan of Union. And no American legislature was ready to surrender its cherished right to tax inhabitants of its own colony—not to a federal council or to any other body. "Everyone cries, a union is necessary," Franklin wrote

Governor Shirley of Massachusetts in disgust; "but when they come to the manner and form of the union, their weak noodles are perfectly distracted." If the Albany Congress proved one thing, it was that American colonials were hopelessly divided.

FORCES OF DIVISION

Franklin, of course, should have known better than to hope for an intercolonial union. A practical man not given to idle dreams, he recognized the many forces of division at work in America. He knew that the colonies were divided by ethnic and regional differences, as well as racial and religious prejudices. Year after year small wooden ships brought a bewildering variety of immigrants to American seaports—especially Philadelphia, where Franklin had lived since 1723. From his efforts to reorganize the post office Franklin knew, too, that Americans were separated by vast distances, poor transportation, and slow communications. He knew how suspicious the frontier districts remained of seaboard communities and how the eastern seaboard disdained the backcountry. Taken all in all, the British settlements in America were, in the eighteenth century, a diverse and divided lot.

Immigration and Natural Increase

One of the largest immigrant groups—250,000 black men, women, and children—had come to the colonies from Africa not by choice but in chains. White arrivals included many English immigrants but also a quarter of a million Scots-Irish, the descendants of seventeenth-century Scots who had regretted settling in northern Ireland; perhaps 135,000 Germans; and a sprinkling of Swiss, Swedes, Highland Scots, and Spanish Jews. Most non-English white immigrants were fleeing lives torn by famine, warfare, and religious persecution. All of the voyagers, English and non-English, risked the hazardous Atlantic crossing (see Daily Lives, page 110–111). Many had paid for passage by signing indentures to work as servants in America.

The immigrants and slaves who arrived in the colonies between 1700 and 1775 swelled an American population that was already growing dramatically from natural increase. The birthrate in eighteenth-century America was triple what it is today. *High birth-rate* Most women bore between five and eight children, and most children survived to maturity. Indeed, the social and political consequences of this population explosion so intrigued Franklin that he wrote an essay on the subject in 1751. He recognized that ethnic and religious diversity, coupled with the hectic pace of westward expansion after 1700, made it hard for colonials to share any common identity. Far from fostering political union, almost every aspect of social development set Americans at odds with one another.

The Settlement of the Backcountry

To white immigrants from Europe weary of war or worn by want, the seaboard's established communities must have seemed havens of order and stability. But by the beginning of the eighteenth century, even the children of longtime settlers could not acquire land along the coast. In older New England towns, three and four genera-

TIME AND TRAVEL

Transatlantic Trials

A mountain of water swelled from the Atlantic, towered over the *Jamaica Packet,* then toppled onto the small wooden passenger ship. The impact hurled Janet Schaw and her maid about their cabin like rag dolls. As seawater surged in, the two women struggled to grasp something, anything, to keep from drowning. The ship pitched wildly, "one moment mounted to the clouds and whirled on the pointed wave," the next plunging prow first into the heaving ocean. Four sailors lashed to the helm fought for control, while the rest of the crew worked with their hands "torn to pieces by the wet ropes." The ship's provisions—hogsheads of water, coops of chickens, and barrels of salted meat—snapped from their fastenings and careened across the deck before bouncing overboard.

For more than two days the *Jamaica Packet* hurtled in the gale's grip. Then its foremast splintered, and the ship flipped onto its side. Passengers, crew, and furniture crashed "heels over head to the side the vessel had laid down on." Schaw found herself "swimming amongst joint-stools, chests, [and] tables" in her cabin and listening to the sound of "our sails fluttering into rags." It would have been the end of the *Jamaica Packet* if, at that moment, its masts

had not washed overboard. With the weight of the masts gone, the ship righted itself.

Schaw, "a lady of quality," as she described herself, was traveling by the finest accommodations from Great Britain to America in the age of sail. For those passengers who could not pay for a private cabin on the *Jamaica Packet,* the storm was worse. Twenty-two or more indentured servants from Scotland in that year of 1774 were bound aboard ship for the West Indies. Those impoverished families of farmers and fishermen had agreed with British merchants to work for American masters in return for the costs of passage. Like thousands of others who came to America in the eighteenth century, they were consigned to steerage, the between-decks area or "upper hold."

Perhaps four to five feet high, that space was crowded with narrow wooden bunks arranged in tiers about two feet apart. It was impossible for most people to stand in steerage or to sit up in a bunk, where as many as four people huddled together at night. Sanitary facilities consisted of a few wooden buckets filled with seawater; candles and fish-oil lanterns supplied the only light. The sole source of air was the hatch opening onto the deck.

When the storm struck, the hatch had been fastened tightly to keep the holds from filling with water. But as waves dashed over

tions were putting pressure on a limited supply of land, while wasteful farming practices had depleted the soil of its fertility. Farther south, earlier settlers had already snatched up the farmland of Philadelphia's outlying counties, the prime Chesapeake tobacco property, and lowcountry rice swamps.

With older rural communities offering few opportunities to either native-born or newly arrived white families, both groups were forced to create new communities on the frontier. The peopling of New England's frontier—Maine, New Hampshire, and the decks, water streamed into steerage, forcing its occupants to stand, clutching their children to keep them from being crushed or suffocated as the storm tumbled everyone from one side of their dark, watery prison to the other. For nine days they stood in water, without a fire or any food except raw potatoes and moldy biscuits. And they were without light or fresh air, except for one young man and his pregnant wife. During the storm the woman miscarried, and her "absolutely distracted" husband, Schaw reported, somehow forced open the hatch and carried her up to the deck, reviv-

ing the unconscious woman and saving her life. When at last the servants were allowed to come up on deck, they discovered that all of their belongings had been swept overboard.

What followed the servants up to the deck, to the horror of all, was a stench "sufficient to raise a plague aboard." But the luck of the *Jamaica Packet* held, for it escaped not only shipwreck but epidemic disease. Passengers on other transatlantic voyages were not so fortunate. Throughout the eighteenth century notices of ships "lost at sea" or of passengers who slipped overboard in storms filled colonial newspapers. Outbreaks of epidemic disease—smallpox, influenza, typhus, and diphtheria—were common. Although there are no reliable statistics for shipboard mortality during the eighteenth century, estimates range from 3 percent of all passengers to as high as 10 to 15 percent, a rate nearly comparable to that for slave ships during the Middle Passage across the Atlantic.

For all who ventured abroad, transatlantic travel was tedious and dirty at best, hazardous and horrific at worst. Those who risked the crossing routinely made out wills and sought the prayers of loved ones. But disease and danger at sea took the greatest toll from the poor, indentured servants, and convict laborers who made up the majority of eighteenth-century emigrants.

Vermont—was left mainly to the descendants of old Yankee families. Better opportunities for new immigrants to acquire land at cheaper prices lay south of New York. By the 1720s German and Scots-Irish immigrants as well as native-born settlers were pouring into western Pennsylvania. Some settled permanently, but others streamed southward into the backcountry of Virginia and the Carolinas, where they encountered native-born southerners pressing westward.

Backcountry settlers endured greater isolation than other colonials. From many

PATTERNS OF SETTLEMENT IN THE EIGHTEENTH CENTURY
The French, English, and Indian nations all jockeyed for power and position across North America during the eighteenth century. The French expanded their fur trade through the interior, while English settlement at midcentury began to press the barrier of the Appalachians. Many non-English settlers spilled into the backcountry: the Scots-Irish and Germans followed the Great Wagon Road through the western parts of the Middle Colonies and southern colonies while the Dutch and Germans moved up the Hudson River valley. Albany, where Franklin journeyed in 1754 for the Albany Congress, was one natural pivotal point in the rivalry—a place were Iroquois, French, and English interests converged.

farmsteads it was a day's ride to the nearest courthouse; taverns and churches were *Isolation* often just as distant. Isolation hindered the formation of strong social bonds, as did *of the* the rapid rate at which people came to and left western communities. Many families *backcountry* pulled up stakes three or four times before settling permanently. Houses reflected that transience: most families crowded into one-room shacks walled with mud, turf, or crude logs.

The backcountry meant economic isolation as well. Large portions of the interior were cut off from water transport because they were located above the fall line, where rivers flowing to the Atlantic became unnavigable. By 1755 several crude wagon roads linked western Pennsylvania and Virginia to towns farther east, including Philadelphia, but transporting crops and driving livestock overland proved prohibitively expensive. Cut off from outside markets, farmers grew only enough to feed their households. Most backcountry inhabitants could not afford to invest in a slave or even a servant, so they relied on family labor alone to cultivate a small fraction of their farms' total acreage. Those conditions made the frontier, more than anywhere else in America, a society of equals.

What the frontier gained in equality it may have lost in stability. In the backcountry there were no southern gentlemen or northern town fathers to supply continuous, experienced local leadership. There was only a handful of farmers in each

This log cabin, built in the North Carolina backcountry in 1782, would have been dark inside, given its lack of windows. The spaces between the logs in such cabins were usually chinked with thin stones or wedges of wood and then daubed with mortar.

county set above their neighbors by owning a few extra acres or a single slave. To these inexperienced and poorly educated men fell the tasks of overseeing public order as justices of the peace or officers in the local militia or representatives to colonial assemblies. It was hard for those with so little authority over their fellows to police sprawling backcountry communities; not surprisingly, coarse and aggressive behavior dominated frontier life. Backcountry men and women mated out of wedlock, swore in public, drank to excess, and brawled at any provocation.

Nor were the churches much help in promoting law and order. Building churches lay beyond the means of many frontier communities, and few ministers were willing to endure the rigors of preaching from one backcountry neighborhood to another. While churches loomed large in the lives of Americans on the coast, most western families, although often deeply pious, had only occasional contact with organized religion.

Frontier women   Hard work dominated the lives of backcountry settlers. Besides doing the usual chores of farm women, western wives and daughters joined male family members in the fields. One traveler from the East expressed his astonishment at seeing German women in western Pennsylvania "at work abroad on the Farm mowing, Hoeing, Loading Dung into a Cart." Perhaps even more difficult to endure than the hard labor was the loneliness of many women's lives. The reactions of women to being resettled on the frontier can be imagined from the promise that one Scottish husband offered his wife: "We would get all these trees cut down . . . [so] that we would see from house to house."

Social Conflict on the Frontier

Despite the discomforts of frontier life, cheap land lured many families to the West. Benjamin Franklin had observed the hordes of Scots-Irish and German immigrants lingering in Philadelphia just long enough to scrape together the purchase price of a frontier farm. From Franklin's point of view, the backcountry performed a valuable service by siphoning off surplus people from congested eastern settlements. But he knew, too, that the frontier was an American Pandora's box. Once opened, the West unleashed discord, especially between the eastern seaboard and the backcountry.

The Paxton Boys   In Pennsylvania, Franklin himself mediated one such contest between east and west. In 1763 a band of Scots-Irish farmers known as "the Paxton Boys" protested the government's inadequate protection of frontier settlers by killing a number of Indians. Then the Paxton Boys took their protests and their guns to Philadelphia, marching as far as Lancaster before Franklin intervened and promised redress of their grievances.

Strife between east and west was even deadlier and more enduring in North and South Carolina. In both colonies legislatures dominated by coastal planters refused to grant inland settlers equitable political representation or even basic legal institutions. In response to those injustices, two protest movements emerged in the Carolina interior, each known as the Regulation.

Regulation movements   Farmers in the South Carolina backcountry organized their Regulation in the 1760s, after that colony's assembly refused to set up courts in the backcountry. Westerners were desperate for protection from outlaws who stole livestock, kidnapped and raped women, and tortured and murdered men. In the absence of courts the Regulators acted as vigilantes, meting out their own brand of grisly frontier justice against these criminals. Regulator threats to march on Charleston itself finally panicked eastern political leaders into extending the court system, but bitter memories lingered among westerners.

Western North Carolinians organized their Regulation to protest not the absence of a legal system but the corruption of local government. Lawyers and merchants, backed by wealthy eastern planters, moved into the western parts of that colony and seized control of politics. Then they used local office to exploit frontier settlers, charging exorbitant fees for legal services, imposing high taxes, and manipulating debt laws. Western farmers responded to these abuses with the Regulation: they seized county courts and finally squared off against an eastern militia led by the governor. Easterners crushed the Regulators at the Battle of Alamance in 1771 but left frontier North Carolinians with an enduring hostility to the seaboard.

Ethnic differences heightened sectional tensions between east and west. While *Ethnic* people of English descent predominated along the Atlantic coast, Germans, Scots- *conflicts* Irish, and other white minorities were concentrated in the interior. Many English colonials regarded these new immigrants as culturally inferior and politically subversive. In 1729 Bostonians greeted the arrival of a boatload of Irish immigrants with a riot. A few years later, a mob in Worcester, Massachusetts, set fire to a Scots-Irish Presbyterian church. Farther south, Charles Woodmason, an Anglican missionary in the Carolina backcountry, lamented the arrival of "5 or 6000 Ignorant, mean, worthless, beggarly Irish Presbyterians, the Scum of the Earth, the Refuse of Mankind," who "delighted in a low, lazy, sluttish, heathenish, hellish life."

German immigrants were generally credited with having steadier work habits, as well as higher standards of sexual morality and personal hygiene. But like the clannish Scots-Irish, the Germans preferred to live, trade, and worship among themselves. By 1751 Franklin was warning that the Germans would retain their separate language and customs: the Pennsylvania English would be overrun by "the Palatine Boors."

Boundary Disputes and Tenant Wars

The settlement of the frontier also triggered disputes between colonies over their boundaries. At the root of the confusion were the old colonial charters and their vague definitions of western borders which allowed groups of settlers and speculators from different colonies to claim the same tract of land. The most serious of these border wars pitted New York against farmers from New England who had settled in present-day Vermont: Ethan Allen and the Green Mountain Boys. In the 1760s, New *Green* York, backed by the Crown, claimed land that Allen and his friends had already pur- *Mountain* chased from New Hampshire. When New York tried to extend its rule over Vermont, *Boys* Allen led a successful guerrilla resistance, harassing Yorker settlers and officials, occupying Yorker courthouses, and setting up a competing judicial system in the Green Mountains.

The spread of settlement also set the stage for mass revolts by tenants in those areas where proprietors controlled vast amounts of land. In eastern New Jersey, proprietors insisted that squatters pay quitrents on land that had become increasingly populated and therefore more valuable. When the squatters, many of them migrants from New England, refused to pay rents, buy the land, or move, the proprietors began evictions, touching off riots in the 1740s. Tenant unrest also raged in New

York's Hudson River valley. In the 1680s the royal governor had granted several prominent merchant families large estates in that region. By the middle of the eighteenth century, there were about 30 manors around New York City and Albany, totaling some 2 million acres and worked by several thousand tenants. Newcomers from New England, however, demanded to own land and preached their ideas to Dutch and German tenants. Armed insurrection exploded in 1757 and again, more violently, in 1766. Tenants refused to pay rents, formed mobs, and stormed the homes of landlords.

Eighteenth-Century Seaports

While most Americans on the move settled on the frontier, others swelled the populations of colonial cities. By present-day standards such cities were small, harboring from 8000 to 22,000 citizens by 1750. The scale of seaports remained intimate, too: all of New York City was clustered at the southern tip of Manhattan Island, and the length of Boston or Charleston could be walked in less than half an hour.

All major colonial cities were seaports, their waterfronts fringed with wharves and shipyards. A jumble of shops, taverns, and homes crowded their streets; the spires of churches studded their skylines. By the 1750s, the grandest and most populous was Philadelphia, which boasted straight, neatly paved streets, flagstone sidewalks, and three-story brick buildings. Older cities like Boston and New York had a more medieval aspect: most of their dwellings and shops were wooden structures with tiny windows and low ceilings, rising no higher than two stories to steeply pitched roofs. The narrow cobblestone streets of Boston and New York also challenged pedestrians, who competed for space with livestock being driven to the butcher, roaming herds of swine and packs of dogs, clattering carts, carriages, and horses.

The commercial classes   Commerce, the lifeblood of seaport economies, was managed by merchants who tapped the wealth of surrounding regions. Traders in New York and Philadelphia shipped the Hudson and Delaware valleys' surplus of grain and livestock to the West Indies. Boston's merchants sent fish to the Caribbean and Catholic Europe, masts to England, and rum to west Africa. Charlestonians exported indigo to English dyemakers and rice to southern Europe. Other merchants specialized in the import trade, selling luxuries and manufactured goods produced in England—fine fabrics, ceramics, tea, and farming implements. Wealth brought many merchants political power: they dominated city governments and shared power in colonial assemblies with lawyers and the largest farmers and planters.

Skilled craftworkers or artisans made up the middling classes of colonial cities. The households of master craftworkers usually included a few younger and less skilled journeymen working in other artisans' shops. Unskilled boy apprentices not only worked but also lived under the watchful eye of their masters. No large-scale domestic industry produced goods for a mass market: instead craft shops filled orders for specific items placed by individual purchasers. Some artisans specialized in the maritime trades as shipbuilders, blacksmiths, and sailmakers. Others, like butchers, millers, and distillers, processed and packed raw materials for export. Still others served the basic needs of city dwellers—the men and, occasionally, women who baked bread, mended shoes, combed and powdered wigs, and tended shops and taverns.

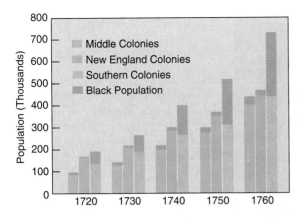

ESTIMATED POPULATION BY REGION,
1720–1760

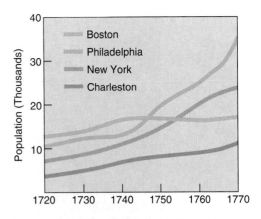

ESTIMATED POPULATION OF COLONIAL
CITIES, 1720–1770
While Boston's population remained stable after
1740, it was surpassed by the sharp growth of
New York and, especially, Philadelphia.

On the lowest rung of a seaport's social hierarchy were free and bound workers. *Free and* *bound* *workers*
Free laborers were mainly young white men and women—journeymen artisans,
sailors, fishermen, domestic workers, seamstresses, and prostitutes. The ranks of unfree workers included apprentices and indentured servants doing menial labor in
shops and on the docks.

Black men and women also made up a substantial part of the bound labor force
of colonial seaports, not only in southern Charleston but in northern cities as well.
While the vast majority of slaves imported from Africa were destined for southern
plantations, a smaller number were sold to urban merchants and craftworkers.
Laboring as porters at the docks, as assistants in craft shops, or as servants in wealthy
households, black residents made up almost 20 percent of the population in New
York City and 10 percent in Boston and Philadelphia.

The character of slavery in northern seaports changed decisively during the mid-
eighteenth century. When wars raging in Europe reduced the supply of white indentured servants, colonial cities imported a larger number of Africans. In the two
decades after 1730, one-third of all immigrants arriving in New York harbor were
black; by 1760, blacks comprised over three-quarters of all bound laborers in
Philadelphia. The preference for importing African men upset what had been an
equal balance of black men and women in colonial seaports, making it difficult for the
newcomers to establish families. Slaves from Africa also lacked immunity to
American diseases, and many did not survive their first winter: the death rate among
urban blacks was double that for whites.

But the survivors brought to urban black culture a new awareness of a common
west African past. The influence of African traditions appeared most vividly in an annual event known as "Negro election day," celebrated in northern seaports. During
the festival, similar to ones held in west Africa, some black men and women paraded
in their masters' clothes or mounted on their horses. An election followed to choose

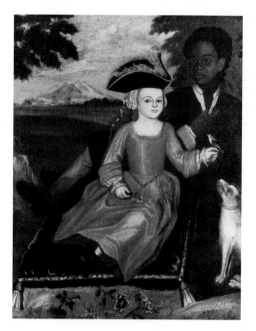

In both eighteenth-century England and America, portraits of prominent white families and individuals sometimes included black slaves who served wealthy households. This portrait depicts a young child of New York's Van Rensselaer family and foretells his future mastery of both the young black male slave and, in the background, a fine estate in the Hudson River valley.

black "kings," "governors," and "judges" who then "held court" and settled minor disputes among white and black members of the community. "Negro election day" did not challenge the established racial order with its temporary reversal of roles, but it did allow the black communities of seaports to honor their own leaders.

Women in cities   The availability of domestic workers, both black and white, made for leisured lives among women from wealthy white families. Even those city women who could not afford household help spent less time on domestic work than farming wives and daughters. Although some housewives grew vegetables in backyard gardens or kept a few chickens, large markets stocked by outlying farmers supplied most of the food for urban families.

For women who had to support themselves, seaports offered a number of employments. Young single women from poorer families worked in wealthier households as maids, cooks, laundresses, seamstresses, or nurses. The highest paying occupations for women, midwifery and dressmaking, both required long apprenticeships and expert skills. The wives of artisans and traders sometimes assisted their husbands and, as widows, often continued to manage groceries, taverns, and print shops. But most women were confined to caring for households, husbands, and children; fewer than 1 out of every 10 women in seaports worked outside their own homes.

Urban diversions and hazards   All seaport dwellers—perhaps 1 out of every 20 Americans—enjoyed a more stimulating environment than other colonials. The wealthiest could attend an occasional ball or concert; those living in New York or Charleston might even see a play performed by touring English actors. The middling classes could converse with other tradespeople at private social clubs and fraternal societies. Men of every class found diversion in drink and cockfighting. Crowds of men, women, and children swarmed to tavern exhibitions of trained dogs and horses or the spectacular waxworks of one

John Dyer, featuring "a lively Representation of Margaret, Countess of Herrinburg, who had 365 Children at one Birth."

But city dwellers, then as now, paid a price for their pleasures. Commerce was riddled with risk: ships sank and wars disrupted trade. When such disasters struck, the lower classes suffered most. The ups and downs of seaport economies, combined with the influx of immigrants, swelled the ranks of the poor in all cities by the mid-eighteenth century. While the major seaports established workhouses to employ the able-bodied poor, city governments continued to aid most of the dependent with small subsidies of money, food, and firewood. Furthermore, epidemics and catastrophic fires occurred with greater frequency and produced higher mortality rates in congested seaports than in the countryside.

Social Conflict in Seaports

The swelling of seaport populations, like the movement of whites to the West, often churned up trouble. English, Scots-Irish, Germans, Swiss, Dutch, French, and Spanish jostled uneasily against one another in the close quarters of Philadelphia and New York. To make matters worse, religious differences heightened ethnic divisions. Jewish funerals in New York, for example, drew crowds of hostile and curious Protestants, who heckled the mourners.

Class resentment also stirred unrest. Some merchant families flaunted their wealth, building imposing town mansions and dressing in the finest imported fashions. During hard times, symbols of merchant wealth like expensive coaches and full warehouses became targets of mob vandalism. Crowds also gathered to intimidate and punish other groups who provoked popular hostility—unresponsive politicians, prostitutes, and "press gangs." Impressment, attempts to force colonials to serve in the British navy, triggered some of the most violent urban riots.

Ashley Bowen, an eighteenth-century New Englander, made a drawing to commemorate his courtship of Dorothy Chadwick. Although she refused him at first (He: "Will thee consent to be my bride"; She: "Sir, I have not that Desire."), Bowen finally prevailed. Ashley's self-portrait, dominating both the sketch and the diminutive Dorothy, underscores colonial views of the relative status of men and women.

SLAVE SOCIETIES IN THE EIGHTEENTH-CENTURY SOUTH

Far starker than the inequalities and divisions among seaport dwellers were those between white and black in the South. By 1775 one out of every five Americans was of African ancestry, and over 90 percent of all black Americans lived in the South, most along the seaboard. Here, on tobacco and rice plantations, slaves fashioned a distinc-

*The
Chesapeake
versus the
Lower South*

tive African American society and culture. But they were able to build stable families and communities only late in the eighteenth century and against enormous odds.

Whether a slave was auctioned off to the Chesapeake or to the Lower South shaped his or her future in important ways. Slaves in the lowcountry of South

THE DISTRIBUTION OF THE AMERICAN POPULATION, 1775
The African American population expanded dramatically during the eighteenth century, especially in the southern colonies. While the high volume of slave imports accounts for most of the growth in the first half of the century, natural increase was responsible for the rising black population during later decades.

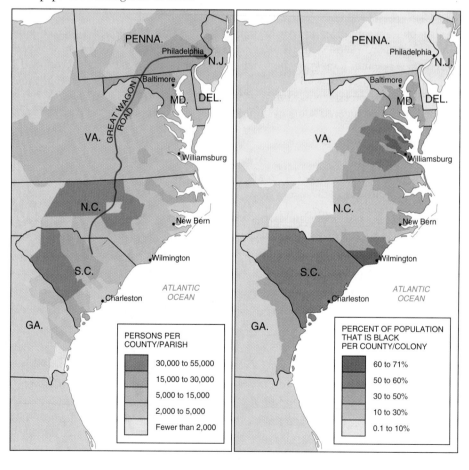

Carolina and Georgia lived on large plantations with as many as 50 other black work-ers, about half of whom were African-born. They had infrequent contact with either their masters or the rest of the sparse white population. "They are as 'twere, a Nation within a Nation," observed Francis LeJau, an Anglican priest in the lowcountry. And their work was arduous, for rice required constant cultivation. Black laborers tended young plants and hoed fields in the sweltering summer heat of the mosquito-infested lowlands. During the winter and early spring, they built dams and canals to regulate the flow of water into the rice fields. But the use of the "task system" rather than gang labor widened the window of freedom within slavery. When a slave had completed his assigned task for the day, one planter explained, "his master feels no right to call upon him."

Many Chesapeake slaves, like those in the Lower South, were African-born, but most lived on smaller plantations with fewer than 20 fellow slaves. Less densely con-centrated than in the lowcountry, Chesapeake slaves also had more contact with whites. Unlike Carolina's absentee owners who left white overseers and black drivers to run their plantations, Chesapeake masters actively managed their estates and sub-jected their slaves to closer scrutiny.

The Slave Family and Community

The four decades following 1700 marked the heaviest years of slave importation into the Chesapeake and Carolina regions. Those Africans had survived the trauma of captivity, the Middle Passage, and sale at slave auctions, only to be thrust into a be-wildering new world: a sea of unfamiliar faces, a clamor of different languages, a host of demands from men and women who called themselves masters.

The newcomers also had to adjust to their fellow slaves. The "new Negroes" hailed from a number of diverse west African tribes, each with a separate language or dialect and distinctive cultures and kinship systems. Often, they had little in com-mon with one another and even less in common with the American-born black mi-nority. Native-born African Americans enjoyed better health, command of English, and experience in dealing with whites. They were also more likely to enjoy a family life, for their advantages probably made them the preferred partners of black women, who were outnumbered two to one by black men. And since immigrant women waited two or three years before marrying, some immigrant men died before they could find a wife, and many never married. Africans resented native-born men as ri-vals in the competition for wives, and some immigrants held in particular contempt native converts to Christianity.

African slaves versus American-born slaves

After the middle of the eighteenth century, a number of changes fostered the growth of black families and the vitality of slave communities. As slave importations began to taper off, the rate of natural reproduction among blacks started to climb. As the proportion of new Africans dropped and the number of native-born black Americans grew, the ratio of men to women in the slave community became more equal. Those changes and the appearance of more large plantations, even in the Chesapeake, created more opportunities for black men and women to find partners and form families. Elaborate kinship networks gradually developed, often extending over several plantations in a single neighborhood. And as the immigrant generations were replaced by native-born offspring, earlier sources of tension and division within the slave community disappeared.

Even so, black families remained vulnerable. If a planter fell on hard times, members of black families might be sold off to different buyers to meet his debts. When a master died, black spouses, parents, and childen might be divided among surviving heirs. Even under the best circumstances, fathers might be hired out to other planters for long periods or sent to work in distant quarters. The migration of slaveholders from the coast to the interior also disrupted black efforts to fashion domestic and communal bonds. Between 1755 and 1782, masters on the move resettled fully one-third of all adult African Americans living in Tidewater, Virginia. Most slaves forced to journey west were men and women in their teens and early twenties, who had to begin again the long process of establishing families and neighborhood networks far from kin and friends.

Influence of African culture

Black families struggling with terrible uncertainties were sustained by the distinctive African American culture evolving in the slave community. The high percentage of native Africans among the eighteenth-century American black population made it easier for slaves to retain the ways of their lost homeland. Christianity won few converts, in part because white masters feared that baptizing slaves might make them more rebellious but also because African Americans preferred their traditional religions. African influence appeared as well in the slaves' agricultural skills and practices, folktales, music, and dances.

Slave Resistance in the Eighteenth Century

Inevitably, slavery forced upon the enslaved a need to cope with the institution's barbarities, and enslaved African Americans both resisted captivity and developed strategies for survival. Among newly arrived Africans, collective attempts at escape were most common. Groups of slaves, often made up of newcomers from the same tribe, fled inland and formed "Maroon" communities of runaways. These efforts were usually unsuccessful because the Maroon settlements were large enough to be easily detected.

More acculturated blacks adopted subtler ways of subverting slavery. Domestics and field hands alike faked illness, feigned stupidity and laziness, broke tools, pilfered from storehouses, hid in the woods for weeks at a time, or simply took off to visit other plantations. Other slaves, usually escaping bondage as solitary individuals, found a new life as craftworkers, dock laborers, or sailors in the relative anonymity of colonial seaports.

More infrequently, black rebellion took direct and violent form. Whites in communities with large numbers of blacks lived in gnawing dread of arson, poisoning, and insurrection. Four slave conspiracies were reported in Virginia during the first half of the eighteenth century. In South Carolina, more than two decades of abortive uprisings and insurrection scares culminated in the Stono Rebellion of 1739, the largest slave revolt of the colonial period. Nearly 100 African Americans, led by a slave named Jemmy, seized arms from a store in the coastal district of Stono and killed several white neighbors before they were caught and killed by the white militia.

The Stono Rebellion

But throughout the eighteenth century, slave rebellions occurred far less frequently on the mainland of North America than in the Caribbean or Brazil. Whites outnumbered blacks in all of Britain's mainland colonies except South Carolina, and only there did rebels have a haven for a quick escape—Spanish Florida. Faced with

The Old Plantation affords a rare glimpse of life in the slave quarters. At this festive gathering, both men and women dance to the music of a molo (a stringed instrument similar to a banjo) and drums. The insets show a stringed kora and a gudugudu drum, instruments common throughout Africa and similar to those depicted in the painting.

those odds, most slaves reasoned that the risks of rebellion outweighed the prospects for success—and most sought opportunities for greater personal freedom within the slave system itself.

Despite the growing rebelliousness of black slaves, southern planters continued to import Africans throughout the eighteenth century. The practice mystified Franklin, revealing at least one gap in his knowledge—the crucial importance of slavery in the southern economy. But unlike some of his Quaker neighbors in Pennsylvania, who were beginning to object to slavery on moral and humanitarian grounds, Franklin's reservations—like his opposition to German immigration—were overtly racist. "Why increase the sons of Africa by planting them in America," he asked, "where we have so fair an opportunity, by excluding all blacks and tawnys, of increasing the lovely white and red?"

COUNTERPOINT

The African American response to enslavement

It is only in the last twenty years that historians have come to appreciate how various and enduring were the ways in which black men and women resisted bondage. In the 1960s, when scholars began to explore the impact of slavery on African Americans, many portrayed blacks as passive victims of a brutal system. They concluded that the experience of captivity left African Americans so disoriented and demoralized that they lost the will to fight back. Indeed, one influential historian compared the regimen of southern plantations to that in Nazi concentration camps during World War II, arguing that both were "total institutions" that utterly transformed the personalities of those subject to such repressive conditions. To survive the horrors of slavery, blacks became docile, submissive, dependent, even childlike.

That interpretation has been sharply challenged since the mid-1970s by other historians who argue for the resourcefulness and resilience of African Americans in bondage. Without denying the harshness of the slave system, these scholars have shown that most southern plantations were not so tightly and efficiently controlled as to cripple the personalities of slaves. On the contrary, they believe that blacks created space within those settings to fashion a sustaining family and communal life, institutions that endowed them with a strong sense of personal and collective identity. They contend, too, that relationships between masters and slaves were often complex interactions in which blacks could negotiate terms for better treatment. There is much evidence to confirm that some slaves became expert at showing masters that their productivity depended on having some measure of freedom—being permitted to set their work schedules, to meet at night for religious services, to choose their mates.

ENLIGHTENMENT AND AWAKENING IN AMERICA

The differences among eighteenth-century colonials resulted in more than clashes between regions, races, classes, and ethnic groups. Those differences also made for diversity in the ways that Americans thought and believed. City dwellers were more attuned to European culture than were people living in small villages or on the frontier. White males from well-to-do families of English ancestry were far more likely to receive college educations than were those from poorer or immigrant households. White women of every class and background were excluded from higher education, and slaves received no formal education at all. Where they lived, how well they lived, whether they were male or female, native-born or immigrant, slave or free—all these variables fostered among colonials distinctive worldviews, differing attitudes and assumptions about the individual's relationship to nature, society, and God.

The Enlightenment in America

The diversity of colonials' inner lives became even more pronounced during the eighteenth century because of the Enlightenment, an intellectual movement that started in Europe during the seventeenth century. The leading figures of the Enlightenment, the "philosophes," stressed the power of human reason to promote progress by revealing the laws that governed both nature and society. In the American colonies the Enlightenment influenced some curious artisans in major seaports, as well as wealthy merchants, lawyers, and landowners with the leisure and education to read the latest books from Europe.

Like many devotees of the Enlightenment, Franklin was most impressed by its emphasis on useful knowledge and experimentation. He pondered air currents and then invented a stove that heated houses more efficiently. He toyed with electricity and then invented lightning rods to protect buildings in thunderstorms. Other amateur colonial scientists constructed simple telescopes, classified animal species native to North America, or sought to explain epidemics in terms of natural causes.

Higher education helped to spread Enlightenment ideas among young colonials from affluent families. While many Americans were still educated at English universities, six colleges had been established in the colonies by 1763. The founders of some of these institutions, such as Harvard (1636) and Yale (1701), had intended them primarily to train ministers, but by the eighteenth century their graduates included lawyers and merchants, doctors and scientists. Most offered courses in mathematics and the natural sciences that taught students algebra and such advanced theories as Copernican astronomy and Newtonian physics.

Some clergy educated at American colleges were touched by the Enlightenment, adopting a more liberal theology that stressed the reasonableness of Christian beliefs. By the middle of the eighteenth century this "rational Christianity" commanded a small following among colonials, usually Anglicans or liberal Congregationalists. Their God was not the Calvinists' awesome deity but a benevolent creator who offered salvation to all, not just to a small, predestined elite. They believed that God's greatest gift to mankind was reason, which enabled all human beings to follow the moral teachings of Jesus. They muted the Calvinist emphasis on human sinfulness and the need for a soul-shattering conversion. *Rational versus traditional Christianity*

Enlightenment philosophy and rational Christianity did not affect the outlook of most colonials. By the middle of the eighteenth century, over half of all white men (and a smaller percentage of white women) were literate. But most colonial readers were not equipped to tackle the learned writings of Enlightenment philosophes. As a result, the outlook of most colonials contrasted sharply with that of the cosmopolitan few. The great majority of Americans still looked for ultimate truth in biblical revelation rather than human reason and explained the workings of the world in terms of divine providence rather than natural law.

Widespread attachment to traditional Christian beliefs was strengthened by the hundreds of new churches built during the first half of the eighteenth century. Church attendance ran highest in the northern colonies, where some 80 percent of the population turned out for public worship on the Sabbath. In the South, because of the greater distances involved and the shortage of clergy, about half of all colonials regularly attended Sunday services.

Despite the prevalence of traditional religious beliefs, many ministers expressed concern about the dangerous influence of rational Christianity. They also worried that the lack of churches might tempt many frontier families to abandon Christianity altogether. Exaggerated as these fears may have been, the consequence was a major religious revival that swept the colonies during the middle decades of the eighteenth century.

The First Great Awakening

The Great Awakening, as the revival came to be called, deepened the influence of older forms of Protestant Christianity and, specifically, Calvinism throughout British America. Participation in the revival was the only experience that a large number of people everywhere in the colonies had in common. But the Great Awakening also heightened religious divisions among Americans.

The first stirrings of revival appeared in the 1730s among Presbyterians and Congregationalists in the Middle Colonies and New England. Many ministers in these churches preached an "evangelical" message, emphasizing the need for individuals to experience "a new birth" through religious conversion. Among them was Jonathan Edwards, the pastor of a Congregational church in Northampton, Massachusetts. Edwards's preaching combined moving descriptions of God's grace with terrifying portrayals of eternal damnation. "The God that holds you over the pit of hell, much as one holds a spider or some loathsome insect over the fire, abhors you and is dreadfully provoked," he declaimed to one congregation; ". . . there is no other reason to be given, why you have not dropped into hell since you arise in the morning, but that God's hand has held you up."

The appeal of George Whitefield

These local revivals of the 1730s were mere tremors compared to the earthquake of religious enthusiasm that shook the colonies with the arrival in the fall of 1739 of George Whitefield. This handsome, cross-eyed "boy preacher" from England electrified crowds from Georgia to New Hampshire during his two-year tour of the

George Whitefield drew critics as well as admirers in both England and America. In this satirical English cartoon, he is depicted as a money-grubbing evangelist who uncharitably condemns other ministers. His audience, which consists mainly of women, is taken in by his pose of sanctity and his youthful good looks.

colonies. He and his many imitators among colonial ministers turned the church into a theater, enlivening sermons with dramatic gestures, flowing tears, and gruesome depictions of hell's torments. The drama of such performances appealed to people of all classes, ethnic groups, and races. By the time Whitefield sailed back to England in 1741, thousands of awakened souls were joining older churches or forming new ones.

The Aftermath of the Great Awakening

Whitefield also left behind a raging storm of controversy. Many "awakened" church members now openly criticized their ministers as cold, unconverted, and uninspiring. To supply the missing fire, some laymen—"and even Women and Common Negroes"—took to "exhorting" any audience willing to listen. The most popular ministers became "itinerants," traveling like Whitefield from one town to another. Throughout the colonies conservative and moderate clergy questioned the unrestrained emotionalism and the disorder that attended the gatherings of lay exhorters and itinerants.

Although Americans had been fighting over religion well before the Great *Religious* Awakening, the new revivals left colonials even more divided along religious lines. *divisions* The largest single group of churchgoers in the northern colonies remained within the Congregational and Presbyterian denominations. But both these groups split into factions that either supported or condemned the revivals. Some conservative Presbyterians and Congregationalists, disgusted with the disorder, defected to the Quakers and the Anglicans, who had shunned the revival. On the other hand the most radical converts joined forces with the warmest champions of the Awakening, the Baptists.

While northern churches splintered and bickered, the fires of revivalism spread *Evangelicalism* to the South and its backcountry. From the mid-1740s until the 1770s, scores of new *on the* Presbyterian and Baptist churches were formed, but conflict often accompanied re- *frontier* ligious zeal. Ardent Presbyterians in the Carolina backcountry disrupted Anglican worship by loosing packs of dogs in local chapels. In northern Virginia, Anglicans took the offensive against the Baptists, whose strict moral code sounded a silent reproach to the hard-drinking, high-stepping, horse-racing, slaveholding gentry. County officials, prodded by resentful Anglican parsons, harassed, fined, and imprisoned Baptist ministers.

While the West was turning toward evangelical Calvinism, the most powerful people on the southeastern coast remained Anglican and, in the Middle Colonies, Quaker. As a result, the seaboard and the backcountry often found themselves quarreling over religious as well as political and ethnic issues. Inevitably, civil governments were drawn into the fight. In colonies where one denomination received state support, other churches lobbied legislatures for disestablishment, an end to the favored status of Congregationalism in Connecticut and Massachusetts and of Anglicanism in the southern colonies.

And so a diverse lot of Americans found themselves continually at odds with one another. Because of differences in religion and education, colonials quarreled over whether rational Christianity enlightened the world or emotional revivalists destroyed its order. Because of ethnic and racial tensions, Spanish Jews found themselves persecuted, and African Americans searched for ways to resist their white masters. Because of westward expansion, Carolina Regulators waged war against coastal planters, while colonial legislatures from Massachusetts to Virginia quarreled over western boundaries.

Benjamin Franklin, a man who made it his business to know, surely understood the depth of those divisions as he made his way toward the Albany Congress in the spring of 1754. He himself had brooded over the boatloads of non-English newcomers. He had lived in two booming seaports and felt the explosive force of the frontier. He personified the Enlightenment—and he had heard George Whitefield himself preach from the steps of the Philadelphia courthouse.

Why, then, could Franklin, who knew how little held the colonials together, sustain his hopes for political unity? The answer may be that even in 1754, the majority of colonials were of English descent. And these free, white Americans liked being English. That much they had in common.

ANGLO-AMERICAN WORLDS OF THE EIGHTEENTH CENTURY

Most Americans prided themselves on being English. When colonials named their towns and counties, they named them after places in their parent country. When colonials established governments, they turned to England for their political models. They frequently claimed "the liberties of freeborn Englishmen" as their birthright. Even in diet, dress, furniture, architecture, and literature colonists adopted English standards of taste.

Yet American society had developed in ways significantly different from that of Great Britain.° Some differences made colonials feel inferior, ashamed of their simplicity when compared with London's sophistication. But colonials also came to appreciate the greater equality of their society and the more representative character of their governments. If it was good to be English, it was better still to be English in America.

English Economic and Social Development

The differences between England and America began with their economies. Large financial institutions like the Bank of England and influential corporations like the East India Company were driving England's commercial development. A growing number of textile factories and mines were deepening its industrial development. Although most English men and women worked at agriculture, it, too, had become a business. Members of the gentry rented their estates to tenants, members of the rural middle class. In turn, these tenants hired men and women from the swollen ranks of England's landless to perform the actual farm labor. By contrast, most colonial farmers owned their land, and most family farms were a few hundred acres. The scale of commerce and manufacturing was equally modest, limited by the preference of colonials to farm instead.

°When England and Scotland were unified in 1707, the nation as a whole became known officially as Great Britain; its citizens, as British.

Coffeehouses like this establishment in London were favorite gathering places for eighteenth-century Americans visiting Britain. Here merchants and mariners, ministers and students, lobbyists and tourists warmed themselves, read newspapers, and exchanged gossip about commerce, politics, and social life.

England's more developed economy fostered the growth of London and other cities. Although three-quarters of England's people lived in the countryside, a considerable number spent some part of their lives in cities. By contrast, 90 percent of all eighteenth-century colonials lived in towns of fewer than 2000.

Americans abroad quickly recognized that even major colonial seaports could not match London, a teeming colossus of 675,000 in 1750. Touring colonials gloried in the British Museum and gawked at cathedrals. They strolled through fashionable shops, fingering fine textiles and inspecting handsome carriages.

Inequality in England and America

But there was an underside to the splendor. London seethed with filth, crime, and desperate poverty. The poor and the unemployed as well as pickpockets and prostitutes crowded into its gin-soaked slums, taverns, and brothels. The contrast between the luxuries enjoyed by a wealthy few Londoners and the misery of the many disquieted colonial observers. Ebenezer Hazard, an American Quaker, knew for certain that he was not in Philadelphia, but instead in "a Sink of Sin."

The opportunities for great wealth provided by England's more developed economy created deep class distinctions, as did the inherited privileges of its aristocracy. The members of the upper class, the landed aristocracy and gentry, made up less than

Class distinctions

2 percent of England's population but owned 70 percent of its land. By right of birth, English aristocrats claimed membership in the House of Lords; by custom, certain powerful gentry families dominated the other branch of Parliament, the House of Commons. England's titled gentlemen shared power and wealth and often family ties with the rich men of the city—major merchants, successful lawyers, and lucky financiers. They too exerted political influence through the House of Commons.

The colonies had their own prominent families but no titled ruling class holding political privilege by hereditary right. And even the wealthiest colonial families lived in far less magnificence than their English counterparts. Probably the finest mansion in eighteenth-century America, William Byrd's Westover plantation, was scarcely a tenth the size of the Marquis of Rockingham's country house, which was longer than two football fields.

If England's upper classes lived more splendidly, its lower classes were larger and worse off than those in the colonies. Less than a third of England's inhabitants belonged to the "middling sort" of traders, professionals, artisans, and tenant farmers. More than two-thirds struggled for survival at the bottom of society. By contrast, the colonial middle class counted for nearly three-quarters of the white population. With land cheap, labor scarce, and wages for both urban and rural workers 100 percent higher in America than in England, it was much easier for colonials to accumulate savings and then buy a farm of their own.

Ambivalent Americans   Colonials were both fascinated and repelled by English society. On the one hand, Benjamin Rush, a Philadelphia physician, felt in the House of Lords as if he "walked on sacred ground." He begged his guide for permission to sit on the throne therein, and then sat "for a considerable time." Other colonials gushed over the grandeur of aristocratic estates and imported suits of livery for their servants, tea services for their wives, and wallpaper for their drawing rooms. They exported their sons to Britain for college educations at Oxford and Cambridge, medical school at Edinburgh, and legal training at London's Inns of Court.

But the aping of English ways made colonials uneasy too. One Philadelphia Quaker ordered an elegant English coach complete with coat of arms—but then reconsidered and removed the crest. Second thoughts also plagued colonial parents when sons educated in England came home wearing dandified silks, affecting foppish manners, and spouting fashionable slang—"Split me, Madam!" "By Gad!" and "Dam me!" Such behavior mirrored the bad habits of some English gentlemen, whose large incomes from renting land encouraged idleness and extravagance.

Colonials recognized that England's ruling classes purchased their luxury and leisure at the cost of the rest of the nation. In his *Autobiography,* Benjamin Franklin painted a devastating portrait of the degraded lives of his fellow workers in a London printshop, who drowned their disappointments by drinking throughout the workday, even more excessively on the Sabbath, and then faithfully observing the holiday of "St. Monday's" to nurse their hangovers. Like Franklin, many colonials believed that gross inequalities of wealth would endanger liberty. They regarded the idle among England's rich and poor alike as ominous signs of a degenerate nation.

A London beggar and her children

Politics in England and America

Colonials were also of two minds about England's government. While they praised the English constitution as the basis of all liberties, they were alarmed by the actual workings of English politics. In theory, England's "balanced constitution" was designed to give every order of English society some voice in the workings of government. While the Crown represented the monarchy and the House of Lords the aristocracy, the House of Commons represented the democracy, the people of England. In fact, the monarch's executive ministers had become dominant by creating support for their policies in Parliament through patronage—or, put more bluntly, bribery. *England's balanced constitution*

Over the course of the eighteenth century, a large executive bureaucracy had evolved in order to enforce laws, collect taxes, and wage the nearly constant wars in Europe and America. The power to appoint all military and treasury officials, customs and tax collectors, judges and justices of the peace lay with the monarch and his or her ministers. By the middle of the eighteenth century, almost half of all members of Parliament held such Crown offices or government contracts. Royal patronage was also used to manipulate parliamentary elections. The executive branch used money or liquor to bribe local voters into selecting their candidates. The small size of England's electorate fostered executive influence. Perhaps one-fourth of all adult males could vote, and many electoral districts were not adjusted to keep pace with *Tools for "managing" Parliament*

This satirical rendering of an English election, by the English artist William Hogarth, mirrored the reservations of many Americans about the political culture of the mother country. The man seated in the foreground of the jostling crowd represents Hogarth's dark view of the typical English voter: much incapacitated by drink, he is being told for whom to vote by the man standing and whispering in his ear. In the background, the overturned carriage suggests that political corruption threatens the stability of England.

population growth and resettlement. The notorious "rotten boroughs" each elected a member of Parliament to represent fewer than 500 easily bribable voters, while some large cities like Manchester and Leeds, newly populous because of industrial growth, had no representation in Parliament at all.

Colonial governments   Americans liked to think that their colonial governments mirrored the ideal English constitution. In terms of formal structure, there were similarities. Most colonies had a royal governor who represented the monarch in America and a bicameral (two-house) legislature made up of a lower house (the assembly) and an upper house (or council). The democratically elected assembly, like the House of Commons, stood for popular interests, while the council, some of which were elected and others appointed, more roughly approximated the House of Lords.

But these formal similarities masked real differences between English and colonial governments. On the face of it, royal governors had much more power than the English Crown. Unlike kings and queens, royal governors could veto laws passed by assemblies; they could dissolve those bodies at will; they could create courts and dismiss judges. However, governors who asserted their full powers quickly met opposition from their assemblies, who objected that such overwhelming authority endangered popular liberty. In any showdown with their assemblies, most royal governors had to give way, for they lacked the government offices and contracts that bought loyalty. The colonial legislatures possessed additional leverage, since all of them retained the sole authority to levy taxes.

Even if the governors had enjoyed greater patronage powers, their efforts to influence colonial legislatures would have been frustrated by the sheer size of the American electorate. There were too many voters in America to bribe. Over half and possibly as many as 70 percent of all white adult colonial men were enfranchised. Property requirements were the same in America as in England, but widespread ownership of land in the colonies allowed most men to meet the qualifications easily.

The colonial electorate was also more watchful. Representatives were required to reside in the districts that they served, and a few even received binding instructions from their constituents about how to vote. Representation was also apportioned according to population far more equitably than in England. Since they were so closely tied to their constituents' wishes, colonial legislators were far less likely than members of Parliament to be swayed by executive pressure.

Most Americans were as pleased with their inexpensive and representative colonial governments as they were horrified by the conduct of politics in England. John Dickinson, a young Pennsylvanian training as a lawyer in London, was scandalized by a Parliamentary election he witnessed in 1754. The king and his ministers had spent over 100,000 pounds sterling to buy support for their candidates, he wrote his father, and "if a man cannot be brought to vote as he is desired, he is made dead drunk and kept in that state, never heard of by his family and friends, till all is over and he can do no harm."

The Imperial System before 1760

Colonials like Dickinson thought long and hard about the condition of England's society and politics. Meanwhile, the English thought about their colonies little, understood them less, and wished neither to think about them more nor to understand them better. It would be hard to exaggerate just how insignificant North America was

OVERSEAS TRADE NETWORKS
Commercial ties to Spain and Portugal, Africa, and the Caribbean sustained the growth of both seaports and commercial farming regions on the British North American mainland and enabled colonials to purchase an increasing volume of finished goods from England. The proceeds from exports in foodstuffs and lumber to the West Indies and trade in fish to Spain and Portugal enabled northern merchants and farmers to buy hardware and clothing from the mother country. Southern planters financed their consumption of English imports and their investment in African slaves with the profits from the sale of tobacco, rice, and indigo abroad.

in the English scheme of things. Those few Britons who thought about America at all believed that colonials resembled the "savage" Indians more than the "civilized" English. As a London acquaintance remarked to Thomas Hancock, it was a pity Mrs. Hancock had to remain in Boston when he could "take her to England and make her happy with Christians."

The same indifference contributed to England's haphazard administration of its colonies. The Board of Trade and Plantations, created from the Lords of Trade in 1696, gathered information about Atlantic trading and fishing, reviewed laws and petitions drawn up by colonial assemblies, and exchanged letters and instructions with royal governors. But the Board of Trade was only an advisory body, reporting to the king's ministers and passing on information to other government agencies.

Real authority over the colonies was divided among an array of other agencies. The Treasury oversaw customs and gathered other royal revenues; the Admiralty Board enforced regulations of trade; the War Office orchestrated colonial defense. But these departments spent most of their hours handling more pressing responsibilities. Colonial affairs stood at the bottom of their agendas. Most British officials in America seemed equally indifferent. Often enough, they had been awarded their jobs in return for political support, not in recognition of administrative ability.

But the branch of England's government most indifferent to America was Parliament. Aside from passing an occasional law to regulate trade, restrict manufacturing, or direct monetary policy, Parliament made no effort to assert its authority in America. Its members assumed that Parliament's sovereignty extended over the entire empire, and nothing had occurred to make them think otherwise.

The benefits of benign neglect

For the colonies, this chaotic and inefficient system of colonial administration worked well enough. The very weakness of imperial oversight left Americans with a great deal of freedom. Even England's regulation of trade rested lightly on the shoulders of most Americans. Southern planters were obliged to send their rice, indigo, and tobacco to Britain only, but they enjoyed favorable credit terms and knowledgeable marketing from English merchants. Colonials were prohibited from finishing iron products and exporting hats and textiles, but they had scant interest in developing domestic industries. Americans were required to import all manufactured goods through England, but by doing so, they acquired high-quality goods at low prices. At little sacrifice, most Americans obeyed imperial regulations. Only sugar, molasses, and tea were routinely smuggled.

Following this policy of benign neglect the British empire muddled on to the satisfaction of most people on both sides of the Atlantic. Economic growth and political autonomy allowed most Americans to like being English, despite their misgivings about their parent nation. The beauty of it was that Americans could be English in America, enjoying greater economic opportunity and political equality. If imperial arrangements had remained as they were in 1754, the empire might have muddled on indefinitely. But because of the French and the Indians on the American frontier, the British empire began to change. And those changes made it increasingly hard for Americans to be English in America.

TOWARD THE SEVEN YEARS' WAR

In the late spring of 1754, while Benjamin Franklin dreamed of unifying Americans, a young Virginian dreamed of military glory. As Franklin rode toward Albany, the young man, an inexperienced officer, led his company of Virginia militia toward Fort Duquesne, the French stronghold on the forks of the Ohio.

Less than a year earlier, the king's ministers had advised royal governors in America to halt the French advance into the Ohio country. The Virginia government organized an expedition against Fort Duquesne, placing at its head the young man who combined an imposing physique with the self-possession of an English gentleman. He wanted, more than anything, to become an officer in the regular British army.

But events in the Ohio country during that spring and summer did not go

George Washington's way. French soldiers easily captured Fort Necessity, his crude outpost near Fort Duquesne. In early July, as the Albany Congress was debating, Washington was surrendering to a French force in the Pennsylvania backcountry and beating a retreat back to Virginia. By the end of 1754, Washington had resigned his militia command and retired to his plantation at Mount Vernon. The disaster at Fort Necessity had dashed his dreams of martial glory and a regular army commission. He had no future as a soldier. *Washington at Fort Necessity*

With the rout of Washington and his troops, the French grew bolder and the Indians more restless. The renewal of war between England and France was certain by the beginning of 1755. This time the contest between the two powers would decide the question of sovereignty over North America. That, at least, was the dream of William Pitt, who was about to become the most powerful man in England.

Even by the standards of English politicians, William Pitt was an odd character. Subject to bouts of illness and depression and loathed for his opportunism and egotism, Pitt surmounted every challenge, buoyed by a strong sense of destiny—his own and that of England. He believed that England must seize the world's trade, for trade meant wealth and wealth meant power. As early as the 1730s, Pitt recognized that the only obstacle between England and its destiny was France—and that the contest between the two for world supremacy would be decided in America. During King George's War, Pitt had mesmerized the House of Commons and the nation with his spellbinding oratory about England's imperial destiny. But the mounting cost of fighting prompted the government to accept peace with France in 1748. In frustration Pitt retired from public life. *The ambitions of William Pitt*

But while Pitt sulked in his library, the rivalry for the American frontier moved toward a showdown. The French pressed their front lines eastward; the English pushed for land westward; the Indians maneuvered for position. Heartened by the news from America, Pitt clung to his dream of English commercial dominion and French defeat. By the late spring of 1754, as Benjamin Franklin and George Washington rode toward their defeats, William Pitt knew that he would have his war with France and his way with the world.

Other dreams would wait longer for fulfillment. The Albany Congress had demonstrated that a few Americans like Franklin had seen beyond the diversity of a divided colonial world to the possibility of union, however unaccustomed and untried. But it would take another war, one that restructured an empire, before some Americans saw in themselves a likeness that was not English.

CHAPTER SUMMARY

From the perspective of 1754 a colonial political union—like that proposed by the Albany Plan—appeared highly improbable. Despite the mounting military threat from the French and the Indians, British colonials remained deeply divided by ethnic and sectional differences. Those differences were intensified by an influx of non-English immigrants, the spread of settlement to the backcountry, and the growth of major seaports. While disorder was not uncommon either on the frontier or in cities, the most serious social and political conflict drew its strength from sectional controversies between east and west, intercolonial contests over boundaries, and quarrels over tenancy. The plantation districts of the eighteenth-century southern coast became more embattled, too, as slave resistance became more frequent and successful. Over the first half of the eighteenth century, a period of massive slave importation, the black community was infused with a more direct exposure to west African culture but divided internally between native-born slaves and newcomers. These differences among African Americans diminished, however, as slave importations tapered off and black population grew through natural increase. After about 1750 the growth of a native-born population strengthened black communal and family life, and black solidarity heightened white fears of slave revolts.

Religious divisions among eighteenth-century colonials compounded the tensions of racial, regional, and ethnic diversity. The two key events that intensified religious conflict were the spread of Enlightenment ideas and the influence of the first Great Awakening. While the Enlightenment prompted some American elites to embrace "rational Christianity," an even larger number of colonials fell under the sway of the evangelical Christianity preached by revivalists. Evangelicals enjoyed great success among the many unchurched men and women of the backcountry regions south of New York, and these conversions sharpened the tensions between westerners and the assemblies of those colonies, which were dominated by Quakers and Anglicans.

Despite their many differences, a majority of white colonials took pride in their common English ancestry. Colonials boasted of their claim to English political liberties, as well as adopting English standards of taste and fashion. Wealthy Americans who crossed the Atlantic gloried in English consumer culture and aped the ways of English aristocrats. Some colonials recognized that the privileged few in England enjoyed leisure and luxury at the expense of the many who endured lives of poverty and toil. Still others criticized England's expensive and corrupt political system, comparing it unfavorably with colonial institutions. But such reservations were quieted by both colonial pride in belonging to a powerful empire and the advantages that an imperial policy of "benign neglect" afforded both sides. Only in the 1760s, in the wake of another war with the French and Indians, would British colonials revise their attitudes toward England and reassess their prospects for unity.

ADDITIONAL READING

There are a number of excellent studies treating broad aspects of American development during the later colonial period. For a comprehensive treatment of economic development, see John McCusker and Russell Menard, *The Economy of British America, 1607–1787* (1985). For the evolution of political institutions, consult Bernard Bailyn, *The Origins of American Politics* (1968). On the subject of religious change, the book to read is Patricia Bonomi, *Under the Cope of Heaven* (1986). For family life, consult Philip Greven's *The Protestant Temperament* (1977). The best studies of the frontier are Charles Grant's work on western Connecticut, *Democracy in the Frontier Town of Kent* (1961), and Rachel Klein's account of the South Carolina backcountry, *The Unification of a Slave State* (1990). The evolution of major seaports is exhaustively chronicled in Gary Nash's *Urban Crucible* (1979), while relations between blacks and whites in the South are ably described by Allan Kulikoff,

Tobacco and Slaves (1987), Rhys Isaac, *The Transformation of Virginia, 1740–1790* (1982), and Mechal Sobel, *The World They Made Together* (1987).

Understanding the impact of immigration and ethnic diversity is essential to appreciating the dynamism of eighteenth-century colonial society. Some especially vivid accounts include Bernard Bailyn, *Voyagers to the West* (1986), Bernard Bailyn and Philip D. Morgan, eds., *Strangers within the Realm* (1991), and Ira Berlin, "Time, Space, and the Evolution of Afro-American Society in British Mainland North America," *American Historical Review,* 85 (1980), 44–78. For a fuller list of readings, see the Bibliography.

SIGNIFICANT EVENTS

1689–1697	King William's War (War of the League of Augsburg)
1702	Anne becomes queen of England
1702–1713	Queen Anne's War (War of the Spanish Succession)
1714	George I becomes king of England, beginning Hanover dynasty
1727	George II becomes king of England
1730s–1740s	Rise in importation of black slaves in northern colonies
1739	George Whitefield's first preaching tour in America; Stono Rebellion in South Carolina
1744–1748	King George's War (War of the Austrian Succession)
1751	Franklin's essay on population
1754	The Albany Congress; Washington surrenders at Fort Necessity
1760–1769	South Carolina Regulation
1763	Paxton Boys march in Pennsylvania
1766	Tenant rebellion in New York
1766–1771	North Carolina Regulation (Battle of Alamance, 1771)

PART TWO THE CREATION OF A NEW REPUBLIC

GLOBAL ESSAY

As the shrewd Benjamin Franklin had observed in 1751, the population of British North America was doubling approximately every 25 years. This astonishing rate was quite possibly the fastest in the world at the time. Even so, the North American surge was merely one part of a more general global rise in population during the second half of the eighteenth century. In sheer numbers China led the way. Its population of 150 million in 1700 had doubled to more than 313 million by the end of the century. Europe's total rose from about 118 million in 1700 to about 187 million a century later, the greatest growth coming on its eastern and western flanks, in Great Britain and Russia. African and Indian populations seem to have increased as well, although historians have analyzed trends there less closely.

This worldwide rise, unprecedented in previous history, occurred for a variety of reasons. Climate may have been one. In Europe, at least, warmer and drier seasons produced generally better harvests. (The population of the already dry Middle East seems not to have expanded, and that region may have been hurt by the climate changes.) Furthermore, health and nutrition improved globally with the spread of Native American crops. Irish farmers discovered that a single acre planted with the lowly American potato could support an entire family. The tomato added crucial vitamins to the Mediterranean diet, while maize provided more calories per acre than any European or African grain. In China the American sweet potato thrived in hilly regions where rice would not grow.

Not only plants but diseases were carried back and forth by European ships. As we have seen, contact between previously isolated peoples produced extreme mortality from epidemics, enabling invaders like Hernando Cortés to conquer populous civilizations. Similarly, the Pilgrims unwittingly blessed Divine Providence for allowing them to take over deserted fields that had been cleared and farmed by Indians only recently struck down by dis-

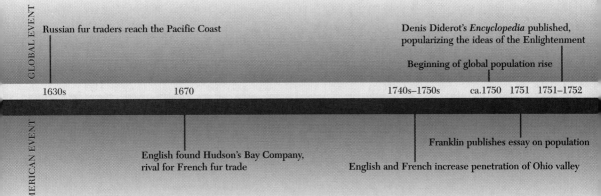

GLOBAL EVENT

Russian fur traders reach the Pacific Coast

Denis Diderot's *Encyclopedia* published,
popularizing the ideas of the Enlightenment

Beginning of global population rise

1630s   1670   1740s–1750s   ca.1750   1751   1751–1752

AMERICAN EVENT

Franklin publishes essay on population

English found Hudson's Bay Company,
rival for French fur trade

English and French increase penetration of Ohio valley

ease. By 1800 the more globally isolated peoples, such as the inhabitants of Australia or the North American plains, remained at risk. But after more than two centuries of sustained contact, Indians developed increased biological resistance to European and African illnesses. The frequent circulation of diseases worldwide led to a more stable environment in which populations began to swell.

During the years that Europeans explored the Atlantic frontiers of North and South America, Slavic and Romanian pioneers were moving eastward into the Eurasian steppes. There they turned sparsely settled pastoral lands into feudal manors and farms. In northern forests unsuitable for farming, Russian fur traders advanced eastward across Siberia until they reached the Pacific in the 1630s. By the 1780s Russian pioneers had pushed into Alaska and down the Pacific American coast, bumping up against western Europeans who were harvesting furs from Canada's forests and streams.

Both flanks of this European thrust often depended on forced labor, especially in agricultural settings. As we have seen, the institution of slavery in North America became increasingly restrictive over the course of the seventeenth century. Furthermore, the number of slaves imported to North America paled when compared to the thousands shipped by the Portuguese to the slave markets of Rio de Janeiro. Similarly, the plight of serfs worsened from 1500 to 1650, as the demand for labor increased in eastern Europe. In 1574 Polish nobles received the right to punish their serfs entirely as they pleased—including execution if they chose. By 1603, Russian peasants were routinely sold along with the land they worked.

The eighteenth-century Enlightenment penetrated eastern Europe too, as it had the urban centers of North America. Russia's Peter the Great absorbed many ideas when he traveled, sometimes incognito, to England and western Europe. As czar (1689–1725), he attempted to put them to use in westernizing Russia. Catherine the Great was even more influenced by the artistic currents of the Enlightenment. During her reign (1762–1796), she imported Western architects, sculptors, and musicians to grace her court.

But Catherine's limits to toleration were made brutally clear in 1773. The same   139

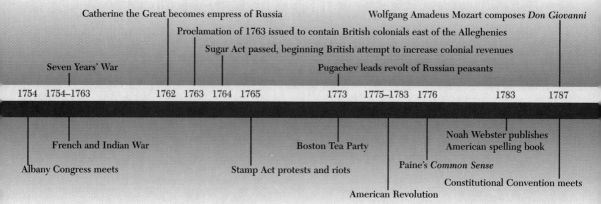

Catherine the Great becomes empress of Russia   Wolfgang Amadeus Mozart composes *Don Giovanni*

Proclamation of 1763 issued to contain British colonials east of the Alleghenies

Sugar Act passed, beginning British attempt to increase colonial revenues

Seven Years' War   Pugachev leads revolt of Russian peasants

1754   1754–1763   1762   1763   1764   1765   1773   1775–1783   1776   1783   1787

French and Indian War   Boston Tea Party   Noah Webster publishes American spelling book

Albany Congress meets   Stamp Act protests and riots   Paine's *Common Sense*

Constitutional Convention meets

American Revolution

year that a group of rowdy Americans were dumping tea into Boston harbor, a Cossack soldier named Emelian Pugachev launched a peasant rebellion. Grandly proclaiming himself emperor, Pugachev issued decrees abolishing serfdom and taxes.

Serfs in the Ural and Volga river valleys flocked to his ragtag army. Catherine ruthlessly imprisoned Pugachev (shown here jailed and chained) and then executed him and scattered his followers. In 1775 she granted Russian nobles even more absolute control over their serfs.

To make the obvious comparison—between a failed Russian revolution for liberty and the triumph of American colonials—would be too smug. Liberty-loving American merchants like John Hancock and genteel tobacco planters like George Washington were hardly in the position of serfs. A more appropriate link might be made between Russian serfs and American slaves, since both groups supplied the forced labor along the frontiers of European expansion. But the slaves, whose African homelands lay thousands of miles away, found the odds of a successful rebellion just as difficult as Russian serfs did. Ironically, white Americans may have been able to fight so vigorously for their liberties precisely because they had made revolt by a class of forced laborers so difficult.

Americans rebelled in 1775 not out of a serf's desperation; quite the opposite. The Seven Years' War ended in 1763 with the French driven from North America and British colonials thriving, thanks to a wartime boom. Thomas Mayhew, a respected Boston minister, voiced the opinion of many when he envisioned a glorious empire spreading across the continent in the century to come. "I do not mean an independent one," he added carefully, but in 1763 the qualification was hardly necessary. Most white Americans were quite pleased with the prospect of being English. With the significant exception of the slave class, the distance between the poorest and richest Americans was smaller than anywhere in Europe. And the British tradition of representative government ensured a broader involvement of citizens in colonial gov-

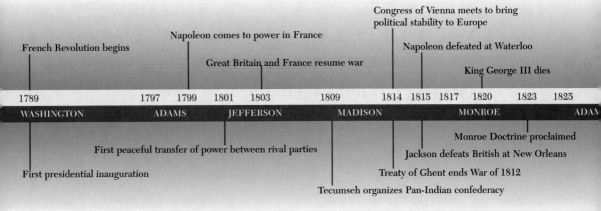

Congress of Vienna meets to bring political stability to Europe

Napoleon comes to power in France

French Revolution begins

Great Britain and France resume war

Napoleon defeated at Waterloo

King George III dies

| 1789 | 1797 | 1799 | 1801 | 1803 | 1809 | 1814 | 1815 | 1817 | 1820 | 1823 | 1825 |

WASHINGTON   ADAMS   JEFFERSON   MADISON   MONROE   ADAM

Monroe Doctrine proclaimed

First peaceful transfer of power between rival parties

Jackson defeats British at New Orleans

First presidential inauguration

Treaty of Ghent ends War of 1812

Tecumseh organizes Pan-Indian confederacy

ernment. Thus, an American Revolution was hardly inevitable in 1776. Most certainly one did not appear likely in 1763. The timing of the break with Great Britain was the result of specific decisions made on both sides of the Atlantic.

America's isolated position on the edge of European expansion certainly created conditions that made separation likely at some point. Most colonials, used to relative social equality among white Americans, blanched at what they saw as English luxury and corruption. English governing elites, when they bothered to notice Americans, usually found them provincial and naive. Under different circumstances the move for independence might have come in 1800, or even 1867, as it did for Canada. But the break came earlier. American colonials, who in 1763 liked being English and gloried in the British empire, gradually came to think of themselves as independent Americans, subject neither to a British monarch nor to Parliament.

5

Toward the War for American Independence

 mericans liked being English. They had liked being English from the beginning of colonial settlement, but they liked it more than ever for a few years after 1759. One wonderful day during those years—September 16, 1762—Bostonians turned out to celebrate belonging to the British empire. Soldiers mustered on the Common; bells pealed from the steeples of local churches; the charge of guns fired from the battery resounded through towns; strains of orchestra music from an outdoor concert floated through the city's crowded streets and narrow alleys. When darkness fell and bonfires illuminated the city, Bostonians consumed "a vast quantity of liquor," drinking "loyal healths" to their young king, George III, and in celebration of Britain's victory in the Seven Years' War.

When the great news of that triumph reached the North American mainland in the fall of 1762, similar celebrations broke out all over the colonies. And with good reason. France's empire in America, which only a few years earlier had appeared so formidable, was now vanquished. Great Britain had become master of Canada, thanks to the joint efforts of British and American colonial troops. In 1763 the Treaty of Paris ratified their victories, making Britain the largest and most powerful empire in the Western world. Americans were among His Majesty's proudest subjects.

Thirteen years after the celebration of 1762, Boston was a different place. Pride in belonging to the empire had shriveled to shrill charges that England conspired to enslave its colonies. Massachusetts led the way, drawing other colonies deep into resistance. Bostonians initiated many of the petitions and resolves against British authority. When words did not work, they ignited riots, harassed British officials, baited British troops, and destroyed British property. In 1775, they were laying plans for rebellion against the British empire.

A process of disillusionment An ironic fate overtook that generation of Americans who loved being English, boasted of their rights as Britons, and celebrated their membership in the all-conquering empire. That very pride drove colonials into rebellion, for the men who ran the British empire after 1763 would not allow Americans to be English. Even before the Seven Years' War, some colonials saw that diverging paths of social and political development made them different from the English. After the Seven Years' War, events demonstrated to even more colonials that they were not considered the polit-

142

To have a standing army!" wrote one Bostonian in 1768. "Good God! What can be worse to a people who have tasted the sweets of liberty! Things are come to an unhappy crisis!" Paul Revere engraved this print of British redcoats arriving in Boston.

ical equals of the English who lived in England. As their disillusionment with the empire deepened, British North Americans from Massachusetts to Georgia slowly discovered a new identity as Americans and declared their independence from being English.

THE SEVEN YEARS' WAR

The Seven Years' War, which actually lasted nine years, pitted Britain and its ally, Prussia, against France, in league with Austria and Spain. The battle raged from 1754 until 1763, ranging over the continent of Europe, the coast of west Africa, India, the Philippines, the Caribbean, and North America.

The Years of Defeat

The war started in 1754 when Virginia sent George Washington and a company of militia into the Ohio River valley to halt French penetration into the area (page 135). Washington's surrender at Fort Necessity only stiffened Britain's resolve to assert its own claims to the Ohio country. In the summer of 1755, as two British regiments led *Braddock's* by Major General Edward Braddock approached the French outpost at Fort *defeat* Duquesne on the forks of the Ohio, they were ambushed and cut to pieces by a party of French and Indians. Washington led the mortally wounded Braddock and the remnants of his army in a retreat.

During the summer of Braddock's defeat, New Englanders fared somewhat better against French forces in Nova Scotia and deported 6000 farmers from that region. The Acadians, as they were known, professed to be neutral in the war between France and Britain. But their ancestors had been French, and the English worried

---

THE SEVEN YEARS' WAR IN AMERICA
After Washington's surrender and Braddock's defeat in the Pennsylvania backcountry, the British and French waged their final contest for supremacy in North America in upstate New York and Canada.

that neighboring Quebec might still persuade them to rebel. Thus the Acadians had their land confiscated, and they were dispersed throughout the colonies.

Still, deporting farmers did little to help win a war. During the opening years of the conflict, Britain mismanaged its forces disastrously. When England and France formally declared war in May 1756, John Campbell, the Earl of Loudoun, took command of the North American theater. American soldiers and colonial assemblies alike hated Lord Loudoun. They balked at his efforts to take command over colonial troops and dragged their heels at his demands for men and supplies. Meanwhile, the French appointed an effective new commanding general of their forces in Canada, Louis Joseph, the marquis de Montcalm. Montcalm drove southward, capturing key British forts and threatening the security of both New York and New England. While he prospered in America, the British were also taking a beating from the French in Europe and in India.

During the years when the French seemed unstoppable, the British looked for help from the strongest tribes of the interior—the Iroquois in the North and the Creek, Choctaw, and Cherokee in the South. Instead, Benjamin Franklin's worst fears were realized: most tribes adopted neutrality or joined the French. As France seemed certain to carry the continent, Indian attacks on English frontier settlements increased.

The Years of Victory

As British fortunes worsened throughout 1756 and 1757, William Pitt resumed his political career and took personal control over the war in his usual bold way. "I know that I can save this country and that no one else can," he announced. Leaving the fighting in Europe to the Prussians, Pitt focused the full strength of the British military on beating the French in America. Pitt also renewed colonial support for the war effort by replacing Lord Loudoun and giving his successor far more limited authority over colonial troops. And Pitt sent requests for men and money directly to each colonial assembly—accompanied by promises of reimbursement in gold and silver.

William Pitt turns the tide

With Pitt now in control, the tide of battle turned. In July of 1758, the British gained control of the St. Lawrence River when the French fortress at Louisbourg fell before the combined force of the Royal Navy and British and colonial troops. In August, a force of New Englanders strangled France's frontier defenses by capturing Fort Frontenac, thereby isolating French forts lining the Great Lakes and the Ohio valley. The Indians, seeing the French routed from the interior, switched their allegiance to the English.

The British succeeded even more brilliantly in 1759. In Canada, Brigadier General James Wolfe gambled on a daring stratagem and won Quebec from Montcalm. Under the cover of darkness, naval squadrons landed Wolfe's men beneath the city's steep bluffs, where they scaled the heights to a plateau known as the Plains of Abraham. Montcalm might have won by holding out behind the walls of his fortress and awaiting reinforcements. Instead, he matched Wolfe's recklessness and offered battle. Five days later both Wolfe and Montcalm lay dead, along with 1400 French soldiers and 600 British and American troops. Quebec had fallen to the British. A year later the French surrender of Montreal ended the fighting in North America, although it continued elsewhere in the world for another two years.

Wolfe and Montcalm battle for Quebec

The Treaty of Paris, signed in February 1763, ended the French presence on the

Before James Wolfe led his troops to fight on the Plains of Abraham, his navy bombarded Quebec in a vain attempt to compel surrender. This French artist's engraving was based on a sketch done by an English crew member of the attacking naval fleet. Both sides were struck by the devastation of the city, with many of its buildings razed to smoldering shells, which presaged the end of France's empire in North America.

continent of North America. The terms confirmed British title to all French territory east of the Mississippi as well as to Spanish Florida. (Spain had made the last-minute mistake of entering the war, against Britain, in 1762.) France ceded to its ally Spain all of its land lying west of the Mississippi and the port of New Orleans.

Postwar Expectations

Britain's victory gave rise to great expectations among Americans. The end of the war, they were sure, meant the end of high taxes. The terms of the peace, they were confident, meant that the fertile lands of the Ohio valley would be thrown open to English settlement. The prosperity of the war years alone made for a mood of optimism. British military spending and William Pitt's subsidies had made money for farmers, merchants, artisans, and anyone else who had anything to do with supplying the army or navy. Colonials also took pride in their contributions of troops and money to the winning of the war. In view of that support, Americans expected to be given more consideration within the British empire. Now, as one anonymous pamphleteer put it, Americans would "not be thought presumptuous, if they consider[ed] themselves upon an equal footing" with English in the parent country.

Colonial pride and optimism

But if Americans took pride in being English, most imperial officials in America thought that they had done a poor job of showing it. British statesmen complained that colonial assemblies had been tightfisted when it came to supplying the army.

English resentments

EUROPEAN CLAIMS IN NORTH AMERICA, 1750 AND 1763
The British victory in the Seven Years' War secured Great Britain's title to a large portion of present-day United States and Canada. While colonials hoped to settle the newly won territory, statesmen in London intended to restrict westward movement with the Proclamation of 1763.

British commanders charged that colonial troops had been lily-livered when it came to fighting the French. Such charges were unjust, but they stuck in the minds of many Britons, who concluded that the Americans were selfish and self-interested, unconcerned with the welfare of the empire as a whole. Britain had accumulated a huge national debt that would saddle the nation with high taxes for years to come. To make matters worse, some Britons suspected that, with the French removed from North America, the colonies would move toward independence. As early as 1755, Josiah Tucker, a respected English economist, had warned that "to drive the French out of all North America would be the most fatal step we could take." Ironically, independence entered the minds of some observers in England long before it was ever entertained by Americans.

Americans in 1763 were not, in truth, revolutionaries in the making. They were loyal British subjects in the flush of postwar patriotism. Americans in 1763, deeply divided among themselves, were not even "Americans." But most postwar English colonials did expect to enjoy a more equal status in the empire. And most Britons had no inclination to accord them that equality. The differing expectations of the colonies' place in the empire poised the postwar generation for crisis.

THE IMPERIAL CRISIS

It was common sense. Great Britain had waged a costly war to secure its empire in America; now it needed to consolidate those gains. The empire's North American territory needed to be protected, its administration tightened, and its colonies made as profitable as possible to the parent nation. In other words, the empire needed to be centralized. That conclusion dictated Britain's decision to leave several thousand troops in America after the Seven Years' War. The British army would prevent France from trying to regain its lost territory.

New Troubles on the Frontier

Keeping troops in North America made sense to the British because of the Indians, too. With the French gone, English traders, speculators, and settlers would swarm into the West. Without the French as trading partners, Indian tribes were in a weaker position to deal with the British. No longer could they count on a steady supply of arms and ammunition from European rivals competing for their furs. The Indians were edgy, expecting the worst, and the British were worried.

Pontiac's Rebellion

Events bore out British fears. In the early 1760s a Lenni Lenape prophet, Neolin, began advising the tribes to return to their native ways and resist the spread of white settlement. Pontiac, an Ottawa chief, embraced Neolin's message of renaissance and rebellion. Other interior tribes joined Pontiac's offensive, and during the summer of 1763 they captured all the British outposts west of Pittsburgh. British troops and American militia finally smothered Pontiac's Rebellion.

Proclamation of 1763

Thereafter British administrators discovered another use for troops in America—to enforce the newly issued Proclamation of 1763. That order, issued by England's Board of Trade, prohibited white settlement past the crest of the Appalachian Mountains. Restricting westward movement might ease Indian fears, the British hoped, and so stave off future conflicts. It might also keep the colonials confined to the seaboard, where they were more easily subject to the control of the empire.

THE APPALACHIAN FRONTIER, 1750–1775

Made bold by the presence of British forts and soldiers, land-hungry colonials spilled into the west through the Cumberland Gap, a notch in the chain of mountains stretching the length of the North American interior. Only Indians and some white hunters knew of the Cumberland Gap before it was scouted in 1750 by Dr. Thomas Walker and a party of Virginians on behalf of a company of land speculators. In 1763, Indians led by Pontiac seized eight British forts before troops under Colonel Henry Bouquet stopped the offensive at Bushy Run, Pennsylvania. In 1775 Daniel Boone took the first large party of pioneers through the Cumberland Gap and established a fort at Boonesborough in present-day Kentucky.

George Grenville's New Measures

A final reason for keeping troops in the colonies occurred to the British by 1764: an armed presence could enforce American acceptance of other new and sensible measures for tightening the empire. Those measures were the solutions of George Grenville, the First Lord of the Treasury, to the financial problems facing England after the Seven Years' War.

Britain's national debt had doubled in the decade after 1754. Adding to that burden was the drain of supporting troops in the colonies. Grenville recognized that English taxpayers alone could not shoulder the costs of winning and maintaining an empire. As matters stood, heavy taxes were already triggering protests among hard-pressed Britons. Americans, by contrast, paid comparatively low taxes to their colonial governments and little in trade duties to the empire. Indeed, Grenville discovered that the colonial customs service paid out four times more in salaries to its collectors than it gathered in duties, operating at a net loss.

Molasses Act of 1733

The income from customs duties was slim because colonial merchants evaded the Molasses Act of 1733. That tariff imposed a hefty duty of six pence on every gallon of molasses imported from the French and Dutch sugar islands. Parliament had designed the duty to encourage colonists to consume more British molasses, which carried a higher price but came duty-free. New England merchants, who distilled molasses into rum and then traded it to the southern colonies and to west Africa, claimed that the British sugar islands could not satisfy the demands of their distilleries. Regrettably, the merchants were forced to import more molasses from the French and Dutch. More regrettably, to keep their costs low and the price of their rum competitive, they had to bribe British customs officials. With the going rate for bribes ranging from a halfpenny to a penny and a half per gallon, the whole regrettable arrangement made handsome profits for both merchants and customs inspectors.

Sugar Act

George Grenville reasoned that if Americans could pay out a little under the table to protect an illegal trade, they would willingly pay a little more to go legitimate. Parliament agreed. In April 1764 it passed the Revenue Act, commonly called the Sugar Act. The legislation actually lowered the duty on foreign molasses from six to three pence a gallon. This time, however, Grenville intended to enforce the new duty and to crack down on smugglers. To do so, the Sugar Act required shipmasters to submit papers listing every item in their cargoes when entering or clearing colonial ports. Even common sailors had to declare the contents of their sea chests. Those caught on the wrong side of the law were to be tried in admiralty courts, where verdicts were handed down by royally appointed judges rather than colonial juries more likely to sympathize with their fellow citizens.

By tightening customs enforcement, Grenville hoped to raise more revenue from the American trade. Unlike the earlier Navigation Acts, which imposed duties mainly to regulate trade, the Sugar Act's duties were intended mainly to yield revenue. Even so, Grenville regarded his demands as modest: he did not expect colonials to help reduce England's national debt or even to cover the entire cost of their defense.

Currency and Quartering Acts

Grenville made other modest proposals, all approved by Parliament. There was the Currency Act of 1764, which prohibited the colonies from making their paper money legal tender. That prevented Americans from paying their debts to British traders in currency that had fallen to less than its face value. There was the Quartering Act of 1765, which obliged any colony in which troops were stationed to provide them with suitable accommodations. That contributed to the cost of keeping British forces in America. Finally, in March of 1765, Parliament passed the Stamp Act.

The Stamp Act placed taxes on legal documents, customs papers, newspapers, almanacs, college diplomas, playing cards, and dice. After November 1, 1765, all these items had to bear a stamp signifying that their possessor had paid the tax. Violators of the Stamp Act, like those disobeying the Sugar Act, were to be tried without juries in admiralty courts. The English had been paying a similar tax for nearly a century, so it seemed to Grenville and Parliament that colonials could have no objections.

Stamp Act

Every packet boat from London that brought news of Parliament passing another one of Grenville's measures dampened postwar optimism. For all of the differences between the colonies and England, Americans still held much in common with the English. Those shared ideas included firm beliefs about why the British constitution, British customs, and British history all served to protect liberty and the rights of the empire's freeborn citizens. For that reason the new measures, which seemed like common sense to Grenville and Parliament, did not make sense at all to Americans.

The Beginning of Colonial Resistance

Like other Britons, colonials in America accepted a maxim laid down by the English philosopher John Locke: property guaranteed liberty. Property, in this view, was not merely real estate, or wealth, or material possessions. It was the source of strength for every individual, providing the freedom to think and act independently. Protecting the

Locke on property and liberty

Visual imagery brought home the urgency of resistance to Americans who could not read political pamphlets or radical newspapers. This detail from an engraving by Paul Revere includes a liberty tree, from which is hung an effigy of the Boston stamp distributor, and a beast busily destroying the Magna Carta while trampling American colonials. The date on the tree, August 14, 1765, marked the first Stamp Act riot in Boston.

individual's right to own property was the main responsibility of government, for if personal property was not sacred, then neither was personal liberty.

It followed from this close connection between property, power, and liberty that no people should be taxed without their consent or that of their elected representatives. The power to tax was the power to destroy by depriving a person of property. Yet both the Sugar Act and the Stamp Act were taxes passed by members of Parliament, none of whom had been elected by colonials.

Like the English, colonials also prized the right of trial by jury as one of their basic constitutional liberties. Yet both the Sugar Act and the Stamp Act would prosecute offenders in the admiralty courts, not in local courts, thus depriving colonials of the freedom claimed by all other English men and women.

Influence of the English Opposition
The concern for protecting individual liberties was only one of the convictions shaping the colonies' response to Britain's new policies. Equally important was their deep suspicion of power itself, a preoccupation that colonials shared with a minority of radical English thinkers. These radicals were known by a variety of names—the "Country Party," the "Commonwealthmen," and "the Opposition." They drew their inspiration from the ancient tradition of classical republicanism, which held that representative government safeguarded liberty more reliably than either monarchy or oligarchy. Underlying that judgment was the belief that human beings were driven by passion and insatiable ambition. One person (a monarch), or even a few people (an oligarchy), could not be entrusted with governing, because they would inevitably become corrupted by power and turn into tyrants. Even in representative governments, the people were obliged to watch those in power at all times. The price of liberty was eternal vigilance.

The Opposition believed that the people of England were not watching their rulers closely enough. During the first half of the eighteenth century, they argued, the entire executive branch of England's government—monarchs and their ministers—had been corrupted by their appetite for power. Proof of their ambition was the executive bureaucracy of military and civil officials that steadily grew larger, interfered more with citizens' lives, and drained increasing amounts of money from taxpayers. Even more alarming, in the Opposition's view, the executive branch's bribery of members of Parliament was corrupting the representative branch of England's government. They warned that a sinister conspiracy originating in the executive branch of government threatened English liberty.

Opposition thinkers commanded little attention in England, where they were dismissed as a discontented radical fringe. But they were revered by political leaders in the American colonies. Especially popular were John Trenchard, a lawyer, and Thomas Gordon, a schoolteacher, who collaborated on a series of scathing essays against the political establishment. Too many "unhappy nations have lost that precious jewel *liberty*," Trenchard warned, because they "have permitted a standing army to be kept amongst them." Why, colonials worried, did Britain insist on keeping troops in America, just when Parliament was putting in place new taxes which had never been approved by American legislatures? Events seemed to confirm all too well the Opposition's description of how powerful rulers turned themselves into tyrants and reduced the people whom they ruled to slaves.

In sum, Grenville's new measures led some colonials to suspect that ambitious men ruling England might be conspiring against American liberties. At the very least, the new measures implied that colonials were not the political equals of the English living in England. They were not entitled to taxation by consent or to trial by jury. To be treated like second-class citizens wounded colonials' pride and mocked their post-war expectations. The heady dreams of the role that the colonies would play in the British empire evaporated, leaving behind the bitter dregs of disappointment.

Britain's determination to centralize its empire after 1763 was a disaster of tim- *Impact of* ing, not just psychologically but also economically. By then, the colonies were in the *postwar* throes of a recession. The boom produced in America by government spending dur- *recession* ing the war had collapsed once subsidies were withdrawn. Colonial merchants were left with full stocks of imported goods gathering dust on their shelves. Farmers lost the brisk and profitable market of the army.

Colonial response to the Sugar Act reflected the painful postwar readjustments. New England merchants led the opposition, objecting to the Sugar Act principally on economic grounds. But with the passage of the Stamp Act, the terms of the imperial debate widened, and resistance intensified within all of the colonies. The Stamp Act hit all colonials, not just New England merchants. It took money from the pockets of anyone who made a will, filed a deed, traded out of a colonial port, bought a news-paper, consulted an almanac, graduated from college, took a chance at dice, or played cards. More important, the Stamp Act served notice that Parliament possessed the rightful authority to tax the colonies directly and for the sole purpose of raising rev-enue.

Riots and Resolves

That unprecedented assertion provoked an unprecedented development: the first display of colonial unity. A nearly unanimous chorus of outrage greeted Parliament's claim that it could tax the colonies. During the spring and summer of 1765, American assemblies passed resolves denying Parliament that authority. The right to tax Americans belonged to colonial assemblies alone, they argued, by the law of nature and by the liberties guaranteed in colonial charters and in the British constitution.

Virginia's assembly, the House of Burgesses, took the lead in protesting the Stamp Act, prodded by Patrick Henry. Just 29 years old in 1765, Henry had tried his hand at planting in western Virginia before recognizing his real talent—demagoguery. Blessed with the eloquence of an evangelical preacher, the dashing charm of a southern gen-tleman, and a mind uncluttered by much learning, Henry parlayed his popularity as a *Patrick* smooth-talking lawyer into a place among the Burgesses. He took his seat just 10 days *Henry's* before introducing the Virginia Resolves against the Stamp Act. *resolves*

The Burgesses passed Henry's resolutions upholding their exclusive right to tax Virginians. They stopped short of adopting those resolves that called for outright re-sistance to the Stamp Act. When news of Virginia's stand spread to the rest of the colonies, other assemblies followed suit, affirming that the sole right to tax Americans resided in their elected representatives. But some colonial newspapers deliberately printed a different story—that the Burgesses had approved all of Henry's resolves, in-

This idealized likeness of Patrick Henry, by the American artist Thomas Sully, conveys his subject's intensity. Henry's eloquence and passion as an orator made a vivid impression on his contemporaries.

cluding one that sanctioned disobedience to any Parliamentary tax. That prompted a few assemblies to endorse resistance. In October 1765 delegates from nine colonies convened in New York, where they prepared a joint statement of the American position and petitioned the king and Parliament to repeal both the Sugar Act and the Stamp Act.

Meanwhile, colonial leaders turned to the press to arouse popular opposition to the Stamp Act. Disposed by the writings of the English Opposition to think of politics in conspiratorial terms, they warned that Grenville and the king's other ministers schemed to deprive the colonies of their liberties by unlawfully taxing their property. The Stamp Act was only the first step in a sinister plan to enslave Americans. Whether or not dark fears of a ministerial conspiracy haunted most colonials in 1765, many resisted the Stamp Act. The merchants of Boston, New York, and Philadelphia agreed to stop importing English goods in order to pressure British traders to lobby for repeal. In every colony, organizations emerged to ensure that the Stamp Act, if not repealed, would never be enforced.

Sons of Liberty

The new resistance groups, which styled themselves the "Sons of Liberty," consisted of traders, lawyers, and prosperous artisans. With great success, they organized the lower classes of seaports in opposition to the Stamp Act. The sailors, dockworkers, poor artisans, apprentices, and servants who poured into the streets resembled mobs that had been organized from time to time earlier in the century. Previous riots against houses of prostitution, merchants who hoarded goods, or supporters of smallpox inoculation had not been spontaneous, uncontrolled outbursts. Crowds chose their targets and their tactics carefully and then carried out the communal will with little violence.

In every colonial city, the mobs of 1765 burnt the stamp distributors in effigy, insulted them on the streets, demolished their offices, and attacked their homes. One hot night in August 1765, a mob went further than the Sons of Liberty had planned. They vandalized the stately mansion of Thomas Hutchinson, the unpopular lieutenant governor of Massachusetts and the brother-in-law of the colony's stamp distributor. By morning Hutchinson's home had been all but leveled. The destruction stunned Bostonians, especially the Sons of Liberty, who resisted Britain in the name of protecting private property. Thereafter they took care to keep crowds under tighter control. In most cases, the mere show of popular force was sufficient: by the first of November, the day that the Stamp Act took effect, most of the stamp distributors had resigned.

Repeal of the Stamp Act

Meanwhile, the repeal of the Stamp Act was already in the works back in England. The man who came—unintentionally—to America's relief was George III. The young king was a good man, industrious and devoted to the empire, but he was also immature and not particularly bright. Insecurity made the young king an irksome master, and he ran through ministers rapidly. By the end of 1765, George had dismissed Grenville for reasons unrelated to the uproar in America and appointed a new first minister, the marquis of Rockingham. Rockingham had opposed the Stamp Act from the outset, and he had no desire to enforce it. He received support from London merchants, who were beginning to feel the pinch of the American nonimportation campaign, and secured repeal of the Stamp Act in March 1766.

The Stamp Act controversy demonstrated to colonials how similar in political outlook they were to one another and how different they were from the British. Americans had found that they shared the same assumptions about the meaning of representation. To counter colonial objections to the Stamp Act, Grenville and his supporters had claimed that Americans *were* represented in Parliament, even though they had elected none of its members. Americans were virtually represented, Grenville insisted, for each member of Parliament stood for the interests of the whole empire, not just those of the particular constituency that had elected him. *Virtual versus actual representation*

Colonials could see no virtue in the theory of virtual representation. After all, the circumstances and interests of colonials, living an ocean away, were so different from those of Britons. The newly recognized consensus among Americans was that colonials could be truly represented only by those whom they had elected. Their view, known as actual representation, emphasized that elected officials were directly accountable to their constituents.

Americans also had discovered that they agreed about the extent of Parliament's authority over the colonies: it stopped at the right to tax. Colonials conceded Parliament's right to legislate and to regulate trade for the good of the whole empire. But taxation, in their view, was the free gift of the people through their representatives—who were not sitting in Parliament.

Members of Parliament had brushed aside colonial petitions and resolves, all but ignoring their constitutional argument. To make its own authority perfectly clear, Parliament accompanied the repeal of the Stamp Act with a Declaratory Act, asserting that it had the power to make laws for the colonies "in all cases whatsoever." In fact, the Declaratory Act clarified nothing. Did Parliament understand the power of legislation to include the power of taxation? *Declaratory Act*

The Townshend Acts

In the summer of 1766 George III—again inadvertently—gave the colonies what should have been an advantage by changing ministers again. The king replaced Rockingham with William Pitt, who enjoyed great favor among colonials for his leadership during the Seven Years' War and for his opposition to the Stamp Act. Almost alone among British politicians, Pitt had grasped and approved the colonists' constitutional objections to taxation. During Parliament's debate over repeal of the Stamp Act, Grenville asked sarcastically, "Tell me when the colonies were emancipated?" Pitt immediately shot back, "I desire to know when they were made slaves!"

If the man who believed that Americans were "the sons not the bastards of England" had been well enough to govern, matters between Great Britain and the colonies might have turned out differently. But almost immediately after Pitt took office, his health collapsed, and power passed into the hands of Charles Townshend, the chancellor of the exchequer. Unlike Pitt, Townshend had little understanding of the colonies and even less sympathy for their constitutional objections to taxation. He wished only to raise more revenue from the Americans. In 1767 he persuaded Parliament to tax the lead, paint, paper, glass, and tea that Americans imported from Britain.

In addition, Townshend was determined to curb the power of the upstart American assemblies. To set a bold example, he singled out for punishment the New York legislature, which was refusing to comply with provisions of the Quartering Act

This 1766 porcelain of *Lord Chatham and America* attests to the popularity of William Pitt, Earl of Chatham, among Americans who resisted the Stamp Act. The artist's representation of "America" as a black kneeling in gratitude echoes the colonists' association of taxation with slavery.

of 1765. The troops that were left on the western frontier after the Seven Years' War had been pulled back into colonial seaports in 1766. In part their movement was meant to economize on costs, but royal officials also hoped the troops' presence would help quiet agitation over the Stamp Act. When the largest contingent came to New York, that colony's assembly protested, claiming that the cost of quartering the troops constituted a form of indirect taxation. But Townshend was determined, and Parliament backed him, suspending the New York assembly in 1767 until it agreed to obey the Quartering Act.

Townshend also dipped into the revenue from his new tariffs in order to make royal officials less dependent on the assemblies. Governors and other officers like customs collectors and judges had previously received their salaries from colonial legislatures. The assemblies lost that crucial leverage when Townshend used the revenues to pay those bureaucrats directly. Finally, in order to ensure more effective enforcement of all the duties on imports, Townshend created an American Board of Customs Commissioners, who appointed a small army of new customs collectors. He also established three new vice-admiralty courts in Boston, New York, and Charleston to bring smugglers to justice.

The Resistance Organizes

John Dickinson and Samuel Adams

In Townshend's efforts to centralize the administration of the British empire, Americans saw new evidence that they were not being treated like the English. In newspapers and pamphlets colonial leaders repeated their earlier arguments against taxation. The most widely read publication, "A Letter from a Farmer in Pennsylvania," was the work of John Dickinson—who was, in fact, a Philadelphia lawyer. He urged Americans to protest the Townshend duties with a show of superior virtue—hard work, thrift, simplicity, and home manufacturing. By consuming fewer imported English luxuries, Dickinson argued, Americans would advance the cause of repeal.

As Dickinson's star rose over Philadelphia, the Townshend Acts also shaped the destiny of another man farther north. By the 1760s Samuel Adams was a leader in the Massachusetts assembly. In some ways his rise had been unlikely. Adams's earlier ventures as a merchant ended in bankruptcy; his stint as a tax collector left all of Boston in the red. But he proved a consummate political organizer and agitator, a man who knew how to exploit every advantage. First his enemies and later his friends claimed that Adams had decided on independence for America as early as 1768. In that year he persuaded the assembly to send to other colonial legislatures a circular letter condemning the Townshend Acts and calling for a united American resistance.

As John Dickinson and Samuel Adams whipped up public outrage, the Sons of Liberty again organized the opposition in the streets. Customs officials, like the stamp distributors before them, became targets of popular hatred. But the customs collectors gave as good as they got. Using the flimsiest excuses, they seized American vessels for violating royal regulations. With cold insolence they shook down American merchants for what amounted to protection money. The racketeering in the customs service brought tensions in Boston to a flashpoint in June 1768 after officials seized and condemned the *Liberty,* a sloop belonging to one of the city's biggest merchants, John Hancock. Several thousand Bostonians vented their anger in a night of rioting, searching out and roughing up customs officials. *The* Liberty *seized*

The new secretary of state for the colonies, Lord Hillsborough, responded to the *Liberty* riot by sending two regiments of troops to Boston. In the fall of 1768 the red-coats, like a conquering army, paraded into town under the cover of warships lying off the harbor. (See Paul Revere's illustration on page 143.) In the months that followed, citizens bristled when challenged on the streets by armed soldiers. Even more disturbing to Bostonians was the execution of British military justice on the Common. British soldiers were whipped savagely for breaking military discipline, and desertion was punished by execution.

The *Liberty* riot and the arrival of British troops in Boston pushed colonial assemblies to coordinate their resistance more closely. Most legislatures endorsed the Massachusetts circular letter sent to them by Samuel Adams. They promptly adopted agreements not to import or to consume British goods. The reluctance among some merchants to revive nonimportation in 1767 gave way to greater enthusiasm by 1768, and by early 1769, such agreements were in effect throughout the colonies.

The Stamp Act crisis had also called forth intercolonial cooperation and tactics like nonimportation. But the protests against the Townshend Acts raised the stakes by creating new institutions to carry forward the resistance. Subscribers to the non-importation agreements established "committees of inspection" to enforce the ban on trade with Britain. The committees publicly denounced merchants who continued to import, vandalized their warehouses, forced them to stand under the gallows, and sometimes resorted to tar and feathers.

After 1768 the resistance also brought a broader range of colonials into the pol-

John Dickinson, a moderate who defended American rights but hoped for reconciliation

PRIVATE SPACE/PUBLIC SPACE

Street Theater

On the first night of November 1765 the narrow, winding streets of New York glowed with unaccustomed light. The Stamp Act was to have taken effect on that date, but the colony's stampmaster had long since resigned his office. What had frightened him into resignation could be seen in the moving shadows of men, women, and children, hundreds of them. The flaring torches and flickering candles that they carried aloft through the city's crooked byways cast on storefronts and doorways dark images of a crowd protesting the "death of Liberty."

Bringing up the rear of the procession was a seaman, bearing atop his head an old chair in which was seated a paper effigy. It represented Cadwallader Colden, "the most hated man in the province," and as New York's temporary governor, the local representative of British authority. The crowd marched to the center of town, shouting insults at Colden's figure and peppering it with pistol shots. When some of the marchers decided that their effigy should evoke the Roman Catholic pope, the chief symbol of tyrannical power to colonial Americans, they broke into Colden's stable and stole his fine coach for a proper papal throne. A second group joined the crowd, bearing their own piece of portable political theater—a gallows illuminated with two lanterns. Hanging from the gallows were effigies of Colden and the devil, the "grand Deceiver of Mankind." The entire assembly climaxed the evening by burning the effigies in a bonfire and then vandalizing the homes of several Stamp Act supporters.

Similar protests had been staged in seaports all over the colonies, following Boston's rioting against the Stamp Act. Some crowds held mock trials of unpopular British officials and then tarred and feathered, beat, hung, or burned their effigies. Other crowds enacted mock funerals, parading effigies in carts or coffins to the accompaniment of tolling church bells. Certain symbols appeared repeatedly: devils and gallows, lanterns and the paraphernalia of papal authority. The "people-out-of-doors," as such crowds were called in the eighteenth century, were making their views known—and their collective power felt.

The frequency and the political focus of street protests were new to the decade preceding the Revolution. Still, the actions taken resembled those of earlier colonial crowds in their direction and restraint. Previous riots against houses of prostitution, merchants who hoarded goods, or supporters of smallpox inoculation had not been spontaneous and uncontrolled outbursts. Crowds chose their targets and their tactics carefully and then carried out the communal will with little violence.

Equally striking, the resistance after 1765 drew on rituals and symbols surrounding traditional forms of protest, punishment, and celebration. For centuries before the Revolution, for example, crowds on both sides of the Atlantic had meted out to prostitutes, adulterers, or henpecked husbands punishments known in England as

itics of protest. Artisans, who recognized that nonimportation would spur domestic manufacturing, began to organize as independent political groups. In many towns, women took an active part in opposing the Townshend duties. The "Daughters of

Daily Lives

A Pope's Day parade in mid-eighteenth-century Boston. Dressed as the devil's imps, boys accompany a cart bearing an effigy of the pope.

"rough music." After being tarred and feathered, the targets of rough music were often ridden "skimmington": placed on the back of a donkey, pelted with mud and dung, and driven through the streets to the accompaniment of hooting laughter and beating drums.

An even more important inspiration for resistance rituals came from Pope's Day, an elaborate annual outdoor celebration of anti-Catholic sentiment that started in Boston early in the eighteenth century. Craftworkers and apprentices from both the North End and the South End of town fashioned a cart bearing a lantern, effigies of the pope and the devil, and signs reading "The devil take the pope" and "North [or South] End Forever." Local boys with blackened faces and jester's caps played the part of the "devil's imps," taunting the pope's effigy as laboring people from both ends of town paraded their carts through the streets. Each group tried to destroy the other's creation

before the final bonfire at the end of the evening.

As colonials adopted the symbols of the past for their street theater of political resistance, the borrowing took an odd twist. Pope's Day, the model for later protests, was in fact a colonial adaptation of an English celebration of monarchy, Guy Fawkes Day. In 1605 Fawkes, a Catholic, had been foiled in his attempt to assassinate James I, a failure that the English annually commemorated with a parade ending with burning the conspirator in effigy. In colonial America an effigy of the pope took the place of the Catholic Fawkes; in resistance rituals after 1765 hated British officials took the place of the pope. Beginning in 1776 Americans celebrated public readings of the Declaration by parading, burning, and burying effigies of George III. Strangely enough, Americans had converted symbols and ceremonies designed to honor monarchy to represent the killing of a king.

Liberty" took to heart John Dickinson's advice: they wore homespun clothing instead of English finery, served coffee instead of tea, and boycotted shops selling British goods.

The Boston Massacre

The situation in Boston deteriorated steadily. British troops found themselves regularly cursed by citizens and occasionally pelted with stones, dirt, and human excrement. The British regulars were particularly unpopular among Boston's laboring classes because they competed with them for jobs. Off-duty soldiers moonlighted as maritime laborers, and they sold their services at cheaper rates than the wages paid to locals. By 1769, brawls between British regulars and waterfront workers broke out with unsettling frequency.

With some 4000 redcoats enduring daily contact with some 15,000 Bostonians under the sway of Samuel Adams, what happened on the night of March 5, 1770, was nearly inevitable. A crowd gathered around the customshouse for the sport of heckling its guard of 10 soldiers. The redcoats panicked and fended off insults and snowballs with live fire, hitting 11 rioters and killing 5. Adams and other propagandists seized upon the incident. Labeling the bloodshed "the Boston Massacre," they publicized that "atrocity" throughout the colonies. The radical *Boston Gazette* framed its account in an eye-catching black-bordered edition headed with a drawing of five coffins.

While Townshend's policies spurred the resistance in America, the obvious finally dawned on Parliament. They recognized that Townshend's duties only discouraged sales to colonials and encouraged them to manufacture at home. The argument for repeal was overwhelming, and the way had been cleared by the unexpected death of Townshend shortly after Parliament adopted his proposals. In 1770 his successor, Lord North, convinced Parliament to repeal all the Townshend duties except the one on tea, allowing that tax to stand as a source of revenue and as a symbol of Parliament's authority.

Resistance Revived

Repeal of the Townshend duties took the wind from the sails of American resistance for more than two years. But the controversy between England and the colonies had not been resolved. Colonials still paid taxes on molasses and tea, taxes to which they had not consented. They were still subject to trial in admiralty courts, which operated without juries. They still lived with a standing army in their midst, a threat to basic freedoms that the English Opposition had continually warned about. Beneath the banked fires of protest smoldered the live embers of Americans' political inequality. Any shift in the wind could fan those embers into flames.

The wind did shift, quite literally, on Narragansett Bay in 1772, running aground the *Gaspee,* a British naval schooner in hot pursuit of Rhode Island smugglers. Residents of nearby Providence quickly celebrated the *Gaspee's* misfortune with a bonfire built on the ship's deck. Outraged British officials sent a special commission to look into the matter, intending once again to bypass the established colonial court system. The arrival of the *Gaspee* Commission reignited the imperial crisis, and in America, once again, resistance flared.

A British grenadier

While the new political activism of some American women often amused male leaders of the resistance, it inspired the scorn of some partisans of British authority. When the women of Edenton, North Carolina, renounced imported tea, this British cartoon mocked them.

It did so through an ingenious mechanism, the committees of correspondence. Established in all the colonies by their assemblies, the committees drew up statements of American rights and grievances, distributed those documents within and among the colonies, and solicited responses from towns and counties. The brainchild of Samuel Adams, the committee structure formed a new communications network, one that fostered an intercolonial agreement on resistance to British measures. The strategy succeeded, and not only between colonies. The committees spread the scope of the resistance from colonial seaports into rural areas, engaging farmers and other country folk in the opposition to Britain.

Committees of correspondence

The committees had much to talk about when Parliament passed the Tea Act in 1773. The law was an effort to bail out the bankrupt East India Company by granting that corporation a monopoly on the tea trade to Americans. Since the company could use agents to sell its product directly, cutting out the middlemen, it could offer a lower price than that charged by colonial merchants. Thus, although the Tea Act would hurt American merchants, it promised to make tea cheaper for ordinary Americans. Still, many colonials saw the act as Parliament's attempt to trick them into accepting its authority to tax the colonies. They set out to deny that power, once and for all.

In early winter of 1773 the tempest over the Tea Act peaked in Boston, with popular leaders calling for the cargoes to be returned immediately to England. On the evening of December 16, thousands of Bostonians, as well as farmers from the surrounding countryside, packed into the Old South Meetinghouse. Some members of the audience knew what Samuel Adams had on the evening's agenda, and they awaited their cue. It came when Adams told the meeting that they could do nothing more to save their country. War whoops rang through the meetinghouse, the crowd spilled onto the streets and out to the waterfront, and the Boston Tea Party commenced. From the throng emerged 50 men dressed as Indians to disguise their identities. The party boarded three vessels docked off Griffin's Wharf, broke open casks

Boston Tea Party

containing 90,000 pounds of tea, and brewed a beverage worth 10,000 pounds sterling in Boston harbor.

The Empire Strikes Back

The Boston Tea Party proved to British satisfaction that the colonies aimed at independence. Lord North's assessment was grim: "We are now to dispute whether we have, or have not, any authority in that country." To reassert its authority, Parliament *Coercive Acts* passed the Coercive Acts, dubbed in the colonies the "Intolerable Acts." The first of these came in March 1774, two months after hearing of the Tea Party, when Parliament passed the Boston Port Bill, closing that harbor to all oceangoing traffic until such time as the king saw fit to reopen it. And George, Parliament announced, would not see fit until colonials paid the East India Company for their losses.

During the next three months, Parliament approved three other "intolerable" laws designed to punish Massachusetts. The Massachusetts Government Act handed over the colony's government to royal officials. Even convening town meetings would require royal permission. The Impartial Administration of Justice Act permitted any royal official accused of a crime in Massachusetts to be tried in England or in another colony. The Quartering Act allowed the housing of British troops in private homes— not only in Massachusetts but in all the colonies.

Many colonials saw the Coercive Acts as proof of a plot to enslave the colonies. In truth, the taxes and duties, laws and regulations of the last decade *were* part of a deliberate design—a commonsensical plan to centralize the administration of the British empire. But those efforts by the king's ministers and Parliament to run the colonies more efficiently and profitably were viewed by more and more Americans as a sinister conspiracy against their liberties.

Fear of For colonials, the study of history confirmed that interpretation, especially their *conspiracy* reading of the histories written by the English Opposition. The Opposition's favorite historical subject was the downfall of republics, whether those of ancient Greece and Rome or more recent republican governments in Venice and Denmark. The lesson of their histories was always the same: power overwhelmed liberty. Those who had power would always seek more, and ambitious politicians would always pursue the same strategies to replace representative government and popular freedom with tyranny. In all places and at all times in the past, the Opposition warned, the conspiracy against liberty unfolded in predictable stages.

First, the people of a republic were impoverished by costly wars—something the colonists could well appreciate after the Seven Years' War. Then the government loaded the people with taxes to pay for those wars—as in the case of the Sugar Act or the Stamp Act or the Townshend duties. Next the government stationed a standing army in the country, pretending to protect the people but actually to lend military force to those in power. And, of course, troops had been unloaded in Boston harbor, were quartered in New York, and were making trouble wherever they appeared. Then wicked men were favored with public offices and patronage to secure their loyalty and support for the foes of liberty. And how else could one describe the royal governors, customs collectors, and judges who now received salaries from the revenues of the Townshend duties? Those in power also deliberately promoted luxury, idleness, and extravagance to weaken the moral fiber of the people—like the consumption encouraged by the low prices ensured by the Tea Act. Finally, those in power attempted to provoke the people to violent action in order to justify new oppression.

Week after week in the spring of 1774, reports of legislative outrages came across the waters. Shortly after approving the Coercive Acts, Parliament passed the Quebec Act, which established a permanent government in what had been French Canada. Ominously, it included no representative assembly. Equally ominous to protestant colonials, the Quebec Act also officially recognized the Roman Catholic church and extended the bounds of the province to include all land between the Mississippi and Ohio rivers. Suddenly New York, Pennsylvania, and Virginia found themselves bordering a British colony whose subjects had no voice in their own government.

Quebec Act

With the passage of the Coercive Acts, many more colonials came to believe not only that ambitious men plotted to enslave the colonies but also that those conspirators included almost all British political leaders. At the time of the Stamp Act and again during the agitation against the Townshend Acts, most colonials had confined their suspicions to the king's ministers. By 1774 those implicated in that conspiracy included members of Parliament—and a few radicals were wondering aloud about George III.

As alarm deepened in the wake of the Coercive Acts, one colony after another called for an intercolonial congress—like the one that had met during the Stamp Act crisis—to determine the best way to defend their freedom. But many also remained unsettled about where the logic of their actions seemed to be taking them: toward a denial that they were any longer English.

First Continental Congress called

COUNTERPOINT

Throughout the twentieth century, some historians have contended that the American Revolution was more than a fight for home rule—it was also a fight over who should rule at home, one that pitted ordinary people against the colonial elite. The most recent advocates of that view have found that American society became more unequal during the course of the eighteenth century, as wealth and political power in every colony grew more concentrated in the hands of leading families of planters, merchants, and lawyers. The result, they contend, was a rising tide of disaffection among humbler folk, whose participation in protests and riots expressed not only their grievances against the British empire but also their hostility to wealthy colonials. In the course of defying Parliament and the king, ordinary farmers and artisans, and even people beneath them in the social structure, developed their own "popular ideology," a political outlook more egalitarian and democratic than the republican views held by gentlemen who led the resistance to Britain.

A revolution within a revolution?

But other historians are more skeptical. While agreeing that mounting inequalities heightened tensions during the decades before the Revolution, they argue that all classes of white colonials embraced a common political outlook—republicanism. What promoted that unity of belief and feeling was that most white men owned land and had the right to vote. As members of a propertied, politically empowered middle class, a majority of white colonials wanted only to throw off their connection with Britain; they had no incentive to seek more drastic changes in their society. Indeed, their moderate political aspirations were ably expressed by republicanism, which spoke directly to the concerns of most white Americans both by upholding property rights as the basis of personal freedom and by warning that any group of people who became too wealthy or powerful posed a threat to the liberty of the people.

TOWARD THE REVOLUTION

By the beginning of September 1774, when 55 delegates to the First Continental Congress gathered in Philadelphia, the news from Massachusetts was bad. The colony verged on anarchy, it was reported, as its inhabitants resisted the enforcement of the Massachusetts Government Act.

In the midst of this atmosphere of crisis, the members of Congress also had to take one another's measure. Many of the delegates had not traveled outside their own colonies. (All but Georgia sent representatives.) Although the delegates encountered a great deal of diversity, they quickly discovered that they esteemed the same traits of character, attributes that they called "civic virtue." These traits included simplicity and self-reliance, industry and thrift, and, above all, an unselfish commitment to the public good. Most members of the Congress also shared a common mistrust of England, associating the mother country with vice, extravagance, and corruption.

Still, the delegates had some misgivings about those from other colonies. Massachusetts in particular brought with it a reputation—well deserved, considering that Samuel Adams was along—for radical action and a willingness to use force to accomplish its ends.

The First Continental Congress

As the delegates settled down to business, their aim was to reach agreement on three key points. How were they to justify the rights they claimed as American colonials? What were the limits of Parliament's power? And what were the proper tactics for resisting the Coercive Acts? Congress quickly agreed on the first point. The delegates affirmed that the law of nature, the colonial charters, and the British constitution provided the foundations of American liberties. This position was what most colonials had argued since 1765. On the two other issues, Congress charted a middle course between the demands of radicals and the reservations of conservatives.

Since the time of the Stamp Act, most colonials had insisted that Parliament had no authority to tax the colonies. But later events had demonstrated that Parliament could undermine colonial liberties by legislation as well as by taxation. The suspension of the New York legislature, the *Gaspee* Commission, and the Coercive Acts all fell into this category. Given those experiences, the delegates adopted a Declaration of Rights and Grievances on October 14, 1774, asserting the right of the colonies to tax and legislate for themselves. The Declaration of Rights thus limited Parliament's power over Americans more strictly than colonials had a decade earlier.

By denying Parliament's power to make laws for the colonies, the Continental Congress blocked efforts of the most conservative delegates to reach an accommodation with England. Their leading advocate, Joseph Galloway of Pennsylvania, proposed a plan of union with Britain similar to the one set forth by the Albany Congress in 1754. Under it, a grand council of the colonies would handle all common concerns, with any laws it passed subject to review and veto by Parliament. For its part, Parliament would

Samuel Adams, a radical who masterminded colonial resistance tactics have to submit for the grand council's approval any acts it passed affecting America. A majority of delegates judged that Galloway's proposal left Parliament too much leeway in legislating for colonials, and they rejected his plan. *Joseph Galloway's plan*

Although the Congress denied Parliament the right to impose taxes or to make laws, delegates stopped short of declaring that it had no authority at all in the colonies. They approved Parliament's regulation of trade, but only because of the interdependent economy of the empire. And although some radical pamphleteers were attacking the king for plotting against American liberties, Congress acknowledged the continuing allegiance of the colonies to George III. In other words, the delegates called for a return to the situation that had existed in the empire before 1763, with Parliament regulating trade and the colonies exercising all powers of taxation and legislation.

On the question of resistance, Congress satisfied the desires of its most radical delegates by drawing up the Continental Association, an agreement to cease all trade with Britain until the Coercive Acts were repealed. They agreed that their fellow citizens would immediately stop drinking East India Company tea and that by December 1, 1774, merchants would no longer import goods of any sort from Britain. A ban on the export of American produce to Britain and the West Indies would go into effect a year later, during September 1775—the lag being a concession to southern rice and tobacco planters, who wanted to market crops already planted. *The Association*

The Association provided for the total cessation of trade, but Samuel Adams and other radicals wanted bolder action. They received help from Paul Revere, a Boston silversmith who had long provided newspapers with many lurid engravings showing British abuses. On September 16, Revere galloped into Philadelphia bearing a copy of resolves drawn up by Bostonians and other residents of Suffolk County. The Suffolk Resolves, as they were called, branded the Coercive Acts as unconstitutional and called for civil disobedience to protest them. Congress endorsed the resolves, as Adams had hoped. But it would not approve another part of the radicals' agenda—preparing for war by authorizing proposals to strengthen and arm colonial militias. *Revere and the Suffolk Resolves*

Thus the First Continental Congress steered a middle course. Although determined to bring about repeal of the Coercive Acts, it held firm in resisting any revolutionary course of action. If British officials had responded to its recommendations and restored the status quo of 1763, the war for independence might have been postponed—perhaps indefinitely. On the other hand, even though the Congress did not go to the extremes urged by the radicals, its decisions drew colonials farther down the road to independence.

The Last Days of the British Empire in America

Most colonials applauded the achievements of the First Continental Congress. They expected that the Association would bring about a speedy repeal of the Coercive Acts. But fear that the colonies were moving toward a break with Britain led others to denounce the doings of the Congress. Conservatives were convinced that if independence was declared, chaos would ensue. Colonials, they argued, would quarrel over land claims and sectional tensions and religious differences, as they had so often in the recent past. Without Britain to referee such disputes, they feared, the result would be civil war, followed by anarchy.

The man in America with the least liking for the Continental Congress sat in the

Thomas Gage in Boston hottest seat in the colonies, that of the governor of Massachusetts. General Thomas Gage now watched as royal authority crumbled in Massachusetts and the rebellion spread to other colonies. In October 1774 a desperate Gage dissolved the Massachusetts legislature, only to see it re-form, on its own, into a Provincial Congress. That new body assumed the government of the colony and began arming the militia. Gage then started to fortify Boston and pleaded for more troops—only to find his fortifications damaged by saboteurs and his requests for reinforcements ignored by Britain.

Collapse of royal authority Outside Boston, royal authority fared no better. Farmers in western Massachusetts forcibly closed the county courts, turning out royally appointed justices and establishing their own tribunals. Popularly elected committees of inspection charged with enforcing the Association took over towns everywhere in Massachusetts, not only restricting trade but also regulating every aspect of local life. The committees called upon townspeople to display civic virtue by renouncing "effeminate" English luxuries like tea and fine clothing and "corrupt" leisure activities like dancing, gambling, and racing. The committees also assigned spies to report on any citizen unfriendly to the resistance. "Enemies of American liberty" risked being roundly condemned in public or beaten and pelted with mud and dung by hooting, raucous mobs.

Throughout the colonies a similar process was under way. During the winter and early spring of 1775, provincial congresses, county conventions, and local committees of inspection were emerging as revolutionary governments, replacing royal authority at every level. As the spectacle unfolded before General Gage, he concluded that only force could subdue the colonies. It would take more than he had at his command, but reinforcements might be on the way. In February of 1775, Parliament had approved an address to the king declaring that the colonies were in rebellion.

The Fighting Begins

As spring came to Boston, the city waited. A band of artisans, organized as spies and express riders by Paul Revere, watched General Gage and waited for him to act. Gage waited for reinforcements from Lord North and watched the hostile town. On April 14 word from North finally arrived: Gage was to seize the leaders of the Provincial Congress. That would behead the rebellion, North said. Gage knew better than to believe North—but he also knew that he had to do something.

On the night of April 18 the sexton of Boston's Christ Church hung two lamps from its steeple. It was a signal that British troops had moved out of Boston and were marching toward the arms and ammunition stored by the Provincial Congress in Concord. As the lamps flashed the signal, Revere and a comrade, William Dawes, rode out to arouse the countryside.

Lexington and Concord When the news of a British march reached Lexington, its militia of about 70 farmers, chilled and sleepy, mustered on the Green at the center of the small rural town. Lexington Green lay directly on the road to Concord. At about four in the morning 700 British troops massed on the Green, and their commander, Major John Pitcairn, ordered the Lexington militia to disperse. The townsmen, outnumbered and overawed, began to obey. Then a shot rang out—whether the British or the Americans fired first is unknown—and then two volleys burst from the ranks of the

The American engraver Amos Doolittle depicted the arrival of British troops in Concord, Massachusetts, just before their fateful encounter with the Minutemen on the North Bridge.

redcoats. With a cheer the British set off for Concord, five miles distant, leaving eight Americans dead on Lexington Green.

By dawn, hundreds of militiamen from nearby towns were surging into Concord. The British entered at about seven in the morning and moved, unopposed, toward their target, a house lying across the bridge that spanned the Concord River. While three companies of British soldiers searched for American guns and ammunition, three others, posted on the bridge itself, had the misfortune to find those American arms—borne by the rebels and being fired with deadly accuracy. By noon, the British were retreating to Boston.

The narrow road from Concord to Boston's outskirts became a corridor of carnage. Pursuing Americans fired on the column of fleeing redcoats from the cover of fences and forests. By the end of April 19, the British had sustained 273 casualties; the Americans, 95. It was only the beginning. By evening of the next day, some 20,000 New England militia had converged on Boston for a long siege.

Common Sense

The bloodshed at Lexington Green and Concord's North Bridge committed colonials to a course of rebellion—and independence. That was the conclusion drawn by Thomas Paine, who urged other Americans to do the same.

Thomas Paine, author of *Common Sense*

Paine himself was hardly an American at all. He was born in England, apprenticed first as a corsetmaker, appointed later a tax collector, and fated finally to become midwife to the age of republican revolutions. Paine came to Philadelphia late in 1774, set up as a journalist, and made the American cause his own. "Where liberty is, there is my country," he declared. In January 1776 he wrote a pamphlet to inform colonials of their identity as a distinct people and their destiny as a nation. *Common Sense* enjoyed tremendous popularity and wide circulation, selling 120,000 copies within three months of its publication.

Thomas Paine argues for independence

After Lexington and Concord, Paine wrote, as the imperial crisis passed "from argument to arms, a new era for politics is struck—a new method of thinking has arisen." That new era of politics for Paine was the age of republicanism. He denounced monarchy as a foolish and dangerous form of government, one that violated the dictates of reason as well as the word of the Bible. By ridicule and remorseless argument, he severed the ties of colonial allegiance to the king. *Common Sense* scorned George III as "the Royal Brute of Britain," who had enslaved the chosen people of the new age—the Americans.

Nor did Paine stop there. He rejected the idea that colonials were or should want to be English. Britain, he told his readers, far from being a tender parent, had bled colonials of their wealth and preyed on their liberties. Why suffer such enslavement? The colonies occupied a huge continent an ocean away from the tiny British Isles—clear proof that nature itself had fashioned America for independence. England lay locked in Europe, doomed to the corruption of an Old World. America had been discovered anew to become an "asylum of liberty."

Many Americans had liked being English, but being English hadn't worked. Perhaps that is another way of saying that over the course of nearly two centuries colonial society and politics had evolved in such a way that the identity between the Americans and the English no longer fit. By the end of the Seven Years' War, the colonies had established political institutions that made the rights of "freeborn Britons" more available to ordinary citizens in America than in the nation that had created those liberties. Perhaps, then, most Americans had succeeded *too* well at becoming English, regarding themselves as political equals entitled to basic constitutional freedoms. In the space of less than a generation, the logic of events made clear that despite all the English and Americans shared, in the distribution of political power they were fundamentally at odds. And the call to arms at Lexington and Concord made retreat impossible.

On that point Paine was clear. It was the destiny of Americans to be republicans, not monarchists. It was the destiny of Americans to be independent, not subject to British dominion. It was the destiny of Americans to be American, not English. That, according to Thomas Paine, was common sense.

CHAPTER SUMMARY

The Seven Years' War resolved the contest for supremacy in North America between the English and the French and set the stage for the conflict over American independence. The war left many English leaders displeased with the colonies; some even anticipated that Americans would exploit their new military security by making a bid for independence. As a result, Britain aimed to impose tighter controls on colonial trade and territory. The new measures of the early 1760s—the Proclamation of 1763, the Sugar Act, the Stamp Act, the Currency Act, the Quartering Act, and the stationing of British troops in the colonies—were all designed to bind the colonies more closely to the empire.

The timing of those new measures was disastrous. They deflated American expectations of a more equal status in the empire and coincided with a postwar downturn in the colonial economy. Perhaps more important, the new measures violated what Americans understood to be their constitutional and political liberties: the right to consent to taxation, the right to trial by jury, the freedom from standing armies. Colonials thus displayed an unprecedented unity in opposing imperial policy, turning to petitions, crowd actions, and boycotts as resistance tactics. Although Parliament repealed the Stamp Act, it reasserted its authority to tax Americans by passing the Townshend Acts in 1767. Americans renewed and institutionalized their resistance, enforcing boycotts with committees of inspection. The stationing of British troops in Boston only deepened colonial hostility, which erupted into violence with the Boston Massacre. With the repeal in 1770 of all of the Townshend duties except for the tax on tea, American resistance subsided until the *Gaspee* incident in 1772 renewed its strength and inspired the formation of the committees of correspondence. When Britain responded to the Boston Tea Party with the Coercive Acts in 1774, many Americans concluded that all British actions in the last decade were part of a deliberate plot to enslave Americans by depriving them of property and liberty. The understanding of history that Americans had learned from the English Opposition— that power inevitably conspires against liberty—colonials now applied to the crisis within the empire.

When the First Continental Congress convened in September 1774, delegates resisted both radical demands to mobilize for war and conservative appeals to reach an accommodation. The Congress denied Parliament any authority in the colonies except the power to regulate trade. It drew up the Continental Association, an agreement to cease all trade with Britain until the Coercive Acts were repealed. Meanwhile, the collapse of royal authority was moving the colonies closer to a showdown with Britain. Intending to make a show of force, General Thomas Gage sent troops from Boston in April of 1775 to seize arms being stored at Concord, and a battle between British soldiers and Massachusetts militiamen resulted. In January of 1776 Thomas Paine's *Common Sense* announced that the imperial crisis had passed from "argument to arms," attacked the rule of kings, and persuaded many Americans of the necessity of independence.

ADDITIONAL READING

The most balanced and readable account of the entire revolutionary era is still Edmund S. Morgan, *The Birth of the Republic* (1956). His study entitled *The Stamp Act Crisis* (1953), coauthored with Helen M. Morgan, remains the clearest and most vivid description of the issues, events, and people involved in that defining moment of the imperial crisis. Good coverage of later developments can be found in Pauline Maier, *From Resistance to Revolution* (1972). To understand the impact of the Seven

Years' War on the attitudes toward Britain among ordinary men in Massachusetts, consult Fred Anderson's excellent *A People's Army* (1984); two equally imaginative interpretations of how the logic of resistance took shape among colonials are Timothy Breen, *Tobacco Culture* (1985) and Robert A. Gross, *The Minutemen and Their World* (1976). Bernard Bailyn, *The Ideological Origins of the American Revolution* (1967) demonstrates the influence of the English Opposition in the evolution of colonial political thought. The most important book on British politics in this period is John Brewer, *Party Ideology and Popular Politics at the Accession of George III* (1976), but for a lively treatment of the monarchy, see J. H. Plumb, *The First Four Georges* (1956).

Biographies shed light on not only their subjects but the times in which they lived. Some of the best chronicle the careers of eighteenth-century Americans who led—or opposed—the resistance to Britain. For the rebels, see Richard R. Beeman, *Patrick Henry* (1974), Eric Foner, *Tom Paine and Revolutionary America* (1976), Pauline Maier, *The Old Revolutionaries* (1980), and Dumas Malone, *Jefferson the Virginian* (1948). For sympathetic treatment of one American loyalist, see Bernard Bailyn, *The Ordeal of Thomas Hutchinson* (1974). For a fuller list of readings, see the Bibliography.

SIGNIFICANT EVENTS

1755	Braddock defeated by French and Indians
1756	England and France declare war
1759	Decisive English victory at Quebec
1760	George III becomes king of England
1763	Treaty of Paris ends the Seven Years' War; Pontiac's Rebellion; royal proclamation prohibits settlement west of the Appalachians
1764	Sugar Act; Currency Act
1765	Stamp Act; Quartering Act
1766	Repeal of the Stamp Act; Declaratory Act
1767	Townshend duties; Parliament suspends New York assembly
1770	Boston Massacre; repeal of most Townshend duties
1772	*Gaspee* Commission
1773	Boston Tea Party
1774	Coercive Acts; First Continental Congress meets at Philadelphia
1775	Battles of Lexington and Concord
1776	Thomas Paine's *Common Sense* published

6

The American People and the American Revolution

rom a high place somewhere in the city—Beacon Hill, perhaps, or Copse Hill—General Thomas Gage looked down on Boston. Through a spyglass his gaze traveled over the church belfries and steeples, the roofs of brick and white frame houses. Finally he fixed his sights on a figure far in the distance across the Charles River. The man was perched atop a crude fortification on Breed's Hill, an elevation lying just below Bunker Hill on the Charlestown peninsula. Gage took the measure of his enemy: an older man, past middle age, a sword swinging beneath his homespun coat, a broad-brimmed hat shading his eyes. As he passed the spyglass to his ally, an American loyalist, Gage asked Abijah Willard if he knew the man on the fort. Willard peered across the Charles and identified his own brother-in-law, Colonel William Prescott. A veteran of the Seven Years' War, Prescott was now a leader in the rebel army laying siege to Boston.

"Will he fight?" Gage wondered aloud.

"I cannot answer for his men," Willard replied, "but Prescott will fight you to the gates of hell."

Battle of Bunker Hill

Fight they did on June 17, 1775, both William Prescott and his men. The evening before, three regiments had followed the colonel from Cambridge to Breed's Hill—soldiers drawn from the thousands of militia who had swarmed to surround British-occupied Boston after the bloodshed at Lexington and Concord. All through the night, they dug deep trenches and built up high earthen walls atop the hill. At the first light of day, a British warship spotted the new rebel outpost and opened fire. By noon barges were ferrying British troops under Major General William Howe across the half mile of river that separated Boston from Charlestown. The 1600 raw rebel troops tensed at the sight of scarlet-coated soldiers streaming ashore, glittering bayonets grasped at the ready. The rebels were farmers and artisans, not professional soldiers, and they were frightened out of their wits.

But Prescott and his men held their ground. The British charged Breed's Hill twice, and Howe watched in horror as streams of fire felled his troops. Finally, during the third British frontal assault, the rebels ran out of ammunition and were forced to withdraw. Redcoats poured into the rebel fort, bayoneting its handful of remaining defenders. By nightfall the British had taken Breed's Hill and the rest of the Charlestown peninsula. They had bought a dark triumph at the cost of 228 dead and 800 wounded.

Eleven years after the event, the American artist John Trumbull painted Battle of Bunker's Hill *(1786), a canvas executed in the currently fashionable mode of grand historical painting, designed to commemorate (and elevate) an occasion of note.*

The cost came high in loyalties as well. The fighting on Breed's Hill fed the hatred of Britain that had been building since April. Throughout America, preparations for war intensified: militia in every colony mustered; communities stockpiled arms and ammunition. Around Charlestown civilians fled the countryside, abandoning homes and shops set afire by the British shelling of Breed's Hill. "The roads filled with frightened women and children, some in carts with their tattered furniture, others on foot fleeing into the woods," recalled Hannah Winthrop, one of their number.

The bloody, indecisive fight on the Charlestown peninsula known as the Battle of Bunker Hill actually took place on Breed's Hill. And the exchange between Thomas Gage and Abijah Willard that is said to have preceded the battle may not have taken place at all. But the story has persisted in the folklore of the American Revolution. Whether it really happened or not, the conversation between Gage and Willard raised the question that both sides wanted answered. Were Americans willing to fight for independence from British rule? It was one thing, after all, to oppose the British ministry's policy of taxation. It was another to support a rebellion for which the ultimate price of failure was hanging for treason. And it was another matter entirely for men to wait nervously atop a hill as the seasoned troops of one's own "mother country" marched toward them with the intent to kill.

Americans react to the Revolution

Indeed, the question "will they fight?" was revolutionary shorthand for a host of other questions concerning how ordinary Americans would react to the tug of loyalties between long-established colonial governments and a long-revered parent nation and monarch. For slaves, the question revolved around their allegiance to masters who spoke of liberty or to their masters' enemies who promised liberation. For those who led the rebels, it was a question of strengthening the resolve of the undecided, coordinating resistance, instilling discipline—translating the *will* to fight into the ability to do so. And for those who believed the rebellion was a madness whipped up by artful politicians, it was a question of whether to remain silent or risk speaking out, whether to take up arms for the king or flee. All these questions were raised, of necessity, by the act of revolution. But the barrel of a rifle shortened them to a single, pointed question: will you fight?

THE DECISION FOR INDEPENDENCE

The delegates to the Second Continental Congress gathered at Philadelphia on May 10, 1775, just one month after the battles at Lexington and Concord. They had to determine whether independence or reconciliation offered the best way to protect the liberties of their colonies.

For a brash, ambitious lawyer from Braintree, Massachusetts, British abuses dictated only one course. "The Cancer [of official corruption] is too deeply rooted," wrote John Adams, "and too far spread to be cured by anything short of cutting it out entire." Yet during the spring and summer of 1775, even strong advocates of independence did not openly seek a separation from Britain. If the radicals' objective of independence was ever to be achieved, greater agreement among Americans had to be attained. Moderates and conservatives harbored deep misgivings about independence: they had to be brought along slowly.

The Second Continental Congress

To bring them along, Congress adopted the "Olive Branch Petition" in July 1775. Drawn up by Pennsylvania's John Dickinson, the document affirmed American loyalty to George III and asked the king to disavow the policies of his principal ministers. At the same time Congress issued a declaration denying that the colonies aimed at independence. Yet, less than a month earlier, Congress had authorized the creation of a rebel military force, the Continental Army, and had issued paper money to pay for the troops.

Aggressive British response

A Congress that sued for peace while preparing for war was a puzzle that British politicians did not even try to understand, least of all Lord George Germain. A tough-minded statesman now charged with overseeing colonial affairs, Germain was determined to subdue the rebellion by force. George III proved just as stubborn: he refused to receive the Olive Branch Petition. By the end of that year Parliament had shut down all trade with the colonies and had ordered the Royal Navy to seize colonial merchant ships on the high seas. In November 1775 Virginia's royal governor,

Lord Dunmore, offered freedom to any slaves who would join the British. During January of the next year, he ordered the shelling of Norfolk, Virginia, reducing that town to a smoldering rubble.

British belligerence withered the cause of reconciliation within Congress and the colonies. Support for independence gained more momentum from the overwhelming reception of *Common Sense* in January 1776. Radicals in Congress realized that the future was theirs and were ready to act. In April 1776 the delegates opened American trade to every nation in the world except Great Britain; a month later Congress advised the colonies to establish new state governments. And on June 7 Virginia's Richard Henry Lee offered the motion "that these United Colonies are, and of right ought to be, free and independent States . . . and that all political connection between them and the State of Great Britain is, and ought to be, totally dissolved."

The Declaration

Congress postponed a final vote on Lee's motion until July. Some opposition still lingered among delegates from the Middle Colonies, and a committee appointed to write a declaration of independence needed time to complete its work. That committee included some of the leading delegates in Congress: John Adams, Benjamin Franklin, Connecticut's Roger Sherman, and New York's Robert Livingston. But the man who did most of the drafting was a young planter and lawyer from western Virginia.

Thomas Jefferson was just 33 years old in the summer of 1776 when he withdrew to his lodgings on the outskirts of Philadelphia, pulled a portable writing desk onto his lap, and wrote the statement that would explain American independence to a "candid world." In the document's brief opening section, Jefferson set forth a general justification of revolution that invoked the "self-evident truths" of human equality and "unalienable rights" to "life, liberty, and the pursuit of happiness." These natural rights had been "endowed" to all persons "by their Creator," the Declaration pointed out; thus there was no need to appeal to the narrower claim of the "rights of Englishmen." *Thomas Jefferson*

While the first part of the Declaration served notice that Americans no longer considered themselves English, its second and longer section denied England any authority in the colonies. In its detailed history of American grievances against the British empire, the Declaration referred only once to Parliament. Instead, it blamed George III for a "long train of abuses and usurpations" designed to achieve "absolute despotism." Unlike *Common Sense,* the Declaration denounced only the reigning king of England; it did not attack the institution of monarchy itself. But like *Common Sense,* the Declaration affirmed that government originated in the consent of the governed and upheld the right of the people to overthrow oppressive rule. *Blaming George III*

Later generations have debated what Jefferson meant by the "pursuit of happiness" and whether he had either women or black Americans in mind when he wrote the famous phrase "all men are created equal." His own contemporaries in Congress did not pause to consider those questions, and surely would have found themselves divided if they had. No matter. By firmly grounding the Declaration on the natural rights due all people, Jefferson placed equality at the center of the new nation's identity, setting the framework for a debate that would continue over the next two centuries. Congress adopted the Declaration of Independence on July 4, 1776.

This painting, which commemorated the signing of the Declaration of Independence, shows Benjamin Franklin (seated center), obviously weighing the consequences of the action he and his colleagues are about to undertake. John Hancock, the president of the Congress, is reported to have remarked, "We must be unanimous; there must be no pulling different ways; we must all hang together." Franklin is said to have rejoined, "Yes, we must indeed all hang together, or most assuredly, we shall all hang separately."

American Loyalists

Colonial political leaders embraced independence because they believed that a majority of Americans would support a revolution. But the sentiment for independence was not universal. Those who would not back the rebellion, supporters of the king and Parliament, numbered perhaps one-fifth of the population in 1775. While they proclaimed themselves "loyalists," their rebel opponents dubbed them "tories"—"a thing whose head is in England, whose body is in America, and whose neck ought to be stretched." That division made the Revolution a conflict pitting Americans against one another as well as the British. In truth, the war for independence was the first American civil war.

PATTERNS OF ALLEGIANCE
While most New Englanders rallied behind the rebel cause, support for the Revolution was not as widespread in the Middle Colonies and southern colonies.

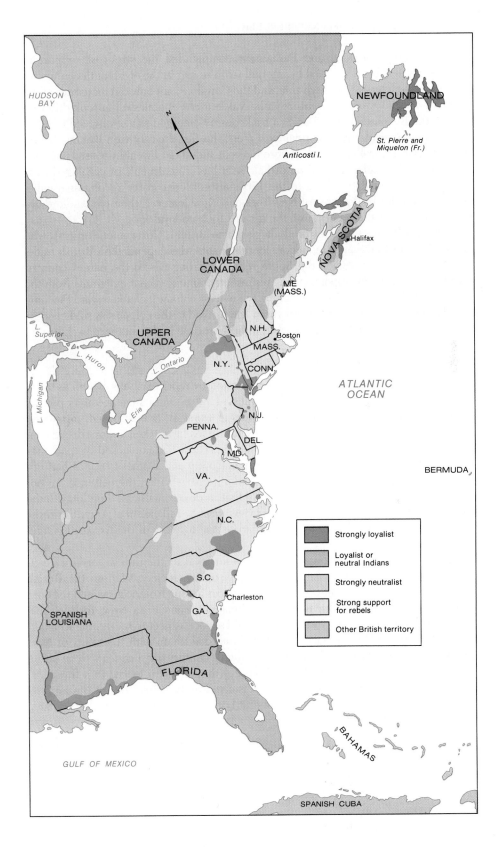

HUDSON BAY

NEWFOUNDLAND

St. Pierre and Miquelon (Fr.)

Anticosti I.

NOVA SCOTIA

Halifax

LOWER CANADA

ME (MASS.)

N.H.

Boston

L. Superior

UPPER CANADA

MASS.

L. Huron

L. Ontario

N.Y.

CONN.

L. Michigan

L. Erie

ATLANTIC OCEAN

N.J.

PENNA.

DEL.

MD.

VA.

BERMUDA

N.C.

SPANISH LOUISIANA

S.C.

Charleston

GA.

Strongly loyalist

Loyalist or neutral Indians

Strongly neutralist

Strong support for rebels

Other British territory

FLORIDA

BAHAMAS

GULF OF MEXICO

SPANISH CUBA

Sources of loyalist support   Predictably, the king and Parliament commanded the strongest support in colonies that had been wracked by internal strife earlier in the eighteenth century. In New York, New Jersey, Pennsylvania, and the Carolinas, not only did memories of old struggles sharpen worries of future upheaval, but old enemies often took different sides in the Revolution. The Carolina backcountry emerged as a stronghold of loyalist sentiment because of influential local men who cast their lot with Britain. To win support against Carolina's rebels, whose ranks included most wealthy coastal planters, western loyalist leaders played on ordinary settlers' resentments of privileged easterners. Grievances dating back to the 1760s also influenced the revolutionary allegiances of former land rioters of New York and New Jersey. If their old landlord opponents opted for the rebel cause, the tenants took up loyalism.

Other influences also fostered allegiance to Britain. Government officials who owed their jobs to the empire, major city merchants who depended on British trade, and Anglicans living outside the South retained strong ties to the parent country. Loyalists were also disproportionately represented among recent emigrants from the British Isles. The inhabitants of Georgia, the newest colony, inclined toward the king, as did the Highland Scots, many of whom had arrived in the colonies as soldiers during the Seven Years' War or had worked for a short time in the southern backcountry as tobacco merchants and Indian traders.

COUNTERPOINT   Histories of the American revolution written by rebel partisans as well as many later chroniclers have not treated the loyalists kindly. Often such accounts portray those who opposed independence as traitors at worst or, at best, timid, misguided souls. But within the last generation, many historians have taken a more dispassionate view, finding that many who took up the king's cause had not lacked sympathy for the resistance. Loyalist leaders like Joseph Galloway and Daniel Leonard had opposed the Stamp Act in 1765 and disapproved of imperial policy thereafter. It was not until the crisis reached a fever pitch in 1774 that more colonials cast their lot with the king. Worse than British taxation, in their view, was the radicalism of American resistance—the dumping of tea into Boston harbor, the forming of the Association, and the defying of royal authority.

Contrasting views of loyalists   Such acts of defiance touched what was for loyalists the rawest nerve: a deep-seated fear of the divisions and instability of colonial society. Without the British around to maintain order, they warned, differences among Americans would result in civil war. On the eve of the Revolution, Jonathan Boucher, a New York loyalist, warned with uncanny foresight that "we should as soon expect to see . . . the wolf and the lamb feed together, as Virginians form a cordial union with the saints of New England." It would take the passage of less than a century for such fears to be borne out by events—the Union divided and the North and South locked in a fratricidal war. In prizing liberty over order, the rebels acted on principle. But as the loyalists predicted, that choice came at a terrible cost both to them and to their descendants.

In any case, although a substantial minority, loyalists never became numerous enough anywhere to pose a serious menace to the Revolution. A more formidable threat was posed by the British army. And the greatest threat of all was posed by those very Americans who claimed that they wanted independence. For the question remained: would they fight?

THE FIGHTING IN THE NORTH

In the summer of 1775 Americans who wished to remain neutral probably outnumbered either loyalists or rebels. From the standpoint of mere survival, staying neutral made more sense than fighting for independence. Even the most ardent advocates of American rights had reason to harbor doubts, given the odds against the rebel colonists defeating the armed forces of the British empire.

Perhaps no friend of American liberty saw more clearly how slim the chances of a rebel victory were than George Washington. But Washington's principles, and his sense of honor, prevailed. June of 1775 found him, then 43 years old, attending the deliberations of the Second Continental Congress and dressed—a bit conspicuously—in his officer's uniform. The other delegates listened closely to his opinions on military matters, for Washington was the most celebrated American veteran of the Seven Years' War who remained young enough to lead a campaign. Better still, as a southerner he could bring his region into what thus far had remained mostly New England's fight. Congress readily appointed him commander-in-chief of a newly created Continental Army.

George Washington, general

The Two Armies at Bay

Thus did Washington find himself, only a month later, looking to bring some order to the rebel forces massing around Boston. He knew he faced a formidable foe.

Highly trained, ably led, and efficiently equipped, the king's troops were seasoned professionals. Rank-and-file soldiers, men drawn mainly from the bottom of British society, were drilled rigorously and disciplined (often savagely) by an aristocratic officer corps. At the height of the campaign in America, reinforcements brought the number of British troops to 50,000, strengthened by some 30,000 Hessian mercenaries from Germany and the support of half the ships in the British navy, the largest in the world.

Washington was more modest about the army under his command, and he had much to be modest about. At first Congress recruited his fighting force of 16,600 rebel "regulars," the Continental Army, from the ranks of local New England militia bands. Although enlistments swelled briefly during the patriotic enthusiasm of 1775, for the rest of the war Washington's Continentals suffered chronic shortages of men and supplies. Even strong supporters of the Revolution hesitated to join the regular army, with its low pay, strict discipline, and the constant threat of disease and danger. Most men preferred to fight instead as members of local militia units, the "irregular" troops who turned out to support the regular army whenever British forces came close to their neighborhoods.

"Regulars" versus the militia

The general reluctance to join the Continental Army created a host of difficulties for its commander and for Congress. Washington wanted and needed an army whose size and military capability could be counted on in long campaigns. He could not create an effective fighting force out of civilians who mustered out occasionally with the militia or enlisted for short stints in the Continental Army. Washington's desire for a professional military establishment clashed with the preferences of most republican leaders. They feared standing armies and idealized "citizen-soldiers"—men of selfless civic virtue who volunteered whenever needed—as the backbone of the

CLOTHING AND FASHION

Radical Chic and the Revolutionary Generation

Women and men of revolutionary America sought to invest themselves with virtue as they escaped British "corruption." The most zealous partisans of colonial rights took that "investiture" to a literal extreme: they made and wore particular clothing as an emblem of political commitment. In the 1760s "homespun," any coarse cloth made in America, became a badge of opposition to British colonial policy.

Clothes sewn from domestic textiles identified the men and women who wore them as friends of liberty, freed from the vanity of British fashion and the humiliating dependence on British imports. As early as 1766 the radical press called for increased domestic industry to offset American reliance on English cloth. It aimed its pleas particularly at the women who managed colonial households.

By 1769 radical propaganda had produced a new ritual of American resistance, the patriotic spinning competition. Wives and daughters from some of the wealthiest and most prominent families, women who had heretofore vied to outdo each other in acquiring the latest English finery, were the featured players in this new form of political theater. Its setting was usually the home of a local minister where, early in the morning, "respectable" young ladies, all dressed in homespun, assembled with their spinning wheels. They spent the day spinning furiously, stopping only to sustain themselves with "American produce ... which was more agreeable to them than any foreign Dainties and Delicacies" and to drink herbal tea. At the end of the day the minister accepted their homespun cloth and delivered an edifying sermon to all present. That was a large group, often including from 20 to 100 "respectable" female spinners as well as hundreds of other townsfolk who had come to watch the competition or to provide food and entertainment.

Women reveled in the new attention and value that the male resistance movement and the radical press now attached to a common and humdrum domestic task. By the beginning of 1769 New England newspapers were highlighting spinning bees and their female participants, sometimes termed the "Daughters of Liberty." Front pages overflowed with praise of female patriotism: "The industry and frugality of American ladies must exalt their character in the Eyes of the World and serve to show how greatly they are contributing to bring about the political salvation of a whole Continent."

Spinning competitions and the vogue of wearing homespun served two political purposes. First, the bees actively enlisted American women in the struggle against common defense. "Oh, that I was a soldier," chubby John Adams fantasized in 1775. "Everyone must and will and shall be a soldier."

But everyone did not become a soldier, and the dwindling number of volunteers gradually overcame republican fears of standing armies. In September 1776 Congress set terms in the Continental Army at a minimum of three years or for the duration of the war and assigned each state to raise a certain number of troops. They offered every man who enlisted in the army a cash bounty and a yearly clothing issue;

180

Daily Lives

Britain. Wives and daughters from families of every rank were made to feel that they could play an important role in the resistance by imitating the elite women showcased in public spinning spectacles. Every woman could display her devotion to liberty by encouraging industry and frugality in her own household. Many women took pride in the new political importance that radical propaganda attributed to domestic pursuits. Writing to her English cousin, Charity Clarke of New York City cast herself as one of America's "fighting army of amazones . . . armed with spinning wheels."

Spinning bees and "dressing down" in homespun also contributed to the solidarity of the resistance by narrowing the visible distance between rich and poor Americans. In accounts of spinning competitions, the radical press emphasized that even the daughters of the elite sacrificed for the cause of resistance by embracing domestic economy and simplicity.

And what genteel women wove, leading men wore. On public occasions throughout the revolutionary crisis, radical leaders appeared in homespun, displaying both their patriotic virtue and their identification with poorer Americans who could not afford British finery. When they returned to their home counties to muster local militia companies, many southern gentlemen adopted homespun "hunting shirts," long, loose, full-sleeved frocks that reached past the thigh. This dress of the frontier united the gentry with ordinary men of the backcountry while declaring their superiority to the corrupt mother country.

Hunting shirts like the one worn by this rifleman (second from right) captured the imagination of the French army officer in America who made these watercolor sketches of revolutionary soldiers. The enlistment of blacks (infantryman at the far left) drew his attention as well.

enlistees for the duration were offered 100 acres of land as well. Still the problem of recruitment persisted. Less than a year later, Congress recommended that the states adopt a draft, but Congress had no authority to compel the states to meet their troop quotas.

Even in the summer of 1775, before enlistments fell off, Washington was worried. As his Continentals laid siege to British-occupied Boston, he measured them against the adversary and found them wanting. Inexperienced officers provided no

181

real leadership, and the men under their command shirked the most basic responsibilities of soldiers. They slipped away from camp at night; they left sentry duty before being relieved; they took potshots at the British; they tolerated filthy conditions in their camps.

Women of the Army

While Washington strove to impose discipline on his Continentals, he also attempted, without success, to rid himself of "the Women of the Army." When American men went off to fight, their wives usually stayed at home. To women then fell the sole responsibility for running farms and businesses, raising children, and keeping households together. They helped to supply the troops by sewing clothing, making blankets, and saving rags and lead weights for bandages and bullets. Other women on the home front organized relief for the widows and orphans of soldiers and protests against merchants who hoarded scarce commodities.

But the wives of poor men who joined the army were often left with no means to support their families. Thousands of such women—1 for every 15 soldiers—drifted after the troops. In return for half-rations, they cooked and washed for the soldiers; and after battles, they nursed the wounded, buried the dead, and scavenged the field for clothing and equipment. An even larger number of women accompanied the redcoats: their presence was the only thing that Washington did not admire about the British army and could barely tolerate in his own. But the services that they performed were indispensable, and women followed the troops throughout the war.

Laying Strategies

At the same time that he tried to discipline the Continentals, Washington designed a defensive strategy to compensate for their weakness. To avoid exposing raw rebel troops on "open ground against their Superiors in number and Discipline," he planned to fight the British from strong fortifications. With that aim in mind, in March 1776, Washington barricaded his army on Dorchester Heights, an elevation commanding Boston harbor from the south. That maneuver, which allowed American artillery to fire on enemy warships, confirmed a decision already made by the British to evacuate their entire army from Boston and sail for Halifax, Nova Scotia.

British assumptions

Britain had hoped to reclaim its colonies with a strategy of strangling the resistance in Massachusetts. But by the spring of 1776 it saw clearly that more was required than a show of force against New England. Instead Britain's leaders chose to wage a conventional war in America, capturing major cities and crushing the Continental forces in a decisive battle. Military victory, the British believed, would enable them to restore political control and reestablish imperial authority.

The first target was New York City. General William Howe and Lord George Germain, the British officials now charged with overseeing the war, chose that seaport for its central location and—they hoped—its large loyalist population. They planned for Howe's army to move from New York City up the Hudson River, meeting ultimately with British troops under General Sir Guy Carleton coming south from Canada. Either the British drive would lure Washington into a major engagement, crushing the Continentals, or, if unopposed, the British offensive would cut America in two, smothering resistance to the south by isolating New England.

Howe brothers

Unfortunately for the British, the strategy was sounder than the men placed in charge of executing it. General Howe took to extremes the conventional wisdom of eighteenth-century European warfare, which aimed as much at avoiding heavy casualties as at winning victories against the enemy. Concern for preserving manpower addicted Howe to caution, when daring more would have carried the day. Howe's brother, Admiral Lord Richard Howe, the head of naval operations in America, also stopped short of pressing the British advantage, owing to his personal desire for reconciliation. The reluctance of the Howe brothers to fight became the formula for British frustration in the two years that followed.

The Campaigns in New York and New Jersey

However cautiously, British forces landed on Staten Island in New York harbor during July 1776. The Continentals marched from Boston and fortified Brooklyn Heights on Long Island, the key to the defenses of New York City on Manhattan Island. By mid-August, 32,000 British troops, including 8000 Hessians, the largest expeditionary force of the eighteenth century, faced Washington's army of 23,000.

At dawn on August 22 the Howe brothers moved on Long Island and easily pushed the rebel army back across the East River to Manhattan. After lingering on Long Island for a month, the Howes again lurched into action, ferrying their forces to Kip's Bay, just a few miles south of Harlem. When the British landed, the handful of rebel defenders at Kip's Bay fled—straight into the towering wrath of Washington, who happened on the scene during the rout. For once the general lost his habitual self-restraint, flogged both officers and men with his riding crop, and came close to being captured himself. But the Howes remained reluctant to hit hard, letting Washington's army escape from Manhattan to Westchester County. *British capture New York City*

Throughout the fall of 1776 General Howe's forces followed as Washington's fled southward into New Jersey. By mid-November, as the British advance picked up speed, the rebels stepped up their retreat and crossed the Delaware River into Pennsylvania on December 7. There Howe stopped, pulling back most of his army to winter in New York City and leaving the Hessians to hold the British line of advance along the New Jersey side of the Delaware River.

Although the retreat through New York and New Jersey had shriveled rebel strength to only 3000 men, Washington decided that the campaign of 1776 was not over. On a snowy Christmas night, the Continentals floated back across the Delaware, picked their way across roads sleeted with ice, and finally slid into Hessian-held Trenton at eight in the morning. One thousand German soldiers, still recovering from their spirited Christmas celebration and caught completely by surprise, quickly surrendered. Washington's luck held on January 3, 1777, when the Continentals defeated British troops on the outskirts of Princeton, New Jersey. *Rebel victories at Trenton and Princeton*

During the winter of 1776–1777 the British lost more than battles: they alienated the very civilians whose loyalties they had hoped to ensure. In New York City the presence of the main body of the British army brought shortages of food and housing and caused constant friction between soldiers and city dwellers. In the New Jersey countryside still held by the Hessians, the situation was more desperate. Forced to live off the land, the Germans aroused resentment among local farmers by seizing "hay, oats, Indian corn, cattle, and horses, which were never or but very seldom paid for," as one loyalist admitted. The Hessians ransacked and destroyed homes and churches; they kidnapped and raped young women.

Many neutrals and loyalists who had had enough of the king's soldiers now took

At the Battle of Princeton, British troops bayoneted the rebel general Hugh Mercer, an assault later commemorated in this painting by George Washington Parke Custis, the adopted step-grandson of George Washington. This rendering draws attention not only to Mercer's courage but to the savagery of the redcoats, both of which helped the rebels win over civilian support.

their allegiance elsewhere. Bands of militia on Long Island, along the Hudson River, and all over New Jersey rallied to support the Continentals.

Capturing Philadelphia

In the summer of 1777 General Howe still hoped to entice the Continentals into a decisive engagement or to seize a major seaport and its surrounding countryside. But he had now decided to goad the Americans into battle by capturing Philadelphia. Rather than risk his army on a march through hostile New Jersey, he approached the rebel capital by sea. In early August the redcoats disembarked on the Maryland shore and headed for Philadelphia, 50 miles away. Washington had hoped to stay on the strategic defensive, holding his smaller army together, harrassing the enemy, but avoiding full-scale battles. Howe's march on Philadelphia made that impossible: Washington's army hurried south from New Jersey to protect the new nation's capi- tal. Washington engaged Howe twice: in September at Brandywine Creek and in October in an early dawn attack at Germantown, but both times the rebels were beaten back. He had been unable to prevent the British occupation of Philadelphia.

Brandywine and Germantown

THE FIGHTING IN THE NORTH, 1775–1777
After the British withdrew from Boston in 1775, they launched an attack on New York City
the following year. Washington was forced to retreat northward, then across the Hudson and
south into New Jersey and Pennsylvania, before surprising the British at Trenton and
Princeton. Burgoyne's surrender at Saratoga in 1777 marked a turning point in the war.

Still, the rebels could take satisfaction from the troubles that beset the British
even in victory. In Philadelphia, as in New York, British occupation jacked up demand and prices for food, fuel, and housing. While inflation hit hardest at the poor,
the wealthy resented British officers who became their uninvited house guests.
Philadelphians complained of redcoats looting their shops, trampling their gardens,

and harassing them on the streets. Elizabeth Drinker, the wife of a Quaker merchant, confided in her diary that "I often feel afraid to go to bed."

Even worse, the British march through Maryland and Pennsylvania had outraged civilians, who fled before the army and then returned to find their homes and barns bare, their crops and livestock gone. Everywhere Howe's men went in the mid-Atlantic, they left in their wake Americans with compelling reasons to support the rebels. Worst of all, just days after Howe marched his occupying army into Philadelphia in the fall of 1777, another British commander in North America was surrendering his entire army to rebel forces at Saratoga, New York.

Disaster at Saratoga

The calamity that befell the British at Saratoga was the doing of a glorymongering general, John "Gentleman Johnny" Burgoyne. After his superior officer, Sir Guy Carleton, bungled a drive into New York during the summer of 1776, Burgoyne won approval to command another attack from Canada. At the end of June 1777 he set out from Quebec with a force of 9500 redcoats, 2000 women and children, and an elaborate baggage train that included the commander's silver dining service, his dress uniforms, and numerous cases of his favorite champagne. As Burgoyne's huge entourage lumbered southward, it was slowed by a rough, winding road that was broken by boulders, felled trees, and ramshackle bridges that swayed over yawning ravines. Meanwhile, a handful of Continentals and a horde of New England militia assembled several miles below Saratoga at Bemis Heights under the command of General Horatio Gates.

Burgoyne surrenders at Saratoga

On September 19 Gates's rebel scouts, nested high in the trees on Bemis Heights, spied the glittering bayonets of Burgoyne's approaching force. Benedict Arnold, a brave young officer, led several thousand rebels into the surrounding woods, meeting Burgoyne's men in a clearing at Freeman's Farm. At the end of the day British reinforcements finally pushed the rebels back from a battlefield piled high with the bodies of soldiers from both sides. Burgoyne tried to flee back to Canada but got no farther than Saratoga, where he surrendered his army to Gates on October 17.

Saratoga changed everything. Burgoyne had not just been nipped in a skirmish; he had lost his entire army. The triumph was enough to convince Britain's old rival France that, with a little help, the Americans might well reap the fruits of victory.

THE TURNING POINT

France had been waiting for revenge against Britain since its humiliating defeat in the Seven Years' War. Over the previous decade, as France's agents in America sent home reports of a rebellion brewing, a scheme for evening the score had been taking shape in the mind of the French foreign minister, Charles Gravier de Vergennes. He reckoned that France might turn discontented colonials into willing allies against Britain.

An Alliance Formed

Vergennes approached the Americans cautiously. He wanted to make certain that the rift between Britain and its colonies would not be reconciled and that the rebels in America stood a fighting chance. Although France had been secretly supplying the Continental Army with guns and ammunition since the spring of 1776, Vergennes would go no further than covert assistance.

Congress approached its former French enemies with equal caution. Would France, the leading Catholic monarchy in Europe, make common cause with the republican rebels? A few years earlier American colonials had fought against the French in Canada. Only recently they had renounced a king. For centuries they had overwhelmingly adhered to Protestantism.

The string of defeats dealt the Continental Army during 1776 convinced Congress that they needed the French enough to accept both the contradictions and the costs of such an alliance. In November Congress appointed a three-member commission to negotiate not only aid from France but also a formal alliance. Its senior member was Benjamin Franklin, who enchanted all of Paris when he arrived in town sporting a simple fur cap and a pair of spectacles (something no fashionable Frenchman wore in public). Hailed as a homespun sage, Franklin played the role of American innocent to the hilt and watched as admiring Parisians stamped his face on everything from the top of commemorative snuffboxes to the bottom of porcelain chamber pots.

Franklin in Paris

Still, Franklin understood that mere popularity could not produce the alliance sought by Congress. It was only news that Britain had surrendered an entire army at Saratoga that finally convinced Vergennes that the rebels could actually win. In February 1778 France signed a treaty of commerce and friendship and a treaty of alliance, which Congress approved in May. Under the terms of the treaties, both par-

The French public's infatuation with Benjamin Franklin knew no bounds. Although Franklin's shrewd habit of dressing simply won him admiration among Parisians as a brilliant "rustic" from the American woods, the artist who painted *The Genius of Franklin* promoted him to godlike status.

ties agreed to accept nothing short of independence for America. France pledged to renounce all future claims in continental North America and to give back any territory captured in the war. The alliance left the British no choice other than to declare war on France. Less than a year later Spain joined France, hoping to recover territory lost to England in earlier wars.

Winding Down the War in the North

The Revolution widened into a global war after 1778. Preparing to fight France and Spain dictated a new British strategy in America. No longer could the British concentrate on crushing the Continental Army. Instead they would disperse their forces to fend off challenges all over the world. In May Sir Henry Clinton replaced William Howe as commander-in-chief and received orders to withdraw from Philadelphia to New York City. There, and in Newport, Rhode Island, Clinton was to maintain defensive bases for harrying northern coastal towns.

Valley Forge   Only 18 miles outside of Philadelphia, at Valley Forge, Washington and his Continentals were assessing their own situation. Some 11,000 rebel soldiers had passed a harrowing winter in that isolated spot, starving for want of food, freezing for lack of clothing, huddling in miserable huts, and hating the British who lay 18 miles away in Philadelphia. The army also cursed their fellow citizens, for the misery of the soldiers resulted from congressional weakness and disorganization and civilian corruption and indifference. Congress lacked both money to pay and maintain the army

The soldiers in this 1777 illustration condemn civilian neglect and the profiteering of private contractors who supplied the Continental Army. Such grievances would provoke mutinies within the army before the end of the fighting.

First Soldier: "Keep up courage, my boys, we will soon bring those villains to terms."

Second Soldier: "These d[amne]d Extortioners are the worst enemies to the country."

Third Soldier: "I serve my country for sixteen pence a day, pinched with cold."

and an efficient system for dispensing provisions to the troops. Most farmers and merchants preferred to supply the British, who could pay handsomely, than to do business with a financially strapped Congress and the Continentals. What little did reach the army often was food too rancid to eat or clothing too rotten to wear. Perhaps 2500 perished at Valley Forge, the victims of cold, hunger, and disease.

Why did civilians who supported the rebel cause allow the army to suffer? Probably because by the winter of 1777, the Continentals came mainly from social classes that received little consideration at any time. The respectable, propertied farmers and artisans who had laid siege to Boston in 1775 had stopped enlisting. Serving in their stead were single men in their teens and early twenties, some who joined the army out of desperation, others who were drafted, still others who were hired as substitutes for the more affluent. The landless sons of farmers, unemployed laborers, drifters, petty criminals, vagrants, indentured servants, slaves, even captured British and Hessian soldiers—all men with no other means and no other choice—were swept into the Continental Army. The social composition of the rebel rank and file had come to resemble that of the British army. It is the great irony of the Revolution: a war to protect liberty and property was waged by those Americans who were poorest and least free. *Social composition of the Continental Army*

The beginning of spring in 1778 brought a reprieve. Supplies arrived at Valley Forge, and so did a fellow calling himself Baron von Steuben, a penniless Prussian soldier of fortune. Although Washington's men had shown spirit and resilience ever since Trenton, they still lacked discipline and training. Those defects and more von Steuben began to remedy. Barking orders and spewing curses in German and French, the baron (and his translators) drilled the rebel regiments to march in formation and to handle their bayonets like proper Prussian soldiers. By the summer of 1778, morale had rebounded as professional pride fused solidarity among Continental ranks in the crucible of Valley Forge.

Spoiling for action after their long winter, Washington's army, now numbering nearly 13,500, set out to harass Clinton's army as it marched overland from Philadelphia to New York. The Continentals caught up with the British force on June 28 at Monmouth Courthouse, where a long, confused battle ended in a draw. After both armies retired for the night, Clinton's forces slipped away to safety in New York City. Washington pursued, longing to launch an all-out assault on New York City, but he lacked the necessary numbers.

While Washington waited outside New York City, his army started to come apart. During the two hard winters that followed, resentments mounted among the rank and file over spoiled food, inadequate clothing, and arrears in pay. The army retaliated with mutinies. Between 1779 and 1780 officers managed to quell uprisings in three New England regiments. But in January 1781 both the Pennsylvania and New Jersey lines mutinied outright and marched on Philadelphia, where Congress had reconvened. Order returned only after Congress promised back pay and provisions and Washington put two ringleaders in front of a firing squad. *Army uprisings*

War in the West

Trouble also loomed on the western frontier. There both the British and the rebels sought support from the Indians because the most powerful tribes determined the balance of power. Most of the tribes remained neutral, but those tribes who took sides most often joined the British, who had tried to stem the tide of colonials taking Indian lands.

While George Rogers Clark and his few hundred rebel troops helped to contain British and Indian raids in the Old Northwest, General John Sullivan led an expedition against the Iroquois in upstate New York. Loyalists under Major John Butler and Iroquois fighters under a Mohawk chief, Thayendanegea (called Joseph Brant by the English), had conducted a series of raids along the New York and Pennsylvania frontiers. Sullivan's expedition routed the marauders and burned over 40 Indian villages.

The Home Front in the North

While fighting flared on the frontier and British troops attacked a few Connecticut coastal towns in 1779, most northern civilians enjoyed a respite from the war. Since the outbreak of the fighting at Lexington and Concord, every rumor of approaching enemy troops had pitched the inhabitants of imperiled neighborhoods into a panic. Refugees on foot and in hastily packed carts filled the roads, fleeing the advancing armies. "By this time the Cannon began to roar," wrote Mary Silliman, a Connecticut mother who escaped a British coastal raid with her two-year-old son Selleck. This "pleased Selleck, and he would mimic them by saying 'bang, bang.' But they were doleful sounds in our ears." Those who remained to protect their homes and property might be caught in the crossfire of contending forces or cut off from supplies of food and firewood. Loyalists who remained in areas occupied by rebel troops faced harassment, imprisonment, or the confiscation of their property. Rebel sympathizers met similar fates in regions held by the British. Disease, however, disregarded political allegiances: military camps and occupied towns spawned epidemics of dysentery and smallpox that devastated civilians as well as soldiers, rebels and loyalists alike.

While plundering armies destroyed civilian property wherever they marched, military demands disrupted family economies throughout the northern countryside. The seasons of intense fighting drew men off into military service just when their *Women and* labor was most needed on family farms. Wives and daughters were left to assume the *the war* work of husbands and sons while coping with loneliness, anxiety, and grief. Often enough, the disruptions, flight, and loss of family members left lasting scars. Two years after she fled before Burgoyne's advance into upstate New York, Ann Eliza Bleecker confessed to a friend, "Alas! the wilderness is within: I muse so long on the dead until I am unfit for the company of the living."

Despite these hardships, many women vigorously supported the revolutionary cause in a variety of ways. The Daughters of Liberty joined in harassing those who opposed the rebel cause. One outspoken loyalist found himself surrounded by angry women who stripped off his shirt, covered him with molasses, and plastered him with flower petals. In more genteel fashion, groups of well-to-do women collected not only money but medicines, food, and pewter to melt for bullets.

THE STRUGGLE IN THE SOUTH

Between the autumn of 1778 and the summer of 1781, while Washington and his restless army waited outside New York City, the British opened another theater in the

American war. Despite their armed presence in the North, the British had come to *Britain's* believe that their most vital aim was to regain their colonies in the mainland South. *southern* The Chesapeake and the Carolinas were more profitable to the empire and more *strategy* strategically important, being so much closer to rich British sugar islands in the West Indies. That new "southern strategy" prompted Clinton to dispatch forces to the Caribbean and Florida. In addition, the British laid plans for a new offensive drive into the Carolinas and Virginia.

English politicians and generals believed that the war could be won in the South. Loyalists were numerous, they believed, especially in the backcountry. Resentment of the seaboard, a rebel stronghold, would breed readiness among frontier folk to take up arms for the king at the first show of British force. And southern rebels—especially the vulnerable planters along the coast—could not afford to turn their guns away from their slaves. So, at least, the British theorized. All that was needed, they concluded, was for the British army to establish a beachhead in the South and then, in league with loyalists, drive northward, pacifying the population while pressing up the coast.

The Siege of Charleston

The southern strategy worked well for a short time in a small place. In November 1778 Clinton sent 3500 troops to Savannah, Georgia. The resistance in the tiny colony quickly collapsed, and a large number of loyalists turned out to help the British. Encouraged by that success, the British moved on to South Carolina.

During the last days of 1779, an expedition under Clinton himself set sail from New York City. Landing off the Georgia coast, his troops mucked through malarial swamps to the peninsula lying between the Ashley and Cooper rivers. At the tip of that neck of land stood Charleston, and the British began to lay siege. By then, an unseasonably warm spring had set in, making the area a heaven for mosquitoes and a hell for human beings. Sweltering and swatting, redcoats weighted down in their woolen uniforms inched their siege works toward the city. By early May Clinton's army closed in, and British shelling was setting fire to houses within the city. On May 12 Charleston surrendered.

Clinton sailed back to New York at the end of June 1780, leaving behind 8300 redcoats to carry the British offensive northward to Virginia. The man charged with leading that campaign was his ambitious and able subordinate, Charles, Lord Cornwallis.

The Partisan Struggle in the South

Cornwallis's task in the Carolinas was complicated by the bitter animosity between rebels and loyalists there. Many Carolinians had taken sides years before Clinton's conquest of Charleston. In the summer and fall of 1775 the supporters of Congress and the new South Carolina revolutionary government mobbed, tortured, and imprisoned supporters of the king in the backcountry. These attacks only hardened loyalist resolve: roving bands seized ammunition, broke their leaders out of jail, and besieged rebel outposts. But within a matter of months, a combined force of rebel militias from the coast and the frontier managed to defeat loyalist forces in the backcountry.

Rebels and loyalists battle for the backcountry

With the fall of Charleston in 1780, the loyalist movement on the frontier returned to life. Out of loyalist vengefulness and rebel desperation issued the brutal civil war that seared the southern backcountry after 1780. Neighbors and even families fought and killed each other as members of roaming rebel and tory militias. The intensity of partisan warfare in the backcountry produced unprecedented destruction. Loyalist militia plundered plantations and assaulted local women; rebel militias whipped suspected British supporters and burned their farms; both sides committed brutal assassinations and tortured prisoners. All of society, observed one minister, "seems to be at an end. Every person keeps close on his own plantation. Robberies and murders are often committed on the public roads. . . . Poverty, want, and hardship appear in almost every countenance."

Cornwallis, when confronted with the chaos, erred fatally. He did nothing to stop his loyalist allies or his own troops from mistreating civilians. A Carolina loyalist admitted that "the lower sort of People, who were in many parts originally attached to the British Government, have suffered so severely . . . that Great Britain has now a hundred enemies, where it had one before." Although rebels and loyalists alike plundered and terrorized the backcountry, Cornwallis's forces bore more of the blame and suffered the consequences.

A growing number of civilians outraged by the king's men cast their lot with the rebels. That upsurge of popular support enabled Francis Marion, the "Swamp Fox," and his band of white and black raiders to cut British lines of communication between Charleston and the interior. It swelled another rebel militia led by "the Gamecock," Thomas Sumter, who bloodied loyalist forces throughout the central part of South Carolina. It mobilized the "over-the-mountain men," a rebel militia in western Carolina who claimed victory at the Battle of King's Mountain in October 1780. By the end of 1780, these successes had persuaded most civilians that only the rebels could restore order.

British victory at Camden

If rebel fortunes prospered in the partisan struggle, they faltered in the conventional warfare being waged at the same time in the South. In August of 1780 the Continentals commanded by Horatio Gates lost a major engagement to the British force at Camden, South Carolina. In the fall of 1780 Congress replaced Gates with Washington's candidate for the southern command, Nathanael Greene, an energetic 38-year-old Rhode Islander and a veteran of the northern campaigns.

Greene Takes Command

Greene bore out Washington's confidence by grasping the military situation in the South. He understood the needs of his 1400 hungry, ragged, and demoralized troops and instructed von Steuben to lobby Virginia for food and clothing. He understood the importance of the rebel militias and sent Lieutenant Colonel Henry "Lighthorse Harry" Lee to assist Marion's raids. He understood the weariness of southern civilians and prevented his men from plundering the countryside.

Above all, Greene understood that his forces could never hold the field against the whole British army. That led him to break the first rule of conventional warfare:

General Nathanael Greene

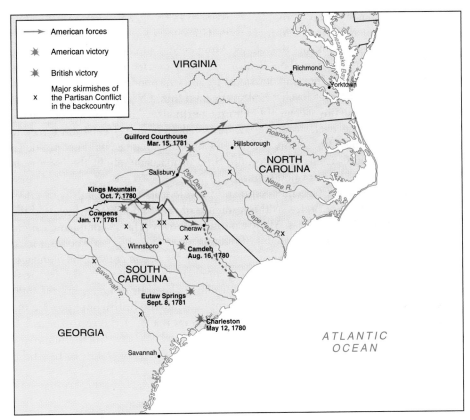

THE FIGHTING IN THE SOUTH, 1780–1781

In December 1780 Nathanael Greene made the crucial decision to split his army, sending Daniel Morgan west, where he defeated the pursuing Banastre Tarleton at Cowpens. Meanwhile Greene regrouped and replenished at Cheraw, keeping Cornwallis off balance with a raid (dotted line) toward Charleston and the coast. Then, with Cornwallis in hot pursuit, Greene and Morgan rejoined at Salisbury, retreating into Virginia. Cornwallis was worn down in this vain pursuit and lost three-quarters of the troops he began with before finally abandoning the Carolina campaign.

he divided his army. In December 1780 he dispatched to western South Carolina a detachment of 600 men under the command of Brigadier General Daniel Morgan of Virginia.

Back at the British camp, Cornwallis worried that Morgan and his rebels, if left unchecked, might rally the entire backcountry against the British. On the other hand, Cornwallis reckoned that he could not commit his entire army to the pursuit of Morgan's men, for then Greene and his troops might retake Charleston. The only solution, unconventional to be sure, was for Cornwallis to divide *his* army. That he did, sending Lieutenant Colonel Banastre Tarleton and 1100 men west after Morgan. Cornwallis had played right into Greene's hands: the rebel troops might be able to defeat a British army split into two pieces. For two weeks Morgan led Tarleton's

Cowpens   troops on a breakneck chase across the Carolina countryside. In January 1781 at an open meadow called Cowpens, Morgan routed Tarleton's force.

Now Cornwallis took up the chase. Morgan and Greene joined forces and agreed to keep going north until the British army wore out. Cornwallis finally stopped at Hillsboro, North Carolina, but few local loyalists responded to his call for reinforcements. To ensure that loyalist ranks remained thin, Greene decided to make a show of force near the tiny village of Guilford Courthouse. On a brisk March day the two sides joined battle, each sustaining severe casualties before Greene was forced to retreat. But the high cost of victory convinced Cornwallis that he could not put down the rebellion in the Carolinas. "I am quite tired of marching about the country in quest of adventures," he informed Clinton.

Value of the militia   Although Nathanael Greene's command provided the Continentals with effective leadership in the South, it was the resilience of rebel militias that thwarted the British offensive in the Carolinas. Many Continental Army officers complained about the militia's lack of discipline, its habit of melting away when homesickness set in or harvest approached, and its record of cowardice under fire in conventional engagements. But when set the task of ambushing supply trains and dispatch riders, harrying bands of local loyalists, or making forays against isolated British outposts, the militia came through. Many southern civilians refused to join the British or to provide the redcoats with food and information because they knew that once the British army left their neighborhoods, the rebel militia would always be back. The Continental Army in the South lost many conventional battles, but the militia kept the British from restoring political control over the backcountry.

African Americans in the Age of Revolution

The British also lost in the Carolinas because they did not seek greater support from those southerners who would have fought for liberty *with* the British—African American slaves.

Black Americans, virtually all in bondage, made up one-third of the population between Delaware and Georgia. Since the beginning of the resistance to Britain, white southerners had worried that the watchwords of liberty and equality would spread to the slave quarters. Gripped by the fear of slave rebellion, southern revolutionaries began to take precautions. Marylanders disarmed black inhabitants and issued extra guns to the white militia. Charlestonians hanged and then burned the body of Thomas Jeremiah, a free black who was convicted of spreading the word to others that the British "were come to help the poor Negroes."

White fears of rebellion   Southern whites fully expected the British to turn slave rebelliousness to their strategic advantage. As early as 1775, Virginia's royal governor, Lord Dunmore, confirmed white fears by offering to free any slave who joined the British. When Clinton invaded the South in 1779, he renewed that offer. Janet Schaw, an English woman visiting her brother's North Carolina plantation, reported that his neighbors had heard that loyalists were "promising every Negro that would murder his master and family he should have his Master's plantation. . . . The Negroes have got it amongst them and believe it to be true."

But in Britain there was overwhelming opposition to organizing support among African Americans. British leaders dismissed Dunmore's ambitious scheme to raise a black army of 10,000 and another plan to create a sanctuary for black loyalists on the southeastern coast. Turning slaves against masters, they recognized, was not the way to conciliate southern whites.

Even so, southern fears of insurrection made the rebels reluctant to enlist black Americans as soldiers. At first, Congress barred African Americans from the Continental Army. But as the rebels became more desperate for manpower, policy changed. Northern states actively encouraged black enlistments, and in the Upper South, some states allowed free men of color to join the army or permitted slaves to substitute for their masters.

Slaves themselves sought freedom from whichever side seemed most likely to grant it. In 1775 more than 800 took up Dunmore's offer and deserted their masters, and thousands more flocked to Clinton's forces after the fall of Charleston. For many runaways the hope of liberation proved an illusion. Although some served the British army as laborers, spies, and soldiers, many died of disease in army camps or were sold back into slavery in the West Indies. An estimated 5000 black soldiers served in the revolutionary army in the hope of gaining freedom. In addition, the number of runaways to the North soared during the Revolution. All told, some 55,000 slaves fled to freedom, some escaping behind British lines, others into the North.

African American quests for liberty

The slave revolts so dreaded by southern whites never materialized. Possibly the boldest slaves were drawn off into the armies; possibly greater white precautions discouraged schemes for black rebellions. In South Carolina, where the potential for revolt was greatest, most slaves chose to remain on plantations rather than risking a collective resistance and escape in the midst of the fierce partisan warfare.

Rebel Americans were able to hold the southern backcountry because of the courage and determination of militias like the one depicted in this nineteenth-century painting. Francis Marion's company was unusual among southern militias because it included blacks.

THE WORLD TURNED UPSIDE DOWN

Despite his losses in the Carolinas, Cornwallis still believed that he could score a de-cisive victory against the Continental Army. The theater he chose for that showdown was the Chesapeake. During the spring of 1781, he had marched his army to the Virginia coast and joined forces with the hero of Saratoga and newly turned loyalist, Benedict Arnold. Embarrassed by debt and disgusted by Congress's shabby treat-ment of the Continental Army, Arnold had started exchanging rebel secrets for British money in 1779 before defecting outright in the fall of 1780. By June of 1781 Arnold and Cornwallis were fortifying a site on the tip of the peninsula formed by the York and James rivers, a place called Yorktown.

Meanwhile, Washington and his French ally, the Comte de Rochambeau, met in Connecticut to plan a major attack. Rochambeau urged a coordinated land–sea as-sault on the Virginia coast. Washington insisted instead on a full-scale offensive against New York City. Just when the rebel commander was about to have his way,

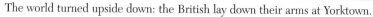

The world turned upside down: the British lay down their arms at Yorktown.

word arrived that a French fleet under the Comte de Grasse was sailing for the Chesapeake to blockade Cornwallis by sea. Washington's Continentals headed south.

Surrender at Yorktown

By the end of September, 7800 Frenchmen, 5700 Continentals, and 3200 militia had sandwiched Yorktown between the devil of an allied army and the deep blue sea of French warships. "If you cannot relieve me very soon," Cornwallis wrote to Clinton, "you must expect to hear the worst." The British navy did arrive—but seven days after Cornwallis surrendered to the rebels on October 19, 1781. When Germain carried the news from Yorktown to the king's first minister, Lord North replied, "Oh, God, it is over." Then North resigned. Germain resigned, and even George III murmured something about abdicating.

It need not have ended at Yorktown, but timing made all the difference. At the end of 1781 and early in 1782, the British army received setbacks in the other theaters of the war: India, the West Indies, and Florida. The French and the Spanish were everywhere in Europe as well, gathering in the English Channel, planning a major offensive against Gibraltar. The cost of the fighting was already enormous. British leaders recognized that the rest of the empire was at stake and set about cutting their losses in America.

Treaty of Paris

The Treaty of Paris, signed on September 3, 1783, was a diplomatic triumph for the American negotiators: Benjamin Franklin, John Adams, and John Jay. They dangled before Britain the possibility that a generous settlement might weaken American ties to France. The British jumped at the bait. They recognized the independence of the United States and agreed to ample boundaries for the new nation: the Mississippi River on the west, the 31st parallel on the south, and the present border of Canada on the north. American negotiators then persuaded a skeptical France to approve the treaty by arguing that, as allies, they were bound to present a united front to the British. When the French finally persuaded Spain, the third member of the alliance, to reduce its demands on Britain for territorial concessions, the treaty became an accomplished fact. The Spanish settled for Florida and Minorca, an island in the Mediterranean.

The Significance of a Revolution

If the Treaty of Paris marked both the end of a war and the recognition of a new nation, the surrender at Yorktown captured the significance of a revolution. Those present at Yorktown on that clear autumn afternoon in 1781 watched as the British second-in-command to Cornwallis (who had sent word that he was "indisposed") surrendered his superior's sword. He offered the sword first, in a face-saving gesture, to the French commander Rochambeau, who politely refused and pointed to Washington. But the American commander-in-chief, out of a mixture of military protocol, nationalistic pride, and perhaps even wit, pointed to *his* second-in-command, Benjamin Lincoln.

Some witnesses recalled that British musicians arrayed on the Yorktown green played "The World Turned Upside Down." Their recollections may have been faulty, but the story has persisted as part of the folklore of the American Revolution—and for good reasons. The world had, it seemed, turned upside down with the coming of American independence. The colonial rebels shocked the British with their answer to the question: would they fight?

Citizen-soldiers fight on their own terms

The answer had been yes—but on their own terms. By 1777 most propertied Americans avoided fighting in the Continental Army. Yet whenever the war reached their homes, farms, and businesses, many Americans gave their allegiance to the new nation by turning out with rifles or supplying homespun clothing, food, or ammunition. They rallied around Washington in New Jersey, Gates in upstate New York, Greene in the Carolinas. Middle-class American men fought, some from idealism, others out of self-interest, but always on their own terms, as members of the militia. These citizen-soldiers turned the world upside down by defeating professional armies.

Of course, the militia did not bear the brunt of the fighting. That responsibility fell to the Continental Army, which by 1777 drew its strength from the poorest ranks of American society. Yet even the Continentals, for all their desperation, managed to fight on their own terms. Some asserted their rights by raising mutinies, until

Congress redressed their grievances. All of them, as the Baron von Steuben observed, behaved differently from European soldiers. Americans followed orders only if the logic of commands was explained to them. The Continentals, held in contempt by most Americans, turned the world upside down by sensing their power and asserting their measure of personal independence.

Thus did a revolutionary generation turn the world upside down. Descended from desperate, idealistic, and self-interested men and women who settled colonies named for kings and queens—ruled by kings and queens who aimed to increase the wealth and power of their dynasties and their nations—these Americans rebelled against a king. They wanted more than a monarch. But what more did they want? What awaited in a world turned upside down by republican revolutionaries?

CHAPTER SUMMARY

Even after the Battle of Bunker Hill and the overwhelming response to Paine's *Common Sense,* the question of whether a majority of Americans favored independence—and would fight for it—remained unresolved. When the Second Continental Congress convened in the spring of 1775, many delegates still hoped for reconciliation. Even as Congress approved the creation of the Continental Army, it dispatched the "Olive Branch Petition" avowing loyalty to George III. But continued British belligerence convinced Congress to adopt the Declaration of Independence on July 4, 1776. If rebel leaders now hoped that they could count on a majority to support the Revolution, they knew that a substantial minority remained loyal to the king and Parliament. Loyalism was especially strong in those places where violent controversies had raged during the decades before 1776.

In 1776 the British under General William Howe evacuated Boston, took New York City, and drove the Continentals into a retreat through New York and New Jersey. But as the winter set in, Washington restored his army's credibility at the battles of Trenton and Princeton. Many civilians in that region, alienated by the British army's harsh treatment, switched their loyalties to the rebel cause. In the summer campaign of 1777, Howe's army took Philadelphia, but British forces under John Burgoyne suffered a disastrous defeat at Saratoga, New York. That marked a turning point in the fighting: in 1778 France openly allied with American rebels, and shortly thereafter, Spain joined France. What had been a colonial rebellion now widened into a European war, forcing the British to fend off challenges all over the world. When the British army, now led by Henry Clinton, pulled back from Philadelphia to New York City, Washington's inactive Continentals erupted in mutinies. Since the end of 1776, the Continental rank and file had been drawn from the poorest Americans; their needs for food, clothing, and shelter had been exploited by military contractors and neglected by a Congress suspicious of standing armies.

While the war in the North stalemated, the British pursued a southern strategy, capturing Savannah, Georgia, and, in 1780, Charleston, South Carolina. But British hopes that southern resistance would collapse were snuffed out by the rebel militia. As a vicious partisan war seared the backcountry, the Continental Army rallied behind Nathanael Greene, who frustrated British efforts to reclaim the Carolinas. The

British also erred by refusing to mobilize one large group of southerners who might have fought with them to win liberty—African American slaves. Cornwallis made one last bid for a victory at Yorktown, Virginia, in 1781 but found himself outflanked by the Continentals and their French allies. With the tide of war in Europe turning against them as well, the British agreed to the Treaty of Paris in 1783. Many Americans had, indeed, been willing to fight for independence, but always on their own terms.

SIGNIFICANT EVENTS

1775 — Second Continental Congress convenes at Philadelphia; Congress creates the Continental Army; Battle of Bunker Hill

1776 — Publication of *Common Sense;* British troops evacuate Boston; Declaration of Independence; British occupy New York City, forcing Washington to retreat through New Jersey into Pennsylvania; Washington counterattacks at Battle of Trenton

1777 — British summer drive to occupy Philadelphia: battles of Brandywine Creek, Germantown; Burgoyne surrenders at Saratoga; Continental Army encamps for winter at Valley Forge

1778 — France allies with rebel Americans; France and Britain declare war; British shift focus to the South: Savannah falls

1780 — British occupy Charleston; partisan warfare of Marion, Sumter; rebel victory at King's Mountain, South Carolina; Nathanael Greene takes southern command

1781 — Engagements at Cowpens, Guilford Courthouse; Cornwallis surrenders at Yorktown

1783 — Treaty of Paris

ADDITIONAL READING

There are two superb overviews of the war for independence: Don Higginbotham, *The American War for Independence* (1971) and Robert Middlekauff, *The Glorious Cause, 1763–1789* (1982). Both provide a wealth of detail about battles, the contending armies, and the roles of the militia and the civilian population. There are also two particularly thoughtful accounts of the relationship between the war and American society: Charles Royster, *A Revolutionary People at War* (1979) and John Shy, *A People Numerous and Armed* (1976). Sylvia Frey offers a fine account of African Americans throughout the years of revolutionary crisis in *Water from the Rock* (1991), while the role of women in wartime America is treated most comprehensively by Mary Beth Norton, *Liberty's Daughters* (1980). An intimate account of the impact of the war on one Connecticut family is Joy Day Buel and Richard Buel, Jr., *The Way of Duty* (1984).

There are now many excellent studies that probe the impact of the American Revolution on the institution of slavery and the lives of African Americans. Among the best are Ira Berlin and Ronald Hoffman, eds., *Slavery and Freedom in the Age of the American Revolution* (1983); Jeffrey Crow, "Slave Rebelliousness and Social Conflict in North Carolina, 1775–1802," *William and Mary Quarterly* (1980); David Brion Davis, *The Problem of Slavery in the Age of Revolution* (1975); and Gary B. Nash, *Race and Revolution* (1990). For a fuller list of readings, see the Bibliography.

7

Crisis and Constitution

 am not a Virginian, but an American," Patrick Henry declared in the Virginia House of Burgesses. Most likely he was lying. Certainly no one listening took him seriously, for the newly independent colonists did not identify themselves as members of a nation. They would have said, as did Thomas Jefferson, "Virginia, Sir, is my country." Or as John Adams wrote to another native son, "Massachusetts is our country." Jefferson and Adams were men of wide political vision and experience: both were leaders in the Continental Congress and more inclined than most to think nationally. But like other members of the revolutionary generation, they identified deeply with their home states and even more deeply with their home counties and towns.

It followed that allegiance to the states, not the Union, determined the shape of the first republican political experiments. For a decade after independence, the revolutionaries were less committed to creating an American nation than to organizing 13 separate state republics. The Declaration of Independence referred explicitly not to *the* United States but to *these* United States. It envisioned not one republic so much as a federation of 13.

How close a union?
Only when peace was restored during the decade of the 1780s were Americans forced to face some unanswered questions raised by their revolution. The Declaration proclaimed that these "free and independent states" had "full power to levy war, conclude peace, contract alliances, establish commerce." Did that mean that New Jersey, as a free and independent state, could sign a trade agreement with France, excluding the other states? If the United States was to be more than a loose federation, how could it assert power on a national scale? Similarly, American borderlands to the west presented problems. If these territories were settled by Americans, would they eventually join the United States? Go their own ways as independent nations? Become new colonies of Spain or England?

Such problems were more than political; they were rooted in social realities. For a political union to succeed, the inhabitants of 13 separate states had to start thinking of themselves as Americans. When it came right down to it, what united a Vermont farmer working his rocky fields and a South Carolina gentleman presiding over a vast rice plantation? What bonds existed between a Kentuckian rafting the Ohio River and a Salem merchant sailing to China for porcelain?

And in a society where all citizens were said to be "created equal," the inevitable social inequalities had to be confronted. How could women participate in the

The portraits of Captain and Mrs. Samuel Chandler, a New England couple,
project the virtuous rectitude of the new republican era. Husband and wife
share the same direct, disarming gaze, a mixture of wariness and resolution.

Revolution's bid for freedom if they were not free to vote or to hold property? How could black Americans feel a bond with white Americans when so often the only existing bonds had been forged with chains? To these questions there were no final answers in 1781. And as the decade progressed, the sense of crisis deepened. Americans worried that factions and selfish interest groups would pull "these" United States apart. The new republican union, which spread out over so many miles, constituted a truly unprecedented venture. A good deal of experimenting would be needed if it was to succeed.

REPUBLICAN EXPERIMENTS

After independence was declared in July 1776, many of America's best political minds turned to draw up constitutions for their individual states. Thomas Jefferson deserted the Continental Congress, leaving the conduct of the war and national affairs to other men, for the more important business of creating Virginia's new government.

In truth, the state constitutions were crucial republican experiments, the first efforts at establishing a government of and by the people. All the revolutionaries agreed that the people—not a king or a few privileged aristocrats—should rule. Yet they were equally certain that republican governments were best suited to small territo-

Belief in the
need for small
republics

ries. They believed that the new United States was too sprawling and its people too diverse to be safely consolidated into a single national republic. They feared, too, that the government of a large republic would inevitably grow indifferent to popular concerns, being distant from many of its citizens. Without being under the watchful eye of the people, representatives would become less accountable to the electorate and turn tyrannical. A federation of small state republics, they reasoned, would stand a far better chance of enduring.

The State Constitutions

The new state constitutions retained the basic form of their old colonial governments, all except Georgia and Pennsylvania providing for a governor and a bicameral legislature. But while most states did not alter the basic structure of their governments, they changed dramatically the balance of power among the different branches of government.

Curbing executive power
    From the republican perspective in 1776, the greatest problem of any government lay in curbing executive power. What had driven Americans into rebellion was the abuse of authority by the king and his appointed officials. To ensure that the executive could never again threaten popular liberty, the new states either accorded almost no power to their governors or abolished that office entirely. The governors had no authority to convene or dissolve the legislature. They could not veto the legislatures' laws, grant land, or erect courts. Most important from the republican point of view, governors had few powers to appoint other state officials. All these limits were designed to deprive the executive of any patronage or other form of influence over the legislature. By reducing the governors' power, Americans hoped to preserve their states from the corruption that they deplored in British political life.

Strengthening legislative powers
    What the state governors lost, the legislatures gained. Sam Adams, the Boston rebel leader, expressed the political consensus when he declared that "every legislature of every colony ought to be the sovereign and uncontrollable Power within its own limits of territory." To ensure that those powerful legislatures truly represented the will of the people, the new state constitutions called for annual elections and required candidates for the legislature to live in the districts they represented. Many states even asserted the right of voters to instruct the men elected to office how to vote on specific issues. Although no state granted universal manhood suffrage, most reduced the amount of property required of qualified voters. Finally, state supreme courts were also either elected by the legislatures or appointed by an elected governor.

By investing all power in popular assemblies, Americans abandoned the British system of mixed government. In one sense, that change was fairly democratic. A majority of voters within a state could do whatever they wanted, unchecked by governors or courts. On the other hand, the arrangement opened the door for legislatures to turn as tyrannical as governors. The revolutionaries brushed that prospect aside: republican theory assured them that the people possessed a generous share of civic virtue, the capacity for selfless pursuit of the general welfare.

Written constitutions
    In an equally momentous change, the revolutionaries insisted on written state constitutions. Whenever government appeared to exceed the limits of its authority, Americans wanted to have at hand the written contract between rulers and ruled. When eighteenth-century Englishmen used the word "constitution," they meant the

Americans responded to independence with rituals of "killing the king," like this New York crowd in 1776, which is pulling down a statue of George III. Americans also expressed their mistrust of monarchs and their ministers by establishing new state governments with weak executive branches.

existing arrangement of government—not an actual document but a collection of parliamentary laws, customs, and precedents. But Americans believed that a constitution should be a written code that stood apart from and above government, a yardstick against which the people measured the performance of their rulers. After all, they reasoned, if Britain's constitution had been written down, available for all to consult, would American rights have been violated?

From Congress to Confederation

While Americans lavished attention on their state constitutions, the national government nearly languished during the decade after 1776. With the coming of independence, the Second Continental Congress conducted the common business of the federated states. It created and maintained the Continental Army, issued currency, and negotiated with foreign powers.

But while Congress acted as a central government by common consent, it lacked any legal basis for its authority. To redress that need, in July 1776 Congress appointed a committee to draft a constitution for a national government. The more urgent business of waging and paying for the war made for delay, as did the consuming interest in framing state constitutions. Congress finally approved the first national constitution in November 1777, but it took four more years for all of the states to ratify these Articles of Confederation.

Articles of
Confederation

The Articles of Confederation provided for a government by a national legislature—essentially a continuation of the Second Continental Congress. That body had the authority to declare war and make peace, conduct diplomacy, regulate Indian affairs, appoint military and naval officers, and requisition men from the states. In affairs of finance it could coin money and issue paper currency. Extensive as these responsibilities were, Congress could not levy taxes or even regulate trade. The crucial power of the purse rested entirely with the states, as did the final power to make and execute laws. Even worse, the national government had no distinct executive branch. Congressional committees, constantly changing in their membership, not only had to make laws but had to administer and enforce them as well. With no executive to carry out the policies of finance, war, and foreign policy, the federal government's influence was extremely limited.

Those weaknesses of the federal government appear more evident in hindsight. For Congress in 1777 it was no easy task to frame a new government in the midst of a war. Besides that distraction, most American leaders of the 1770s had given little thought to federalism, the organization of a United States. Political leaders had not yet recognized the need for dividing power between the states and the national government. With the new nation in the midst of a military crisis, Congress assumed—correctly in most cases—that the states did not have to be forced to contribute men and money to the common defense. To have given significant powers to the national government would only have aroused opposition among the states, each jealous of its independence. Creating a strong national government would also have antagonized many Americans, who after all had just rebelled against the distant, centralized authority of Britain's king and Parliament.

Guided by republican political theory and by their colonial experience, American revolutionaries created a loose confederation of 13 independent state republics under a nearly powerless national government. They succeeded so well that the United States almost failed to survive the first decade of its independence. The problem was that republican theory and lessons from the colonial past were not always useful guides to postwar realities. Only when events forced Americans to think nationally did they begin to consider the possibility of reinventing "these United States"—this time under the yoke of a truly federal republic.

THE TEMPTATIONS OF PEACE

The surrender of Cornwallis at Yorktown in 1781 marked the end of military crisis in America. But as the threat from Britain receded, so did the source of American unity. The many differences among Americans, most of which lay submerged during the struggle for independence, surfaced in full force. Those domestic divisions, combined with challenges to the new nation from Britain and Spain, created conflicts that neither the states nor the national government proved equal to handling.

The Temptations of the West

The greatest opportunities and the greatest problems for postwar Americans awaited in the rapidly expanding West. With the boundary of the new United States now set at the Mississippi River, more settlers spilled across the Appalachians, planting farm-steads and raw frontier towns throughout Ohio, Kentucky, and Tennessee. By 1790 places that had been almost uninhabited by whites in 1760 held more than 2.25 million people, one-third of the nation's population.

After the Revolution, as before, western settlement fostered intense conflict. American claims that its territory stretched all the way to the Mississippi were by no means taken for granted by European and Indian powers. The West also confronted Americans with questions about their own national identity. Would the newly settled territories enter the nation as states on an equal footing with the original 13 states? Would they be ruled as dependent colonies? Could the federal government reconcile conflicting interests, cultures, and traditions over so great an area? The fate of the West, in other words, constituted a crucial test of whether "these" United States could grow and still remain united.

Foreign Intrigues

Both the British from their base in Canada and the Spanish in Florida and Louisiana hoped to chisel away at American borders. Their considerable success in the 1780s exposed the weakness of Confederation diplomacy.

Before the ink was dry on the Treaty of Paris, Britain's ministers were secretly instructing Canadians to maintain their forts and trading posts inside the United States' northwestern frontier. They reckoned—correctly—that with the Continental Army disbanded, the Confederation could not force the British to withdraw.

The British also made mischief along the Confederation's northern borders, mainly with Vermont. For decades, Ethan Allen and his Green Mountain Boys had waged a war of nerves with neighboring New York, which claimed Vermont as part of its territory. After the Revolution the Vermonters petitioned Congress for statehood, demanding independence of both New York and New Hampshire. When Congress dragged its feet, the British tried to woo Vermont into their empire as a province of Canada. That flirtation with the British pressured Congress into granting Vermont statehood in 1791.

The loyalty of the southwestern frontier was even less certain. By 1790 more than 100,000 settlers had poured through the Cumberland Gap to reach Kentucky and Tennessee. Along with the farmers came speculators, who bought up large tracts of land from the Indians. But the commercial possibilities of the region depended entirely on access to the Mississippi and the port of New Orleans, since it was far too costly to ship southwestern produce over the rough trails east across the Appalachians. And the Mississippi route was still dominated by the Spanish, who controlled Louisiana as well as forts along western Mississippi shores as far north as St. Louis. The Spanish, seeing their opportunity, closed the Mississippi to American navigation in 1784. That action prompted serious talk among southwesterners about seceding from the United States and joining Spain's empire.

Spanish designs on the Southwest

The Spanish also tried to strengthen their hold on North America by making common cause with the Indians. Of particular concern to both groups was protecting Florida, which had reverted to Spain's possession, from the encroachment of American settlers filtering south from Georgia. Florida's governor alerted his superiors back in Spain to the threat posed by those backwoodsmen who were "nomadic like Arabs and . . . distinguished from savages only in their color, language, and the

William Augustus Bowles typified the British traders who sought to profit from Spain's eagerness to supply the southeastern Indian tribes with finished goods. Born in Maryland, he joined the British army during the American Revolution and was sent to Florida. There he began a long association with the Creek Nation, lived among them for nearly a decade, and intrigued constantly to promote their ties to Britain. At one point, British merchants, rivals of the firm of Panton and Leslie, hired him to break that company's monopoly on the Indian trade.

superiority of their depraved cunning and untrustworthiness." So Spanish colonial officials responded eagerly to the overtures of Alexander McGillivray, a young Indian leader whose mother was of French-Creek descent and whose father was a Scots trader. His efforts brought about a treaty of alliance between the Creeks and the Spanish in 1784, quickly followed by similar alliances with the Choctaws and the Chickasaws. What cemented such treaties were the trade goods that the Spanish agreed to supply the tribes, for, as McGillivray explained, "Indians will attach themselves to and serve them best who supply their necessities." Securing European gunpowder and guns had become essential to southeastern Indians, because their entire economies now revolved around hunting and selling deerskins to white traders. So eager were the Spanish to "serve" the Indians in that matter that they even permitted British merchants, who could command a steady supply of manufactured goods, to monopolize the Indian trade. The largest dealers, William Panton and John Leslie, two loyalists who had fled to Florida in the wake of the Revolution, developed a trading network with southeastern tribes that reached all the way to the Mississippi by the 1790s. This flood of British merchandise sustained the alliance between the Spanish and the Indians, while British guns enabled the Creeks to defend their hunting territory from American invaders.

Disputes among the States

As if foreign intrigues were not divisive enough, the states continued to argue among themselves over western land claims. The old royal charters for some colonies had extended their boundaries all the way to the Mississippi and beyond. (See the map, below.) But the charters were often vague, granting both Massachusetts and Virginia, for example, undisputed possession of present-day Wisconsin. In contrast, other charters limited state boundaries to within a few hundred miles of the Atlantic coast. "Landed" states like Virginia wanted to secure control over the large territory granted them by their charters. "Landless" states (which included Maryland, Delaware, *Landed versus landless states*

WESTERN LAND CLAIMS, 1782–1802
The Confederation's settlement of conflicting western land claims was an achievement essential to the consolidation of political union. Some states asserted that their original charters extended their western borders to the Mississippi River. A few states, like Virginia, claimed western borders on the Pacific Ocean.

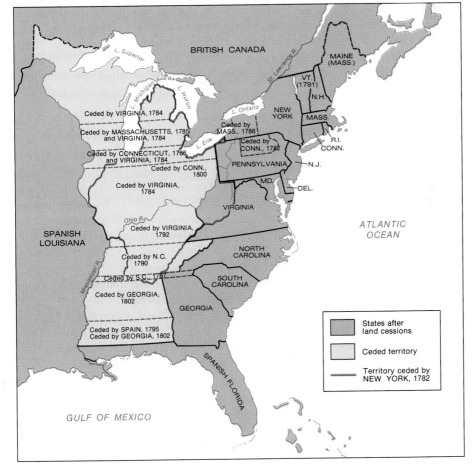

Pennsylvania, Rhode Island, and New Jersey) called on Congress to restrict the boundaries of landed states and to convert western lands into a domain administered by the Confederation.

The landless states argued that the landed states enjoyed an unfair advantage from the money they could raise selling their western claims. That revenue would allow landed states to reduce taxes, and lower taxes would lure settlers from the landless states. Meanwhile, landless states would have to raise taxes to make up for the departed taxpayers, causing even more residents to leave. Speculators were also eager to see Congress control the western lands. Before the Revolution, many prominent citizens of landless Pennsylvania, Maryland, and New Jersey had purchased tracts in the West from Indians. These speculators now joined forces with the political leaders of the landless states to lobby for congressional ownership of all western lands—except those tracts that they had already purchased from the Indians.

The landless states lost the opening round of the contest over ownership of the West. The Articles of Confederation acknowledged the old charter claims of the landed states. Then Maryland, one of the smallest landless states, retaliated by refusing to ratify the Articles. Since every state had to approve the Articles before they were formally accepted, the fate of the United States hung in the balance. One by one the landed states relented. The last holdout, Virginia, in January 1781 ceded its charter rights to land north of the Ohio River. In a moment of uncharacteristic modesty, the Virginians conceded that they might have trouble extending a republican government over the entire territory allotted them in their charter—a substantial portion of the North American continent. Once Virginia ceded, Maryland ratified the Articles in February 1781, four long years after Congress had first approved them.

The More Democratic West

More bitterly disputed than western land claims was the issue concerning the sort of men westerners elected to political office. The state legislatures of the 1780s were both larger and more democratic in their membership than the old colonial assemblies. Before the Revolution no more than a fifth of the men serving in the assemblies were middle-class farmers or artisans. Government was almost exclusively the domain of the wealthiest merchants, lawyers, and planters. After the Revolution twice as many state legislators were men of moderate wealth. The shift was more marked in the North, where middle-class men predominated among representatives. But in every state, some men of modest means, humble background, and little formal education attained political power.

Changing composition of state legislatures   State legislatures became more democratic in their membership mainly because as backcountry districts grew, so too did the number of their representatives. Since western districts tended to be less developed economically and culturally, their leading men were less rich and cultivated than the eastern seaboard elite. Wealthy, well-educated gentlemen thus became a much smaller and less powerful group within the legislatures because of greater western representation and influence.

But many republican gentlemen, while endorsing government by popular consent, doubted whether ordinary people were fit to rule. The problem, they contended, was that the new western legislators concerned themselves only with the narrow interests of their constituents, not with the good of the whole state. As Ezra Stiles, the president of Yale College, observed, the new breed of politicians were

This sketch of an "American New Cleared Farm" idealizes many aspects of life on the late eighteenth-century frontier. Although western farmers first sought to "improve" their acreage by felling trees, as the stumps dotting the landscape indicate, their dwellings were far less substantial than those depicted in the background above. And while Indians sometimes guided parties of white surveyors and settlers into the West, as shown in the foreground, Indians more often resisted white encroachment. For that reason, dogs, here perched placidly in canoes, were trained to alert their white masters to the approach of Indians.

those with "the all-prevailing popular talent of coaxing and flattering," who "whenever a bill is read in the legislature . . . instantly thinks how it will affect his constituents." And if state legislatures could not rise above petty bickering and narrow self-interest, how long would it be before civic virtue and a concern for the general welfare simply withered away?

The Northwest Territory

Such fears of "democratic excess" also influenced policy when Congress finally came to decide what to do with the Northwest Territory. Carved out of the land ceded by the states to the national government, the Northwest Territory comprised the present-day states of Ohio, Indiana, Illinois, Michigan, and Wisconsin. With so many white settlers moving into these lands, Congress was faced with a crucial test of its federal system. If an orderly way could not be devised to expand the confederation of states beyond the original 13 colonies, the new territories might well become independent countries or even colonies of Spain or Britain. Congress dealt with the issue of expansion by adopting three ordinances.

The first, drafted by Thomas Jefferson in 1784, divided the Northwest Territory

Jefferson's plan for the Northwest

into 10 states, each to be admitted to the Union on equal terms as soon as its population equaled that in any of the existing states. In the meantime, Jefferson provided for democratic self-government of the territory by all free adult males. A second ordinance of 1785 set up an efficient mechanism for dividing and selling public lands. The Northwest Territory was surveyed into townships six miles square. Each township was then divided into 36 lots of one square mile, or 640 acres.

Congress waited in vain for buyers to flock to the land offices it established. The cost of even a single lot—$640—was too steep for most farmers. Disappointed by the shortage of buyers and desperate for money, Congress finally accepted a proposition submitted by a private company of land speculators who offered to buy some 6 million acres in present-day southeastern Ohio. That several members of Congress numbered among the company's stockholders no doubt added to enthusiasm for the deal.

The transaction concluded, Congress calmed the speculators' worries that incoming settlers might enjoy too much self-government by scrapping Jefferson's dem-

Northwest Ordinance

ocratic design and substituting the Northwest Ordinance of 1787. That ordinance provided for a period in which Congress held sway in the territory through its appointees—a governor, a secretary, and three judges. When the population reached 5000 free adult males, a legislature was to be established, although its laws required the governor's approval. A representative could sit in Congress but had no vote. When the population reached 60,000, the inhabitants might apply for statehood, and the whole Northwest Territory was to be divided into not less than three or more than five states. The ordinance also guaranteed basic rights—freedom of religion and trial by jury—and provided for the support of public education.

Congress's plan completely ignored the rights of the Shawnee, Chippewa, and other Indian peoples who lived in the region. To them, it made no difference that the British had ceded their lands to the Americans. And in terms of Jefferson's democratic ideals for white inhabitants, the ordinance of 1787 also fell short. Still, Congress had succeeded in extending republican government to the West and incorporating the frontier into the new nation. Congress also outlawed slavery throughout the territory.

That decision had an unexpected, almost ironic consequence. The Northwest Ordinance went a long way toward establishing a federal system that would minimize tensions between the East and the West, a major source of postwar conflict. The Republic now had a peaceful, orderly way to expand its federation of states. Yet by limiting the spread of slavery in the northern states, Congress deepened the critical social and economic differences between North and South, evident already in the 1780s.

Slavery and Sectionalism

When white Americans declared their independence, they owned nearly half a million black Americans. African Americans of the revolutionary generation, most of them enslaved, constituted 20 percent of the total population of the colonies in 1775, and nearly 90 percent of them lived in the South. Yet few political leaders directly confronted the issue of whether slavery should be permitted to exist in a truly republican society.

Republicanism and slavery

When political discussion did stray toward the subject of slavery, southerners—especially ardent republicans—bristled defensively. Theirs was a difficult position,

THE ORDINANCE OF 1785
Surveyors entered the Northwest Territory in September of 1785, imposing on the land regular grids of six square miles to define new townships, as shown on this range map of a portion of Ohio. Farmers purchased blocks of land within townships, each one mile square, from the federal government or from land speculators. This pattern was followed in mapping and settling public lands all the way to the Pacific coast.

riddled with contradictions. On the one hand, they had condemned parliamentary taxation as tantamount to political "slavery" and had rebelled, declaring that all men were "created equal." On the other hand, enslaved African Americans formed the basis of the South's plantation economy. To surrender slavery, southerners believed, would be to usher in economic ruin.

Some planters in the Upper South resolved the dilemma by freeing their slaves. Such decisions were made easier by changing economic conditions in the Chesapeake. As planters shifted from tobacco toward wheat, a crop demanding a good deal less labor, Virginia and Maryland liberalized their manumission statutes, laws providing for freeing slaves. Between 1776 and 1789, most southern states also joined the North in prohibiting the importation of slaves, and a few antislavery societies appeared in the Upper South. But no southern state legally abolished slavery. Masters defended their right to hold human property in the name of republicanism.

Eighteenth-century republicans regarded property as crucial, for it provided a man and his family with security, status, and wealth. More important, it provided a measure of independence: to be able to act freely, without fear or favor of others. People without property were dangerous, republicans believed, because the poor could never be politically independent. Southern defenders of slavery thus argued that free, propertyless black people would pose a political threat to the liberty of propertied white citizens. Subordinating the human rights of blacks to the property rights of whites, southern republicans reached the paradoxical conclusion that their freedom depended on keeping African Americans in bondage.

The North followed a different course. Because its economy depended far less on slave labor, black emancipation did not run counter to powerful economic interests. Antislavery societies, the first founded by the Quakers in 1775, spread throughout the northern states during the next quarter century. Over the same period the legislatures of most northern states provided for the immediate or gradual abolition

Negro Methodists Holding a Meeting in a Philadelphia Alley evokes the vibrancy of African American religious life in the city that became a haven for free blacks. The artist, Pavel Petrovich Svinin, was a Russian diplomat who traveled throughout America, praised its religious freedom, and predicted the end of slavery. (Metropolitan Museum of Art, New York)

of slavery. Freedom for most northern African Americans came slowly, but by 1830 there were fewer than 3000 slaves out of a total northern black population of 125,000.

The Revolution, which had been fought for liberty and equality, did little to change the status of most black Americans. By 1800 more enslaved African Americans lived in the United States than had lived there in 1776. Slavery continued to grow in the Lower South as the rice culture of the Carolinas and Georgia expanded and as the new cotton culture spread westward.

Still, a larger number of slaves than ever before became free during the war and in the following decades, whether through military service, successful escape, manumission, or gradual emancipation. All these developments fostered the growth of free black communities, especially in the Upper South and in northern cities. By 1810 free African Americans made up 10 percent of the total population of Maryland and Virginia. The composition of the postwar free community changed as well. Before independence most free blacks had been either mulattoes—the offspring of interracial unions—or former slaves too sick or aged to have value as laborers. By contrast, the free population of the 1780s became darker skinned, younger, and healthier. This group injected new vitality into black communal life, organizing independent schools, churches, and mutual benefit societies for the growing number of "free people of color." *Growth of the free black community*

After the Revolution slavery ceased to be a national institution. It became the "peculiar institution" of a single region, the American South. The isolation of slavery in one section set North and South on radically different courses of social development, sharpening economic and political divisions.

Wartime Economic Disruption

With the outbreak of the Revolution, Americans had suffered an immediate economic loss. Formerly, Britain had supplied manufactured goods, markets for American exports, and credit that enabled commerce to flourish. The war changed all that. Hardest hit were southern planters, who had to seek new customers for their tobacco, cotton, and rice as well as find new sources of capital to finance production. Northerners too faced difficulties, for their major seaports were occupied for a time by British troops, whose presence disrupted commercial activity.

Matters did not improve with the coming of peace. France and Britain flooded the new states with their manufactures, and postwar Americans, eager for luxuries, indulged in a most unrepublican spending spree. The flurry of buying left some American merchants and consumers as deeply in debt as their governments. When loans from private citizens and foreign creditors like France proved insufficient to finance the fighting, both Congress and the states printed paper money—a whopping total of $400 million. The paper currency was backed only by the government's promise to redeem the bills with money from future taxes, since legislatures balked at the unpopular alternative of levying taxes during the war. For the bills to be redeemed, the United States had to survive, so by the end of 1776, when Continental forces sustained a series of defeats, paper money started to depreciate dramatically. By 1781 it was virtually without value, and Americans coined the expression "not worth a Continental." *Public and private debt*

The printing of paper money, combined with a wartime shortage of goods, triggered an inflationary spiral. As goods became scarcer and scarcer, they cost more and *Postwar inflation* more worthless dollars. In this spiral, creditors were gouged by debtors, who paid them back with depreciated currency. At the same time soaring prices for food and manufactured goods eroded the buying power of wage earners and small farmers. And the end of the war brought on demands for prompt repayment from the new nation's foreign creditors as well as from soldiers seeking back pay and pensions.

Congress could do nothing. With no power to regulate trade, it could neither dam the stream of imported goods rushing into the states nor stanch the flow of gold and silver to Europe to pay for these items. With no power to prohibit the states from issuing paper money, it could not halt depreciation. With no power to regulate wages or prices, it could not curb inflation. With no power to tax, it could not reduce the public debt. Efforts to grant Congress greater powers met with determined resistance from the states. They refused Congress any revenue of its own, fearing the first steps toward "arbitrary" government.

Political divisions over economic policy

Within states, too, economic problems aroused discord. Some major merchants, creditors, and large commercial farmers had profited handsomely during the war by selling supplies to the American, British, and French armies at high prices or by preying on enemy vessels as privateers. Eager to protect their windfall, they lobbied state legislatures for an end to inflationary monetary policies. That meant passing high taxes to pay wartime debts, a paper currency that was backed up with gold and silver, and an active policy to encourage foreign trade.

Less affluent men fought back, pressing legislatures for programs that met their needs. Western farmers, often in debt, urged the states to print more paper money and to pass laws lowering taxes and postponing the foreclosure of mortgages. Artisans opposed merchants by calling for protection from low-priced foreign imports that competed with the goods they produced. They set themselves against farmers as well by demanding price regulation of the farm products they consumed. In the continuing struggle, the state legislatures became the battleground of competing economic factions, each bent on gaining its own particular advantage.

As the 1780s wore on, conflicts mounted. So long as the individual states remained sovereign, the Confederation was crippled—unable to conduct foreign affairs effectively, unable to set coherent economic policy, unable to deal with discontent in the West. Equally dismaying was the discovery that many Americans, instead of being selflessly concerned for the public good, selfishly pursued their private interests.

REPUBLICAN SOCIETY

The war for independence transformed not only America's government and economy but also its society and culture. Inspired by the Declaration's ideal of equality, some Americans rejected the subordinate position assigned to them under the old colonial order. Westerners, newly wealthy entrepreneurs, urban artisans, and women all claimed greater freedom, power, and recognition. The authority of the traditional leaders of government, society, and the family came under a new scrutiny; the impulse to defer to social superiors became less automatic. The new assertiveness demonstrated how deeply egalitarian assumptions were taking root in American culture.

Gilbert Stuart's *The Skater* captures one American gentleman's characteristic sense of mastery over himself, nature, and society. But the Revolution instilled in many people of humbler status a new sense of pride and potential. Typical of such groups were New York's Society of Pewterers, whose banner proclaimed them "solid and pure" — the equals of those gentlemen who prided themselves on being society's "natural leaders."

The New Men of the Revolution

The Revolution gave rise to a new sense of social identity and a new set of ambitions among several groups of men who had once accepted a humbler status. The more democratic society of the frontier emboldened westerners to believe themselves the equals of easterners. As one Kentuckian explained to James Madison, the western migrants "must make a very different mass from one which is composed of men born and raised on the same spot. . . . They see none about them to whom or to whose families they have been accustomed to think themselves inferior."

The war also offered opportunities to aspiring entrepreneurs everywhere, and often they were not the same men who had prospered before the war. At a stroke, independence swept away the political prominence of loyalists, whose ranks included an especially high number of government officials, large landowners, and major merchants. And while loyalists found their properties confiscated by revolutionary governments, other Americans grew rich. Many northern merchants gained newfound wealth from privateering or military contracts. Commercial farmers in the mid-Atlantic states prospered from the high food prices caused by wartime scarcity and army demand.

Winners and losers

The Revolution effected no dramatic redistribution of wealth. Indeed, the gap between rich and poor increased during the 1780s. But those families newly enriched by the Revolution came to demand and receive greater social recognition and political influence. The republican ideal of "an aristocracy of merit" justified their ambitions.

Urban artisans

City craftworkers pushed for recognition too. Their experience in organizing boycotts against British goods during the imperial crisis gave artisans a greater taste of politics. With the Revolution accomplished, they clamored for men of their own kind to represent them in government. Their assertiveness came as a rude shock to gentlemen like South Carolina's William Henry Drayton, who balked at sharing power with men "who never were in a way to study" anything except "how to cut up a beast in the market to the best advantage, to cobble an old shoe in the neatest manner, or to build a necessary house."

While master craftworkers competed for political office, the laborers who worked for them also exhibited a new sense of independence. As domestic manufacturing expanded after the Revolution, journeymen and even apprentices moved out of their masters' households and away from the supervision of their masters. Recognizing that their interests were often distinct from those of masters, journeymen formed new organizations to secure higher wages. Between 1786 and 1816 skilled urban laborers organized the first major strikes in American history.

The New Women of the Revolution

Not long after the fighting with Britain had broken out, Margaret Livingston of New York wrote to her sister Catherine, "You know that our Sex are doomed to be obedient in every stage of life so that we shant be great gainers by this contest." By war's end, however, Eliza Wilkinson from rural South Carolina was complaining boldly to a woman friend: "The men say we have no business with political matters . . . it's not our sphere. . . . [But] I won't have it thought that because we are the weaker Sex (as to bodily strength my dear) we are Capable of nothing more, than minding the Dairy . . . surely we may have enough sense to give our Opinions."

What separated Margaret Livingston's resignation from Eliza Wilkinson's assertion of personal worth and independence was the Revolution. Eliza Wilkinson had managed her parents' plantation during the war and defended it from British marauders. Other women discovered similar reserves of skill and resourcefulness. When soldiers returned home, some were surprised to find their wives and daughters, who had been running family farms and businesses, less submissive and more self-confident.

Exclusion of women from politics

But American men had not fought a revolution for the equality of American women. In fact, male revolutionaries gave no thought whatsoever to the role of women in the new nation, assuming that those of the "weaker sex" were incapable of making informed and independent political decisions. Most women of the revolutionary generation agreed that the proper female domain was the home, not the public arena of politics. Still, the currents of the Revolution occasionally left gaps that allowed women to display their keen political interests. When a loosely worded

Mrs. John McAllister of Philadelphia

provision in the New Jersey state constitution gave the vote to "all free inhabitants" owning a specified amount of property, white widows and single women went to the polls. Only in 1807 did the state legislature close the loophole.

"Republican Motherhood" and Education

Even though women's primary sphere remained the home, the Revolution brought about changes. Reformers like Benjamin Rush and Judith Sargent Murray argued that only educated and independent-minded women could raise the informed and self-reliant citizens that a republican government required. The notion of "republican motherhood" contributed to the most dramatic change in the lives of women after the war—the spread of female literacy.

Between 1780 and 1830 the number of American colleges and secondary academies rose dramatically, and some of these new institutions were devoted to educating women. Not only did the number of schools for women increase, these schools also offered a solid academic curriculum. By 1850—for the first time in American history—there were as many literate women as there were men. To counter popular prejudices, the defenders of female education contended that schooling for women would produce the ideal republican mother. An educated woman, as one graduate of a female academy claimed, would "inspire her brothers, her husband, or her sons with such a love of virtue, such just ideas of the true value of civil liberty . . . that future heroes and statesmen shall exaltingly declare, it is to my mother that I owe this elevation." *Improved schooling and literacy rates*

The Revolution also prompted some states to reform their marriage laws, making divorce somewhat easier, although it remained extremely rare. But while women won greater freedom to divorce, courts became less concerned to enforce a widow's traditional legal claim to one-third of her spouse's real estate. And married women still could not sue or be sued, make wills or contracts, or buy and sell property. Any wages that they earned went to their husbands; so did all personal property that wives brought into a marriage; so did the rents and profits of any real estate they owned. Despite the high ideals of "republican motherhood," most women remained confined to the "domestic sphere" of the home and deprived of the most basic legal and political rights. *Women's legal status*

The Attack on Aristocracy

Why wasn't the American Revolution more revolutionary? Independence secured the full political equality of white men who owned property, but women were still deprived of political rights, African Americans of human rights. Why did the revolutionaries stop short of extending equality to the most unequal groups in American society—and with so little sense that they were being inconsistent?

In part, the lack of concern was rooted in republican ideas themselves. Republican ideology viewed property as the key to independence and power. Lacking property, women and black Americans were easily consigned to the custody of husbands and masters. Then, too, prejudice played its part: the perception of women and blacks as naturally inferior beings. *Republican view of equality*

But revolutionary leaders also failed to press for greater equality because they conceived their crusade in terms of eliminating the evils of a European past domi-

Daily Lives

FOOD/DRINK/DRUGS

The Spirits of Independence

If God had intended man to drink water, Ben Franklin remarked, He would not have made him with an elbow capable of raising a wineglass. Colonials from all across America agreed with Franklin on the virtues of drink. The ruddy glow of colonial cheeks (still visible in the portraits hung in museums) reflected not only good health and ardent republican virtue but also substantial daily doses of alcohol. Colonials consumed about twice as much alcohol as Americans today, though in different forms. Beer was not popular, the only sort consumed being a weak, homemade "small beer" containing about one percent alcohol. Only the wealthy, like Franklin, could afford imported Madeira and port wines. On the other hand, the produce of apple orchards allowed Americans northward from Virginia to drink their fill of hard cider. Far and away the most popular distilled liquor was rum, a potent 90 proof beverage (45 percent alcohol) that they sipped straight or mixed with water and sugar to make "toddies."

Special occasions were particularly convivial. The liquor flowed freely at ministerial ordinations in New England towns, at court days in the South, at house-raisings, corn-huskings, and quilting bees on the frontier, and at weddings, elections, and militia musters everywhere in the colonies. But Americans did not confine their drinking to occasional celebrations. Some, like John Adams, started the day with a tankard of hard cider. Others, merchants and craftworkers, broke the boredom of late mornings and early afternoons by sending the youngest apprentice in the shop out for spirits. Laborers in seaport docks and shipyards, fishermen and sailors at sea, and farm workers in the countryside commonly received a daily allotment of liquor as part of their wages. And at night, men of every class enjoyed a solitary glass at home or a sociable one at a local tavern.

Socialization into the drinking culture started in childhood. Parents permitted youngsters to sip the sweet dregs of a glass of rum, and when young men entered their teens, they joined their fathers at the tavern. Women drank too, although more often at home, and they sometimes explained their use of distilled liquor as serving some "medicinal" purpose. Slaves got around laws restricting their consumption of alcohol by stealing from masters or bartering with white peddlers.

Until the middle of the eighteenth century, most colonials (and Europeans) considered spirits a source of physical strength and an essential supplement to their diet, as well as a remedy for colds, fevers, snakebite, and, ironically, depression. They did not condone public drunkenness, but they saw nothing amiss in the regular use of alcohol or even in occasional intoxication.

The easy acceptance of drinking prevailed for most of the colonial period for two reasons. First, until about the 1760s, nated by kings and aristocrats. They believed that the great obstacle to equality was monarchy—kings and queens who bestowed hereditary honors and political office on favored individuals and granted legal privileges and monopolies to favored churches and businesses. These artificial inequalities posed the real threat to liberty, most republicans concluded. In other words, the men of the Revolution were intent on attaining equality by leveling off the top of society. It did not occur to most republicans that the cause of equality could also be served by raising up the bottom—by attack-

220

Daily Lives

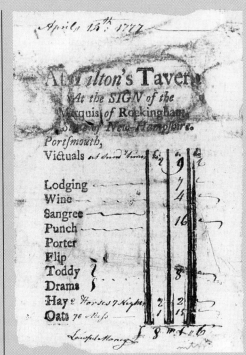

This tavern bill from New Hampshire indicates that in 1777 whiskey was still too rare to be listed.

frequent access to the strongest spirits, rum, lay beyond the means of most Americans. Second, the leaders of local communities were able to oversee most public drinking and to keep disorder to a minimum. But by the middle of the eighteenth century some Americans developed misgivings about the drinking culture. Increased production and importation led the price of rum to drop so sharply that an ordinary laborer could earn enough in a day to stay "drunk as a lord" for the rest of the week. Taverns proliferated, making it impossible for community leaders to monitor the popular consumption of alcohol.

The new concern that the drinking of rum fostered crime and social disruption prompted the first steps toward temperance reform. By the 1770s, Quakers like Anthony Benezet were urging that alcohol, like slavery, was an "unrepublican vice," for both forms of bondage deprived their victims of liberty and the capacity for rationality and self-control. Some members of the medical profession also joined early temperance ranks, most notably Benjamin Rush.

While the advocates of more moderate consumption won support among some educated elites, most Americans altered their drinking habits by consuming *more* hard liquor. Rum, the liquor of choice before the Revolution, lost much of its ground to a new rival, whiskey. Whiskey was democratic and cheap, for it could be made in the lowliest backcountry farmhouse. It was patriotic, since it did not depend on imports from the Caribbean. Gradually these "spirits of independence" supplanted rum not only in the frontier West but also in the urban East. Consumption of alcohol was on a steady rise that would finally result, half a century after the Revolution, in louder calls for temperance reform.

ing the laws and prejudices that kept African Americans enslaved and women dependent.

The most significant reform of the republican campaign against artificial privilege was the dismantling of state-supported churches. Most states had a religious establishment. In New York and the South, it was the Anglican church; in New England, the Congregational church. Since the 1740s, dissenters who did not worship at state churches had protested laws that taxed all citizens to support the clergy

Disestablishment

221

of established denominations. After the Revolution dissenters argued that equality required ending such privileges. As more dissenters became voters, state legislators gradually abolished state support for Anglican and Congregational churches.

Not only in religious life but in all aspects of their culture, Americans rejected inequalities associated with a monarchical past. In that spirit reformers attacked the *Society of Cincinnati*, a group organized by former officers of the Continental Army in 1783. The society, which was merely a social club for veterans, was forced to disband for its policy of passing on its membership rights to eldest sons. In this way, critics charged, the Cincinnati was creating artificial distinctions and perpetuating a hereditary warrior nobility.

Society of Cincinnati

Today, many of the republican efforts at reform seem misdirected. While only a handful of revolutionaries worked for the education of women and the emancipation of slaves, enormous zeal went into fighting threats from a monarchical past that had never existed in America. Yet the threat from kings and aristocrats was real to the revolutionaries—and indeed remained real in many parts of Europe. Their determination to sweep away every shred of formal privilege ensured that these forms of inequality never took root in America. And if eighteenth-century Americans did not extend equality to women and racial minorities, it was a failure that they shared with later revolutionary movements that promised more.

COUNTERPOINT   Not all historians agree that the American Revolution was an essentially conservative movement, one that effected little fundamental social change. On the contrary, some argue that the Revolution had radical consequences, dramatically transforming not only government but society. True, unlike later revolutions in France and Russia, the American Revolution did not involve the violent overthrow of a ruling class by a nonruling class. Even so, these scholars believe that the birth of republican government not only created a more egalitarian culture in the new United States than existed anywhere else in the world but also spurred the rise of a liberal, democratic, and capitalist society.

Radicalism and the American Revolution

The real radicalism of the American Revolution, in this view, lay in its challenging the age-old belief that gentlemen and common men were two separate kinds of human beings. For many previous centuries, most people of every social rank in both the Old World and the New had accepted as a simple truth the notion that gentlefolk were innately superior because of their high birth, classical learning, polite refinements, and leisured existences. Ordinary people were held to be naturally ignorant and narrow-minded, driven by the basest desires and needs, and so dulled by lives of hard work that they were incapable of elevated thought or noble behavior. But the republicanism of American revolutionaries shattered that hierarchical way of thinking by celebrating the common sense of the common man and asserting that all human beings are naturally equal in their moral capacity to judge right from wrong. Indeed, revolutionaries went even further, endowing ordinary people and their labor with dignity by elevating the importance of productive work and by depicting industrious farmers and artisans as more virtuous citizens than the idle rich.

In short, historians contending for the radicalism of the American Revolution believe that to emphasize the inequalities of race and gender that persisted in the new United States is to overlook the very real change that republicanism achieved. It accorded common white men unprecedented respect and power at the same time that it created a government dedicated to promoting their liberty, security, and prosperity.

FROM CONFEDERATION TO CONSTITUTIONS

While Americans in many walks of life sought to realize the republican commitment to equality, leaders in Congress wrestled with the problem of preserving the nation itself. With the new republic slowly rending itself to pieces, some political leaders concluded that neither the Confederation nor the state legislatures were able to remedy the basic difficulties facing the nation. But how could the states be convinced to surrender their sovereign powers? The answer came in the wake of two events—one foreign, one domestic—that lent momentum to the cause of strengthening the central government.

The Jay–Gardoqui Treaty

The international episode that threatened to leave the Confederation in shambles was a debate over a proposed treaty with Spain. In 1785 southwesterners still could not legally navigate the Mississippi and were still threatening to secede from the union and annex their territory to Spain's American empire. To shore up southwestern loyalties, Congress instructed its secretary of foreign affairs, John Jay, to negotiate an agreement with Spain preserving American rights to navigate on the Mississippi River. But the Spanish emissary, Don Diego de Gardoqui, sweet-talked Jay into accepting a treaty by which the United States would give up all rights to the Mississippi for 25 years. In return, Spain agreed to grant trading privileges to American merchants.

Jay, a New Yorker, knew more than a few northern merchants who were eager to open new markets. But when the proposed treaty became public knowledge, southwesterners denounced it as nothing short of betrayal. The treaty was never ratified, but the hostility stirred up during the debate revealed the strength of sectional feelings.

Shays' Rebellion

On the heels of this humiliation by Spain came an internal conflict that challenged the notion that individual states could maintain order in their own territories. The trouble erupted in western Massachusetts, where many small farmers were close to ruin. By 1786 farm wages and prices had fallen sharply and farmers were selling little produce. Yet they still had to pay mortgages on their farms, still had other debts, and were perpetually short of money. In 1786 the lower house of the Massachusetts legislature obliged the farmers with a package of relief measures. But creditors in eastern Massachusetts, determined to safeguard their own investments, persuaded the upper house to defeat the measures.

In the summer of 1786 western farmers responded, demanding that the upper house of the legislature be abolished and that the relief measures go into effect. That autumn 2000 farmers rose in armed rebellion, led by Captain Daniel Shays, a veteran of the Revolution. They closed the county courts to halt creditors from foreclosing on their farms and marched on the federal arsenal at Springfield. The state militia quelled the uprising by February 1787, but the insurrection left many in Massachusetts and the rest of the country thoroughly shaken.

Response to agrarian unrest

Alarmed conservatives saw Shays' Rebellion as the consequence of radical democracy. "The natural effects of pure democracy are already produced among us," lamented one republican gentleman; "it is a war against virtue, talents, and property carried on by the dregs and scum of mankind." He was wrong. The rebels with Daniel Shays were no impoverished rabble. They were reputable members of western communities who wanted their property protected and believed that government existed to provide that protection. The Massachusetts state legislature had been unable to safeguard the property of farmers from the inroads of recession or to protect the property of creditors from the armed debtors who closed the courts. It had failed, in other words, to fulfill the most basic aim of republican government.

What if such violent tactics spread? Other states with discontented debtors feared what the example of western Massachusetts might mean for the future of the Confederation itself. But by 1786 Shays' Rebellion supplied only the sharpest jolt to a movement for reform that was already under way. Even before the rebellion, a group of Virginians had proposed a meeting of the states to adopt a uniform system of commercial regulations. Once assembled at Annapolis in September 1786, the delegates from five states agreed to a more ambitious undertaking. They called for a second, broader meeting in Philadelphia, which Congress approved, for the "express purpose of revising the Articles of Confederation."

Framing a Federal Constitution

It was the wettest spring anyone could remember. The 55 men who traveled over muddy roads to Philadelphia in May 1787 arrived drenched and bespattered. Fortunately, most of the travelers were men in their thirties and forties, young enough to survive a good soaking. Since most were gentlemen of some means— planters, merchants, and lawyers with powdered wigs and prosperous paunches— they could recover from the rigors of their journey in the best accommodations offered by America's largest city.

The delegates came from all the states except Rhode Island. The rest of New England supplied shrewd backroom politicians—Roger Sherman and Oliver Ellsworth from Connecticut and Rufus King and Elbridge Gerry, Massachusetts men who had learned a trick or two from Sam Adams. The middle states marshaled much of the intellectual might: two Philadelphia lawyers, John Dickinson and James Wilson; one Philadelphia financier, Robert Morris; and the aristocratic Gouverneur Morris. From New York there was Alexander Hamilton, the mercurial and ambitious young protégé of Washington. South Carolina provided fiery orators, Charles Pinckney and John Rutledge.

It was "an assembly of the demi-gods," gushed Thomas Jefferson, who, along with John Adams, was serving as a diplomat in Europe when the convention met. In fact, the only delegate who looked even remotely divine was the convention's presiding deity. Towering a full half foot taller than most of his colleagues, George Washington displayed his usual self-possession from a chair elevated on the speaker's platform where the delegates met, in the Pennsylvania State House. At first glance, the delegate of least commanding presence was Washington's fellow Virginian, James Madison. Short and slightly built, the 36-year-old Madison had no profession except hypochondria; he read a great deal and dressed in black. But he was an astute politi-

James Madison

James Madison, the scholar and statesman whose ideas and political skill shaped the Constitution

cian and a brilliant political thinker who, more than anyone else, shaped the framing of the federal Constitution.

The delegates from 12 different states had two things in common. They were all men of considerable political experience, and they all recognized the need for a stronger national union. So when the Virginia delegation introduced Madison's outline for a new central government, the convention was ready to listen.

The Virginia and New Jersey Plans

What Madison had in mind was a truly national republic, not a confederation of independent states. His "Virginia Plan" proposed a central government with three branches: legislative, executive, and judicial. Furthermore, the legislative branch, Congress, would possess the power to veto all state legislation. In place of the Confederation's single assembly, Madison substituted a bicameral legislature, with a lower house elected directly by the people and an upper house chosen by the lower, from nominations made by state legislatures. Representatives to both houses would be apportioned according to population—a change from practice under the Articles, in which each state had a single vote in Congress. Madison also revised the structure of government that had existed under the Articles by adding an executive, who would be elected by Congress, and an independent federal judiciary.

Madison's Virginia Plan

After two weeks of debate over the Virginia Plan, William Paterson, a lawyer from New Jersey, presented a less radical counterproposal. While his "New Jersey Plan" increased Congress's power to tax and to regulate trade, it kept the national government as a unicameral assembly, with each state receiving one vote in Congress under the policy of equal representation. The delegates took just four days to reject Paterson's plan. Most endorsed Madison's design for a stronger central government.

Paterson's New Jersey Plan

Even so, the issue of apportioning representation continued to divide the delegates. While smaller states pressed for each state having an equal vote in Congress, larger states backed Madison's provision for basing representation on population. Underlying the dispute over representation was an even deeper rivalry between southern and northern states. While northern and southern populations were nearly equal in the 1780s, and the South's population was growing more rapidly, the northern states were more numerous. Giving the states equal votes would put the South at a disadvantage. Southerners feared being outvoted in Congress by the northern states and felt that only proportional representation would protect the interests of their section.

That division turned into a deadlock as the wet spring burned off into a blazing summer. Delegates suffered the daily torture of staring at a large sun painted on the speaker's chair occupied by Washington. The stifling heat was made even worse because the windows remained shut to keep any news of the proceedings from drifting out onto the Philadelphia streets.

The Deadlock Broken

Compromise over representation

Finally, as the heat wave broke, so did the political stalemate. On July 2 a committee headed by Benjamin Franklin suggested a compromise. States would be equally represented in the upper house of Congress, each state legislature appointing two senators to six-year terms. That satisfied the smaller states. In the lower house of Congress, which alone could initiate money bills, representation was to be apportioned according to population. Every 30,000 inhabitants would elect one representative for a two-year term. A slave was to count as three-fifths of a free person in the calculation of population, and the slave trade was to continue until 1808. That satisfied the larger states and the South.

Electoral College

By the end of August the convention was prepared to approve the final draft of the Constitution. The delegates agreed that the executive, now called the president, would be chosen every four years. Direct election seemed out of the question—after all, how could citizens in South Carolina know anything about a presidential candidate who happened to live in distant Massachusetts, or vice versa? But if voters instead chose presidential electors, those eminent men would likely have been involved in national politics, have known the candidates personally, and be prepared to vote wisely. Thus the Electoral College was established, with each state's total number of senators and representatives determining its share of electoral votes.

Separation of powers

An array of other powers ensured that the executive would remain independent and strong. He would have command over the armed forces, authority to conduct diplomatic relations, responsibility to nominate judges and officials in the executive branch, and the power to veto congressional legislation. Just as the executive branch was made independent, so too the federal judiciary was separated from the other two branches of government. Madison believed that this clear separation of powers was essential to a balanced republican government.

Madison's only real defeat came when the convention refused to give Congress veto power over state legislation. Still, the new bicameral national legislature enjoyed much broader authority than Congress had under the Confederation, including the power to tax and to regulate commerce. The Constitution also limited the powers of state legislatures, prohibiting them from levying duties on trade, coining money or issuing paper currency, and conducting foreign relations. The Constitution and the acts

As the Constitution is signed, Benjamin Franklin (second from left) looks on; Washington presides. "The business being closed," Washington wrote, "the members adjourned to the City Tavern, dined together and took cordial leave of each other."

passed by Congress were declared the supreme law of the land, taking precedence over any legislation passed by the states. And changing the Constitution would not be easy. Amendments could be proposed only by a two-thirds vote of both houses of Congress or in a convention requested by two-thirds of the state legislatures. Ratification of amendments required approval by three-quarters of the states.

Amending the Constitution

On September 17, 1787, thirty-nine of the forty-two delegates remaining in Philadelphia signed the Constitution. It was fortunate that the signatories included so many lawyers, for the summer's proceedings had been of such dubious legality that many skilled attorneys would be needed to make them seem otherwise. Charged only to revise the Articles, the delegates had instead written a completely new frame of government. And to speed up ratification, the convention decided that the Constitution would go into effect after only nine states had approved it, overlooking the fact that even a revision of the Articles would have required the assent of all state legislatures. They further declared that the people themselves—not the state legislatures—would pass judgment on the Constitution in special ratifying conventions. To serve final notice that the new central government was a republic of the people and not merely another confederation of states, Gouverneur Morris of Pennsylvania hit on a happy turn of phrase to introduce the Constitution. "We the People," the document begins, "in order to form a more perfect union. . . ."

Ratification

With grave misgivings on the part of many, the states called for conventions to decide whether to ratify the new Constitution. Those with the gravest misgivings—the Anti-Federalists as they came to be called—voiced familiar republican fears. Older and less cosmopolitan than their Federalist opponents, the Anti-Federalists drew upon

The Anti-Federalists

their memories of the struggle with England to frame their criticisms of the Constitution. Expanding the power of the central government at the expense of the states, they warned, would lead to corrupt and arbitrary rule by new aristocrats. Extending a republic over a large territory, they cautioned, would separate national legislators from the interests and close oversight of their constituents.

The Federalist Papers

Madison responded to these objections in *The Federalist Papers*, a series of 85 essays written with Alexander Hamilton and John Jay during the winter of 1787–1788. He countered Anti-Federalist concerns over the centralization of power by pointing out that each separate branch of the national government would keep the others within the limits of their legal authority. That mechanism of checks and balances would prevent the executive from oppressing the people while preventing the people from oppressing themselves.

To answer Anti-Federalist objections to a national republic, Madison drew on the ideas of an English philosopher, David Hume. In his famous tenth essay in *The Federalist Papers*, Madison argued that in a great republic, "the Society becomes broken into a greater variety of interests, of pursuits, of passions, which check each other." The larger the territory, the more likely it was to contain multiple political interests and parties, so that no single faction could dominate. Instead, each would cancel out the others.

Bill of Rights

The one Anti-Federalist criticism Madison could not get around was the absence of a national bill of rights. Opponents insisted on an explicit statement of rights to secure the freedoms of individuals and minorities from being violated by the federal government. Madison finally promised to place a bill of rights before Congress immediately after the Constitution was ratified.

Throughout the early months of 1788, Anti-Federalists continued their opposition. But they lacked the articulate and influential leadership that rallied behind the Constitution and commanded greater access to the public press. In the end, too, Anti-Federalist fears of centralized power proved less compelling than Federalist prophecies of the chaos that would follow if the Constitution was not adopted.

Ratification of the Constitution

STATE	DATE	VOTE FOR	VOTE AGAINST
Delaware	December 8, 1787	30	0
Pennsylvania	December 12, 1787	46	23
New Jersey	December 18, 1787	38	0
Georgia	January 2, 1788	26	0
Connecticut	January 9, 1788	128	40
Massachusetts	February 16, 1788	187	168
Maryland	April 26, 1788	63	11
South Carolina	May 23, 1788	149	73
New Hampshire	June 21, 1788	57	47
Virginia	June 25, 1788	89	79
New York	July 26, 1788	30	27
North Carolina	November 21, 1789	194	77
Rhode Island	May 29, 1790	34	32

By June 1788 all but three states had voted in favor of ratification. The last hold-out—to no one's surprise Rhode Island—finally came aboard in May 1790, after Madison had carried through on his pledge to submit a bill of rights to the new Congress. Indeed, these 10 amendments proved to be the Anti-Federalists' most impressive legacy.

Changing Revolutionary Ideals

Within the life span of a single generation, Americans had declared their independence twice. In many ways the political freedom claimed from Britain in 1776 was less remarkable than the intellectual freedom that Americans achieved by agreeing to the Constitution. The Constitution represented both a triumph of imagination and common sense and a rejection of some older, long-cherished republican beliefs.

Americans thought long and hard before changing their minds, but many did. Committed at first to limiting executive power by making legislatures supreme, they at last ratified a constitution that provided for an independent executive and a balanced government. Committed at first to preserving the sovereignty of the states, they at last established a national government with authority independent of the states. Committed at first to the proposition that a national republic was impossible, they at last created an impossibility that still endures.

Rejected republican beliefs

What, then, became of the last tenet of the old republican creed—the belief that civic virtue would sustain popular liberty? The hard lessons of the war and the crises of the 1780s withered confidence in the capacity of Americans to sacrifice their private interests for the public welfare. Many came to share Washington's sober view that "the few . . . who act upon Principles of disinterestedness are, comparatively speaking, no more than a drop in the Ocean." The Constitution reflected the new recognition that interest rather than virtue shaped the behavior of most people most of the time and that the clash of diverse interest groups would remain a constant of public life.

Behavior shaped by interest rather than virtue

Yet Madison and many other Federalists did not believe that the competition between private interests would somehow result in policies fostering public welfare. That goal would be met instead by the new national government acting as "a disinterested and dispassionate umpire in disputes between different passions and interests in the State." The Federalists looked to the national government to fulfill that role because they trusted that a large republic, with its millions of citizens, would yield more of that scarce resource—disinterested gentlemen dedicated to serving the public good. Such gentlemen, in Madison's words, "whose enlightened views and virtuous sentiments render them superior to local prejudices," would fill the small number of national offices.

Not all the old revolutionaries agreed. Anti-Federalists drawn from the ranks of ordinary Americans still believed that common people were more virtuous and gentlemen more interested than the Federalists allowed. "These lawyers and men of learning, and moneyed men, that talk so finely," complained one Anti-Federalist, would "get all the power and all of the money into their own hands, and then they will swallow up all us little folks." Instead of being dominated by enlightened gentlemen, the national government should be composed of representatives from every social class and occupational group.

The narrow majorities by which the Constitution was ratified reflected the continuing influence of such sentiments, as well as fear that the states were surrendering too much power. That fear made Patrick Henry so ardent an Anti-Federalist that he refused to attend the Constitutional Convention in 1787, saying that he "smelt a rat." "I am not a Virginian, but an American," Henry had once declared. Most likely he was lying. Or perhaps Patrick Henry, a southerner and a slaveholder, could see his way clear to being an "American" only so long as sovereignty remained firmly in the hands of the individual states. Henry's convictions, 70 years hence, would rise again to haunt the Union.

CHAPTER SUMMARY

The American Revolution did not create an American national identity. For a decade after independence, the revolutionaries were less committed to creating a single national republic than to organizing 13 separate state republics. Popularly elected legislatures became the dominant force in state governments, controlling not only weak executives but also the judiciary. While Americans lavished attention on their state constitutions, the national government received little attention. The Articles of Confederation provided for a government by a national legislature, essentially a continuation of the Second Continental Congress. But it left the crucial power of the purse, as well as all final power to make and execute laws, entirely to the states. Leading Americans would give more thought to federalism, the organization of a United States, as the events of the postrevolutionary period revealed the weaknesses of the state and national governments.

Many conflicts arose from westward expansion, which posed international difficulties and internal problems. As the British tried to lure Vermonters into Canada and the Spanish encouraged secession among southwesterners, "landless" and "landed" states squabbled over how to administer the large tracts of land to the west. The settlement of the West also triggered controversy by democratizing state legislatures, a development disdained by some conservatives. Their fears of democratic excess shaped the Northwest Ordinance of 1787, which withheld full self-government from new territories until they had attained statehood. In the wake of the Revolution, ordinary Americans struggled to define a new republican society too. Newly rich families came to demand and receive greater status; workers began to organize; some women claimed a right to greater political consideration, more freedom to divorce, and better educational opportunities; religious dissenters clamored for disestablishment. Northern laws abolishing slavery, along with an increase in manumissions in the Upper South, swelled the growth of the free black community. In the South as a whole, however, slavery continued to expand along with the cotton economy.

In the mid-1780s the political crisis of the Confederation came to a head, prompted by the controversy over the Jay–Gardoqui Treaty and Shays' Rebellion. The response was the Constitutional Convention of 1787, which produced an entirely new frame of government establishing a truly national republic. Based largely on James Madison's Virginia Plan, the new Constitution provided for a separation of powers among a judiciary, a bicameral national legislature, and a strong executive. Most opponents of the Constitution, the Anti-Federalists, softened their objections when promised a bill of rights after ratification. By May of 1790, all of the states had accepted the Constitution, thereby repudiating their earlier commitment to legislative supremacy and revising their former insistence upon state sovereignty.

SIGNIFICANT EVENTS

1777	Continental Congress approves the Articles of Confederation
1781	Articles of Confederation ratified
1784	Spain closes the Mississippi River to American navigation
1785	Jay–Gardoqui Treaty negotiated but not ratified
1786	Shays' Rebellion; Annapolis convention calls for revising the Articles
1787	Congress adopts the Northwest Ordinance; Constitutional Convention
1787–1788	Publication of *The Federalist Papers*
1788	New Hampshire becomes ninth state to ratify Constitution
1791	Bill of Rights adopted

ADDITIONAL READING

Gordon Wood's two books, *The Creation of the American Republic* (1969) and *The Radicalism of the American Revolution* (1992), tell a compelling story about the transformation of American society, culture, and politics in the latter half of the eighteenth century. Forrest MacDonald's accounts of the Confederation period and the Constitution are also excellent, *E Pluribus Unum* (1965) and *Novus Ordo Seclorum* (1985), as is Linda Kerber's study of the relevance of republicanism for American women, *Women of the Republic* (1980). The liveliest account of the framing of the Constitution is still Clinton Rossiter, *1787: The Grand Convention* (1973), while the best single introduction to the Anti-Federalists remains Cecilia Kenyon's "Men of Little Faith: The Anti-Federalists and the Nature of Representative Government," *William and Mary Quarterly*, 12 (1955).

Historians are developing a new and deeper appreciation for the ways in which the Revolutionary era transformed society and politics in the early republic, particularly in the North. For a vivid sense of how that change affected a single community in western Massachusetts, see John Brooke, *The Heart of the Commonwealth* (1991), and, for a fascinating tale of how the Revolution made one ordinary man's life extraordinary, see Alan Taylor, *William Cooper's Town* (1995). Probably the best single account of how the Revolution's legacy affected one African American community in the North is Shane White, *Somewhat More Independent* (1991). For a fuller list of readings, see the Bibliography

White and Black Southerners Worshiping Together

During the 50 years before 1800, evangelicals introduced southerners to new ways of being religious. Those attending their worship services were men and women drawn into the earliest southern Baptist, Methodist, and Presbyterian churches by the First Great Awakening and other local revivals that followed in its wake. These early services were held in private homes, others in crudely constructed churches, and still others in open fields. In such settings, evangelical preachers stressed the importance of being "reborn" by faith in Jesus Christ—and some southerners responded. They wept and confessed their sins; they encouraged one another with hopeful words and warm embraces. Those who came to such gatherings engaged in the most intimate kind of sharing and self-revelation.

But what made these services even more extraordinary is that some who participated were white, and some were black. These were truly biracial religious fellowships, and so they re-mained until after the Civil War. That remarkable fact has intrigued historians. Evangelical churches were one of the few southern institutions that brought blacks and whites together rather than keeping them apart. How did members behave toward each other daily? Were born-again converts from both races treated equally? How was authority within such churches distributed among black and white members?

The questions are tantalizing, but the answers by no means easy to come by. Some letters and diaries survive from the last half of the eighteenth century, among them the daily journals and correspondence of ministers. A few preachers even published autobiographies of their experiences. But even more valuable information can be gathered from what might seem at first a rather drab source. There are scores of church records dating from this period, most of them kept by Virginia Baptists. The members of each Baptist church elected a clerk, always a white male "brother," whose duty it was to record all of the business transacted at their monthly meetings, often in a ledger-sized bound volume called the "church book." Church books provide an insight into relations between whites and blacks in part because their clerks are *not* consciously trying to write about race relations. They are simply recording the everyday business of the church, week in, week out.

Sometimes practical concerns dominated the meeting. Should the church building be repaired? Who among the brethren will be permitted to preach? (Many Baptist churches boasted several preachers besides the pastor.) On other occasions, members debated about what the Bible taught was the holiest way to govern their churches. But at most meetings, members fixed their attention on admitting new converts to their fellowship and "disciplining" older members suspected of sexual misconduct or theft, slander or swearing, drinking or fighting. Church clerks duly noted all those accepted as new members, as well as the names of wayward brothers and sisters—and whether they were merely scolded for their faults or expelled.

Such records offer the most direct and vivid sense of African Americans' presence and participation in early evangelical churches. First, they show that blacks made up a substantial minority—perhaps one-fifth to one-quarter—of the members in most churches. In a few, they comprised a majority. Many churches, too, authorized at least one African American brother to preach, sometimes permitting him that "liberty" only among other

blacks but in other instances allowing him to address racially mixed gatherings. There were even a few predominantly white churches in early Virginia that black preachers served as pastors.

In some churches, too, black men and, more rarely, black women were permitted to vote in meetings, and in all of them, African American members could participate in church deliberations and give testimony in discipline cases. Indeed, there are several instances of masters

Churchbook record: "Names of Black Members"

Note the treatment of black names.

being disciplined after slave members complained of being abused. Black members, too, were sometimes charged with wrongdoing, but white men were far more likely than any group of members to be hauled before the church for re-

233

"Uncle Jack," shown in this 1849 engraving, preaches informally to a white congregation. He began his career as a minister in the 1790s and continued until 1832.

discussed the mundane matter of church repair reveal, for example, that the Baptists segregated seating at public worship. African Americans were consigned to the least choice spots at the back of the church or in "sheds" attached to the side. Moreover, when white members filled every available seat, black members were ordered outdoors to listen from underneath open windows. The attitude that such practices convey—that whites regarded African Americans as "second-class" members—is also suggested by the manner in which many clerks recorded new church members. While they always entered the full names of white converts, new African American members are usually listed last and often collectively as "several Negroes."

Church discussions about who might preach also show a growing concern on the part of white members to restrict the activities of black preachers. Increasingly after 1750 those allowed that "liberty" were given ever stricter instructions about whom they might preach to, at which times, and from what texts of the Bible. At meetings where the rules of conducting church business were discussed, white members also began to express concern about whether African American members should be allowed to vote. Most churches revoked that right before the end of the eighteenth century. Tracing how churches dealt with black members accused of misbehavior suggests a similar anxiety among white members, which increased over time. While African Americans continued to make up only a tiny minority of church members suspected of misbehavior, those convicted of wrongdoing were far more likely than white members to be expelled rather than to receive a milder punishment.

In other words, a closer inspection of church records suggests that white evangelicals drifted toward more racially restrictive policies over the latter half of the eighteenth century. Why? The numbers in the church books are suggestive. After the Revolution, increasing numbers of African Americans were entering Baptist (and other evangelical) churches. As the percentage of black members rose, white evangelicals feared that the "freedoms" given to black worshipers

ported misdeeds. In short, evangelical churches like these Baptist fellowships were among the most racially egalitarian institutions in early southern society. They offered African Americans unusual opportunities to hold positions of authority, to voice their opinions, and to gain leverage over their masters.

Yet these same church records also reveal the limits of racial equality among early evangelicals. Like all evidence mined by historians, the sources yield data that are sometimes complex and contradictory.

Records of those meetings at which members

might detract from the church's ability to win converts among slaveholders.

Clearly, evangelicals were winning converts among African Americans. Yet other evidence suggests that black members were left unsatisfied by their treatment in white churches. The diaries and letters of white evangelicals reveal that many black members of biracial churches had also begun conducting their own separate devotions. Even by the 1790s, African American Christians were meeting nightly in the slave quarters to pray, sing, and hear the sermons of black preachers. Such "shadow churches" served as the crucible of Afro-Christianity, a melding of evangelical Protestant and west African religious traditions. John Antrobus's painting *Plantation Burial* (below, also on page 413) reflects the situation that prevailed by the mid-nineteenth century. While blacks attended white services in greater numbers, their most vital worship often took place elsewhere. White masters and preachers were like the shadowy couple Antrobus painted on the right: divorced from the Christian worship of their slaves.

BIBLIOGRAPHY. Historians disagree about the extent to which early evangelical churches were egalitarian. The strongest arguments in favor are presented by Mechal Sobel, *The World They Made Together* (1987); the most forceful challenge to Sobel is Jewel Spangeler, "Salvation Was Not Liberty: Baptists and Slavery in Revolutionary Virginia," *American Baptist Quarterly*, 13 (1994). Other studies that treat the dynamics of these early biracial churches and the experience of the first black southern evangelicals are Albert J. Raboteau, *Slave Religion* (1978), the best introduction to this subject; Sylvia R. Frey, *Water from the Rock* (1991), which usefully updates Raboteau; and, most recently, Christine Leigh Heyrman, *Southern Cross* (1997). The evolving views of race and slavery among early white evangelicals is thoughtfully analyzed in James Essig, *The Bonds of Wickedness* (1982), while the most eloquent descriptions of Afro-Christianity in the slave quarters appear in Eugene Genovese, *Roll, Jordan, Roll* (1972) and Lawrence Levine, *Black Culture and Black Consciousness* (1977).

8

The Republic Launched

ne spring evening in 1794 General John Neville was riding home from Pittsburgh with his wife and granddaughter. While going up a hill his wife's saddle started to slip, so Neville dismounted to tighten the girth. As he adjusted the strap, he heard the clip-clop of approaching horses. A rider galloped up and in a gruff voice asked, "Are you Neville the excise officer?"

Still busy with his wife's saddle, Neville replied "yes," without turning around.

"Then I must give you a whipping!" cried the rider as he leaped from his horse. He grabbed the startled Neville by the hair and lunged at his throat, and the two began tussling. Breaking free, Neville finally managed to knock the man down and subdue him. He recognized his assailant as Jacob Long, a local farmer. After Long fled, the badly shaken Neville resumed his journey.

John Neville was not accustomed to such treatment. As one of the wealthiest men in the area, his estate near Pittsburgh, "Bower Hill," boasted fine European furnishings that presented a sharp contrast with the humble log cabins of his neighbors. Neville expected respect from those of lower social rank—and had received it; at least he had until becoming embroiled in a controversy over the new "whiskey tax" on distilled spirits. In a frontier district like western Pennsylvania, farmers regularly distilled their grain into whiskey for barter and sale. Not surprisingly, the excise tax, passed by Congress in 1791, was notoriously unpopular. Still, Neville had accepted an appointment to be one of the tax's regional inspectors. For three years he had endured threats as he tried to enforce the law, but this roadside assault clearly indicated that popular hostility was rising.

As spring turned to summer, the grain ripened, and so did the people's anger. In mid-July, a federal marshal arrived to serve summonses to a number of farmer-distillers who had not paid taxes. One, William Miller, squinted at the paper and was amazed to find the government ordering him to set aside "all manner of business and excuses" and appear in court—hundreds of miles away in Philadelphia—in little more than a month. Even worse, the papers claimed he owed $250.

And there, next to this unknown federal marshal, stood the stiff-backed, unyielding John Neville.

"I felt myself mad with passion," recalled Miller. "I thought $250 would ruin me; and . . . I felt my blood boil at seeing General Neville along to pilot the sheriff to my very door." Meanwhile word of the marshal's presence brought 30 or 40 laborers swarming from a nearby field. Armed with muskets and pitchforks, they were both

Frontier farmers in Pennsylvania tar and feather a federal tax collector during the Whiskey Rebellion. The political violence of the 1790s led Americans to wonder whether the new government would succeed in uniting a socially diverse nation.

angry and well-liquored. When a shot rang out, Neville and the marshal beat a hasty retreat.

Within hours, news of Neville's doings spread to a nearby militia company. Enraged by what they considered this latest trampling on individual liberty, the militia marched to Neville's fortified house the next morning. A battle ensued, and the general, aided by his slaves, beat back the attackers. A larger group, numbering 500 to 700, returned the following day to find Neville fled and his home garrisoned by a group of soldiers from nearby Fort Pitt. The mob burned down most of the outbuildings and, after the soldiers surrendered, torched Neville's well-furnished home.

Throughout the region that summer, marauding bands roamed the countryside, burning homes, banishing individuals, and attacking tax collectors and other enemies. To many citizens who learned of the disturbances, such echoes of the revolutionary

1760s and 1770s were deeply distressing. In the space of only 15 years, Americans had already overturned two governments: England's colonial administration and the Articles of Confederation. As the aged Benjamin Franklin remarked in 1788, although Americans were quite skilled at overthrowing governments, it remained to be seen whether they were any good at sustaining them. Now, Franklin's warning seemed prophetic.

Yet Federalists—supporters of the Constitution—had recognized from the beginning how risky it was to unite a territory as large as the United States' 890,000 square miles. Yankee merchants living along Boston wharves had economic interests and cultural traditions quite different from those of backcountry farmers who raised hogs, tended a few acres of corn, and distilled whiskey. Even among farmers, there was a world of difference between a South Carolina planter who shipped tons of rice to European markets and a New Hampshire family whose stony fields yielded barely enough to survive. Could the new government established by the Constitution provide a framework strong enough to unite such a socially diverse nation?

1789: A SOCIAL PORTRAIT

When the Constitution went into effect, the United States stretched from the Atlantic Ocean to the Mississippi River. The first federal census, compiled in 1790, counted approximately 4 million people, divided about evenly between the northern and southern states. The Republic's population was overwhelmingly concentrated along the eastern seaboard. Only about 100,000 settlers lived beyond the Appalachians in the Tennessee and Kentucky territories, which were soon to become states. In limited parts of this region, commercial agriculture based on slavery had begun to take root. But full-scale operations could not develop in the trans-Appalachian West so long as Spain controlled the mouth of the Mississippi River. The area north of the Ohio River was virtually unsettled by whites.

Within the Republic's boundaries were two major racial groups that lacked effective political influence: African Americans and Indians. In 1790 black Americans numbered 750,000, almost one-fifth of the total population. Over 90 percent lived in the southern states from Maryland to Georgia; most were slaves who worked on tobacco and rice plantations. But there were free blacks as well, their numbers increased by the ideals of the Revolution. Indeed, the free black population in 1790 was larger, relative to the total African American population, than it would be at any time before the Civil War. The census did not count the number of Indians living east of the Mississippi. North of the Ohio, the powerful Miami Confederacy discouraged settlement, while to the south, five strong, well-organized tribes—the Creeks, Cherokees, Chickasaws, Choctaws, and Seminoles—dominated the region from the Appalachians to the Mississippi River.

Population growth   That situation would change, however, as the white population continued to double approximately every 22 years. Immigration contributed only a small part to this astonishing growth. On average, fewer than 10,000 Europeans arrived annually between 1790 and 1820. The primary cause was natural increase, since the average American white woman gave birth to nearly eight children. As a consequence, the United States had an unusually youthful population: in 1790 almost half of all white Americans were under 16 years old.° The age at first marriage was about 25 for men, 24 for women; but it was significantly lower in newly settled areas (on average perhaps 21 for males and younger for females), which contributed to the high birthrate.

This youthful, growing population remained overwhelmingly rural. Only 24 towns and cities boasted 2500 or more residents, and 19 out of 20 Americans lived outside them. In fact, in 1800 over 80 percent of American families were engaged in agriculture. In such a rural environment the movement of people, goods, and information was slow. Few individuals used the expensive postal system, and most roads were still little more than dirt paths hacked through the forest, with stumps cut off at 16 inches (so axles would just clear them) and large trees sometimes left in the roadway. The roads choked with dust during dry spells and became a sea of mud after rains. In 1790 the country had 92 newspapers, published weekly or semiweekly, mostly in towns and cities along major avenues of transportation. Americans off the beaten path only occasionally heard news of the outside world.

Poor transportation

Life in isolated regions contrasted markedly with bustling urban centers like New York and Philadelphia. But the most basic division in American society was not between the cities and the countryside, important as that was. What would divide Americans most broadly over the coming decades was the contrast between semisubsistence and commercial ways of life. Semisubsistence farmers lived on the produce of their own land and labor. Americans in the commercial economy were tied more closely to the larger markets of a far-flung world. As the United States began its life under the new federal union, the distinction between a semisubsistence economy and a commercial economy was a crucial one.

The Semisubsistence Economy of Crèvecoeur's America

Most rural white Americans lived off the produce of their own land in a barter economy. It was this world that a French writer, Hector St. John de Crèvecoeur, described so well.

Crèvecoeur arrived in the British colonies in 1759 and almost immediately began wandering: riding over the rutted roads that led to the farms of New England and New York, fording the streams between the scattered settlements of Ohio and Kentucky, knocking the dust of Virginia off his clothes, stopping to talk at taverns along the roads to Philadelphia, and finally settling for a number of years as a farmer in the Hudson River valley. He published in 1783 his *Letters from an American Farmer*, asking in them the question that had so often occurred to him: "What then is the American, this new man?"

For Crèvecoeur what distinguished American society was the widespread equality of its people, especially the rural farmers. Americans were hostile to social pretensions and anything that smacked of aristocratic privilege. Furthermore, the conditions of the country promoted equality. Land was abundant and widely distributed, citizens lived decently, and the population was not divided into the wealthy few and the desperate many. (Like most of his contemporaries, Crèvecoeur glided rather quickly over the plight of black slaves.) "We are the most perfect society now existing in the world," he boasted.

Equality

°Because the 1790 census did not include significant data on the black population, many of the statistical figures quoted for this era apply only to white Americans.

Work in semisubsistence rural families was done by both sexes and often involved coopera-tion among neighbors. While a woman milks the cow, a group of men assist in the difficult labor of burning felled trees and plowing a new field with an eight-ox team.

Although Crèvecoeur waxed romantic about the conditions of American life, he painted a reasonably accurate portrait of most of the interior of the northern states and the backcountry of the South. Wealth in those areas, while not distributed equally, was spread fairly broadly. And subsistence remained the goal of most white families. "The great effort was for every farmer to produce anything he required within his own family," one European visitor noted. In such an economy women played a key role. Wives and daughters had to be skilled in making articles such as candles, soap, clothing, and hats, since the cost of buying such items was steep.

Barter economy   With labor scarce and expensive, farmers also depended on the help of their neighbors in clearing fields, building homes, and harvesting crops. If a farm family produced a small surplus, they usually exchanged it locally rather than selling it for cash in a distant market. In this barter economy money was seldom seen and was used primarily to pay taxes and purchase imported goods. "Instead of money going inces-santly backwards and forwards into the same hands," a French traveler recorded, res-idents in the countryside "supply their needs . . . by direct reciprocal exchanges. . . . They write down what they give and receive on both sides and at the end of the year they settle a large variety of exchanges with a very small quantity of coin."

Indian economies were also based primarily on subsistence. In the division of labor women raised crops, while men fished or hunted—not only for meat but also for skins to make clothing. Indians did not domesticate cattle, sheep, or pigs, but they managed and "harvested" deer by burning the surrounding forests once or twice a year to produce an environment free of underbrush, full of large, well-spaced trees and open meadows. Because Indians followed game more seasonally than white set-tlers, their villages were moved to several different locations over the course of a year. But both whites and Indians in a semisubsistence economy moved periodically to new fields after the old ones were exhausted. Indians consumed more firewood than whites and were forced to relocate villages near new supplies of timber. But they exhausted agricultural lands less quickly because they planted beans, corn, and squash in the same field, a technique that better conserved soil nutrients.

Despite the popular image of both the independent "noble savage" and the self-reliant yeoman farmer, virtually no one in the backcountry operated within a truly subsistence economy. While farmers tried to grow most of the food their families ate, they normally bought salt, sugar, and coffee, and they often traded with their neighbors for food and other items. In addition, necessities such as iron, glass, lead, and gunpowder had to be purchased, usually at a country store, and many farmers hired artisans to make items such as shoes and to weave cloth. Similarly, Indians quickly became enmeshed in the wider world of European commerce, exchanging furs for iron tools or clothing and ornamental materials.

The Commercial Economy of Franklin's America

Outside the backcountry, Americans were tied much more closely to a commercial economy. Here, merchants, artisans, and even farmers did not subsist on what they produced but instead sold goods or services in a wider market and lived on their earnings. Cities and towns, of course, played a key part in the commercial economy. But so did the agricultural regions near the seaboard and along navigable rivers.

For commerce to flourish, goods had to move from producers to market cheaply enough to reap profits. Water offered the only cost-effective transportation over any distance; indeed, it cost as much to ship goods a mere 30 miles over primitive roads as to ship by boat 3000 miles across the Atlantic to London. Cost-effective transportation was available to the planters of the Tidewater South, and city merchants used their access to the sea to establish trading ties to the West Indies and Europe. But urban artisans and workers were also linked to this market economy, as were many farm families in the Hudson valley, southeastern Pennsylvania, and southern New England. Where transportation was limited or prohibitively expensive, farmers had no incentive to increase production, and an economy of barter and semisubsistence persisted.

Commercial society differed from Crèvecoeur's world in another important way: its wealth was less equally distributed. By 1790, the richest 10 percent of those living in cities and in the plantation districts of the Tidewater South owned about 50 percent of the wealth. In the backcountry the top 10 percent was likely to own 25 to 35 percent of the wealth. *Inequality of wealth*

Crèvecoeur argued that the American belief in equality sustained this society of small farm families, bound together in a community of relative equals. But he failed to see how much that equality rested on isolation. Without access to market, one could aspire only so high. Where the market economy operated more fully, however, Americans were more acquisitive and materialistic. Europeans were struck by Americans' desire for wealth. "Man here weighs everything, calculates everything, and sacrifices everything to his interest," one foreign visitor reported. Although semisubsistence farm families were eager to rise in life and acquire material goods, only those in the commercial economy could realistically pursue these dreams.

The man who gained international renown as a self-made citizen of commercial America was Benjamin Franklin. In his writings and in the example of his own life, *Commercial values*

SEMISUBSISTENCE AND COMMERCIAL AMERICA, 1790
To prosper, a commercial economy demanded relatively cheap transportation to move goods. Thus in 1790 American commerce was confined largely to settled areas along the coast and to navigable rivers below the fall line. Since commerce depended on an efficient flow of information and goods, newspapers flourished in these areas.

Franklin offered a vision of the new nation that contrasted with Crèvecoeur's ideal of a subsistence America. He had arrived in Philadelphia as a runaway apprentice who by hard work and talent rose to be one of the leading citizens of his adopted city. The preface to Franklin's popular *Poor Richard's Almanack*, as well as his countless essays, spelled out simple maxims for Americans seeking the upward path. "The way to wealth is as plain as the way to market," he noted. "It depends chiefly on two words, industry and frugality." Those anxious to succeed should "remember that time is money." The kind of success he preached depended on taking advantage of commerce and a wider market. As a printer, Franklin was able to lead a life of acquisition and social mobility because he could distribute his almanacs and newspapers to ever-greater audiences.

The ethics of Franklin's marketplace, which looked forward to the opening up of opportunity in American society, threatened to destroy Crèvecoeur's egalitarian America. At the time of Franklin's death in 1790, the ideal that Crèvecoeur had so eloquently described still held sway across much of America. But the political debate of the 1790s showed clearly that Franklin's world of commerce and markets was slowly transforming the nation.

Philadelphia was the largest and most prosperous city in the country in 1789. Its growth fueled the development of commercial agriculture in the surrounding countryside, as more and more farmers hauled their surplus to town for sale in the city's busy markets. In this scene, both men and women buy fresh foods on the streets, along with Indians who also participated in the commercial economy.

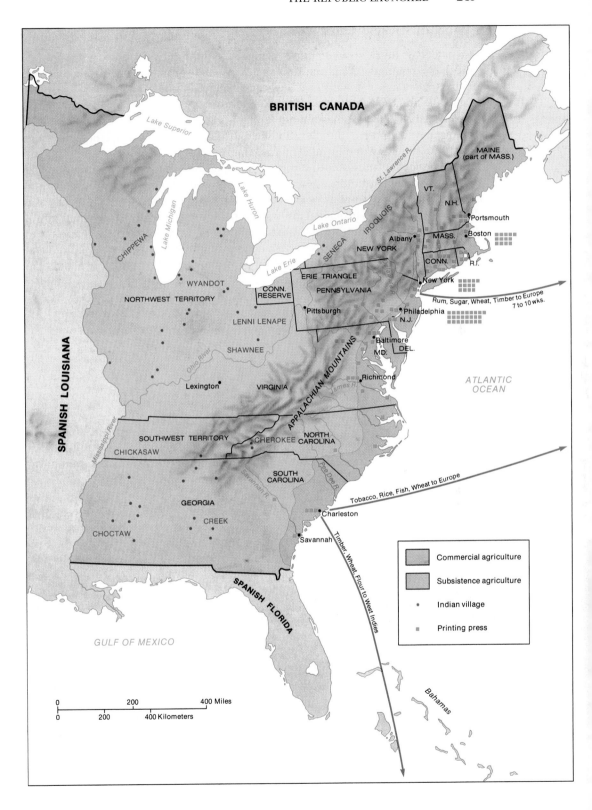

BRITISH CANADA

Lake Superior

Lake Michigan

Lake Huron

St. Lawrence R.

MAINE
(part of MASS.)

VT.

N.H.

Lake Ontario

Portsmouth

IROQUOIS

SENECA

Albany

MASS.

Boston

CHIPPEWA

Lake Erie

NEW YORK

CONN.

R.I.

WYANDOT

ERIE TRIANGLE

New York

NORTHWEST TERRITORY

CONN.
RESERVE

PENNSYLVANIA

Rum, Sugar, Wheat, Timber to Europe
7 to 10 wks.

LENNI LENAPE

Pittsburgh

Philadelphia

N.J.

SPANISH LOUISIANA

Ohio River

SHAWNEE

Baltimore

DEL.

MD.

Richmond

APPALACHIAN MOUNTAINS

James R.

ATLANTIC
OCEAN

Lexington

VIRGINIA

SOUTHWEST TERRITORY

CHEROKEE

NORTH
CAROLINA

CHICKASAW

SOUTH
CAROLINA

Pee Dee R.

Tobacco, Rice, Fish, Wheat to Europe

Mississippi River

GEORGIA

CREEK

Savannah R.

Charleston

CHOCTAW

Savannah

Timber, Wheat, Flour to West Indies

SPANISH FLORIDA

GULF OF MEXICO

Commercial agriculture

Subsistence agriculture

• Indian village

▪ Printing press

Bahamas

0   200   400 Miles

0   200   400 Kilometers

The Constitution and Commerce

In many ways the fight over ratification of the Constitution represented a struggle be-tween the commercial and the subsistence-oriented elements of American society. Urban merchants and workers as well as commercial farmers and planters generally rallied behind the Constitution. They took a broader, more cosmopolitan view of the nation's future, and they had a more favorable view of government power. Franklin, predictably, supported the Constitution. So did Madison and Washington, both planters whose wealth depended on trade and commerce.

Americans who remained a part of the semisubsistence barter economy tended to oppose the Constitution. More provincial in outlook, they feared concentrated power, were suspicious of cities and commercial institutions, opposed aristocracy and special privilege, and in general just wanted to be left alone. They were a majority of the population, but they were not easily mobilized, lacked prestigious leaders, and did not have the access to communication that their opponents enjoyed. In defeat they remained suspicious that a powerful government would tax them to benefit the commercial sectors of the economy.

And so in 1789 the United States embarked on its new national course, with two rival visions of the direction that the fledgling Republic should take. Which vision would prevail—a question that was as much social as it was political—increasingly di-vided the generation of revolutionary leaders during the 1790s.

THE NEW GOVERNMENT

Whatever the Republic was to become, Americans agreed that George Washington personified it. When the first Electoral College cast its votes, Washington was unan-imously elected, the only president in history so honored. John Adams became vice president.

Failure of past republics

The Federalists—supporters of the Constitution—called the new government "the great experiment." They were intensely aware that throughout history demo-cratic republics had in the end degenerated into quarreling factions, as with the city-states of ancient Greece, or ushered in dictatorships, as had happened in Cromwell's England. No republic—not England, or Rome, or the Swiss city-states—had stretched over a territory as large as the United States. Loyalty to the new Republic, with its untried form of government and diversity of peoples and interests, rested to a great degree on the trust and respect Americans gave Washington.

Washington's Character

Time has transformed Washington from a man into a monument: remote and unknow-able, stiff, unbowing, impenetrable. Even during his own life, he had no close friends in public life and discouraged familiarity. "I could never be on familiar terms with the General — a man so cold, so cautious," one foreigner testified after visiting Mount Vernon. He learned with age to control his temper and tried to endure criticism pa-tiently, yet he bitterly resented it. In an age of brilliant political thinkers, Washington

Washington's trip from Virginia to New York City to assume the presidency was a triumphant procession as Americans enthusiastically greeted him with cheers and even flowers strewn along his path. In New York harbor Washington traveled in a festively decorated barge, manned by 13 pilots dressed in white, as ships with flags and banners flying fired a salute in the background.

was intellectually cautious and deliberate. As president he usually asked for written advice and made his decision only after weighing the options carefully.

The president also provoked criticism by the pomp with which he conducted the government. Washington, who was one of the richest men in America, enjoyed the luxuries that wealth brought. Critics complained about his formal public receptions, the large number of servants, and the coach emblazoned with his coat of arms—all aristocratic habits. Still, as much as Washington craved honor and military fame, he did not hunger for power and accepted the office of the presidency only reluctantly.

Organizing the Government

Washington realized that as the first occupant of the executive office, everything he did was fraught with significance. "I walk on untrodden ground," he commented. "There is scarcely any part of my conduct which may not hereafter be drawn into precedent."

The Constitution made no mention of a cabinet. Yet the drafters of the Constitution, aware of the experience of the Continental Congress under the Articles of Confederation, clearly assumed that the president would have some system of advisers. Congress authorized the creation of four departments—War, Treasury, State, and Attorney General—whose heads were to be appointed with the consent of the

The cabinet

Senate. Washington's most important choices were Alexander Hamilton as secretary of the treasury and Thomas Jefferson to head the State Department. At first the president did not meet regularly with his advisers as a group, but the idea of a cabinet that met to discuss policy matters eventually evolved. Washington gradually excluded Adams from cabinet discussions, and any meaningful role for the vice president, whose duties were largely undefined by the Constitution, soon disappeared.

Federal judiciary   The Constitution created a federal Supreme Court but beyond that was silent about the court system. The Judiciary Act of 1789 set the size of the Supreme Court at 6 members; it also established 13 federal district courts and 3 circuit courts of appeal. Supreme Court justices spent much of their time serving on these circuit courts, a distasteful duty whose long hours "riding the circuit" caused one justice to grumble that Congress had made him a "traveling postboy." The Judiciary Act made it clear that federal courts had the right to review decisions of the state courts and specified cases over which the Supreme Court would have original jurisdiction. Washington appointed John Jay of New York, a staunch Federalist, as the first chief justice.

The Bill of Rights

Congress also confronted the demand for a bill of rights, which had become an issue during the debate over ratification. At that time, nearly 200 amendments had been put forward in one form or another. Supporters of the Constitution were particularly alarmed over proposals to restrict the federal power to tax. As leader of the Federalist forces in the House of Representatives, James Madison moved to head off any large-scale changes that would weaken federal power by submitting a bill of rights that focused on civil liberties.

Ultimately Congress sent 12 amendments to the states. By December 1791, 10 had been ratified and incorporated into the Constitution.° Their passage by Congress helped persuade North Carolina (1789) and Rhode Island (1790), the two holdouts, to join the Union. At the same time, the advocates of strong federal power, like Hamilton, were relieved that "the structure of the government, and the mass and distribution of its powers," remained unchanged.

Protected rights   These first 10 amendments, known as the Bill of Rights, were destined to be of crucial importance in defining personal liberty in the United States. Among the rights guaranteed were freedom of religion, the press, and speech, as well as the right to assemble and petition and the right to bear arms. The amendments also established clear procedural safeguards, including the right to a trial by jury and protection against illegal searches and seizures. They prohibited excessive bail, cruel and unusual punishment, and the quartering of troops in private homes. The last two amendments were intended to calm fears about the federal government having unlimited power. Madison was careful, however, to phrase these particular amendments in very general terms. At the same time, an attempt in Congress to apply these same guarantees to state governments failed, and almost a century would pass before Congress moved, during Reconstruction, to prevent states from interfering with certain basic rights.

°Of the two proposed amendments that were not initially approved, one was ratified in 1992 as the Twenty-seventh Amendment. It stipulates that there must be an intervening election before a congressional pay raise goes into effect.

Hamilton's Financial Program

Before adjourning, Congress called on Alexander Hamilton, as secretary of the treasury, to prepare a report on the nation's finances. Hamilton undertook the assignment eagerly, for he did not intend to be a minor figure in the new administration.

Hamilton never forgot that he was a self-made man. He grew up on the islands of the West Indies, scarred by the stigmas of poverty and illegitimacy. To compensate, he was driven constantly to seek respectability and money. He served as a military aide to Washington during the Revolution, and marriage to the daughter of a wealthy New York politician gave him influential connections he could draw on in his political career. Nevertheless, his haughty manner, jealousy, and penchant for intrigue made him many enemies. He was a brilliant thinker, yet he felt out of place in the increasingly democratic society emerging around him. "All communities divide themselves into the few and the many," he declared. "The first are rich and wellborn, the other the mass of the people. . . . The people are turbulent and changing; they seldom judge or determine right." *Hamilton's character*

While Hamilton was not a monarchist, his experience in the army, which impressed on him the necessity of a vigorous government, made him more inclined to use force than most of his colleagues. Convinced that human nature was fundamentally selfish, Hamilton believed that the government needed to appeal to the self-interest of the rich and wellborn in order to succeed. "Men," he observed succinctly, "will naturally go to those who pay them best." He took as his model Great Britain, whose greatness he attributed to its system of public finance and its preeminence in commerce and manufacturing. Thus Hamilton set out to achieve two goals. He intended to use federal power to encourage manufacturing and commerce in order to make the United States economically strong and independent of Europe. And he was determined to link the interests of the wealthy with those of the new government.

Neither goal could be achieved until the federal government solved its two most pressing financial problems: revenue and credit. Without revenue it could not be effective. Without credit—the faith of merchants and other nations that the government would repay its debts—it would lack the ability to borrow. Hamilton proposed that all $52 million of the federal debt be paid in full (or funded). He also recommended that the federal government assume responsibility for the remaining $25 million in debts that individual states owed. He intended with these twin policies to put the new federal government on a sound financial footing and enhance its power by increasing its need for revenue and making the wealthy look to the national government, not the states. Hamilton also proposed a series of excise taxes, including a controversial 25 percent levy on whiskey, to help meet government expenses. *Funding and assumption*

After heated debate, Congress deadlocked over funding and assumption. Finally, over dinner with Hamilton, Jefferson and Madison of Virginia agreed to support his proposal if, after 10 years in Philadelphia, the permanent seat of government was located in the South, on the Potomac River between Virginia and Maryland. Aided by this understanding, funding and assumption passed Congress. In 1791 Congress also approved a 20-year charter for the first Bank of the United States. The bank would hold government deposits and issue banknotes that would be received in payment of all debts owed the federal government. Congress proved less receptive to the rest of Hamilton's program, although a limited tariff to encourage manufacturing and several excise taxes, including the one on whiskey, won approval. *Location of the capital*

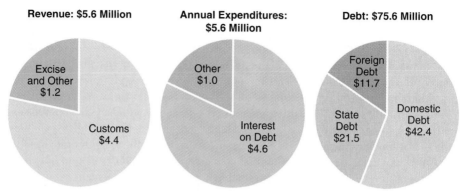

HAMILTON'S FINANCIAL SYSTEM
Under Hamilton's financial system, over 80 percent of federal revenues went to pay the interest on the national debt. Note that most of the revenue came from tariff duties.

Opposition to Hamilton's Program

The passage of Hamilton's program caused a permanent rupture among supporters of the Constitution. Madison, who had collaborated closely with Hamilton in the 1780s, broke with his former ally over funding and assumption. Jefferson finally went over to the opposition when Hamilton announced plans for a national bank. Eventually the two warring factions organized themselves into political parties: the Republicans, led by Jefferson and Madison, and the Federalists, led by Hamilton and Adams.° But the division emerged slowly over several years.

Fears of a financial aristocracy

Hamilton's program promoted the commercial sector at the expense of semi-subsistence farmers. Thus it rekindled many of the concerns that had surfaced during the struggle over ratification of the Constitution. The ideology of the Revolution had stressed that republics inevitably contained groups who sought power in order to destroy popular liberties and overthrow the republic. To some Americans, Hamilton's program seemed a clear threat to establish a privileged and powerful financial aristocracy—perhaps even a monarchy.

Who, after all, would benefit from the funding proposal? During and after the Revolution, the value of notes issued by the Continental Congress dropped sharply. Speculators had bought up most of these notes for a fraction of their face value from small farmers and workers. If the government ultimately redeemed the debt, speculators would profit accordingly. Equally disturbing, members of Congress had been purchasing the notes before the adoption of Hamilton's program. Nearly half of the members of the House owned U.S. securities. Madison urged that only the original holders of the debt be reimbursed in full, but Hamilton rejected this idea, since commercial speculators were precisely the class of people he hoped to bind to the new government.

Similarly, when stock in the Bank of the United States went on sale, speculators snapped up all the shares in an hour. The price of a share skyrocketed from $25 to

---

°The Republican party of the 1790s, sometimes referred to as the Jeffersonian Republicans, is not to be confused with the modern-day Republican party, which originated in the 1850s.

A study in contrasts, Jefferson and Hamilton increasingly came into conflict in Washington's administration. Despite his aristocratic upbringing, Jefferson (left) was awkward, loose-jointed, reserved, and ill-at-ease in public. Testifying before a congressional committee, he casually lounged in a chair and spoke in a rambling, nonstop manner. "Yet he scattered information wherever he went," conceded Senator Maclay of Pennsylvania, "and some even brilliant sentiments sparkled from him." Hamilton, though short of stature, cut a dashing figure with his erect bearing, strutting manner, meticulous dress, and carefully powdered hair. Declared the wife of the British ambassador: "I have scarcely ever been more charmed with the vivacity and conversation of any man."

$300 in two months. Jefferson was appalled by the mania Hamilton's program encouraged. "The spirit of gambling, once it has seized a subject, is incurable," he asserted. "The taylor who has made thousands in one day, tho he has lost them the next, can never again be content with the slow and moderate earnings of his needle."

The national bank struck its critics as a dangerous mimicking of English corruption. Indeed, in Great Britain the Bank of England played a powerful role. Its investments not only helped fuel the economy, its loans to many members of Parliament gave it great political influence. Jefferson warned that the same thing would happen in the United States. English-style corruption seemed to be taking root as "paper men" became rich not by producing anything substantial with their own hard work but by shuffling paper, trading notes, and benefiting from the financial legislation they themselves passed. These fears were heightened because Americans

System of corruption

had little experience with banks: only three existed in the country when the Bank of the United States was chartered. One member of Congress expressed a common attitude when he said that he would no more be caught entering a bank than a house of prostitution.

Then, too, banks and commerce were a part of the urban environment that rural Americans so distrusted. Although Hamilton's opponents generally granted that a certain amount of commerce was necessary, they believed that it should remain subordinate. Hamilton's program, in contrast, encouraged manufacturing and urbanization, developments that history had shown to be incompatible with liberty and equality. Moreover, the tariff favored one group in society—manufacturers—at the expense of other groups.

After Congress approved the bank bill, Washington hesitated to sign it. When he consulted his cabinet, Jefferson stressed that the Constitution did not specifically authorize Congress to charter a bank. Both he and Madison upheld the idea of strict construction—that the Constitution should be interpreted narrowly and the federal government restricted to powers expressly delegated to it. Otherwise, the federal government would be the judge of its own powers, and there would be no safeguard against the abuse of power.

Strict construction

Hamilton countered that the Constitution contained implied as well as enumerated powers. He particularly emphasized the clause that permitted Congress to make all laws "necessary and proper" to carry out its duties. A bank would be useful in carrying out the enumerated powers of regulating commerce and maintaining the public credit; therefore, Congress had a right to decide whether to establish one. Since the Constitution could not anticipate all future developments, the government needed flexibility to meet its responsibilities. In the end Washington accepted Hamilton's forceful arguments and signed the bill.

Implied powers

The Specter of Aristocracy

The threat posed by a powerful bank heightened the fears of Hamilton's opponents that an aristocracy was developing in the United States. While Americans did not insist on an equal division of property and wealth, they were hostile to any haughtiness among the upper classes and to Europe's aristocratic traditions. Because Hamilton's program deliberately aided the rich and created a class of citizens whose wealth derived from the federal government, it strengthened these traditional fears. "Money will be put under the direction of government," charged Philip Freneau, a leading Republican editor, "and the government will be put under the direction of money."

Many who opposed Hamilton's financial program had also been against the Constitution, but leadership of the opposition fell to Jefferson and Madison, who had staunchly worked for ratification. Although Jefferson and Madison were planters, well accustomed to the workings of the marketplace, they still distrusted cities and commerce and Hamilton's aristocratic ways.

Hamilton's success

Economically Hamilton's program was a success. The government's credit was restored, and the national bank ended the inflation of the previous two decades and created a sound currency. At the same time the administration demonstrated that the federal government would not be paralyzed as it had been under the Articles. And Hamilton's theory of implied powers and broad construction gave the nation the flexibility necessary to respond to unanticipated crises.

EXPANSION AND TURMOIL IN THE WEST

In the peace treaty of 1783, Britain ceded to the United States the territory between the Appalachian Mountains and the Mississippi River. Even so, British troops continued to hold the forts in the Northwest and Indian tribes controlled most of this region. To demonstrate the government's effectiveness, Washington moved to extend control over the West.

The Resistance of the Miamis

In principle, the United States recognized the rights of Indians to their lands. Furthermore, it had promised that any purchase of Indian land would be made only by treaty and not through private purchases by land companies and individual settlers. Nevertheless, the government was determined to buy out Indian titles in order to promote white settlement.

By 1790 the United States had negotiated purchase of Indian lands in most of Kentucky and about one-quarter of Tennessee. North of the Ohio, however, the Miami Confederacy (composed of eight western tribes headed by the Miami) stoutly refused to sell territory and soundly defeated two American military expeditions. In response, Washington dispatched an army of 2000, commanded by "Mad Anthony" Wayne, an accomplished general and hero of the Revolution, to the Ohio Valley. At the Battle of Fallen Timbers in August 1794 Wayne won a decisive victory, breaking the Indians' hold on the Northwest. In the Treaty of Greenville (1795), he forced the tribes to cede the southern two-thirds of the area between Lake Erie and the Ohio River, thus opening up the Northwest to white settlement. *Treaty of Greenville*

The Whiskey Rebellion

Westerners approved of the administration's military policy against the Indians. They were far less pleased that in 1791 Congress had passed a new excise tax on distilled liquors. In the barter economy west of the Appalachians, barrels of whiskey were sometimes used as currency. Furthermore, about the only way farmers could profitably export surplus grain was to distill it and bring the liquor to market. So the whiskey tax brought the question of federal power quite directly to the attention of the ordinary citizen.

The West during the 1790s was a society in turmoil. Most property owners along the frontier found it hard to make ends meet. In response, a number were forced to sell their land and fell into the ranks of tenant farmers. Thus wealth became more concentrated in the hands of fewer individuals. While the whiskey tax was unpopular in many rural areas, frontier settlers resisted most fiercely, since for them the sale of whiskey made the greatest difference in providing a bit of extra income. Tenant farmers protested loudly too, resenting the more commercially minded larger landowners of their region. Many of these poor farmers turned out at mass meetings to condemn the tax and protest against having to support government officials and the burdensome national debt. Beset by economic dislocation, they directed their resentment not just at the authorities but also at wealthy landowners and merchants. *Western society*

Farmers in the western districts of several states defied federal officials and refused to pay, launching a "whiskey rebellion." The greatest unrest flared in western Pennsylvania, where General Neville was burned out of his home (page 237). That summer an even larger gathering of impoverished farmers threatened to march on Pittsburgh. For rural residents, the city had become a symbol of the corrupt cosmopolitan influences that threatened their liberty. Many in the crowd relished the idea of looting the property of wealthy residents. "I have a bad hat now, but I expect to have a better one soon," shouted one of the mob.

Collapse of resistance

To distant easterners, the Whiskey Rebellion at first appeared serious. Hamilton, who had pushed the whiskey tax in order to demonstrate the power of the new government, saw the matter as a question of authority. "Shall there be government, or no government?" he asked. An alarmed Washington led an army of 13,000 men—larger than he had commanded at Yorktown—into the Pennsylvania countryside to overawe the populace and subdue the rebels. Hamilton soon took charge, but to his disappointment the troops met no organized resistance. "An insurrection was announced and proclaimed and armed against," Jefferson scoffed, "but could never be found." Even some of Hamilton's allies conceded that he had overreacted. "Elective rulers can scarcely ever employ the physical force of a democracy," one remarked, "without turning the moral force, or the power of public opinion, against the government."

Pinckney's Treaty

Navigation of the Mississippi

Western unhappiness was also eased somewhat when Washington sent Thomas Pinckney to negotiate a treaty with Spain. That nation still controlled Florida and the mouth of the Mississippi and had never agreed to a northern boundary between its possessions and the United States. Pinckney's Treaty, which the Senate unanimously ratified in 1796, set the 31st parallel as the southern boundary of the United States and granted Americans free navigation of the Mississippi, with the right to deposit goods at New Orleans for reshipment to ports in the East and abroad. No longer could Spain try to detach the western settlements from American control by promising to open the Mississippi to their trade.

THE EMERGENCE OF POLITICAL PARTIES

Members of the Revolutionary generation fervently hoped that political parties would not take root in the United States. "If I could not go to heaven but with a party, I would not go at all," remarked Jefferson. Influenced by radical English republican thought, American critics condemned parties as narrow interest groups that routinely placed selfishness and party loyalty above a concern for the public good. In fact, many members of Britain's Parliament did in effect sell their votes in return for offices, pensions, and profitable contracts. Yet despite Americans' distrust of such institutions, the United States became the first nation to establish truly popular parties.

Social conditions and parties

Social conditions encouraged the rise of parties. Because property ownership was widespread, the nation had a broad suffrage. Furthermore, during the Revolution legislatures lowered property requirements in many states, increasing the number of voters still further. If party members hoped to hold office, they had to offer a program attractive to the broader voting public. When parties acted as representatives of economic and social interest groups, they became one means by which a large electorate could make its feelings known. In addition, the United States had the highest literacy rate in the world and the largest number of newspapers, further encouraging political interest and participation. Finally, the fact that well-known patriots of the Revolution headed both the Federalists and the Republicans helped defuse the charge that either party was hostile to the Revolution or the Constitution.

The French Revolution

While domestic issues at first split the supporters of the Constitution, a crisis in Europe propelled Americans further toward political parties. When the French Revolution began in 1789, Americans hailed it as the first stirring of liberty on the European continent. Each new ship from overseas brought exciting news: the Bastille prison had been stormed in July; the new National Assembly had abolished feudal privileges and adopted the Declaration of the Rights of Man. France seemed on the way to establishing its own just society.

By 1793, however, enthusiasm for the French Revolution began to cool when radical elements instituted a reign of terror, executing the king and queen and many of the nobility. The French republic even outlawed Christianity and substituted the worship of Reason. Finally in 1793 republican France and monarchical England went to war. Americans were deeply divided over whether the United States should continue its old alliance with France or support Great Britain.

Hamilton and his allies viewed the French Revolution as sheer anarchy. Its leaders seemed to be destroying the very institutions that held civilization together: the church, social classes, property, law and order. The United States, Hamilton argued, should renounce the 1778 treaty of alliance with France and side with Britain. "Behold France, an open hell," warned Fisher Ames, a member of Congress from Massachusetts, ". . . still smoking with suffering and crimes, in which we see perhaps our future state." For Jefferson and his followers, the issue was republicanism versus monarchy. France was a sister republic, and despite deplorable excesses, its revolution was spreading the doctrine of liberty. Britain remained repressive and corrupt, presided over by the same tyrannical king who had made war on the colonies. Jefferson argued that the United States should maintain its treaty of alliance with France and insist that as neutrals, Americans had every right to trade with France as much as with England.

Differing views of the Revolution

As tempers flared, each faction suspected the worst of the other. To the Jeffersonians, Hamilton and his friends seemed part of a monarchist conspiracy. "The ultimate object of all this," Jefferson said of Hamilton's policies, "is to prepare the way for a change, from the present republican forms of Government, to that of a monarchy." As for the Hamiltonians, they viewed Jefferson and his faction as disciples of French radicals, conspiring to establish mob rule in the United States. Years later, when calm reflection was possible, John Adams conceded that both parties had "excited artificial terrors." But during the 1790s, each side believed that the destiny of the American republic was threatened by events abroad.

Washington's Neutral Course

Washington, for his part, was convinced that in order to prosper, the United States must remain independent of Europe and its unending quarrels and wars. Thus the president issued a proclamation of American neutrality and tempered Jefferson's efforts to support France.

Neutral rights   Under international law, neutrals could trade with belligerents—nations at war—so long as the trade had existed before the outbreak of hostilities and did not involve war supplies. But both France and Great Britain refused to respect the rights of neutrals in the midst of their desperate struggle. They began intercepting American ships and confiscating cargoes. In addition, Britain, which badly needed manpower to maintain its powerful navy, impressed into service American sailors it suspected of being British subjects. Despite these abuses, Hamilton continued to support a friendly policy toward Britain. He recognized, as did Washington, that the United States was not strong enough to challenge Britain militarily.

Moreover, Hamilton's domestic program depended on trade with the British, who purchased 75 percent of America's exports (mostly foodstuffs and naval supplies), as well as provided 90 percent of imports. With Europe torn by war, the demand for American grains rose sharply, driving up the price on the world market. During the decade, American exports nearly quadrupled, and American ships almost completely took over the carrying trade between the United States and Europe. All parts of the commercial economy shared in this unprecedented prosperity, not only merchants but also urban workers and businessmen, sailors, the shipbuilding industry, and farmers who sold their surplus at high prices.

In addition to violating neutral rights and impressment, Great Britain continued to maintain the western forts it had promised to evacuate in 1783, and it closed the West Indies, a traditional source of trade, to American ships. Washington sent John Jay to Britain as a special minister to negotiate the differences between the two coun-

Jay's Treaty   tries. In the end, Jay persuaded the British only to withdraw their troops from the Northwest. The West Indies remained closed to American shipping. In essence, Jay's Treaty reinforced the United States' position as an economic satellite of Britain. Only reluctantly did Washington submit it to the Senate.

The treaty debate was extremely bitter. Republicans denounced Jay and hanged him in effigy while a mob stoned Hamilton in the streets. In June 1795 the Senate finally approved Jay's Treaty by a vote of 20 to 10, the bare two-thirds margin required.

The Federalists and Republicans Organize

Thus events in Europe contributed directly to the rise of parties in the United States by stimulating fears over the course of American development. The war, Jefferson commented, "kindled and brought forward the two parties with an ardour which our own interests merely, could never excite." By the mid-1790s both sides were organizing on a national basis. Hamilton took the lead in coordinating the Federalist party, which grew out of the voting bloc in Congress that enacted his economic program. Increasingly, Washington drew closer to Federalist advisers and policies and became the symbol of the party, although he clung to the vision of a nonpartisan administration and never recognized the extent to which he had become a party leader.

The guiding genius of the opposition movement was Hamilton's onetime col-

Silhouette of Washington, 1795

league James Madison. Jefferson, who resigned as secretary of state at the end of 1793, became the symbolic head of the party, much as Washington headed the Federalists. Unconvinced of the wisdom and necessity of such a party, he was reluctant to lead it. But Madison acted more vigorously, conferring over strategy and lining up the Republican voting bloc in the House. The disputes over Jay's Treaty and the whiskey tax in 1794 and 1795 gave the Republicans popular issues, and they began organizing on the state and local levels. Unlike the Federalists, who cloaked themselves in Washington's mantle and claimed to uphold the government and the Constitution, the Republicans had to overcome the ingrained idea that an opposition party was seditious and therefore illegitimate. Because of broad support for the Constitution, Republican leaders had to be careful to distinguish between opposing the administration and opposing the Constitution. Indeed, it was by no means clear that an opposition party could arise without threatening the government itself.

Organization of an opposition party

As more and more members of Congress allied themselves with one faction or the other, voting became increasingly partisan. In the first two Congresses, party votes occurred mostly on Hamilton's economic program and organization of the government. In the third and fourth Congresses, party questions included foreign affairs and domestic issues, such as the Whiskey Rebellion. By 1796 even minor matters were decided by partisan votes. Gradually, party organization filtered downward to local communities.

Typifying the rising party spirit of the 1790s, this anti-Republican cartoon portrays Washington with American troops repulsing an invasion of bloodthirsty French radicals. Jefferson attempts to hold his chariot back, while a dog (presumably an ardent Federalist) sprays a Republican newspaper. This cartoon appealed to American nationalism by linking the opposition with foreign influence and disloyalty.

The 1796 Election

As long as Washington remained head of the Federalists, they enjoyed an insurmountable advantage. But in 1796 the weary president, stung by the abuse heaped on him by the opposition press, announced he would not accept a third term, thereby setting a two-term precedent that other presidents would follow until Franklin Roosevelt. In his Farewell Address Washington warned against the dangers of parties and urged a return to the earlier nonpartisan system. But that vision had become obsolete. Parties were an effective way of expressing the interests of different social and economic groups within the nation. When the Republicans chose Thomas Jefferson to oppose John Adams, the possibility of a nonparty constitutional system ended.

The framers of the Constitution did not anticipate that political parties would run competing candidates for both the presidency and the vice presidency. Thus they provided that, of those running for president, the candidate with the most electoral votes would win and the second highest would become vice president. But Hamilton strongly disliked both Adams and Jefferson. Ever the intriguer, he tried to manipulate the electoral vote so that the Federalist vice-presidential candidate, Thomas Pinckney of South Carolina, would be elected president. In the ensuing confusion, Adams won with 71 electoral votes, and his rival, Jefferson, gained the vice presidency with 68 votes.

Support for the two parties The fault line between the two parties reflected basic divisions in American life. Geographically, the Federalists were strongest in New England, with its commercial ties to Great Britain and its powerful tradition of hierarchy and order. Moving farther south, the party became progressively weaker. Of the southernmost states, the Federalists enjoyed significant strength only in aristocratic South Carolina. The Republicans won solid support in semisubsistence areas like the West, where Crèvecoeur's farmers were only weakly involved with commerce. The middle states were closely contested, although the most cosmopolitan and commercially oriented elements remained the core of Federalist strength.

The Republicans won over most of the old Anti-Federalist opponents of the Constitution, as well as a number of Americans who had firmly backed the new union. These supporters included some commercial farmers in the North and planters in the South and, increasingly, urban workers and small shopkeepers who were repelled by the aristocratic tone of the Federalists. The Republicans were often led by ambitious men of new wealth who felt excluded by the entrenched Federalist elite. For similar reasons Jefferson attracted the support of immigrants from France and Ireland, who felt culturally excluded, as well as members of religious sects such as the Baptists and Methodists, who resented the power and privileges of New England's established Congregational church.

Federalist and Republican Ideologies

In different ways, each party looked both forward and backward: toward certain traditions of the past as well as toward newer social currents that would shape America in the nineteenth century.

Federalist ideas Most Federalists viewed themselves as a kind of natural aristocracy making a last desperate stand against the excesses of democracy. They clung to the notion that the upper class should rule over its social and economic inferiors. In supporting the established social order, most Federalists opposed unbridled individualism. They believed that society's needs were more important than the individual's. In their view, government should regulate individual behavior for the good of society and protect property from the violent and unruly. Pessimistic about human nature, Federalists were almost obsessed by fear of the "mob." In a republic, they argued, government had to restrain popular power.

Although the Federalists resolutely opposed the rising tide of democracy and individualism, they were remarkably forward-looking in their economic ideas. They sensed that the United States would become the major economic and military power of their vision only by prospering through commerce and economic development. To that end, they argued, the government ought to use its power actively, to encourage the growth of commerce and manufacturing.

The Republicans, in contrast, looked backward to the traditional Revolutionary fear that government power threatened liberty. Over and over Republicans emphasized the threat of corruption. The Treasury, they warned, was corrupting Congress, the army would enslave the people, and broad construction of the Constitution would make the federal government all-powerful. To them, Federalist attitudes and policies illustrated the corruption eating away at American morals, just as England had become corrupt before 1776. *Republican ideas*

Nor did their economic ideals anticipate future American development. For Republicans, agriculture and not commerce stood as the centerpiece of American liberty and virtue. To be sure, leaders like Jefferson and Madison recognized that some commercial activity was necessary, especially to sell America's agricultural surplus abroad. But Jefferson and his followers believed that republican values would be preserved only by limiting commerce and promoting household manufacturing instead of industry. Furthermore, Republicans failed to appreciate the role of financial institutions in promoting economic development. Instead, Republicans focused on the abuses of "paper wealth" and those who manipulated it—speculators, bank directors, and holders of the public debt. Economically, they rejected the forward-looking ideals of urban commerce and industry that would dominate American society in the nineteenth century.

On the other hand, the Jeffersonians were more farsighted in matters of equality and personal liberty. Their faith in the people put them in tune with the emerging egalitarian temper of society. Eagerly they embraced the virtues of individualism, hoping to reduce government to the bare essentials in order to free individuals to develop their potential without interference. And they looked to the West—the land of small farms and a more equal society—as the means to preserve opportunity and American values.

Historians have offered varying interpretations of the conflict between the Federalist and Republican parties in the 1790s. Some paint the conflict as a clash between aristocracy and democracy. The Federalists, in their view, at bottom tried to create and sustain an American aristocracy that combined social, economic, and political prestige and thus were hostile to the mass of Americans. The Jeffersonians, in contrast, represented the democratic impulses in the country and thus enjoyed far wider popular support. **COUNTERPOINT** *Key differences between Republicans and Federalists*

Despite its wide appeal, this interpretation overlooks the fact that the leaders of both parties were hardly ordinary citizens but instead men of great wealth and privilege. Moreover, Jefferson's party was especially strong in the more aristocratic South. Indeed, his victory in 1800 depended on the three-fifths clause, which increased the South's electoral votes by counting slaves in apportioning representation in the House of Representatives. Without the additional representation that slavery gave the southern states, John Adams, the supposedly aristocratic candidate, would have won.

Other historians trace party divisions back to the republican ideology of the Revolution. In their view, both parties favored republican government, but they held quite different views of the relationship between economic growth and republicanism. The Jeffersonians upheld the traditional attitude that republicanism rested on public virtue and that wealth, luxury, idleness, and speculation would undermine the moral fiber of the people and thus destroy the Republic. The Federalists also wanted a government elected by and responsible to the people. But to them commerce was not a threat to the Republic but the means to strengthen it, by stimulating Americans to think nationally rather than locally. Thus the two parties differed not over republican institutions but over the role commerce should play in a republic.

THE PRESIDENCY OF JOHN ADAMS

As president, John Adams became the nominal head of the Federalists. In many ways, though, he was out of step with his party. Unlike Hamilton, Adams felt no pressing need to aid the wealthy, nor was he fully committed to Hamilton's commercial–industrial vision. As a crusty revolutionary leader who in the 1780s had served as American minister to England, Adams also opposed any alliance with Britain.

Increasingly Adams and Hamilton clashed over policies and party leadership. Part of the problem stemmed from personalities. Adams was so abrasive and thin-skinned, it was difficult for anyone to get along with him, and Hamilton's intrigues in the 1796 election had not improved relations between the two men. Although Hamilton had resigned from the Treasury Department in 1795, key members of Adams's cabinet regularly turned to the former secretary for advice. Indeed, they opposed Adams so often that the frustrated president sometimes dealt with them, according to Jefferson, "by dashing and trampling his wig on the floor." The feud between the two rivals did not bode well for the Federalist party.

The Quasi-War with France

Adams began his term trying to balance relations with both Great Britain and France. Since the terms of Jay's Treaty had been so favorable to the British, the French in retaliation set their navy and privateers to raiding American shipping. To resolve the conflict, Adams dispatched three envoys to France in 1797, but the French foreign minister demanded a bribe before negotiations could even begin. The American representatives refused, and when news of these discussions became public, it was known as the XYZ Affair (because in the official documents the Adams administration substituted the letters X, Y, and Z for the names of the French officials involved). A tremendous outcry ensued.

XYZ Affair

Confronted with such deeply felt anger, Federalist leaders saw a chance to retain power by exploiting the national emergency and going to war with France. With war fever running high, Congress in 1798 repudiated the French treaty of 1778 and enlarged the army and navy. Republicans suspected that the real purpose of the army was not to fight the French army—none existed in North America—but to crush the opposition party and establish a military despotism. All that remained was for Adams to whip up popular feeling and lead the nation into war.

But Adams hesitated, afraid he would become a scapegoat if his policies failed. Furthermore, he distrusted standing armies and preferred the navy as the nation's primary defense. So an unofficial naval war broke out—the so-called Quasi-War—as ships in each navy openly and freely raided the fleets of the other, while Britain continued to impress American sailors and seize ships suspected of trading with France. *The Quasi-War*

Eager for war, Hamilton dreamed of using the army to seize Louisiana and Florida from Spain, France's ally. He even toyed with provoking resistance in Virginia in order to justify suppression of the Republican party. Urging that Virginia be put "to the test of resistance," he disclosed that he was ready to use the army "to subdue a *refractory and powerful State.*" Hamilton's hotheaded behavior, however, only helped to cool Adams's willingness to go to war.

Suppression at Home

Meanwhile, Federalist leaders attempted to suppress disloyalty at home. In the summer of 1798 Congress passed several measures known together as the Alien and *Alien and Sedition Acts*

John Adams, who believed that pageantry and pomp were essential to government, aroused fears of monarchy and European corruption by proposing in 1789 that the president's title be "His Highness the President of the United States and Protector of the Rights of the Same." Of distinctly unmilitary bearing, he wore this sword at his inauguration in the vain hope that it would lend dignity. Sarcastic Republicans, noting his paunchy figure, gleefully bestowed a title of their own: "His Rotundity."

Daily Lives

POPULAR ENTERTAINMENT

Exploring the Wondrous World

In 1786 Charles Willson Peale, painter and jack-of-all-trades, opened a museum of natural history in his home on Lombard Street in Philadelphia. Americans had always been fascinated by freaks of nature and "remarkable providences" (see Daily Lives, "A World of Wonders and Witchcraft," pages 92–93). But unlike seventeenth-century colonials, Peale was not searching for signs of the supernatural in everyday life. A child of the Enlightenment, Peale intended his museum to be "a school of useful knowledge" that would attract men and women of all ages and social ranks. By studying natural history, Peale believed, citizens would gain an understanding of themselves, their country, and the world and thereby help sustain civilization in the United States. The sign over the door read, "Whoso would learn wisdom, let him enter here!"

Inside, the visitor found a wide assortment of items from around the world. Peale displayed nearly a hundred paintings he had completed of leading Americans, stuffed birds and animals, busts of famous scientists, cases of minerals, and wax figures representing the races of the world. Among the technological innovations that were showcased, a machine called a *physiognotrace* produced precise silhouettes. Moses Williams, a former slave, operated the machine and did a thriving business, selling 8880 profiles in the first year. Peale's backyard soon contained a

zoo with a bewildering assortment of animals, including two grizzly bear cubs, an eagle, numerous snakes, monkeys, and a hyena. Prominent acquaintances such as Benjamin Franklin, George Washington, and Thomas Jefferson sent specimens, and the collection eventually totaled some 100,000 items.

Peale's most famous exhibit was a skeleton of a mastodon (he misnamed it a mammoth, thereby adding a synonym for *huge* to the American vocabulary). Assembled from several digs he had conducted with great publicity in upstate New York, it stood 11 feet high at the shoulder and was the first complete mastodon skeleton ever mounted. Billed "the ninth wonder of the world," it was housed in a special "Mammoth Room" that required a separate admission fee.

In gathering and mounting his specimens, Peale sought "to bring into one view a world in miniature." He carefully labeled plants, animals, insects, and birds and arranged them according to accepted scientific classifications. He also pioneered the grouping of animals in their natural habitat. Stuffed tigers and deers stood on a plaster mountainside, while below, a glass pond was filled with fish, reptiles, and birds. For the safety of visitors who could not resist handling the exhibits, the birds, whose feathers were covered with arsenic, were eventually put in glass-fronted cases with painted habitats behind them.

Peale refused to indulge the popular

Sedition Acts. The Alien Act authorized the president to arrest and deport aliens suspected of "treasonable" leanings. Although never used, the act directly threatened nonnaturalized immigrants, many of whom were prominent Jeffersonians. To limit the number of immigrant voters—again, most of them Republicans—the Naturalization Act increased the period of residence required to become a naturalized citizen from 5 to 14 years. But the most controversial law was the Sedition Act,

Daily Lives

In this self-portrait, Charles Willson Peale lifts a curtain to reveal the famous Long Room of his museum. Partially visible on the right behind Peale is the great mastodon skeleton, at which a woman gazes in awe, while in the rear a father instructs his son on the wonders of nature.

taste for showmanship and freaks. He hesitated before accepting a five-legged cow with two tails, fearing it would lower the dignity of and compromise his institution's serious purpose. He declined to display a blue sash belonging to George Washington, since it had no educational value, and only after Peale's death was it exhibited. He put curiosities away in cabinets and showed them only on request.

Peale's museum was an expression of its founder's republican ideals of order, stability, and harmony. It was, in his mind, an institute of eternal laws, laid bare for the masses to see and understand. Peale hoped the museum would instill civic responsibility in its patrons, and he often told the story of how two hostile Indian chiefs, meeting by accident in the museum, were so impressed with its harmony that they agreed to sign a peace treaty.

The museum attracted thousands of curious customers and prospered in its early years. It was one of the major attractions in Philadelphia and became famous throughout the nation. Yet Peale's vast collection soon overwhelmed his scientific classification scheme, and his grandiose plans always outran his funds and soon his space as well. Refusing to slow his collection efforts, Peale moved his museum in 1794 to Philosophical Hall, and then in 1802 he took over the second floor of Independence Hall.

Before he retired in 1810, Peale tried vainly to interest the national government in acquiring his collection and creating a national museum. Under the direction of his son, the museum struggled on, but it was unable to satisfy the growing popular appetite for showmanship rather than education. The museum finally closed its doors in 1850, but during the Republic's formative years it offered thousands of Americans a unique opportunity, as the ticket of admission promised, to "explore the wondrous world."

which established heavy fines and even imprisonment for writing, speaking, or publishing anything of "a false, scandalous and malicious" nature against the government or any officer of the government. To cries that such censorship violated the First Amendment's guarantees of freedom of speech and the press, Federalists replied that sedition and libel were not protected by the Constitution.

Because of the heavy-handed way it was enforced, the Sedition Act quickly became a symbol of tyranny. Federalists convicted and imprisoned a number of prominent Republican editors, and several Republican papers ceased publication. The act even brought to justice one unfortunate tippler who had proclaimed his fervent hope that a cannonball might hit the president in his rear. In all, 25 were arrested under the law and 10 convicted and imprisoned, including Matthew Lyon, a Republican member of Congress from Vermont. Unpopular by any measure, the Sedition Act became doubly obnoxious because Federalists used it in such a partisan manner.

Freedom of the press

The crisis over the Sedition Act forced Republicans to develop a broader conception of freedom of the press. Previously, most Americans had agreed that newspapers should not be restrained before publication but that they could be punished afterward for sedition. Jefferson and others now argued that the American government was uniquely based on the free expression of public opinion, and thus criticism of the government was not a sign of criminal intent. Only overtly seditious acts, not opinions, should be subject to prosecution. The courts eventually endorsed this view, adopting a new, more absolute view of freedom of speech guaranteed by the First Amendment.

Virginia and Kentucky resolutions

The Republican-controlled legislatures of Virginia and Kentucky responded to the crisis of 1798 by each passing a set of resolutions. Madison secretly wrote those for Virginia, and Jefferson those for Kentucky. These resolutions proclaimed that the Constitution was a compact among sovereign states, which delegated strictly limited powers to the federal government. When the government exceeded those limits and threatened the liberties of citizens, states had the right to interpose their authority.

But Jefferson and Madison were not ready to rend a union that had so recently been forged. Jefferson and Madison intended for the Virginia and Kentucky resolutions only to rally public opinion to the Republican cause. They opposed any effort to resist federal authority by force. Furthermore, other states openly rejected the doctrine of "interposition." During the last year of the Adams administration, the Alien and Sedition Acts quietly expired. Once in power, the Republicans repealed the Naturalization Act.

The Election of 1800

With a naval war raging on the high seas and the Alien and Sedition Acts sparking debate at home, Adams suddenly shocked his party by negotiating a peace treaty with

Federalist split

France. It was a courageous act, for Adams not only split his party in two but also ruined his own chances for reelection by forcing Hamilton's pro-British wing of the party into open opposition. The nation benefited, however, for France signed a peace treaty ending its undeclared war. Adams, who bristled with pride and independence, termed this act "the most disinterested, the most determined and the most successful of my whole life."

With the Federalist party split, Republican prospects for 1800 brightened. Again the party chose Jefferson to run against Adams, along with Aaron Burr for vice president. The Republicans' efficient party organization mobilized supporters, whereas the Federalists' high-handed policies and disdain for the "mob" doomed them in a republic where so many citizens could vote. The political journalist Noah Webster put his finger on the problem of his fellow Federalists when he commented, "They have attempted to resist the force of public opinion, instead of falling into the current with a view to direct it."

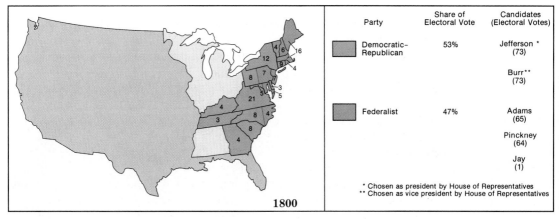

Party	Share of Electoral Vote	Candidates (Electoral Votes)
Democratic–Republican	53%	Jefferson * (73)
		Burr** (73)
Federalist	47%	Adams (65)
		Pinckney (64)
		Jay (1)

* Chosen as president by House of Representatives
** Chosen as vice president by House of Representatives

1800

ELECTION OF 1800

Sweeping to victory, the Republicans won control of both houses of Congress for the first time. Adams ran ahead of his party, but Jefferson outdistanced him, 73 electoral votes to 65. Once again, the election demonstrated the fragility of the fledgling political system. Jefferson and Burr received an equal number of votes, but the Constitution, with no provision for political parties, did not distinguish between the votes for president and vice president. With the election tied, the decision lay with the House of Representatives, where each state was allotted one vote. Since Burr refused to step aside for Jefferson, the election remained deadlocked for almost a week, until the Federalists eventually decided that Jefferson represented the lesser of two evils. They allowed his election on the thirty-sixth ballot. In 1804 the Twelfth Amendment corrected the problem, specifying that electors were to vote separately for president and vice president.

Jefferson's election

Political Violence in the Early Republic

It had been a tense moment: the leadership of the Republic hanging on bitter party votes in the House. Some Federalists even swore they would "go without a constitution and take the risk of civil war." Indeed, it is easy to forget how violent and unpredictable the politics of the 1790s had been.

Some of the violence was physical. The leading Republican newspaper editor in Philadelphia plunged into a street brawl with his Federalist rival; Representatives Matthew Lyon and Roger Griswold slugged it out on the floor of Congress. Mobs threatened the leaders of both parties, and at the height of the crisis of 1798–1799, President John Adams actually smuggled guns into his home for protection. The political rhetoric of the era was equally abusive and violent. Republicans accused patriots like Washington and Hamilton of being British agents and monarchists; Federalists portrayed Jefferson as an irreligious radical and the Republicans as "blood-drinking cannibals." Washington complained that he was abused "in such exaggerated and indecent terms as could scarcely be applied . . . to a common pickpocket." By 1797, reported Jefferson sadly, "men who have been intimate all their

Generating strong popular emotions, elections in the early Republic involved many more voters than ever before. In this detail of an early nineteenth-century painting by John Lewis Krimmel, party workers bring electors to the Philadelphia polls in carriages, while voters heatedly argue about candidates and celebrate.

lives, cross the streets to avoid meeting, and turn their heads another way, lest they should be obliged to touch their hats."

Ideology of republicanism

What accounted for this torrent of violence—both real and rhetorical—in the first decade of the Republic? For one thing, Federalists and Republicans alike recognized how fragile a form of government republicanism had proved over the long course of history. Its repeated failure left political leaders uneasy and uncertain about the American experiment. Then, too, the ideology of the American Revolution stressed the need to guard constantly against conspiracies to subvert liberty. All too quickly, turbulent foreign events like the French Revolution heightened domestic suspicions.

In such overheated circumstances, both Republicans and Federalists readily assumed the worst of one another. Neither side grasped that political parties were essential in a democracy to express and resolve peacefully differences among competing social, geographic, and economic interests. Instead, each party considered the other a faction and therefore illegitimate. Each longed to reestablish a one-party system. Not until after 1815 did a political ideology develop that recognized the need for parties.

Federalist achievements

As John Adams prepared to leave office, he looked back with mixed feelings on the 12 years that the Federalist party had held power. Under Washington's firm leadership and his own, his party had made the Constitution a workable instrument of government. The Federalists had proved that republicanism was compatible with stability and order, and they had established economic policies and principles of foreign affairs that even their opponents would continue. The Union had been strengthened, the Constitution had been accepted, and prosperity had returned.

But most Federalists took no solace in such reflections, for the forces of history seemed to be running against them. As the champions of order and hierarchy, of government by the well-born, of a society in which social betters guided their respectful inferiors, they had waged one last desperate battle to save their disintegrating world—and had lost. Power had fallen into the hands of the ignorant and unwashed rabble, led by that demagogue Thomas Jefferson. Federalists shared fully the view of the British minister who concluded in 1800 that the entire American political system was "tottering to its foundations."

The great American experiment in republicanism had failed. Of this most Federalists were certain. And surely, if history was any judge, the destruction of liberty and order would soon follow.

CHAPTER SUMMARY

In 1789 when the new government went into operation under the Constitution, the United States was divided between the commercial and semisubsistence areas of the country. The commercial sector of the economy, located in and around cities and in the plantation regions of the South, was tied to international trade and depended on the widespread exchange of goods and services. Families in the semisubsistence economy, in contrast, tried to produce most of what they consumed and did not buy and sell in an extensive market. Americans who participated in the commercial economy held different attitudes about wealth and opportunity than residents in the semisubsistence areas. These attitudes produced contrasting concepts about the role of government in society.

Politics in the early Republic was rooted in this fundamental social division. Eventually two parties crystallized in the 1790s: the Federalists, led by Alexander Hamilton and George Washington, and the Republicans, led by James Madison and Thomas Jefferson. Divisions over domestic issues, especially Hamilton's policies as secretary of the treasury, stimulated the formation of rival political parties. The Federalists' belief in order and hierarchy, their support for loose construction of the Constitution, and their desire to establish a powerful central government that actively promoted economic growth aroused deeply ingrained popular fears of power and privilege. The Republican party, in contrast, endorsed strict construction of the Constitution, wanted a less active federal government, and harbored a strong fear of aristocracy.

Foreign policy also stimulated the formation of parties. The French Revolution, which began in 1789 and became progressively more radical, was the focus of controversy in the United States. When monarchical England and republican France went to war, the Federalists favored Britain while the Jeffersonians backed France. Party differences over America's relations with France and England continued during the administration of John Adams, also a Federalist. The major events of Adams's presidency—the XYZ Affair, the Quasi-War, and the Alien and Sedition Acts—were all linked to the debate over foreign policy. In the presidential election of 1800, Thomas Jefferson became the first leader of an opposition party to be elected president. During their 12 years in power, the Federalists had shown that the new government could meet its responsibilities and would be a more active force in American society, but their controversial domestic and foreign policies, internal divisions, and open hostility to the masses eventually led to their defeat.

SIGNIFICANT EVENTS

1789	First session of Congress; Washington inaugurated president; French Revolution begins; Judiciary Act passed
1790	Funding and assumption approved
1791	Bank of the United States chartered; first 10 amendments (Bill of Rights) ratified
1792	Washington reelected
1793	Execution of Louis XVI; war breaks out between France and England; Washington issues Neutrality Proclamation
1794	Battle of Fallen Timbers; Whiskey Rebellion
1795	Jay's Treaty ratified; Treaty of Greenville signed
1796	Pinckney's Treaty ratified; first contested presidential election— Adams defeats Jefferson
1798–1799	Quasi-War with France
1798	XYZ Affair; Alien and Sedition Acts passed; Virginia and Kentucky resolutions
1800	Adams sends new mission to France; Jefferson defeats Adams
1801	The House elects Jefferson president

ADDITIONAL READING

Once the subject of considerable controversy, political developments in this period have attracted less attention from historians in recent years. Much of the scholarship, while older, is nevertheless sound. The most recent overview is Stanley Elkins and Eric McKitrick's massively detailed study, *The Age of Federalism* (1993). James Roger Sharp, *American Politics in the Early Republic* (1993) is a brief, up-to-date survey. Jacob E. Cooke, *Alexander Hamilton* (1982) is a good short biography, while Stephen G. Kurtz, *The Presidency of John Adams* (1957) analyzes the growing split in the party under Adams. Some of the most imaginative work has focused on the ideology of republicanism. Lance Banning, *The Jeffersonian Persuasion* (1978) and Drew R. McCoy, *The Elusive Republic* (1980) are both excellent treatments of the ideology of the Jeffersonians. There is no equivalent study of Federalist ideology. The best account of the Republican party's formation is Noble Cunningham, *The Jeffersonian Republicans* (1963).

Historians are beginning to examine American society in these years. Useful works include Jack Larkin, *The Reshaping of Everyday Life, 1790–1840* (1988), Reginald Horsman, *The Frontier in the Formative Years, 1783–1815* (1970), Howard Rock, *Artisans of the New Republic* (1979), and Laurel Thatcher Ulrich, *A Midwife's Tale* (1990). Crèvecoeur's and Franklin's writings are available in many editions. For a fuller list of readings, see the Bibliography.

9

The Jeffersonian Republic

O n September 29, 1800, following a rather rocky courtship, Margaret Bayard married Samuel H. Smith. Even though Samuel was well educated and from a socially prominent family, Margaret's father consented to the marriage reluctantly, for the Bayards were staunch Federalists and Smith was an ardent Republican. Indeed, Thomas Jefferson had asked Smith, a Republican editor in Philadelphia, to follow the government to Washington, D.C., and establish a party newspaper in the new capital. After the wedding, the couple traveled to the new seat of government on the banks of the Potomac River.

When the Smiths arrived in Washington, they found a raw village of 3200 souls. Samuel began publishing the *National Intelligencer,* the first national newspaper in the United States, while Margaret's social charm and keen intelligence made their home a center of Washington society. When she met Jefferson about a month after her arrival, she found herself captivated by his gracious manners, sparkling conversation, and gentlemanly bearing. Whatever remained of her Federalist sympathies vanished, and she became (perhaps as her father feared) a devoted supporter of the Republican leader.

Jefferson's inauguration
In eager anticipation she went to the Senate on March 4, 1801, to witness Jefferson's inauguration. The chamber was packed, but the members of Congress nonetheless reserved one side for the ladies present. To emphasize the change in attitude of the new administration, the president-elect walked to the capitol with only a small escort. Absent were the elaborate ceremonies of the years of Federalist rule. Since the new president delivered his inaugural address in almost a whisper, few in the assembled crowd heard much of what he said. Then Chief Justice John Marshall, a Virginian but a Federalist whom Jefferson deeply distrusted, administered the oath of office. When the swearing in was completed, the new president returned to his lodgings at Conrad and McMunn's boardinghouse, where he declined a place of honor and instead took his accustomed seat at the foot of the table. Only several weeks later did he finally move to his official residence.

As Margaret Smith proudly watched the proceedings, she could not help thinking of the most striking feature of this transfer of power: it was peaceful. "The changes of administration," she commented, "which in every government and in every age have most generally been epochs of confusion, villainy and bloodshed, in

We Owe Allegiance to No Crown, *by John A. Woodside, reflects the growing*
nationalism in American life after 1815.

our happy country take place without any species of distraction, or disorder." After the fierce controversies of the previous decade and the harsh rhetoric of the election of 1800, to see the opposition party take power peacefully—the first such occurrence in the nation's history—was indeed remarkable.

Once in power, Jefferson set out to reshape the government and society into closer harmony with Republican principles. He later referred to his election as "the Revolution of 1800," asserting that it "was as real a revolution in the principles of our government as that of 1776 was in its form." That statement is an exaggeration, perhaps. But the rule of the Republican party during the following two decades set the nation on a distinctly more democratic tack. And in working out its relationship with Britain and France, as well as with the Indian nations of the West, America achieved a sense of its own nationhood that came only with time and with the passing of the Revolutionary generation.

JEFFERSON IN POWER

Thomas Jefferson was the first president to be inaugurated in the new capital of Washington, D.C. In 1791 George Washington had commissioned Pierre Charles L'Enfant, a French architect and engineer who had served in the American Revolution, to draw up plans for the new seat of government. L'Enfant designed a city with broad avenues, statues and fountains, parks and plazas, and a central mall. Because the Federalists believed that government was the paramount power in a nation, they had intended that the city would be a new Rome—a cultural, intellectual, and commercial center of the Republic.

The New Capital City

Crude condition of capital

The new city, however, fell far short of this grandiose dream. It was located in a swampy river bottom near the head of navigation on the Potomac, and the surrounding low-lying hills rendered the spot oppressively hot and muggy during the summer. Removed from the thriving commercial centers of the country, the capital had no business or society independent of the government. The streets were filled with tree stumps and became impenetrable seas of mud after a rain. Much of the District was wooded, and virtually all of it remained unoccupied.

When the government moved to its new residence in 1800, the Senate chamber, where Jefferson took the oath of office, was the only part of the capitol that had been completed. The executive mansion was unfinished as well, although it had been occupied since November, when the Adamses had moved in for the last few months of John Adams's presidency. Except for its classical architecture, the city gave no hint of imitating the great centers of antiquity. A British diplomat grumbled at having to leave Philadelphia, the previous capital, with its bustling commerce, regular communication with the outside world, and lively society, to conduct business in "a mere swamp."

Yet the isolated and unimpressive capital reflected the new president's attitude toward government. Distrustful of centralized power of any kind, Jefferson deliberately set out to remake the national government into one of limited scope that

Washington in 1800 barely resembled L'Enfant's grand design. When Jefferson was inaugurated, only one wing of the capitol was complete, and a primitive Pennsylvania Avenue ran more than a mile through the woods before it connected with the unfinished executive mansion.

touched few people's daily lives. He took as his ideal precisely what the Federalists had striven to avoid—a government, in Hamilton's words, "at a distance and out of sight," which commanded little popular attention.

Jefferson's Character and Philosophy

Jefferson himself reflected that vision of modesty. Even standing nearly 6 feet, 3 inches, the 57-year-old president lacked an imposing presence. He dressed so carelessly in frequently ill-fitting clothes that William Plumer, a New Hampshire Federalist, mistook him for a servant when he called at the executive mansion. Despite his wealth and genteel birth into Virginia society, Jefferson disliked pomp and maintained an image of republican simplicity. His informal manners and habit of conducting business in a frayed coat and slippers dismayed dignitaries who called on him decked out in ribbons and lace.

Jefferson was a product of the Enlightenment, with its faith in the power of human reason to improve society and decipher the universe. While afflicted with occasional bouts of despair, he was on the whole an unshakable optimist. "I steer my bark with Hope in the head," he once declared, "leaving fear astern." An elegant writer but ineffective public speaker, he preferred to accomplish his political business in private conferences or at his renowned dinner parties, where he charmed his guests with his easy conversation.

Thomas Jefferson, about 1799

Jefferson considered "the will of the majority" to be "the only sure guardian of the rights of man," which he defined as "life, liberty, and the pursuit of happiness." Although he conceded that the masses might err, he was confident they would soon return to correct principles. His faith in human virtue exceeded that of most of the founding generation, yet in good republican fashion, he feared those in power, even if they had been elected by the people. Government seemed to Jefferson at best a necessary evil.

Agrarian values

To Jefferson, agriculture was a morally superior way of life. "Those who labour in the earth are the chosen people of God, if ever he had a chosen people," he wrote in *Notes on the State of Virginia* (1787). Like Crèvecoeur, Jefferson praised rural life for nourishing the honesty, independence, and virtue so essential in a republic. Government would "remain virtuous . . . as long as [the American people] are chiefly agricultural," he assured James Madison. Rather than encouraging large-scale factories, Jefferson wanted to preserve small household manufacturing, which was an essential part of the rural economy. Commerce should exist primarily to sell America's agricultural surplus. He was never able to overcome his earlier belief, rooted in the republican ideology of the Revolution, that cities and commerce promoted speculation, greed, and useless luxury and self-indulgence.

Jefferson's radicalism exaggerated

Although Jefferson asserted that "the tree of liberty must be refreshed from time to time by the blood of patriots and tyrants," his reputation as a radical was undeserved. While he wanted to extend the suffrage to a greater number of Americans, he clung to the traditional republican idea that voters should own property and thus be economically independent. One of the largest slaveholders in the country, he increasingly muffled his once-bold condemnation of slavery, and in the last years of his life he reproached critics of the institution who sought to prevent it from expanding westward. Nor did his belief in free speech mean that he had any qualms about state governments punishing political criticism.

Slaveholding aristocrat and apostle of democracy, lofty theorist and pragmatic politician, Jefferson was an exceedingly complex, at times contradictory, personality. But like most politicians, he was flexible in his approach to problems and tried to balance means and ends. And like most leaders, he quickly discovered that he confronted very different problems in power than he had in opposition.

Republican Principles

Limited government

Once Jefferson settled into the executive mansion, he took steps to return the government to the republican ideals of simplicity and frugality. The states rather than the federal government were "the most competent administrators for our domestic concerns," he asserted in his inaugural address. Ever the individualist, he recommended a government that left people "free to regulate their own pursuits of industry and improvement."

Jefferson also went out of his way to soothe the feelings of defeated Federalists. Acknowledging Hamilton's fiscal policies, he promised to uphold the government's credit and protect commerce as the "handmaiden" of agriculture—both Federalist concerns. Agreeing with Washington, he proposed friendship with all nations and "entangling alliances" with none. Finally, he called on Americans to unite for the common good: "We have called by different names brethren of the same principles. We are all republicans—we are all federalists."

The election of 1800 established the legitimacy of an opposition party in American politics, and Jefferson, in his inaugural address, seemed to endorse the validity of a party system. In reality, however, he hoped to restore one-party rule to the country by winning over moderate and honest Federalists and isolating the party's extremists, whom he still attacked as monarchists.

Jefferson's Economic Policies

But what would Jefferson do about Hamilton's economic program? As he promised in his inaugural address, the new president proceeded to cut spending, reduce the size of the government, and begin paying off the national debt. Unless the debt was paid, he warned Albert Gallatin, his talented secretary of the treasury, "we shall be committed to the English career of debt, corruption and rottenness, closing with revolution." He abolished the internal taxes enacted by the Federalists, including the controversial levy on whiskey, and thus was able to get rid of all tax collectors and inspectors. "What farmer, what mechanic, what laborer, ever sees a tax gatherer in the United States?" boasted Jefferson in 1805. Land sales and the tariff duties would supply the funds needed to run the government.

The most serious spending cuts were made in the military branches. Jefferson slashed the army budget in half, reducing the army to 3000 men. In a national emergency, he reasoned, the militia could defend the country. Jefferson reduced the navy even more, halting work on powerful frigates authorized during the Quasi-War with France and replacing them with a fleet of small gunboats, which captured Jefferson's fancy because they were cheap. In the long term, however, they proved totally inadequate to defend the nation's coasts in war.

By such steps, Jefferson made significant progress toward paying off Hamilton's hated national debt. He lowered it from $83 million to only $57 million by the end of his two terms in office, despite the added financial burden of the Louisiana Purchase (page 277). Still, Jefferson did not entirely dismantle the Federalists' economic program. Funding and assumption could not be reversed—the nation's honor was pledged to paying these debts, and Jefferson fully understood the importance of maintaining the nation's credit. The tariff had to be retained as a source of revenue to meet government expenses. More surprising, Jefferson argued that the national bank should be left to run its course until 1811, when its charter would expire. In reality, he expanded the bank's operations and, in words reminiscent of Hamilton, advocated tying banks and members of the business class to the government by rewarding those who supported the Republican party. *Failure to abolish Hamilton's program*

In effect, practical politics had triumphed over agrarian economics. Throughout his presidency, Jefferson often put pragmatic considerations above unyielding principles. As he himself expressed it, "What is practicable must often control what is pure theory."

John Marshall and Judicial Review

Having lost both the presidency and control of Congress in 1800, the Federalists took steps to shore up their power before Jefferson took office. They did so by expanding the size of the federal court system, the one branch of the federal government that they still controlled. The Judiciary Act of 1801 created 6 circuit courts and 16 new judgeships, along with a number of marshals, attorneys, and clerks. Federalists justified these "midnight appointments" (executed by Adams in the last weeks of his term) on the grounds that the expanding nation required a larger judiciary.

Jefferson, however, saw matters differently. "The Federalists, defeated at the polls, have retired into the Judiciary," he fumed, "and from that barricade . . . hope to batter down all the bulwarks of Republicanism." In 1802, by a strict party vote, Congress repealed the 1801 law and eliminated the new courts and their officers.

Marbury v. Madison

Among Adams's last-minute appointments was that of William Marbury as justice of the peace for the District of Columbia. When James Madison assumed the office of secretary of state under the new administration, he found a batch of undelivered commissions, including Marbury's. Wishing to appoint loyal Republicans to these posts, Jefferson instructed Madison not to hand over the commissions, whereupon Marbury sued under the Judiciary Act of 1789. Since that act gave the Supreme Court original jurisdiction in cases against federal officials, the case of *Marbury v. Madison* went directly to the Court in 1803.

Chief Justice John Marshall, a Federalist and one of Adams's late-term appointments, seized on this case to affirm the Court's greatest power, the right to review statutes and interpret the meaning of the Constitution. "It is emphatically the province of and duty of the judicial department to say what the law is," he wrote in upholding the doctrine of judicial review. This idea meant that the Court "must of necessity expound and interpret" the Constitution and the laws when one statute conflicted with another or when a law violated the framework of the Constitution. Marshall found that the section of the Judiciary Act of 1789 that granted the Supreme Court original jurisdiction in the case was unconstitutional. Since the Constitution specified those cases in which the Court had such jurisdiction, they could not be enlarged by statute. *Marbury v. Madison* was so critical to the development of the American constitutional system that it has been called the keystone of the constitutional arch.

Judicial review

Marshall and his colleagues later asserted the power of the Court to review the constitutionality of state laws in *Fletcher v. Peck* (1810) when it struck down a Georgia law. It also brought state courts under the scrutiny of the Supreme Court in *Martin v. Hunter's Lessee* (1816), denying the claim of the Virginia Supreme Court that it was not subject to the authority of the federal judiciary, and in *Cohens v. Virginia* (1821), in which it asserted its right to review decisions of state courts on issues arising under the Constitution. In fact, during his tenure on the bench, Marshall extended judicial review to all acts of government. It took time for the doctrine to be accepted, but since Marshall's time the Supreme Court has successfully defended its position as the final judge of the meaning of the Constitution.

The Jeffersonian Attack on the Judiciary

Having disposed of the bulk of Adams's recent appointments, the Republicans proceeded to attack Federalist judges who had been particularly obnoxious during the party battles of the 1790s. Jefferson argued that impeachment was not limited to

John Marshall

criminal acts but was an appropriate political device to remove any judge who proved unacceptable to two-thirds of the Senate. In 1803, after the House had impeached federal district judge John Pickering of New Hampshire, who was both insane and an alcoholic, he was convicted and removed by the Senate.

Encouraged by this success, the administration turned its attention to Associate Justice Samuel Chase of the Supreme Court. An ultra-Federalist, Chase had interpreted the Sedition Act in a blatantly partisan fashion to ensure convictions against Republicans. After the House impeached Chase, a majority of senators voted to convict, but since a two-thirds vote was necessary for removal, Chase was acquitted. In the end, Republicans decided to wait for death and retirement to give them eventual control of the remaining branch of the government through presidential appointments.

JEFFERSON AND WESTERN EXPANSION

The Federalists feared the West as a threat to social order and stability. Frontiersmen, sneered New Englander Timothy Dwight, were "too idle; too talkative; too passionate . . . and too shiftless to acquire either property or character." Farther south, another observer referred to squatters on western lands as "ragged, dirty, brawling, browbeating monsters, six feet high, whose vocation is robbing, drinking, fighting, and terrifying every peaceable man in the community." Thus when Federalists passed an act in 1796 authorizing the sale of federal land, they viewed it as a revenue measure rather than the means to develop the country and kept the price of land high. It sold for a minimum of $2 an acre, with a required purchase of at least 640 acres, over four times the size of the typical American farm.

Jefferson, on the other hand, viewed the West as the means to preserve the values of an agrarian republic. He anticipated that as settled regions of the country became crowded, many rural residents would migrate to the cities in search of work unless cheap land beckoned farther west. America's vast spaces provided land that would last for a thousand generations, he predicted in his inaugural address, enough to transform the United States into "an empire of liberty." *Empire of liberty*

In 1801 the Republican Congress reduced the minimum tract to 320 acres and established a four-year credit system to pay (page 320). The intention was to encourage rapid settlement of the interior, and in fact, land sales boomed under the new law. Most of the sales, however, were to speculators and land companies rather than individual settlers. Nevertheless, the West remained overwhelmingly Republican. The admission of new western states strengthened Jefferson's party and hastened the decline of the Federalists. From Jefferson's perspective, western expansion was a blessing economically, socially, and politically.

The Louisiana Purchase

Because Spain's colonial empire was disintegrating, Americans were confident that before long they would gain control of Florida and the rest of the Mississippi, either through purchase or by military occupation. This comforting prospect was shattered, however, when Spain secretly ceded Louisiana—the territory lying between the

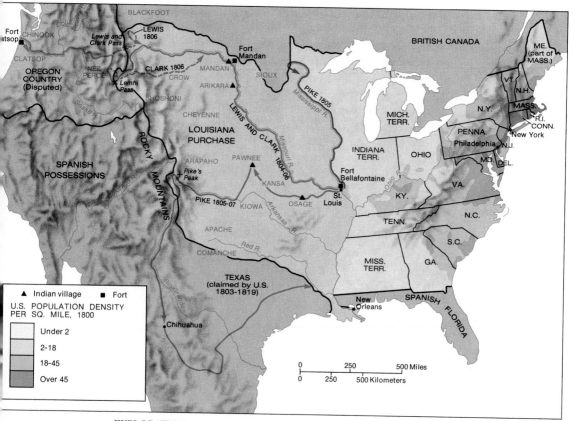

EXPLORATION AND EXPANSION: THE LOUISIANA PURCHASE
The vast, largely uncharted Louisiana Purchase lay well beyond the most densely populated areas of the United States. The Lewis and Clark expedition along with Lieutenant Zebulon Pike's exploration of the upper Mississippi River and the Southwest opened the way for westward expansion.

Mississippi River and the Rocky Mountains—to France. Under the leadership of Napoleon Bonaparte, France had become the most powerful nation on the European continent, with the military might to protect its new colony and block American expansion. American anxiety intensified when Spain, while still in control of Louisiana, abruptly revoked Americans' right to navigate the lower Mississippi guaranteed by Pinckney's Treaty (page 252). Western farmers, who were suddenly denied access to the sea, angrily protested Spain's high-handed action.

Jefferson dispatched James Monroe to Paris to join Robert Livingston, the American minister, to negotiate the purchase of New Orleans and West Florida from the French and thus secure control of the Mississippi. "There is on the globe one single spot, the [possessor] of which is our natural and habitual enemy," Jefferson reminded them. "It is New Orleans."

Sale of Louisiana

In the meantime, however, Napoleon lost interest in Louisiana. With war looming again in Europe, he needed money, and so in April 1803 he offered to sell not just

New Orleans but all of Louisiana to the United States. This proposal flabbergasted Livingston and Monroe. Their instructions said nothing about acquiring all of Louisiana, and they had not been authorized to spend what the French demanded. On the other hand, here was an unprecedented opportunity to expand dramatically the boundaries of the United States. Pressed for an immediate answer, Livingston and Monroe wanted to consult Jefferson but worried that the French might withdraw the offer as suddenly as they had made it. So after haggling over a few details, the American ministers agreed to purchase Louisiana for approximately $15 million.

The millions of acres of fertile farmland, untold natural resources, and control of the vital Mississippi River and its tributaries were one of the most extraordinary bargains in the history of the United States. In one fell swoop, the American negotiators had doubled the country's size by adding some 830,000 square miles. "From this day," Livingston asserted, "the United States take their place among the powers of the first rank."

Jefferson, naturally, was immensely pleased at the prospect of acquiring so much territory, which seemed to guarantee the survival of his agrarian republic. At the same time, as someone who favored the doctrine of strict construction, he found the legality of the act deeply troubling. The Constitution, after all, did not specifically authorize the acquisition of territory by treaty. Livingston and Monroe urged haste, however, and in the end, Jefferson sent the treaty to the Senate for ratification, noting privately, "The less we say about constitutional difficulties the better." Once again pragmatism had triumphed over theory. *Jefferson's pragmatism*

The purchase of Louisiana was generally popular, and the Senate ratified the treaty 24 to 7. West Florida, which bordered part of the lower Mississippi, remained in Spanish hands, and Jefferson's efforts to acquire this region were unsuccessful. Nevertheless, western commerce could flow down the Mississippi unhindered to the sea. The Louisiana Purchase would rank as the greatest achievement of Jefferson's presidency.

Lewis and Clark

Early in 1803, even before the Louisiana Purchase was completed, Congress secretly appropriated $2500 to send an exploring party up the Missouri River to the Pacific. This expedition was led by Meriwether Lewis, Jefferson's secretary, and William Clark, a younger brother of Revolutionary War hero George Rogers Clark.

Jefferson instructed Lewis and Clark to map the region and make detailed observations of the soil, climate, rivers, minerals, and plant and animal life. They were also to investigate the practicability of an overland route to the Pacific and engage in diplomacy with the Indians along the way. Equally important, by pushing onward to the Pacific, Lewis and Clark would strengthen the American title to Oregon, which several nations claimed but none effectively occupied.

In the spring of 1804 Lewis and Clark left St. Louis and headed up the Missouri with 48 men. They laboriously pushed their boats up the Missouri River to present-day North Dakota, where they spent the winter with the Mandan Indians. The next spring, they headed west again. Only with great difficulty did the expedition pass the rugged mountains ahead of the winter snows and then float down first the Snake and then the Columbia River to the Pacific. *Exploration of the West*

After spending a bleak winter in Oregon, vainly awaiting a ship that would take them back, the company returned in 1806 over the Rockies. Having traveled across half the continent in both directions, navigated countless rapids, and conducted negotiations with numerous tribes, Lewis and Clark arrived in St. Louis in September, two and a half years after they had departed. The expedition fired the imagination of Americans about the exotic lands of the newly acquired Louisiana Purchase, as well as the Pacific Northwest. Lewis and Clark had collected thousands of useful plant and animal specimens, discovered several passes through the Rockies, and produced a remarkably accurate map, their most valuable contribution to western exploration.

WHITES AND INDIANS ON THE FRONTIER

In February 1803, as American diplomats prepared to leave for France in hopes of gaining title to western lands, another delegation was visiting Washington with a similar purpose. Black Hoof, a Shawnee chief from the Ohio River valley, asked Secretary of War Henry Dearborn to issue a deed to the lands that legally belonged to the Shawnee in western Ohio. The deed, said Black Hoof, would ensure that his people could "raise good Grain and cut Hay for our Cattle" and guarantee "that nobody would take advantage" of them. The astonished Dearborn was not about to give the Shawnee any document that would strengthen their title to land in Ohio. But he did promise to provide some plows and cattle.

Indian attempts at assimilation
Unlike many Shawnees, Black Hoof had decided that the best way to get along with white Americans was to adopt their ways. For a number of years he and his tribe settled along the Auglaize River, built log houses, wore garments like those of whites, cleared land to raise corn, potatoes, cabbage, and turnips, and even planted an apple orchard. But in 1808, after the government refused to pay a Quaker missionary who was providing technical support, Black Hoof's followers became increasingly dependent on government payments. Even Black Hoof admitted, "The white people . . . have been our ruin."

The Shawnee along the Auglaize were only one of many Indian tribes forced to make hard choices as white Americans streamed into the fertile lands of the Ohio River valley. In 1790 only about 100,000 whites lived in the West. By 1800 that number had jumped to almost 400,000 and, a decade later, to more than a million. By 1820 more than 2 million whites lived in a region they had first entered only 50 years earlier.

In this backcountry, where white and Indian cultures mixed and often clashed, both peoples experienced the breakdown of traditional cultural systems. White immigrants pushing into Indian territory often lacked the structures of community such as churches, schools, and legal institutions. But Indian cultures were also severely stressed by the availability of white trade goods and by the more settled agricultural ways of white farmers, with their domesticated animals and fenced-in fields. Above all, Indians had to deal with the unceasing hunger of whites for Indian lands.

The Course of White Settlement

Following the Treaty of Greenville (page 251), white settlers poured into the Ohio Territory by wagon and flatboat. "From what I have seen and heard," one girl wrote while crossing Pennsylvania bound for the West, "I think the State of Ohio will be well fill'd before winter,—Waggons without number, every day go on." The pattern of settlement remained the same: in the first wave came backwoods families who laboriously cleared a few acres of forest by girdling the trees, removing the brush, and planting corn between the dead trunks. Their isolated one-room log cabins were crude, dark, and windowless, with mud stuffed between the chinks; the furniture and utensils were sparse and homemade. Such settlers were mostly squatters without legal title to their land. As a region began to fill up, these restless pioneers usually sold their improvements and headed west again.

Many of those who replaced them were young unmarried men who left crowded regions in the East seeking new opportunities. Their migration, which relieved population pressures back home, contributed to the imbalance of males and females on the frontier. Once established, they quickly married and started families. Like the pioneers before them, most engaged in semisubsistence agriculture. As their numbers increased and a local market developed, they switched to surplus agriculture, growing and making much of what the family needed while selling or exchanging the surplus to obtain essential items. "The woman told me that they spun and wove all the cotton and woolen garments of the family, and knit all the stockings," a visitor to an Ohio farm wrote. "Her husband, though not a shoemaker by trade, made all the shoes. She manufactured all the soap and candles they used." The wife sold butter and chickens to get money to buy coffee, tea, and whiskey. *Maturing society*

A Changing Environment

The inrush of new settlers significantly reduced the amount of original forest west of the Appalachian Mountains. Americans, who equated clearing the forest with progress, "have an unconquerable aversion to trees," one observer noted, "and whenever a settlement is made they cut away all before them without mercy; not one is spared; all share the same fate and are involved in the same general havoc. . . ." By 1850 they had cleared at least 100 million acres. In newly cleared areas the resulting landscape was often bleak, according to one traveler. "The trees are cut over at the height of three or four feet from the ground and the stumps are left for many years till the roots rot;—the edge of the forest, opened for the first time to the light of the sun looks cold and raw;—the ground rugged and ill-dressed . . . as if nothing could ever be made to spring from it."

This rapid cutting of the forest altered plant and animal life in significant ways. Large animals, such as the deer and bears, became scarce, and the bison soon disappeared east of the Mississippi River. The loss of forest cover, combined with the new plowing of the land, increased the amount of runoff after rains, which lowered the water table and caused many streams to dry up for a good part of the year. At the same time increased runoff made rivers more destructive and floods more common. Clearing the land also produced serious soil erosion, particularly on hillsides, and silted many previously navigable streams and rivers. The climate changed as well: it was hotter in the summer and the winds blew more fiercely, causing erosion in the summer and chilling gusts in the winter. *Effects of deforestation*

Deforestation also made the Ohio valley more unhealthy. Malaria was not unknown in the region previously, but the growing population density and the cutting of forests made the disease more common. In clearing the land, settlers often created wasteland with pools of stagnant water from the increased runoff, which became breeding places for mosquitoes that spread the disease. Observers remarked on the greater prevalence of malaria and other summer diseases in the region as the forests came down.

The Second Great Awakening

It was the sparsely settled regions that became famous for a second wave of revivals, known collectively as the Second Great Awakening, that swept across the nation beginning in the late 1790s. Like the first national outpouring of religious enthusiasm 50 years earlier, these revivals were fanned by ministers who traveled the countryside preaching to groups anywhere they could. Beginning in the late 1790s Congregationalists, Presbyterians, and Baptists all participated. The Methodists, however, had the most effective organization for spreading the gospel in remote areas with their system of circuit riders. One competing Presbyterian minister ruefully noted that "into every hovel I entered I learned that the Methodist missionary had been there before me."

Cane Ridge

News of several revivals in Kentucky in the summer of 1800 quickly spread, and people came from 50 and 100 miles around, camping in makeshift tents and holding services out of doors. This new form of worship, the camp meeting, reached its climax at Cane Ridge, Kentucky, in August 1801. At a time when the largest city in the state had only 2000 people, over 10,000 gathered for a week to hear dozens of ministers.

Men and women earnestly examined their hearts; scoffers came, half-mocking, half-fearful of what they might see. For rural folk accustomed to going to bed soon after dark, the sight of hundreds of campfires flickering throughout the woods far into the night, reinforced by the endless singing, praying, and crying, was a powerful tonic indeed. "The vast sea of human beings seemed to be agitated as if by storm," recalled one skeptic, who himself was converted at Cane Ridge.

> I counted seven ministers all preaching at once. . . . Some of the people were singing, others praying, some crying for mercy in the most piteous accents. . . . At one time I saw at least 500 swept down in a moment as if a battery of a thousand guns had been opened upon them, and then immediately followed shrieks and shouts that rent the very heavens.

Although the clergy at camp meetings were male, women played prominent roles, often pressing husbands to convert. In the overwhelming emotion of the moment, converts might dance, bark, laugh hysterically, or jerk uncontrollably, hair flying, the whole body shaking, as they sought to gain assurance of their salvation. (See Daily Lives, "The Frontier Camp Meeting," pages 282–283.)

African Americans and revivals

In the South, African Americans, including slaves, attended camp meetings and enthusiastically participated in the tumultuous services. Indeed, revivals were a major force in spreading Christianity to African Americans and producing slave conversions. Revivalists' clear and vivid speech, their acceptance of the moral worth of every individual regardless of race, and their emphasis on the conversion experience rather than abstract theology had the same appeal to black listeners, who had little formal schooling, as they did to poorly educated white churchgoers. Blacks worshiped separately from and sometimes together with whites. The revivals also produced black preachers, who exhorted white as well as black audiences. Some slaveholders, espe-

Men and women witness the baptism of a female worshiper. A European observer said of such baptisms, "Barefoot and bareheaded, with flowing hair, they step solemnly into the river, while a choir sings." Like camp meetings and revivals, such scenes were an emotional experience for the congregation as well as the converts. Several members kneel in prayer or shout praises to the Lord while the rest of the group gaze with rapt attention.

cially in eastern plantation districts, worried that camp meetings might foster racial egalitarianism, but revivalists concentrated on bringing slaves to Christ rather than questioning society's institutions. As with white worshipers, the Baptist and Methodist churches received the bulk of African American converts.

The revivals quickly found critics who decried the emotionalism and hysteria they produced. For a time Presbyterians and Baptists withdrew from camp meetings, leaving the field to the Methodists. Eventually even the Methodists sought to dampen excessive emotion by restricting admittance and patrolling the meeting grounds.

Revivals like Cane Ridge provided an emotional release from the hard, isolated life on the frontier. Pioneers could momentarily forget the drabness of their lives, the pains and sorrows they endured as they struggled to carve an existence out of the forest. For families with few neighbors, camp meetings offered a chance to participate in a wider social gathering while relieving pent-up emotions. And for those at the bottom of the social hierarchy, the revivalists' message emphasized an individual's ability to gain personal triumph and salvation regardless of his or her station in life. In the swiftly changing borderlands north and south of the Ohio River, where society seemed constantly in flux, revivals brought a sense of uplift and comfort.

Attraction of revivals

PUBLIC SPACE/PRIVATE SPACE

The Frontier Camp Meeting

The Cane Ridge revival, one of the earliest along the frontier, was a chaotic, disorganized affair. But as western clergy became more experienced with outdoor camp meetings, they standardized the format. About a week in advance, organizers chose a forest clearing, removed nearby underbrush, erected pulpits, and constructed benches. Usually the camp went up near an established church, which provided lodging for the ministers. Since a water supply was essential, camps were located near springs, creeks, or rivers. A good site needed dry ground, shade so worshipers could escape the blazing sun, and pasturage for the horses.

The site might be laid out in a horseshoe, a rectangle, or, most popularly, a broad circle. In each case the tents of the worshipers formed a ring around the outdoor auditorium where services were held. As participants arrived, a supervisor directed drivers where to park wagons, tether animals, and pitch tents. At a large meeting, where as many as 200 tents covered the site, they were set up in several rows with streets in between to allow easy access. To help people find their lodgings, the streets were sometimes even named. This outer perimeter constituted the meeting's private space. Here, beneath tents of sailcloth or even shelters patched together from old blankets and sheets, individuals could withdraw from the larger group to find relative solitude, cook meals in front of campfires, and sleep on rude beds of straw or simply on the ground.

Worshipers were naturally drawn toward the central public space, where they filled bench after bench at the periodic call of a bugle. Rising above the listeners, at one or both ends of the clearing, stood the preachers' pulpit. Sometimes it was merely a 10-foot-square platform on stilts; other times it was more elaborate, with several levels and a roof. Services were held in the open, where neither rain nor thunderstorms would interrupt them. At night, the dancing light and shadows produced by the candles, torches, campfires, and fire altars (earthen-covered platforms) at each corner heightened the feeling of awe.

The democracy of the frontier did not automatically break down customary social constraints. For reasons of authority as well as practicality, the ministers' pulpit rose above the congregation. And the audience itself was segregated: women on one side of the clearing, men on the other. In the South, black worshipers were seated in an area behind the pulpit, where they set up their own camp and conducted separate services.

Since the purpose of camp meetings was to "revive" religion and stir listeners' hearts, several rows of planks were set aside directly in front of the pulpit as an "anxious bench," for those whose souls struggled in the agony of conversion. The design of the space thus focused the attention of both congregation and ministers on the "mourn-

Pressure on Indian Lands and Culture

As white settlers continued to pour into the backcountry, the pressure to acquire Indian lands increased. Jefferson endorsed the policy that Indian tribes would either have to assimilate into American culture by becoming farmers and abandoning their seminomadic hunting or would have to move west of the Mississippi River. There, isolated from white settlement, they could gradually develop the skills and values

Daily Lives

CODE
X Cooking fires—illumination also from candles in trees
△ Tents
🛒 Wagons
🟰 Horses
1. Speakers' stand—candles for illumination
2. Earthen covered fire platforms
3. Mourners' bench
4. Blacks' worship area
5. Seats—women's side
6. Seats—men's side
7. Preachers' tent
8. Boarding tent

Source: Adapted from Charles A. Johnson, *The Frontier Camp Meeting: Religion's Harvest Time* (Dallas: SMU Press, 1955), pp. 43 and 47.

public and private, male and female, and even black and white could be broken down. As excitement grew, several services might be held at once, some people praying, others singing, shouting, or listening to ministers who stood on wagons or makeshift platforms of felled trees. And when formal services ended, men and women often continued singing and exhorting in small groups, going into the woods to pray, and searching one another's souls by campfires late into the night. Indeed, the social mixing and spontaneous excitement were great enough that meeting sponsors quickly learned that supervision was necessary to prevent unseemly activities. The nearby forest, the numerous tents, and nightfall all offered temptations for drinking, carousing, or lovemaking. Therefore, official patrols were set up to regularly investigate suspicious activities and to monitor sleeping arrangements.

On the final day white and black worshipers joined together in a singing and marching festival before disbanding to their more humdrum daily routines. Successful camp meetings depended on more than the talents of the clergy and the enthusiasm of participants. In their layout they were carefully planned and regulated communities in the forest, designed to reduce the distance between public and private space and thereby instill a sense of religion in all of the activities that took place in the meeting, as well as those that would be resumed in the regular world.

ers," who were exhorted and prayed over in hopes that they would receive a new birth in Christ. As camp meetings became increasingly organized, separate mourning tents were set up on the edge of the arena near the anxious benches. (Again, curtains separated the male and female sections, and black participants had their own mourning tents.)

But the social boundaries between

necessary to fit into American society. Jefferson defended these alternatives as in the best interests of the Indians, since otherwise he believed that they faced extermination. But he also recognized that by becoming farmers they would need less land. "While they are learning to do better on less land," he noted, "our increasing numbers will be calling for more land."

The hard truth about white policies toward Indians was that however enlightened individuals might be, the demographic pressure of high birthrates and aggressive expansion ensured conflict between the two cultures. Anglo-Americans never doubted the superiority of their ways. As William Henry Harrison, governor of the new Indiana Territory, confessed in 1801, "A great many of the Inhabitants of the Fronteers consider the murdering of the Indians in the highest degree meritorious." Even a student of the Enlightenment like Jefferson could become cynical and encourage the policy of selling goods on credit in order to lure Indians into debt. "When these debts get beyond what the individuals can pay," the president observed, "they become willing to lop them off by a cession of lands." Between 1800 and 1810 whites pressed Indians into ceding more than 100 million acres in the Ohio River valley.

Destruction of Indian cultures

The loss of so much land to white settlement devastated traditional Indian cultures by reducing hunting grounds and making game and food scarce. "Stop your people from killing our game," the Shawnees complained in 1802 to federal Indian agents. "They would be angry if we were to kill a cow or hog of theirs, the little game that remains is very dear to us." Tribes also became dependent on white trade to obtain blankets, guns, metal utensils, alcohol, and decorative beads. To pay for these goods with furs, Indians often overtrapped, which forced them to invade the lands of neighboring tribes, provoking wars. The debilitating effects of alcohol, which Indians turned to as a means of coping with cultural stress, were especially marked during these years, and increased production in white backcountry settlements during the 1790s and early 1800s made whiskey readily available. Indeed, white consumption of alcohol was also rising during these years, a symptom of the adjustment of white society to cultural stress.

Among the Shawnees in the Ohio River valley, the strain produced by white expansion led to alcoholism, growing violence among tribe members, family disintegration, and the collapse of the clan system designed to regulate relations among different villages. These problems might have been lessened by separation from white culture, but the Shawnees had become dependent on trade for articles they could not produce themselves. The question of how to deal with white culture became a matter of anguished debate. Black Hoof, as we have seen, attempted to take up farming and accommodate to white ways. But for most Indians, the course of assimilation proved unappealing and fraught with risk.

The Prophet, Tecumseh, and the Pan-Indian Movement

Other Shawnees decided not to adopt white ways but to revitalize their culture by severing all ties with the white world. In such efforts Indian religion often played a central role. During the 1790s a revival of religious fervor led by Handsome Lake took hold among the Iroquois, following the loss of most of the Iroquois lands and the collapse of their military power in western New York. Subsequently, Lalawethika, also known as the Prophet, sparked a religious revival among the Shawnees. The Prophet's early life was undistinguished: he was a poor hunter and as a child accidentally blinded himself in the right eye with an arrow. His portly build and homely looks reinforced his unsightly appearance, and the ridicule of his fellow tribe members drove him to alcoholism. Then suddenly in April 1805 he lapsed into a trance so deep that he was given up for dead. When he revived, he spoke of having died and been reborn. In this vision and others he later received, he outlined a new creed for the Shawnee. Renouncing alcohol, he took a new name, Tenskwatawa (the Open

Door), to express his mission to "reclaim the Indians from bad habits and to cause them to live in peace with all mankind."

Tenskwatawa urged the Shawnee to renounce whiskey and white goods and return to their old ways of hunting with bows and arrows, eating customary foods like corn and beans, and wearing traditional garb. Seeking to revitalize Shawnee culture, the Prophet condemned intertribal violence, promoted monogamous marriage, and denounced the idea of private instead of communal property. Except for guns, which could be used in self-defense, his followers were to discard all items made by whites.

Prophet's message

Not only was trade forbidden with white settlers, so was intermarriage. Indian wives of white men were to leave their husbands and return to the tribe, and children of mixed parentage were to be barred from the village. Setting up headquarters at the newly built village of Prophetstown in Indiana in 1808, Tenskwatawa led a religious revival among the tribes of the Northwest, who were increasingly concerned about the loss of their lands. Just as thousands of white settlers traveled to Methodist or Baptist camp meetings in the woods, where preachers denounced the evils of liquor and called for a return to a purer way of life, so thousands from northern tribes traveled to the Prophet's village for inspiration.

While Tenskwatawa's strategy of revitalization was primarily religious, his older brother Tecumseh turned to political and military solutions. William Henry Harrison described Tecumseh as "one of those uncommon geniuses which spring up occasion-

Tecumseh's movement

Tenskwatawa (left), "the Open Door," shown in traditional dress, led a religious movement to revitalize Shawnee culture and attracted a large following among the northwestern tribes. After the Battle of Tippecanoe, he was supplanted as leader of the Indian revitalization movement by his brother Tecumseh (right), who advocated political unity to preserve Indian lands and cultures. Tecumseh was the dominant figure among the western tribes until he died fighting alongside the British in the War of 1812.

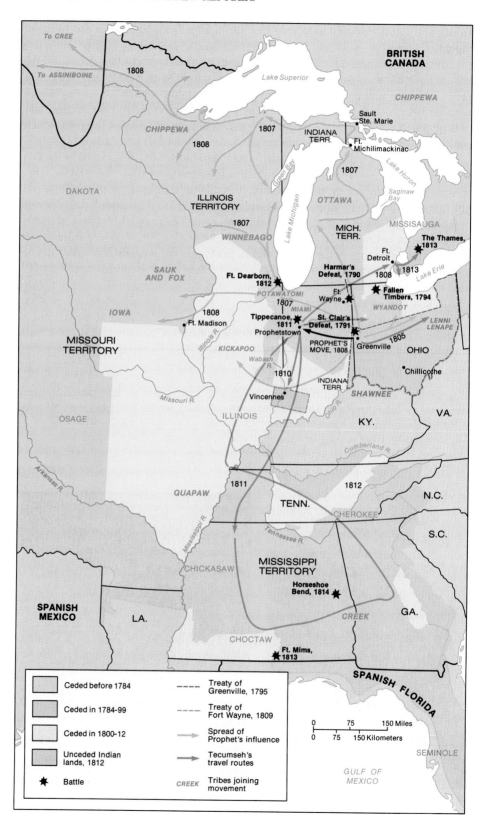

THE INDIAN RESPONSE TO WHITE ENCROACHMENT

With land cessions and white western migration placing increased pressure on Indian cultures after 1790, news of the Prophet's revival fell on eager ears. It spread especially quickly northward along the shores of Lake Michigan and westward along Lake Superior and the interior of Wisconsin. Following the Battle of Tippecanoe, Tecumseh eclipsed the Prophet as the major leader of Indian resistance, but his trips south to forge political alliances met with less success.

ally to produce revolutions and overturn the established order of things." Tall and athletic, an accomplished hunter and a renowned warrior, Tecumseh became active in 1809, after the Lenni Lenape and Miami tribes ceded yet another 3 million acres in Indiana and Illinois under the Treaty of Fort Wayne. Repudiating the treaty, he traveled throughout the Northwest, urging tribes to forget their ancient rivalries and unite under his leadership to protect their lands from white incursions. Tecumseh's confederacy brought together the Wyandot, Chippewa, Sauk and Fox, Winnebago, Potawatomi, and other tribes. As Tecumseh began to overshadow the Prophet, William Harrison aptly termed him "really the efficient man—the Moses of the family."

Tecumseh's message of Pan-Indian unity and centralized authority ran counter to many facets of traditional Indian cultures. He asked villages to pay less attention to their local leaders and join his larger movement; he also called on tribes to unite with their traditional enemies in a common cause. While the amount of support he received was impressive, his following never matched that of the Prophet's earlier revivals. After recruiting allies among the northwestern tribes, Tecumseh in 1811 *Tecumseh's* headed south, where he encountered greater resistance. In general, the southern *failure in the* tribes were more prosperous, were more acculturated, and felt less immediate pres- *South* sure on their land from whites. In addition, the Choctaws and Chickasaws refused to forget long-standing feuds with northern tribes. So Tecumseh's southern mission ended largely in failure.

To compound Tecumseh's problems, while he was away a force of Americans under Governor Harrison defeated the Prophet's forces at the Battle of Tippecanoe in November and then destroyed Prophetstown. As a result, Tecumseh became convinced that the best way to contain white expansion was to play off the Americans against the British in the Great Lakes region. Indeed, by 1811, the two nations were on the brink of war.

COUNTERPOINT

Inevitably, the contrast between the tactics of the Prophet and Tecumseh have invited comparisons. For many years, historians saw Tecumseh as a towering figure *Tecumseh* who advocated the most effective response to white pressure on tribal lands. Perhaps *versus the* because white historians lived in a nation whose story centered on the union of one *Prophet* nation from out of many, they tended to sympathize with Tecumseh's ideas of a Pan-Indian confederacy and military resistance under a centralized authority. From this perspective, the Prophet was a minor figure whose ideas were irrelevant and doomed to failure.

More recently, historians have challenged the prominence given to Tecumseh over his brother. The Prophet's religious message, these revisionists point out, was much more in harmony with Indian cultures. As a result, the Prophet attracted a much larger following. Tecumseh's idea of a Pan-Indian confederacy, in contrast, ran counter to Indian cultures, bypassed traditional sources of authority within individual tribes, and ignored long-standing hostility among various tribes. Ironically, his ideas were closer to those of white society. Indeed, it was for precisely this reason that American officials had a high opinion of Tecumseh and historians since have been sympathetic: he responded to the northwestern tribes' situation the way whites would have. But within the context of tribal cultures, the Prophet's movement had a much greater impact.

THE SECOND WAR FOR AMERICAN INDEPENDENCE

As Tecumseh was working to create a Pan-Indian alliance, Jefferson was looking to restore American political unity by wooing all but the most extreme Federalists into the Republican camp. The president easily won reelection in 1804 over Federalist Charles Cotesworth Pinckney, carrying 15 of 17 states. With the Republicans controlling three-quarters of the seats in Congress, Jefferson's goal of one-party rule seemed at hand.

That unity was threatened, however, by renewed fighting in Europe. Only two weeks after Napoleon agreed to sell Louisiana to the United States, war broke out between France and Great Britain. As in the 1790s, the United States found itself caught between the world's two greatest powers. In his struggle to maintain American neutrality, Jefferson's controversial policies momentarily revived the two-party system.

Neutral Rights

At first the war benefited American trade because of the disruption in European agriculture. That stimulated demand for American foodstuffs and other raw materials. As the fighting drove most nonneutral ships from the seas, American shipping dominated the carrying trade, and the nation's foreign trade doubled between 1803 and 1805. But after 1805 the British navy began seizing American ships with increasing frequency, as it tightened its blockade of Europe.

Impressment   Adding to American anger, the British navy also resumed its impressment of sailors and even passengers from American ships. British authorities refused to recognize the right of its citizens to emigrate and become American citizens, insisting that even if naturalized by the United States they remained subjects of the Crown. Anywhere from 4000 to 10,000 sailors were impressed by British naval officers, who did not always bother to distinguish naturalized from native-born Americans.

Isaac Clark, for example, was a native of Randolph, Massachusetts, yet he was taken from the American ship *Jane* in June 1809 after it was stopped by the British. When he presented papers attesting to his American citizenship, the English captain tore them up and threw them overboard. Refusing to work, he was put in irons, given a daily allowance of a biscuit and a pint of water, and once a week received two dozen lashes. Finally, half-starved and physically broken, Clark gave in. He served in the

British navy for over two and a half years until wounded in action against a French frigate. While in a hospital he was freed through the intervention of the American consul. Voicing American indignation, John Quincy Adams characterized impressment as an "authorized system of kidnapping upon the ocean."

By 1805, the war had demonstrated the British navy's clear superiority at sea, while Napoleon's army enjoyed a decisive edge on land. Adopting a strategy of attrition, each country began to raid America's ocean commerce with the other side. Between 1803 and 1807, Britain seized over 500 American ships; France, over 300. Britain issued new regulations in 1807, known as the Orders in Council, that required any ship trading with France or its satellites to put in first at a British port, pay a duty, and get a license. Napoleon retaliated with the Milan Decree of 1807, which announced that any ship that stopped in Britain in conformity with the Orders in Council would be treated as a British ship, subject to seizure. American merchants, caught in the middle, saw the number of seized ships again increase. An irate Jefferson complained of France and England, "The one is a den of robbers, the other of pirates." When in June 1807 a British frigate fired on the U.S. warship *Chesapeake* in American waters and seized four deserters from the Royal Navy, public opinion clamored for military retaliation.

American ships seized

Orders in Council

Impressment was a major controversy between the United States and Great Britain before the War of 1812. Short of men, the hard-pressed Royal Navy searched American ships for deserters but often seized native-born American sailors instead, including many free blacks.

The Embargo

Yet Jefferson shrank from declaring war. He announced instead a program of "peaceable coercion," designed to protect neutral rights without war. The plan not only prohibited American ships from trading with foreign ports, it stopped the export of all American goods. Jefferson was confident that American exports were so essential to the two belligerents, they would quickly agree to respect American neutral rights. In December 1807 Congress passed the Embargo Act.

The president had seriously miscalculated. France did not depend on American trade and so managed well enough, while British ships quickly took over the carrying trade as American vessels lay idle. Under the embargo, American exports plunged from $108 million in 1807 to a mere $22 million a year later. At the same time, imports fell from almost $145 million to about $58 million. As the center of American shipping, New England port cities were hurt the most and protested the loudest. And when their merchants were not protesting, they were smuggling behind American officials' backs. During his last months in office Jefferson simply gave up trying to enforce the act.

Madison and the Young Republicans

Following Washington's example, Jefferson did not seek a third term. A caucus of Republican members of Congress selected James Madison to run against Federalist Charles Cotesworth Pinckney. Although Madison triumphed easily, Pinckney swept all of New England, where feeling against the embargo was highest, and the Federalists picked up 24 seats in Congress. The party seemed on the verge of a revival.

AMERICAN IMPORTS AND EXPORTS, 1790–1820
The prosperity of the 1790s is reflected in steadily rising foreign trade. Note the sharp drop after the Embargo Act and during the war.

Few men have assumed the presidency with more experience than James Madison. A leading nationalist in the 1780s, the father of the Constitution, a key floor leader in Congress, the founder of the Republican party, Jefferson's secretary of state and closest adviser, Madison had spent over a quarter of a century in public life. Yet his tenure as president proved disappointing, for despite his intellectual brilliance, he lacked the force of leadership and the inner strength to impose his will on less capable men. *Madison's character*

With a president reluctant to fight for what he wanted, leadership passed from the executive branch to Congress. The elections of 1810 swept in a new generation of Republicans, led by the adroit and magnetic 34-year-old Henry Clay of Kentucky, who gained the rare distinction of being elected Speaker in his first term. These younger Republicans were much more nationalistic than the generation led by Jefferson and Madison. They sought an ambitious program of economic development and were aggressive expansionists, especially those from frontier districts. Their feisty willingness to go to war earned them the name of War Hawks. Though they numbered fewer than 30 in Congress, they quickly became the driving force in the Republican party. *War Hawks*

The Decision for War

During Jefferson's final week in office in early 1809, Congress repealed the Embargo Act. To encourage the two great powers to respect neutral rights, the new act reopened trade with all nations except Britain and France and authorized the president to resume trade with either nation that lifted its restrictions. The following year it authorized trade with France and England but decreed that if one of the two belligerents agreed to stop interfering with American shipping, trade with the other would be prohibited.

In this situation, Napoleon cleverly outmaneuvered the British by announcing that he would set aside the French trade regulations. Madison eagerly took the French emperor at his word and reimposed a ban on trade with England. But as French raiders continued to seize American ships, it became clear that Napoleon had no intention of lifting restrictions. Madison, who had boxed himself into a corner, refused to rescind his order unless the British revoked the Orders in Council. In the disputes that followed, American anger focused on the British, who seized many more ships than the French and continued to impress American sailors. Westerners also accused the British of stirring up hostility among the Indian tribes.

The embargo produced hard times in Britain, and finally on June 16, 1812, the British ministry suspended the Orders in Council. But it was too late. Two days earlier, unaware of the change in policy, the United States had declared war on Britain.

Angered by the continued violations of American neutrality and pressed by the War Hawks to defend American honor, Madison on June 1 asked for a declaration of war. The vote was 79 to 49 in the House and 19 to 13 in the Senate, mostly along party lines, with every Federalist voting against war. As the representatives of commercial interests, particularly in New England, Federalists were convinced that war would ruin American commerce. They also still identified with Britain as the champion of order and conservatism. The handful of Republicans who joined the Federalists represented coastal districts, which were most vulnerable to the Royal Navy. *Declaration of war*

Clearly, the vote for war could not be explained as a matter of outraged

Americans protecting neutral rights. The coastal areas, which were most affected, preferred trade over high principle. On the other hand, members of Congress from the South and the West, regions that had a less direct interest in the issue, clamored most strongly for war. Their constituents were consumed with a desire to seize additional territory in Canada or in Florida (owned by Britain's ally Spain). In addition, they were outraged by British intrigues with Indians along the frontier.

Perhaps most important, the War Hawks were convinced that Britain had never truly accepted the verdict of the American Revolution. To them, American independence—and with it republicanism—hung in the balance. For insecure Americans, hungering for acceptance in the community of nations, nothing rankled more than being treated by the British as colonials. John Quincy Adams expressed this point of view when he declared: "In this question something besides dollars and cents is concerned and no alternative [is] left but war or the abandonment of our rights as an independent nation."

National Unpreparedness

With Britain preoccupied by Napoleon, the War Hawks expected that the United States would win an easy victory. In truth, the United States was totally unprepared for war. Crippled by Jefferson's cutbacks, the navy was unable to lift the British blockade of the American coast, which bottled up the country's merchant marine and most of its navy. But the Great Lakes, which were inaccessible to the British navy, held the key to the naval war, and when hostilities began, neither side had an advantage on these waters. As for the U.S. army, it was small and poorly led. When Congress moved to increase its size to 75,000, even the most hawkish states failed to meet their quotas. Congress was also reluctant to levy taxes to finance the war.

Battle of Lake Erie   A three-pronged American invasion of Canada from Detroit, Niagara, and Lake Champlain failed dismally in 1812. Americans fared better the following year, as both sides raced to build a navy on the strategically located Lake Erie. Led by Commander Oliver Hazard Perry, American forces won a decisive victory at Put-In Bay in 1813. Perry's triumph gave the United States control of Lake Erie and greatly strengthened the American position in the Northwest.

"A Chance Such as Will Never Occur Again"

As the United States struggled to organize its forces, Tecumseh sensed that his long-awaited opportunity had come to drive Americans out of the western territories. "Here is a chance . . . such as will never occur again," he told a war council, "for us Indians of North America to form ourselves into one great combination." Joining up with the British, Tecumseh traveled south in the fall to talk again with his Creek allies. To coordinate a concerted Indian offensive for the following summer, he left a bundle of red sticks with eager Creek soldiers. They were to remove one stick each day from the bundle and attack when the sticks had run out.

Defeat of the Creeks   A number of the older Creeks were more acculturated and preferred an American alliance. But about 2000 younger "Red Stick" Creeks launched a series of attacks, climaxed by the destruction of Fort Mims along the Alabama River in August 1813. Once again, the Indians' lack of unity was a serious handicap, as warriors from the Cherokee, Choctaw, and Chickasaw tribes, traditional Creek enemies, allied with the Americans.

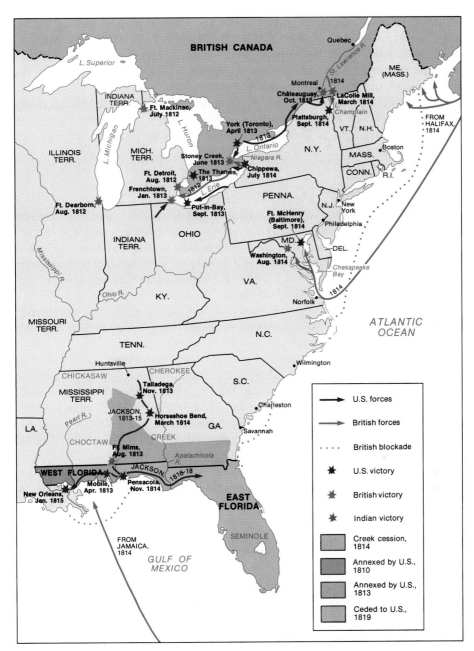

THE WAR OF 1812
After the American victory on Lake Erie and the defeat of the western Indians at the Battle of the Thames, the British adopted a three-pronged strategy to invade the United States, culminating with an attempt on New Orleans. But they met their match in Andrew Jackson, whose troops marched to New Orleans after fighting a series of battles against the Creeks and forcing them to cede a massive tract of land.

At the Battle of Horseshoe Bend in March 1814, General Andrew Jackson and his Tennessee militia soundly defeated the Red Stick Creeks. Jackson promptly dictated a peace treaty under which the Creeks ceded 22 million acres of land in the Mississippi Territory. They and the other southern tribes still retained significant landholdings, but Indian military power had been broken in the Southwest.

Tecumseh's death

Farther north, in October 1813 American forces under General William Henry Harrison defeated the British and their Indian allies at the Battle of the Thames. In the midst of heavy fighting Tecumseh was slain—and with him died any hope of a Pan-Indian movement.

The British Invasion

As long as the war against Napoleon continued, the British were unwilling to divert army units to North America. But in 1814 Napoleon was at last defeated. Free to concentrate on America, the British devised a coordinated strategy to invade the United States in the northern, central, and southern parts of the country. The main army headed south from Montreal but was checked when Captain Thomas Macdonough destroyed the British fleet on Lake Champlain.

Meantime, a smaller British force captured Washington and burned several public buildings, including the capitol and the president's home. To cover the scars of this destruction, the executive mansion was painted with whitewash and became known as the White House. The burning of the capital was a humiliating event; President Madison and his wife Dolley were abruptly forced to flee, leaving their dinner to be eaten by the British. But the defeat had little military significance. The principal British objective was Baltimore, where for 25 hours their fleet bombarded Fort McHenry in the city's harbor. When he saw the American flag still flying above the fort at dawn, Francis Scott Key hurriedly penned the verses of "The Star Spangled Banner," which was eventually adopted as the national anthem.

Jackson's victory at New Orleans

The third British target was New Orleans, where a formidable army of 7500 British troops was opposed by a hastily assembled American force commanded by Major General Andrew Jackson. The Americans included regular soldiers; frontiersmen from Kentucky and Tennessee; citizens of New Orleans, including several companies of free African Americans; Choctaw Indians; and—for an added dash of color—a group of pirates. Jackson's outnumbered and ill-equipped forces won a stunning victory, which made the general an overnight hero. The Battle of New Orleans enabled Americans to forget the war's many failures and to boast that once again the United States had humbled the world's greatest military power.

The Hartford Convention

In December 1814, while Jackson was organizing the defense of New Orleans, New England Federalists met in Hartford to map strategy against the war. Yankee merchants, contemptuous of "Mr. Madison's War," had continued to trade with the enemy, while New England governors declined to make available the state militias. Finally the Massachusetts legislature called for a convention to discuss New England's grievances. Massachusetts, Connecticut, and Rhode Island sent delegates, but only three counties in New Hampshire and one in Vermont were represented.

Rejecting calls for secession, the delegates endorsed a series of proposed

During the Battle of New Orleans, American troops under Jackson entrenched behind breastworks, while their artillery raked the advancing British forces with deadly fire. The ladders needed to scale the American works quickly became entangled in the disorganized British assault.

amendments to the Constitution that showed their displeasure with the government's economic policies and their resentment of the South's national political power. To their dismay, however, the committee sent to Washington to present the convention's demands arrived in the capital just as news of Andrew Jackson's victory was being trumpeted on the streets. The burst of national pride following Jackson's victory badly undercut the Hartford Convention's position, as did news from across the Atlantic that American negotiators in Ghent, Belgium, had signed a treaty ending the war. Hostilities had ceased, technically, on Christmas Eve 1814, two weeks before the Battle of New Orleans.

Like the war itself, the Treaty of Ghent accomplished little. All the major issues between the two countries, including impressment, neutral rights, trade, and the boundary between the United States and Canada, were either ignored or referred to future commissions for settlement. As John Quincy Adams commented, "Nothing was adjusted, nothing was settled—nothing in substance but an indefinite suspension of hostilities was agreed to." Both sides were simply relieved to end the conflict.

Treaty of Ghent

AMERICA TURNS INWARD

Adams was right in concluding that, in terms of international relations, the war had settled nothing. Psychologically, however, the nation's mood had changed perceptibly. "Let any man look at the degraded condition of this country before the war," declaimed young Henry Clay, a leading War Hawk. "The scorn of the universe, the con-

National pride tempt of ourselves. . . . What is our present situation? Respectability and character abroad—security and confidence at home." Indeed, the return of peace hard on the heels of Jackson's victory sparked a new confidence in their country's destiny. "We have stood the contest, single-handed, against the conqueror of Europe," wrote Supreme Court Justice Joseph Story to a friend, "and we are at peace, with all our blushing victories thick crowding on us."

Death of the Federalist party The upsurge in nationalism sounded the death knell of the Federalist party. The resistance of New England Federalists to the embargo and their disloyalty during the war had already weakened the party elsewhere, and the Hartford Convention tainted it with disunion and treason. Although the party had made its best showing in years in 1812, when Madison narrowly defeated his Federalist opponent, its support collapsed in the 1816 election. Madison's secretary of state, James Monroe, resoundingly defeated Federalist Rufus King of New York. Four years later Monroe ran for re-election unopposed.

Monroe's Presidency

The spirit of postwar harmony produced the so-called Era of Good Feelings, presided over by James Monroe, the last president of the Revolutionary generation. Monroe, like Jefferson before him, hoped to eliminate political parties, which he considered unnecessary in a free government. Like Washington, he thought of himself as the head of the nation rather than of a party.

Monroe's greatest achievements were diplomatic, accomplished largely by his talented secretary of state, John Quincy Adams, the son of President John Adams. An experienced diplomat, Adams thought of the Republic in continental terms and was intent on promoting expansion to the Pacific. Such a vision required dealing with Spain, which had never recognized the legality of the Louisiana Purchase. In addition, between 1810 and 1813 the United States had occupied and unilaterally annexed Spanish West Florida.

Spain, however, was preoccupied with events farther south in the Americas. In the first quarter of the nineteenth century, its colonies one after another had revolted and established themselves as independent nations. These revolutions increased the pressure on the Spanish minister to America, Luis de Onís, to come to terms with the United States. Furthermore, in 1818 Andrew Jackson marched into East Florida and captured several Spanish forts. Jackson had exceeded his instructions, but Adams understood well enough the additional pressure this aggression put on Onís and refused to disavow it.

Transcontinental Treaty Fearful that the United States might next invade Texas or other Spanish territory, Spain agreed to the Transcontinental, or Adams–Onís, Treaty in February 1819. Its terms set the boundary between American and Spanish territory all the way to the Pacific (map, page 339). Spain not only gave up its claims to the Pacific Northwest, it ceded Florida in exchange for the U.S. government assuming $5 million in claims against Spain by American citizens. In exchange for the line to the Pacific, the United States abandoned its contention that Texas was part of the Louisiana Purchase. Adams had wanted Texas, but he wanted the line to the Pacific even more. Understanding the strategic commitment to expanding across the continent, Adams wrote in his diary, "The acknowledgement of a definite line of boundary to the South Sea [the Pacific] forms a great epoch in our history."

The upsurge in national pride after the War of 1812 is reflected in the proud demeanor of these American soldiers, as portrayed by Paul Svinin, an artist visiting from Russia. Fourth of July parades routinely allowed soldiers to parade, drums beating and flags flying for the entertainment of civilians.

The Monroe Doctrine

The United States came to terms not only with Spain but, even more important, with Great Britain as well. Following the War of 1812, the British abandoned their connections with the western Indian tribes and no longer attempted to block American expansion to the Rocky Mountains. In a growing spirit of cooperation, the Rush–Bagot Agreement in 1817 limited naval forces on the Great Lakes and on Lake Champlain. In 1818 the countries agreed to the 49th parallel as the northern boundary of the Louisiana Purchase and also to joint control of the Oregon Territory for 10 years, subject to renewal.

Improved relations with Britain

In this atmosphere of good will, George Canning, the British foreign secretary, proposed in August 1823 that the United States and Britain issue a joint statement disavowing any expansionist aims in Latin America and opposing the transfer of Spain's colonies to any foreign power. Monroe was inclined to accept the British offer, and both Jefferson and Madison urged him to do so. But John Quincy Adams forcefully argued that the United States should not make any pledge against acquiring territory in the future, particularly in Texas, Mexico, and the Caribbean. Adams also worried that in any joint statement the United States would appear to be merely a junior partner, coming along "as a cock-boat in the wake of a British man-of-war." Monroe finally agreed to make an independent statement.

Monroe Doctrine

He included it in his annual message to Congress, on December 2, 1823. Monroe reaffirmed that the United States would not intervene in European affairs, a principle of American foreign policy since Washington's Farewell Address. And he also announced that the United States would not interfere with already established European colonies in the Western Hemisphere. But any intervention, he warned, in the new republics of Latin America would be considered a hostile act: "The American continents . . . are henceforth not to be considered as subjects for future colonization by any European powers." The essence of this policy, which was Adams's handiwork, was the concept of two worlds, one old and one new, each refraining from interfering in the other's affairs.

American public opinion hailed Monroe's statement and then promptly forgot it. Only years later would it be referred to as the Monroe Doctrine. Still, it represented the culmination of the American quest since 1776 for independence and sovereignty. The very fact that Britain had proposed a joint declaration demonstrated that, at last, the parent nation recognized its offspring as a legitimate and sovereign nation. Monroe's declaration underlined the United States' determination not to act in world affairs as a satellite of Britain. Ever since the adoption of the Constitution, the issue of independence had been at the center of American politics. It had surfaced during the 1790s, in Hamilton's quarrel with Jefferson over whether to favor Britain or France and in the differing responses of Americans to the French Revolution. It colored the debates over the embargo and finally once again came to a head in 1812 with the second war for American independence.

The End of an Era

End of foreign threat

The growing reconciliation with Great Britain ended the external threat to the Republic. Isolated from Europe and protected by the British fleet, the United States was free to turn its attention inward, to concentrate on expanding across the vast continent and on developing its resources. Yet how would the nation be developed? Jefferson had dreamed of an "empire of liberty," delighting in western expansion as the means to preserve a nation of small farmers like those Crèvecoeur had written about during the 1780s.

Younger, more nationalistic Republicans had a different vision. They spoke of internal improvements, protective tariffs to help foster American industries, better roads and canals to link farmers with towns, cities, and wider markets. The tone of these new Republicans was not aristocratic, like the Federalists of old. Still, their dream of a national, commercial republic resembled Franklin's and Hamilton's more than Jefferson's. They looked to profit from speculation in land, from the increasing market for cotton, from the new methods of industrial manufacturing. If they represented the rising generation, what would be the fate of Crèvecoeur's semisubsistence farm communities? The answer was not yet clear.

In one of those remarkable coincidences that Americans hailed as a sign of Providence's favor, Thomas Jefferson and John Adams died within hours of each other on July 4, 1826, the fiftieth anniversary of the adoption of the Declaration of Independence. The lives of these two giants of the Revolution—Jefferson, the ever-hopeful, self-styled revolutionary Virginia gentleman, and Adams, the prickly, independent Federalist of Braintree—intertwined with one another in the fabric of the nation's development. Partners in the struggle to secure American independence, these revolutionary giants had become bitter foes in the heated party battles of the 1790s and resumed a warm friendship only after they had retired from public life. Their reconciliation was in tune with the surge of American nationalism, but their time was past. Leadership belonged now to a new generation of Americans who confronted different problems and challenges. Revolutionary America had passed from the scene. The dawn of a new nation was at hand.

CHAPTER SUMMARY

Prior to becoming president, Thomas Jefferson advocated the principles of agrarianism, limited government, and strict construction of the Constitution. Once in power, however, Jefferson failed to dismantle Hamilton's economic program. Instead, he increasingly abandoned his earlier ideals in favor of nationalism, a trend that continued under his successors, James Madison and James Monroe.

By upholding the principle of judicial review, or the right of the courts to interpret the meaning of the Constitution, the judiciary emerged as an equal branch of government in this period. This development was the work of Chief Justice John Marshall, a staunch Federalist. In a series of decisions the Supreme Court, under Marshall's leadership, asserted its right to determine the constitutionality of laws passed by Congress and state legislatures, as well as review decisions on constitutional matters by state courts.

Believing that it would preserve his agrarian republic for generations, Jefferson promoted western expansion by acquiring Louisiana from France despite his constitutional principles. As white settlers pushed westward, tensions with the Indian tribes in the Ohio Valley steadily increased. Many northern tribes rallied to a religious movement led by the Shawnee prophet Tenskwatawa, which aimed to revive traditional Indian cultures. When the Prophet's religious movement failed to prevent the erosion of tribes' traditional land holdings, Tecumseh emerged as the most important Indian leader. Tecumseh advocated a political and military confederacy to protect Indians' lands, but a number of important tribes refused to support him. His movement collapsed with his death during the War of 1812.

When war resumed between Britain and France, foreign affairs became increasingly important in American politics. Neither power was willing to respect America's neutral rights, and eventually the United States went to war against Britain in 1812. The war achieved little militarily, but in the years after 1815 there was a surge in American nationalism. During the administration of James Monroe, Madison's successor, this nationalism was particularly manifested in foreign policy. Under the leadership of secretary of state John Quincy Adams, the United States negotiated the Transcontinental Treaty with Spain and proclaimed the Monroe Doctrine. Britain's recognition of American sovereignty after 1815 ended the threat of foreign interference in America's internal affairs and brought to successful fulfillment the quest for independence from British control that had commenced with the American Revolution.

SIGNIFICANT EVENTS

1790s	Second Great Awakening begins
1801	Adams's "midnight" appointments; Marshall becomes chief justice; Jefferson inaugurated in Washington; Cane Ridge revival
1802	Judiciary Act of 1801 repealed
1803	*Marbury v. Madison;* Louisiana Purchase; war resumes between Great Britain and France
1804–1806	Lewis and Clark expedition
1805	Prophet's revivals begin
1807	*Chesapeake* affair; Embargo Act passed
1808	Madison elected president
1809	Tecumseh's confederacy organized
1810	*Fletcher v. Peck*
1810–1813	West Florida annexed
1811	Battle of Tippecanoe
1812	War declared against Great Britain
1813	Battle of Lake Erie; Tecumseh killed
1813–1814	Creek War
1814	Washington burned; Hartford Convention; Treaty of Ghent signed
1815	Battle of New Orleans
1816	Monroe elected president
1818	United States–Canada boundary fixed to the Rockies; joint occupation of Oregon established
1819	Transcontinental Treaty with Spain; United States acquires Florida
1823	Monroe Doctrine proclaimed

ADDITIONAL READING

A good survey of the presidencies of Jefferson and Madison is Marshall Smelser, *The Democratic Republic* (1968). Drew R. McCoy, *The Elusive Republic* (1980) skillfully analyzes the dilemmas Jefferson and Madison confronted in power. An important study of the Federalist party is David Hackett Fischer, *The Revolution of American Conservatism* (1965). For the origins of the War of 1812, see Roger H. Brown, *The Republic in Peril* (1964). The biographies of Jefferson and Madison examine political developments in this period in detail.

Malcolm J. Rohrbough, *The Trans-Appalachian Frontier* (1978) traces the process of western settlement, while other aspects of western society are treated in John Boles, *The Great Revival in the South* (1972) and R. David Edmunds, *The Shawnee Prophet* (1983). Donald Jackson, *Thomas Jefferson and the Stony Mountains: Exploring the West from Monticello* (1979) is a fascinating analysis of western exploration in this period. The journals of the Lewis and Clark expedition, which have been published in several editions, are invaluable; a recent history is Stephen E. Ambrose, *Undaunted Courage* (1996).

The first part of George Dangerfield, *The Awakening of American Nationalism*

(1965), capably covers Monroe's administration. Samuel F. Bemis traces American foreign policy during and after the war in *John Quincy Adams and the Foundations of American Foreign Policy* (1949). Ernest R. May, *The Making of the Monroe Doctrine* (1976), is the best study of the subject. For a fuller list of readings, see the Bibliography.

PART THREE

THE REPUBLIC TRANSFORMED AND TESTED

GLOBAL ESSAY

Two remarkable transformations began sweeping the world in the late eighteenth century. So wrenching and far-reaching were these changes that both have been called revolutions. The first was a cascade of political revolts that led to increased democratic participation in the governing of many nation-states. The other was the application of machine labor and technological innovation to agricultural and commercial economies, known as the industrial revolution.

Proclaiming the values of liberty and equality, Americans in 1776 led the way with their own democratic revolution. As we have seen, the act of revolution itself did not solve the question of how regional and economic antagonisms could be adjusted peacefully in the new nation-state. Not until the Republicans succeeded the Federalists was a tradition of peaceful political change established within the framework of the Constitution. And not until a new generation of leaders arrived on the scene during the second war for independence did a national consciousness fully bloom.

These were notable milestones, but internationally, the center of revolutionary attention had shifted in 1789 to France. There, as in America, the ideals of the Enlightenment played a part in justifying the rejection of rule by monarchy. French liberals like the Marquis de Lafayette were inspired by the example of the United States. Still, the crowds marching through the streets of Paris adopted a more radical and violent stance, reflecting the burdens on peasants and workers of the harsh feudal system as well as other social pressures. The worldwide rise in population of the previous half century had left the French capital overcrowded, underfed, and thoroughly unruly. The French citizenry proved that much more willing to arm themselves and march on the Bastille, on the palace at Versailles, against any perceived enemies of the Revolution. The countryside, too, suffering from a series of bad harvests, rose up

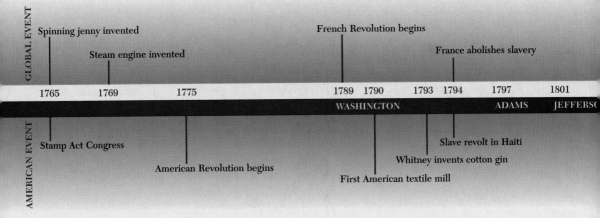

Spinning jenny invented

French Revolution begins

Steam engine invented

France abolishes slavery

| 1765 | 1769 | 1775 | | 1789 | 1790 | 1793 | 1794 | 1797 | 1801 |

WASHINGTON   ADAMS   JEFFERS(

Stamp Act Congress

Slave revolt in Haiti

Whitney invents cotton gin

American Revolution begins

First American textile mill

in protest, sometimes brutally. Paradoxically, the population pressure that had pushed matters to a crisis was relieved as the Revolution gave way to the emperor Napoleon, whose wars of conquest killed almost as many French soldiers as the natural increase of the nation's population. When Napoleon was at last defeated at the Battle of Waterloo in 1815, Louis XVIII reestablished the French monarchy.

In Latin America, however, movements of democracy and nationalism spread. Just as Great Britain had attempted to pay for its colonial defenses with additional revenue from its colonies, so the Spanish Crown raised taxes in the Americas, with predictable results. The Creole class—Spanish who had been born in America—resented the preferential treatment and administrative positions given the *peninsulares*—colonial residents born in Spain. Although the Spanish colonies lacked the tradition of representative assemblies found in North America, the writings of Jefferson and Thomas Paine circulated, as did translations of the French *Declaration of the Rights of Man*. From 1808 to 1821 Spain's American provinces declared their independence one by one. Democracy did not always root itself in the aftermath of these revolutions, but democratic ideology remained a powerful social catalyst.

The industrial revolution was less violent but no less dramatic in its effects. It began in Great Britain, where canals built toward the end of the eighteenth century improved the transportation network, just as they would in the United States during the 1820s and 1830s. In Britain, too, James Watt in 1769 invented an engine that harnessed the power of steam, while innovations in textile production led to the use of water and later steam power to drive mechanical looms. At about the same time, steam power, along with other innovations, made it possible for coal mining and the manufacture of iron to be accomplished on a larger scale. (The British miner, shown here, was drawn in 1814.)

As steam power was applied to ships and rail locomotives, the reach of commercial markets widened. Regular shipping made it possible to bring Egyptian cotton from Alexandria to factories in British Manchester and American cotton from the Arkansas Red River country to New England. Just as skilled workers like Samuel Slater smuggled the new technology out of England to the United States, others like

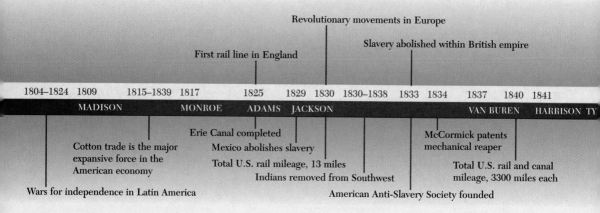

Revolutionary movements in Europe

Slavery abolished within British empire

First rail line in England

| 1804–1824 | 1809 | 1815–1839 | 1817 | 1825 | 1829 | 1830 | 1830–1838 | 1833 | 1834 | 1837 | 1840 | 1841 |

MADISON · MONROE · ADAMS · JACKSON · VAN BUREN · HARRISON TY

Erie Canal completed

Cotton trade is the major expansive force in the American economy

Mexico abolishes slavery

Total U.S. rail mileage, 13 miles

Indians removed from Southwest

McCormick patents mechanical reaper

Total U.S. rail and canal mileage, 3300 miles each

Wars for independence in Latin America

American Anti-Slavery Society founded

William Cockerill set up factories in Europe, as the capabilities of steam and industrial manufacturing spread to the continent.

In many ways the narrative of the young American republic is the story of how one nation worked out the implications of these twin revolutions, industrial and democratic. It was only after the War of 1812 that a market economy began rapidly to transform the agricultural practices of Crèvecoeur's semisubsistence America. Urban areas of the North became more diversified and industrial as young women took jobs in textile mills and young men labored in flour mills processing grain to be shipped east. The impact of industry on the North is probably clear enough in the popular imagination.

What is sometimes less appreciated is how the industrial revolution transformed the rural South. Cotton would never have become king there without the demand for it created by textile factories or without the ability to "gin" the seeds out of cotton by Eli Whitney's invention. (The "gin" in *cotton gin* is a clipped southern pronunciation of the word "engine.") Nor could cotton production have flourished without industrial advances in transportation, which allowed raw materials and factory goods to be shipped worldwide.

As the industrial and democratic revolutions developed side by side, the United States had to resolve the conflicts that the two presented each other. On the one hand, the advances in industry and commerce made it possible for resourceful entrepreneurs to reap profits on a scale that Americans of Crèvecoeur's day could never

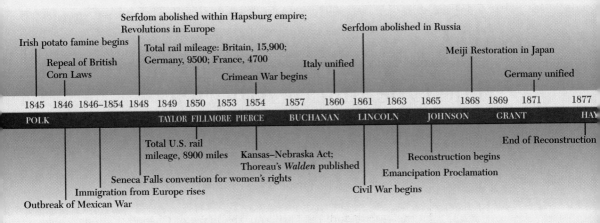

Serfdom abolished within Hapsburg empire; Revolutions in Europe

Serfdom abolished in Russia

Irish potato famine begins

Repeal of British Corn Laws

Total rail mileage: Britain, 15,900; Germany, 9500; France, 4700

Italy unified

Crimean War begins

Meiji Restoration in Japan

Germany unified

| 1845 | 1846 | 1846–1854 | 1848 | 1849 | 1850 | 1853 | 1854 | 1857 | 1860 | 1861 | 1863 | 1865 | 1868 | 1869 | 1871 | 1877 |

POLK   TAYLOR FILLMORE PIERCE   BUCHANAN   LINCOLN   JOHNSON   GRANT   HAY

Total U.S. rail mileage, 8900 miles

Kansas–Nebraska Act; Thoreau's *Walden* published

End of Reconstruction

Reconstruction begins

Emancipation Proclamation

Seneca Falls convention for women's rights

Civil War begins

Immigration from Europe rises

Outbreak of Mexican War

have imagined. They also created a labor force more impoverished than most Americans had been. In the North, factory workers found the conditions of labor increasingly harsh as the century progressed. In the South, the institution of slavery became even more economically entrenched because of the profits to be made using slave labor to raise cotton. The industrial revolution, in other words, made possible a society in which Americans could become both richer and poorer than they had ever been before—a society more stratified and more unequal. At the same time, the democratic revolution spreading across America was calling for greater equality among all citizens. This potential contradiction was one Americans wrestled with throughout the era.

The industrial revolution thus transformed both the North and the South—but in conflicting ways. Although the economies of the two regions depended on one another, slavery came increasingly to be the focus of disputes between them. The industrial revolution's demand for cotton increased both southern profits and the demand for slave labor. Yet the spread of democratic ideology worldwide was creating increased pressure to abolish slavery everywhere. In France the revolutionary government struck it down in 1794. The British empire outlawed it in 1833, about the time that American abolitionists, influenced by their British friends, became more active in opposing it. In eastern Europe the near slavery of feudal serfdom was being eliminated as well: in 1848 within the Hapsburg empire; in 1861 in Russia; in 1864 in Romania.

If the purpose of a democratic republic is to resolve conflicts among its members in a nonviolent manner, then in 1861 the American republic failed. It took four years of bitter fighting to reconcile the twin paths of democracy and industrial development. Given the massive size of the territory involved and the depth of sectional divisions, it is perhaps not surprising that a union so diverse did not hold without the force of arms. That the separation was not final—that, in the end, reunion emerged out of conflict—is perhaps one reason why the tale is so gripping.

10

The Opening of America

I n the years before the Civil War, the name of Chauncey Jerome could be found traced in neat, sharp letters in a thousand different places across the globe: everywhere from the fireplace mantels of southern planters to the log huts of Illinois prairie farmers and even in Chinese trading houses in Canton. For Chauncey Jerome was a New England clockmaker, whose clever, inexpensive, and addictive machines had conquered the markets of the world.

Jerome, the son of a Connecticut blacksmith, had apprenticed himself to a carpenter during his boyhood, but after serving in the War of 1812 he decided to try his luck as a clockmaker. For several years he eked out a living peddling his products from farmhouse to farmhouse. Then in 1824 his career took off thanks to a "very showy" bronze looking-glass clock. The new model he had designed sold as fast as the clocks could be manufactured. Between 1827 and 1837 Jerome's factory produced more clocks than any other in the country. But when the Panic of 1837 struck, Jerome had to scramble to avoid financial ruin.

Looking for a new opportunity, he set out to produce an inexpensive brass "one-day" clock—so called because its winding mechanism kept it running that long. Traditionally, the works of these clocks were made of wood, and the wheels and teeth had to be painstakingly cut by hand. Furthermore, wooden clocks could not be exported overseas because the humidity on board ship swelled the wood and ruined them. Jerome's brass version proved more accurate than earlier types and cheaper to boot. Costs came down further when he began to use interchangeable parts and combined his operations for making cases and movements within a single factory in New Haven, Connecticut. By systematically organizing the production process, Jerome brought the price of a good clock within the reach of ordinary people. So popular were the new models that desperate competitors began attaching Jerome labels to their own inferior imitations.

Disaster struck again in 1855, when Jerome went into partnership with several unreliable associates. Within a few years his business faltered, then failed. At the age of 62, the once-prominent business leader found himself working again in a clock factory as an ordinary mechanic. He lived his last years in poverty.

Jerome rose higher than most Americans of his generation, and he fell further. Yet his fellow citizens shared his dreams of success, just as they were haunted by the fear of losing everything. For Jerome, not only material comforts vanished; so did respect. "One of the most trying things to me now," he confessed in his autobiography,

Under the wings of a proud eagle, the nation prospers with new forms of transportation, including steamboats, canals, and railroads. A bobbin, representing industry, is in the foreground, along with the traditional symbols of an anvil and a plow.

"is to see how I am looked upon by the community since I lost my property. I never was any better when I owned it than I am now, and never behaved any better. But how different is the feeling towards you, when your neighbors can make nothing more out of you. . . . You are passed by without notice."

Chauncey Jerome's life spanned the transition from the master-apprentice system of production to the beginnings of mechanization and the rise of the factory system. Crèvecoeur's vision of independent American farmers living mainly on what they themselves produced had, by 1850, become a dream of the past. In its place stood a commercial republic in which a full-blown national market drew together most settled areas of the country.

Market economy

The concept of the market is crucial here. Americans tied themselves to one another eagerly, even aggressively, through the mechanism of the free market. They sold cotton or wheat and bought manufactured cloth or brass one-day clocks. They borrowed money not merely to buy a house or farm but also to speculate and profit. They relied, even in many rural villages, on cash and paper money instead of bartering for goods and services. American life moved from less to more specialized forms of labor. It moved from face-to-face local dealings to impersonal, distant transactions. It shifted from the mechanically simple to the technologically complex and from less dense patterns of settlement on farms to more complex arrangements in cities and towns. Such were the changes Chauncey Jerome witnessed—indeed, changes he helped to bring about himself, with his clocks that divided the working days of Americans into more disciplined, orderly segments.

As these changes occurred about him, Jerome sensed that society had taken on a different tone—that the marketplace and its ethos had become dominant. "It is all money and business, business and money which make the man now-a-days," he complained. "Success is every thing, and it makes very little difference how, or what means he uses to obtain it." The United States, according to one foreign traveler, had become "one gigantic workshop, over the entrance of which there is the blazing inscription '*No admission here except on business.*'"

THE MARKET REVOLUTION

A truly national system of markets began to grow following the War of 1812, when the United States entered a period of unprecedented economic expansion. As it grew, the economy became varied enough to sustain and even accelerate its growth. Before the war it had been tied largely to international trade. The United States exported staples like cotton, wheat, tobacco, and timber; if the nations that bought these commodities suddenly stopped doing so, the domestic economy suffered. That happened during the European wars of the 1790s and again after 1803. Since so many Americans remained rural and primarily self-sufficient, they could not absorb any increase in goods produced by American manufacturers.

Growth of a domestic market

But the War of 1812 marked the turning point in the creation and expansion of a domestic market. First the embargo and then the war itself stimulated the growth of manufacturing, particularly in textiles. In 1808 the United States had 8000 spindles spinning cotton thread; by the end of the war the number had jumped to around 130,000. In addition, war had also bottled up capital in Europe. When peace was restored, this capital flowed into the United States, seeking investments. Finally, the war experience led the federal government to adopt policies designed to spur economic expansion.

The New Nationalism

After the war with Britain, leadership passed to a new generation of the Republic—younger men like Henry Clay, John C. Calhoun, and John Quincy Adams. All were

Chauncey Jerome's brass clock revolutionized clock-making and made him wealthy. The label displaying Jerome's name, the equivalent of a modern trademark, is visible inside the case.

ardent nationalists eager to use federal power to promote rapid development of the nation. Increasingly dominant within the Republican party, they advocated the "New Nationalism," a set of economic policies designed to foster the prosperity of all regions of the country and bind the nation more tightly together.

Even James Madison saw the need for increased federal activity, given the problems the government experienced during the war. The national bank had closed its doors in 1811 when its charter expired. Without it the country had fallen into financial chaos. Madison had opposed Hamilton's national bank in 1791, but now with his approval, Congress in 1816 chartered the Second Bank of the United States for a period of 20 years. Madison also agreed to a mildly protective tariff to aid budding American industries by raising the price of competing foreign goods. Passed in 1816, it set an average duty of 20 percent on imported woolen and cotton cloth, iron, and sugar. The measure enjoyed wide support in the North and West, while a number of southern representatives voted against it since most of its benefits went to northern manufacturers. *National bank*

Protective tariff

Madison also recommended that the government promote internal improvements such as roads, canals, and bridges. The war had demonstrated how cumbersome it was to move troops or supplies overland. While Madison did not believe that federal funds could be used for merely local projects, he was willing to support projects broader in scope. His successor, James Monroe, approved additional ones.

The Cotton Trade

Cotton proved to be the key to American economic development after 1815. By the end of the eighteenth century, southern planters had discovered that short-fibered cotton would grow in the lower part of the South. But the cotton contained sticky green seeds that could not be easily separated from the lint by hand. The needed breakthrough came in 1793, when Eli Whitney invented the cotton gin, a mechanical device that removed the seeds from the lint. The gin allowed a laborer to clean 50 pounds of cotton a day, compared with only one pound by hand. With prices high on the world market, cotton production in the Lower South soared. By 1840 the South produced more than 60 percent of the world supply, which accounted for almost two-thirds of all American exports.

The cotton trade was the major expansive force in the economy until the depression of 1839. Northern factories increasingly made money by turning raw cotton into cloth, while northern merchants reaped profits from shipping the cotton and then reshipping the textiles. Planters used the income they earned to purchase foodstuffs from the West and goods and services from the Northeast.

The Transportation Revolution

To become truly national, a market economy needed an efficient transportation network linking various regions of the nation. The economy had not become self-sustaining earlier partly because the only means of transporting goods cheaply was by water. Thus trade was limited largely to coastal and international markets, for even on rivers, bulky goods moved easily in only one direction—downstream.

All that changed, however, after 1815. From 1825 to 1855—the span of a single generation—the cost of transportation on land fell 95 percent, while its speed increased fivefold. As a result, new regions were drawn quickly into the market.

The Canal Age

Erie Canal

Canals attracted considerable investment capital, especially after the success of the wondrous Erie Canal. Built between 1818 and 1825, the canal stretched 364 miles from Albany on the Hudson River to Buffalo on Lake Erie. Its construction by the state was an act of faith, for in 1816 the United States had only 100 miles of canals, none longer than 28 miles. Then, too, the proposed route ran through forests, disease-ridden swamps, and unsettled wilderness. The canal's engineers lacked experience, but they made up for that by sheer ingenuity. Improving on European tools, they devised a cable and screw that allowed one man to pull down even the largest trees and a stump-puller that removed up to 40 stumps a day.

The project paid for itself within a few years. The Erie Canal reduced the cost of shipping a ton of goods from Buffalo to New York City from more than 19 cents a mile to less than 3 cents a mile. By 1860 the cost had fallen to less than a penny a mile. Where its busy traffic passed, settlers flocked, and towns like Rochester and Lockport sprang up and thrived by moving goods and serving markets. "Everything in this bustling place appears to be in motion," wrote one English traveler about Rochester in 1827. The steady flow of goods eastward gave New York City the dominant position in the scramble for control of western trade.

Whitney's cotton gin

The Erie Canal promoted urban growth, economic development, and feverish activity along its route. Here boatmen guiding their craft past busy laborers on the shore provide an indication of the commerce that quickly flourished on the waterway.

New York's commercial rivals, like Philadelphia and Baltimore, were soon frantically trying to build their own canals to the West. Western states like Ohio and Indiana, convinced that prosperity depended on cheap transportation, constructed canals to link interior regions with the Great Lakes. By 1840 the nation had completed more than 3300 miles of canals—a length greater than the distance from New York City to Seattle—at a cost of about $125 million. Almost half of that amount came from state governments.

By 1850 the canal era was over. The depression of 1839 caused several states to halt or slow their construction, especially since many poorly planned canals lost money. Still, whether profitable or not, canals sharply reduced transportation costs and stimulated economic development in a broad belt along their routes.

End of canal era

Steamboats and Railroads

Because of its vast expanse, the United States was particularly dependent on river transportation. But shipping goods downstream from Pittsburgh to New Orleans took 6 weeks, and the return journey required 17 weeks or more. Steamboats reduced the time of a trip from New Orleans to Louisville from 90 to 8 days, while cutting upstream costs by 90 percent.

*Western
steamboats*

Robert Fulton demonstrated the commercial possibilities of propelling a boat with steam when his ship, the *Clermont,* traveled in 1807 from New York City to Albany on the Hudson River. But steamboats had the greatest effect on transportation on western rivers, where the flat-bottomed boats could haul heavy loads even when the water level was low. The number of steamboats operating in those waters jumped from 17 in 1817 to 727 in 1855. Since steamboats could make many more voyages annually, the carrying capacity on the western rivers increased 100-fold between 1820 and 1860.

Governments did not invest heavily in steamboats as they had in canals; instead, their main assistance was removing fallen trees and other obstacles to navigation. Although railroads would end the steamboat's dominance by 1860, it was the major form of western transportation during the years in which the national market economy grew up, and it proved the most important factor in the rise of manufacturing in the Ohio and upper Mississippi valleys.

*Railroads'
later influence*

In 1830 the nation had only 13 miles of railroad track, and most of the lines constructed in the following decade served as feeder lines to canals. But soon enough, cities and towns saw that their economic future depended on having good rail links, so that by 1840 railroad and canal mileage were almost exactly equal (3325 miles). By 1850, the nation had a total of 8879 miles of track. Railroad rates were usually higher than canal or steamboat charges, but the new iron roads operated year-round, offered more direct routes, and moved goods about twice as fast. Even so, not until the 1850s did they come to dominate the transportation system.

TIME OF TRAVEL, 1800 AND 1830

1800 TRAVEL TIMES

1830 TRAVEL TIMES

PROFILE OF ERIE CANAL

Buffalo · Lockport · Rochester · Syracuse · Rome · Utica · Little Falls · Canajoharie · Schenectady · Albany

Lake Erie

570 FT.

Mohawk R.

Hudson R.

0 · 50 · 100 Miles
0 · 50 · 100 Kilometers

Lake Superior

BRITISH CANADA

ME.

WIS. TERR.

Lake Michigan

Lake Huron

MICH.

Lake Ontario

N.Y.

VT. · N.H.

Erie Canal

Lockport · Rochester · Albany · MASS. · Boston

Buffalo

R.I. · CONN.

IOWA TERR.

Lake Erie

PENNA.

Hudson R.

New York

Cleveland · RAIL LINK

Philadelphia

OHIO

N.J.

Wheeling · Pittsburgh

IND.

NATIONAL ROAD

Cumberland · Baltimore

MD. · DEL.

Potomac R.

Mississippi R.

Illinois R.

ILL.

Wabash R.

Vandalia · Louisville

VA.

St. Louis

James R.

MO.

KY.

Richmond

Cumberland R.

Missouri R.

Nashville

N.C.

ATLANTIC OCEAN

ARK.

TENN.

Arkansas R.

Memphis

Tennessee R.

S.C.

Savannah R.

GA.

Charleston

MISS.

ALA.

Savannah

Alabama R.

Natchez

Red R.

LA.

Mobile

New Orleans

FLA. TERR.

GULF OF MEXICO

0 · 100 · 200 Miles
0 · 100 · 200 Kilometers

—— Main roads

┴┴┴┴ Main canals

- - - Canals under construction

—— Navigable section of river

THE TRANSPORTATION NETWORK OF A MARKET ECONOMY, 1840

Canals played their most important role in the Northeast, where they linked eastern cities to western rivers and the Great Lakes. On the Erie Canal, a system of locks raised and lowered boats in a series of steps along the route. Steamboats were most crucial in the extensive river systems of the South and the West.

Agriculture in the Market Economy

The new forms of transportation had a remarkable effect on Crèvecoeur's yeoman farm families: they became linked ever more tightly to a national market system. Before the canal era, wheat could be shipped at a profit no farther than 50 miles. But given cheap transportation, farmers eagerly grew more grain and sold the surplus at distant markets.

Commercial agriculture   In this shift toward commercial agriculture, farmers began cultivating more acres, working longer hours, and adopting scientific farming methods, including crop rotation and the use of manures as fertilizer. Instead of bartering goods with friends and neighbors, they more often paid cash or depended on banks to extend them credit. Instead of taking the crops to market themselves, they began to rely on regional merchants, middlemen in a far-flung distribution system. Like southern planters, western wheat farmers increasingly sold in a world market. Banks and distributors advanced credit to farmers, who more and more competed in a market controlled by impersonal forces centered in distant locations.

As transportation and market networks connected more areas of the nation, they encouraged regional specialization. The South increasingly concentrated on staple crops for export, and the West grew foodstuffs, particularly grain. By 1850, Wisconsin and Illinois were major wheat-producing states. Eastern farmers, unable to compete with wheat yields from fertile western farms, shifted to grazing sheep or producing fruits, vegetables, and dairy products for rapidly growing urban areas.

Although foreign commerce expanded too, it was overshadowed by the dramatic growth in domestic markets, which absorbed more and more of the goods and services being produced. The cities of the East no longer looked primarily to the sea for their trade; they looked to southern and western markets. That, indeed, was a revolution in markets.

John Marshall and the Promotion of Enterprise

For a national market system to flourish, a climate favorable to investment had to exist. Under the leadership of Chief Justice John Marshall the Supreme Court became the branch of the federal government most aggressive in protecting the new forms of business central to the growing market economy.

Marshall, who presided over the Court from 1801 to 1835, at first glance seemed an unlikely leader. Informal in manners and almost sloppy in dress, he was nonetheless a commanding figure: tall and slender, with twinkling eyes and a contagious, hearty laugh. His forceful intellect was reinforced by his genial ability to persuade. Time after time he convinced his colleagues to uphold the sanctity of private property and the power of the federal government to promote economic growth.

Constitutionality of the national bank   In the case of *McCulloch v. Maryland* (1819) the Court upheld the constitutionality of the Second Bank of the United States. Maryland had levied a tax on the Baltimore branch of the national bank, which the bank refused to pay, and the case went to the Supreme Court. The Court struck down the tax. Just as Alexander Hamilton had argued in the debate over the first national bank, Marshall emphasized that the Constitution gave Congress the power to make all "necessary and proper" laws to carry out its delegated powers. If Congress believed that a bank would help it meet its responsibilities, such as maintaining the public credit and regulating the currency, then it was constitutional. The bank only had to be useful, not essential. "Let the end be legitimate," Marshall wrote, "let it be within the scope of the Constitution, and all means which are appropriate, which are plainly adapted to that end, which are not prohibited . . . are constitutional." By upholding Hamilton's doctrine of implied powers, Marshall enlarged federal power to an extraordinary degree.

He also encouraged a more freewheeling commerce in *Gibbons v. Ogden* (1824). *Interstate commerce* Under a New York law Aaron Ogden held a monopoly on steamboat traffic on the Hudson River between New Jersey and New York City. Gibbons, who had a federal license to operate a steamboat, set up a competing line and Ogden sued. The case gave Marshall a chance to define the greatest power of the federal government in peacetime, the right to regulate interstate commerce. In striking down a steamboat monopoly granted by the state of New York, the chief justice gave the term "commerce" the broadest possible definition, declaring that it covered all commercial dealings and that Congress's power over interstate commerce could be "exercised to its utmost extent." The result was increased business competition throughout society.

At the heart of most commercial agreements were private contracts, made between individuals or companies. Marshall took an active role in defining contract law, *Protection of contracts* which was then in its infancy. The case of *Fletcher v. Peck* (1810) showed how far he was willing to go to protect private property. The justices unanimously struck down a Georgia law taking back a land grant that a group of speculators had obtained by bribing members of the legislature. A grant was a contract, Marshall declared, and since the Constitution forbade states from impairing "the obligation of contracts," the legislature could not interfere with the grant once it had been made. Although the framers of the Constitution probably meant contracts to refer only to agreements between private parties, Marshall made no distinction between public and private agreements, thereby greatly expanding the meaning of the contract clause.

The most celebrated decision Marshall wrote on the contract clause was in *Dartmouth College v. Woodward*, decided in 1819. This case arose out of the attempt by New Hampshire to alter the college's charter granted by George III in 1769. The Court overturned the state law on the grounds that state charters were also contracts and could not be altered by later legislatures. By this ruling Marshall intended to protect corporations, which conducted business under charters granted by individual states.

Thus the Marshall Court encouraged economic risk taking. Its decisions protected property and contracts, limited state interference in business affairs, and created a climate of business confidence.

General Incorporation Laws

Corporations were not new in American business, but as the economy expanded, they grew in numbers. Corporations had the advantage of continuing beyond the lives of *Importance of corporations* the individuals who created them. By pooling investors' resources, they also provided a way to raise capital for large-scale undertakings. Then, too, corporations offered the advantage of limited liability: that is, an investor was liable only for the amount he or she had invested, which limited a person's financial risk. Small and medium-sized

Daily Lives

TIME AND TRAVEL

Floating Palaces of the West

Plying the Mississippi River and its tributaries, the steamboat carried both freight and passengers, but it won its greatest fame as a mode of travel. The most luxurious boats, dubbed "floating palaces," offered accommodations far beyond the experience of the average American. Steamboats also provided the cheapest form of inland transportation up to the Civil War. By midcentury, cabin passage for the 1400-mile trip from Louisville to New Orleans was only $12 to $15.

On the earliest steamboats passengers were housed on the main deck along with the cargo, but as the boats became larger, designers added a second, or boiler, deck (which, despite its name, was not where the boilers were located). Eventually a third level was added, the hurricane or texas, with additional accommodations. The boiler deck's saloon was the center of society, with the ladies' parlor at one end and the barroom at the other. Besides serving as a dining room and lounge, the saloon sometimes provided the sleeping quarters for men. Berths were arranged in two tiers on both sides and, at least on the better boats, contained bedding and a mattress. Women entered the saloon only for meals.

Steamboats also offered passage on the main deck for about one-fifth the price of a regular ticket. These passengers received no living quarters or toilet facilities and had to provide their own food. Then, too, boiler explosions, collisions, and sinkings from a snag took a much higher loss of life among lower deck passengers, who were primarily the poor, immigrants, and African Americans. Between 1811 and 1851, 44 steamboats collided, 166 burned, 209 exploded, and 576 hit obstructions and sank, costing thousands of lives.

The steamboat was, as many travelers remarked, a "world in miniature," conveying slaves and planters, farmers and manufacturers, merchants and frontier families, soldiers and Indians, ministers and professional gamblers. As fares steadily dropped, people of widely different wealth and position were thrown together in the main cabin and mingled with a democratic familiarity. Women spent their time talking, sewing, caring for children, and strolling the deck. Men passed the time in conversation about politics, the weather, business, and crops. The bar was the center of their social world, and gambling was rife.

The most famous vessels on the rivers boasted intricately carved gingerbread facings, painted a glistening white and trimmed in gold leaf—an architectural style known as "Steamboat Gothic." For all their luxurious veneer, however, steamboats lacked many amenities. Most six-by-six staterooms had two narrow shelves to sleep on and no light-

---

businesses continued to be run as partnerships and individual ventures, but ventures such as banks, insurance companies, railroads, and manufacturing firms—which all required a large amount of capital—increasingly were incorporated.

Originally, state legislatures were required to approve a special charter for each

Daily Lives

The luxurious saloon furnishings of a Mississippi steamboat, the *Princess*

James Audubon journeyed from Louisville to St. Louis on what he described as "the very filthiest of all filthy old rattraps I ever traveled in." He grumbled particularly about a leaky roof, threadbare sheets, and pillows filled with corn husks.

In maintaining law and order, the captain was aided by the passengers, who in the tradition of the frontier sometimes formed their own courts to deal with those charged with minor offenses. Travelers accused of theft, illicit sexual relations, or gambling disputes might find themselves flogged or put ashore at some desolate spot. In one case, when a young man and woman traveling together as "cousins" aroused suspicion, the passengers insisted on an investigation by the boat's officers, who discovered the pair sharing a berth. At the next stop, while the boat waited, indignant passengers marched the couple ashore, rounded up a minister, and compelled them to get married.

Despite the discomforts of swarming mosquitoes, heat from the boilers, and noisy engines at all hours of the night, observers agreed that journeying by steamboat was far more pleasant than taking a stagecoach, the principal alternative in the West before 1850. With their churning paddlewheels, gingerbread decks, and belching smokestacks, these gaudy vessels became the grandest showpieces of life along the commercial waterways of the Mississippi.

ing or heat. The washrooms in the main cabin contained tin basins and pitchers of cold water, a comb and brush, and a communal toothbrush. One traveler complained that there were only two towels for 70 men on one boat. Water, for both drinking and washing, came directly from the river and was laden with silt. Steamboat food was ample but often poorly prepared and saturated with grease. Furthermore, the average riverboat hardly lived up to the standards of the most famous packets. In 1843 John

new corporation. Beginning in the 1830s, states adopted general incorporation laws that automatically granted a corporation charter to any applicant who met certain minimum qualifications. This reform made it much easier and faster to secure a charter and stimulated organization of the national market.

A RESTLESS TEMPER

"Eating on the first of May," contended one New York City resident, "is entirely out of the question." For that was "moving day," when all the leases in the city expired. On that date nearly everyone, it seemed, moved to a new residence or place of business. Bedlam prevailed as furniture and personal belongings cluttered the sidewalks and people, movers, and horses crowded the streets. To Frances Trollope, it looked as if the whole population was "flying from the plague." Whereas in Europe millions of ordinary folk had never ventured beyond their local village, a Boston paper commented in 1828, "here, the whole population is in motion. . . ."

A People in Motion

Between 1815 and 1850, the nation reverberated with almost explosive energy. "An American . . . wants to perform within a year what others do within a much longer period," observed Francis Lieber, a noted political scientist who emigrated from Germany. The famous French commentator Alexis de Tocqueville was astonished, like most Europeans, at the restless mobility of the average American. "Born often under another sky, placed in the middle of an always moving scene, . . . the American . . . grows accustomed only to change, and ends by regarding it as the natural state of man."

A high-speed society   This emphasis on speed affected nearly every aspect of American life. Americans ate so quickly that one disgruntled European insisted food was "pitchforked down." Steamboat captains risked boiler explosions for the honor of having the fastest boat on the river, prompting the visiting English novelist Charles Dickens to

---

Europeans were shocked that Americans bolted their food or gorged themselves on anything within reach, as this English drawing indicates. Such habits reflected both the indifferent preparation of food and the frenetic tempo of American life.

comment that traveling under these conditions was like taking up "lodgings on the first floor of a powder mill." American technology emphasized speed over longevity. Unlike European railroads, American railroads were lightweight, hastily constructed, and paid little heed to the safety or comfort of passengers. Even so, Americans quickly embraced this new mode of transportation because of its speed. Eighteen-year-old Caroline Fitch of Boston likened her first ride on a railroad to a "lightning flash": "It was 'whew!' and we were there, and 'whew!' and we were back again."

Even within railroad cars Americans were too fidgety to adapt to the European system of individual passenger compartments. Instead, American cars had a center aisle, allowing ever-restless passengers to wander the length of the train. Riding the rails in Texas, an English visitor was astounded that the passengers were "constantly jumping on and off whilst the train is in motion, and larking from one car to the other."

Horatio Greenough, a sculptor who returned to the United States in 1836 after an extended stay abroad, was amazed and a bit frightened by the pace he witnessed. "Go ahead! is the order of the day," he observed. "The whole continent presents a scene of scrambling and roars with greedy hurry." In the economic arena, the growth of a national market increased the sense of motion and restlessness. But social factors also contributed to this high-speed society.

Population Growth

The American population continued to double about every 22 years—more than twice the birthrate of Great Britain. The census, which counted fewer than 4 million Americans in 1790, surpassed 23 million in 1850. Although the birthrate peaked in 1800, it declined only slowly before 1840. During the 1840s, as urban areas grew rapidly, it dropped about 10 percent, the first significant decrease in American history. In cities, families were smaller, in part because the labor of children was not as critical to the family's economic welfare.

At the same time, many basic population characteristics changed little throughout the first half of the nineteenth century. Life expectancy did not improve significantly, the population remained quite young, and early marriage remained the norm, especially in rural areas.

From 1790 to 1820 natural increase accounted for virtually all of the country's population growth. But immigration, which had been disrupted by the Napoleonic Wars in Europe, revived after 1815. In the 1830s some 600,000 immigrants arrived, more than double the number in the quarter century after 1790. And these new-comers proved to be merely a foretaste of the flood of immigrants that reached America beginning in the late 1840s.

Immigration rises after 1830

The Federal Land Rush

The vast areas of land available for settlement absorbed much of the growing population. By 1850 almost half of all Americans lived outside the original 13 states. Well over 2 million lived beyond the Mississippi River. As settlers streamed west, speculation in western lands reached frenzied proportions. In the single year of 1818, at the peak of land-buying fever, the United States sold 3.5 million acres of its public domain. (In contrast, only 68,000 acres were sold in 1800.)

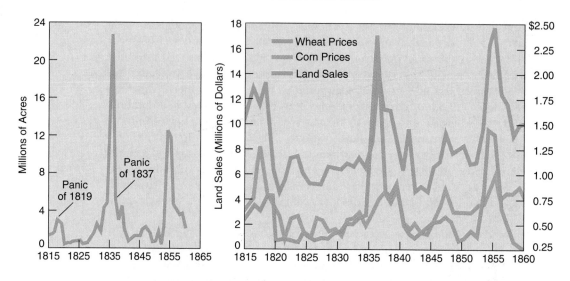

Purchases of Public Land			
YEAR	PRICE PER ACRE	MINIMUM ACREAGE	TERMS OF SALE
1785	$1.00	640	Cash
1796	2.00	640	One-half cash; 1 year to pay balance
1800	2.00	320	Payment over 4 years
1804	2.00	160	Payment over 4 years
1820	1.25	80	Cash
1832	1.25	40	Cash
1841	Preemption (squatter could buy up to 160 acres at minimum price of $1.25 per acre)		
1854	Graduation (price of unsold lands reduced over time to a minimum of 12.5 cents per acre)		

WESTERN LAND SALES AND THE PRICE OF CORN AND WHEAT
Western farmers' expectations of future income were tied to the price of corn and wheat. As commodity prices rose, farmers eagerly bought land on credit, anticipating that future profits would enable them to pay off their mortgages. As the graph illustrates, when wheat and corn prices fell sharply in the Panic of 1819, land sales plummeted, and many farmers who had purchased on credit found themselves unable to pay their debts; a similar pattern is apparent in the 1830s. In the South there was a comparable relationship between land sales and the price of cotton. In order to encourage settlement, the terms to purchase public land (table, bottom) were made increasingly favorable, so that eventually a squatter could acquire the traditional 80-acre family farm on good land for only $100. Nevertheless, speculators continued to hold vast tracts of the public domain.

The Panic of 1819 sent sales and prices crashing, and in the depression that followed many farmers lost their farms. Congress reacted by abolishing credit sales and demanding payment in cash, but it tempered this policy by lowering the price of the cheapest lands to $1.25 an acre. (The best lands, sold at auction, fetched considerably higher prices, however.) The government also reduced the minimum tract to 80 acres, which meant that an ordinary farm could be purchased for $100.

Even so, speculators purchased most of the public lands sold, since the law put no limit on how many acres an individual or a land company could buy. These land speculators played a leading role in settlement of the West. To hasten sales, they usually sold land partially on credit—a vital aid to poorer farmers. They also provided loans to purchase needed tools and supplies, since the cost of establishing a farm was beyond the means of many young men. Many farmers became speculators themselves, buying up property in the neighborhood and selling it to latecomers at a tidy profit. "Speculation in real estate has been the ruling idea and occupation of the Western mind," one Englishman reported in the 1840s. "Clerks, labourers, farmers, storekeepers merely followed their callings for a living while they were speculating for their fortunes." *Speculators help settle western lands*

Geographic Mobility

Given such rapid settlement, geographic mobility became one of the most striking characteristics of the American people. The 1850 census revealed that nearly half of all native-born free Americans lived outside the state where they had been born. In Boston from 1830 to 1860 perhaps one-third of the inhabitants changed their place of residence each year. Some owners, dissatisfied with their location, moved their houses instead. An astonished Charles Dickens recounted he once met a house "coming downhill at a good round trot, drawn by some twenty oxen!" The typical American "has no root in the soil," visiting Frenchman Michel Chevalier observed, but "is always in the mood to move on, always ready to start in the first steamer that comes along from the place where he had just now landed." Indeed, Americans were so mobile that Chevalier thought the national emblem should be a steamboat or locomotive. *On the road again*

It was the search for opportunity, more than anything else, that accounted for such restlessness. An American moved, noted one British observer, "if by so doing he can make $10 where before he made $8." Often, the influence of the market uprooted Americans too. In 1851, a new railroad line bypassed the village of Auburn, Illinois, on the way to Springfield. "It seemed a pity," wrote one resident, "that so pretty a site as that of the old town should be abandoned for so unpromising a one . . . much of it mere swamp—but railroad corporations possess no bowels of compassion, the practical more than the beautiful being their object." After residents quickly moved to the new town that sprang up around the depot, a neighboring farmer purchased the site, plowed up the streets, and Auburn reverted to a cornfield.

Urbanization

Even with the growth of a national market, the United States remained a rural nation. Nevertheless, the four decades after 1820 witnessed the fastest rate of urbanization in American history. In 1820 there were only 12 cities with a population of more than 5000; by 1850 there were nearly 150. The 1820 census classified only about 9 percent of the American people as urban (living in towns with a population of 2500 or more). Forty years later the number had risen to 20 percent. As a result,

St. Louis, a major urban center that developed in the West, depended on the steamboat to sustain its commerce, as this 1859 illustration makes clear.

the ratio of farmers to city dwellers steadily dropped from 15 to 1 in 1800 to 5.5 to 1 in 1850. Improved transportation, the declining productivity of many eastern farms, the beginnings of industrialization, and the arrival of immigrants all stimulated the growth of cities.

Urban centers, old and new

The most heavily urbanized area of the country was the Northeast, where in 1860 more than a third of the population lived in cities.° The nation's largest city was New York, with more than half a million people, and older cities like Philadelphia, Boston, Baltimore, and New Orleans continued to be major urban centers. Equally significant, important urban centers such as St. Louis and Cincinnati arose in the West. Remarkably, by the century's midpoint, 40 percent of the nation's total urban population resided in interior cities. The South, with only 10 percent of its people living in cities, was the least urbanized region.

All of these changes—the amazing growth of the population, the quickening movement westward, and the rising migration to the cities—pointed to a fundamental reorientation of American development. Expansion was the keynote of the new America, and the prospects it offered both excited and unsettled Americans.

°The Northeast included New England and the mid-Atlantic states (New York, Pennsylvania, and New Jersey). The South comprised the slave states plus the District of Columbia.

THE RISE OF FACTORIES

It was an isolated life, growing up in a rural, hilly Vermont. But stories of the textile factories that had sprung up in Lowell and other towns in Massachusetts reached even small villages like Barnard. Fifteen-year-old Mary Paul was working there as a domestic servant when she asked her father for permission to move to Lowell. "I am in need of clothes which I cannot get about here," she explained. In 1845 two friends from Barnard helped her find a job at the Lowell mills, from which she earned $128 in 11 months. After four years she returned home but now found "countryfied" life too confining. This time she left her rural hometown for good. She moved about and supported herself at several occupations before finally marrying and settling down in nearby Lynn.

Mary Paul was one of thousands of rural Americans whose lives were fundamentally altered by the economic transformation of the young republic. The changes in her lifestyle and her working habits demonstrated that the new factories and industries needed more than technological innovation to run smoothly. Equally crucial, the labor used to manufacture these goods needed to be reorganized.

Technological Advances

Small-scale manufacturing

Before 1815 manufacturing had been done in homes or shops by skilled artisans who turned out a small number of finished goods, often made to order for local customers. As master craftworkers, they taught their trades to apprentices and journeymen. In addition, women often worked in their homes part-time under the putting-out system, making finished articles from raw material supplied by merchant capitalists. During the winter months many farm families manufactured items such as brooms and fans to supplement their income.

After 1815 this older form of manufacturing began to give way to factories with machinery tended by unskilled or semiskilled laborers. Cheap transportation networks, the rise of cities, and the availability of capital and credit all stimulated the shift to factory production.

Acceptance of technology

From England came many of the earliest technological innovations. But Americans often improved on the British machines or adapted them to more extensive uses. In contrast to the more traditional societies of Europe, "everything new is quickly introduced here," one visitor commented in 1820. "There is no clinging to old ways; the moment an American hears the word 'invention' he pricks up his ears." From 1790 to 1860 the United States Patent Office granted more patents than England and France combined.

To protect their economic advantage, the British forbade the export of any textile machinery or emigration of any craftworker trained in their construction. But in 1790 a mill worker named Samuel Slater slipped by English authorities and built the first textile mill in America. Two decades later, the Boston merchant Francis Cabot Lowell imitated British designs for a power loom and then improved on them.

Interchangeable parts

The first machines required highly skilled workers to both build and repair them. Eli Whitney had a better idea. Having won a contract to produce 10,000 muskets for the government, he developed machinery that would mass-produce parts that were interchangeable from one gun to another. Such parts had to be manufactured to rigid specifications that Whitney had difficulty attaining, but once the process was perfected after his death, a worker could assemble a musket quickly with only a few tools. Simeon North applied the same principle to the production of clocks, and Chauncey Jerome followed North's example and soon surpassed him.

Communi-
cation

What rail and steam engines did for transportation, Samuel F. B. Morse's telegraph did for communications. Morse patented a device that sent electrical pulses over a wire in 1837, and before long telegraph lines fanned out in all directions, linking various parts of the country instantaneously. By 1860 there were more than 50,000 miles of telegraph lines laid. The new telegraph sped business information, helped link the transportation network, and allowed newspapers to provide readers with up-to-date news.

Indeed, the invention of the telegraph and the perfection of a power press (1847) by Robert Hoe and his son Richard revolutionized journalism. The mechanical press sharply increased the speed with which sheets could be printed over the old hand method. Mass-produced newspapers, often selling for only a penny, gained huge circulations since ordinary families could afford them. Hoe's press had a similar impact on book publishing, as thousands of copies could be printed at affordable prices.

Textile Factories

The factory system originated in the Northeast, where capital, water power, and transportation facilities were available. As in England, the production of cloth was the first manufacturing process to make significant use of the new technology on a large scale. Eventually all the processes of manufacturing cloth were brought together in a single location, from opening the cotton bales to weaving the cloth, and machines did virtually all the work.

Lowell

In 1813 a group of wealthy Boston merchants chartered the Boston Manufacturing Company and established the first fully integrated textile factory at Waltham, Massachusetts. Expanding their highly profitable operations, these investors, known as the Boston Associates, set up operations in 1820 at Chelmsford, Massachusetts, which they renamed Lowell. Intended as a model community, Lowell soon became the nation's most famous center of textile manufacturing.

Its founders sought to avoid the wretched misery that characterized the factory system in England by combining paternalism with high profits. Instead of relying primarily on child labor or a permanent working class, the Lowell mills employed daughters of New England farm families. Thus women were the first factory workers in the United States. They lived in company boardinghouses under the watchful eye of a matron. To its many visitors, Lowell presented an impressive sight: huge factories, well-kept houses, bustling shops. Female employees were encouraged to attend lectures and use the library. They even published their own magazine, the *Lowell Offering*.

Hard work in
the mills

In reality, factory life involved strict rules and long hours of tedious, repetitive work. At Lowell, for example, workers could be fined for lateness or misconduct, including talking on the job. Alcohol, cards, and gambling were forbidden in the shop or mill yard. The women's morals in the boardinghouses were strictly guarded; male visitors were supervised, and there was a 10 p.m. curfew. Work typically began at 7 a.m. (earlier in the summer) and continued until 7 at night, six days a week. With only

"There are very many young ladies at work in the factories that given up milinary dressmaking and school-keeping for to work in the mill," wrote Malenda Edwards in 1839. This young woman was one of them.

30 minutes for the noon meal, many workers had to run to the boardinghouse and back to avoid being late. Winter was the "lighting up" season, when work began before daylight and ended after dark. The only light after sunset came from whale oil lamps that filled the long rooms with smoke. Even in summer the factories were poorly lit and badly ventilated.

Female workers

Although the labor was hard, the female operators earned from $2.40 to $3.20 a week, wages that were considered good at the time. (Domestic servants and seamstresses, two of the most common jobs women held, were paid less than a dollar a week.) The average "mill girl," as they were called, was between 16 and 30 years old. Most were not working to support their families back home on the farm; instead they wanted to save some money for perhaps the first time in their lives and sample some of life's pleasures. "I must . . . have something of my own before many more years have passed," Sally Rice wrote when her parents asked her to return home to Somerset, Vermont. "And where is that something coming from if I go home and earn nothing?"

The sense of sisterhood that united women in the boardinghouses made it easier for farm daughters to adjust to the stress and regimen the factory imposed on them. So did their view of the situation as temporary rather than permanent, for most women worked in the mills no more than five years before getting married.

As competition in the textile industry intensified, factory managers looked to raise productivity. In the mid-1830s the mills began to increase the workloads and speed up the machinery. Even these changes failed to maintain previous profits, and on several occasions factories cut wages. The ever-quickening pace of work finally provoked resistance among the mill workers. Several times in the 1830s wage cuts sparked strikes in which a minority of workers walked out. Management retaliated by firing strike leaders, hiring new workers, and blacklisting women who refused to return. In the 1840s workers' protests focused on the demand for a 10-hour day.

Transforma-
tion of Lowell

The quest for profits also undercut the owners' paternalism. As the mills expanded, a smaller proportion of the workers lived in company boardinghouses and moral regulations were relaxed. But the greatest change was a shift in the workforce from native-born women to Irish immigrants. In 1845 the Irish made up only 8 percent of the Lowell workforce. By 1860 they amounted to almost half, many of them men and children. Because these new workers were poor and desperate for work, wages declined further. And because they did not view their situation as temporary, a permanent working class began to take shape.

Lowell and the Environment

Lowell was a city built on water power. Early settlers had used the power of the Merrimack River to run mills, but never on the scale used by the new textile factories. As the market spread, Americans came to link progress with the fullest use of the natural resources of the environment. Just as they had done in Lowell itself, the Boston Associates sought to impose a sense of order and regularity on the surrounding physical environment in order to efficiently use its natural resources. In the process, they fundamentally reshaped the area's waterscape.

Reshaping the
area's
waterscape

As more and more mills were built, the Boston Associates sought to harness water for energy. By 1836, Lowell had seven canals, with a supporting network of locks and dams, to govern the Merrimack's flow and distribute water to the city's twenty-six mills. The Associates also built dams at several points along the river to store water and divert it into power canals for factories. At Lawrence, they constructed the largest dam in the world at the time, a 32-foot-high granite structure that spanned 1600 feet across the river. But even dammed, the Merrimack's waters proved insufficient. So the Associates gained control of a series of lakes in New Hampshire covering over 100 square miles that fed into the river system. By damming these lakes, they could provide a regular flow of water down the river, especially in the drier summer months. In the course of establishing this elaborate water-control system, they came to see water as a form of property, divorced from the ownership of land along the river. Water became a commodity that was measured in terms of its power to operate a certain number of spindles and looms.

Damaging
effects

By regulating the river's waters, the Boston Associates made the Merrimack Valley the greatest industrial center in the country in the first half of the nineteenth century. But not all who lived in the valley benefited. By raising water levels, the dams flooded farm lands, blocked the transportation of logs downstream, and damaged mills upstream by reducing the current and creating backwater that impeded waterwheels. The dams also devastated the fish population by preventing upstream spawning, while factories routinely dumped their wastes into the river to be carried downstream. These wastes, combined with sewage from the growing population, eventually contaminated water supplies. Epidemics of typhoid, cholera, and dysentery occurred with increasing frequency, so that by midcentury Lowell had a reputation as a particularly unhealthy community.

In the end, the factory system fundamentally transformed the environment. Far from existing in harmony with its rural surroundings, Lowell, with its clattering machines and dammed rivers, presented a glaring contrast to rural life. The founding vision of Lowell had disappeared.

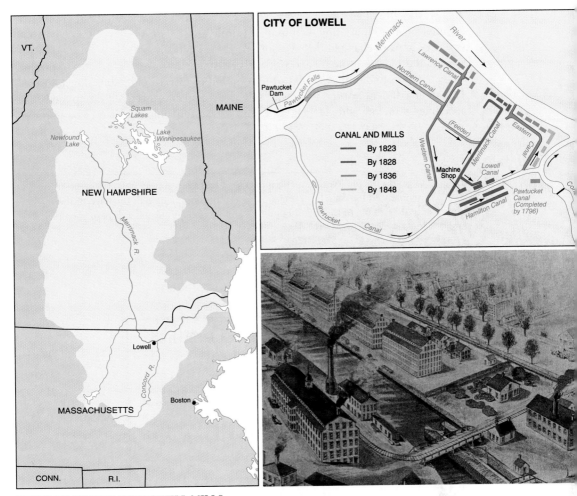

DEVELOPMENT OF THE LOWELL MILLS
As more mills were built at Lowell, the demand increased for water to power them. By 1859 the mills drew water from lakes 80 to 100 miles upstream, including Winnipesaukee, Squam, and Newfound. The map at left shows the watersheds affected. In the city of Lowell (right), a system of canals was enlarged over several decades. In the painting (done in 1845), the machine shop can be seen at left, with a row of mills alongside a canal. Rail links tied Lowell and Boston together.

Industrial Work

For most workers, adaptation to the disciplined work routine of the factory did not happen easily. Traditionally, artisans had worked within the home. Apprentices were considered part of the family, and masters were responsible not only for teaching their apprentices a trade but also for providing them some education and for supervising their moral behavior. Journeymen took pride in their work, knowing that if they perfected their skill, they could become respected master artisans with their own

Artisan system

shops. Nor did skilled artisans work by the clock, at a steady pace, but rather in bursts of intense labor alternating with more leisurely time.

Transforma-
tion of work

The factory changed that. Factory-produced goods were not as finished or elegant as those done by hand, and pride in craftsmanship gave way to rates of productivity. At the same time, workers were required to discard old habits, for industrialism demanded a worker who was sober, dependable, and self-disciplined. The machines, whirring and clacking away, set a strict schedule that had to be followed.

Long hours and punctuality: that is the message of this Lowell timetable. Often accustomed to a less regimented life on a farm, machine operators complained of the pace of the machines and the tyranny of the factory bell that summoned and dismissed them each day. A song, "The Lowell Factory Girl," described factory life:

> "The factory bell begins to ring,
> and we must all obey,
> And to our old employment go,
> or else be turned away."

TIME TABLE OF THE LOWELL MILLS,

To take effect on and after Oct. 21st, 1851.

The Standard time being that of the meridian of Lowell, as shown by the regulator clock of JOSEPH RAYNES, 43 Central Street

	From 1st to 10th inclusive.				From 11th to 20th inclusive.				From 21st to last day of month.			
	1st Bell	2d Bell	3d Bell	Eve. Bell	1st Bell	2d Bell	3d Bell	Eve. Bell	1st Bell	2d Bell	3d Bell	Eve. Bell
January,	5.00	6.00	6.50	•7.30	5.00	6 00	6.50	•7.30	5.00	6.00	6.50	•7.30
February,	4.30	5.30	6.40	•7.30	4.30	5.30	6.25	•7.30	4.30	5.30	6.15	•7.30
March,	5.40	6.00		•7.30	5.20	5.40		•7.30	5.05	5.25		6.35
April,	4.45	5.05		6.45	4.30	4.50		6.55	4.30	4.50		7.00
May,	4 30	4.50		7·00	4.30	4.50		7.00	4.30	4.50		7 00
June,	"	"		"	"	"		"	"	"		"
July,	"	"		"	"	"		"	"	"		"
August,	"	"		"	"	"		"	"	"		"
September,	4.40	5.00		6.45	4.50	5.10		6.30	5.00	5.20		•7.30
October,	5.10	5.30		•7.30	5.20	5.40		•7.30	5.35	5.55		•7.30
November,	4.30	5.30	6.10	•7.30	4.30	5.30	6.20	•7.30	5.00	6.00	6.35	•7.30
December,	5.00	6.00	6.45	•7.30	5.00	6.00	6.50	•7.30	5.00	6·00	6.50	•7.30

• Excepting on Saturdays from Sept. 21st to March 20th inclusive, when it is rung at 20 minutes after sunset.

YARD GATES,

Will be opened at ringing of last morning bell, of meal bells, and of evening bells; and kept open Ten minutes.

MILL GATES.

Commence hoisting Mill Gates, Two minutes before commencing work.

WORK COMMENCES,

At Ten minutes after last morning bell, and at Ten minutes after bell which "rings in" from Meals.

BREAKFAST BELLS.

During March "Ring out".........at....7.30 a. m........."Ring in" at 8:05 a. m.
April 1st to Sept. 20th inclusive.....at....7 00 " " .... " " at 7.35 " "
Sept. 21st to Oct. 31st inclusive.....at....7.30 " " .... " " at 8.05 " "
Remainder of year work commences after Breakfast.

DINNER BELLS.

"Ring out"..................................12.30 p. m........."Ring in".... 1.05 p. m.

In all cases, the *first* stroke of the bell is considered as marking the time.

Absenteeism, lateness, and drunkenness hurt productivity and, since work was specialized, disrupted the regular factory routine. Thus industrialization not only produced a fundamental change in the way work was organized, it transformed the very nature of work.

For newcomers to industrial ways, the factory clock became the symbol of the new order. One mill worker who finally quit complained of "obedience to the ding-dong of the bell—just as though we are so many living machines." Along with the loss of personal freedom came the loss of standing in the community. Unlike the master-apprentice relationship, factories sharply separated workers from management. Few workers rose through the ranks to supervisory positions, and even fewer could achieve the artisan's dream of setting up one's own business. Even well-paid workers sensed their decline in status.

The Shoe Industry

Shoemaking illustrated the process at work. Traditionally, a skilled cobbler knew how to judge the quality of leather, cut out the various parts of a shoe, and stitch and glue the parts together. He then sold the shoes in the same shop where he and his apprentices made them. Unlike the textile industry, shoemaking was not rapidly transformed in this period by a shift to heavy machinery. Even so, expanding national markets fundamentally altered the business.

Following in his father's footsteps, Micajah Pratt, a cobbler from Lynn, Massachusetts, began selling shoes in 1812 to customers in New England. He found, however, that there were ready markets in the South and West for cheaply made shoes. So he hired workers to produce shoes in larger and larger central shops. Pratt cut costs further by using new production techniques, such as standardized patterns and sole-cutting machines. He eventually employed as many as 500 men and women and produced about a quarter million pairs of shoes annually. Other shoe manufacturers adopted similar strategies, and Lynn soon became the nation's shoe manufacturing center.

With the shoe industry booming, Lynn's population doubled every 20 years. Yet so great was the national market that manufacturers could not keep pace with demand. Increasingly they hired nearby farmers, fishermen, and their families to do part-time work at home. Women and girls sewed the upper parts of a shoe, men and boys attached the bottoms. While slow, this mode of production allowed wages to be reduced still further. A few highly paid workers performed critical tasks like cutting the leather, but most work was done either in large central shops or in homes. With workers no longer able to make an entire shoe, in little more than a generation shoemaking ceased to be a craft. Though not organized in a factory setting, it had become essentially an assembly-line process.

Lynn as the center of shoemaking

The Labor Movement

In this newly emerging economic order, workers sometimes organized to protect their rights and traditional ways of life. Craftworkers like carpenters, printers, and tailors formed unions, and in 1834 individual unions came together in the National Trades' Union.

The leaders of these groups argued that labor was degraded in America: workers endured long hours, low pay, and low status. Workers were not being rewarded according to the value of their labor, they argued; instead, the idle rich lived off the industrious poor. Unlike most American social thinkers of the day, a number of labor leaders accepted the idea of conflict between different classes. They did not believe that the interests of workers and employers could be reconciled, and they blamed the plight of labor on monopolies, especially banking and paper money, and on machines and the factory system.

If the unions' rhetoric sounded radical, the solutions they proposed were moderate. Reformers agitated for public education and abolition of imprisonment for debt to provide better opportunities for workers. Leaders saw effective unions and political action as the means to restore labor to its former honored position. Proclaiming the republican virtues of freedom and equality, they attacked special privilege and decried workers' loss of independence.

The labor movement gathered some momentum in the decade before the Panic of 1837, but in the depression that followed, its strength collapsed. During hard times, few workers were willing to strike or engage in collective action. Nor did skilled craftworkers, who spearheaded the union movement, feel a particularly strong bond with semiskilled factory workers and unskilled laborers. More than a decade of agitation did finally gain the 10-hour day for some workers by the 1850s, and the courts also recognized workers' right to strike, but these gains had little immediate impact.

Workers were united in resenting the industrial system and their loss of status. But they found themselves divided by a host of other factors: ethnic and racial antagonisms, gender, conflicting religious perspectives, occupational differences, party loyalties, and disagreements over tactics. For most workers, the factory and industrialism were not agents of opportunity but reminders of their loss of independence and a measure of control over their lives.

COUNTERPOINT

Workers and industriali- zation

The process of industrialization was both sweeping and complex, so it is not surprising that historians have disagreed over its impact on the lives of workers. Economic historians generally emphasize industrialization's benefits. Focusing on wages and the standard of living, they estimate that between 1820 and 1860 real wages rose anywhere from 60 to 100 percent. Even unskilled workers enjoyed a rise in income, thanks partly to higher wages but mostly due to the lower cost of consumer items, which were now mass-produced. At the beginning of the century only prosperous families could enjoy items like matched chairs, finished furniture, carpets, clocks, silverware, and dishes. Historians examining estate inventories, however, have found that by midcentury such items were well within reach of workers and their families. Inexpensive textiles enlarged personal wardrobes, allowed for more frequent changes of clothing, and thus promoted cleanliness. Workers' diets also improved as the variety of foods available in stores greatly increased. These gains spread throughout all ranks of free white society.

Labor historians, who emphasize instead workers' attitudes, have painted a bleaker picture. As workers ceased to be skilled craftspeople, they sensed that manual labor no longer commanded respect in the community. Moreover, even though their standard of living might be increasing, workers were receiving a smaller *pro-*

portion of the wealth their labor produced. Given this increasingly unequal distribution of wealth, they were not as well off as employers and professionals, who no longer did manual labor. Furthermore, they faced a lifetime of hard and tedious work with only a limited chance of rising into the middle class. From this perspective, industrialization took a heavy psychological toll on factory laborers by weakening their pride and independence and hardening class lines. Their despair was voiced by a group of cotton mill workers who protested that workers were becoming "mere machine[s] producing wealth by perpetual exertion, yet living a life of unceasing anxiety and want. . . ."

SOCIAL STRUCTURES OF THE MARKET SOCIETY

Farmers, workers, and merchants—all these Americans were affected, as individuals, by the revolution in markets. Equally critical, the market revolution restructured American society as a whole. It created greater extremes between the rich and the poor, contributed to the rise of a growing middle class, placed greater emphasis on material goods, and even changed the way Americans thought about time.

Economic Specialization

To begin with, the spread of the market produced greater specialization. As we have seen, transportation networks made it possible for farmers to concentrate on producing certain crops, while factories could focus on making a single item such as cloth or shoes. Within factories, the division of labor broke down the manufacture of an item into smaller, more specialized (and less skilled) tasks. As we have seen, no longer did one cobbler produce a pair of shoes from start to finish.

This process evolved at different rates. Textiles and milling were completely mechanized. Other sectors of the economy, like shoes and men's clothing, depended little on machinery. Indeed, large factories were the exception rather than the rule. Much manufacturing was still done in smaller shops with few employees. Even so, the tendency was toward more technology, greater efficiency, and increasing specialization.

Specialization had consequences at home as well. The average eighteenth-century American woman produced thread, cloth, clothing, and candles in the home for family use. With the growth of factories, however, household manufacturing all but disappeared. As a result, women lost many of the economic functions they had once performed at home. Again, textiles are a striking example. Between 1815 and 1860, the price of cotton cloth fell from 18 to 2 cents a yard. Because manufactured cloth was also smoother and more brightly colored than homespun, most women purchased cloth rather than made it themselves. Similarly, the new ready-made men's clothing reduced the amount of sewing women did, especially in cities, where more men purchased clothing from retail stores. As Chapter 12 will make clearer, the growth of industry led to an economic reorganization of the family and a new definition of women's role in society.

Decline of women's traditional work

Materialism

Europeans who visited the United States during these years were struck by how hard Americans worked and how preoccupied they were with material goods and achievements. The new generation did not invent materialism, but the spread of the market after 1815 made it much more evident. "I know of no country, indeed," Tocqueville commented, "where the love of money has taken stronger hold on the affections of men." And in 1836 the American writer Washington Irving coined the classic phrase that captured the spirit of the age when he spoke, in one of his stories, of "the almighty dollar, that great object of universal devotion throughout the land."

Wealth and status

In a nation that had no legally recognized aristocracy, no established church, and class lines that were only informally drawn, wealth became the most obvious symbol of status. Dismissing birth as "a mere idea," one magazine explained, "Wealth is something substantial. Everybody knows that and feels it." Materialism reflected more than a desire for goods and physical comfort. It represented a quest for respect and recognition. "Americans boast of their skill in money making," one contemporary observed, "and as it is the only standard of dignity and nobility and worth, they endeavor to obtain it by every possible means."

The emphasis on money and material goods left its mark on the American character. Often enough, it encouraged sharp business practices and promoted a greater tolerance of wealth acquired by questionable means. Families were rated by the size, not the source, of their fortunes. Americans also emphasized practicality over theory. The esteem of the founding generation for intellectual achievement was mostly lost in the scramble for wealth that seemed to consume the new generation.

The Emerging Middle Class

In the years after 1815, a new middle class took shape in American society. A small class of shopkeepers, professionals, and master artisans had existed earlier, but the creation of a national market economy greatly expanded its size and influence. As

Separation of middle class from manual laborers

specialization increased, manual and nonmanual labor were more often physically separated. Office work and selling became removed from the production and handling of merchandise. More frequently, businessmen, professionals, storekeepers, clerks, office workers, and supervisors began to think of themselves as a distinct social group. "In America it is customary to denominate as 'clerk' all young men engaged in commercial pursuits," wrote one observer at midcentury. "Of course, the term is not applied to those engaged in mechanical trades." Members of the growing middle class had access to more education and enjoyed greater social mobility. They were paid not only more but differently. A manual worker might earn $300 a year, paid as wages computed on an hourly basis. Professionals received a yearly salary and might make $1000 a year or more.

Middle-class neighborhoods, segregated along income and occupational lines, also began to develop in towns and cities. Moreover, in large urban areas the separation of work from place of residence along with improvements in transportation made it possible for many middle-class residents to live in surrounding suburbs and commute to work. Leisure also became segregated as separate working-class and middle-class social organizations and institutions emerged.

This traffic jam in New York City conveys the rapid pace and impatient quality of American life in the first half of the nineteenth century. "In the streets all is hurry and bustle," one European visitor to the city reported. "Carts, instead of being drawn by horses at a walking pace, are often met at a gallop, and always in a brisk trot. . . . The whole population seen in the streets seem to enjoy this bustle and add to it by their own rapid pace, as if they were all going to some place of appointment, and were hurrying on under the apprehension of being too late."

During these years, a distinct middle-class way of life evolved based in part on levels of consumption. Greater wealth meant the ability to consume more. Someone like Joseph Engles, a Philadelphia publishing agent, might boast a house furnished with not one but two sofas, a looking glass, thirteen chairs, five yards of ingrain carpet on the floors, and even a piano and stool. Material goods became emblems of success and status—as clockmaker Chauncey Jerome sadly discovered when his business failed and his wealth vanished. Indeed, this materialistic ethos was most apparent in the middle class, as they strove to set themselves apart from other groups in society.

Material goods as emblems of success

The rise of a middle class would soon launch far-reaching changes in American society, as we will see in Chapter 12. The middle class came to embrace a new concept of marriage, the family, and the home. Along with occupation and income, moral outlook also marked class boundaries during this period.

The Distribution of Wealth

As American society became more specialized and differentiated, greater extremes of wealth appeared. After 1815, local tax records reveal a growing concentration of wealth at the top of the social pyramid. The concentration was greatest in large eastern cities and in the cotton kingdom of the South, but everywhere the tendency was for the rich to get richer and own a larger share of the community's total wealth. In New York, Brooklyn, Boston, and Philadelphia, the top 1 percent of the wealth holders owned a quarter of the total wealth in 1825; by 1850 they owned half. Similar trends appeared in western cities, such as Cincinnati and St. Louis. By 1860, 5 percent of American families owned more than 50 percent of the nation's wealth.

In contrast, those at the base of the social pyramid held a smaller percentage of a community's wealth. In Connecticut towns between 1831 and 1851 the number of inhabitants listed as having no property increased by 33 percent. In Cincinnati the bottom half of the city's taxpayers held 10 percent of the wealth in 1817; in 1860 their share had dropped to less than 3 percent.

In a market society, the rich were able to build up their assets because those with capital were in a position to increase it dramatically by taking advantage of new investment opportunities. Although a few men, such as Cornelius Vanderbilt and John Jacob Astor, vaulted from the bottom ranks of society to the top, most of the nation's richest individuals came from wealthy families.

Social Mobility

The existence of great fortunes is not necessarily inconsistent with the idea of social mobility or property accumulation. Although the gap between the rich and the poor widened after 1820, even the incomes of most poor Americans rose, because the total amount of wealth produced in America had become much larger. From about 1825 to 1860 the average per capita income almost doubled to $300. Voicing the popular belief, a New York judge proclaimed, "In this favored land of liberty, the road to advancement is open to all."

Limits of social mobility   Social mobility existed in these years, but not as much as contemporaries boasted. Most laborers—or more often their sons—did manage to move up the social ladder, but only a rung or two. Few unskilled workers rose higher than to a semiskilled occupation. Even the children of skilled workers normally did not escape the laboring classes and enter the middle-class ranks of clerks, managers, or lawyers. For most workers, improved status came in the form of a savings account or home ownership, which gave them some security during economic downswings and in old age.

A New Sensitivity to Time

It was no accident that Chauncey Jerome's clocks spread throughout the nation along with the market economy. The new methods of doing business involved a new and stricter sense of time. Factory life required a more regimented schedule, where work began at the sound of a bell, workers kept machines going at a constant pace, and the day was divided into hours and even minutes.

Clocks began to invade private as well as public space. Before Jerome and his competitors began using standardized parts, only the wealthy owned clocks, but with mass production ordinary families could afford them. Even farmers became more sensitive to time as they became integrated into the marketplace. As one frontier traveler reported in 1844, "In Kentucky, in Indiana, in Illinois, in Missouri, and here in every dale in Arkansas, and in cabins where there was not a chair to sit on, there was sure to be a Connecticut clock."

The Market at Work: Three Examples

To sense how much America was leaving behind Crèvecoeur's vision of a land of subsistence farmers, consider three examples of the new market economy, from a small city on the East Coast to the distant frontier of the Rocky Mountains.

In 1820 Kingston, New York, was a small, rural-oriented community of 1000 people, located along the Hudson River halfway between New York City and Albany. But in 1828 the Delaware and Hudson Canal linked Kingston with the Pennsylvania coal fields, jolting the town out of its economic lethargy. The rise of the coal trade stimulated local commerce and greatly increased the number of banks and the variety of businesses. The rhythm of life in Kingston now focused on the docks, stores, and canal boats rather than on planting and harvest. By 1850 Kingston had a population of 10,000, ten times that in 1820.

The market transforms Kingston, New York

Its landscape changed too. In 1820 most storekeepers and craftworkers had conducted business from their homes. By 1850 a commercial district boasted specialized stores, some handling china and glassware, others dry goods, clothing, or jewelry and watches. In addition, most manufacturing facilities were confined to two sections on the city's outskirts. Residential areas were separate from the commercial center and had become segregated along class lines, with different neighborhoods for the elite of the community, for skilled workers, and for unskilled laborers. By midcentury, street signs and gas lamps were going up, and numbers were being assigned to buildings. Kingston had become an urban center.

A thousand miles west lay the small prairie settlement of Sugar Creek, Illinois. The first white settlers had moved to Sugar Creek in 1817, as the market revolution was getting under way. The village's pioneers were primarily concerned about simply surviving. The land they plowed was on the edge of the forest, where girdled trees often remained standing among the crops until they could be cleared. The roads to larger towns like Springfield were mere cart paths, winding hither and yon among the trees.

Sugar Creek, Illinois

By the 1840s and 1850s the market economy had made inroads at Sugar Creek. True, a farmer like Eddin Lewis might still keep an account book noting that James Wilson came by for "six days work planting corn [$]3.00." That was the traditional barter system in action, for no cash actually changed hands. Lewis was simply keeping tabs, noting also when he helped Wilson, so that eventually the account could be balanced. But Lewis had also begun to drive hogs to St. Louis, where he received cash in return. By 1848 he was shipping south 6000 pounds of barreled pork, as well as lard and 350 bushels of corn. Wealth had become more concentrated in Sugar Creek, too. The richest farmers concentrated on a few money-making crops and rented their surplus land to poorer tenants; their wives no longer had to produce large amounts of butter for market to make ends meet. Sugar Creek, in other words, was becoming more specialized, more stratified in its wealth, and more tied into regional and national markets.

Another thousand miles west a different sort of American roamed, who might at first seem unconnected to the bustle of urban markets. These were the legendary mountain men. Traveling across the Great Plains, along upland streams, and over the passes of the Rockies, hard-bitten outdoorsmen like Jim Bridger, Jedediah Smith, and James Walker wore buckskin hunting shirts, let their unkempt hair grow to their shoulders, and stuck pistols and tomahawks in their belts. In good times they feasted on raw buffalo liver and roasted hump; when game was scarce, some were not above holding their hands "in an anthill until they were covered with ants, then greedily [licking] them off," as one trapper recalled. Wild and exotic, the mountain men quickly became romantic symbols of the American quest for individual freedom.

Yet these wanderers too were tied to the market. During their heyday, from the mid-1820s to the early 1840s, they trapped beaver, whose pelts were shipped east and turned into fancy hats for gentlemen. The fur trade was not a sporting event but a business, dominated by organizations like John Jacob Astor's American Fur Company, and the trapper was part of a vast economic structure that stretched from the mountains to the eastern cities and on to Europe. The majority of these men went into the wilderness not to flee civilization but to make money. Their ultimate goal was

---

Thomas Hicks's painting, *Calculating*, captures the spirit of the United States as the market revolution unfolded. Americans, one foreign visitor reported, were a "guessing, reckoning, expecting and calculating people." During this period the phrase "I calculate" came to mean "I think." The man carefully going over his figures wears a beaver hat, the end product of the fur trade. Indeed, business attitudes shaped and controlled the fur trade, and many mountain men ended up as calculating businessmen. (M. and M. Karolik Collection of American Paintings, 1815–1865. Courtesy, Museum of Fine Arts, Boston.)

to accumulate capital in order to set themselves up in society. Of those who survived the fur trade, almost none remained permanently outside the bounds of civilization but returned and took up new careers. Far from repudiating society's values, the mountain men sought respectability and success as defined by the society they had temporarily left. They, like farmers, were expectant capitalists for whom the West was a land of opportunity.

PROSPERITY AND ANXIETY

The mountain men, the farmers of Sugar Creek, and the workers of Kingston were all alert to the possibilities of the market. As Americans saw their nation's frontiers expand and its economy grow, many began to view history in terms of an inevitable and continuous improvement. The path of commerce, however, was not steadily upward. Rather it advanced in a series of wrenching boom–bust cycles: accelerating growth and overheated expansion, followed by a crash and then depression.

The country remained extraordinarily prosperous from 1815 until 1819, only to sink into a depression that lasted from 1819 to 1823. During the next cycle, slow economic expansion in the 1820s gave way to almost frenzied speculation and investment in the 1830s. Then came the inevitable contraction in 1837, and the country suffered an even more severe depression from 1839 to 1843. The third cycle again followed the familiar pattern: gradual economic growth during the 1840s, frantic expansion in the 1850s, and a third depression that began in 1857 and lasted until the Civil War. In each of these depressions, thousands of workers were thrown out of work, overextended farmers lost their farms, and many businesses closed their doors.

Boom–bust cycle

The impact of the boom–bust cycle can be seen in the contrasting fates of two Americans who moved west in search of opportunity. In 1820, 17-year-old Benjamin Remington left Hancock, Massachusetts, for western New York, which was just being opened to white settlement. Possessing little money and no property, he tried his hand at several jobs before purchasing on credit a 150-acre farm near the growing city of Rochester. Remington's timing was ideal. In 1823, two years after his arrival, the new Erie Canal was completed as far as Rochester. Wheat prices rose, flour shipments from the region shot up, and Remington prospered supplying food for eastern markets. Over the years, he added to his acreage, built a comfortable house for his family, and was elected town supervisor. For Remington, the West was indeed a land of opportunity.

Somewhat younger, Addison Ward moved west when he came of age in 1831, leaving Virginia for Indiana. Unfortunately, by the time Ward arrived in Greene County, the best land had already been claimed. All he could afford was 80 acres of rough government land, which he bought in 1837 largely on credit. The region lacked adequate transportation to outside markets, but the economy was booming, land values were soaring, and the state had begun an ambitious internal improvements program. Ward's timing, however, could not have been worse. Almost immediately the country entered a depression, driving farm prices and land values downward. Overwhelmed by debts, Ward sold his farm and fell into the ranks of tenant farmers. He eventually moved on but never recovered financially. Catching the wrong end of the boom–bust cycle, Ward never achieved economic success and social respectability. As his experience demonstrated, the market revolution wore a double face, and the bright side did not shine on everyone.

In such an environment, prosperity, like personal success, seemed all too fleeting. Because Americans believed that the good times would not last—that the bubble would burst and another "panic" would set in—their optimism was often tinged by insecurity and anxiety. They knew too many individuals like Chauncey Jerome, who had been rich and then lost all their wealth in a downturn.

Popular anxiety

The Panic of 1819

The initial shock of this boom-and-bust psychology came with the Panic of 1819, the first major depression in the nation's history. From 1815 to 1818 cotton had commanded truly fabulous prices on the Liverpool market, reaching 32.5 cents a pound in 1818. In this heady prosperity, the federal government extended liberal credit for land purchases, and the new national bank encouraged merchants and farmers to expand their operations by borrowing in order to catch the rising tide.

National depression

But in 1819 the price of cotton collapsed and took the rest of the economy with it. Once the inflationary bubble burst, land values, which had been driven to new heights by the speculative fever, plummeted 50 to 75 percent almost overnight. As the economy went slack, so did the demand for western foodstuffs and eastern manufactured goods and services, pushing the nation into a severe depression.

Because the market economy had spread to new areas, the downturn affected not only city folk but rural Americans as well. Many farmers, especially in newly settled regions, had bought their land on credit, and farmers in established areas had expanded their operations, looking to future profits. When prices fell, both groups were hardpressed to pay their debts. New cotton planters in the Southwest, who were most vulnerable to the ups and downs of the world market, were especially hard hit.

The Missouri Crisis

The Panic of 1819 brought an end to the optimism that had followed the War of 1812 as the New Nationalism's spirit of cooperation gave way to jealousy and conflict between competing interests and social groups. Scrambling to weather the economic storm, southern planters, Yankee merchants, and western farmers looked first to their own welfare. So it was probably not surprising that sectional tensions flared in 1819, when the Missouri Territory applied for admission as a slave state. As the economy spiraled downward, northerners linked control of western lands to their economic self-interest; in the same manner, southerners saw the expansion of slavery as vital to their economic welfare.

Before the controversy over Missouri erupted, slavery had not been a major issue in American politics. Congress had debated the institution when it prohibited the African slave trade in 1808, the earliest year this could be done under the Constitution. In the absence of any specific federal legislation, however, slavery had crossed the Mississippi River into the Louisiana Purchase. Louisiana entered the Union in 1812 as a slave state, and in 1818 Missouri, which had about 10,000 slaves in its population, asked permission to come in too.

In 1818 the Union contained 11 free and 11 slave states. As the federal government became stronger and more active, both the North and the South became increasingly anxious about maintaining their political power. The North's greater population gave it a majority in the House of Representatives, 105 to 81. The Senate, of course, was evenly balanced, since each state had two senators regardless of population. But Maine, which previously had been part of Massachusetts, requested admission as a free state. That would upset the balance unless Missouri came in as a slave state.

Representative James Tallmadge of New York disturbed this delicate state of affairs when in 1819 he suddenly introduced an amendment designed to establish a program of gradual emancipation in Missouri. The debate that followed was bitter, as for the first time Congress directly debated the morality of slavery. The House approved the Tallmadge amendment, but the Senate refused to accept it, and the two houses deadlocked.

When Congress reconvened in 1820, Henry Clay of Kentucky promoted what came to be known as the Missouri Compromise. Under its terms Missouri was admitted as a slave state and Maine as a free state. In addition, slavery was forever prohibited in the remainder of the Louisiana Purchase north of 36°30′ (the southern boundary of Missouri). Clay's proposal, the first of several sectional compromises he would engineer in his long career, won congressional approval, ending the crisis. But southern fears for the security of slavery and northern fears about its spread remained. As Thomas Jefferson had gloomily predicted, "A geographical line, coinciding with a marked principle, moral and political, once conceived and held up to angry passions of men, will never be obliterated; and every new irritation will mark it deeper and deeper."

Missouri Compromise

Yet sectional tensions, though ominous, tended to ebb and flow with events. Meanwhile, the Panic of 1819 affected the political life of the nation in even more direct ways. As the depression deepened and hardship spread, Americans viewed government policies as at least partly to blame. The postwar nationalism, after all, had been based on the belief that government should stimulate economic development

---

THE MISSOURI COMPROMISE AND THE UNION'S BOUNDARIES IN 1820

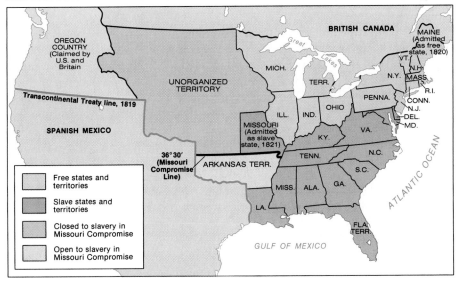

through a national bank and protective tariff, by improving transportation, and by opening up new lands. As Americans struggled to make sense of their new economic order, they looked to take more direct control of the government that was so actively shaping their lives. During the 1820s, the popular response to the market and the Panic of 1819 produced a strikingly new kind of politics in the Republic.

CHAPTER SUMMARY

The market revolution, which united the country in a single market, transformed the United States during the quarter century after 1815. Government action was critical for the creation and expansion of a domestic market; so was the development of new forms of transportation, including canals, steamboats, and eventually railroads, which allowed goods to be transported cheaply on land. By adopting a pro-business stance that encouraged investment and risk taking, the Supreme Court under John Marshall played a vital role as well.

Economic expansion generated greater national wealth, but it also brought social and intellectual change. Restless Americans poured steadily westward or flocked to the growing cities in search of opportunity. They were impatient to achieve their objectives and were convinced that change was the normal order of things. In its values this generation placed heavy emphasis on materialism, and wealth became the primary determinant of status.

Entrepreneurs reorganized their operations to increase production and sell in a wider market. Stimulated by technological advances, factories appeared for the first time, beginning with the textile industry, which employed large numbers of young women from rural families. Factory work was done by machines tended by semiskilled operators; it imposed a new discipline, based on a precise sense of time and schedule, on previously rural residents. Protesting the pace of work, the strict routine, and their declining status, workers formed unions and resorted to strikes to promote their demands, but the depression that began in 1837 destroyed these organizations.

With the restructuring of work and opportunity by the market revolution, wealth became much more unevenly distributed in American society. Social mobility still existed, but it was more limited than boosters of the day claimed. As the economy lurched up and down in the years after 1815, individuals were at the mercy of economic forces beyond their control. In hard times when the economy went bust, Americans looked to the government to relieve economic distress. The Missouri crisis of 1819–1821, which erupted in the wake of the first national depression in American history, was an early demonstration of this concern.

ADDITIONAL READING

Charles Sellers, *The Market Revolution* (1991) is the most ambitious synthesis of social, economic, and political developments in this period, but it is marred by an overly romantic view of preindustrial society and a pronounced ideological bias. For a critique of Sellers's interpretation, see William E. Gienapp, "The Myth of Class in Jacksonian America," *Journal of Policy History*, 6 (1994), 232–281, with comments and a rejoinder. Additional assessments are offered in Melvin Stokes and Stephen Conway, eds., *The Market Revolution in America* (1996). Insightful discussions of a number of relevant topics can be found in Mary Kupiec Cayton et al., eds., *Encyclopedia of American Social History* (3 vols., 1993), a superb and wide-ranging collection based on the latest scholarship.

A very important overview of economic change is Douglass C. North, *The Economic Growth of the United States, 1790–1860* (1961). George Rogers Taylor, *The Transportation Revolution, 1815–1860* (1951) is the classic survey. Many of the social consequences of the new market economy are described in Jack Larkin, *The Reshaping of Everyday Life, 1790–1840* (1988) and more analytically in Christopher Clark, *The Roots of Rural Capitalism* (1990). Significant community studies include Stuart M. Blumin, *The Urban Threshold* (1976) and John Mack Faragher, *Sugar Creek* (1986). Workers' experiences are sympathetically examined in Thomas Dublin, *Women at Work* (1979), Paul G. Faler, *Mechanics and Manufacturers in the Early Industrial Revolution* (1981), and Sean Wilentz, *Chants Democratic: New York City and the Rise of the American Working Class, 1788–1850* (1984). Stuart Blumin's *The Emergence of the Middle Class* (1989) is an excellent treatment of a critical subject. For a fuller list of readings, see the Bibliography.

SIGNIFICANT EVENTS

1790	Slater's textile mill opens
1793	Eli Whitney invents the cotton gin
1798	Whitney begins work on a system of interchangeable parts
1807	Fulton's *Clermont* begins regular steamboat service on the Hudson River
1810	*Fletcher v. Peck*
1810–1820	Cotton boom begins in the South
1811	First steamboat trip from Pittsburgh to New Orleans
1813	Waltham system established
1816	Second Bank of the United States chartered; protective tariff enacted
1818–1825	Erie Canal constructed
1819	*Dartmouth College v. Woodward*; *McCulloch v. Maryland*
1819–1823	Panic and depression
1820	Missouri Compromise enacted; Lowell mills established
1824	*Gibbons v. Ogden*
1825–1850	Canal era
1830	Baltimore and Ohio Railroad begins passenger service
1834	National Trades' Union founded
1837	Panic
1839–1843	Depression
1844	Samuel F. B. Morse sends first intercity telegraphic message
1847	Rotary printing press invented

11

The Rise of Democracy

The notice, printed in a local newspaper, made the rounds in the rural Pearl River district of Mississippi. A traveler, the advertisement announced, had lost a suitcase while fording the Tallahala River. The contents included "6 ruffled shirts, 6 cambric handkerchiefs, 1 hair-brush, 1 tooth-brush, 1 nail-brush. . . ."

As the list went on, the popular reaction would inevitably shift from amusement to disdain: "1 pair curling tongs, 2 sticks pomatum . . . 1 box pearl powder, 1 bottle Cologne, 1 [bottle] rose-water, 4 pairs silk stockings, and 2 pairs kid gloves." The howls of derision that filled the air could only have increased upon learning that anyone finding said trunk was requested to contact the owner—Mr. Powhatan Ellis of Natchez.

Powhatan Ellis was no ordinary backcountry traveler. Born into a genteel Virginia family, Ellis had moved in 1816 to the raw Southwest to seek his fortune. With his cultivated tastes, careful dress, and stately dignity, he upheld the tradition of the gentleman politician. In Virginia he would have commanded respect: indeed, in Mississippi he had been appointed district judge and U.S. senator. But for the voters along the Pearl River, the advertisement for his trunk of ruffled shirts, hair oils, and fancy "skunkwater" proved to be the political kiss of death. His opponents branded him an aristocrat and a dandy, and his support among the piney woods farmers evaporated faster than a morning mist along Old Muddy on a sweltering summer's day.

No one was more satisfied with this outcome than the resourceful Franklin E. Plummer, one of Ellis's political enemies. In truth, while the unfortunate Powhatan Ellis had lost a trunk fording a stream, he had never placed the advertisement trying to locate it. That was the handiwork of Plummer, who well understood the new playing field of American politics in the 1820s. If Powhatan Ellis typified the passing political world of the Revolutionary era, Plummer was a product of the raucous democratic system emerging in its place. Leaving his home in New England, Plummer had made his way as a young man to the new state of Mississippi, where he set himself up as an attorney, complete with a law library of three books. Plummer's shrewdness and oratorical talent made up for his lack of legal training, however, and he was quickly elected to the legislature.

Champion of the people

In 1830 Plummer's ambition led him to announce a run for Congress. At first few observers took his candidacy seriously. But Plummer boldly portrayed himself as the champion of the people battling against the aristocrats of Natchez. Contrasting

342

A Whig parade in Philadelphia, 1840, by Francis H. Schell. "It seems as though every man, woman, and child preferred politics to anything else," wrote one politician at the end of the campaign.

his humble background with that of his wealthy opponent, Plummer proclaimed: "We are taught that the highway to office, distinction and honor, is as free to the *meritorious poor* man, as to the *rich;* to the man who has risen from obscurity by his own individual exertions, as to him who has inherited a high and elevated standing in society. . . ." Taking as his slogan "Plummer for the People, and the People for Plummer," he was easily elected.

On the campaign trail Plummer knew how to affect the common touch. Once, while canvassing the district with his opponent, the pair stopped at a farmhouse. When his opponent, seeking the farmer's vote, kissed the daughter, Plummer picked up a toddling boy and began picking red bugs off him, telling the enchanted mother, "They are powerful bad, and mighty hard on babies." On another occasion, while his opponent slept, Plummer rose at dawn to help milk the family's cow—and won another vote.

As long as Plummer maintained his image as one of the people, fighting their battles against aristocrats, he remained invincible. But in 1835 when he became a candidate for the U.S. Senate, his touch deserted him. Borrowing money from a Natchez bank, he purchased a stylish coach, put his servant in a uniform, and campaigned across the state. Aghast at such pretensions, his followers promptly abandoned him, and he was soundly defeated. He died in 1852 in obscurity and poverty. Ah, Plummer! Even the staunchest of nature's noblemen may stumble, prey to the temptations of power and commerce!

Franklin Plummer was being pulled two ways by the forces transforming American society. As the previous chapter explained, the growth of commerce and new markets opened up opportunities for more and more Americans during these years. "Opportunity" was one of the bywords of the age. Through his connections

In the new democratic political system, politicians resorted to new techniques to win support. Here a candidate seeking votes helps—not very successfully— with the chores on a backwoods farm in Mississippi. An amused farm woman looks on.

with bankers and the well-to-do, Plummer saw the opportunity to accumulate wealth and to gain status and respect.

Yet at the same time that new markets were producing a more stratified, unequal society, the nation's politics were becoming more democratic. The new political system that developed after 1820 differed strikingly from that of the early Republic. Just as national markets linked the regions of America economically, the new system of national politics with its mass electioneering techniques involved more voters than ever before and created a new class of politicians. Plummer's world reflected that new political culture. And its central feature—another byword on everyone's lips—was "equality." In truth, the relation between the new equalities of politics and the new opportunities of the market was an uneasy one.

EQUALITY AND OPPORTUNITY

Middle- and upper-class Europeans who visited the United States during these decades were especially sensitive to the egalitarian quality of American life. Coming from the more stratified society of Europe, they were immediately struck by the "democratic spirit" that had become "infused into all the national habits and all the customs of society." Europeans spent only a few days traveling American roads before the blunt contours of Franklin Plummer's world were brought home to them.

To begin with, they discovered that only one class of seats was available on stagecoaches and rail cars. These were filled according to the rough-and-ready rule of first come, first served. In steamboat dining rooms or at country taverns, everyone ate at a common table, sharing food from the same serving plates. As one upper-class gentleman complained, "The rich and the poor, the educated and the ignorant, the polite and the vulgar, all herd on the cabin floor, feed at the same table, sit in each others laps, as it were."

Indeed, the democratic "manners" of Americans seemed positively shocking. Europeans were used to social inferiors speaking only if spoken to. But Americans felt free to strike up a conversation with anyone, including total strangers. Frances Trollope was offended by the "coarse familiarity of address" between classes, while another visitor complained that in a nation where every citizen felt free to shake the hand of another, it was impossible to know anyone's social station. This informality—a forward, even *rude* attitude—could also be seen in the American custom of chewing tobacco and spitting everywhere: in the national capitol, in courts and hospitals, even in private homes. Fanny Kemble, an English actress, reported that on an American steamboat "it was a perfect shower of saliva all the time."

Americans were self-consciously proud of such democratic behavior, which they viewed as a valued heritage of the Revolution. The keelboaters who carried the future King Louis-Philippe of France on a trip down the Mississippi made their republican feelings plain when the keelboat ran aground. "You kings down there!" bellowed the captain. "Show yourselves and do a man's work, and help us three-spots pull off this bar!" The ideology of the Revolution made it clear that, in the American deck of cards at least, "three-spots" counted as much as jacks, kings, and queens. Kings were not allowed to forget that—and neither was Franklin Plummer.

Daily Lives

CLOTHING AND FASHION

The Plain Dark Democracy of Broadcloth

The emergence of democracy in American life was accompanied by a dramatic change in men's clothing. In the eighteenth century clothing was a prime indicator of social rank and set members of the upper class apart from ordinary citizens. A gentleman's finely tailored apparel—ruffled shirts, lace cuffs, silk stockings, decorative garters, and buckled shoes—was a mark of status since only elites could afford these expensive items. Because of the cost and extensive labor involved, most Americans owned only a few clothes, and these usually were made out of homespun—cloth woven from thread spun in the household. With a quick glance an observer could tell a person's social rank.

In the Jacksonian era, however, fashionable clothing became cheaper and much more widely available, and as a result dress no longer revealed social standing. By significantly lowering the cost, textile mills made good quality cloth accessible to ordinary families. "All sorts of cotton fabrics are now so cheap that there is no excuse of any person's not being well provided," commented *The Young Lady's Friend* in 1836. Poor families and slaves did not share in this abundance, but most Americans' basic wardrobe expanded: now women usually owned more than a couple of dresses, and

men ordinarily had more than a single jacket and one or two pairs of pants.

The colorful shirts, rude trousers, leather aprons, frocks, and heavy boots and shoes worn by farmers and mechanics while working were readily distinguishable from the coats and trousers of middle-class merchants, professionals, managers, and clerks. Outside the workplace, however, differences in clothing style, if not workmanship, largely disappeared. British traveler John Fowler in 1831 was amazed to see American workers, decked out in their Sunday best, walking the streets wearing "sleek coats, glossy hats, watchguards, and deerskin gloves!" Unlike the eighteenth century, men dressed in somber colors. By the 1830s "black was the prevailing color," one New Yorker recalled. "It was worn for promenade, parlor, church, ball, business," and "in such uniformity of style, as effectively to destroy all individuality."

The emergence after 1840 of the ready-made clothing industry also had a decisive impact on men's fashions. A growing number of men in middle-class positions were anxious to create a proper image but could not afford the expert tailoring required to make a business suit. In response to this demand, tailors developed standardized patterns and a proportional sizing system and began mass-producing affordable ready-made clothing. Decently made, fashionable suits could be purchased off the rack, and thus clerks began wearing clothing identical in style to that

The Tension between Equality and Opportunity

Opportunity and inequality of wealth

While Americans praised both opportunity and equality, a fundamental tension existed between the two values. Inevitably, widespread opportunity would produce inequality of wealth. In Crèvecoeur's America, a rough equality of wealth and status had prevailed because of the lack of access to the market. In 1800 shoemakers in Lynn, with no way to ship large quantities of shoes across the country, could not be-

346

Daily Lives

As this nattily dressed butcher suggests, clothes were not much help in sorting out social status in America. Although the clothing of the upper class was often made of finer material and was more skillfully tailored, by the 1820s less prosperous Americans wore similar styles. "The washerwoman's Sunday attire is now as nearly like that of the merchant's wife as it can be," commented one astonished observer.

worn by their employer. By eliminating the distinction between homemade clothing and that sewed by a tailor, ready-made clothing further democratized men's clothing.

New ways of dressing began with the urban middle class and gradually spread throughout most of society. Ill-fitting clothes were increasingly a sign not of poverty but of isolation from the main avenues of transportation, commerce, and information.

Rather than distinguishing one class from another, democratic fashions increasingly set men apart from women. Fashion came to be considered a female concern, and ornamentation and bright colors now were associated with women's clothing. Ready-made clothing was not available for women, since female styles required a close fit in the bodice. Nevertheless, the style of women's clothing also became standardized. American women sought to keep abreast of the latest Paris fashions, and if they could not afford a dressmakers' fitting, they sewed their own clothing. Illustrated magazines such as *Godey's Lady's Book* publicized the latest fashions, and even young women working in the mills at Lowell joined together to buy a subscription.

An English visitor reported that in the United States "men dress after the same type, differing only in finer or coarser material; every man would wear, if he could, a black satin waistcoat and a large diamond pin stick in the front of his shirt, as he certainly has a watch or a gild or gold chain of some sort or other. The mean white affects the style of the large proprietor of . . . capital as closely as he can. . . ." As one newspaper commented, Americans in the Jacksonian era were citizens of the "plain dark democracy of broadcloth."

---

come wealthy. Without steamboats or canals, farmers in Jefferson's day could not market surplus grain for profit. But by the 1820s and 1830s, as the opportunities of the market expanded, wealth became much more unevenly distributed. Thus the new generation had to confront contradictions in the American creed that their parents had been able to conveniently ignore.

By equality, Americans did not mean equality of wealth or property. "I know of no country where profounder contempt is expressed for the theory of permanent

Meaning of equality

equality of property," Alexis de Tocqueville wrote. Nor did equality mean that all citizens had equal talent or capacity. Americans realized that individuals possessed widely differing abilities, which inevitably produced differences in wealth. "Distinctions in society will always exist under every just government," Andrew Jackson declared. "Equality of talents, or education, or of wealth cannot be produced by human institutions."

In the end, what Americans upheld was the equality of opportunity, not equality of condition. "True republicanism requires that every man shall have an equal chance—that every man shall be free to become as unequal as he can," one American commented. In an economy that could go bust as well as boom, Americans agreed that one primary objective of government was to safeguard opportunity. Thus the new politics of democracy walked hand in hand with the new opportunities of the market.

THE NEW POLITICAL CULTURE OF DEMOCRACY

The stately James Monroe, with his powdered hair and buckled shoes and breeches, was not part of the new politics. But in 1824 as he neared the end of his second term, a host of new leaders in the Republican party looked to succeed him. Traditionally, a congressional caucus selected the party's presidential nominee, and the Republican caucus finally settled on Secretary of Treasury William H. Crawford of Georgia. Condemning "King Caucus" as undemocratic, three other Republicans, all ardent nationalists, refused to withdraw from the race: Secretary of State John Quincy Adams, John C. Calhoun, Monroe's secretary of war, and Henry Clay, the Speaker of the House.

Death of the caucus system

None of these men bargained on the sudden emergence of another Republican candidate, Andrew Jackson, the hero of the Battle of New Orleans. Because of his limited political experience, no one took Jackson's candidacy seriously at first, including Jackson himself. But soon the general's supporters and rivals began receiving reports of his popularity. From Cincinnati an observer wrote, "Strange! Wild! Infatuated! All for Jackson!" Savvy politicians soon flocked to his standard, but it was the people who first made Jackson a serious candidate.

The Election of 1824

Calhoun eventually dropped out of the race, but that still left four candidates, none of whom received a majority of the popular vote. Jackson led the field, however, and finished first in the Electoral College with 99 votes. Adams had 84, Crawford 41, and Clay 37. Under the Twelfth Amendment, the House was to select a president from the top three candidates. Clay, though himself eliminated, held enough influence as Speaker of the House to name the winner. After he met privately with Adams, he rallied the votes in the House needed to put Adams over the top.

Corrupt bargain

Two days later, Adams announced that Clay would be his new secretary of state, the usual steppingstone to the presidency. Jackson and his supporters promptly charged that there had been a "corrupt bargain" between Adams and Clay. Before Adams had even assumed office, the 1828 race was under way.

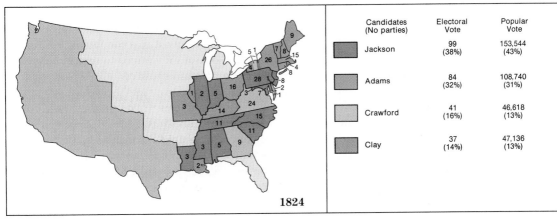

Candidates (No parties)	Electoral Vote	Popular Vote
Jackson	99 (38%)	153,544 (43%)
Adams	84 (32%)	108,740 (31%)
Crawford	41 (16%)	46,618 (13%)
Clay	37 (14%)	47,136 (13%)

ELECTION OF 1824

Even more significant, the election of 1824 shattered the old party system. Henry Clay and John Quincy Adams began to organize a new party, known as the National Republicans, to distinguish it from Jefferson's old party. Jackson's disappointed supporters eventually called themselves Democrats. To muddy the waters even further, a third party arose out of a controversy that erupted in 1826 over a secret organization known as the Freemasons.

Anti-Masonry and the Defense of Equality

The Freemasons (or simply Masons) were a secret fraternal group whose chapters had spread through Europe and America during the eighteenth century. Members like George Washington and Benjamin Franklin shared the Enlightenment's belief in the power of reason and the idea of progress, while also embracing the Masons' moral commitment to temperance, charity, and hard work. By 1826 the 150,000 American Masons were predominantly business leaders, manufacturers, and professionals. While Masons were often above average in wealth, their power and prestige stemmed more from the number of public offices they held.

It was in western New York along the Erie Canal that William Morgan, a disgruntled Mason, announced in 1826 that he intended to publish a book exposing the secrets of the order. Not long after, he was seized by a group of Masons, forced into a closed carriage, and spirited off into the night. Morgan was never seen again, and little doubt exists that he was murdered, allegedly near Niagara Falls. When prominent Masons used their power to thwart any investigation, the Anti-Masonic movement began. Anti-Masons demanded that the Masonic order be rooted out and eliminated. By 1830, they had organized in 10 states as a political party. Two years later they ran a presidential ticket. *Origins of the Anti-Masonic movement*

In national terms Morgan's disappearance was a relatively minor incident, but it touched raw nerves in an egalitarian society. The shadowy Masons seemed a sinister threat to equality and opportunity, since the members swore an oath to advance a "brother's" interests over those of nonmembers. Confronted with the power of such *Appeal of Anti-Masonry* an "aristocratic" order, how could ordinary citizens compete? "The direct object of freemasonry," one Anti-Masonic writer charged, "is to benefit the few at the expense of the many, by creating a privileged class, in the midst of a community entitled to enjoy equal rights and privileges." The Anti-Masons undertook to reform society by arousing public opinion and involving more citizens in politics.

As a rule, Anti-Masonry was strongest in populous, rapidly developing, market-oriented towns. Poor farmers who lacked access to markets and desired new roads or canal lines were often suspicious of Masonic officeholders. So were farmers in newly opened areas who had become dependent on city banks and merchants for credit. By attacking Masonry as an infidel society that exalted reason over traditional religion, the Anti-Masonic movement also represented a fervent desire to Christianize society. As such it represented a protest against the increasingly secular aspects of American life, which the spread of the market had strengthened.

Second party system

The new parties were one indication of how much the political system was in flux. By the mid-1830s, the National Republicans gave way to the Whigs, a new party that absorbed many members of the fading Anti-Masons. The Democrats, the other major party, came together under the leadership of Andrew Jackson. Once established, this second American party system dominated the nation's politics until the 1850s.

Social Sources of the New Politics

New attitudes toward government

Why was it that a new style and new system of politics emerged in the 1820s? We have already seen that a revolution in markets, stimulated by new transportation networks, was under way. We have seen, too, that the scramble to bring western lands into the market generated a speculative land boom that collapsed in the Panic of 1819. The rise of the new political culture was rooted in these social conditions. During the sharp depression that followed, many Americans became convinced that government policy had aggravated, if not actually produced, hard times. As a result, they decided that the government had a responsibility to relieve distress and promote prosperity.

For the first time, large numbers of Americans saw politics as relevant to their daily lives. Agitation mounted, especially at the state level, for government to enact relief for those in debt and provide other assistance. Elections soon became the means through which the majority expressed its policy preferences by voting for candidates pledged to specific programs. The older idea that representatives should be independent and vote their best judgment gave way to the notion that representatives were to carry out the will of the people, as expressed in the outcomes of elections.

Democratic reforms

With more citizens championing the "will of the people," pressure mounted to open up the political process. Most states eliminated property qualifications for voting in favor of white manhood suffrage, under which all adult white males were allowed to vote. Similarly, property requirements for officeholders were reduced or dropped.

Presidential elections became more democratic as well. By 1832 South Carolina was the only state where the legislature rather than the voters still chose presidential electors. The Anti-Masons pioneered a convention as a more democratic method of nominating party candidates and approving a platform, and the other parties soon followed suit. And because a presidential candidate had to carry a number of states in different sections of the country, the backing of a national party, with effective state and local organizations, became essential.

As the new reforms went into effect, voter turnout soared. Whereas in the 1824 presidential election only 27 percent of eligible voters bothered to go to the polls, four years later the proportion had more than doubled to 56 percent. In 1840, 78 percent of eligible voters cast ballots, probably the highest turnout in American history.

Voter turnout

The Acceptance of Parties

All these developments worked to favor the rise of a new type of politician: one whose life was devoted to party service and who often depended for his living on public office. As the number of state-sponsored internal improvement projects increased during the 1820s, so did the number of government jobs that could support party workers. No longer was politics primarily the province of the wealthy, who spent only part of their time on public affairs. Instead, political leaders were more likely to come from the middle ranks of society, especially outside the South. Many became economically established after entering politics, but as Franklin Plummer demonstrated, large sums of money were not required to conduct a campaign. Indeed, a successful politician now had to mingle with the masses and voice their feelings—requirements that put the wealthy elite at a disadvantage.

Rise of the professional politician

In many ways, Martin Van Buren epitomized the new breed of politician. The son of a New York tavern keeper, Van Buren lacked a magnetic personality. But he was a master organizer and tactician, highly skilled at using the new party system. His abilities eventually carried him to the Senate and even the White House. Unlike the older Revolutionary generation, who regarded political parties as dangerous and destructive, Van Buren argued that they were not only "inseparable from free governments" but "in many and material respects . . . highly useful to the country." While conceding they were subject to abuse, he stressed that competing parties would watch each other and check abuses at the same time that they kept the masses informed.

Acceptance of parties

The Politics of the Common Man

Andrew Jackson was one of the first political leaders to grasp the new politics, in which the ordinary citizen was celebrated as never before. "Never for a moment believe that the great body of the citizens . . . can deliberately intend to do wrong," he proclaimed. Party leaders everywhere avoided aristocratic airs when on the stump. "I have always dressed chiefly in *Home spun* when among the people," one North Carolina member of Congress explained. "If a Candidate be dressed Farmerlike he is well received and kindly remembered by the inmates of the Log Cabin, and there is no sensation among the children or the *chickens*."

New style of politics

Politics became mass entertainment, in which campaign hoopla often overshadowed the issues. Parades, glee clubs, massive rallies, and barbecues were used to rouse voters, and treating to drinks became an almost universal campaign tactic. ("The way to men's hearts is down their throats," quipped one Kentucky vote-getter.) Although politicians often talked about principles, political parties were pragmatic organizations, intent on gaining and holding power.

The Jacksonian era has been called the Age of the Common Man, but such demo-

Limitations of the democratic political system

cratic tendencies had distinct limits. Women and slaves were not allowed to vote, nor could free African Americans (except in a few states) and Indians. Nor did the parties always deal effectively with (or even address) basic problems in society. Still, Van Buren's insight was perceptive. Popular political parties provided an essential mechanism for peacefully resolving differences among competing interest groups, regions, and social classes.

COUNTERPOINT

How democratic was Jacksonian democracy?

How democratic was the new political system? Some historians have painted these reforms as truly dramatic. With the caucus system replaced by political conventions, ordinary citizens like Franklin Plummer found it easier to run for office. With more Americans able to vote, party leaders could not so easily ignore the wishes of their constituents. These historians conclude that whatever the new political sys-

"The Will of the People the Supreme Law" reads the banner at this county election. One of the few occasions when most of the men would assemble at the village, election day remained an all-male event, as well as a time of excitement, heated debate, and boisterous celebration. As citizens give their oath to an election judge, diligent party workers dispense free drinks, solicit support, offer party tickets, and keep a careful tally of who has voted. Liquor and drinking are prominently featured: one elector enjoys another round, a prospective voter who is too drunk to stand is held up by a faithful party member, and on the right a groggy partisan sports a bandage as a result of a political brawl.

tem's limitations, the party system addressed responsibly many of the major problems confronting the country. Public policy reflected public opinion rather than the wishes of the elites.

Other historians have been more skeptical. Despite the tide of democratic reforms, both race and gender still defined citizenship, depriving women and minorities of political power. Whatever their power, "the people" referred only to adult white males. Other critics have insisted that democratic reform can be seen as meaningful only if it actually changes the distribution of power in society. Even with more Americans voting, the leaders of both parties generally remained wealthier and better educated than their constituents. Neither party was led by ordinary farmers and workers, the two largest groups in society. Privileged men ambitious for office, like Andrew Jackson and Henry Clay, simply adopted new campaign techniques to win popular support. The result, according to these historians, was that under the leadership of such men the political system evaded the real problems of privilege and the growing concentration of wealth in society. Politicians' self-proclaimed identity with the people was more symbolic than real.

JACKSON'S RISE TO POWER

The new democratic style of politics first appeared on the state and local levels: Van Buren deftly working behind the scenes in New York; Amos Kendall of Kentucky campaigning in favor of debtor relief; Davy Crockett of Tennessee carefully dressed in frontier garb and offering voters a drink from a jug of whiskey and a chew from a large plug of tobacco. The national implications of these changes, however, were not immediately clear.

John Quincy Adams's Presidency

When he assumed the presidency in 1825, John Quincy Adams might have worked to create a mass-based party. But Adams, a talented diplomat and a great secretary of state, possessed hardly a political bone in his body. Cold and tactless, he could build no popular support for the ambitious and often farsighted programs he proposed. His desire to promote not only manufacturing and agriculture but also the arts, literature, and science left his opponents aghast.

Nor would Adams take any steps to gain reelection, though he earnestly desired it. Despite urgent pleas from Henry Clay and other advisers, he declined to remove from federal office men who actively opposed him. Since Adams refused to be a party leader, Clay undertook to organize the National Republicans. But with a reluctant candidate at the top of the ticket, Clay labored under serious handicaps. The new style of politics came into its own nationally only when Andrew Jackson swept to power at the head of a new party, the Democrats.

Building a new party was a tricky business. Because Jackson's coalition was made up of conflicting interests, "Old Hickory" remained vague about his own position on many issues. Thus the campaign of 1828 soon degenerated into a series of personal   *Jackson's election* attacks, splattering mud on all involved. Aided by enormous majorities in the South, Jackson won handily.

In one sense, the significance of the election was clear. It marked the beginning of politics as Americans have practiced it ever since, with two disciplined national parties actively competing for votes, an emphasis on personalities over issues, and the resort to mass electioneering techniques. Yet in terms of public policy, the meaning of the election was anything but clear. The people had voted for Jackson as a national hero without any real sense of what he would do with his newly won power.

President of the People

Certainly the people looked for change. "I never saw such a crowd here before," Daniel Webster wrote as inauguration day approached. "Persons have come 500 miles to see General Jackson, and they really seem to think that the country is rescued from some dreadful danger!" Some 15,000 supporters cheered wildly after Jackson was sworn in.

At the White House reception pandemonium reigned. Elbowing aside the invited dignitaries, thousands of ordinary citizens pushed inside to catch a glimpse of their idol. The new president had to flee after being nearly crushed to death by wellwishers. The crowd trampled on the furniture, broke glass, smashed mirrors, and ruined carpets and draperies. "It was a proud day for the people," boasted Amos Kendall, one of the new president's advisers. "General Jackson is their own president." Supreme Court Justice Joseph Story was less enraptured: "I never saw such a mixture. The reign of King Mob seemed triumphant."

Jackson's stubborn determination shines through clearly in this portrait by Asher Durand, painted in 1835. "His passions are terrible," Jefferson noted. "When I was President of the Senate, he was Senator, and he could never speak on account of the rashness of his feelings. I have seen him attempt it repeatedly, and as often choke with rage. His passions are, no doubt, cooler now; he has been much tried since I knew him, but he is a dangerous man." (Collection of the New-York Historical Society.)

Whether loved as a man of the people or hated as a demagogue leading the mob, *Jackson's* Jackson was the representative of the new democracy. The first president from west *character* of the Appalachians, he moved as a young lawyer to the Tennessee frontier. He had a quick mind but limited schooling and little use for learning; after his death a family friend acknowledged that the general had never believed that the Earth was round. A man of action, his decisiveness served him well as a soldier and also in the booming economy around Nashville, where he established himself as a large landowner and slaveholder. Tall and wiry, with flowing white hair, Jackson carried himself with a soldier's bearing. His troops had nicknamed him Old Hickory out of respect for his toughness, but that strength sometimes became arrogance, and he could be vindictive and a bully. He was not a man to provoke, as his reputation for dueling indicated.

For all these flaws, Jackson was a shrewd politician. He knew how to manipulate men and could be affable or abusive as the occasion demanded. He would sometimes burst into a rage to get his way with a hostile delegation, only to chuckle afterward, "They thought I was mad." He also displayed a keen sense of public opinion, skillfully reading the shifting national mood.

As the nation's chief executive, Jackson defended the spoils system, under which *Spoils system* public offices were awarded to political supporters, as a democratic reform. Rotation in office, he declared, would guard against insensitive bureaucrats who presumed that they held their positions by right. The cabinet, he believed, existed more to carry out his will than to offer counsel, and throughout his term he remained a strong executive who insisted on his way—and usually got it.

The Political Agenda in the Market Economy

Jackson took office at a time when the market economy was spreading through America and the nation's borders were expanding geographically. The three major problems his administration faced were directly caused by the resulting growing pains.

First, the demand for new lands put continuing pressure on Indians, whose valuable cornfields and hunting grounds could produce marketable commodities like cotton and wheat. Second, as the economies of the North, South, and West became more specialized, their rival interests forced a confrontation over the tariff. And finally, the booming economy focused attention on the role of credit and banking in society and on the new commercial attitudes that were a central part of the developing market economy. The president attacked all three issues in his characteristically combative style.

DEMOCRACY AND RACE

As a planter, Jackson benefited from the international demand for cotton that was drawing new lands into the market. He had gone off to the Tennessee frontier in 1788, a rowdy, ambitious young man who could afford to purchase only one slave. Caught up in the get-rich-quick mania of the frontier, he became a prominent land speculator, established himself as a planter, and by the time he became president owned nearly 100 slaves. His popularity derived not only from defeating the British but also from opening extensive tracts of valuable Indian lands to white settlement. Through military fighting and treaty negotiating, he was personally responsible for obtaining about a third of Tennessee for the United States, three-quarters of Florida and Alabama, a fifth of Georgia and Mississippi, and a tenth of Kentucky and North Carolina.

Even so, in 1820 an estimated 125,000 Indians remained east of the Mississippi River. In the Southwest the Choctaws, Creeks, Cherokees, Chickasaws, and Seminoles retained millions of acres of prime land in the heart of the cotton kingdom. Led by Georgia, southern states demanded that the federal government clear these titles. In response, Monroe in 1824 proposed to Congress that the remaining eastern tribes be relocated west of the Mississippi River.

New attitudes toward race   As white pressure for removal intensified, a shift in the attitude toward Indians and race increasingly occurred. Previously whites had generally attributed cultural differences among whites, blacks, and Indians to the environment. After 1815 the dominant white culture stressed "innate" racial differences that could never be erased. A growing number of Americans began to argue that the Indian was a permanently inferior savage who blocked progress.

Accommodate or Resist?

The clamor among southern whites for removal placed the southwestern tribes in a difficult situation. Understandably, they strongly rejected the idea of abandoning their lands. They diverged, however, over how to respond. Among the Seminoles, mixed-bloods (those with white as well as Indian ancestry) took the lead in urging military resistance to any attempt to expel them. In the Cherokee nation, on the other hand, mixed-bloods led by John Ross advocated a program of accommodation by adopting white ways to prevent removal. After a bitter struggle Ross prevailed, and *Cherokee government* in 1827 the Cherokees adopted a written constitution modeled after that of the United States. They also enacted the death penalty for any member who sold tribal lands to whites without consent of the governing general council. Developing their own alphabet, they published a bilingual newspaper, *The Cherokee Phoenix.* Similarly, the neighboring Creeks moved to centralize authority by strengthening the power of the governing council at the expense of local towns. They too made it illegal for individual chiefs to sell any more land to whites.

The division between traditionalists and those favoring accommodation reflected the fact that Indians too had been drawn into a web of market relationships. As more Cherokee families began to sell their surplus crops, they ceased to share property communally as in the past. Cherokee society became more stratified and unequal, just as white society had, and economic elites dominated the tribal government. Women's traditional economic role was transformed as well, as men now took over farming operations, previously a female responsibility. Nor were the Cherokees untouched by the cotton boom. Some of the tribe's leaders, particularly half-bloods

The leader of the antiremoval faction, Cherokee chief John Ross was the son of a mixed-blood mother and a Scottish trader.

INDIAN REMOVAL
During Jackson's presidency, the federal government concluded nearly 70 treaties with Indian tribes, in the Old Northwest as well as in the South. Under their terms, the United States acquired approximately 100 million acres of Indian land.

who could deal easily with white culture, became substantial planters who owned large numbers of slaves and thousands of acres of cotton land. Largely of mixed ancestry, slaveholders were wealthier, had investments in other enterprises such as gristmills and ferries, raised crops for market, were more likely to read English, and were the driving force behind acculturation.

Changing nature of Cherokee society

As cotton cultivation expanded among the Cherokees, slavery became harsher and a primary means of determining status, just as in southern white society. The general council passed several laws forbidding intermarriage with African Americans and excluding African Americans and mulattoes from voting or holding office. Ironically, at the same time that white racial attitudes toward Indians were deteriorating, the Cherokees' racial attitudes toward black Americans were also hardening, paralleling the increased racism among white Americans.

Trail of Tears

Pressure for Indian removal

As western land fever increased and racial attitudes hardened, Jackson prodded Congress to provide funds for Indian removal. He watched sympathetically as the Georgia legislature overturned the Cherokee constitution, declared Cherokee laws null and void, and decreed that tribal members would be tried in state courts. In 1830 Congress finally passed a removal bill.

But the Cherokees brought suit in federal court against Georgia's actions. In 1832 in the case of *Worcester v. Georgia,* the Supreme Court sided with the Cherokees. Indian tribes had full authority over their lands, wrote Chief Justice John Marshall in the opinion. Thus Georgia had no right to extend its laws over Cherokee territory. Pronouncing Marshall's decision "stillborn," Jackson ignored the Court's edict and went ahead with plans for removal.

Although Jackson assured Indians that they could be removed only voluntarily, he paid no heed when state governments harassed tribes into surrendering lands. Under the threat of coercion, the Choctaws, Chickasaws, and Creeks reluctantly agreed to move to tracts in present-day Oklahoma. In the process, Indians unaccustomed to white law and notions of property fell victim to shameful frauds, as land-hungry schemers cheated countless tribal members out of their lands. As much as 90 percent of the land allotments may have fallen into the hands of speculators.

Removal of the Cherokees

The Cherokees held out longest, but to no avail. In order to deal with more pliant leaders of the tribe, Georgia authorities kidnapped Chief John Ross, who led the resistance to relocation, and threw him into jail. Ross was finally released but not allowed to negotiate the treaty, which stipulated that the Cherokees leave their lands no later than 1838. When that time came, most refused to go. In response, President Martin Van Buren had the U.S. Army round up resistant members and force them, at bayonet point, to join the westward march. Of the 15,000 who traveled this Trail of Tears, approximately one-quarter died along the way of exposure, disease, and exhaustion, including Ross's wife. As for the western tracts awaiting the survivors, they were smaller and generally inferior to the rich lands that had been taken from the Cherokees.

Military resistance

Some Indians chose resistance. In the Old Northwest a group of the Sauk and Fox led by Black Hawk recrossed the Mississippi into Illinois in 1832 and were crushed by federal troops and the militia. More successful was the military resistance of a minority of Seminoles under the leadership of Osceola. Despite his death, they held out until 1842 in the Everglades of Florida before being subdued and removed. In the end, only a small number of southern tribe members were able to escape removal. Most were shunted off onto worthless lands that whites did not want.

Except for a few missionaries and eastern reformers, Americans expressed little regret over the treatment of the eastern tribes. In his Farewell Address in 1837, Jackson defended his policy by piously asserting that the eastern tribes had been fi-

The Choctaws were one of the southern tribes forcibly removed by the United States government in the 1830s. Here a Choctaw family, led by a proud male, walks along a Louisiana bayou. Tocqueville watched one group, which included the sick and wounded, newborn babies, and elderly members near death, cross the Mississippi in the middle of winter. "They possessed neither tents nor wagons, but only their arms and some provisions. . . . No cry, no sob, was heard among the assembled crowd. . . . Their calamities were of ancient date, and they knew them to be irremediable."

nally "placed beyond the reach of injury or oppression, and that [the] paternal care of the General Government will hereafter watch over them and protect them." Indians, however, knew the bitter truth of the matter. Without effective political power, they found themselves at the mercy of the pressures of the marketplace and the hardening racial attitudes of white Americans.

Free Blacks in the North

Unlike Indian removal, the rising discrimination against free African Americans during this period did not depend directly on presidential action. Still, it was Jackson's Democratic party, which so loudly trumpeted its belief in democracy, that was also the most strongly proslavery and the most hostile to black rights. The intensifying racism that accompanied the emergence of democracy in American life bore down with particular force on free African Americans. "The policy and power of the national and state governments are against them," commented one northerner. "The popular feeling is against them—the interests of our citizens are against them. Their prospects . . . are dreary, and comfortless."

In the years before the Civil War, the free states never had a significant free black population. Only about 171,000 lived in the North in 1840, about a quarter of whom were mulattoes. Although free African Americans made up less than 2 percent of the North's population, most states enacted a series of laws to keep them in an inferior position. (For a discussion of free African Americans in the South, see Chapter 13.)

THE SPREAD OF WHITE MANHOOD SUFFRAGE
Although white manhood suffrage became the norm during the Jacksonian era, in a number of states free black males who had been voting by law or by custom lost the right to vote. After 1821 a $250 property requirement disfranchised about 90 percent of adult black males in New York.

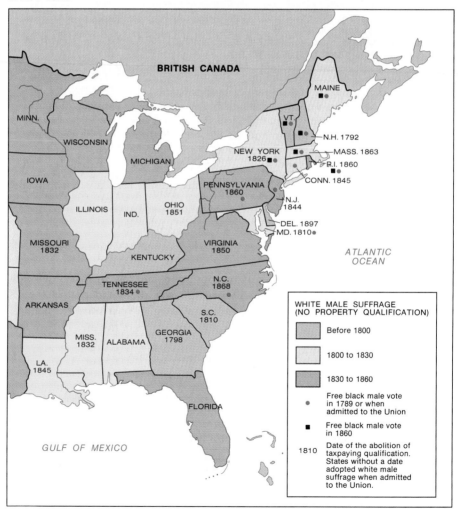

Most black northerners lacked any meaningful political rights. Black men could *Discrimination* vote on equal terms with whites in only five New England states. New York imposed *against free* a property requirement only on black voters, which disfranchised all but a handful of *blacks* African American males. Moreover, in New Jersey, Pennsylvania, and Connecticut, African American men lost the right to vote after having previously enjoyed that privilege.

Black northerners were also denied basic civil rights that whites enjoyed. Five states prohibited them from testifying against whites, and either law or custom excluded African Americans from juries everywhere except Massachusetts. In addition, several western states passed black exclusion laws prohibiting free African Americans from immigrating into the state. These laws were seldom enforced, but they were available to harass the African American population in times of social stress.

Segregation, or the physical separation of the races, was widely practiced in the free states. African Americans were assigned to special, separate sections on public transportation. Throughout the North they could not go into most hotels and restaurants, and if permitted to enter theaters and lecture halls, they sat in the corners and balconies. In white churches, they were put in separate pews and took communion after white members. In virtually every community, black children were excluded from the public schools or forced to attend overcrowded and poorly funded separate schools. Commented one English visitor: "We see, in effect, two nations—one white and another black—growing up together . . . but never mingling on a principle of equality."

Discrimination pushed African American males into the lowest paying and most *Black poverty* unskilled jobs in society: servants, sailors, waiters, and common laborers. In Philadelphia in 1838, 80 percent of employed black males were unskilled laborers, and three of five black families had less than $60 total wealth. African American women normally continued working after marriage, mostly as servants, cooks, laundresses, and seamstresses, since their wages were critical to the family's economic survival. Blacks were willing strikebreakers, because white workers, fearing economic competition and loss of status, were overtly hostile and excluded them from trade unions. A number of antiblack riots erupted in northern cities during these years. "Whenever the interests of the white man and the black come into collision," one foreign observer noted, "the black man goes to the wall. It is certain that, wherever labor is scarce, there he is readily employed; when it becomes plentiful, he is the first to be discharged." Forced into abject poverty, free blacks in the North suffered from an inadequate diet, were more susceptible to disease, and in 1850 had a life expectancy 8 to 10 years less than that of whites.

"None but those who experience it can know what it is—this constant, galling sense of cruel injustice and wrong," grieved Charlotte Forten, a free African American from Philadelphia.

The African American Community

African Americans responded to this oppression by founding self-help societies, and the black community centered on institutions such as black churches, schools, and mutual aid societies. They also agitated against slavery in the South and for equal rights in the North. After 1840 black frustration generated a nationalist movement that emphasized racial unity, self-help, and, for some, renewal of ties with Africa.

Because of limited economic opportunity, the African American community was not as diversified as white society in terms of occupation and wealth. There were distinctions, nevertheless, that rested on wealth and skin color. In general, mulattoes (lighter-skinned blacks) had greater opportunities to become more literate and skilled, were better off economically, and were more likely to be community leaders. Mulattoes' feelings of superiority were reflected in marriage choices, as they usually shunned darker-skinned blacks. "They have as much caste among themselves as we have," lamented the abolitionist Sarah Grimké, "and despise the poor as much I fear as their pale brethren."

The Minstrel Show

Appeal of minstrelsy

The racist attitudes of the day were very much reflected in popular culture, nowhere more than in minstrel shows, the most popular form of entertainment in Jacksonian America. Originating in the 1830s and 1840s and playing to packed houses in cities and towns throughout the nation, minstrel shows featured white actors performing in blackface. They dealt in the broadest of racial stereotypes, ridiculing blacks as physically different and portraying them as buffoons.

Although popular throughout the country, minstrelsy's primary audience was in northern cities. Its basic message was that African Americans could not cope with freedom and therefore did not belong in the North. Enslaved African Americans were portrayed as happy and contented, whereas free black Americans were carica-

---

Minstrel sheet music (left) illustrates the racist attitudes that pervaded Jacksonian democracy. Blacks, played by whites, were made to appear ridiculous through grotesque physical features, exaggerated poses, and pretentious airs. In contrast, the black sawyer (right) working in New York City evidences the dignity free blacks maintained in the face of unrelenting hostility and discrimination.

tured either as strutting dandies or as helpless ignoramuses. Drawing its patrons from workers, Irish immigrants, and the poorer elements in society, minstrelsy assured these white champions of democracy that they remained superior.

The unsettling economic, social, and political changes of the Jacksonian era heightened white Americans' fear of failure, which stimulated racism. The popular yet unrealistic expectation was that any white man might become rich. Yet in fact, 20 percent or more of white adult males of this era never accumulated any property. Their lack of success encouraged them to relieve personal tensions through increased hostility to their black neighbors. Subjecting black Americans to legal disabilities ensured that even the poorest whites would enjoy an advantage in the race for wealth and status. "The prejudice of race appears to be stronger in the states that have abolished slavery than in those where it still exists," Tocqueville noted, "and nowhere is it so intolerant as in those states where servitude has never been known." The power of racism in Jacksonian America stemmed in part, at least, from the fact that equality remained part of the nation's creed, while it steadily receded as a social reality.

Deepening racism

THE NULLIFICATION CRISIS

Indian removal and antiblack discrimination provided one answer to the question of who would be given equality of opportunity in America's new democratic society. Indians and African Americans would not. The issue of nullification raised a different, equally pressing question. As the market revolution pushed the economies of the North, South, and West to become increasingly specialized, how would various regions or interest groups accommodate their differences?

The Growing Crisis in South Carolina

South Carolina had been particularly hard hit by the depression of 1819. When prosperity returned to the rest of the nation, many of the state's cotton planters remained economically depressed. With lands exhausted from years of cultivation, they could not compete with the fabulous yields of frontier planters in Alabama and Mississippi.

Increasingly, South Carolinians viewed federal tariffs as the cause of their miseries. When Congress raised the duty rates in 1824, they assailed the tariff as an unfair tax that raised the prices of goods they imported while benefiting other regions of the nation. Other southern states opposed the 1824 tariff as well, though none so vehemently as South Carolina.

The one southern state in which black inhabitants outnumbered whites, South Carolina, had also been growing more sensitive about the institution of slavery. In 1822 a slave conspiracy led by Denmark Vesey, a free black carpenter in Charleston, had been thwarted only at the last moment. A brilliant leader, literate, and well traveled, Vesey argued that slavery violated the principles of both republicanism and Christianity. He devised a well-coordinated plan to seize control of the city and raise the standard of black liberty, but several slaves betrayed the conspiracy at the last moment. Charleston authorities hurried to arrest Vesey and his lieutenants, who were tried, convicted, and either executed or banished. Even so, white South Carolinians were convinced that other undetected conspirators lurked in their midst.

Denmark Vesey's conspiracy

As an additional measure of security, the state's leaders pushed for stronger constitutional protection of slavery. After all, supporters of high tariffs had already claimed that the "implied powers" of the Constitution gave them the right to promote manufacturing. What was to stop these same broad claims from being used to end slavery? "In contending against the tariff, I have always felt that we were combatting against the symptom instead of the disease," argued Chancellor William Harper of South Carolina. "Tomorrow may witness [an attempt] to relieve . . . your slaves."

Other southern states opposed the 1824 tariff, though none so heatedly as South Carolina. When Congress raised the duty rates still higher in 1828 with the so-called Tariff of Abominations, South Carolina's legislature published the *South Carolina Exposition and Protest*, which outlined for the first time the theory of nullification. Only later was it revealed that its author was Jackson's own vice president, John C. Calhoun.

Calhoun's Theory of Nullification

Educated at Yale and at the most distinguished law school in the country, Calhoun was the most impressive intellect of his political generation. During the 1820s the South Carolina leader made a slow but steady journey away from nationalism toward an extreme states' rights position. When he was elected Jackson's vice president, South Carolinians assumed that tariff reform would be soon enacted. But Jackson and Calhoun quarreled, and Calhoun lost all influence in the administration.

Minority rights versus majority rule

In his theory of nullification, Calhoun addressed the problem of how to protect the rights of a minority in a political system based on the rule of the majority. The Union, he argued, was a compact between sovereign states. Thus the people of each state, acting in special popular conventions, had the right to nullify any federal law that exceeded the powers granted to Congress under the Constitution. The law would then become null and void in that state. In response, Congress could either repeal the law or propose a constitutional amendment expressly giving it the power in question. If the amendment was ratified, the nullifying state could either accept the decision or exercise its ultimate right as a sovereign state and secede from the Union.

Nationalists' theory of the Union

When Senator Robert Hayne of South Carolina outlined Calhoun's theory in the Senate in 1830, Senator Daniel Webster of Massachusetts replied sharply that the Union was not a compact of sovereign states. The people, and not the states, he argued, had created the Constitution. "It is the people's constitution, the people's government, made for the people, made by the people, and answerable to the people." Webster also insisted that the federal government did not merely act as the agent of the states but had sovereign powers in those areas where it had been delegated responsibility. Finally, Webster endorsed the doctrine of judicial review, which gave the Supreme Court authority to determine the meaning of the Constitution.

The Nullifiers Nullified

When Congress passed another tariff in 1832 that failed to give the state any relief, South Carolina's legislature called for the election of delegates to a popular convention, which overwhelmingly adopted an ordinance in November that declared the tariffs of 1828 and 1832 "null, void, and no law, nor binding upon this state, its officers or citizens" after February 1, 1833.

As Daniel Webster outlines his nationalist theory of the Constitution and the Union, Senator Robert Hayne of South Carolina sits (front, left) with his hands together. The Senate gallery is filled, with most of the seats occupied by women, evidence of the widespread interest in politics.

Jackson, who had spent much of his life defending the nation, was not about to tolerate any defiance of his authority or the federal government's. In his Proclamation on Nullification, issued in December 1832, he insisted that the Union was perpetual. *Idea of a* Under the Constitution, there was no right of secession. Surprisingly, it had taken 40 *perpetual* years since the adoption of the Constitution to develop this point. To reinforce his an- *Union* nounced determination to enforce the tariff laws, Congress passed the Force Bill, reaffirming the president's military powers.

Yet Jackson was also a skillful politician. At the same time that he threatened South Carolina, he urged Congress to reduce the tariff rates. By holding out the hope of tariff reform, he managed to isolate South Carolina from the rest of the southern states. With no other state willing to follow South Carolina's lead, Calhoun reluctantly *Compromise* joined forces with Henry Clay to work out a compromise tariff, which Jackson signed *of 1833* on March 1, 1833, the same day he signed the Force Bill. South Carolina's convention repealed the nullifying ordinance, and the crisis came to an end.

Calhoun's doctrine had proved too radical for the rest of the South. Yet at the same time the controversy convinced many southerners that they were becoming a permanent minority. "It is useless and impracticable to disguise the fact," concluded nullifier William Harper, "that we are divided into slave-holding and non-slaveholding states, and this is the broad and marked distinction that must separate us at last." As that feeling of isolation grew, it was not nullification but the threat of secession that ultimately became the South's primary weapon.

THE BANK WAR

Jackson understood well the political ties that bound the nation. He grasped much less firmly the economic and financial connections that linked different regions of the country through banks and national markets. In particular, the president was suspicious of the national bank and the power it possessed. His clash with the Second Bank of the United States brought on the greatest crisis of his presidency.

The National Bank and the Panic of 1819

Monster bank   Chartered by Congress in 1816 for a 20-year period, the Second Bank of the United States suffered initially from woeful mismanagement. At first it helped fuel the speculative pressures in the economy. Then it turned about-face and sharply contracted credit by calling in loans when the depression hit in 1819. The Bank regained a sound financial footing, but William Gouge, a Philadelphia journalist and economist, charged, "The Bank was saved and the people were ruined." Critics viewed the Bank's policies not as a consequence but as the cause of the financial downswing. To many Americans, the Bank had already become a monster.

The psychological effects of the Panic of 1819 were almost as momentous as the economic. In the midst of dizzying prosperity and unbounded optimism, Americans were suddenly plunged into privation, despair, and economic depression. That shock convinced many uneasy farmers and workers that the hard times were punishment for having lost sight of the old virtues of simplicity, frugality, and hard work. For them banks became a symbol of the commercialization of American society and the rapid passing of a simpler way of life.

Biddle's Bank

In 1823 Nicholas Biddle, a rich 37-year-old Philadelphia businessman, became president of the national bank. Biddle was intelligent and thoroughly familiar with the banking system, but he was also impossibly arrogant. Seeking boldly to restore the

Function as a
central bank   Bank's damaged reputation, he set out to use the Bank to regulate the amount of credit available in the economy and thereby provide the nation with a sound currency.

Government revenues were paid largely in banknotes (paper money) issued by state-chartered banks. Because the Treasury Department regularly deposited U.S.

funds in the national bank, the notes of state banks from all across the Union came into its possession. If Biddle believed that a state bank was overextended and had issued more notes than was safe, he presented them to that bank and demanded they be redeemed in specie (gold or silver). Because banks did not have enough specie reserves to back all the paper money they issued, the only way a state bank could continue to redeem its notes was to call in its loans and reduce the amount of its notes in circulation. This action had the effect of lessening the amount of credit in the economy.

On the other hand, if Biddle felt that a bank's credit policies were reasonable, he simply returned the state banknotes to circulation without presenting them for redemption. Being the government's official depository gave Biddle's bank enormous power over state banks and over the economy. As Biddle tactlessly admitted, "There are very few [state banks] which might not have been destroyed by an exertion of the powers of the bank." Under Biddle's direction the Bank became a financial colossus: it had 29 branches and made 20 percent of the country's loans, issued one-fifth of the total banknotes, and held fully a third of all deposits and specie. Yet for the most part, Biddle used the Bank's enormous power responsibly to provide the United States a sound paper currency, which the expanding economy needed.

Although the Bank had strong support in the business community, workers complained that they were often paid in depreciated state banknotes. Such notes could be redeemed for only a portion of their face value, a practice that in effect cheated workers out of part of their wages. They called for a "hard money" currency of only gold and silver. Hard money advocates viewed bankers and financiers as profiteers who manipulated the paper money system to enrich themselves at the expense of honest, hardworking farmers and laborers.

Opposition to paper money

The Clash between Jackson and Biddle

Jackson's own experiences left him with a deep distrust of banks and paper money. In 1804 his Tennessee land speculations had brought him to the brink of bankruptcy, from which it took years of painful struggle to free himself. Reflecting on his personal situation, he became convinced that banks and paper money threatened to corrupt the Republic.

As president, Jackson called for reform of the banking system from time to time, but Biddle refused even to consider curbing the Bank's powers. Already distracted by the nullification controversy, Jackson warned Biddle not to inject the bank issue into the 1832 campaign. When Biddle went ahead and applied for a renewal of the Bank's charter in 1832, four years early, Jackson was furious. "The Bank is trying to kill me," he stormed to Van Buren, *"but I will kill it."*

Despite the president's opposition, Congress passed a recharter bill in the summer of 1832. Immediately Jackson vetoed it as unconstitutional (rejecting Chief Justice Marshall's ruling in favor of the bank in *McCulloch v. Maryland*). The president went on to condemn the Bank as an agent of special privilege and as inconsistent with the republican principle of equality, because it made "the rich richer and the potent more powerful." Holding up the national bank as a symbol of aristocracy, the president pledged to protect "the humble members of society—the farmer, mechanics, and laborers" against "the advancement of the few at the expense of the many." The message completely ignored the Bank's vital services in the economy.

Jackson's veto

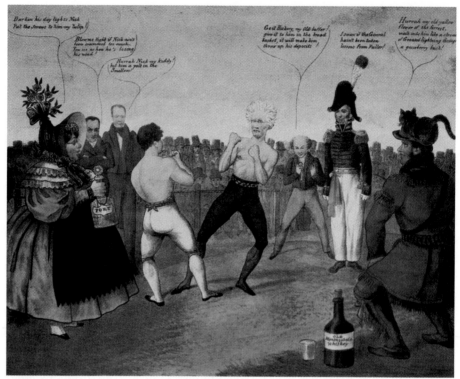

In this Bank War cartoon, Jackson boxes Biddle as Webster and Clay urge Biddle on and Van Buren shouts instructions from Old Hickory's corner. The heavyset woman holding a bottle of port (an upper-class beverage) represents the national bank, bloated with privilege and wealth, while a plain American in frontier garb holds Jackson's bottle of whiskey, the drink of the masses.

As Jackson's veto message revealed, the struggle over the national bank tended to pit traditional farmers and workers against the world of commerce and national markets. Jackson's strongest supporters were workers and farmers outside the commercial economy and those who were disturbed by the changes that the market produced in their lives. Individuals who were more comfortable with the new commercial ethos rallied to the Bank's defense. In the end, most of them would end up as members of the opposing Whig party.

The Bank Destroyed

When Congress failed to override Jackson's veto, the recharter of the Bank became a central issue of the 1832 campaign. Jackson's opponent was Henry Clay, a National Republican who eagerly accepted the financial support of Biddle and the national bank. Clay went down to defeat, and once reelected, Jackson was determined to destroy the Bank. He believed that as a private corporation the Bank wielded a dangerous influence over government policy and the economy, and he was justly incensed over its heavy-handed attempt to influence the election.

To cripple the Bank, the president simply ordered all the government's federal deposits withdrawn. Since such an act clearly violated federal law, Jackson was forced to transfer one secretary of the treasury and fire another before he finally found in Roger Taney someone willing to take the job and carry out the edict. Taney (pronounced "Taw-ney") began drawing against the government's funds to pay its debts while depositing new revenues in selected state banks. *Removal of the deposits*

Biddle fought back by deliberately precipitating a brief financial panic in 1833. "Go to Biddle," Jackson snapped to businessmen seeking relief. "I never will restore the deposits. I never will recharter the United States Bank, or sign a charter for any other bank." Eventually Biddle had to relent, and Jackson's victory was complete. When the Bank's charter expired in 1836, no national banking system replaced it. Instead, Jackson continued depositing federal revenues in selected state banks. A large majority of these "Pet Banks" were controlled by Democrats.

Jackson's Impact on the Presidency

Jackson approached the end of his administration in triumph. Indian removal was well on its way to completion, the nullifiers had been confounded, and the "Monster Bank" had been destroyed. In the process, Jackson immeasurably enlarged the power of the presidency. "The President is the direct representative of the American people," he lectured the Senate when it opposed him. "He was elected by the people, and is responsible to them." With this declaration, Jackson redefined the character of the presidential office and its relationship to the people. *Strengthening of presidential powers*

Jackson also converted the veto into an effective presidential power. During his two terms in office, he vetoed 12 bills, compared with only 9 for all previous presidents combined. Moreover, where his predecessors had vetoed bills only on strict constitutional grounds, Jackson felt free to block laws simply because he thought them bad policy. The threat of such action became an effective way to shape pending legislation to his liking, which fundamentally strengthened the power of the president over Congress. The development of the modern presidency began with Andrew Jackson.

VAN BUREN AND DEPRESSION

With the controls of the national bank removed, state banks rapidly expanded the amount of paper money in circulation. The total value of banknotes jumped from $82 million in January 1835 to $120 million in December 1836. As the currency expanded, so did the number of banks: from 329 in 1829 to 788 in 1837. A spiraling inflation set in as prices rose 50 percent after 1830 and interest rates by half as much.

As prices rose sharply, so did speculative fever. By 1836 land sales, which had been only $2.6 million four years earlier, approached $25 million. Almost all of these lands were bought entirely on credit with banknotes, many of which had little value. Men seeking land poured into the Southwest, and as one observer wryly commented,

Specie Circular

"under this stimulating process prices rose like smoke." In July 1836 in an attempt to apply the brakes to the economy, Jackson issued the Specie Circular, which decreed that the government would accept only specie for the purchase of public land. Land sales drastically declined, but the speculative pressures in the economy were by now too great to be reversed. Congress finally repealed the Specie Circular in 1838.

"Van Ruin's" Depression

Whig party

During Jackson's second term, his opponents had gradually come together in a new party, the Whigs. Led by Henry Clay, they charged that "King Andrew I" had dangerously concentrated power in the presidency. The Whigs also embraced Clay's "American System," designed to spur national economic development and particularly manufacturing. To do this the Whigs advocated a protective tariff, a national bank, and federal aid for internal improvements. In 1836 the Democrats nominated Martin Van Buren, who triumphed over three Whig sectional candidates.

This Whig cartoon blames the Democratic party for the depression that began during Van Buren's administration. Barefoot workers go unemployed, and women and children beg and sleep in the streets. Depositors clamor for their money from a bank that has suspended specie payments, while the pawnbroker and liquor store do a thriving business and the sheriff rounds up debtors.

Van Buren had less than two months in office to savor his triumph before the *Depression*
speculative mania collapsed, and with it the economy. After a brief recovery, the bottom fell out of the international cotton market in 1839 and the country entered a serious depression. Arising from causes that were worldwide, the depression demonstrated how deeply the market economy had penetrated American society. It was not until 1843 that the economy revived.

Public opinion identified hard times with the policies of the Democratic party. Since he strongly opposed a new national bank, Van Buren instead persuaded Congress in 1840 to create an Independent Treasury to keep the government's funds. *Independent* Its offices were forbidden to accept paper currency, issue any banknotes, or make any *Treasury* loans. The government's money would be safe, but it would also remain unavailable to banks to make loans and stimulate the economy.

As the depression deepened, thousands of workers were unemployed and countless businesses failed. Urban workers and their families were among the hardest hit. Nationally wages fell 30 to 50 percent. "Business of all kinds is completely at a stand," wrote one business leader in 1840, "and the whole body politic sick and infirm, and calling aloud for a remedy."

The Whigs' Triumph

By 1840 the Whigs had done much to perfect their party's national organization, and with the nation stuck in the worst depression of the century, they approached the election of 1840 in high spirits. To oppose Van Buren, they turned to William Henry Harrison, the military leader who had won fame defeating the Shawnee Indians at Tippecanoe (page 287). Using the democratic electioneering techniques that Jackson's *First modern* supporters had first perfected, they portrayed Harrison as a man of the people while *presidential* painting Van Buren as a dandy and an aristocrat who wore a corset, ate off gold plates *campaign* with silver spoons, and used cologne. Shades of Franklin Plummer!

Whig rallies featured hard cider and log cabins to reinforce Harrison's image as a man of the people. Ironically, Harrison had been born into one of Virginia's most aristocratic families and was living in a 16-room mansion in Ohio. But the Whig campaign, by portraying the election as a contest between aristocracy and democracy, was perfectly attuned to the prevailing national spirit.

Both parties used parades, barbecues, liberty pole raisings, party songs, and mass meetings to stir up enthusiasm. But the Whigs pioneered a new aspect of mass political campaigning: they prominently involved women. Deeming themselves the party of morality, Whigs appealed directly to women for support, urging them to be- *Women take a* come politically informed in order to morally instruct their husbands. Women at- *new political* tended Whig rallies, conducted meetings, made speeches, and wrote campaign pam- *role* phlets, activities that before had been solely the duties of men. "I never took so much interest in politics in my life," Mary Steger of Richmond confessed to a friend. Uncertain what to make of this new Whig tactic, one Democrat observed, "This way of making politicians of their women is something new under the sun. . . ." Democrats had no choice but to eventually follow suit. Women's role in national pol-

William Henry Harrison's supposed "rustic" home, complete with hard cider.

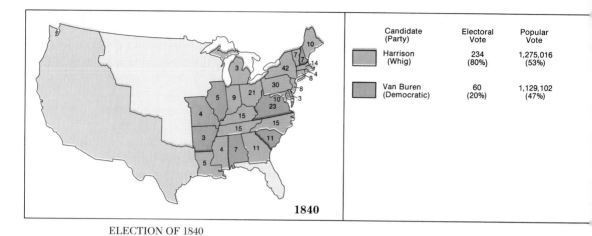

Candidate (Party)	Electoral Vote	Popular Vote
Harrison (Whig)	234 (80%)	1,275,016 (53%)
Van Buren (Democratic)	60 (20%)	1,129,102 (47%)

1840

ELECTION OF 1840

itics began in 1840, and within a few years their presence at party rallies was commonplace.

Just as the Panic of 1819 had roused the voters to action, the depression and the two parties' response to it sparked interest. The result was a record turnout, as some 900,000 new voters were mobilized between 1836 and 1840 and nearly four-fifths of the eligible voters went to the polls. Although the popular vote was fairly close (Harrison led by about 150,000 votes out of 2.4 million cast), in the Electoral College he won an easy victory, 234 to 60.

The "log cabin" campaign marked the final transition from the deferential politics of the Federalist era to the egalitarian politics that had emerged in the wake of the Panic of 1819. "We have been sung down, lied down, drunk down!" protested one indignant Democratic journal. As the *Democratic Review* conceded after the Whigs' victory in 1840, "We have taught them how to conquer us."

THE JACKSONIAN PARTY SYSTEM

It is easy, given the hoopla of democratic campaigning, to be distracted from the central fact that the new political system was directly shaped by the social and economic strains of an expanding nation. Whigs and Democrats held different attitudes toward the changes brought about by the market, banks, and commerce.

Democrats, Whigs, and the Market

Democratic ideology

The Democrats tended to view society as a continuing conflict between "the people"—farmers, planters, and workers—and a set of greedy aristocrats. These were not Europe's landed aristocrats, of course, but a "paper money aristocracy" of bankers, stock jobbers, and investors. This new class manipulated the banking system for its own profit, Democrats claimed, and sapped the nation's virtue by encouraging speculation and the desire for quickly gained, unearned wealth. For Democrats, the Bank War became a battle to restore the old Jeffersonian Republic with its values of simplicity, frugality, hard work, and independence. This is what Jackson meant when he said that removal of the deposits from Biddle's Bank would "preserve the morals of the people."

Jackson understood the dangers private banks posed to a democratic society. Yet Democrats, in effect, wanted the rewards of the market without sacrificing the features of a simple agrarian republic. They wanted the wealth and goods that the market offered without the competitive, changing society, the complex dealings, the dominance of urban centers, and the loss of independence that came with it.

Whigs, on the other hand, were more comfortable with the market. For them, commerce and economic development were agents of civilization. Nor did the Whigs envision any conflict in society between farmers and mechanics on the one hand and businesspeople and bankers on the other. Economic growth would benefit everyone by creating jobs, stimulating demand for agricultural products, raising national income, and expanding opportunity. The government's responsibility was to provide a well-regulated economy that guaranteed opportunity for citizens of ability. In such an economy, banks and corporations were not only useful but necessary. A North Carolina Whig well expressed the party's vision of society: "All should be mutual friends and helpers to each other, and who ever aids and assists his fellow men from good motives, by lending money, by affording employment by precept or example, is a benefactor to his fellow men."

Whig ideology

Whigs and Democrats differed not only in their attitudes toward the market but also about how active government should be. Despite Andrew Jackson's inclination to be a strong president, Democrats as a rule believed in limited government. Government's role in the economy was to promote competition by destroying monopolies and special privileges. As one New Jersey Democratic newspaper declared, "All Bank charters, all laws conferring special privileges, with all acts of incorporation, for purposes of private gain, are monopolies, in as much as they are calculated to enhance the power of wealth, produce inequalities among the people and to subvert liberty."

Democrats' belief in limited government

In *Charles River Bridge v. Warren Bridge* (1837) the Supreme Court strengthened the vision of an expanding capitalistic society undergirded by free competition. The opinion was written by Chief Justice Roger Taney, whom Jackson had appointed in 1835 to succeed John Marshall. At issue was whether in authorizing construction of a free bridge Massachusetts violated the rights of the owners of an adjacent toll bridge. Declaring that the public interest was the overriding concern, Taney's opinion struck down the idea of implied monopolies. In this decision, the Court sought to promote equality of opportunity and economic progress.

Opposition to monopolies

In keeping with this philosophy of limited government, Democrats also rejected the idea that moral beliefs were the proper sphere of government action. Religion and politics, they believed, should be kept clearly separate, and they generally opposed humanitarian legislation as an interference with personal freedom. On the other hand, they supported debtor relief, which in their view curbed the wealthy aristocrats who tyrannized the common worker.

The Whigs, in contrast, viewed government power positively. They believed that it should be used to protect individual rights and public liberty and that it had a special role where individual effort was ineffective. By regulating the economy and com-

Whigs' belief in active government

petition, the government could ensure equal opportunity. Indeed, for Whigs the concept of government promoting the general welfare went beyond the economy. Northern Whigs in particular also believed that government power should be used to foster the moral welfare of the country. They were much more likely to favor temperance or antislavery legislation and aid to education. Whigs portrayed themselves not only as the party of prosperity but also as the party of respectability and proper behavior.

The Social Bases of the Two Parties

In some ways the social makeup of the two parties was similar. To be competitive, Whigs and Democrats both had to have significant support among farmers, the largest group in society, and workers. Neither party could carry an election by appealing exclusively to the rich or the poor.

Attitudes toward the market economy

The Whigs, however, enjoyed disproportionate strength among the business and commercial classes, especially following the Bank War. Whigs appealed to planters who needed credit to finance their cotton and rice trade in the world market, to farmers who were eager to sell their surpluses, and to workers who wished to improve themselves. Democrats attracted farmers isolated from the market or uncomfortable with it, workers alienated from the emerging industrial system, and rising entrepreneurs who wanted to break monopolies and open the economy to newcomers like themselves. The Whigs were strongest in the towns, cities, and rural areas that were fully integrated into the market economy, whereas Democrats dominated areas of semisubsistence farming that were more isolated and languishing economically. Attitude toward the market, rather than economic position, was more important in determining party affiliation.

Religious and ethnic factors

Religion and ethnic identities also shaped partisanship. As the self-proclaimed "party of respectability," Whigs attracted the support of high-status native-born church groups, including the Congregationalists and Unitarians in New England and Presbyterians and Episcopalians elsewhere. The party also attracted immigrant groups that most easily merged into the dominant Anglo-Protestant culture, such as the English, Welsh, and Scots. Democrats, on the other hand, recruited more Germans and Irish, whose more lenient observance of the Sabbath and (among Catholics) use of parochial schools generated native-born hostility. Democrats appealed to the lower-status Baptists and Methodists, particularly in states where they earlier had been subjected to disabilities. Both parties also attracted freethinkers and the unchurched, but the Democrats had the advantage because they resisted demands for temperance and sabbatarian laws, such as the prohibition of Sunday travel. In states where they could vote, African Americans were solidly Whig in reaction to the Democratic party's strong racism and hostility to black rights.

The Triumph of the Market

Clearly, Jacksonian politics evolved out of the social and economic dislocation produced by rapidly expanding economic opportunity. Yet efforts to avoid the costs of the market while preserving its benefits were doomed to failure. In states where the Democrats eliminated all banks, so much hardship and financial chaos ensued that some system of banking was soon restored. The expansion of the economy after 1815 had caught farmers as well as urban residents in an international network of trade and finance, tying them with a tightening grip to the price of cotton in Liverpool or the interest rates of the Bank of England. There was no rolling back the market in a return to the ideals of Crèvecoeur.

Still, Americans had evolved a system of democratic politics to deal with the conflicts that the new order produced. The new national parties—like the new markets spreading across the nation—had become essential structures uniting the American nation. They advanced an ideology of equality and opportunity, which stood as a goal for the nation even though women, African Americans, and Indians were excluded. The new politics developed a system of truly national parties, competing with one another, involving large numbers of ordinary Americans resolving differences through compromise and negotiation. Along with the market, democracy had become an integral part of American life.

CHAPTER SUMMARY

The rise of democracy was stimulated by the Panic of 1819. In the wake of hard times Americans turned more quickly to their government for solutions and politicians courted voters more actively. The new political culture of democracy included the use of conventions to make nominations, the celebration of the wisdom of the people, the adoption of white manhood suffrage, and the acceptance of political parties as essential for the working of the constitutional system. Andrew Jackson came to personify these changes in national politics.

The new system had distinct limits for racial minorities, however, as democratic politics intensified racism in American society. The drive to remove the Indian tribes east of the Mississippi River accelerated after Jackson's election as president. Tribes adopted various strategies to resist removal, but eventually virtually all of the eastern Indians were forced to move to new lands in the West. The position of free blacks also deteriorated as they were subject to increasingly harsh discrimination and exclusion.

The two major crises of Jackson's presidency were the nullification crisis and the Bank War. In response to John C. Calhoun's theory of nullification, that a state convention could nullify a federal law, nationalists advanced the idea of the perpetual Union. When South Carolina attempted to nullify the federal tariff in 1832, Jackson threatened to use force against the state, until Henry Clay worked out a compromise gradually lowering the tariff. Jackson also clashed with Nicholas Biddle, head of the Second Bank of the United States. Jackson vetoed a bill in 1832 to recharter the Bank, and following his reelection he destroyed the Bank by removing its federal deposits. No national banking system replaced the Bank when its charter expired in 1836. By his forceful leadership, Jackson significantly expanded the powers of the presidency.

Shortly after Martin Van Buren took office the nation entered a severe depression, and most of his term was devoted to economic problems. Capitalizing on the hard times and employing the democratic political techniques that Jackson and the Democrats had pioneered, the Whigs gained national power in 1840. By the time of the Whigs' triumph, the two parties had developed different ideologies concerning banking, the commercialization of American society, and the role of government in the economy and in regulating moral behavior. The Whigs were more comfortable with the mechanisms of the market and linked commerce with progress. The Democrats harked back to a simpler, less complex age. Yet their efforts to escape the consequences of the market, while preserving its benefits, were doomed to failure.

SIGNIFICANT EVENTS

1819–1823	Panic and depression
1822	Denmark Vesey conspiracy
1823	Biddle becomes president of the Bank of the United States
1824	Tariff duties raised; Jackson finishes first in presidential race
1825	House elects John Quincy Adams president
1826	William Morgan kidnapped
1827	Cherokees adopt written constitution
1828	Tariff of Abominations; *South Carolina Exposition and Protest;* Jackson elected president
1830	Webster–Hayne debate; Indian Removal Act
1830–1838	Indian removal
1831	Anti-Masonic party holds first nominating convention
1832	*Worcester v. Georgia;* Jackson vetoes recharter of the national bank; Jackson reelected; South Carolina nullifies tariff; Jackson's Proclamation on Nullification
1833	Force Bill; tariff duties reduced; Jackson removes deposits from the Bank of the United States
1833–1834	Biddle's panic
1834	Whig party organized
1835–1842	Second Seminole war
1836	Specie Circular; Van Buren elected president
1837	*Charles River Bridge* case; economic panic
1838	Trail of Tears
1839–1843	Depression
1840	Independent Treasury Act; Harrison elected president
1842	First professional minstrel troupe

ADDITIONAL READING

Arthur M. Schlesinger, Jr., *The Age of Jackson* (1945), marks the beginning of modern historiography on the Jacksonian era. Locating the main sources of Jacksonianism among eastern workers, he emphasized the banking and currency issue as the defining issue of Jacksonian politics. Lightly researched, overwritten, and partisan in its analysis, Schlesinger's book provoked a flurry of works challenging its interpretation. Among the most important is the chapter on Jackson in Richard Hofstadter, *The*

American Political Tradition (1948). Despite this withering criticism, Schlesinger is not without defenders. Charles Sellers, *The Market Revolution* (1991), offers an updated—and equally flawed—version of Schlesinger's argument.

A good recent interpretation of Jacksonian politics is Harry Watson, *Liberty and Power* (1990). Robert Remini places the features of the new democratic political system in bold relief in *The Election of Andrew Jackson* (1963). Important discussions of party ideologies include Marvin Meyers, *The Jacksonian Persuasion* (1957), Daniel Walker Howe, *The Political Culture of the American Whigs* (1979), and Lawrence Frederick Kohl, *The Politics of Individualism* (1988). The best account of the nullification crisis is William W. Freehling, *Prelude to Civil War* (1966), while Robert Remini offers a succinct analysis of the banking issue in *Andrew Jackson and the Bank War* (1967). Paul Goodman, *Towards a Christian Republic* (1988) is the most valuable study of Anti-Masonry. For differing views on Indian removal, see Michael D. Green, *The Politics of Indian Removal* (1982), which deals with Creek society, and Robert Remini, *The Legacy of Andrew Jackson* (1988). For a fuller list of readings, see the Bibliography.

12

The Fires of Perfection

I n 1826 the Reverend Lyman Beecher was probably the most celebrated minister of the Republic, and the pulpit of Hanover Street Church was his to command. Beecher looked and spoke like a pious farmer, but every Sunday he was transformed when he mounted the pulpit of Boston's most imposing church. From there, he would blaze forth denunciations of dancing, drinking, dueling, or "infidelity," all the while punctuating his sermon with pump-handle strokes of the right hand.

Nor were Beecher's ambitions small. His goal was nothing less than to bring the kingdom of Christ to the nation and the world. Like many ministers, Beecher had studied the intriguing final book of the New Testament, the Revelation to John. The *Prophecies* Revelation foretold in the latter days of the Earth a glorious millennium—a thousand *of the* years of peace and triumph—when the saints would rule and evil would be banished *millennium* from the world. Beecher was convinced that the long-awaited millennium might well begin in the United States.

Personal experience reinforced this optimism. Born to a sturdy line of New England blacksmiths in 1775, Beecher entered Yale College during the high tide of postwar nationalism—and, some said, the lowest ebb of religion among young people. In the revivals of the Second Great Awakening that came to many colleges in 1802, Beecher had been one of those converted.

But he was hardly a stodgy Puritan. Much of Beecher's boundless energy went into raising a family of 11 children, every one of whom he prayed would take leading roles in bringing the kingdom of God to America. He loved to wrestle on the floor with his sons, climb the highest trees, or go "berrying" with his daughters. Still, the religious dimension of their lives was constant. The family attended two services on Sunday, a weekly prayer meeting, and a monthly "concert of prayer," where the devout met to pray for the conversion of the world. Beecher's son Thomas remembered his father commanding: "Overturn and overturn till He whose right it is shall come and reign, King of nations and King of saints."

To usher in the kingdom of God entire communities and even nations would have to be swept with a divine fire. Toward that end Beecher joined other Protestant *Benevolent* ministers in supporting a host of religious reforms and missionary efforts. In 1810 the *associations* American Board of Commissioners for Foreign Missions was established, followed by the American Bible Society (1816) and the American Tract Society (1825), whose

Bibles and religious pamphlets blanketed every sleepy hamlet in the country.

In The Way of Good and Evil *devout Christians are all helped on the path (right) to millennial perfection by the virtues of family, religion, education, and hard work. Sinners on the left, however, take the path of disobedience, intemperance, and lying—straight to hell.*

Societies sprang up to promote Sunday schools and minister to sailors and the poor. By 1830 the most important of these organizations made up the loosely united "Benevolent Empire." To Beecher these were signs of the coming kingdom.

As the new pastor at Hanover Street, Beecher also directed his righteous artillery on a host of evils that seemed to be obstructing God's kingdom. With scorn he attacked Unitarians, whose liberal, rational creed rejected the divinity of Jesus. In Boston, they were mainly upper-class and cultured. But he also denounced what he viewed as sinful pastimes of the lower class: playing cards, gambling, and drinking. And he denounced Roman Catholic priests and nuns as superstitious, devious agents of "Antichrist."

Lyman Beecher (center) with his family in 1855. Five of his six sons, all of whom were ministers, stand in back. In front, daughters Catharine (holding his arm to steady it for the long exposure) and Isabella are on the left; Harriet, the author of *Uncle Tom's Cabin,* is at the far right.

Beecher's efforts at "moral reform" antagonized many immigrants and other working people who enjoyed liquor or lotteries. Thus when a blaze broke out in the basement of his church in 1830, unsympathetic local firefighters stood by while the splendid structure burned to the ground. The fires of spiritual reform had been halted, temporarily, by a blaze of a literal sort.

Differing goals of reform   Any fire, real or spiritual, is unpredictable as it spreads from one scrap of tinder to the next. That proved to be the case with reform movements of the 1820s and 1830s, as they moved in diverging, sometimes contradictory ways. What did it mean, after all, to bring in Christ's kingdom? The goals of the early reform societies were moral rather than social. Leaders like Beecher sought to convert individuals and to church the unchurched, with the help of religious revivals and benevolent associations. Their conservative aim, as he expressed it, was to restore America to "the moral government of God."

Other Christians, however, began to focus on social issues like slavery, the inequality of women, and the operation of prisons. To these problems they demanded more radical solutions. Ironically, many of Beecher's children went well beyond his more conservative strategies for hastening the millennium. They spoke out for abolition, women's rights, and education in ways that left their father distinctly uncomfortable. In their activities the Beechers reflected the diversity of the reform impulse itself.

REVIVALISM AND THE SOCIAL ORDER

Society during the Jacksonian era was undergoing deep and rapid changes. The revolution in markets brought both economic expansion and periodic depressions, as its citizens competed—often anxiously—for status and wealth. In a nation where fortunes could be won and lost almost overnight, some reformers sought stability and moral order in religious community. The bonds of unity created by a revival brought a sense of peace in the midst of a society in change. Revivals could reinforce strength and discipline, too, in an emerging industrial culture that demanded sobriety and regular working habits.

Other reformers, however, sought to check the excesses of Jacksonian America by radically remaking institutions or devising utopian, experimental ways of living and working together. The drive for renewal, in other words, led reformers sometimes to preserve social institutions, other times to overturn them. It led them sometimes to liberate, other times to control. And the conflicting ways in which these dynamics operated could be seen in the electric career of Charles Grandison Finney.

Finney's New Measures

As a young man, Finney experienced a soul-shattering conversion in 1821 that led him to give up his law practice to become an itinerant minister. Eventually he was ordained in the Presbyterian church, although he lacked any formal theological training. He first attracted national attention when in the mid-1820s and early 1830s he conducted a series of spectacular revivals in the booming port cities along the new Erie Canal.

Like George Whitefield before him, Finney had an entrancing voice that carried great distances. His power over an audience was such that when he described the descent of a sinner into hell, those in the back of the hall rose to witness the final plunge. His success, however, resulted as much from his use of special techniques—"the new measures"—and his casual attitude toward religious doctrine.

Protracted meetings and the anxious bench

These new measures had been developed during the frontier revivals of the Second Great Awakening (page 280). Finney's contribution was to popularize the techniques and use them systematically. He held "protracted meetings" night after night to build up excitement. Speaking boldly and bluntly, he prayed for sinners by name, encouraged women to testify in public gatherings, and placed those struggling with conversion on the "anxious bench" at the front of the church. "A revival is not a miracle," he coolly declared, "it is a purely scientific result of the right use of constituted means."

Finney and other evangelical° revivalists stressed the need for individuals to undergo an emotionally wrenching conversion experience and be reborn. Not all con-

°The word *evangelical* derives from a Greek word meaning the bringing of good news—in this case the Gospel. Protestant evangelicals stressed the need for individual conversion and rebirth stemming from an awareness of sinful guilt and Christ's act of atoning, through his death, for their sins.

Charles Finney, about 1834

Conversion experience version experiences, however, occurred during revivals, prayer meetings, and religious gatherings. The slave Mortimer, for example, first heard a voice calling his name while he was in the field plowing. As he started to run, the cry "I am blessed but you are damned!" reverberated around him. Begging for mercy, Morte began to pray when a soft voice reassured him, "You are this day made alive and freed from hell." Deeply impressed by Morte's experience, his master told him henceforth he could preach on the plantation, and thus commenced his lifelong career as a preacher. Like Mortimer, born again Christians could describe in detail their feelings and experiences when they were reborn. And as in his case, religion could bring both peace and a sense of purpose in one's life.

The Philosophy of the New Revivals

Finney also rejected many religious doctrines of Calvinism, including predestination, which maintained that God had already determined which individuals were destined to be saved or damned, and no human effort could change this decision. But by the 1820s such a proposition seemed unreasonable to a generation that condemned hereditary distinctions, celebrated personal dignity, and praised human ability and activity. Leaving the Lord little role in the drama of human deliverance, Finney em-*Free will and* braced the doctrine of free will. All men and women who wanted to could be saved. *perfectionism* To those anxious about their salvation, he thundered, "Do it!" Finney's approach also made emotion paramount. While his revivals were not as tumultuous as those on the southern frontier, agonized prayers, groans, and uncontrolled crying often resounded through the hall.

With salvation within reach of every individual, what might be in store for society at large? "If the church would do her duty," Finney confidently predicted, "the millennium may come in this country in three years." By the 1830s Finney had taken to preaching not merely faith in human progress but something more—human perfectibility. Embracing this new theology of "perfectionism," he boldly asserted that all Christians should "aim at being holy and not rest satisfied until they are as perfect as God." And a true Christian would not rest until society was made perfect as well.

By preaching an optimistic message of free will and salvation to all, Finney and his eager imitators transformed Protestantism. But not all clergy applauded. For Lyman Beecher, as well as many supporters of the Second Great Awakening, Finney's new measures went too far in generating excessive emotionalism, while his theology of perfectionism verged on heresy. Undaunted by such criticism, Finney continued his revivals. As for Lyman Beecher, he decided in 1832 to outflank his adversaries by moving west to become the president of Lane Seminary in Cincinnati. There he planned to train the right sort of revivalists to save the frontier for true religion and to bring about the kingdom of God in America.

Religion and the Market Economy

Revival audiences responded to the call for reform partly because they were unsettled by the era's rapid social changes. In the North, evangelical religion proved strongest not in isolated backwaters but in frontier areas just entering the market economy. Rochester, New York, a booming flour-milling center on the Erie Canal, epitomized that social environment.

When Charles Finney came to town in the winter of 1830–1831, Rochester was *Finney's* a community in crisis. It had grown in a decade and a half from a village of 300 souls *Rochester* to a commercial city of more than 20,000. That wrenching expansion produced sharp *revival* divisions among the town's leaders, a large working class that increasingly lived apart from employers and beyond their moral control, and a rowdy saloon culture catering to canal boatmen and other transients.

Finney preached almost daily in Rochester for six months. Assisted by local ministers, his revivals brought thousands to accept his message of voluntary salvation and doubled church membership. Religion helped bring order to what had been a chaotic and fragmented city.

Although revivals like Finney's Rochester triumph drew converts from all seg- *Revivalism's* ments of American society, they appealed especially to the middle class. Lawyers, *appeal to the* merchants, retailers, and manufacturers all played central roles in the larger market *middle class* economy and invested in factories and railroads. The market put intense pressure on these upwardly mobile citizens. They viewed success as a reflection of moral character, yet they also feared that with the ups and downs of the economy—boom, then bust—they would lose their wealth. Religion provided a way in which to cope with the tensions and uncertainties of their own lives.

Workers, too, were among the converted. Conversions among workers dramati- *Workers and* cally increased during the depression that began in 1839, as revivalists preached from *church* street corners and held meetings in the workplace and homes. The Methodist *membership* church, which lacked the social respectability of some of the other evangelical churches, was particularly important in instilling the values of sobriety, frugality, and hard work in the urban working class.

Among other things, joining a church reflected a desire to get ahead in the new economy by accepting moral self-discipline. To a striking degree, social mobility and church membership were linked. In Rochester two-thirds of the male workers who were church members improved their occupational status in a decade. By contrast, workers who did not join a church rarely stayed in town more than a few years, and those who stayed were likely to decline in status.

Revivalists like Finney were interested in saving souls, not money, and their converts were most concerned with their spiritual state. Even so, evangelical Protestantism reinforced values needed to succeed in the new competitive economy. Churchgoers embraced the values of hard work, punctuality, and sobriety; they internalized the demand for self-control. In that sense, religion was one means of social control in a disordered society. And many employers put pressure on workers to give up their drinking habits, on and off the job, and to embrace religion.

The Rise of African American Churches

Independent black churches grew in size and importance as well as African Americans in urban areas increasingly resented being treated as second-class worshipers. In 1787, only a month after the close of the Constitutional Convention in Philadelphia, Richard Allen was praying at St. George's Church. Allen was not only a devout churchgoer but also a popular black preacher. But this Sunday morning his prayers were interrupted. "You must get up—you must not kneel here," a white usher whispered to Allen, who was not in the area reserved for black parishoners. Several white ushers roughly pulled him to his feet. Allen and other black members of the congregation walked out. In 1794 he organized the Bethel Church, where African Americans would be free to worship without discrimination.

In the early nineteenth century, similar tensions led to the formation of black Methodist and Baptist churches in a number of northern and southern cities. The most important was the African Methodist Episcopal (AME) Church. Growing fears for the security of slavery caused southern white communities, especially in the Deep South, to suppress independent black churches after 1820. But these churches, which were strongly evangelical, continued to grow in the North. In 1836 the AME Church, first organized in 1816, had 7,500 members. Twenty years later its membership was about 20,000. Like the black Baptist church, however, its major growth lay in the future and in the South following emancipation.

The Significance of the Second Great Awakening

As a result of the Second Great Awakening, the dominant form of Christianity in America became evangelical Protestantism. Membership in the major Protestant churches—Congregational, Presbyterian, Baptist, and Methodist—soared during the first half of the nineteenth century. By 1840 an estimated half of the adult population was nominally connected to some church, with the Methodists emerging as the largest Protestant denomination in both the North and the South.

Evangelicalism bolsters individualism and equality

Evangelicalism was in harmony with the basic values of early nineteenth-century Americans. Its emphasis on the ability of everyone to bring about his or her salvation upheld the American belief in individualism. By catering to a mass audience without social distinctions, the revivals reinforced the American belief in democracy and equality. And Finney's invincibly optimistic doctrine of perfectionism was exactly attuned to the spirit of the age.

WOMEN'S SPHERE

But not all—or even a majority—of Americans who flocked to revivals or joined reform societies were men. On the contrary, female converts outnumbered males by about three to two. Usually the initial convert in a family was a woman, and many men who converted were related to women who had come forward earlier.

Women and Revivalism

Women's changing lives

Women played such an important role in the Awakening partly because of changes in their own social universe. Instead of parents arranging the marriages of their children, couples were beginning to wed more often on the basis of affection. Under such conditions, a woman's prospects for marriage became less certain, and in older areas like New England, the migration of so many young men to the West compounded this uncertainty. Yet marriage was deemed important for a woman's happiness, and it remained essential for her economic security.

The unpredictability of these social circumstances drew young women toward religion. Women between the ages of 12 and 25 were especially susceptible to conversion. Joining a church heightened a young woman's feeling of initiative and gave her a sense of purpose. By establishing respectability and widening her social circle of friends, church membership also enhanced her chances of marriage.

The Ideal of Domesticity

The era's changing economic order brought other pressures to bear on wives and mothers. Most men now worked outside the home, while the rise of factories led to a decline in part-time work such as spinning, which women had once performed to supplement family income. Moreover, except on the frontier, home manufacturing was no longer essential, for the family purchased articles that women previously had made, such as cloth, soap, and candles. "The transition from mother-and-daughter power to water-and-steam power," one New England minister noted, produced "a complete revolution of domestic life."

This growing separation of the household from the workplace meant that the home took on a new social identity. It was idealized as a place of "domesticity," a haven away from the competitive, workaday world, with the mother firmly at its center. This new view of women's role was elaborated largely by clergy and female authors in sermons, advice manuals, and pieces of sentimental fiction for an urban middle-class audience. But the ideal's significance and acceptance had far-reaching consequences. The idea of domesticity was based on the notion of separate sexual

Separate spheres of influence

As business affairs grew increasingly separate from the family in the nineteenth century, the middle-class home became a female domain. As a wife and mother, a woman was to dispense love and moral guidance to her husband and her children.

spheres. If men's sphere was the world of factories, offices, and fields, women's sphere was the home, where they were to dispense love and comfort and teach moral values to husbands and children. "Love is our life our reality, business yours," Mollie Clark told one suitor.

Women, who were considered morally stronger, were also held to a higher standard of sexual purity. A man's sexual infidelity, while hardly condoned, brought no lasting shame. But a woman who engaged in sexual relations before marriage or was unfaithful afterward was threatened with everlasting disgrace. Under this double standard, women were to be passive and submerge their identities in those of their husbands.

Catharine Beecher and women's role

Most women of the era did not see this ideology as a rationale for male dominance. On the contrary, women played an important role in creating the ideal of domesticity, none more than Lyman Beecher's daughter Catharine. Like the earlier advocates of "republican motherhood," Catharine Beecher argued that women exercised power as moral guardians of the nation's future. The proper care of a middle-class household was also a crucial responsibility, and Beecher wrote several books on efficient home management. "There is no one thing more necessary to a housekeeper in performing her varied duties, than a habit of system and order," she told readers. "For all the time afforded us, we must give account to God."

Catharine Beecher was also a leading advocate of giving women greater educational opportunities in order to become schoolteachers. Conceiving of the school as an extension of the home, she maintained that teachers, like mothers, should instill sound moral values in children. She argued that women's naturally pious character and their affection for children made them ideally suited to be teachers.

"Sisterhood" and social networks

Women also exerted their moral authority through the growing number of benevolent organizations, which fostered close friendships among women. Women gave emotionally much more to other family members than they received in exchange, and they turned to other women for comfort and support. This "sisterhood"—the common sense of identity and shared experiences—helped sustain reform movements launched by women to aid females of the lower classes.

The majority of white women hardly had time to make the ideal of domesticity the center of their lives. Farmers' wives had to work constantly, while lower-class families could not get by without the wages of female members. Still, most middle-class women tried to live up to the ideal, though many found the effort confining. "The great trial is that I have nothing to do," one complained. "Here I am with abundant leisure and capable, I believe, of accomplishing some good, and yet with no object on which to expend my energies."

Women's socially defined role as guardians of morality helps explain their prominence among revival converts. Religious activity was one way that women could exert influence over society and one area where wives need not be subordinate to their husbands. For some male critics, Finney's policy of giving women a prominent role in revivals threatened to bring about a dangerous equality between the sexes. One unhappy man in Rochester complained about the effect of Finney's visit to his home: "He *stuffed* my wife with tracts, and alarmed her fears, and nothing short of meetings, night and day, could atone for the many fold sins my poor, simple spouse had committed." Then, getting to the heart of the matter, he added, "She made the miraculous discovery, that she had been 'unevenly yoked.' From this unhappy period, peace, quiet, and happiness have fled from my dwelling, never, I fear, to return."

The Middle-Class Family in Transition

As the middle-class family adapted to the pressures of competitive society by becoming a haven of moral virtue, it developed a new structure and new set of attitudes closer in spirit to the modern family. One basic change was the rise of privacy. The family was increasingly seen as a sheltered retreat from the outside world. (See Daily Lives, pages 388–389.) In addition, the pressures to achieve success led middle-class young adults to delay marriage, since a husband was expected to have the financial means to support his wife.

Smaller family size was a result of the delay in marriage as well, since wives began bearing children later. But especially among the urban middle class, women began to use birth control to space children further apart and minimize the risks of pregnancy. In addition, it has been estimated that before 1860 one abortion was performed for every five or six live births. These practices contributed to a decline in the birthrate, from slightly more than 7 children per family in 1800 to 5.4 in 1850—a 25 percent drop. Although the birthrate had been falling gradually since the turn of the century, it dropped more abruptly beginning in the 1830s. Family size was directly related to the success ethic. On the farm, children had been an economic asset, able to work in the fields as well as around the house. In the new, market-oriented society, by contrast, children needed an extended education and special training in order to succeed. Thus they were a greater financial burden upon their parents.

Decline in the birthrate

With smaller families, however, parents were able to show greater concern about providing their children with advantages in the race for success. Middle-class families increasingly took on the expense of additional education to prepare their sons for a career in business. Middle-class families also frequently equalized inheritances rather than giving priority to the eldest son or favoring sons over daughters.

AMERICAN ROMANTICISM

The rational-minded Unitarians in Boston had become accustomed to being attacked by evangelical ministers like Lyman Beecher. They were less prepared to be criticized by one of their own—and on their own home ground, no less. Yet that was what happened when a Unitarian minister named Ralph Waldo Emerson addressed the students of Harvard Divinity School on a warm summer evening in July 1838.

Emerson warned his listeners that the true church seemed "to totter to its fall, almost all life extinct." Outside, nature's world was alive and vibrant: "The grass grows, the buds burst, the meadow is spotted with fire and gold in the tint of flowers." But from the pulpits of too many congregations came lifeless preaching. "In how many churches, by how many prophets, tell me," Emerson demanded, "is man made sensible that he is an infinite Soul?" Leaving the shocked audience to ponder his message, Emerson and his wife drove home beneath a night sky illuminated by the northern lights.

Emerson's Divinity School Address glowed much like that July aurora. The address lacked the searing fire of Finney's revivals. Yet it was bold in its own way, because it reflected a second major current of thought that shaped the reform movements of the era. That was the intellectual movement known as Romanticism.

PUBLIC SPACE/PRIVATE SPACE

Privacy Begins at Home

In 1831 Olive Walkley made a significant decision: she moved the bed in which she and her husband Stephen slept out of the parlor and replaced it with a carpet. She also had the unfinished upstairs plastered and partitioned into bedrooms for their children. The Walkleys were farmers in Southington, Connecticut, but like middle-class urban families they were influenced by the new movement to separate public and private space in the home.

When the Walkleys were married in 1811, Americans were accustomed to living in close quarters, for most houses had few rooms. Further, the limited light and heat forced members to congregate together. Parents and sometimes the entire family slept in the parlor, where visitors were also entertained and the family's most valuable possessions, including its best bed, were proudly displayed. Even in the wealthiest households, usually only the parents enjoyed separate sleeping quarters, and in most homes beds could be found in virtually every room.

In the years after 1820, however, the American home was reshaped to create specialized regions of privacy, service, and socializing. While houses increasingly faced the road, new designs provided greater privacy by creating an entry hall that served as a transition space from the outside world to the various parts of the house and by separating living and cooking quarters from areas for entertainment.

A sitting room was for the family's everyday use, while the parlor was reserved for public activity, including receiving company, giving recitals, and performing ceremonies such as weddings and funerals. As Americans developed a new sense of privacy, the parents' bed and the intimate activities associated with it were placed out of sight. In more prosperous homes an upholstered mahogany sofa replaced the bed in the parlor, and the floor was covered with a carpet, as much a symbol of the family's refinement as the mantle clock was of its modern outlook.

Food preparation and domestic work were done in a separate kitchen and adjoining back rooms. While rural families often continued to eat in the sitting room, houses more frequently contained a separate dining room. Stoves, which enlarged usable space by radiating heat, became common in more affluent homes, while the hearth and its fire—once the main source of food, heat, and light—ceased to be the center of the family's life together. In addition, sleeping space became increasingly private and individual. Larger homes now contained bedrooms, normally on the second floor, and if space permitted adolescent and grown unmarried children were given separate bedrooms, where they could

Romantic movement   Romanticism began in Europe as a reaction against the Enlightenment. The Enlightenment had placed reason at the center of human achievement; Romanticism instead emphasized the importance of emotion and intuition as sources of truth. It gloried in the unlimited potential of the individual, who might soar if freed from the restraints of institutions. Romanticism extolled humanitarianism and sympathized with the oppressed.

In elevating inner feelings and heartfelt convictions, Romanticism reinforced the emotionalism of religious revivals. Philosophically, its influence was strongest

Daily Lives

An architect confers with builders about the plans as a new house goes up in the background. (Metropolitan Museum of Art, New York)

withdraw from the rest of the family. Smaller family size as well as higher income enabled middle-class families to create new private space within the home.

The newer homes projected a sense of order as well, in sharp contrast to the run-down appearance of older houses, especially in the countryside. These were rarely painted, doors often did not fit, broken windows were patched with rags, and front yards remained unenclosed. Often enough, trash and garbage were simply tossed out the nearest window or door. However, as middle-class families became increasingly sensitive to the home's exterior public face (especially in the North), they began to paint their houses and keep them in good repair. They also erected whitewashed fences around their front yards, planted ornamental trees and shrubs, trimmed the grass, and put their refuse in pits.

The new standards of domestic life also emphasized cleanliness and decoration. Lydia Maria Child's popular *The American Frugal Housewife* offered families of modest means numerous tips on cleaning and scouring as well as decorating. The market for brooms soared as wives sought to keep their homes clean. In 1798 only a few hundred broomcorn brooms were manufactured; in 1840 almost 2 million were sold. At the same time, women increasingly decorated their homes with mass-produced carpets, wallpaper, mirrors, lithographs, and curtains (which enhanced privacy from passersby).

A home's floor plan and furnishings not only determined comfort; they defined a family's status and aspirations. These signs of refinement were most often found in homes of professionals, prosperous farmers, and upwardly mobile skilled workers. The new domestic ideal of the home, which required additional floor space and the ownership of consumer goods, widened the gap between the middle and poorer ranks of society.

---

among intellectuals who took part in the Transcendental movement and in the dramatic flowering of American literature. And like revivalism, Romanticism offered its own paths toward perfectionism.

Emerson and Transcendentalism

Above all, Romanticism produced individualists. Thus Transcendentalism is difficult to define, for its members resisted being lumped together. It blossomed in the mid-

In the summer of 1858 members of the cultural Saturday Club of Boston made an excursion to the Adirondacks to observe nature. In *Philosopher's Camp,* painted by William J. Stillman, who organized the expedition, a group on the left dissects a fish under the supervision of the famous scientist Louis Agassiz, while on the right others practice firing rifles. Symbolically, Ralph Waldo Emerson stands alone in the center contemplating the world in solitude.

1830s, when a number of Unitarian clergy like George Ripley and Ralph Waldo Emerson resigned their pulpits, loudly protesting the church's smug, lifeless teachings. The new "Transcendentalist Club" attracted a small following among other discontented Boston intellectuals, including Margaret Fuller, Bronson Alcott, and Orestes Brownson.

Transcenden-
talist ideas
Like European Romantics, American Transcendentalists emphasized feeling over reason, seeking a spiritual communion with nature. By *transcend* they meant to go beyond or to rise above—specifically above reason and beyond the material world. As part of creation, every human being contained a spark of divinity, Emerson avowed. Transcendentalists also shared in Romanticism's glorification of the individual. "Trust thyself. Every heart vibrates to that iron string," Emerson advised. "The root and seed of democracy is the doctrine, judge for yourself." If freed from the constraints of traditional authority, the individual had infinite potential. So optimistic was Transcendentalism in its view of human nature, it essentially denied the existence of evil.

Transcendentalism had much in common with Jacksonian America—optimism, individualism, and an egalitarian spirit. Like the devout at Finney's revivals, who sought to perfect themselves and society, listeners who flocked to Emerson's lectures were infused with the spirit of optimistic reform.

As the currents of Romanticism percolated through American society, the country's literature came of age. In 1820 educated Americans still tended to ape the fashions of Europe and read English books. But as the population grew, education increased, and the country's literary market expanded, American writers looked with greater interest at the customs and character of their own society. Improved printing presses made possible cheaper, mass-produced American books, and better transportation led to a wider distribution of printed material. By 1850 for every British book, two American books were sold in the United States.

Emergence of American literature

Emerson's address "The American Scholar" (1837) constituted a declaration of literary independence. "Our long dependence, our long apprenticeship to the learning of other lands draws to a close," he proclaimed. "Events, actions arise, that must be sung, that will sing themselves."

The Clash between Nature and Civilization

At the time Emerson spoke, James Fenimore Cooper was already making his mark as the first distinctive American novelist. In the Leatherstocking Tales, a series of five novels written between 1823 and 1841, he focused on the clash between nature and civilization. Cooper clearly admired his hero, Natty Bumppo, a self-reliant frontiersman who represented the nobility and innocence of the wilderness. At the same time, the novels portrayed the culture of the frontier as a threat to the civilization Cooper prized so highly.

Cooper and wilderness

In one scene in *The Pioneers* (1823), as frontier villagers slaughter thousands of pigeons, Leatherstocking laments the wanton destruction, only to hear a townsman express surprise that anyone would "grumble at the loss of a few pigeons. . . . If you had to sow your wheat twice, and three times, as I have done," he continues, "you wouldn't be so massyfully feeling'd toward the devils." As Americans began to exploit the resources of the hinterlands, many of the country's new Romantic writers betrayed a concern that the advance of civilization, with its market economy and crowded urban centers, might destroy the natural simplicity of the land. Natty Bumppo stood halfway between the savage and civilized worlds, not comfortable embracing either.

Henry David Thoreau, too, used nature as a backdrop to explore the conflict between the unfettered individual and the constraints of society. Thoreau grew up in Concord, Massachusetts, where he became part of Emerson's circle. In 1845 he built a cabin on the edge of Walden Pond, living in relative solitude for 16 months to demonstrate the advantages of self-reliance. His experiences became the basis for one of the classics in American literature, *Walden* (1854).

Thoreau and individualism

Thoreau argued that only in nature could one find true independence. By living simply, it was possible to master oneself and the world. Thoreau's own isolation, however, was less than total. When lonely or hungry, he walked to Emerson's home nearby for conversation and a slice of Lidia Emerson's apple pie, and most of the materials he used to build his "wilderness" cabin were store-bought. Still, *Walden* eloquently denounced Americans' frantic competition for material goods and wealth. "Money is not required to buy one necessity of the soul," Thoreau maintained. "I see my townsmen, whose misfortune it is to have inherited farms, houses, barns, cattle, and farming tools. . . . Who made them serfs of the soil?" It seemed only too clear that "the mass of men lead lives of quiet desperation."

Thoreau's individualism was so extreme that he rejected any institution that contradicted his personal sense of right. "The only obligation which I have a right to assume, is to do at any time what I think right," he wrote in his essay "On Civil Disobedience." Voicing the anti-institutional impulse of Romanticism, he took individualism to its antisocial extreme.

Songs of the Self-Reliant and Darker Loomings

In contrast to Thoreau's exclusiveness, Walt Whitman was all-inclusive, embracing American society in its infinite variety. A journalist and laborer in the New York City area, Whitman was inspired by the common people, whose "manners, speech, dress, friendships . . . are unrhymed poetry." In taking their measure in *Leaves of Grass* (1855), he pioneered a new, modern form of poetry, unconcerned with meter and rhyme and filled with frank imagery and sexual references.

Whitman and democracy
        Conceiving himself the representative of all Americans, Whitman exuberantly titled his first major poem "Song of Myself."

> I am your voice—It was tied in you—In me it began to talk.
> I celebrate myself to celebrate every man and woman alive.

Emerson and other critics were put off by his rough-hewn methods, but Whitman, like the Transcendentalists, exalted the emotions, nature, and the individual. At the same time, he endowed these ideas with a more joyous, democratic spirit.

        More brooding in temperament was Nathaniel Hawthorne, who lived for a time in Concord. Unable to partake of Emerson's sunny optimism and repelled by the self-centered outlook of Thoreau, Hawthorne wrote of the power of the past to shape future generations and the consequences of pride, selfishness, envy, and secret guilt. In *The Scarlet Letter* (1850), set in New England's Puritan era, Hawthorne spun the tale of Hester Prynne, who bore an illegitimate child, as well as the Puritan neighbors who harshly condemned her. Like the Puritans, Hawthorne had no illusions about creating a world without evil, and he rejected the American belief that a person or nation could free itself from the past.

Melville and Nature's destructive power
        Hawthorne found a soul mate in Herman Melville, whose dark masterpiece, *Moby-Dick* (1851), drew on his youthful experiences aboard a whaling ship. The novel's Captain Ahab relentlessly drives his ship in pursuit of the great white whale Moby-Dick. In Melville's telling, Ahab becomes a powerful symbol of American character: the prototype of the ruthless businessman despoiling nature's resources in his ferocious pursuit of success. "Swerve me?" he asks at one point. "The path to my fixed purpose is laid with iron rails, whereon my soul is grooved to run. Over unsound gorges, through the rifled hearts of mountains, under torrents' beds, unerringly I rush!" Ahab is Emerson's self-reliant man, but in him, self-reliance is transformed into a dangerous monomania that eventually destroys his ship, its crew, and himself.

        More clearly than any other writer, Melville recognized the dilemma created by Romanticism's emphasis on the individual. Liberated from institutional restraints, human possibilities seemed unlimited to Romantic philosophers. Yet as older tradi-

Walt Whitman, poet of democracy

Herman Melville

tions and institutions dropped away, the new individualism also led to a competitive materialism devoid of the older sense of community. How, Melville asked, could American society be made perfect, if it was based on self-interested materialism and individualism?

But awash in the many opportunities opening before them, most Americans were not attuned to such searching criticism. They preferred to celebrate, with Emerson, the glories of democracy and the individual's quest for perfection.

THE AGE OF REFORM

In the glowing fires of a fervent camp meeting, the quest for perfection often proved hard to control. At the Cane Ridge revival of 1800, the Methodist Peter Cartwright had his hands full trying to stop less orthodox preachers from gathering converts. Quite a few worshipers had joined a group known as the Shakers. Cartwright had to ride around the neighborhood "from cabin to cabin" trying to cure people of the Shaker "delusion."

The Shakers were only one group that demonstrated more radical possibilities for democratic change. While the mainline benevolent societies aimed at a more conservative reformation of individual sinners, the more radical offshoots of Romanticism and perfectionism sought to remake society at large.

Some schemers and dreamers for a better world harbored decidedly eccentric notions. Sylvester Graham, who argued that diet determined character, won lasting fame by inventing a cracker named after him. While he gained a small following, most Americans ignored him—except commercial bakers, who, knowing a threat when they saw one, mobbed this champion of homemade bread. Other reformers, however, decided that the best way to test untried ideas was to withdraw from the everyday world in order to demonstrate the possibilities of perfection.

Utopian Communities

Utopian communities aimed at reforming the world through example. They looked to replace the competitive individualism of American society with a purer spiritual unity and group cooperation. Some were directly linked to religion, but even the secular communities shared the optimism of perfectionism and millennialism.

The Shakers proved to be one of the most long-lived utopian experiments. Ann Lee, the illiterate daughter of an English blacksmith, believed that God had a dual nature, part male and part female. Through a series of religious visions Lee became convinced that her own life would reveal the female side of the divinity, just as Christ had come to earth exemplifying the male side. In 1774 she led a small band of followers to America.

The Shaker movement's greatest growth, however, came after Lee's death, when

The Shakers

Dancing was an integral part of the Shakers' religion, as this picture of a service at Lebanon, New York, indicates. In worshiping, men and women formed separate lines with their hands held out and moved back and forth in rhythm while singing religious songs. One Shaker hymn proclaimed, "With ev'ry gift I will unite,/And join in sweet devotion/To worship God is my delight,/With hands and feet in motion." Note the presence of African Americans in the community.

her followers recruited converts at revivals like Cane Ridge. The new disciples founded about 20 communal settlements based on the teachings of Mother Ann, as she was known. Her followers sometimes shook in the fervent public demonstration of their faith—hence the name Shakers. Convinced that the end of the world was at hand and that there was no need to perpetuate the human race, Shakers practiced celibacy, separating the sexes as far as practical. Men and women normally worked apart, ate at separate tables in silence, entered separate doorways, and had separate living quarters.

Shaker communities accorded women unusual authority and equality. Community tasks were generally assigned along sexual lines, with women performing household chores and men laboring in the fields. Leadership of the church, however, was split equally between men and women. By the mid-nineteenth century, a majority of members were female.

Property in Shaker settlements was owned communally and controlled by the church hierarchy. The sect's members worked hard, lived simply, and impressed outsiders with their cleanliness and order. Lacking any natural increase, however, membership began to decline after 1850, from a peak of about 6000 members.

The Oneida Community and complex marriage

The Oneida Community, founded by John Humphrey Noyes, also set out to alter the relationship between the sexes, though in a markedly different way. Noyes, a convert of Charles Finney, took the doctrine of perfection to extremes. While

Finney argued that men and women should strive to achieve perfection, Noyes announced that he had actually reached this blessed state. Settling in Putney, Vermont, and, after 1848, in Oneida, New York, Noyes set out to create a community organized on his religious ideals.

In pursuit of greater freedom, Noyes relieved women of what he termed "kitchen slavery." Female members cooked only at breakfast and thereafter were free from household duties until the next morning. Noyes's ideas of liberation, however, went beyond the kitchen. Under his doctrine of "complex marriage," commune members were permitted to have sexual relations with one another, but only with the approval of the community and after a searching examination of the couple's motives. Noyes eventually undertook experiments in planned reproduction by selecting "scientific" combinations of parents to produce morally perfect children.

Under his charismatic leadership the Oneida Community grew to more than 200 members in 1851. But in 1879 an internal dispute drove him from power, and without his guiding hand the community soon fell apart. In 1881 its members reorganized as a business enterprise.

The Mormon Experience

The Church of Jesus Christ of Latter-day Saints, whose members were generally known as Mormons, was founded by a young man named Joseph Smith in Palmyra, in western New York, where the religious fires of revivalism flared up regularly. The son of a poor farmer, Smith was robust, charming, almost hypnotic in his appeal. In 1827, at the age of only 22, he announced that he had discovered a set of golden tablets on which was written the *Book of Mormon*. The tablets, which Smith claimed to have translated, told the story of some lost tribes of Israel, who came to America and established a Christian civilization, only to be exterminated by the Indians. Proclaiming that he had a commission from God to reestablish the true church, Smith gathered about him a group of devoted followers.

Like Charles Finney's more liberal theology, Mormonism placed little emphasis on predestination and proclaimed that salvation was available to all. Moreover, Mormon culture upheld the middle-class values of hard work, thrift, and self-control. It partook of the optimistic, materialist attitudes of American society. And by teaching that Christ would return to rule the earth, it shared in the hope of a coming millennial kingdom.

Mormonism was less an outgrowth of evangelicalism, however, than of the primitive gospel movement, which sought to reestablish the ancient church. Indeed, having seen the consequences of excessive emotion in the revivals of his youth, Smith soon curbed enthusiasm among his followers and downplayed the experience of conversion. In restoring what Smith called "the ancient order of things," he drew upon both the Old and New Testaments. Thus Mormons created a theocracy uniting church and state, reestablished biblical priesthoods and titles, and adopted temple rituals. With its claims of continuing divine revelation, Mormonism attracted weary seekers of spiritual certainty and the true church.

Movement to restore the ancient church

After a revelation told Smith to gather the saints in the city of Zion in preparation for Christ's return to earth, he undertook to create a spiritual community first in Ohio and then in Missouri. But his unorthodox teachings provoked bitter persecution wherever he went, and mob violence finally hounded him out of Missouri in 1839. In response, Smith established a new holy city, which he named Nauvoo, located on the Mississippi River in Illinois.

City of Zion: Nauvoo

Reinforced by a steady stream of converts from Britain, Nauvoo became the largest and fastest growing city in Illinois, with a population of 10,000 by the mid-1840s. There, Smith introduced the most distinctive features of Mormon theology, including baptism for the dead, eternal marriage, and polygamy, or plural marriage. He also established the secret ceremonies of the Mormon temple, modified from the rituals of the Masonic order. As a result, Mormonism increasingly diverged from traditional Christianity and became a distinct new religion. Nauvoo's political organization was unorthodox too. To bolster his authority as a prophet, Smith established a theocratic government, under which church leaders controlled political offices and governed the community, with Smith as mayor.

Discarding his earlier ideas of community property, Smith embraced private enterprise at Nauvoo. But speculation in land soon overran the city, rival neighborhoods vied to become the main commercial district, and dissident groups in the city challenged Smith's power. Neighboring residents, alarmed by the Mormons' growing political power and reports that Smith had adopted polygamy, demanded that Nauvoo's charter be revoked and the church suppressed. In 1844, while in jail for destroying his opponents' press in Nauvoo, Smith was murdered by an anti-Mormon mob. In 1846 the Mormons abandoned Nauvoo, and the following year Brigham Young, Smith's successor, led them westward to Utah. Nauvoo ceased to be a holy community.

Socialist Communities

Not all utopian experiments were based on religious teachings. The hardship and poverty that accompanied the growth of industrial factories also inspired utopian communities based on science and reason. Robert Owen, a Scottish industrialist, came to the United States in 1824 committed to creating a society that balanced agriculture and manufacturing. Owen believed that the character of individuals was shaped by their surroundings and that by changing those surroundings, one could change human character.

Robert Owen and New Harmony

Unfortunately, most of the 900 or so volunteers who flocked to Owen's community in New Harmony, Indiana, lacked the skills and commitment needed to make it a success. Bitter factions soon split the settlement. Having lost most of his own fortune, Owen dissolved the community in 1827. More than 20 other American communities were founded on Owen's theories, none particularly successful.

Brook Farm

In 1841 Emerson's friend George Ripley organized Brook Farm, a Transcendentalist community and socialist experiment near Boston where members could live "a more wholesome and simple life than can be led amidst the pressure of our competitive institutions." Brook Farm attracted a number of prominent New England intellectuals, who remained for varying lengths of time. Its most important achievements were a magazine, *The Dial*, edited by Margaret Fuller, and its innovative school, whose curriculum included modern subjects such as history, art, and literature. The school's success, however, was overshadowed by the economic failure of the farm, and in 1847 the community disbanded.

The experiences of Brook Farm, New Harmony, and other similar communities demonstrated that the United States was poor soil for socialistic experiments. Wages were too high and land too cheap to interest most Americans in collectivist ventures. And individualism was too strong to create a commitment to cooperative action.

The Temperance Movement

The most significant reform movements of the period sought not to withdraw from society but to change it directly. One of the most determined of these was the temperance movement.

The origins of the campaign against alcohol lay in the era's heavy drinking. *Attack on* Alcohol consumption soared after the Revolution, so that by 1830 the average *drinking* American consumed four gallons of absolute alcohol a year, the highest level in American history and nearly triple present-day levels. Anne Royale, whose travels took her cross-country by stage, reported, "When I was in Virginia, it was too much whiskey—in Ohio, too much whiskey—in Tennessee, it is too, too much whiskey!" The social costs for such habits were high: broken families, abused and neglected wives and children, sickness and disability, poverty, and crime. The temperance movement undertook to eliminate these problems by curbing drinking.

Led largely by clergy, the movement at first focused on drunkenness and did not oppose moderate drinking. But in 1826 the American Temperance Society was founded, taking voluntary abstinence as its goal. During the next decade approximately 5000 local temperance societies were founded. As the movement gained momentum, annual per capita consumption of alcohol dropped sharply. By 1845 it had fallen below two gallons a year.

The temperance movement lasted longer and attracted many more supporters *Temperance's* than other reforms. It appealed to young and old, to urban and rural residents, to *broad appeal* workers and businesspeople. Moreover, it was one of the few reform movements with significant support in the South. Its success came partly for social reasons. Democracy necessitated sober voters; factories required sober workers. In addition, temperance attracted the upwardly mobile—professionals, small businesspeople,

ANNUAL CONSUMPTION OF DISTILLED SPIRITS, PER CAPITA, 1710–1920
Beginning in 1790, per capita levels of drinking steadily rose until 1830, when the temperance movement produced a sharp decline over the next two decades.

and skilled artisans anxious to improve their social standing. Finally, temperance advocates stressed the suffering that men inflicted on women and children, and thus the movement appealed to women as a means to defend the home and carry out their domestic mission.

Educational Reform

Common school movement

In 1800 Massachusetts was the only state that required free public schools supported by community funds. The call for tax-supported education arose first among workers, as a way to restore their deteriorating position in society. But middle-class reformers quickly took control of the movement, looking to uplift the masses, make them responsible citizens, and preserve equal opportunity. Horace Mann, the leading proponent of common schools, hailed education as "the great equalizer of the conditions of men" and contended that it would eliminate poverty. Reformers appealed to business leaders by arguing that the new economic order needed educated workers.

Mann convinced Massachusetts to create a state board of education, which he oversaw from 1837 to 1848. Under his leadership, the state adopted a minimum-length school year, provided for training of teachers, and expanded the curriculum to include subjects such as history, geography, and various applied skills. Massachusetts also took the lead in requiring every town with a population of 500 or more to establish a high school. This innovation was slow to catch on elsewhere; by 1860 the nation could count only about 300 high schools, fully a third of them in Massachusetts. Moreover, compulsory attendance was rarely instated. Many poor parents out of necessity sent their children to work instead of school. Still, by the 1850s the number of schools, attendance figures, and school budgets had all increased sharply. School reformers enjoyed their greatest success in the Northeast and the least in the South, where planters opposed paying taxes to educate poorer white children.

Female education

Educational opportunities for women also expanded. Teachers like Catharine Beecher and Emma Hunt Willard established a number of private girls' schools, putting to rest the objection of many male educators that fragile female minds could not absorb large doses of mathematics, physics, or geography. In 1833 Oberlin became the nation's first coeducational college. Four years later Mary Lyon founded Mount Holyoke, the first American college for women.

COUNTERPOINT   What motivated advocates like Emma Willard, Charles Finney, or the Beechers?

Reform and social control

Some historians have doubted whether "social uplift" truly motivated middle-class reformers. Instead, they suggest, the real purpose of the Jacksonian reform movements was to instill middle-class values in the working class in order to make them diligent (and submissive) workers. In so doing, the reformers undercut any real threat the working class might pose to society. These historians pay particular attention to the educational reform movement, which aimed in the classroom to teach good behavior to lower-class students. The curriculum of the common schools emphasized middle-class values and behavior, and textbooks such as the famous McGuffey Readers stressed the virtues of self-control, punctuality, hard work, patriotism, and Protestantism. Emerson satirized the more extreme arguments of school reformers as "we must educate them or they will be at our throats."

This social control thesis has been criticized by historians who place greater emphasis on the role of religion. In their view, reformers' perfectionism sprang out of the ideals of the Second Great Awakening. Viewing social problems as manifestations of individual sin, reformers looked to create a morally perfect society. They also warned that a decline in public virtue would undermine republicanism. Education did become a way to instill proper moral values in the masses—values including self-reliance, responsible citizenship, and Christianity. But reformers saw tax-supported public schools as a means to expand rather than restrict opportunity in American life, including opportunities for lower-class children, who otherwise would have no access to education. These historians contend that middle-class reformers were hardly indifferent to the welfare of less privileged groups in society.

The Asylum Movement

After 1820 there was also a dramatic increase in the number of asylums of every sort—orphanages, jails, and hospitals. Advocates of asylums called for isolating and separating the criminal, the insane, the ill, and the dependent from outside society. The goal of care in asylums, which had earlier focused on confinement, shifted to the reform of personal character.

Prison reformers believed that rigid discipline, extensive rules, and (in some programs) solitary confinement were necessary to rehabilitate criminals. Here prisoners in Sing Sing march in lockstep, their hands on the shoulders in front of them, under the strict supervision of the guards. These programs had only limited success in reforming wrongdoers.

American efforts to rehabilitate prisoners attracted international attention. Pennsylvania and New York developed systems to isolate prisoners, introducing the measures of solitary confinement and absolute silence to give inmates time to reflect on their past errors. The reformers assumed that environment produced criminal behavior and that the new prison routines would rehabilitate criminals. The new measures were not very effective, however, and under the strain of isolation some inmates went insane or committed suicide.

Dorothea Dix and the insane

Dorothea Dix, a Boston schoolteacher, took the lead in advocating state-supported asylums for the mentally ill. She attracted much attention to the movement by her report detailing the horrors to which the mentally ill were subjected, including being chained, kept in cages and closets, and beaten with rods. In response to her efforts, 28 states maintained mental institutions by 1860.

Like other reform movements, the push for new asylums and better educational facilities reflected overtones of both liberation and control. Asylums freed prisoners and the mentally ill from the harsh punishments and abuses of the past, but the new techniques of "rehabilitation" forced prisoners to march in lockstep. Education brought with it the freedom to question and to acquire knowledge, but some enthusiastic reformers hoped that schools would become as orderly as prisons. Louis Dwight, who advocated solitary confinement for prisoners at night and total silence by day, suggested eagerly that such methods "would greatly promote order, seriousness, and purity in large families, male and female boarding schools, and colleges."

ABOLITIONISM

Late in the fall of 1834, Lyman Beecher was in the midst of his continuing efforts to "overturn and overturn" on behalf of the kingdom of God. As planned, he had gone to Cincinnati to assume leadership of Lane Seminary. The school had everything that an institution for training ministers to convert the West needed—everything, that is, except students. In October 1834 all but 8 of Lane's 100 scholars had departed after months of bitter fighting with Beecher and the trustees over the issue of abolition.

Beecher knew the source of his troubles: a scruffy yet magnetic student named Theodore Dwight Weld. Weld had been firing up his classmates over the need to immediately free the slaves. Beecher was not surprised, for Weld had been converted by that firebrand Finney. He knew, too, that Weld had been influenced by the arguments of William Lloyd Garrison, whose abolitionist writings had sent shock waves across the entire nation. Indeed, Beecher's troubles at Lane Seminary provided only one example of how the flames of reform, when fanned, could spread along paths not anticipated by those who first kindled them.

The Beginnings of the Abolitionist Movement

William Lloyd Garrison symbolized the transition from a moderate antislavery movement to the more militant abolitionism of the 1830s. A sober, religious youngster deeply influenced by his Baptist mother, Garrison apprenticed as a printer and in the 1820s edited a newspaper sympathetic to many of the new reforms. In 1829 he was enlisted in the antislavery cause by Benjamin Lundy, a Quaker who edited a

William Lloyd Garrison (shown, left, at age 30) and Theodore Dwight Weld represented different wings of the abolitionist movement. Garrison's growing radicalism led him to repudiate organized religion in the struggle against slavery. Weld, on the other hand, preferred to work through the evangelical churches and cooperate with the clergy.

Baltimore antislavery newspaper, *The Genius of Universal Emancipation.* Calling for a gradual end to slavery, Lundy supported colonization, a strategy for overcoming southern fears of emancipation by transporting free black Americans to Africa.

Embracing colonization, Garrison went to Baltimore to help edit Lundy's paper. It was there that Garrison first encountered the opinions of free African Americans, who played a major role in the genesis of the abolitionist movement. To his surprise, Garrison discovered that most of them strongly opposed the colonization movement as proslavery and antiblack. "This is our home, and this is our country," a free black convention proclaimed in 1831. "Beneath its sod lie the bones of our fathers; for it some of them fought, bled, and died. Here we were born, and here we will die." Under their influence, Garrison soon developed views far more radical than Lundy's, and within a year of moving to Baltimore, the young firebrand was convicted of libel and imprisoned. Upon his release Garrison hurried back to Boston, determined to publish a new kind of antislavery journal.

Free blacks oppose colonization

On January 1, 1831, the first issue of *The Liberator* appeared, and abolitionism was born. In appearance, the bespectacled Garrison seemed frail, almost mousy. In print, however, he was abrasive, withering, and uncompromising. "On this subject, I do not wish to think, or speak, or write with moderation," he proclaimed. "I am in earnest—I will not equivocate—I will not excuse—I will not retreat a single inch—AND I WILL BE HEARD." Repudiating gradual emancipation and embracing "immediatism," Garrison insisted that slavery end at once. He denounced colonization as a racist, antiblack movement and upheld the principle of racial equality. To those who suggested that slaveowners should be compensated for freeing their slaves, Garrison was firm. Southerners ought to be convinced by "moral suasion" to renounce slavery as a sin. Virtue was its own reward.

Garrison's immediatism

Garrison attracted the most attention, but other abolitionists spoke with equal conviction. Wendell Phillips, from a socially prominent Boston family, held listeners spellbound with his speeches. Lewis Tappan and his brother Arthur, two New York City silk merchants, boldly placed their wealth behind a number of humanitarian causes, including abolitionism. James G. Birney, an Alabama slaveholder, converted to abolitionism after wrestling with his conscience, and Angelina and Sarah Grimké, the daughters of a South Carolina planter, left their native state to speak against the institution. And there was Angelina's future husband, Theodore Weld, the restless student at Lane Seminary who had fallen so dramatically under Garrison's influence.

To abolitionists, slavery was a moral, not an economic, question. The institution seemed a contradiction of the principle of the American Revolution that all human beings had been created with natural rights. Then, too, it went against the Romantic spirit of the age, which celebrated the individual's freedom and self-reliance. Abolitionists condemned slavery because of the breakup of marriages and families by sale, the harsh punishment of the lash, slaves' lack of access to education, and the sexual abuse of black women. Most of all, they denounced slavery as outrageously contrary to Christian teaching. As one Ohio antislavery paper declared, "We believe slavery to be a sin, always, everywhere, and only, sin—sin, in itself." So persistent were abolitionists in their religious objections, they forced the churches to face the question of slavery head on. In the 1840s the Methodist and Baptist churches each split into northern and southern organizations over the issue.

The Spread of Abolitionism

After helping organize the New England Anti-Slavery Society in 1832, Garrison joined with Lewis Tappan and Theodore Weld the following year to establish a national organization, the American Anti-Slavery Society. It coordinated a loosely affiliated network of state and local societies. During the years before the Civil War, perhaps 200,000 northerners belonged to an abolitionist society.

Geography of abolitionism

Abolitionists were concentrated in the East, especially New England, and in areas that had been settled by New Englanders, such as western New York and northern Ohio. The movement was not strong in cities or among businesspeople and workers. Most abolitionists were young, being generally in their twenties and thirties when the movement began, and had grown up in rural areas and small towns in middle-class families. Intensely religious, many had been profoundly affected by the revivals of the Second Great Awakening. Whatever their background, they shared a deep alienation from American society—its crass materialism, its shallow politics, and its lack of religion. More and more they came to feel that slavery was the fundamental cause of the Republic's degraded condition.

Certainly Theodore Weld was cut from this mold. After enrolling in Lane Seminary in 1833, he promoted immediate abolitionism among his fellow students. When Lyman Beecher assumed the Lane presidency a year later, he confronted a student body dominated by committed abolitionists, impatient of any position that stopped short of Garrison's immediatism.

Lane Seminary rebellion

The radicalism of Lane students was also made clear in their commitment to racial equality. Unlike some abolitionists, who opposed slavery but disdained blacks as inferior, Lane students mingled freely with Cincinnati's free black community. Alarmed by rumors in the summer of 1834 that the town's residents intended to demolish the school, Beecher and Lane's trustees forbade any discussion of slavery on campus, restricted contact with the black community, and ordered students to return to their studies. "Who that has an opinion and a soul will enter L. Sem now?" one rebel asked. "Who can do it without degrading himself?" All except a few left the school and enrolled at Oberlin College. That debt-ridden institution agreed to their demands for guaranteeing freedom of speech, admitting black students, and hiring Charles Finney as professor of theology.

But Finney fared no better than Beecher with the Lane rebels. In the end, he too concluded that reform generated discord, distracting Christians from the greater good of promoting revivals. Both men conceived of sin in terms of individual immorality, not unjust social institutions and prejudices. To the abolitionists, however, America could never become a godly nation until slavery was abolished. "Revivals, moral Reform, etc. will remain stationary until the temple is cleansed," concluded Weld bluntly.

Free African Americans, who made up the majority of subscribers to Garrison's *Liberator,* provided important support and leadership for the movement. Frederick Douglass assumed the greatest prominence. Having escaped from slavery in Maryland, he became an eloquent critic of its evils. Initially a follower of Garrison, Douglass eventually broke with him and started his own newspaper in Rochester. Other important black abolitionists included Martin Delany, William Wells Brown, William Still, and Sojourner Truth. Most black Americans endorsed peaceful means to end slavery, but David Walker in his *Appeal to the Colored Citizens of the World* (1829) urged slaves to use violence to end bondage. Aided by many other African Americans, these men and women battled against racial discrimination in the North as well as slavery in the South.

Black abolitionists

A network of antislavery sympathizers also developed in the North to convey runaway slaves to Canada and freedom. While not as extensive or as tightly organized as contemporaries claimed, the Underground Railroad hid fugitives and transported them northward from one station to the next. Free African Americans, who were more readily trusted by wary slaves, played a leading role in the Underground Railroad. One of its most famous conductors was Harriet Tubman, an escaped slave who repeatedly returned to the South and eventually escorted to freedom more than 200 slaves.

Opponents and Divisions

The drive for immediate abolition faced massive obstacles within American society. With slavery increasingly important to the South's economy, Southerners forced opponents of slavery to flee the region. In the North, where racism was equally entrenched, abolitionism provoked bitter resistance. Even abolitionists like Garrison treated blacks paternalistically, contending that they should occupy a subordinate place in the antislavery movement.

On occasion, northern resistance turned violent. A hostile Boston mob seized Garrison in 1835 and paraded him with a rope around his body before he was finally rescued. Another anti-abolitionist mob burned down the headquarters of the American Anti-Slavery Society in Philadelphia. And in 1837 in Alton, Illinois, Elijah Lovejoy was murdered when he tried to protect his printing press from an angry crowd. The leaders of these mobs were not from the bottom of society but, as one of

An escaped slave, Harriet Tubman (far left) made several forays into the South as a "conductor" on the Underground Railroad. Shown here with one group that she led to freedom, she was noted for her stealth and firm determination, qualities that helped her repeatedly to outwit her pursuers.

their victims noted, were "gentlemen of property and standing." Prominent leaders in the community, they reacted vigorously to the threat that abolitionists posed to their power and prosperity and to the established order.

Divisions among abolitionists   But abolitionists were also hindered by divisions among reformers. At Oberlin College Charles Finney preferred revivalism over Theodore Weld's abolitionism. Even more conservative than Finney, Lyman Beecher was shocked to hear that his son Edward had stood guard over Elijah Lovejoy's printing press the evening before the editor was murdered. Within another decade, Beecher would see his daughter Harriet Beecher Stowe write the most successful piece of antislavery literature in the nation's history, *Uncle Tom's Cabin*. Even the abolitionists themselves splintered, shaken by the opposition they encountered and unable to agree on the most effective response. More conservative reformers wanted to work within established institutions, using the churches and political action to end slavery. But for Garrison and his followers, the mob violence demonstrated that slavery was only part of a deeper national disease, whose cure required the overthrow of American institutions and values.

By the end of the decade, Garrison had worked out a program for the total reform of society. He embraced perfectionism and pacifism, denounced the clergy, urged members to leave the churches, and called for an end to all government. Condemning the Constitution as proslavery—"a covenant with death and an agreement with hell"—he publicly burned a copy one July 4th. No person of conscience, he

argued, could vote or otherwise participate in the corrupt political system. This platform was radical enough on all counts, but the final straw for Garrison's opponents was
his endorsement of women's rights as an inseparable part of abolitionism.

The Women's Rights Movement

Women faced many disadvantages in American society. They were kept out of most
jobs, denied political rights, and given only limited access to education beyond the el-
ementary grades. When a woman married, her husband became the legal representative of the marriage and gained complete control of her property. If a marriage
ended in divorce, the husband was awarded custody of the children. Any unmarried
woman was made the ward of a male relative.

When abolitionists divided over the issue of female participation, women found
it easy to identify with the situation of slaves, since both were victims of male tyranny.
Sarah and Angelina Grimké took up the cause of women's rights after they were criticized for speaking to audiences that included men as well as women. Sarah responded with *Letters on the Condition of Women and the Equality of the Sexes*
(1838), arguing that women deserved the same rights as men. Abby Kelly, another
abolitionist, remarked that women "have good cause to be grateful to the slave," for
in "striving to strike his irons off, we found most surely, that we were manacled *ourselves.*"

Two abolitionists, Elizabeth Cady Stanton and Lucretia Mott, launched the
women's rights movement after they were forced to sit behind a curtain at a world an-

Elizabeth Cady Stanton, one of
the instigators and guiding spirits at the Seneca Falls convention, photographed with two of
her children about that time.

Seneca Falls convention

tislavery convention in London. In 1848 Stanton and Mott organized a conference in Seneca Falls, New York, that attracted about a hundred supporters. The meeting issued a Declaration of Sentiments, modeled after the Declaration of Independence, that began, "All men and women are created equal."

The Seneca Falls convention approved resolutions calling for educational and professional opportunities for women, laws giving them control of their property, recognition of legal equality, and repeal of laws awarding the father custody of the children in divorce. The most controversial proposal, and the only resolution that did not pass unanimously, was one demanding the right to vote. The Seneca Falls convention established the arguments and the program for the women's rights movement for the remainder of the century.

The women's rights movement won few victories before 1860. Several states gave women greater control over their property, and a few made divorce easier or granted women the right to sue in courts. But disappointments and defeats outweighed these early victories. Still, many of the important leaders in the crusade for women's rights that emerged after the Civil War had already taken their places at the forefront of the movement. They included Stanton, Susan B. Anthony, Lucy Stone, and—as Lyman Beecher by now must have expected, one of his daughters—Isabella Beecher Hooker.

The Schism of 1840

It was Garrison's position on women's rights that finally split antislavery ranks already divided over other aspects of his growing radicalism. The showdown came in 1840 at the national meeting of the American Anti-Slavery Society, when delegates debated whether women could hold office in the organization. Some of Garrison's opponents favored women's rights but opposed linking the question to the slavery issue, insisting that it would drive off potential supporters. By packing the convention, Garrison carried the day. His opponents, led by Lewis Tappan, resigned to found the rival American and Foreign Anti-Slavery Society.

The schism of 1840 lessened the influence of abolitionism as a benevolent reform movement in American society. Although abolitionism heightened moral concern about slavery, it failed to convert the North to its program, and its supporters remained a tiny minority. For all the considerable courage they showed, their movement suffered from the lack of a realistic, long-range plan for eliminating so deeply entrenched an institution. Garrison even boasted that "the genius of the abolitionist movement is to have *no* plan." Abolitionism demonstrated the severe limits of moral suasion and individual conversions as a solution to deeply rooted social problems.

REFORM SHAKES THE PARTY SYSTEM

"What a fog-bank we are in politically! Do you see any head-land or light—or can you get an observation—or soundings?" The words came from a puzzled Whig politician writing a friend after the Massachusetts state elections of 1853. He was in such a confused state because reformers were increasingly entering the political arena to achieve results.

The crusading idealism of revivalists and reformers inevitably collided with the   *Reform enters*
hard reality that society could not be perfected by converting individuals. In   *politics*
America's democratic society, politics and government coercion promised a more effective means to impose a new moral vision on the nation. Several movements, including those to establish public schools and erect asylums, had operated within the
political system from the beginning. A growing number of other frustrated reformers
abandoned the principle of voluntary persuasion and looked to governmental coercion to achieve their goals.

Politicians did not particularly welcome the new interest. Because the Whig and
Democratic parties both drew on evangelical and nonevangelical voters, heated
moral debates over the harmful effects of drink or the evils of slavery threatened to
detach regular party members from their old loyalties and disrupt each party's unity.
The strong opposition of German and Irish immigrants to temperance stimulated an-
tiforeign sentiment among reformers and further divided both party coalitions, particularly the Democrats. "The temperance question is playing havock in the old party
lines," commented one Indiana politician. The issue of abolition seemed even more
disruptive.

Women and the Right to Vote

As the reform impulse shifted toward the political arena, women in particular lost influence. As major participants in the benevolent organizations of the 1820s and
1830s, they had used their efforts on behalf of "moral suasion." But since women
could not vote, they felt excluded when the temperance and abolitionist movements
turned to electoral action to accomplish their goals. By the 1840s female reformers
increasingly demanded the right to vote as the means to change society. Nor were
men blind to what was at stake: one reason they so strongly resisted female suffrage
was because it would give women real power.

Previously, many female reformers had accepted the right of petition as their
most appropriate political activity. But *The Lily*, a women's rights paper, soon
changed its tack. "Why shall [women] be left only the poor resource of petition?" it
asked. "For even petitions, when they are from women, without the elective franchise
to give them backbone, are of but little consequence."

The Maine Law

The political parties could resist the women's suffrage movement, since most of its
advocates lacked the right to vote. Less easily put off were temperance reformers.   *Struggle over*
Although drinking had significantly declined in American society by 1840, it had   *prohibition*
hardly been eliminated. After 1845 the arrival of large numbers of German and Irish
immigrants, who were accustomed to consuming alcohol, made voluntary prohibition
even more remote. In response, temperance advocates proposed state laws that
would outlaw the manufacture and sale of alcoholic beverages. If liquor was unavailable, reformers reasoned, drinkers would be forced to reform whether they wanted
to or not.

Party leaders tried to dodge the question of prohibition, since large numbers of
Whigs and Democrats were found on both sides of the question. Temperance advocates countered with a strategy of endorsing the legislative candidates who pledged

to support a prohibitory law. To win additional recruits, temperance leaders adopted techniques used in political campaigns, including house-to-house canvasses, parades and processions, bands and singing, banners, picnics, and mass rallies.

The movement's first major triumph came in 1851 in Maine. The Maine Law, as it was known, authorized search and seizure of private property and provided stiff penalties for selling liquor. In the next few years a number of states enacted similar laws, although most were struck down by the courts or later repealed. Prohibition remained a controversial political issue throughout the century.

Although prohibition was temporarily defeated, the issue badly disrupted the Whig and Democratic parties. It detached a number of voters from both coalitions, greatly increased the extent of party switching, and brought to the polls a large number of new voters, including many "wets" who wanted to preserve their right to drink. By dissolving the ties between so many voters and their parties, the temperance issue played a major role in the eventual collapse of the Jacksonian party system in the 1850s.

Abolitionism and the Party System

Abolition was the most divisive issue to come out of the benevolent reform movement. In 1835 abolitionists distributed over a million pamphlets through the post office. A wave of excitement swept the South when the first batches arrived addressed to white southerners. Former senator Robert Hayne led a Charleston mob that burned sacks of U.S. mail containing abolitionist literature, and postmasters in other southern cities refused to deliver the material. The Jackson administration allowed southern states to censor the mail, leading abolitionists to protest that their civil rights had been violated. In reaction, the number of antislavery societies in the North nearly tripled.

Censorship of the mails

With access to the mails impaired, abolitionists began flooding Congress with petitions against slavery. Asserting that Congress had no power over the institution, angry southern representatives demanded action, and the House in response adopted the so-called gag rule in 1836. It automatically tabled without consideration any petition dealing with slavery. But southern leaders had made a tactical blunder. The gag rule allowed abolitionists not only to attack slavery but also to speak out as defenders of white civil liberties. The appeal of the antislavery movement was broadened, and in 1844 the House finally repealed the controversial rule.

Gag rule

Many abolitionists outside Garrison's extreme circle began to feel that an antislavery third party offered a more effective means of attacking slavery. In 1840 these political abolitionists founded the Liberty party and nominated for president James Birney, a former slaveholder who had converted to abolitionism. Birney received only 7000 votes, but the Liberty party was the seed from which a stronger antislavery political movement would grow. From 1840 onward, abolitionism's importance would be in the political arena rather than as a voluntary reform organization.

After two decades of fiery revivals, benevolent crusades, utopian experiments, and Transcendental philosophizing, the ferment of reform had spread through urban streets, canal town churches, frontier clearings, and the halls of Congress. Abolition, potentially the most dangerous issue, seemed still under control in 1840. Birney's small vote, coupled with the disputes between the two national antislavery societies, encouraged political leaders to believe that the party system had turned back this latest threat of sectionalism. But the growing northern concern about slavery highlighted differences between the two sections. Despite the strength of evangelicalism in the South, the reform impulse spawned by the revivals found little support there, since reform movements were discredited by their association with abolitionism. The party system confronted the difficult challenge of holding together sections that, although sharing much, were also diverging in important ways. To the residents of both sections, the South increasingly appeared to be a unique society with its own distinctive way of life.

CHAPTER SUMMARY

The Jacksonian era produced the greatest number of significant reform movements in American history. These movements grew out of the revivals of the Second Great Awakening. Rejecting traditional Calvinism and the doctrine of predestination, revivalists led by Charles Grandison Finney preached the optimistic doctrine of good works and salvation available to all, and they eventually endorsed the ideals of perfectionism and millennialism as well. The revivalists' new doctrines helped Americans adjust to the new market economy and deal with the pressures they felt in their daily lives. Romanticism also strengthened reform, with its emphasis on the unlimited potential of each individual and, like the revivals, on emotion as a source of truth.

At the same time, women's lives were reshaped as the market economy expanded and as a middle class grew. The new ideal of domesticity proclaimed that women's lives should center on the home and the family. Denied employment opportunities and political rights, middle-class women turned to religion and reform as ways to shape society. Women dominated church membership and played a critical role in reform movements.

Utopian communities represented one variety of reform for those who wished to establish a model society for the rest of the world to follow. More within the mainstream of American society, humanitarian movements sought to save individuals by combating social evils. Temperance, educational reform, and the establishment of asylums all gained advocates, but abolitionism became the most significant, and most divisive, cause to emerge. Because abolitionism challenged powerful groups in American society and championed the cause of enslaved African Americans—the least powerful social class—it precipitated strong and often violent opposition, and the movement split in 1840. Frustrated over their limited success through voluntary action, reformers increasingly turned to political action. Advocates of temperance, antislavery, and women's rights all became active in politics. The intrusion of these moral questions into the political system threatened to disrupt the two national parties; antislavery especially made it difficult to preserve support in both sections. Although still intact, the party system was seriously weakened by these reform movements.

SIGNIFICANT EVENTS

1787	First Shaker commune established
1821	New York constructs first penitentiary
1824	New Harmony established
1824–1837	Peak of revivals
1826	James Fenimore Cooper's *The Last of the Mohicans* published; American Temperance Society founded
1829	David Walker's *Appeal to the Colored Citizens of the World* published
1830	*Book of Mormon* published
1830–1831	Charles Finney's revival at Rochester
1831	*The Liberator* established
1833	American Anti-Slavery Society founded; Oberlin College admits women
1834	Lane Seminary rebellion
1835	Abolitionists' postal campaign
1836	Transcendental Club organized; gag rule passed
1837	Massachusetts establishes state board of education; Ralph Waldo Emerson delivers "The American Scholar" address; Mount Holyoke Seminary commences classes; Elijah Lovejoy killed
1838	Sarah Grimké's *Letters on the Condition of Women and the Equality of the Sexes* published
1839	Nauvoo founded
1840	Schism of American Anti-Slavery Society; Liberty party organized
1841	Brook Farm founded
1843	Dorothea Dix's report on treatment of the insane
1844	Joseph Smith murdered; gag rule repealed
1846	Mormons abandon Nauvoo
1848	Oneida Community established; Seneca Falls convention
1850	Nathaniel Hawthorne's *The Scarlet Letter* published
1851	Maine adopts prohibition law; Herman Melville's *Moby-Dick* published
1854	Henry David Thoreau's *Walden* published
1855	Walt Whitman's *Leaves of Grass* published

ADDITIONAL READING

Considerable work has been done in recent years on the relationship between evangelical religion and society. Nathan O. Hatch, *The Democratization of American Christianity* (1989) is a good starting point. Whitney Cross, *The Burned Over District* (1950) explores the revivals of western New York, where evangelicalism was particularly strong. Paul Johnson's, *A Shopkeeper's Millennium* (1978) is an interesting, well-written community study, but it strains the evidence somewhat to push its thesis that revivalism was a form of class domination. George H. Thomas, *Revivalism and*

Cultural Change (1989) also examines the relationship between religion and the new market economy.

Ronald G. Walters, *American Reformers, 1815–1860* (1978) presents a general history of the reform impulse. A fuller treatment, with more emphasis on evangelical religion, is Alice Felt Tyler, *Freedom's Ferment* (1944), which captures the era's heady optimism. Good discussions of the concept of domesticity and women's lives can be found in Carl Degler, *At Odds* (1977) and Nancy Cott, *The Bonds of Womanhood* (1977). Mary P. Ryan, *The Cradle of the Middle Class* (1981) skillfully traces the connection between economic transformation and family structure. Specific reform movements are analyzed in Carl F. Kaestle, *Pillars of the Republic* (1983) on the common school movement, Ellen C. DuBois, *Feminism and Suffrage* (1978), and James B. Stewart, *Holy Warriors* (1976), which is the best study of abolitionism. Lori D. Ginzberg, *Women and the Work of Benevolence* (1990) and Barbara Epstein, *The Politics of Domesticity* (1981) examine women's participation in reform. For a fuller list of readings, see the Bibliography.

13

The Old South

The impeccably dressed Colonel Daniel Jordan, master of 261 slaves at Laurel Hill, strolls down his oak-lined lawn to the dock along the Waccamaw River, a day's journey north of Charleston, to board the steamship *Nina.* On Fridays, it is Colonel Jordan's custom to visit the exclusive Hot and Hot Fish Club, founded by his fellow lowcountry planters, to play a game of lawn bowling or billiards and be waited on by black servants in livery as he sips a mint julep in the refined atmosphere that for him is the South.

Several hundred miles to the west another steamboat, the *Fashion,* makes its way along the Alabama River near the village of Claiborne. One of the passengers is upset by the boat's slow pace. He has been away from his plantation in the Red River country of Texas and is eager to get back. "Time's money, time's money!" he mutters to anyone who will listen. "Time's worth more'n money to me now; a hundred percent more, 'cause I left my niggers all alone; not a damn white man within four mile on 'em." When asked what they are doing, since the cotton crop has already been picked, he says, "I set 'em to clairin', but they ain't doin' a damn thing. . . . I know that as well as you do. . . . But I'll make it up, I'll make it up when I get thar, now you'd better believe." For this Red River planter, time is money and cotton is his world—indeed, cotton is what the South is all about. "I am a cotton man, I am, and I don't car who knows it," he proclaims. "I know cotton, I do. I'm dam' if I know anythin' but cotton."

At the other end of the South, the slave Sam Williams works in the intense heat of Buffalo Forge, an iron-making factory nine miles from Lexington, Virginia, in the Shenandoah Valley. As a refiner, Williams has the most important job at the forge, alternately heating pig iron in the white-hot coals, then slinging the ball of glowing metal on an anvil, where he pounds it with huge, water-powered hammers to remove the impurities. Ambitious and hard working, he earns extra money (at the same rate paid to whites) for any iron he produces beyond his weekly quota. In some years his extra income is over $100. His wife Nancy, who is in charge of the dairy, earns extra money as well, and their savings accounts at the local bank total more than $150. Additional income allows them to buy extra food and items for themselves and their four daughters, but more important, it helps keep their family intact in an unstable environment. They know that their owner is very unlikely to sell away slaves who work so hard. For Sam and Nancy Williams, family ties, worship at the local Baptist church, and socializing with their fellow slaves are what make life important.

Plantation Burial, *painted about 1860 by John Antrobus, portrays the black slave community from a Louisiana plantation burying a loved one. Religion played a central role in the life of slaves.*

In the bayous of the Deep South, only a few miles from where the Mississippi Delta meets the Gulf, Octave Johnson hears the dogs coming. For over a year now Johnson has been a runaway slave. He fled from a Louisiana plantation in St. James Parish when the work bell rang before daybreak and the overseer threatened to whip him for staying in bed. To survive, he hides in the swamps four miles behind the plantation—stealing turkeys, chickens, and pigs and trading with other slaves. As uncertain as this life is, nearly 30 other slaves have joined him over the past year.

The sound of the dogs warns Johnson and his companions that the hound master Eugene Jardeau is out again. This time when the pack bursts upon them, the slaves do not flee but kill as many dogs as possible. Then they plunge into the bayou, and as the hounds follow, alligators make short work of another six. For Octave Johnson the real South is a matter of weighing one's prospects between the uncertainties of alligators and the overseer's whip—and deciding when to say no.

Ferdinand Steel and his family are not forced, by the flick of the lash, to rise at five in the morning. They rise because the land demands it. Steel, in his twenties, owns 170 acres of land in Carroll County, Mississippi. Unmarried, he moved there from Tennessee with his widowed mother, sister, and brother in 1836, only a few years after the Choctaws had been forced to give up the region and march west. His life is one of continuous hard work, caring for the animals and tending the crops. His mother Eliza and sister Julia have plenty to keep them busy: making soap, fashioning dippers out of gourds, or sewing.

The Steel family grows cotton, too, but not with the single-minded devotion of the planter aboard the *Fashion*. Self-sufficiency and family security always come first, and Steel's total crop amounts to only five or six bales. His profit is never sufficient to consider buying even one slave. In fact, he would have preferred not to raise any cotton—"We are to[o] weak handed," he says—but the five bales mean cash, and cash means that when he goes to market in nearby Grenada, he can buy sugar and coffee, gunpowder and lead, a yard or two of calico, and quinine to treat the malaria that is so common in those parts. Though fiercely independent, Steel and his scattered neighbors help each other raise houses, clear fields, shuck corn, or quilt. They depend on one another and are bound together by blood, religion, obligation, and honor. For small farmers like Ferdinand Steel, these ties constitute the real South.

Diversity of the South

The portraits could go on: different people, different Souths, all of them real. Such contrasts underscore the difficulty of trying to define a regional identity. Encompassing in 1860 the 15 slave states plus the District of Columbia, the South was a land of great geographic diversity. It extended from the Tidewater coastal plain along the Atlantic seaboard to the prairies of Texas, from the Kentucky Bluegrass region to the Gulf coast, from the mountains of western Virginia to the swamps of the Mississippi Delta with its semitropical climate. The only geographic feature that separated the North and South was the Ohio River, and it was an avenue of trade rather than a source of division.

Factors unifying the South

Yet despite its many differences of people and geography, the South was bonded by ties so strong, they eventually outpulled those of the nation itself. At the heart of this unity was an agricultural system that took advantage of the region's warm climate and long growing season. Cotton required 200 frost-free days, and rice and sugar even more, which meant that in the United States these staples could be grown only in the South. Most important, this rural agricultural economy was based on the institution of slavery, which had far-reaching effects on all aspects of southern society. It shaped not only the culture of the slaves themselves but the lives of their masters and mistresses, and even of farm families and herders in the hills and backwoods who saw few slaves in their day-to-day existence. To understand the Old South, then, we must understand how the southern agricultural economy and the institution of slavery affected the social class structure of both white and black southerners.

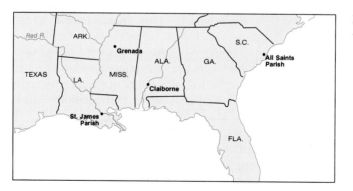

THE DIVERSE SOUTH

THE SOCIAL STRUCTURE OF THE COTTON KINGDOM

We have already seen (in Chapter 10) that the spread of cotton stimulated the nation's remarkable economic growth after the War of 1812. Demand spurred by the textile industry sent the price of cotton soaring on the international market, and white southerners scrambled into the fresh lands of the Southwest to reap the profits to be made in the cotton sweepstakes.

The Boom Country Economy

Letters, newspapers, and word of mouth all brought tales of the black belt region of Alabama, where the dark soil was particularly suited to growing cotton, and of the tremendous yields from the soils along the Mississippi River's broad reaches. "The *Alabama Feaver* rages here with great violence and has *carried off* vast numbers of our Citizens," a North Carolinian wrote in 1817. "I am apprehensive if it continues to spread as it has done, it will almost depopulate the country." A generation later, as the removal of the southern Indian tribes opened vast tracts of land to white settlement, immigrants were still "pouring in with a ceaseless tide," one observer reported, "including 'Land Sharks' ready to swallow up the home of the redmen, or the white, as oportunity might offer."

Cotton pushes westward

By the 1840s planters even began to leave Mississippi and Alabama—virgin territory at the turn of the century—to head for the new cotton frontier along the Red River and up into Texas. A decade later the northern visitor Frederick Law Olmsted came across many abandoned southern homesteads, which he called "Gone to Texas" farms. Amazingly, by the eve of the Civil War nearly a third of the total cotton crop came from *west* of the Mississippi River.

As Senator James Henry Hammond of South Carolina boasted in 1858, cotton was king in the Old South. True, the region devoted more acreage to corn, but cotton was the primary export and the major source of southern wealth. By 1860 the United States produced three-fourths of the world's supply of cotton. This boom fueled the southern economy so strongly that following the depression of 1839–1843, the southern economy grew faster than that in the North. Even so, per capita income in the South remained below that of the free states, and wealth was not as evenly distributed in the plantation South as in northern agricultural areas.

Southern prosperity

The single-crop agriculture practice by southern farmers rapidly wore out the soil. Tobacco was a particularly exhaustive crop, and corn also rapidly drained nutrients. To restore their soils, planters and farmers in the Upper South increasingly shifted to wheat production, but because they now plowed their fields rather than using a hoe, this shift intensified soil erosion. Destruction of the forests, particularly in the Piedmont where commercial agriculture now took hold, had the same effect, and many streams quickly silted up and were no longer navigable. Row-crop agriculture made floods and droughts more common. In addition, reliance on a single crop increased toxins and parasites in the soil, making southern agriculture more vulnerable to destruction than varied agriculture.

Environmental impact of single-crop agriculture

Only the South's low population density mitigated the impact on the environment. More remote areas remained heavily forested, wetlands were still common, and as late as 1860 eighty percent of the region was uncultivated (cattle and hogs, however, ranged over much of this acreage). Throughout much of the South, farmers

W.A.Walker. 1883.

fired the woods in the spring to destroy insects, burn off brush, and increase grass for their browsing stock.

Perhaps the most striking environmental consequence of the expansion of southern society was the increase in disease. The South, especially the Lower South, enjoyed a reputation for unhealthiness. Epidemic diseases such as malaria, yellow fever, and cholera were brought to the area by Europeans. The clearing of land—which increased runoff, precipitated floods, and produced pools of stagnant water—along with the growing white and black population, facilitated the spread of these diseases. In notoriously unhealthy areas, such as the coastal swamps of South Carolina's rice district, wealthy whites fled during the sickly summer months and were only part-time residents.

The Upper South's New Orientation

As cotton transformed the boom country of the Deep South, agriculture in the Upper South also adjusted.° Improved varieties and more scientific agricultural practices reversed the decline in tobacco, which had begun in the 1790s. More important, however, farmers in the Upper South made wheat and corn their major crops. As early as 1840 the value of wheat grown in Virginia was twice that of tobacco.

°The Upper South included the border states (Delaware, Maryland, Kentucky, and Missouri) and Virginia, North Carolina, Tennessee, and Arkansas. The states of the Deep South were South Carolina, Georgia, Florida, Alabama, Mississippi, Louisiana, and Texas.

In this romanticized Currier and Ives print of a cotton plantation, field hands are waist-deep in cotton while other slaves haul the picked cotton to be ginned and then pressed into bales. Looking on are the owner and his wife. Picking began as early as August and continued in some areas until late January. Because the bolls ripened at different times, a field had to be picked several times.

Slave trade

Because the new crops required less labor, planters in the Upper South regularly sold their surplus slaves to cotton and sugar planters in the Deep South. Indeed, some planters in the Upper South maintained a profit margin only by these sales. The demand in the Deep South for field hands drove their price steadily up, so that by the late 1850s a prime field hand, who would have sold for $600 in the early 1840s, commanded $1500. Even with increased labor costs, southern agriculture flourished.

The Rural South

The Old South, then, was dynamic, expanding, and booming economically. But the region remained overwhelmingly rural, with 84 percent of its labor force engaged in agriculture in 1860, compared with 40 percent in the North. Conversely, the South lagged in manufacturing, producing only 9 percent of the nation's manufactured goods. During the 1850s some southern propagandists urged greater investment in industry to diversify the South's economy. But as long as high profits from cotton continued, these advocates made little headway.

Lack of manufacturing

With so little industry, few cities developed in the South. New Orleans, with a

Absence of cities

population of 169,000 in 1860, was the only truly southern city of significant size. Only 1 in 10 southerners lived in cities and towns in 1860, compared with 1 out of 3 persons in the North. North Carolina, Alabama, Mississippi, Arkansas, and Texas did not contain a single city with a population of 10,000.

As a rural society, the South evidenced far less interest in education. Southern colleges were inferior to those in the North, and public secondary schools were virtually nonexistent. Wealthy planters, who hired tutors or sent their children to private academies, generally opposed a state-supported school system. Thus free public schools were rare, especially in the rural districts that made up most of the South. Georgia in 1860 had only one county with a free school system, and Mississippi had no public schools outside its few cities. On average southern white children spent only one-fifth as much time in school as did their northern counterparts.

The net result was that illiteracy rates were much higher in the South. Among

---

COTTON AND OTHER CROPS OF THE SOUTH

By 1860, the cotton kingdom extended across the Lower South into the Texas prairie and up the Mississippi River valley. Tobacco and hemp were the staple crops of the Upper South, where they competed with corn and wheat. Rice production was concentrated in the swampy coastal region of South Carolina and Georgia as well as the lower tip of Louisiana. The sugar district was in southern Louisiana.

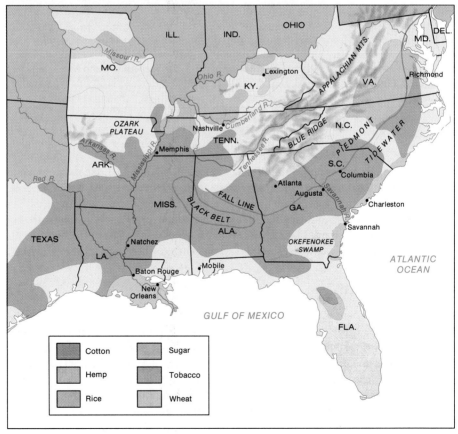

native-born white citizens, the 1850 census showed that 20 percent were unable to read and write. The comparable figure was 3 percent in the middle states and 0.4 percent in New England. In some areas of the South, over a third of all white residents were illiterate.

White illiteracy

Distribution of Slavery

Even more than agrarian ways, slavery set the South apart. Whereas in 1776 slavery had been a national institution, by 1820 slavery was confined to the states south of Pennsylvania and the Ohio River. The South's "peculiar institution" bound white and black southerners together in a multitude of ways.

Slaves were not evenly distributed throughout the region. More than half lived in the Deep South, where African Americans outnumbered white southerners in both South Carolina and Mississippi by the 1850s. Elsewhere in the Deep South, the black population exceeded 40 percent in all states except Texas. In the Upper South, on the other hand, whites greatly outnumbered blacks. Only in Virginia and North Carolina did the slave population top 30 percent.

The distribution of slaves showed striking geographic variations within individual states as well. In areas of fertile soil, flat or rolling countryside, and good transportation, slavery and the plantation system dominated. In the pine barrens, areas isolated by lack of transportation, and hilly and mountainous regions, small family farms and few slaves were the rule.

Almost all enslaved African Americans, male and female, worked in agricultural pursuits, with only about 10 percent living in cities and towns. On large plantations, a few slaves were domestic servants and others were skilled artisans—blacksmiths, carpenters, or bricklayers—but most toiled in the fields. Only about 5 percent of the South's manufacturing employees in the 1850s were slaves like Sam Williams.

Slave occupations

Slavery as a Labor System

Slavery was, first and foremost, a system to manage and control labor. The plantation system, with its extensive estates and large labor forces, could never have developed without slavery, nor could it have met the world demand for cotton and other staples. Slaves represented an enormous capital investment, worth more than all the land in the Old South.

Furthermore, slavery remained a highly profitable investment. The average slaveowner spent perhaps $30 to $35 a year to support an adult slave; some expended as little as half that. Allowing for the cost of land, equipment, and other expenses, a planter could expect one of his slaves to produce more than $78 worth of cotton—which meant that even at the higher cost of support, a slaveowner took about 60 percent of the wealth produced by a slave's labor. For those who pinched pennies and drove slaves harder, the profits were even greater.

Profitability of slavery

By concentrating wealth and power in the hands of the planter class, slavery shaped the tone of southern society. Planters were not aristocrats in the European sense of having special legal privileges or formal titles of rank. Still, the system encouraged southern planters to think of themselves as a landed gentry upholding the aristocratic values of pride, honor, family, and hospitality.

Slavery and aristocratic values

Whereas slavery had existed throughout most of the Americas at the beginning of the century, by the 1850s the United States, Cuba, and Brazil were the only slave-

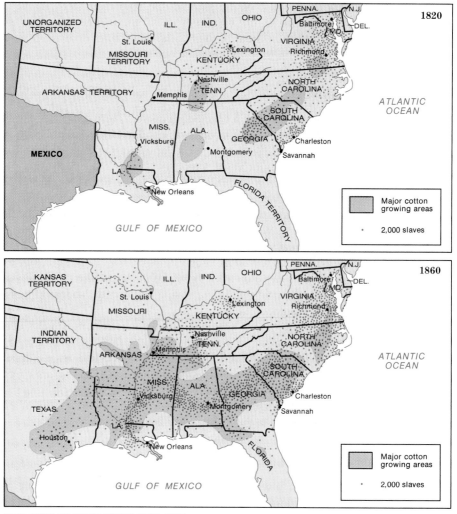

THE SPREAD OF SLAVERY, 1820–1860
Between 1820 and 1860, the slave population of the South shifted southward and westward, concentrating especially heavily in coastal South Carolina and Georgia, in the black belt of central Alabama and Mississippi (so named because of its rich soil), and in the Mississippi valley. Small farms with few slaves predominated in cotton-growing areas that lacked good transportation, such as northern Georgia, and in regions with poor soil, such as the piney woods of southern Mississippi.

holding nations left in the region. Public opinion in Europe and in the North had grown more and more hostile to the peculiar institution, causing white southerners to feel increasingly like an embattled minority. Yet they clung tenaciously to slavery, for it was the base on which the South's economic growth and way of life rested. As one Georgian observed on the eve of the Civil War, slavery was "so intimately mingled with our social conditions that it would be impossible to eradicate it."

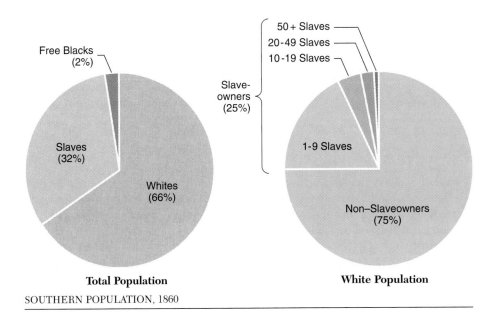

Total Population   **White Population**

SOUTHERN POPULATION, 1860

CLASS STRUCTURE OF THE WHITE SOUTH

In 1860 the region's 15 states had a population of 12 million, of which roughly two-thirds were white, one-third were black slaves, and about 2 percent were free African Americans. Because of the institution of slavery, the social structure of the antebellum South differed in important ways from that of the North. Even so, southern society was remarkably fluid; as a result, class lines were not rigid.

The Slaveowners

Of the 8 million white southerners in 1860, only about 2 million (one-quarter) either owned slaves or were members of slaveowning families. Moreover, most slaveowners owned only a few slaves. If one uses the census definition of a planter as a person who owned 20 or more slaves, only about 1 out of every 30 white southerners belonged to families of the planter class.

A planter of consequence, however, needed to own at least 50 slaves, and there were only about 10,000 such families—less than 1 percent of the white population. This privileged group made up the aristocracy at the top of the southern class structure. Owners of large numbers of slaves were very rare; only about 2000 southerners like Colonel Daniel Jordan owned 100 or more slaves. Although limited in size, the planter class nevertheless owned more than half of all slaves and controlled more than 90 percent of the region's total wealth.

The typical plantation had 20 to 50 slaves and 800 to 1000 acres of land. On an estate larger than that, slaves would have to walk more than an hour to reach the farthest fields, losing valuable work time. Thus larger slaveowners usually owned several

Plantation administration

plantations, with an overseer to manage the slaves on each, while the owner attended to administrative and business matters. The slaves were divided into field hands, skilled workers, and house servants, with one or more slaves serving as "drivers" to assist the overseer. While planters pioneered the application of capitalistic methods, including specialization and division of labor, to agriculture, plantations remained labor-intensive operations. Of the southern staples, only the production of sugar was heavily mechanized.

Tidewater and Frontier

Southern planters shared a commitment to preserve slavery as the source of their wealth and stature. Yet in other ways they were a diverse group. On the one hand, the tobacco and rice planters of the Atlantic Tidewater were part of a settled region and a culture that reached back 150 to 200 years. States such as Mississippi and Arkansas, by contrast, were at or just emerging from the frontier stage, since most residents had arrived after 1815. Consequently, the society of the Southwest was rawer and more volatile.

Tidewater society

It was along the Tidewater, especially the bays of the Chesapeake and the South Carolina coast, that the legendary "Old South" was born. Here, masters erected substantial homes, some—especially between Charleston and Columbia—the classic white-pillared mansions in the Greek revival style. Here, more than a few planters were urbane and polished.

The ideal of the Tidewater South was the country gentleman of the English tradition. An Irish visitor observed that in Maryland and Virginia the great planters lived in "a style which approaches nearer to that of the English country gentleman than what is to be met with anywhere else on the continent." As in England, the local gentry often served as justices of the peace, and the Episcopal church remained the socially accepted road to heaven. Here, too, family names continued to be important in politics.

Society in the cotton kingdom

While the newer regions of the South boasted planters with cultivated manners, as a group the cotton lords were a different breed. They were basically entrepreneurs who had moved west for the same reason so many other Americans had: to make their fortunes. Some were planters like Thomas Dabney, fleeing the exhausted soils of the Tidewater; others were the sons of planters seeking to improve their lot. Not a few were northerners with an eye for opportunity, such as Henry Watson, who went south as a young tutor, settled in Greensboro, Alabama, and became a leading planter. Overseers sometimes rose into the ranks of slaveowners, as Ephraim Beanland of Mississippi did. Merchants and businessmen like Maunsel White of New Orleans invested their profits in a plantation; land speculators rode the land grabs of the 1830s into the ranks of the elite. But by and large, the wealthy planters of the cotton gentry were self-made men, who through hard work, aggressive business tactics, and good luck had risen from ordinary backgrounds. For them, the cotton boom and the exploitation of enslaved men and women offered the opportunity to move up in a new society that lacked an entrenched elite.

Slaveholders' values

"Time's money, time's money." For men like the impatient Texan, time was indeed money, slaves were capital, and cotton by the bale signified cash in hand. This business orientation was especially apparent in the cotton kingdom, where planters sought to maximize their profits and constantly reinvested their returns in land and slaves. As one visitor said of Mississippi slaveholders: "To sell cotton in order to buy

A PLANTATION LAYOUT
Often covering a thousand acres or more, a plantation contained several fields and usually extensive uncleared woods. Service buildings might include a smokehouse, stables, a gin house (for cotton) or a rice mill, and an overseer's dwelling. Like most large plantations, Hopeton produced a considerable amount of foodstuffs, but it grew both rice and cotton as staples. Most plantations concentrated on a single cash crop.

negroes—to make more cotton to buy more negroes, 'ad infinitum,' is the aim and direct tendency of all the operations of the thorough-going cotton planter: his whole soul is wrapped up in the pursuit." One shocked Virginian who visited Vicksburg claimed that its citizens ran "mad with speculation" and did business "in a kind of phrenzy." And indeed there was money to be made. The combined annual income of the richest thousand families of the cotton kingdom approached $50 million, while the wealth of the remaining 666,000 families amounted to only about $60 million.

Stately mansions could be found in a few areas of the cotton South. In general, though, most planters lived humbly. Although they ranked among the richest citizens in America, their homes were often simple one- or two-story unpainted wooden frame houses, and some were log cabins. A visitor to one Georgia plantation reported that the house did not have a pane of glass in the windows, a door between the rooms, or a ceiling other than the roof. "If you wish to see people worth millions living as [if] they were not worth hundreds," advised one southwestern planter in 1839, "come to the land of cotton and negroes."

Practical men, few of the new cotton lords had absorbed the culture and learning of the traditional country gentleman. During his extensive journeys in the South, the noted New Yorker Frederick Law Olmsted declared that he "did not see, except perhaps in one or two towns, a thermometer, nor a book of Shakespeare, nor a piano or sheet of music, nor a good reading lamp, nor an engraving or copy of any kind, or a work of art of the slightest merit. A large majority of all these houses were residences of slaveholders, a considerable proportion cotton planters."

The Master at Home

Whether supervising a Tidewater plantation or creating a cotton estate on the Texas frontier, the master had to coordinate a complex agricultural operation. He gave daily instructions concerning the work to be done, settled disputes between slaves and the overseer, and generally handed out rewards and penalties. In addition, the owner made the critical decisions concerning the planting, harvesting, and marketing of the crops. Planters also watched investments and expenditures, and they often sought to expand their production by clearing additional fields, buying more land or slaves, or investing in machinery such as cotton gins. As in any business, these decisions required a sound understanding of the domestic and international market as well as anticipation of future swings.

Paternalism   In performing his duties, the plantation owner was supposed to be the "master" of his crops, his family, and his slaves. Defenders of slavery often held up this paternalistic ideal—the care and guidance of dependent "children"—and maintained that slavery promoted a genuine bond of affection between the caring master and his loyal slaves.

In real life, however, the forces of the market made this paternalistic ideal less evident. Even in the Tidewater, planters were concerned with money and profits. Indeed, some of the most brutal forms of slavery existed on rice plantations, where the absenteeism of many owners, combined with the sheer numbers of slaves, made close personal ties impossible. Except for a few domestic servants, owners of large plantations generally had little contact with their slaves. Nor could paternalism mask the reality that slavery everywhere rested on violence, racism, and exploitation.

The Plantation Mistress

Upper-class southern white women, like those in the North, grew up with the ideal of domesticity, reinforced by the notion of a paternalistic master who was lord of the plantation. But the plantation mistress soon discovered that, given the demands placed on her, the ideal was hard to fulfill.

Mistress's   Growing up, a young genteel lady enjoyed a certain amount of leisure. But once
duties   she married and became a plantation mistress, a southern woman was often shocked by the magnitude of her responsibilities. Nursing the sick, making clothing, tending the garden, caring for the poultry, and overseeing every aspect of food preparation were all her domain. She also had to supervise and plan the work of the domestic servants and distribute clothing. After taking care of breakfast, one harried Carolina mistress recounted that she "had the [sewing] work cut out, gave orders about dinner, had the horse feed fixed in hot water, had the box filled with cork: went to see the carpenters working on the negro houses . . . now I have to cut out the flannel jackets." Sarah Williams, the New York bride of a North Carolina planter, admitted that her mother-in-law "works harder than any Northern farmer's wife I know."

This skillful portrait of John Stock, a wealthy South Carolina rice planter, depicts his self-confidence and aristocratic tastes.

Sarah Pierce Vick, the mistress of a plantation near Vicksburg, Mississippi, pauses to speak to one of her slaves, who may be holding feed for her horse. A plantation mistress had many duties and, while enjoying the comforts brought by wealth and status, often found her life more difficult than she had anticipated before marriage.

Mistress's discontent

Unlike female reformers in the North, upper-class southern women did not openly challenge their role, but there is evidence that they found their sphere confining. The greatest unhappiness stemmed from the never-ending task of managing slaves. One southern mistress confessed, "I do not see how I can live my life amid these people! To be always among people whom I do not understand and whom I must guide, and teach and lead on like children. It frightens me." Yet without the labor of slaves, the lifestyle of these women was an impossibility.

Some women drew a parallel between their situation and that of the slaves. Both were subject to male dominance, and independent-minded women found the subordination of marriage difficult. Susan Dabney Smedes, in her recollection of growing up on an Alabama plantation, recalled that "it was a saying that the mistress of a plantation was the most complete slave on it." Some women particularly bristled at their lack of independence and at the necessity of obeying men. "How men can go blustering around, making everybody uncomfortable, simply to show that they are masters and we are only women and children at their mercy!" exclaimed Mary Chesnut, the wife of a South Carolina planter who termed her father-in-law "as absolute a tyrant as the Czar of Russia . . . or the Sultan of Turkey."

Many women were deeply discontented, too, with the widespread double stan-

Miscegenation   dard for sexual behavior and with the daily reminders of miscegenation some had to face. A man who fathered illegitimate children by slave women suffered no social or legal penalties, even in the case of rape (southern law did not recognize such a crime against slave women). On the other hand, a white woman guilty of adultery lost all social respectability.

Mary Chesnut, who knew the reality of miscegenation firsthand from her father-in-law's liaisons with slave women and discussed it more frankly than most, sneered in her diary at the assumptions of male superiority. "All the time they seem to think themselves patterns—models of husbands and fathers," she fumed, bitter at the enforced silence among wives. "Like the patriarchs of old, our men live all in one house with their wives and concubines; and the mulattoes one sees in every family partly resemble the white children. Any lady is ready to tell you who is the father of all the mulattoes one sees in everybody's household but her own. Those, she seems to think, drop from the clouds. My disgust sometimes is boiling over." One planter's wife spoke of "violations of the moral law that made mulattoes as common as blackberries," and another recalled, "I saw slavery in its bearing on my sex. I saw that it teemed with injustice and shame to all womankind and I hated it."

Still, only a small minority of women questioned either their place in southern society or the corrosive influence of slavery. Even fewer were willing to forgo the material comforts that slavery made possible. Moreover, racism was so pervasive within American society that the few white southern women who privately criticized the institution displayed little empathy for the plight of slaves themselves, including black women. Whatever the burdens of the plantation mistress, they were hardly akin to the bondage of slavery itself.

Yeoman Farmers

In terms of numbers, yeoman farm families were the backbone of southern society, accounting for well over half the southern white population. They owned no slaves and farmed the traditional 80 to 160 acres, like northern farmers. About 80 percent
Farmers and   owned their own land, and the rest were tenant farmers who hoped one day to ac-
herders   quire a homestead. They settled almost everywhere in the South, except in the rice and sugar districts and valuable river bottomlands of the Deep South, which were monopolized by large slaveowners. Like Ferdinand Steel, most were semisubsistence farmers who raised primarily corn and hogs, along with perhaps a few bales of cotton or some tobacco, which they sold to obtain the cash needed to buy items like sugar, coffee, and salt. Some were not so much farmers as herdsmen, who set large herds of scrawny cattle or pigs to forage in the woods until it was time for the annual drive to market. Yeoman farmers lacked the wealth of planters, but they had a pride and dignity that earned them the respect of their richer neighbors.

Southern farmers led more isolated lives than their northern counterparts. Yet the social activities of these people were not much different from those of northern farmers. Religion played an important role at camp meetings held in late summer after the crops were laid by and before harvest time. As in the North, neighbors also met to exchange labor and tools, always managing to combine work with fun. The men rolled logs to clear fields of dead trees, turning the activity into a contest. Women met for quilting bees, and adults and children alike would gather to shuck corn. A Tennessee plain farmer recalled that his neighbors "seem to take delight in helping each other sutch as lay[ing] railings, cornshucking and house raising[.] they tried to help each other all they could and dancet all night." Court sessions, militia musters, political rallies—these too were occasions that brought rural folk together.

Since yeoman farmers lacked cheap slave labor, good transportation, and access to credit, they could not compete with planters in the production of staples. When it came to selling their corn and wheat, small farmers conducted only limited business with planters, who usually grew as much of their own foodstuffs as possible. In the North urban centers became a market for small farmers, but in the South the lack of towns limited this internal market. *Limits to economic opportunity*

Thus while southern yeoman farmers were not poor, they suffered from a chronic lack of money and the absence of conveniences that northern farm families enjoyed, such as cast-iron stoves, sewing machines, specialized tools, and good furniture. A few chafed at the absence of public schools and greater opportunities. Josiah Hinds, who hacked a farm out of the isolated woods of northern Mississippi, worried that his children were growing up "wild." He complained that "education is but little prized by my neighbours," who were satisfied "if the corn and cotton grows to perfection . . . [and] brings a fare price, and hog meat is at hand to boil with the greens."

In some ways, then, the worlds of yeoman farmers and upper-class planters were not only different but also in conflict. Still, a hostility between the two classes did not emerge. Yeoman farmers admired planters and hoped that one day they would join the gentry themselves. And even white southerners who owned no slaves accepted *Absence of class conflict*

A majority of white southerners were members of nonslaveholding yeoman farm families. Ruggedly independent, these families depended on their own labor and lived under more primitive conditions. They lacked many comforts, and a number, such as in this painting by George Caleb Bingham, lived in log cabins. (Courtesy, Museum of Fine Arts, Boston)

slavery as a means of controlling African Americans as members of an inferior social caste based on race. "Now suppose they was free," one poor farmer told Frederick Law Olmsted. "You see they'd all think themselves as good as we." Racism and fear of black people were sufficient to keep nonslaveholders loyal to southern institutions.

Poor Whites

The poorest white southerners were confined to land that no one else wanted: the wiregrass region of southeastern Georgia, the sand hills of central South Carolina, the pine barrens of the coastal plains from Virginia to southeastern Mississippi. In their backgrounds they were similar to other southerners, but they were the least efficient, the least enterprising, and the least lucky of the rural white population. Their numbers are difficult to estimate. A rough guess would be perhaps half a million, or a little more than 5 percent of the white population. Poverty-stricken, they lived in rough, unchinked, windowless log cabins located in the remotest areas and were often squatters without title to the land they were on. The men spent their time hunting and fishing, while women did the domestic work and what farming they could manage.

Lives of poor whites   Circumstances made their poverty difficult to escape. Largely illiterate, they suffered from malnutrition stemming from a monotonous diet of corn, pork, and whiskey, and they were afflicted with malaria and hookworm, diseases that sapped their energy. Contemporaries repeatedly commented on their sickly cast, liberal use of whiskey and snuff, sexual immorality, and prematurely aged appearance. Encountering one woman of this class in a piney woods cabin, Olmsted described her as "apparently young" but with a face "dry and impassive as a dead man's. . . . Once in about a minute, [she] would suddenly throw up her chin, and spit with perfect precision into the hottest embers of the fire." Other white southerners scornfully referred to poor whites as crackers, white trash, sandhillers, and clay eaters.

Relations with planters   Because poor whites traded with slaves, exchanging whiskey for stolen goods, contemptuous planters often bought them out simply to rid the neighborhood of them. For their part, poor whites keenly resented planters, but their hostility toward African Americans was even stronger. Poor whites refused to work alongside slaves or perform any work commonly done by them and vehemently opposed ending slavery. Emancipation would remove one of the few symbols of their status—that they were, at least, free.

THE PECULIAR INSTITUTION

Slaves were not free. That overwhelming fact must be understood before anything is said about the kindness or the cruelty individual slaves experienced; before any consideration of healthy or unhealthy living conditions; before any discussion of how slave families coped with hardship, rejoiced in shared pleasures, or worshiped in prayer. The lives of slaves were affected day in and day out, in big ways and small, by the basic reality that slaves were not their own masters. If a slave's workload was reasonable, it remained so only at the master's discretion, not because the slave determined it to be. If slaves married or visited family or friends on a nearby plantation, they could do so only with the master's permission. If they raised a family, they could remain together only so long as the master did not separate them by sale. Whatever slaves wanted to do, they had always to consider the response of their masters.

When power was distributed as unequally as it was between masters and slaves, every action on the part of the enslaved involved a certain calculation, conscious or unconscious. The consequences of every act, of every expression or gesture, had to be considered. In that sense, the line between freedom and slavery penetrated every corner of a slave's life, and it was an absolute and overwhelming distinction.

One other stark fact reinforced the sharp line between freedom and slavery: slaves were distinguished on the basis of color. While the peculiar institution was an economic system of labor, it was also a caste system based on race. The color line of slavery made it much easier to brand black people as somehow different. It made it easier to defend the institution and win the support of yeoman farmers and poor white southerners, even though in many ways the system held them back. Hence slavery must be understood on many levels: not only as an economic system but also as a racial and cultural one, not only in terms of its outward conditions of life and labor but also through the inner demands it made on the soul.

Slavery and race

Work and Discipline

The conditions slaves encountered varied widely, depending on the size of the farm or plantation, the crop being grown, the personality of the master, and whether he was an absentee owner. On small farms slaves worked in the fields with the owners and had much closer contact with whites. On plantations, in contrast, most slaves dealt primarily with the overseer, who was paid by the size of the harvest he brought in and was therefore often harsh in his approach. The largest plantations, which raised rice and sugar, also required the longest hours and the most grueling labor.

House servants and the drivers, who supervised the field hands, were accorded the highest status, and skilled artisans such as carpenters and blacksmiths were also given special recognition. The hardest work was done by the field hands, both men and women, who sometimes were divided into plowhands and hoe gangs. In the summer of 1854 Olmsted watched a group of Mississippi slaves return to work in the fields after a thunderstorm. "First came, led by an old driver carrying a whip, forty of the largest and strongest women I ever saw together; . . . they carried themselves loftily, each having a hoe over the shoulder, and walking with a free, powerful swing like [soldiers] on the march." Behind them were the plowhands on the mules, "the cavalry, thirty strong, mostly men, but a few of them women." Bringing up the rear was "a lean and vigilant white overseer, on a brisk pony."

Organization of slave labor

Some planters organized their slaves by the gang system, in which a white overseer or a black driver supervised gangs of 20 to 25 adults. Although this approach extracted long hours of reasonably hard labor, the slaves had to be constantly supervised and shirkers were difficult to detect. Other planters preferred the task system, under which each slave was given a specific daily assignment to complete, after which he or she was finished for the day. This system allowed slaves to work at their own pace, gave them an incentive to do careful work, and freed overseers from having to closely supervise the work. On the other hand, slaves resisted vigorously if masters tried to

Black slave driver

increase the workload. The task system was most common in the rice fields, whereas the gang system predominated in the cotton districts. Many planters used a combination of the two.

Slaves' workday

Toil began just before sunrise and continued until dusk. During cultivation and harvest, slaves were in the field 15 to 16 hours a day, eating a noonday meal there and resting before resuming labor. Work was uncommon on Sundays, and frequently only a half day was required on Saturdays. Even so, the routine was taxing. "We . . . have everybody at work before day dawns," an Arkansas cotton planter reported. "I am never caught in bed after day light nor is any body else on the place, and we continue in the cotton fields when we can have fair weather till it is so dark we can't see to work."

Rewards and punishment

Often masters gave money, additional food, gifts, and time off to slaves who worked diligently, but the threat of punishment was always present. Slaves could be denied passes; their food allowance could be reduced; and if all else failed, they could be sold. The most common instrument of punishment, however, was the whip. The frequency of its use varied from plantation to plantation, but few slaves escaped the lash entirely. "We have to rely more and more on the power of fear," the planter James Henry Hammond acknowledged. "We are determined to continue masters, and to do so we have to draw the reign tighter and tighter day by day to be assured that we hold them in complete check."

Slave Maintenance

Clothing and housing

Planters generally bought rough, cheap cloth for slave clothing and each year gave adults at most only a couple of outfits and a pair of shoes that were worn out by the end of the year. Few had enough clothing or blankets to keep warm when the weather dipped below freezing. Some planters provided well-built housing, but more commonly slaves lived in cramped, poorly built cabins that were leaky in wet weather, drafty in cold, and furnished with only a few crude chairs, benches and a table, perhaps a mattress filled with corn husks or straw, and a few pots and dishes.

Sickness among the hands was a persistent problem. In order to keep medical expenses down, slaveowners treated sick slaves themselves and called in a doctor only for serious cases. Even conscientious masters often employed harmful treatments and dispensed quack patent medicines. Conditions varied widely, but on average, a slaveowner spent less than a dollar a year on medical care for each slave.

Slaves' lower life expectancy

Even so, the United States was the only slave society in the Americas where the slave population increased naturally—indeed, at about the same rate as the white population. Nevertheless, a deficient diet, inadequate clothing and shelter, long hours of hard toil, and poor medical care resulted in a lower life expectancy among slaves. Infant mortality was more than double that of the free white population; for every 1000 live births among southern slaves, more than 200 died before the age of 5. As late as 1860, fewer than two-thirds of slave children lived to age 10. For those who survived infancy, enslaved African Americans had a life expectancy about 8 years less than white Americans.

Resistance

Given the wide gulf between freedom and slavery, it was only natural that slaves resisted the bondage imposed on them. The most radical form of resistance was rebellion. Unlike Latin America, slave revolts were rare in the southern United States, where whites outnumbered blacks, the government was much more powerful, a majority of slaves were native-born, and family life was much stronger. Slaves recognized the odds against them, and many potential leaders became fugitives instead. What is remarkable is that American slaves revolted at all. *Infrequency of revolts*

Early in the nineteenth century several well-organized uprisings were barely thwarted. In 1800 Gabriel Prosser, a slave blacksmith, recruited perhaps a couple hundred slaves in a plan to march on Richmond and capture the governor. But a heavy thunderstorm postponed the attack and a few slaves then betrayed the plot. Prosser and other leaders were eventually captured and executed. Denmark Vesey's conspiracy in Charleston in 1822 met a similar fate (page 363).

The most famous slave revolt, led by a literate slave preacher named Nat Turner, was smaller and more spontaneous. Turner, who lived on a farm in southeastern Virginia, enjoyed unusual privileges. His master, whom he described as a kind and trusting man, encouraged him to study the Bible and preach to other slaves on Sundays and gave him great personal freedom. Spurred on by an almost fanatic mysticism, Turner became convinced from visions of white and black angels fighting that God intended to punish white people and that he had been selected "to carry terror and devastation" throughout the countryside. One night in 1831 following an eclipse of the sun, he and six confederates stole out and murdered Turner's master and family. Gaining some 70 recruits as they went, Turner's band eventually killed 57 white men, women, and children. Along the way, the members voiced their grievances against slavery and announced that they intended to confiscate their masters' wealth. *Nat Turner's rebellion*

The revolt lasted only 48 hours before being crushed. Turner himself eluded pursuers for over two months but finally was captured, tried, and executed. While the uprising was quickly put down, it left white southerners throughout the region with a haunting uneasiness. Turner seemed a model slave, yet who could read a slave's true emotions behind the mask of obedience?

Few slaves followed Turner's violent example. But there were other, more subtle ways of resisting a master's authority. Most dramatically, they could do as Octave Johnson did and run away. With the odds stacked heavily against them, few runaways escaped safely to freedom except from the border states. More frequently, slaves fled to nearby woods or swamps to avoid punishment or protest their treatment. Some runaways stayed out only a few days; others, like Johnson, held out for months. *Day-to-day resistance*

Many slaves resisted by abusing their masters' property. They mishandled animals, broke tools and machinery, misplaced items, and worked carelessly in the fields. Olmsted observed one field gang that stopped hoeing every time the overseer turned his back. Slaves also sought to trick the master by feigning illness or injury and by hiding rocks in the cotton they picked. Slaves complained directly to the owner about an overseer's mistreatment, thereby attempting to drive a wedge between the two.

The most common form of resistance, and a persistent annoyance to slaveowners, was theft. Slaves took produce from the garden, raided the master's smokehouse, secretly slaughtered his stock, and killed his poultry. Slaves often distinguished between "stealing" from each other and merely "taking" from white masters. "Dey allus done tell us it am wrong to lie and steal," recalled Josephine Howard, a former slave in Texas, "but why did de white folks steal my mammy and her mammy? Dey lives . . . over in Africy. . . . Dat de sinfulles' stealin' dey is."

Slaves learned to outwit their masters by wearing an "impenetrable mask" around whites, one bondsman recalled. "How much of joy, of sorrow, of misery and *Slaves' hidden feelings* anguish have they hidden from their tormentors." Frederick Douglass, the most famous fugitive slave, explained that "as the master studies to keep the slave ignorant, the slave is cunning enough to make the master think he succeeds."

SLAVE CULTURE

Trapped in bondage, faced with the futility of revolt, slaves could at least forge a culture of their own. By the nineteenth century, American slaves had been separated from much of their traditional African heritage, but that did not mean they had fully accepted the dominant white culture. Instead, slaves combined strands from their African past with customs that evolved from their life in America. This slave culture was most distinct on big plantations, where the slave population was large and slaves had more opportunity to live apart from white scrutiny.

The Slave Family

Breakup of families

Maintaining a sense of family was one of the most remarkable achievements of African Americans in bondage, given the obstacles that faced them. Southern law did not recognize slave marriages as legally binding, nor did it allow slave parents complete authority over their children. Black women faced the possibility of rape by the master or overseer without legal recourse, and husbands, wives, and children had to live with the fear of being sold and separated. From 1820 to 1860 more than 2 million slaves were sold in the interstate slave trade. Perhaps 600,000 husbands and wives were separated by such sales. The chance that a slave family would be broken up—children taken from parents, brothers separated from sisters—was even greater. A slave mother whose three children had all been sold away grieved to Fredrika Bremer: "When they took from me the last little girl . . . I believed I never should have got over it! It almost broke my heart!"

Family ties in slavery

Still, family ties remained strong, as slave culture demonstrated. The marriage ceremony among slaves varied from a formal religious service to jumping over a broomstick in front of the slave community to nothing more than the master giving verbal approval. Whatever the ceremony, slaves viewed the ritual as a public affirmation of the couple's commitment to their new duties and responsibilities. Rather than adopting white norms, slaves developed their own moral code concerning sexual relations and marriage. Although young slaves often engaged in premarital sex, they were expected to choose a partner and become part of a stable family. It has been estimated that at least one in five slave women had one or more children before marriage, but most of these mothers eventually married. "The negroes had their own ideas of morality, and they held them very strictly," the daughter of a Georgia planter recalled. "They did not consider it wrong for a girl to have a child before she married, but afterwards were very strict upon anything like infidelity on her part." Black churches played a leading role in condemning adultery.

Gender roles

The traditional nuclear family of father, mother, and children was the rule, not the exception, among slaves. Within the marriage the father was viewed as the traditional head of the family; wives were to be submissive and obey their husbands. Labor in the quarters was divided according to sex. Women did the indoor work, such

Slaves who have been sold are being loaded into boxcars to be transported from Richmond to plantations farther south. As they say their final sad good-byes to family and friends, a slave trader completes his business. Once while walking with a European visitor, Mary Chesnut, an upper-class South Carolinian, passed a sidewalk slave sale. "If you can stand that," she acidly remarked, "no other Southern thing need choke you."

as cooking, washing, and sewing, and men performed outdoor chores, such as gathering firewood, hauling water, and tending the animals and garden plots. The men also hunted and fished to supplement the spare weekly rations. "My old daddy . . . caught rabbits, coons an' possums," recalled Louisa Adams of North Carolina. "He would work all day and hunt at night." (See Daily Lives, "A Slave's Daily Bread," pages 436–437.)

Beyond the nuclear family, slaves developed strong kinship networks that promoted a sense of community. Aunts and uncles were expected to look after children who lost their parents through death or sale. When children were sold to a new plantation, a family in the slave quarters took them in. Thus all members of the slave society drew together in an extended network of mutual obligation.

Slave Songs and Stories

In the songs they sang, slaves expressed some of their deepest feelings about love and work and the joys and pain of life. "The songs of the slave represent the sorrows of his heart," commented Frederick Douglass. Surely there was bitterness as well as sorrow when slaves sang:

Protest and celebration

Lewis Miller of York, Pennsylvania, painted this picture of Virginia slaves dancing in 1853. Dancing and music were important components of slave culture and provided a welcome respite from work under slavery. Declared one runaway slave, "The sternest . . . master cannot frighten or whip the fun out of us."

We raise the wheat
They give us the corn
We bake the bread
They give us the crust
We sift the meal
They give us the husk
We peel the meat
They give us the skin
And that's the way
They take us in

Yet songs were also central to the celebrations held in the slave quarters: for marriages, Christmas revels, and after harvest time. And a slave on the way to the fields might sing:

Saturday night and Sunday too
Young gals on my mind.
Monday morning 'way 'fore day,
Old master's got me gwine.
Peggy does you love me now?

Folktales   Slaves expressed themselves through stories as well as song. Most often these folktales used animals as symbolic models for the predicaments in which slaves found themselves. In the best known of these, the cunning Brer Rabbit was a weak fellow who defeated larger animals like Brer Fox and Brer Bear by using his wits. Sometimes the identity of the trickster was no longer symbolic, but the slave. Because these latter stories contained more overt hostility to white people, slaves usually told them only among themselves. But the message, whether direct or symbolic, was much the same: to laugh at the master's shortcomings and teach the young how to survive in a hostile world.

Steal Away to Jesus

At the center of slave culture was religion. The Second Great Awakening, which had begun on the southern frontier (page 280), converted many slaves, most of whom joined the Methodist and Baptist churches. Slaves constituted more than a quarter of the members of both of these southern churches.

Slaveowners encouraged a certain amount of religion among slaves as an effective means of social control. Masters provided slaves with a minister (often white), set the time and place of services, and usually insisted that a white person be present. "Church was what they called it," one former slave protested, "but all that preacher talked about was for us slaves to obey our masters and not to lie and steal. Nothing about Jesus was ever said and the overseer stood there to see that the preacher talked as he wanted him to talk." In response, some slaves rejected all religion, while others continued to believe in conjuring, voodoo, and various practices derived from African religion.

Most slaves, however, sought a Christianity firmly their own, beyond the control *Slave religion* of the master. On many plantations they met secretly at night, in the quarters or at "hush harbors" in the safety of the woods, where they broke into rhythmic singing and dancing, modeled on the ring shout of African religion. Even regular services were characterized by intense enthusiasm. "The way in which we worshiped is almost indescribable," one slave preacher recalled. "The singing was accompanied by a certain ecstasy of motion, clapping of hands, tossing of heads, which would continue without cessation about half an hour. The old house partook of the ecstasy; it rang with their jubilant shouts, and shook in all its joints." In an environment where slaves, for most of the day, were prevented from expressing their deepest feelings, such meetings served as a satisfying emotional release.

Religion also provided slaves with values to guide them through their daily experiences and give them a sense of self-worth. Slaves learned that God would redeem the poor and downtrodden and raise them one day to honor and glory. Rejecting the teaching of some white ministers that slavery was punishment, slave preachers assured their congregations that they were the chosen people of God. Just as certainly, on the final Day of Judgment, masters would be punished for their sins. "This is one reason why I believe in hell," a former slave declared. "I don't believe a just God is going to take no such man as my former master into His Kingdom."

Again, song played a central role. Slaves sang religious "spirituals" at work and *Slave* at play as well as in religious services. Seemingly meek and otherworldly, the songs *spirituals* often contained a hidden element of protest. Frederick Douglass disclosed that when slaves sang longingly of "Canaan, sweet Canaan," they were thinking not only of the Bible's Promised Land but of the North and freedom. When slaves heard "Steal Away to Jesus" sung in the fields, they knew that a secret devotional meeting was scheduled that evening. Songs became one of the few ways slaves could openly express their

FOOD/DRINK/DRUGS

A Slave's Daily Bread

Once a week on most plantations, slaves lined up to receive their rations from the master. Although quantities might vary, each adult could expect to receive about a peck of cornmeal, three or four pounds of bacon or salt pork, and some molasses for sweetener. Some masters added vegetables, fruits, or sweet potatoes in season, but only on rare occasions did slaves receive wheat flour, beef, lean meat, poultry, or eggs. Milk, when available at all, was reserved for children and was usually sour.

In terms of simple calories, this ration was ample enough to sustain life. A careful modern study of the slave diet has concluded that on the eve of the Civil War, adult slaves received almost 5400 calories, which exceeds today's recommended levels of consumption. But more than 80 percent of the calories came from corn and pork. This monotonous fare of hog-and-hominy lacked several essential nutrients as well as enough protein, afflicting many slaves with diet-related diseases like pellagra and beriberi. The malnutrition was due more to ignorance than miserliness or willful neglect on the part of masters. Although slaveowners and their families enjoyed more variety in their food and better cuts of meat, they too lacked a balanced diet.

On some plantations masters left all cooking to the slaves, who would make breakfast and their noon meal before going to work in the morning, taking dinner with them to eat in the fields. At night, they came home to fix a light supper. Other masters established a plantation kitchen where cooks prepared breakfast and dinner, though supper remained the responsibility of the individual slave or family. On these plantations a noon meal was brought to the fields. In general, the quality of food preparation was better under this system because slaves were often too exhausted after work to put much time or care into cooking. Naturally enough, however, slaves preferred to fix meals according to their own taste and eat as a family in some privacy. Fanny Kemble reported that on her husband's Georgia plantation the slaves sat "on the earth or doorsteps, and ate out of their little cedar tubs or an iron pot, some few with broken iron spoons, more with pieces of wood, and all the children with their fingers." The cooking itself was done in front of a large fireplace.

Wherever their masters permitted it, slaves tended their own vegetable gardens after work or raised chickens and other animals. Not only did this practice provide eggs and other items not included in the weekly rations, it also enabled slaves to sell their surplus to the master or in town and use their earnings to buy occasional luxuries such as coffee, sugar, and tobacco. Slaves also raided the master's smokehouse, secretly slaughtered his stock and killed his

yearning for freedom, in the approved language of Christianity. While a song's lyrics might speak of an otherworldly freedom from sin in heaven, their hearts were considering a this-worldly escape from physical bondage.

Religion, then, served not only to comfort slaves after days of toil and sorrow. It

When slaves working in the fields became dizzy from the heat, they sometimes called out, "I see a monkey." "Monkey pots" like this one brought water and relief.

poultry, and stole from neighboring plantations. Richard Carruthers, a former slave, recalled, "If they didn't provision you 'nough, you just had to slip round and get a chicken."

Slaves who worked all day still had plenty of incentive to stir out at night to fish or to hunt raccoon or opossum. "The flesh of the coon is palatable," admitted Solomon Northup, a northern free black kidnapped into slavery, "but verily there is nothing in all butcherdom so delicious as a roasted 'possum." Possum was parboiled to soften it and then roasted with lard over the fire, along with sweet potatoes. Squirrel meat, though tougher, could be boiled long enough to soften it for squirrel pie served with dumplings. Rabbits, especially young ones, were tender enough to fry.

Along with such meat might come "hoe-cakes," a popular dish made by slapping cornmeal dough on the blade of a hoe and holding it over the coals. Vegetables were boiled in a pot with a bit of hog jowl, each new vegetable thrown in at the appropriate cooking time: beans first, then cabbage when the beans were half done, then squash, and finally okra. Whenever they could get them, slave cooks used spices to flavor their dishes. Some spices, such as sesame seeds, had come from Africa with the slaves. Red pepper, native to the Americas, added zing to innumerable dishes.

On holidays the master usually provided a banquet for all hands on the plantation. Slaves eagerly filled up on beef, mutton, roast pig, coffee, wheat bread, pies, and other dishes only rarely tasted. Although masters generally tried to keep whiskey away from their slaves, some slaveowners made an exception at Christmas. Feasting was one of the slaves' "principle sources of comfort," one ex-slave testified. "Only the slave who has lived all the year on his scanty allowance of meal and bacon, can appreciate such suppers."

also strengthened the sense of togetherness and common purpose and held out the promise of eventual freedom in this world and the next. The faith that "some ob dese days my time will come" was one of the most important ways that slaves coped with bondage and resisted its pressure to rob them of their self-esteem.

437

The Slave Community

Hierarchy

While slaves managed with remarkable success to preserve a sense of self-worth in a culture of their own, the hard reality of slavery made it impossible to escape fully from white control. Even the social hierarchy within the slave quarters never was entirely free from the white world. Slave preachers, conjurers, and herb doctors held status that no white conferred, but the prestige of a slave driver rested ultimately on the authority of the white master. Similarly, skilled slaves and house servants often felt superior to other slaves, an attitude masters consciously promoted. "We house slaves thought we was better'n the others what worked in the field," one personal servant confessed. Light-skinned slaves sometimes deemed their color a badge of superiority. Fanny Kemble recorded that one woman begged to be relieved of field labor, which she considered degrading, "on *'account of her color.'*"

The daughter of a driver who had been educated by her mistress, Lucy Skipworth was a member of the slave elite. At Hopewell plantation in Alabama, she was in full charge of the main residence during her master's frequent absences. She ran a plantation school (despite white opposition) and, as a devout Baptist, supervised her fellow slaves' religious life. Eager for her master's approval, Skipworth on several occasions reported slave disobedience, which temporarily estranged her from the slave community. Yet in the end she was always welcomed back. While Skipworth never rebelled or apparently ever considered running away, she was far from submissive. She defied white authority, protected her family, and used her influence to get rid of an overseer the slaves disliked. Like many house servants, she lived between two worlds—her master's and the slave quarters—and was never entirely comfortable in either.

But the realities of slavery and white racism inevitably drove black people closer together in a common bond and forced them to depend on each other to survive. New slaves on a plantation were immediately instructed in the mysteries of the quarters, including such vital matters as the best strategies for avoiding punishment. Walled in from the individualistic white society beyond, slaves out of necessity created a community of their own.

COUNTERPOINT

The role of religion in the lives of slaves

Modern studies of slavery recognize that religion was one of the most crucial components of slave culture. Historians have disagreed, however, over the role those religious beliefs played. Some historians have argued that slaves took the evangelical religion of white Protestants and adapted it, creating in essense a new version of Christianity that strongly reflected their African heritage. The role of communal singing and dancing in slave services represented a continuation of African forms. The African view that gods spoke to individuals by possessing their spirit was akin to the conversion experience in evangelical churches, and the African concept of a creator god was easily adapted to the Christian concept of an all-powerful deity. This interpretation of slave religion places primary emphasis on independent black services in the quarters and secret ones held in the woods. In this view, religion helped create a distinctive African American culture, nurtured racial self-esteem, and weakened the forces of accommodation within slavery.

Other historians emphasize that the religious experiences of most enslaved African Americans occurred within the regular white-controlled churches of the South. It has been estimated that one million slaves were included in the southern churches before the Civil War. Black worshipers were especially numerous in the Methodist and Baptist churches; indeed, in some areas, slaves were a majority in local congregations. As a result, most slaves worshiped together with their masters rather than in separate services. At one point during the regular service ministers delivered a special message to the slaves who were present, but they also heard the same sermon as whites, with its emphasis on faith and salvation. According to this view, secret services in the quarters and elsewhere were an extension of regular worship, not an alternative. Thus they did not provide a fundamentally different message. "The church," one historian concludes, "was the single most important institution in the 'Americanization' of the bondsman."

Free Black Southerners

Of the 4 million African Americans living in the South in 1860, only 260,000—about 7 percent—were free. More than 85 percent of them lived in the Upper South, with almost 200,000 in Maryland, Virginia, and North Carolina alone. Free black south-

This painting shows a free African American market woman in Baltimore performing her daily tasks. Urban blacks in the South, including slaves, enjoyed greater personal freedom and access to more social activities but had only limited economic opportunity.

erners were also much more urban than the southern white and slave populations. In 1860 almost a third of the free African Americans in the Upper South, and more than half in the Lower South, lived in towns and cities. As a rule, free African Americans were more literate than slaves, and they were disproportionately female and much more likely to be of mixed ancestry. Only 10 percent of all slaves were classified as mulattoes, compared to four times as many free African Americans.

Lives of free blacks

Still, most free black southerners lived in rural areas, although usually not near plantations. A majority eked out a living farming or in low-paying unskilled jobs, but some did well enough to own slaves themselves. In 1830 about 3600 did, although commonly their "property" was their own wives or children, purchased because they could not be emancipated under state laws. A few, however, were full-blown slave-owners.

Tightening control

Following Nat Turner's rebellion of 1831, southern legislatures increased the restrictions on free African Americans. Most states in the Deep South prohibited residents from freeing slaves in their wills, and some required any emancipated slaves to leave the state. All states forbade the entry of free African Americans, and those already living there were subject to ever greater restrictions. They had to carry their free papers, could not assemble when they wished, were subject to a curfew, often had to post a bond and be licensed to work, and could not vote, hold office, or testify in court against white people.

Lighter-skinned black southerners who were free, like their counterparts in the North, tended to set themselves apart from darker-skinned African Americans, free or slave. In such cities as Charleston and New Orleans, they established separate social and cultural organizations and maintained their own exclusive social network. Economically dependent on white customers, they developed close connections with white southerners yet were never accepted in the white world. Free African Americans occupied an uncertain position in southern society, well above black slaves but distinctly beneath even poorer white southerners. They were victims of a society that had no place for them.

SOUTHERN SOCIETY AND THE DEFENSE OF SLAVERY

From wealthy planters to yeoman farmers, from free black slaveholders to white mountaineers, from cotton field hands to urban craftworkers, the South was a remarkably diverse region. Yet it was united by its dependence on staple crops and above all by the institution of slavery. As the South's economy became more and more dependent on slave-produced staples, slavery became more central to the life of the South, to its culture and its identity.

The Virginia Debate of 1832

At the time of the Revolution, the leading critics of slavery had been southerners—Jefferson, Washington, Madison, and Patrick Henry among them. But beginning in the 1820s, in the wake of the controversy over admitting Missouri as a slave state (page 339), southern leaders became less apologetic about slavery and more aggressive in defending it. The turning point occurred in the early 1830s, when the South found itself increasingly under attack. It was in 1831 that William Lloyd Garrison began publishing his abolitionist newspaper, *The Liberator.* In that year too Nat Turner launched his revolt, which frightened so many white southerners.

In response to the Turner insurrection, a number of Virginia's western counties, where there were few slaves, petitioned the legislature to adopt a program for gradual emancipation. Between January 16 and 25, 1832, the House of Delegates engaged in a remarkable debate over the merits of slavery. In the end, however, the legislature refused, by a vote of 73 to 58, to consider legislation to end slavery.

The Virginia debate represented the last significant attempt of white southerners to take action against the peculiar institution. In its aftermath, most felt that the subject was no longer open to debate. Instead, during the 1830s and 1840s, southern leaders defended slavery as a positive good, not just for white people but for black people as well. As John C. Calhoun proclaimed in 1837, "I hold that in the present state of civilization, where two races . . . distinguished by color and other physical differences, as well as intellectual, are brought together, the relation now existing in the slaveholding states between the two is, instead of an evil, a good—a positive good." *Significance of the Virginia debate*

The Proslavery Argument

Politicians like Calhoun were not alone. White southern leaders justified slavery in a variety of ways. Ministers argued that under the law of Moses, Jews were authorized to enslave heathens and emphasized that none of the Biblical prophets or Christ himself had ever condemned slavery. They traced slavery's origins to the curse of Canaan, *Religious arguments*

This 1841 proslavery cartoon contrasts the treatment of American slaves, who are allegedly well fed, well clothed, and well cared for, with the plight of English factory workers. Defenders of slavery made the same comparisons to northern laborers.

in which Canaan (the allegedly black grandson of Noah) was made a servant in punishment for his father's sin.

Social and racial arguments

Defenders of the institution also pointed out that classical Greece and Rome depended on slavery. They even cited John Locke, that giant of the Enlightenment, who had recognized slavery in the constitution he drafted for the colony of Carolina. African Americans belonged to an intellectually and emotionally inferior race, slavery's defenders argued, and therefore lacked the ability to care for themselves and required white guardianship. "Providence has placed [the black man] in our hands for his good, and has paid us from his labor for our guardianship," contended James Henry Hammond, an eminent planter and senator from South Carolina whose "guardianship" of several hundred slaves had netted him a tidy fortune.

Proslavery writers sometimes argued that slaves in the South lived better than factory workers in the North. Masters cared for slaves for life, whereas northern workers had no claim on their employer when they were unemployed, old, or no longer able to work. In advancing this argument, white southerners exaggerated the material comforts of slavery and minimized the average worker's standard of living—to say nothing, of course, about the incalculable psychological value of freedom. Still, to many white southerners, slavery seemed a more humane system of labor relations.

Defenders of slavery did not really expect to influence public opinion in the North. Their target was more often slaveowners themselves. As Duff Green, a southern editor and one of Calhoun's advisers, explained, "We must satisfy the consciences, we must allay the fears of our own people. We must satisfy them that slavery is of itself right—that it is not a sin against God—that it is not an evil, moral or political. In this way only," he went on, "can we prepare our own people to defend their institutions."

Closing Ranks

Not all white southerners could quell their doubts. To take only one example, Robert Scott, an antislavery advocate in the Virginia debate of 1832, was publicly calling slavery "an institution reprobated by the world" as late as 1849. Still, a striking change in southern opinion seems to have occurred in the three decades before the Civil War. Outside the border states, few white southerners after 1840 would admit even in private that slavery was wrong. Those who continued to oppose slavery found themselves harassed, assaulted, and driven into exile. Southern mobs destroyed the presses of antislavery papers and threatened the editors into either keeping silent or leaving the state. Southern mails were forcibly closed to abolitionist propaganda, and defenders of the South's institutions carefully scrutinized textbooks and faculty members in southern schools. Southerners like James Birney and Sarah and Angelina Grimké had to go to the free states to continue their fight against slavery.

Increasingly, too, the debate over slavery spread to the national political arena. Before 1836 Andrew Jackson's enormous popularity in the South blocked the formation of a competitive two-party system there. The rise of the abolitionist movement in the 1830s, however, left many southerners uneasy, and when the Democrats nominated the northerner Martin Van Buren in 1836, southern Whigs seized on the issue of the security of slavery and charged that Van Buren could not be counted on to meet the abolitionist threat. The Whigs made impressive gains in the South in 1836, carrying several states and significantly narrowing the margin between the two parties.

In later presidential elections, both parties in the South attacked the opposing party through its northern supporters as unreliable on slavery. This tactic was less successful in state elections, however, since both parties were led by slaveholders and were committed to protecting slavery. In addition, the depression that began in 1837 focused the attention of southern voters on economic matters. Southern Whigs appealed to the commercially oriented members of society: planters, business leaders and merchants, bankers, professionals, residents of cities and the plantation black belts. Democrats won their share of slaveowners, but the party's greatest support came from small independent farmers in more isolated regions. As in the North, class and occupation were less important than one's economic and moral outlook. Southern voters most comfortable with the market and the changes it brought gravitated toward the Whig party. On the other hand, those farmers who feared the loss of personal independence that banks and commercial development brought with them tended to support the Democratic party.

Economics and party affiliation

During the Jacksonian era, most southern political battles did not revolve around slavery. Even so, southern politicians in both parties had to be careful to avoid the stigma of antislavery, since they were under mounting pressure from John Calhoun and his followers. Frustrated in his presidential hopes by the nullification crisis in 1832–1833, Calhoun sought to unite the South behind his leadership by agitating the slavery issue, introducing inflammatory resolutions in Congress upholding slavery, seizing on the abolitionist mailing campaign to demand censorship of the mails, and leaping to his feet to insist on a gag rule to block antislavery petitions. During the 1830s and early 1840s, few southern politicians followed his lead, but they did become extremely careful about being in the least critical of slavery or southern institutions. They knew quite well that even if their constituents were not as fanatical as Calhoun, southern voters overwhelmingly supported slavery.

Sections and the Nation

Viewing the events of the 1830s and 1840s with the benefit of hindsight, one cannot help but concentrate on the Civil War looming in the distance and focus on the differences dividing the North and the South. Yet free white northerners and southerners had much in common as Americans.

The largest group in both sections was composed of independent farmers who cultivated their own land with their own labor and were devoted to the principles of personal independence and social egalitarianism. Although southern society was more aristocratic in tone, both sections were driven forcefully by the quest for material wealth. The Texas Red River planter for whom time was money did not take a backseat to the Yankee clockmaker Chauncey Jerome in the scramble for success and status. White Americans in both sections aspired to rise in society, and they looked to the expanding opportunities of the market to help them do so. Moreover, both northerners and southerners linked geographic mobility to opportunity, and both pushed westward in search of better land and a new start.

Forces of national unity

Many Americans, North and South, also adhered to the teachings of evangelical Protestantism. Southern churches were less open to social reform, primarily because of its association with abolitionism, and southern churches, unlike most in the North, defended slavery as a Christian institution. Eventually both the Methodist and the Baptist churches split into separate northern and southern organizations over this issue, but their attitudes on other matters often coincided.

Finally, white northerners and southerners shared a belief in democracy and white equality. To be sure, the existence of the planter class created greater tensions in southern society between democracy and aristocracy. But southern as well as northern states embraced the democratic reforms of the 1820s and 1830s, and the electorate in both sections favored giving all white males the vote and making public officeholders responsible to the people. Southerners insisted that the equality proclaimed in the Declaration of Independence applied only to white Americans (and really only to white males), but the vast majority of northerners in practice took no exception to this attitude. Both sections agreed on the necessity of safeguarding equality of opportunity rather than promoting equality of wealth.

With so much in common, it was not inevitable that the two sections would come to blows. Certainly, before 1840 few politicians believed that the differences between the two sections were decisive. It was only in the mid-1840s, when the United States embarked on a new program of westward expansion, that the slavery issue began to loom ominously in American life and Americans began to question whether the Union could permanently endure, half slave and half free.

CHAPTER SUMMARY

The Old South was a complex society in which whites and blacks, slaveholders and yeoman farmers, and men and women lived together. In the years before the Civil War the South developed a regional identity based on a culture that was in some ways distinct. Southerners placed heavy emphasis on agriculture and upheld the superiority of the rural way of life. Southern commercial agriculture produced several staple crops for sale in northern and European markets, of which cotton was the most important. As southern agriculture expanded into the fresh lands of the Deep South, the slave population moved steadily westward and southward, and the Upper South became more diversified agriculturally. The prosperity of southern agriculture helped keep the South overwhelmingly rural. Few cities and towns developed, and southern wealth depended heavily on agricultural exports.

Slavery played a major role in shaping the class structure of the Old South. Ownership of slaves brought privilege and status, and the largest slaveowners were extraordinarily wealthy, although planters on the older eastern seaboard enjoyed a more refined lifestyle than those on the new cotton frontier. Most slaveowners, however, owned only a few slaves, and the majority of southern whites were non-slave-owning yeoman farmers, who owned their own farm and worked it with their family's labor. At the bottom of the white class structure were the poor whites. Slavery hurt nonslaveholding whites economically, but class tensions were muted in the Old South because of racial fears.

The institution of slavery was both a labor system and a system of regulating relations between the races. Yet slaves were far from passive victims. Slaves resisted bondage in many ways, ranging from the subtle to the overt, although slave revolts, the most spectacular form of resistance, were rare. Excluded from white society, slaves developed their own culture, which helped them cope with the pressures of bondage. The family, religion, and songs were important parts of slave culture. Out of their shared experiences, slaves created a community based on a common identity and mutual values.

Slavery increasingly set the South apart from the rest of the nation. As slavery came under mounting attack, white southerners rallied to protect their peculiar institution and developed a set of arguments defending slavery as a positive good. The slavery issue also shaped and influenced southern politics, and both parties in the South strongly defended the institution and southern rights. In the years before 1860 there were still important similarities between the North and the South, but some significant differences had emerged.

SIGNIFICANT EVENTS

1800	Gabriel's Rebellion
1815–1860	Spread of the cotton kingdom
1822	Denmark Vesey conspiracy
1830–1840	Proslavery argument developed
1830–1860	Agricultural reform movement in Upper South
1831	Nat Turner's rebellion
1832	Virginia debate on slavery
1844	Methodist church divides into northern and southern organizations
1845	Baptist church divides

ADDITIONAL READING

Few topics have received more historical attention than slavery and the Old South. The economics of slavery, the values of slaveowners, the nature of the region's social structure, and the content of slave culture are all matters of great controversy. The reports of Frederick Law Olmsted, conveniently available in Lawrence Powell, ed., *The Cotton Kingdom* (1984), provide a fascinating introduction to antebellum southern society. James Oakes, *Slavery and Freedom* (1990) is a good synthesis of the contradictions between slavery and freedom in southern life.

William W. Freehling, *The Road to Disunion* (1990) is a wide-ranging examination of the South to 1854 that emphasizes the diversity and divisions in southern society. James Oakes, *The Ruling Race* (1982) is a controversial study of slaveowners that emphasizes their capitalist orientation. While old, Frank Owsley's *Plain Folk of the Old South* (1949) has not been superseded on southern yeoman farmers. The lives of upper-class southern white women and their servants are analyzed in Elizabeth Fox-Genovese, *Within the Plantation Household* (1988), while Victoria E. Bynum, *Unruly Women* (1992) deals with white and black women of lower status. The impact of geographic mobility on southern society can be studied in Joan E. Cashin, *A Family Venture* (1991). The best exploration of slavery as a labor system still remains Kenneth M. Stampp, *The Peculiar Institution* (1956), but the most perceptive treatment of slave culture is Eugene D. Genovese, *Roll, Jordon, Roll* (1974). Charles Joyner, *Down by the Riverside* (1984) is a very sensitive recreation of slave culture in the rice districts. Ira Berlin, *Slaves without Masters* (1974) is an excellent account of southern free blacks. Drew Faust, *A Sacred Circle* (1977) is a stimulating discussion of proslavery thought, while William J. Cooper, Jr., *The Politics of Slavery* (1978) stresses the role of the slavery issue in southern politics. For a fuller list of readings, see the Bibliography.

14

Western Expansion and the Rise of the Slavery Issue

At first the Crows, Arapahos, and other Indians of the Great Plains paid little attention to the new people moving out from the forests far to the east. After all, for as long as they could remember, nations like the Crow had called the plains their own. But the new arrivals were not to be taken lightly. Armed with superior weapons and bringing a great many women and children, their appetite for land seemed unlimited. They attacked the villages of the Plains Indians, ruthlessly massacred women and children, and forced defeated tribes to live on reservations and serve their economic interests. In little more than a century and a half—from the first days when only a handful of their hunters and trappers had come into the land—they had become the masters of the plains.

The invaders who established this political and military dominance were *not* the strange "white men," who also came from the forest. During the 1830s and early 1840s, whites were still few in number. The more dangerous people—the ones who truly worried the Plains tribes—were the Sioux.

Cultural interaction

Westward expansion is usually told as a one-dimensional tale, centering on the wagon trains pressing on toward the Pacific. But frontiers, after all, are the boundary lines between contrasting cultures or environments, and during the nineteenth century, those in the West were constantly shifting and adapting. Frontier lines moved not only east to west, as with the white and Sioux migrations, but also south to north, as Spanish culture diffused, and west to east, as Asian immigrants came to California. Furthermore, frontiers marked not only human but also animal boundaries. Horses, cattle, and pigs, all of which had been imported from Europe, moved across the continent, usually in advance of European settlers. Often they transformed the way Indian peoples lived. Frontiers could also be technological, as in the case of trade goods and firearms. Moreover, as we have already seen, disease moved across the continent, with disastrous consequences for natives who had not acquired immunity to European microorganisms.

Three frontiers altered the lives of the Sioux: those of the horse, the gun, and disease. The horse frontier spread ahead of white settlement from the southwest, where horses had first been imported by the Spanish. On the other hand, the Spanish, unlike English and French traders, refused to sell firearms to Indians, so the gun frontier moved in the opposite direction, from northeast to southwest. The two

The cultures of the Plains Indians depended on the large buffalo herds that roamed the plains. Here two Plains Indians mounted on horses hunt buffalo with bows and arrows.

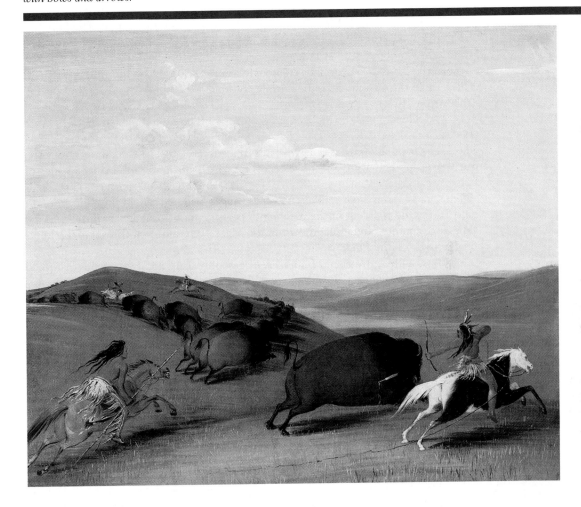

waves met and crossed along the upper Missouri during the first half of the eighteenth century. For the tribes that possessed them, horses provided greater mobility, both for hunting bison and for fighting. Guns, too, conferred obvious advantages, and the arrival of these new elements inaugurated an extremely unsettled era for Plains Indian cultures.

The Sioux were first lured from the forest onto the Minnesota prairie during the early 1700s to hunt beaver, whose pelts could be exchanged with white traders for manufactured goods. Having obtained guns in exchange for furs, the Sioux drove the Omahas, Otos, Cheyennes, and Missouris (who had not yet acquired guns) south and west. But by the 1770s their advantage in guns had disappeared, and any farther advance was blocked by powerful tribes like the Mandans and Arikaras. These peoples were primarily horticultural, raising corn, beans, and squash and living in well-forti-fied towns. They also owned more horses than the Sioux, which made it easier for them to resist attacks.

But the third frontier, disease, threw the balance of power toward the Sioux after 1779. European traders brought smallpox with them onto the prairie. The horticul-tural tribes were hit especially hard because they lived in densely populated villages, where the epidemic spread more easily. The Sioux embarked on a second wave of westward expansion in the late eighteenth century, so that by the time Lewis and Clark came through in 1804, they firmly controlled the upper Missouri as far as the Yellowstone River.

The Sioux's nomadic life, centered on the buffalo hunt, enabled them to avoid the worst ravages of disease, especially the smallpox epidemic of 1837, which reduced the plains population by as much as half. Indeed, the Sioux became the largest tribe on the plains and were the only one whose high birthrate approximated that of whites. From an estimated 5000 in 1804, they grew to 25,000 in the 1850s. Their numbers increased Sioux military power as well as the need for new hunting grounds, and during the first half of the nineteenth century, they pushed even farther up the Missouri, conquered the plains west of the Black Hills, and won control of the hunt-ing grounds on the Platte River.

These shifting frontiers of animals, disease, firearms, and trade goods disrupted the political and cultural life of the Great Plains. And as white Americans moved west-ward, their own frontier lines produced similar disruptions, not only between white settlers and Indians but also between Anglo-American and Hispanic cultures.

Ironically, perhaps the greatest instability created by the moving frontiers oc-curred in established American society. As the political system of the United States struggled to incorporate territories, the North and South engaged in a fierce debate over whether the new lands should become slave or free. Just as the Sioux's cultural identity was brought into question by the moving frontier, so too was the identity of the American Republic.

MANIFEST (AND NOT SO MANIFEST) DESTINIES

"Make way . . . for the young American Buffalo—he has not yet got land enough," roared one American politician in 1844. In the space of a few years, the United States acquired Texas, California, the lower half of the Oregon Territory, and the lands be-tween the Rockies and California: nearly 1.5 million square miles in all. John L. O'Sullivan, a prominent Democratic editor in New York, struck a responsive chord when he declared that it had become the United States' "manifest destiny to over-spread the continent allotted by Providence for the free development of our yearly multiplying millions." The cry of "Manifest Destiny" soon echoed in other editorial pages and in the halls of Congress.

Manifest Destiny

The Roots of the Doctrine

Many Americans had long believed that their country had a special, even divine mis-sion, which could be traced back to the Puritans' attempt to build a "city on a hill."

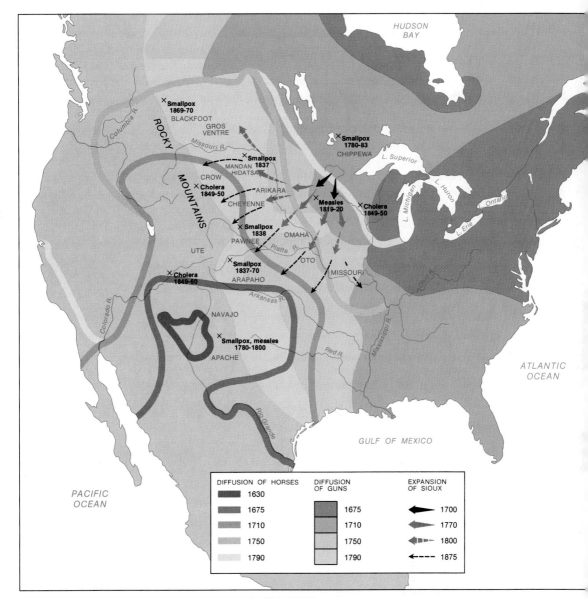

SIOUX EXPANSION AND THE HORSE AND GUN FRONTIER
In 1710 the horse and gun frontiers had not yet crossed, but by 1750 the two waves began to overlap. The Sioux pushed west during the early eighteenth century thanks to firearms; they were checked from further expansion until the 1770s, when smallpox epidemics again turned the balance in their favor.

Manifest Destiny also contained a political component, inherited from the ideology of the Revolution. In the mid-nineteenth century, Americans spoke of extending democracy, with widespread suffrage among white males, no king or aristocracy, and no established church, "over the whole North American continent."

Americans believed that their social and economic system, too, should spread around the globe. They pointed to its broad ownership of land, individualism, and free play of economic opportunity as superior features of American life. Of course, Manifest Destiny had its self-interested side. American business interests recognized the value of the fine harbors along the Pacific Coast, which promised a lucrative trade with Asia, and they hoped to make them American.

Finally, underlying the doctrine of Manifest Destiny was a widespread racism. The same belief in racial superiority that was used to justify Indian removal under Jackson, to uphold slavery in the South, and to excuse segregation in the North also proved handy to defend expansion westward. The United States had a duty to regenerate the backward peoples of America, declared politicians and propagandists. Their reference was not so much to Indians—who refused to assimilate into American society—but to Mexicans, whose Christian nation had its roots in European culture. The Mexican race "must amalgamate and be lost, in the superior vigor of the Anglo-Saxon race," proclaimed O'Sullivan's *Democratic Review*, "or they must utterly perish."

Before 1845 most Americans assumed that expansion would be achieved peace-

With the Star of Empire blazing from her forehead, the Spirit of Progress dominates John Gast's painting *Manifest Destiny*. Indians and wild animals retreat in the face of the advance of progress, as white settlers and farmers, railroads and other forms of transportation, telegraph lines, schools symbolized by a book, and, in the distance, cities follow. In reality, the movement of the frontier was hardly one-dimensional, as Hispanic, Indian, Asian, and white cultures clashed.

fully. American settlement would spread westward, and when the time was right, neighboring provinces, like ripe fruit, would fall naturally into American hands. Texas, New Mexico, Oregon, and California—areas that were sparsely populated and weakly defended—dominated the American expansionist imagination. With time, Americans became less willing to wait patiently for the fruit to fall.

The Mexican Borderlands

The heart of Spain's American empire was Mexico City, where spacious boulevards spread out through the center of the city and the University of Mexico, the oldest university in North America, had been accepting students since 1553, a full 85 years longer than Harvard. From the Mexican point of view, the frontier was 1000 miles to the north, a four-week journey to Texas, another two weeks to New Mexico, and three months by land and sea to the missions of California. Being so isolated, these provinces developed largely free from supervision.

California's settlements were anchored by four coastal *presidios,* or forts, at San Diego, Santa Barbara, Monterey, and San Francisco. Between them lay 21 Catholic missions run by a handful of Franciscans (there were only 36 in 1821). The missions controlled enormous tracts of land on which grazed gigantic herds of cattle, sheep, and horses. The animals and irrigated fields were tended by about 20,000 Indians, who worked for all practical purposes as slaves.

California society

Although most Indians worked both on Spanish missions and on *ranchos* in conditions of near slavery, Indians were encouraged to adopt Spanish religion and customs. This Indian choir at Mission San Buenaventura sang in the mass. The Indians often made their own instruments, including flutes, violins, drums, guitars, and triangles.

When Mexico won its independence from Spain in 1821, California at first was little affected. But in 1833 the Mexican Congress freed the Indians of California and stripped the Catholic church of its lands. These were turned over to Mexican cattle ranchers, usually in massive grants of 50,000 acres or more. The new *rancheros* ruled their estates much like great planters of the Old South. Labor was provided by Indians, who once again were forced to work for little more than room and board. Indeed, the mortality rate of Indian workers was twice that of southern slaves and four times that of the Mexican Californians. At this time the Mexican population of California was approximately 4000. During the 1820s and 1830s Yankee traders set up shop in California in order to buy cattle hides for the growing shoe industry at Lynn and elsewhere. Still, in 1845 the American population in California amounted to only 700.

New Mexico   Spanish settlement of New Mexico was more dense: the province had about 44,000 inhabitants in 1827. But like California, its society was dominated by *ranchero* families who grazed large herds of sheep along the upper Rio Grande valley between El Paso and Taos. A few individuals controlled most of the wealth, while their workers eked out a meager living. Mining of copper and gold was also important, and here, too, the profits enriched a small upper class. Spain had long outlawed any commerce with Americans, but after Mexico declared its independence in 1821, yearly caravans from the United States began making the long journey along the Santa Fe Trail. While this trade flourished over the next two decades, developments in the third Mexican borderland, neighboring Texas, worsened relations between Mexico and the United States.

The Texas Revolution

American   At first, the new government in Mexico encouraged American immigration to Texas,
immigration   where only about 3000 Mexicans, mostly ranchers, lived. In 1821 Moses Austin, an
to Texas   American, received a grant from the Spanish government to establish a colony. After his death, his son Stephen took over the project, laying out the little town of San Felipe de Austin along the Brazos River and offering large grants of land at almost no cost. By 1824 the colony's population exceeded 2000. Stephen Austin was only the first of a new wave of American land agents, or *empresarios,* who obtained permission from Mexican authorities to settle families in Texas. Ninety percent of the new arrivals came from the South. Some, intending to grow cotton, brought slaves.

Cultural   Tensions between Mexicans and American immigrants grew with the Texas
conflict   economy. Most settlers from the States were Protestant. Although the Mexican government did not enforce its law that all citizens become Catholic, it barred Protestant churches. In 1829 Mexico abolished slavery, then looked the other way when Texas slaveholders evaded the law. In the 1830s the Mexican government began to have second thoughts about American settlement and passed laws prohibiting any new immigration. But Texans were most disturbed because they had little say in their government, whose legislature lay about 700 miles to the south.

For a time the Mexican authorities enforced these policies only erratically and in 1833 allowed American immigration to resume. But the flood of new settlers only made the situation worse. By middecade the American white population of 30,000 was nearly 10 times the number of Mexicans in the territory. Mexico also seemed determined to enforce the abolition of slavery. Even more disturbing to the American

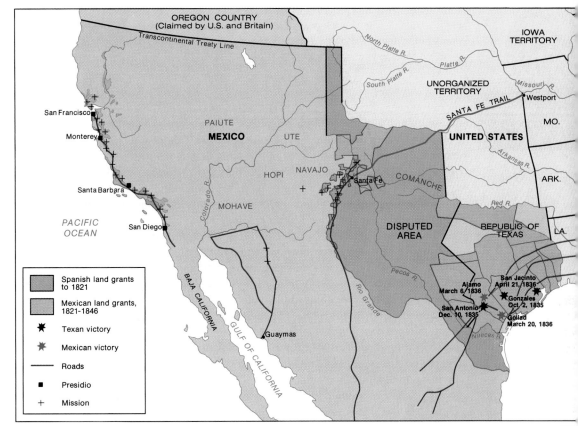

THE MEXICAN BORDERLANDS

newcomers, in 1834 General Antonio Lopez de Santa Anna dissolved the Mexican Congress and proclaimed himself dictator. When Santa Anna led a military expedition north to enforce his new regime, a ragtag Texas army drove back the advance party and then captured Mexican troops in nearby San Antonio. A full-scale revolution was under way.

The Texas Republic

As Santa Anna massed his forces, a provisional government on March 2, 1836, proclaimed Texan independence. The constitution of the new Republic of Texas borrowed heavily from the U.S. Constitution, except that it explicitly prohibited the new Texas Congress from interfering with slavery. Meanwhile, Santa Anna's troops overran a Texan garrison at an old mission in San Antonio, known as the Alamo, and killed all of its 187 defenders. The Mexicans, however, paid dearly for the victory, losing more than 1500 men. The massacre of another force at Goliad after it surrendered further inflamed American resistance.

But anger was one thing; organized resistance was another. The commander of the Texas forces was Sam Houston, a former governor of Tennessee. Of striking

Sam Houston, the first president of the Texas Republic, once set tongues wagging by appearing at a ball in a suit of black velvet lined with white satin and sporting a large hat trailing plumes of feathers. This daguerreotype, taken about 1850, shows the aging lion's firm determination. (Courtesy George Eastman House.)

physique and something of an eccentric, Houston had a flair for wearing colorful clothing to attract attention. His political career in Tennessee might have continued, except that the failure of his marriage led him to resign abruptly as governor and go live with the Indians. Eventually he made his way to Texas, where his intellectual ability and unexcelled talent as a stump speaker propelled him to the forefront of the independence movement. Steadily retreating eastward, Houston adeptly forged his ragged army into a disciplined fighting force.

By late April Houston was ready to fight. Reinforced by eager volunteers from the United States, Houston's army surprised the Mexican army camped along the San Jacinto River. With the first Mexican volley rattling overhead, the Texans charged, shouting "Remember the Alamo!" In only 15 minutes they overwhelmed the Mexicans (who had been enjoying an afternoon siesta) and captured Santa Anna.

Threatened with execution, the Mexican commander signed treaties recognizing Texan independence and establishing the Rio Grande as the southern boundary of the Texas Republic. The Mexican Congress (which had been reestablished in 1835) repudiated this agreement and launched several unsuccessful invasions into Texas. In the meantime, Houston assumed office in October 1836 as the first president of the new republic, determined to bring Texas into the Union as quickly as possible.

As an old Tennessee crony of Andrew Jackson, Houston assumed that the United States would quickly annex such a rich and inviting territory. But Jackson worried that any such move would revive sectional tensions and hurt Martin Van Buren's chances in the 1836 presidential election. Only on his last day in office did he extend formal diplomatic recognition to the Texas Republic. Van Buren, distracted by the economic panic that broke out shortly after he entered office, took no action during his term.

Texan independence   Rebuffed, Texans decided to go their own way. In the 10 years following independence, the Lone Star Republic attracted more than 100,000 immigrants by offering free land to settlers. Mexico, however, refused to recognize Texan independence, and the vast majority of its citizens still wished to join the United States, where most of them, after all, had been born. There matters stood when the Whigs and William Henry Harrison won the presidency in 1840.

THE TREK WEST

As thousands of Americans were moving into Texas, a much smaller trickle headed toward the Oregon country. Since 1818 the United States and Great Britain had occupied that territory jointly, as far north as latitude 54°40′. Although white settlement remained sparse, by 1836 American settlers outnumbered the British in the Willamette valley.

Pushed by the Panic of 1837 and six years of depression and pulled by tales of Oregon's lush, fertile valleys and the healthy, frost-free climate along California's Sacramento River, many American farmers struck out for the West Coast. Missouri was "cleaned" out of money, worried farmer Daniel Waldo, and his wife was even more adamant about heading west: "If you want to stay here another summer and shake your liver out with the fever and ague, you can do it," she announced to her husband, "but in the spring I am going to take the children and go to Oregon, Indians or no Indians." The wagon trains began rolling west.

The Overland Trail

Only a few hundred emigrants reached the West in 1841 and 1842, but in 1843 more than 800 followed the Overland Trail across the mountains to Oregon. From then on, they came by the thousands. Every spring brought a new rush of families to Independence or later to St. Joseph, Missouri, or to Council Bluffs, Iowa, where they waited for the spring rains to end and the trails to become passable. The migration was primarily a family enterprise, and many couples had only recently married. Most adults were between 20 and 50, since the hard journey discouraged the elderly. Furthermore, a family of four needed about $600 to outfit its journey, an amount that excluded the poor.

Migration west

Caravans of 20 to 30 wagons were not uncommon the first few years, but after 1845 parties traveled in smaller trains of 8 to 10 wagons. Large companies used up the grass quickly, disagreements were more likely, and breakdowns (and hence halts) were more frequent. The trip itself lasted about 6 months, since the wagons normally covered only 15 miles a day, and the weather, repairs, deaths, and other eventualities necessitated occasional halts.

Women on the Overland Trail

The journey west placed a special strain on women, for the rugged life along the trail disrupted their traditional sense of the home. Few wives were as eager as Dan Waldo's to undertake the journey. "Poor Ma said only this morning, 'Oh I wish we never had started,'" one daughter reported, "and she looks so sorrowful and dejected." In one study of Oregon-bound parties, three-fourths of the women did not want to make the move.

At first, parties divided work by gender, as had been done back home. Women cooked, washed, sewed, and took care of the children, while men drove the wagons, cared for the stock, stood guard, and did the heavy labor. Necessity placed new demands on women, however, and eventually altered their roles. Within a few weeks, they found themselves helping to repair wagons and construct bridges. When men became exhausted, sick, or injured, women stood guard and drove the oxen. The change in work assignments proceeded only in one direction, however, for few men undertook "women's work."

Breakdown of women's traditional role

The extra labor did not bring women new authority or power within the family. Nor, by and large, did they seek it. Women resisted efforts to blur the division between male and female work and struggled to preserve their traditional role and image. Quarrels over work assignments often brought into the open long-simmering family tensions. One woman reported that there was "not a little fighting" in their

TIME AND TRAVEL

Seeing the Elephant on the Overland Trail

In an era when traveling circuses proved a welcome though rare attraction, Americans used the expression "I have seen the elephant" to indicate they had gotten all—or considerably more—than they had bargained for. To the quarter of a million men and women who migrated overland to the Pacific coast, "seeing the elephant" meant ceasing to be a greenhorn by overcoming hardship and succeeding. The greeting "Have you seen the elephant?" became the unofficial password of the Overland Trail.

Some walked, rode horseback, or accompanied mule pack trains, but the overwhelming majority of emigrants traveled in wagons. Wagons could haul more pounds per animal, did not have to be packed each day, could carry the sick and injured, and could be arranged in a defensive circle at night. Most often, emigrants modified a common farm wagon, about 10 feet long. The wooden wagon bed, made of seasoned hardwood to withstand extreme heat, cold, and moisture, was arched over by cloth or waterproofed canvas that could be closed at each end. Many owners adorned their wagon covers with personal information and slogans or decorated them with paintings and pictures of animals (the elephant was a popular choice) so they would stand out in the crowd.

Pulled usually by four to six oxen, one wagon could carry provisions and gear for a family of four. Most farm families were larger, however, and took at least one additional wagon. Packed within was a supply of bacon, breadstuffs (mostly flour), and coffee. For sleeping, families brought blankets and frequently a tent; a well-equipped wagon might have a feather bed laid over the packed possessions in the wagon. Parents normally slept there for privacy while children used the tent.

Before starting, the adult male members of a company elected their leaders. In the first years, when trains often ran to 30 wagons or more, a complex set of rules and procedures was adopted. With experience these were simplified. Still, disputes inevitably arose, and leaders were sometimes deposed midjourney. Samuel Tetherow recalled that his father, the captain of an 1845 train, "was capable as well as popular.... But if you think it's any snap to run a wagon train of 66 wagons with every man in the train having a different idea of what is the best thing to do, all I can say is that some day you ought to try it."

At first, overlanders were gripped by a spirit of adventure; this feeling soon passed, however, as the monotonous daily routine set in. Women rose before daybreak to cook breakfast and food for lunch; the men followed at around five to care for the animals; the train was off at seven with the call of a bugle. Men and older sons walked alongside

company, which was "invariably the outcome of disputes over divisions of labor." The conflicting pressures a woman might feel were well illustrated by Mary Ellen Todd, a teenaged daughter who spent hours practicing how to crack the bullwhip. "How my heart bounded," she recalled, "when I chanced to hear father say to mother, 'Do you know that Mary Ellen is beginning to crack the whip.' Then how it fell again when mother replied, 'I am afraid it isn't a very lady-like thing for a girl to do.' After this, while I felt a secret joy in being able to have a power that set things going, there was also a sense of shame over this new accomplishment."

Daily Lives

Joseph Goldsborough Bruff, who traveled the Overland Trail to California, drew this picture of a Platte River crossing.

a guard was posted, the exhausted emigrants turned in for the night.

Once the Great Plains were crossed and the Rockies loomed, mutual assistance was critical. The final third of the route lay across deserts, along twisting rivers with difficult crossings, on paths barely wide enough for a wagon. Wagons had to be double- and triple-teamed up steep grades and hoisted over canyon walls with ropes, chains, and winches. Since most wagons lacked brakes, drivers locked the wheels when going down steep slopes, dragged a weight behind, or lowered the wagon by a rope attached to a tree. At some desert crossings, a tradition developed: travelers used supplies left by earlier groups, then hauled water and grass back, after they had safely crossed, for the next party.

Improvements in the 1850s shortened the trip and reduced the hardships. Still, it required considerable courage to embark on the journey and fortitude to complete it. "To enjoy such a trip," an anonymous overlander testified, "a man must be able to endure heat like a Salamander, . . . dust like a toad, and labor like a jackass. He must learn to eat with his unwashed fingers, drink out of the same vessel with his mules, sleep on the ground when it rains, and share his blanket with vermin. . . . It is a hardship without glory." When they reached their new homes, those who traveled the Overland Trail could boast that they had, indeed, seen the elephant.

the team or herded stock in the rear. Women and children could ride in the wagon as it jolted along, but before long they walked as much as possible to conserve the animals' strength. After a noonday stop for a cold lunch, the journey resumed; by midafternoon the men seemed almost asleep as they plodded under the baking sun beside their teams. At evening camp the men attended to the animals while the women and children collected buffalo dung for fuel and hauled water. Women cooked the evening meal and afterward washed the dishes, took care of the bedding, cleaned the wagons, aired provisions, and mended clothes. After

As women strove to maintain a semblance of home on the trail, they often experienced a profound sense of loss. Trains often worked or traveled on the Sabbath, which had been ladies' day back home and an emblem of women's moral authority. Women also felt the lack of close companions to whom they could turn for comfort. One woman, whose husband separated their wagon from the train after a dispute, sadly watched the other wagons pull away: "I felt that indeed I had left all my friends to journey over the dreaded plains without one female acquaintance even for a companion—of course I wept and grieved about it but to no purpose."

Women's sense of loss

Often fatigued, their sense of moral authority eroded, and their ultimate home uncertain, women complained, as one put it, that "we had left all civilization behind us." Civilization to women meant more than law, government, and schools; it also meant their homes and domestic mission. Once settled in the West, they strove to reestablish that order.

COUNTERPOINT

Women in the West

For many years historians, caught up in the trailblazing heroics of "frontiersmen," gave little attention to women in the West. But except for the mining frontier, white migration westward was largely a family process. Yet even as historians have come to recognize that women were central to western history, they continue to disagree about the effect of the western experience on white women.

Some historians have argued that women enjoyed greater freedom and status in the West. They see western women as crucial to the family economy in a way they no longer were in the industrializing market economy of the East. Thus women's wages were higher in the West, where labor was scarce and women a minority. To a much greater extent, western schoolteachers were women; a surprising number ended up making teaching a career. Far from helpless or passive, women actively accepted frontier challenges, were economic partners with their husbands, refused to surrender their domestic mission, and took pride in their achievements. Some historians have even argued that western women's greater opportunities and more equal status explain why divorce was more common in the West and why women gained political and legal rights more quickly there.

Other historians portray the impact of the western experience quite differently. Drawing on diaries women kept on the Overland Trail, they contend that the decision to migrate was almost always made by the husband and that wives often opposed the move. Moreover, many women who made the trek westward regretted going. These historians argue that the domestic work women performed was more akin to drudgery than liberating and no different from women's work in preindustrial society. They do not see western society according women greater power, and they emphasize that western women were equally subject to male dominance. "This is the Paradise of men," Martha Hitchcock wrote home in 1851. "I wonder if a paradize for poor *Women* will ever be discovered."

Indians and the Trail Experience

Pressures on the Plains Indians

The nations whose lands were crossed by white wagon trains reacted in a number of ways to the westward tide. The Sioux, who had long been trading with whites, were among the tribes who regularly visited overlanders to trade for blankets, clothes, cows, rifles, and knives. On the other hand, white migrants took a heavy toll on the Plains Indians' way of life: the emigrant parties scared off game and reduced buffalo herds, overgrazed the grass, and depleted the supply of wood. Having petitioned unsuccessfully in 1846 for government compensation, the Sioux decided to demand payment from the wagon trains crossing their lands. Whether parties paid or not depended on the relative strength of the two groups, but whites complained bitterly of what seemed to them naked robbery.

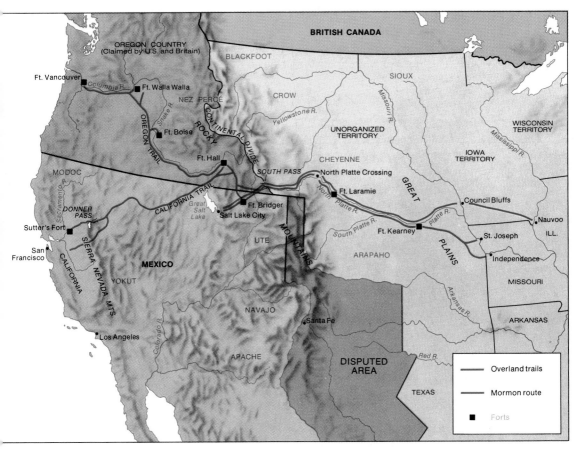

THE OVERLAND TRAIL
Beginning at several different points, the Overland Trail followed the Platte and Sweetwater rivers across the plains to South Pass, where it crossed the Continental Divide. The trail split again near Fort Hall. Between 1840 and 1860 more than a quarter of a million emigrants made the trek. Following news of the gold strikes in 1848, the flow of westward emigrants increased and shifted toward California.

Their fears aroused by sensational stories, overland parties were wary of Indians, but this menace was greatly exaggerated, especially on the plains. Few wagon trains were attacked by Indians, and less than 4 percent of deaths on the trail were caused by Indians. In truth, emigrants killed more Indians than Indians killed emigrants. For overlanders the most aggravating problem posed by Indians was theft of stock. Many companies received valuable assistance from Indians, who acted as guides, directed them to grass and water, and transported stock and wagons across rivers.

As trail congestion and conflict increased, the government constructed a string of protective forts and in 1851 summoned the Plains Indians to a conference at Fort Laramie. The U.S. government agreed to make an annual payment as compensation for the damages caused by the wagon trains but also required tribes to confine them-selves to areas north or south of a corridor through which the Overland Trail ran. Some tribes were unwilling to surrender their freedom of movement and refused to agree. The Sioux, the most powerful tribe on the plains, signed and then ignored the terms.

THE POLITICAL ORIGINS OF EXPANSION

President William Henry Harrison made the gravest mistake of his brief presidential career when he ventured out one raw spring day, bareheaded and without an over-coat, to buy groceries at the Washington markets. He caught pneumonia and died only one month after his inauguration.

Tyler becomes president

For the first time in the nation's history, a vice president succeeded to the nation's highest office upon the death of the president. John Tyler of Virginia had been a Democrat who supported states' rights so strongly that, during the nullification crisis, he was the only senator to vote against the Force Bill (page 365). After that, Jackson and the Democrats would have nothing to do with him, so Tyler joined the Whigs de-spite his strict constructionist principles. In 1840 the Whigs put him on the ticket with Old Tip in order to balance the ticket sectionally. In the rollicking 1840 campaign, the Whigs sang all too accurately: "And we'll vote for Tyler, therefore,/Without a why or wherefore."

Tyler's Texas Ploy

Tyler's courteous manner and personal warmth masked a rigid mind. Repeatedly, when Henry Clay and the Whigs in Congress passed a major bill, Tyler opposed it.

Tyler breaks with the Whigs

After Tyler twice vetoed bills to charter a new national bank, disgusted congressional Whigs formally expelled their president from the party. Most Democrats, too, avoided him as an untrustworthy "renegade."

Tyler, in short, was a man without a party. Surrounded by a group of flatterers, the president could claim almost no support except among federal officeholders, who could be fired if they did not endorse him. Still, Tyler's ambition led him to believe that he might win another four years in the White House if only he latched onto the right popular issue. Nursing their own personal and political dreams, his advisers began to whisper in his ear that that issue was the annexation of Texas.

The Texas movement

That advice came mostly from Democrats disgruntled with Martin Van Buren. Jackson's successor was, in their eyes, an ineffective leader who had stumbled through a depression and in 1840 gone down in ignominious defeat. "They mean to throw Van overboard," reported one delighted Whig, who caught wind of the plans. Meanwhile, Tyler's allies launched rumors designed to frighten southerners into pushing for annexation. Britain was ready to offer economic aid if Texas would abol-ish slavery, they claimed. (The rumor was false.) In April 1844 Tyler sent to the Senate for ratification a treaty he had secretly negotiated to bring Texas into the Union.

Van Overboard

The front runners for the Whig and Democratic presidential nominations were Clay and Van Buren. Although rivals, they were both moderates who feared the slavery issue. Apparently by prearrangement, both men issued letters opposing annexation on the grounds that it threatened the Union and would provoke war with Mexico.

As expected, the Whigs unanimously nominated Clay on a platform that ignored the expansion issue entirely. The Democrats, however, had a more difficult time. Those who opposed Van Buren persuaded the Democratic convention to adopt a rule requiring a two-thirds vote to nominate a candidate. That blocked Van Buren's nomi- *Polk's* nation. On the ninth ballot the delegates finally turned to James K. Polk of Tennessee, *nomination* who was pro-Texas. The 1844 Democratic platform called for the "reannexation" of Texas (under the claim it had been part of the Louisiana Purchase) and the "reoccupation" of Oregon, all the way to its northernmost boundary at 54°40′.

Angered by the convention's outcome, Van Buren's supporters in the Senate joined the Whigs in decisively defeating Tyler's treaty of annexation. Tyler eventually withdrew from the race as an independent candidate, but the Texas issue would not go away. Henry Clay found many southerners slipping out of his camp because he opposed annexation; backtracking, he announced that he would be glad to see Texas annexed if it could be done without war or dishonor and without threatening the Union. And in the North, a few antislavery Whigs turned to James G. Birney, running on the Liberty party ticket.

In the end, Polk squeaked through by 38,000 votes out of nearly 3 million cast. *Polk's narrow* If just half of Birney's 15,000 ballots in New York had gone to Clay, he would have *victory* carried the state and been narrowly elected president. Indignant Whigs charged that by refusing to support Clay, political abolitionists had made the annexation of Texas, and hence the addition of slave territory to the Union, inevitable. And indeed, Tyler again asked Congress to annex Texas—this time by a joint resolution, which required only a majority in both houses rather than a two-thirds vote for a treaty in the Senate. In the new atmosphere following Polk's victory, the resolution passed, and on March 3, 1845, his last day in office, Tyler invited Texas to enter the Union.

ELECTION OF 1844

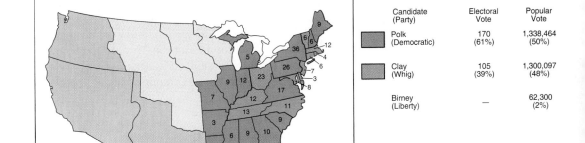

Candidate (Party)	Electoral Vote	Popular Vote
Polk (Democratic)	170 (61%)	1,338,464 (50%)
Clay (Whig)	105 (39%)	1,300,097 (48%)
Birney (Liberty)	—	62,300 (2%)

1844

To the Pacific

Polk pursued his objectives as president with a dogged determination. Humorless, calculating, and often deceitful, he was not particularly brilliant in his maneuvering. But the life of politics consumed him, he knew his mind, and he could take the political pounding. Embracing a continental vision of the United States, Polk not only endorsed Tyler's offer of annexation but looked beyond, hoping to gain the three best harbors on the Pacific: San Diego, San Francisco, and Puget Sound. That meant wresting Oregon from Britain and California from Mexico.

Compromise on Oregon   Claiming that the American title was "clear and unquestionable," the new president brushed aside any notion of continuing joint occupation of Oregon with Britain. To pressure the British, he induced Congress to give the required one-year notice terminating the joint occupation of Oregon. His blustering was reinforced by the knowledge that American settlers in Oregon outnumbered the British 5000 to 750. On the other hand, Polk hardly wanted war with a nation as powerful as Great Britain. So when the British offered, in June 1846, to divide the Oregon Territory along the 49th parallel, he readily agreed (see map, page 479). Britain retained Vancouver Island, where the Hudson's Bay Company's headquarters was located. But the arrangement gave the United States Puget Sound, which had been the president's objective all along.

The Mexican War

The Oregon settlement left Polk free to deal with Mexico. In 1845 Congress admitted Texas to the Union as a slave state, but Mexico had never formally recognized Texas's independence. It insisted, moreover, that Texas's southern boundary was the Nueces River, not the Rio Grande, 130 miles to the south, as claimed by Texas. In reality, Texas had never controlled the disputed region, the Nueces had always been Texas's boundary when it was a Mexican province, and if taken literally, the Rio Grande border incorporated New Mexican territory all the way to Santa Fe—lands still controlled by Mexico. Polk, already looking toward the Pacific, supported the Rio Grande boundary.

Disputed boundary of Texas

When Mexico broke off diplomatic relations after Texas came into the Union, Polk countered by sending American troops under General Zachary Taylor across the Nueces. At the same time, knowing that the unstable Mexican government desperately needed money, he attempted to buy territory to the Pacific. Sending John Slidell of Louisiana to Mexico as his special minister, Polk was prepared to offer $2 million in return for clear title to the Rio Grande boundary, $5 million for the remaining part of New Mexico, and up to $25 million for California. But the Mexican public overwhelmingly opposed ceding any more territory to the land-hungry Yankees, and the government refused to receive Slidell. "Depend upon it," reported Slidell, as he departed from Mexico in March 1846, "we can never get along well with them, until we have given them a good drubbing."

James K. Polk, continentalist (detail from an 1846 portrait by George Healy)

THE MEXICAN WAR

Blocked on the diplomatic front, Polk ordered Taylor, who had already crossed the Nueces with 4000 troops, to proceed south to the Rio Grande. From the Mexican standpoint, the Americans had invaded their country and occupied their territory. For his part, Polk wanted to be in position to defend the disputed region if the two countries went to war. He also hoped that the Mexican army might attack Taylor's force and make war inevitable.

On May 9 Polk had already begun work on a declaration of war, when word arrived that on April 25 Mexican forces had crossed the Rio Grande and attacked some of Taylor's troops, killing 11 Americans. The president quickly revised his war message, placing the entire blame for the war on Mexico. "Mexico has passed the boundary of the United States, has invaded our territory, and shed American blood upon American soil," he told Congress on May 11. "War exists, and notwithstanding all our efforts to avoid it, exists by the act of Mexico herself." The administration sent a bill to Congress calling for volunteers and requesting money to supply American troops.

Opposition to the War

The war with Mexico posed a dilemma for Whigs. They were convinced (correctly) that Polk had provoked the conflict in order to acquire more territory from Mexico, and many northern Whigs accused the president of seeking to extend slavery. But they remembered, too, that the Federalist party had doomed itself to extinction by opposing the War of 1812. Throughout the conflict, they therefore voted in favor of bills supplying American troops. At the same time they strenuously attacked the conduct of "Mr. Polk's War."

Sentiment for the war was strongest in the Old Southwest and most of the Old Northwest. It was much weaker in the East, where antislavery "Conscience Whigs" were prominent. "If I were a Mexican," Senator Thomas Corwin of Ohio affirmed in the Senate, "I would tell you, . . . 'we will greet you with bloody hands and welcome you to hospitable graves.'" With their party deeply divided over the issue of the expansion of slavery, Whigs opposed the acquisition of any territory from Mexico.

The Price of Victory

Even before any word of hostilities arrived in California, a group of impetuous American settlers around Sacramento launched the "Bear Flag Revolt." In June 1846 they proclaimed California an independent republic. American forces in the area soon put down any Mexican resistance, and by the following January California was safely in American hands.

Conquest of Mexico   Meanwhile, Taylor moved south from the Rio Grande and won several battles, culminating in the decisive victory at Buena Vista which ended the war in Mexico's northern provinces. Polk had gained the territory he sought to reach the Pacific; now he wanted only peace. But the Mexican people refused to support any government that sued for peace, so Polk ordered an invasion into the heart of Mexico. After an American army commanded by General Winfield Scott captured Mexico City on September 14, 1847, Mexico surrendered.

The war had cost $97 million and 13,000 American lives, mostly as a result of disease. Yet the real cost was even higher. By bringing vast new territories into the Union, the war forced the explosive slavery issue to the center of national politics and threatened to upset the balance of power between North and South. Ralph Waldo Emerson had been prophetic: "The United States will conquer Mexico," he wrote when the Mexican War began, "but it will be as the man who swallows the arsenic which brings him down in turn. Mexico will poison us."

The Rise of the Slavery Issue

When the second party system emerged during the 1820s, Martin Van Buren had championed political parties as one way to forge links between North and South that would strengthen the Union. But the Texas movement increased sectional suspicions, and President Polk did nothing to ease this problem.

Polk was a politician to his bones: constantly maneuvering, promising one thing, doing another, making a pledge, taking it back—using any means to accomplish his ends. As his term wore on, the pro-southern bent of this Tennessee slaveholder em-

The fortified heights of Chapultepec fell in 1847 to Winfield Scott's invading forces, but not without fierce resistance by young Mexican cadets. Like the partisans of the Alamo, who gained fame in Texas lore, the defenders of Chapultepec won an honored place in Mexican history.

bittered Democrats from the North and West. Western Democrats were furious when Polk vetoed a bill to improve rivers and harbors. Northerners complained that Polk had compromised with the British on Oregon, which was suitable for northern agriculture, at the same time that he had used military force to defend Texas's absurd boundary claims. *Northern discontent*

This festering discontent finally erupted in August 1846 when Polk requested $2 million from Congress, as he vaguely explained, to "facilitate negotiations" with Mexico. It was widely understood that the money was to be used to bribe the Mexican government to cede territory to the United States. On August 8 David Wilmot, an obscure Pennsylvania congressman, startled Democratic leaders by introducing an amendment to the bill that barred slavery from any territory acquired from Mexico. The Wilmot Proviso, as the amendment became known, passed the northern-controlled House of Representatives several times, only to be rejected in the Senate, where the South had more power. As such, it revealed mounting sectional tensions. *Wilmot Proviso*

Wilmot himself was hardly an abolitionist. Indeed, he hoped to keep not only slaves but all black people out of the territories. Denying any "morbid sympathy for the slave," he declared, "I would preserve for white free labor a fair country . . .

where the sons of toil, of my own race and color, can live without the disgrace which association with negro slavery brings upon free labor." The Wilmot Proviso aimed not to destroy slavery in the South but to confine the institution to those states where it already existed. Still, abolitionists had long contended that southern slaveholders—the "Slave Power"—were plotting to extend their sway over the rest of the country. The political maneuverings of slaveholders like Tyler, and especially Polk, convinced growing numbers of northerners that the Slave Power did indeed exist and that it was aggressively looking to expand its influence.

Peace treaty with Mexico

The status of slavery in the territories became more than an abstract question when the Senate in 1848 ratified the Treaty of Guadalupe Hidalgo. Under its terms the United States acquired Mexico's provinces of New Mexico and Upper California in return for approximately $18 million. That translated into a half million square miles of territory along with about 75,000 Spanish-speaking inhabitants. With the United States in control of the Pacific Coast from San Diego to Puget Sound, Polk's continental vision had become a reality.

NEW SOCIETIES IN THE WEST

As Hispanic, Indian, Asian, and Anglo-American cultures mixed, the patterns of settlement along the frontier varied widely. Some recreated the farm economies and small towns of the Anglo-American East; others continued the cattle-ranching life of the Hispanic West. In California the new settlements were overwhelmingly shaped by the rush for gold after 1848. And in the Great Basin around Salt Lake, the Mormons established a society whose sense of religious mission was as strong as that of the Puritans.

Farming in the West

The overlanders expected to replicate the societies they had left behind. Once a wagon train arrived at its destination, members had usually exhausted their resources and thus quickly scattered in search of employment or a good farm site. "Friday, October 27.—Arrived at Oregon City at the falls of the Willamette," read one pioneer diary. "Saturday, October 28.—Went to work."

Evolution of western society

In a process repeated over and over, settlers in a new area set up the machinery of government. Although violence was common on the frontier, farming communities tended to resolve problems by traditional means. Churches took longer to establish, for ministers were hard to recruit and congregations were often not large enough to support a church. As the population grew, however, a more conventional society evolved. Towns and a middle class developed, the proportion of women increased, schools were established, and the residents became less mobile.

While opportunity was greater on the frontier and early arrivals had a special advantage, more and more the agricultural frontier of the West resembled the older society of the East. With the development of markets and transportation, wealth became concentrated, some families fell to the lower rungs of society, and those who were less successful left, seeking yet another fresh start.

The Gold Rush

In January 1848, while constructing a sawmill along the American River, James Marshall noticed gold flecks in the millrace. More discoveries followed, and when the news reached the East, it spread like wildfire. The following spring the Overland Trail was jammed with eager "forty-niners." Some 80,000 emigrants journeyed to California that year, about 55,000 of whom took the overland route. In only two years, from 1848 to the end of 1849, California's population jumped from 14,000 to 100,000. By 1860 it stood at 380,000.

Among those who went to California was William Swain, a 27-year-old farmer in western New York. Deciding that he had had enough of the hard work of farming, he bid good-bye to his wife and daughter in 1849 and set off for the gold fields to make his fortune. Upon his arrival in November, he entered a partnership and staked a claim along the Feather River, but after several months of back-breaking work in icy waters, he and his partners discovered that their claim was "worth nothing." He sold out and joined another company, but early rains soon forced them to stop work. In October 1850, after less than a year in the diggings, Swain decided to return home. With only a few hundred dollars to show for his labor, he counted himself one of the vast majority of miners who had seen "their bright daydreams of golden wealth vanish like the dreams of night." He arrived home the following February and resumed farming.

Those like Swain intent on making a fortune and returning home gave no thought to putting down roots. Most agreements were made by the month. Mining camps literally appeared and died overnight, as word of a new strike sent miners racing off to another canyon, valley, or streambed. Most settlements were hardly more than a single street, littered with debris and lined with stores, buildings, and miners' shacks—often no more than blankets or cloth tacked to a wooden frame. A saloon and gambling hall, which might double as a hotel and sometimes a brothel, was usually the most prominent building in town. More than 80 percent of the prospectors who poured into the gold country were Americans, including free blacks. Mexicans, Australians, Hawaiians, Chinese, French, English, and Irish also came. Whatever their nationality, the new arrivals were overwhelmingly unmarried men in their twenties and thirties.

Life in the mining camps

The constant movement, the hard labor of mining, the ready cash, and the rootlessness all made camp society unstable. "There is an excitement connected with the pursuit of gold which renders one restless and uneasy—ever hoping to do something better," explained one forty-niner. Removed from the traditional forms of social control, miners engaged in gambling, swearing, drinking, and fighting. One startled minister reported from the California gold fields that unlike back home, immorality "is in the open, unmasked, makes no apologies and asks none. It unfurls its flag in the most public and conspicuous places."

Only about 5 percent of gold rush emigrants were women or children; given this relative scarcity, men were willing to pay top dollar for women's domestic skills. Women supported themselves by cooking, sewing, and washing, as well as by running hotels and boardinghouses. "A smart woman can do very well in this country," one woman informed a friend in the East. "It is the only country I ever was in where a woman received anything like a just compensation for work." Likewise, they suffered no shortage of suitors. "I had men come forty miles over the mountains, just to look

Women in the camps

at me," Eliza Wilson recalled, "and I never was called a handsome woman, in my best days, even by my most ardent admirers." Women went to the mining frontier to be with their husbands, to make money, or to find adventure. But the class most frequently seen in the diggings were prostitutes, who numbered perhaps 20 percent of female Californians in 1850.

Predictably, mining the miners offered one of the more reliable roads to prosperity. Perhaps half the inhabitants of a mining town were shopkeepers, businesspeople, and professionals who provided services for prospectors. Also conspicuous were gamblers, card sharks, and other outcasts, all bent on separating the miner from his riches. In such an atmosphere, violence was prevalent, so when a new camp opened, miners adopted a set of rules and regulations. Justice was dispensed promptly, either by a vote of all the miners or by an elected jury. While effective when administered fairly, the system at times degenerated into lynch law.

Nativist and racial prejudices

Observers praised the diggings' democratic spirit. Yet such assertions overlooked strongly held nativist prejudices: when frustrated by a lack of success, American miners directed their hostility toward foreigners. The miners ruthlessly exterminated the Indians in the area, mob violence drove Mexicans out of nearly every camp, and the Chinese were confined to claims abandoned by Americans as unprofitable. The state eventually enacted a foreign miners' tax that fell largely on the Chinese. Free African Americans felt the sting of discrimination as well, both in the camps and in state law. White American miners proclaimed that "colored men were not privileged to work in a country intended only for American citizens."

With their distinctive clothing and bamboo hats, Chinese miners could be seen throughout the diggings. Chinese immigration reached a peak in 1852, when 20,000 arrived in California. In the heyday of the mining camps, perhaps 20 percent of the miners were Chinese. Confronted with intense hostility from other miners, they worked abandoned claims and unpromising sites with primitive and less expensive equipment.

Before long, the most easily worked claims had been played out, and competition steadily drove down the average earnings from $20 a day in 1848 to $6 in 1852. That was still higher than eastern wages, but goods and services cost significantly more too. As gold became increasingly difficult to extract, larger corporations using heavy equipment and employing miners working for wages came to dominate the industry. Men who had come to California filled with visions of wealth usually found only shovels of mud. As the era of the individual miner passed, so too did mining camps and the unique society they spawned.

The damage mining did to the land endured longer. Abandoned prospect holes and diggings pockmarked the gold fields and created piles of debris that heavy rains would wash down the valley, choking streams and ruining lands below. Excavation of hillsides, construction of dams to divert rivers, and the destruction of the forest cover to meet the heavy demand for lumber and firewood caused serious erosion of the soil and spring floods. The attitude of the individual miners differed little from the capitalists who succeeded them: both sought to exploit the environment as rapidly as possible with little thought to long-term consequences. Untempered by any sense of restraint, the quest for rapid wealth left long-lasting scars on the landscape of the gold country. *Environmental impact of mining*

Instant City: San Francisco

When the United States assumed control of California, San Francisco had a population of perhaps 200. But thousands of emigrants took the water route west, passing through San Francisco's harbor on their way to the diggings. By 1856 the city's population had jumped to an astonishing 50,000. In a mere 8 years the city had attained the size New York had taken 190 years to reach.

The product of economic self-interest, San Francisco developed in helter-skelter fashion. Land prices soared, speculation was rampant, and commercial forces became paramount. Residents lived in tents or poorly constructed, half-finished buildings. To enlarge the commercial district, hills began to be leveled, with the dirt used to fill in the bay (thereby creating more usable land). Since the city government took virtually no role in directing development, almost no land was reserved for public use. Property owners defeated a proposal to widen the streets, prompting the city's leading newspaper to complain, "To sell a few more feet of lots, the streets were compressed like a cheese, into half their width." An amazing assortment of languages could be heard on the city's streets; indeed, in 1860 San Francisco was 50 percent foreign-born. *San Francisco's chaotic growth*

The most distinctive of the ethnic groups was the Chinese. They had come to *Gum San,* the land of the golden mountain, because China in the 1840s had experienced considerable economic distress. Between 1849 and 1854, some 45,000 Chinese went to California. Like the other gold seekers, they were overwhelmingly young and male, and they wanted only to accumulate savings and return home to their families. (Indeed, only 16 Chinese women arrived before 1854.) Sixteen-year-old Lee Chew left for California after a man from his village returned with great wealth from the "country of the American wizards." Generally poor, Chinese immigrants arrived already in debt, having borrowed the price of their steamship tickets; they fell further into debt to Chinese merchants in San Francisco, who loaned them money to purchase needed supplies. *Chinese experience*

San Francisco in 1852 (Collection of the New-York Historical Society.)

When the Chinese were harassed in the mines, many opened laundries in San Francisco and elsewhere, since little capital was required—soap, scrub board, iron, and ironing board. The going rate at the time for washing, ironing, and starching shirts was an exorbitant $8 per dozen. Many early San Franciscans actually found it cheaper to send their dirty laundry to Canton or Honolulu, to be returned several months later. Other Chinese around San Francisco set up restaurants or worked in the fishing industry. In these early years they found Americans less hostile, so long as they stayed away from the gold fields. As immigration and the competition for jobs increased, however, anti-Chinese sentiment intensified.

Gradually, San Francisco took on the trappings of a more orderly community. The city government established a public school system, erected streetlights, created a municipal water system, and halted further filling in of the bay. Industry was confined to the area south of the city; several new working-class neighborhoods grew up near the downtown section. Fashionable neighborhoods sprouted on several hills, as high rents drove many residents from the developing commercial center, and churches and families became more common. By 1856, the city of the gold rush had been replaced by a new city whose stone and brick buildings gave it a new sense of permanence.

The Mormons in Utah

The makeshift, often chaotic society spawned by the gold rush was a product of largely uncontrolled economic forces. By contrast, the society evolving in the Great Basin of Utah exhibited an entirely different but equally remarkable growth. Salt Lake City became the center of a religious kingdom established by the Church of Jesus Christ of Latter-day Saints.

After Joseph Smith's death in 1844 (page 326), the Mormon church was led by Brigham Young, who lacked Smith's religious mysticism but was a brilliant organizer. Young decided to move his followers to the Great Basin, an isolated area a thousand miles from the settled parts of the United States. In 1847 the first thousand settlers arrived, the vanguard of thousands more who extended Mormon settlement throughout the valley of the Great Salt Lake and the West. Church officials also held the government positions, and Young had supreme power in legislative, executive, and judicial matters as well as religious affairs. In 1849 the state of Deseret was officially established, with Brigham Young as governor. It applied for admission to the Union.

State of Deseret

The most controversial church teaching was the doctrine of polygamy, or plural marriage, which Young finally sanctioned publicly in 1852. Visitors reported with surprise that few Mormon wives seemed to rebel against the practice. Some plural wives developed close friendships; indeed, in one sample almost a third of plural marriages included at least two sisters. If the wives lived together, the system allowed them to share domestic work. When the husband established separate households, wives enjoyed greater freedom, since the husband was not constantly present. Moreover, because polygamy distinguished Mormonism from other religions, plural wives saw it as an expression of their religious faith. "I want to be assured of *position in God's estimation,*" one such wife explained. "If polygamy is the Lord's order, we must carry it out."

Polygamy

The Mormons connected control of water to their sense of mission and respect for hierarchy. The Salt Lake valley, where the Mormons established their holy community, lacked significant rivers or abundant sources of water. Thus success depended on irrigating the region, something never before attempted. When the first Mormons arrived from the East, they had no experience with irrigation and little capital. But they made up for that lack with a strong sense of unity bolstered by a religious commission to exploit the environment and make it fruitful. By constructing a coordinated series of dams, aqueducts, and ditches, they brought life-giving water to the valleys of the region. Fanning out from their original settlement, they founded a series of colonies throughout the West, all tied to Salt Lake City and joined by ribbons of water. Mormon farmers grew corn, wheat, hay, and an assortment of fruits and vegetables. By 1850, there were more than 16,000 irrigated acres in what would eventually become the state of Utah. The Mormons were the first Anglos to extensively use irrigation in North America.

Irrigation and community

Manipulation of water reinforced the Mormons' sense of hierarchy and group discipline. Centralization of authority in the hands of church officials made possible an overall plan of development, allowed for maximum exploitation of resources, and freed communities from the disputes over water rights that plagued many settlements in the arid West. In a radical departure from American ideals, church leaders insisted that water belonged to the community, not individuals, and vested this authority in the hands of the local bishop. Control of water resources, which were vital for survival in the desert, reinforced the power of the church hierarchy over not just the faithful but dissidents as well. Community needs, as interpreted by church leaders, took precedent over individual rights. Thus irrigation did more than make the desert bloom. By checking the Jeffersonian ideal of an independent, self-sufficient farmer, it also made possible a centralized, well-regulated society under the firm control of the church.

Temple City: Salt Lake City

In laying out the Mormons' "temple city" of Salt Lake, Young was also determined to avoid the commercial worldliness and competitive individualism that had plagued the Mormons at Nauvoo (page 326). City lots, which were distributed by lottery, could not be subdivided for sale, and real estate speculation was forbidden.

Salt Lake City's orderly growth

The city itself was laid out in a checkerboard grid well suited to the level terrain. Streets were 132 feet wide (compared with 60 feet in San Francisco), and each square block contained eight home lots of 1.25 acres each. Unlike early San Francisco, the family was the basic social unit in Salt Lake City, and almost from the beginning the city had an equal balance of men and women. The planners also provided for four public squares in various parts of the city. The city lacked any traditional secular authority: it was divided into 18 wards, each under the supervision of a bishop, who held civil as well as religious power.

As the city expanded, the original plan had to be modified to accommodate the developing commercial district by dividing lots into sizes more suitable for stores. Experience and growth also eventually dictated smaller blocks and narrower streets, but the city still retained its spacious appearance and regular design. Through religious and economic discipline church leaders succeeded in preserving a sense of common purpose.

Shadows on the Moving Frontier

Transformations like Salt Lake City and San Francisco were truly remarkable. But it is important to remember that Americans were not coming into a trackless, unsettled wilderness. As frontier lines crossed, 75,000 Mexicans had to adapt to American rule.

The Treaty of Guadalupe Hidalgo guaranteed Mexicans in the ceded territory

Salt Lake City in 1853

"the free enjoyment of their liberty and property." So long as Mexicans continued to be a sizable majority in a given area, their influence was strong. But wherever Anglos became more numerous, they demanded conformity to American customs. When Mexicans remained faithful to their heritage, language, and religion, these cultural differences worked to reinforce Hispanic powerlessness, social isolation, and economic exploitation.

New Mexico had the largest Hispanic population as well as the fewest Anglos in the Mexican cession. As a result, the upper-class Mexicans who owned the land and employed large numbers of mixed-blood workers on their ranches managed to maintain their position. This class had cultivated American allies during the Santa Fe trade, and their connections grew stronger as American businessmen slowly entered the territory in the 1850s. Neither group had much interest in the lower-class Hispanics, whom both exploited.

The rush of American emigrants quickly overwhelmed Hispanic settlers in California. Even in 1848, before the discovery of gold, Americans in California outnumbered Mexicans two to one, and by 1860 Hispanics amounted to only 2 percent of the population. At the time of the American conquest, the 200 or so *ranchero* families owned about 14 million acres, but changes in California land law required verification of their original land grants by a federal commission. Since the average claim took 17 years to complete and imposed complex procedures and hefty legal fees, many *rancheros* lost large tracts of land to Americans.

Hispanic–Anglo conflict

Lower-class Mexicans scratched out a bare existence on ranches and farms or in the growing cities and towns. Scorned by the dominant Anglo majority and without skills and resources, they were often reduced to extreme poverty. As the Hispanic population in California became primarily urban, women assumed a larger role in the family. Many men were seasonal workers who were absent part of the year, and thus women played a greater role in sustaining the family economically.

Town plazas, such as this one in San Antonio, were commercial centers in the Mexican Southwest. Traders from outlying *ranchos* enjoy refreshments while their goods, loaded on oxcarts, await sale. (Courtesy of the Witte Museum and the San Antonio Museum Association, San Antonio, Texas)

Mexicans in Texas were also greatly outnumbered: they totaled only 6 percent of the population in 1860. Stigmatized as inferior, they were the poorest group in free society. One response to this dislocation, an option commonly taken by persecuted minorities, was social banditry. An example was the folk hero Juan Cortina. A member of a displaced landed family in southern Texas, Cortina was driven into resistance in the 1850s by American harassment. He began stealing from wealthy Anglos to aid poor Mexicans, proclaiming, "To me is entrusted the breaking of the chains of your slavery." Cortina continued to raid Texas border settlements until finally imprisoned by Mexican authorities. While failing to produce any lasting change, Cortina demonstrated the depth of frustration and resentment among Hispanics over their abuse at the hands of the new Anglo majority.

ESCAPE FROM CRISIS

Issue of slavery's extension

With the return of peace, Congress confronted the problem of whether to allow slavery in the newly acquired territories. David Wilmot, in his controversial proviso, had already proposed to outlaw slavery throughout the Mexican cession. John C. Calhoun, representing the extreme southern position, countered that slavery was legal in all territories. The federal government had acted as the agent of all the states in acquiring the land, he argued, and southerners had a right to take their property there, including slaves. Only when the residents of a territory drafted a state constitution could they decide the question of slavery.

Between these extremes were two moderate positions. One proposed extending the Missouri Compromise line of 36°30′ to the Pacific, which would have continued the earlier policy of dividing the national domain between the North and the South. The other proposal, championed by Senator Lewis Cass of Michigan and Senator Stephen A. Douglas of Illinois, was to allow the people of the territory rather than Congress to decide the status of slavery. This solution, which became known as popular sovereignty, was deliberately ambiguous, since its supporters refused to specify whether the residents could make this decision at any time or only when drafting a state constitution, as Calhoun insisted.

When Congress organized the Oregon Territory in 1848, it prohibited slavery there, since even southerners admitted that the region was too far north to grow the South's staple crops. But this seemingly straightforward decision made it impossible to apply the Missouri Compromise line to the other territories. Without Oregon as a part of the package, the bulk of the remaining land would be open to slavery, something at which the North balked. Almost inadvertently, one of the two moderate solutions had been discarded by the summer of 1848.

A Two-Faced Campaign

In the election of 1848 both major parties tried to avoid the slavery issue. The Democrats nominated Lewis Cass, a supporter of popular sovereignty, while the Whigs bypassed all their prominent leaders and selected General Zachary Taylor, who had taken no position on any public issue and who remained silent throughout the campaign. The Whigs adopted no platform and planned instead to emphasize the general's war record.

But the slavery issue would not quietly go away. Instead, a new antislavery coalition, the Free Soil party, came together. Alienated by Polk's policies and still angry over the 1844 convention, northern Democrats loyal to Van Buren spearheaded its creation. They were joined by "Conscience Whigs," who disavowed Taylor's nomination because he was a slaveholder. Furthermore, political abolitionists like Salmon P. Chase left the Liberty party in favor of this broader coalition. To widen its appeal, the Free Soil platform focused on the dangers of extending slavery rather than on the evil of slavery itself. Ironically, the party's convention named as its candidate Martin Van Buren—the man who for years had struggled to keep the slavery issue out of politics.

Free Soil party

With the Free Soilers strongly supporting the Wilmot Proviso, the Whigs and Democrats could not ignore the slavery question. The two major parties responded by running different campaigns in the North and the South. To southern audiences, each party promised that it would protect slavery in the territories; to northern voters, each claimed that it would keep the territories free. In this two-faced, sectional campaign, the Whigs won their second national victory. Taylor held on to the core of Whig voters in both sections (Van Buren as well as Cass, after all, had long been Democrats). But in the South, where the contest pitted a southern slaveholder against two northerners, Taylor won many more votes than Clay had in 1844. As one southern Democrat complained, "We have lost hundreds of votes, solely on the ground that General Cass was a Northerner and General Taylor a Southern man."

Furthermore, Van Buren polled five times as many votes as the Liberty party had four years earlier. It seemed that the national system of political parties was being gradually pulled apart.

The Compromise of 1850

Once he became president, Taylor could no longer remain silent. The territories gained from Mexico had to be organized; furthermore, by 1849 California had gained enough residents to be admitted as a state. In the Senate the balance of power between North and South stood at 15 states each. California's admission would break the sectional balance.

Taylor's plan   Called "Old Rough and Ready" by his troops, Taylor was a forthright man of action, but he was politically inexperienced and oversimplified complex problems. Since even Calhoun conceded that entering states had the right to ban slavery, Taylor proposed that the way to end the sectional crisis was to skip the territorial stage by combining all the Mexican cession into two very large states, New Mexico and California. So the president sent agents to California and New Mexico with instructions to set the machinery in motion for both territories to draft constitutions and apply for statehood directly. Even more shocking to southern Whigs, he proposed to apply the Wilmot Proviso to the entire area, since he was convinced that slavery would never flourish there. By the time Congress convened in December 1849, California had drafted a constitution and applied for admission as a free state. Taylor reported that New Mexico (which included most of Arizona, Utah, and Colorado) would soon do the same and recommended that both be admitted as free states. The president's plan touched off the most serious sectional crisis the Union had yet confronted.

Into this turmoil stepped Henry Clay, now 73 years old and nearing the end of his career. A savvy card player all his life, Clay loved politics: the bargaining, the wheeling and dealing, the late-night trade-offs eased along by a bottle of bourbon. Thirty years earlier he had engineered the Missouri Compromise, and in 1833 he had helped defuse the nullification crisis. Clay decided that a grand compromise was needed to save the Union. Already, Mississippi had summoned other southern states to meet in a convention at Nashville to discuss the crisis, and southern extremists were pushing for secession. The points of disagreement went beyond the question of the western territories. Many northerners considered it disgraceful that slaves were bought and sold in the nation's capital, where slavery was still permitted. Southerners complained bitterly that northern states ignored the 1793 fugitive slave law and prevented them from reclaiming runaway slaves.

Clay's compromise   Clay's compromise, submitted in January 1850, addressed all these concerns. California, he proposed, should be admitted as a free state, which represented the clear wishes of most settlers there. The rest of the Mexican cession would be organized as two territories, New Mexico and Utah, under the doctrine of popular sovereignty. Thus slavery would not be prohibited from these regions. Clay also proposed that Congress abolish the slave trade but not slavery itself in the District of Columbia and that a new, more rigorous fugitive slave law be passed to enable southerners to reclaim runaway slaves. To reinforce the idea that both North and South were yielding ground, Clay combined those provisions that dealt with the former Mexican ter-

The Great Triumvirate, Clay, Webster, and Calhoun, served together in public life for almost four decades. Clay (left) and Webster (center) supported the Compromise of 1850, whereas in his last speech in the Senate, the dying Calhoun opposed it. By midcentury, power was passing to a new generation of politicians more accustomed to sectional conflict and less amenable to compromise.

ritory and several others adjusting the Texas–New Mexico boundary in a larger package known as the Omnibus Bill.

With the stakes so high, the Senate debated the bill for six months. Daniel Webster of Massachusetts, always deep-voiced, seemed more somber than usual when he delivered a pro-compromise speech on the seventh of March. "I wish to speak today not as a Massachusetts man, not as a Northern man, but as an American. . . . I speak today for the preservation of the Union. Hear me for my cause." Calhoun, whose aged, crevassed face mirrored the lines that had been drawn so deeply between the two sections, was near death and too ill to deliver his final speech to the Senate, which a colleague read for him as he listened silently. The "cords of Union," he warned—those ties of interest and affection that held the nation together—were snapping one by one. Only equal rights for the South and an end to the agitation against slavery could preserve the Union.

Clay, wracked by a hacking cough, spent long hours trying to line up the needed votes. But for once, the great whist enthusiast had misplayed his hand. The Omnibus Bill required that the components of the compromise be approved as a package. Extremists in Congress from both regions, however, combined against the moderates and rejected the bill.

With Clay exhausted and his strategy in shambles, Democrat Stephen A. Douglas assumed leadership of the pro-compromise forces. The sudden death in July of President Taylor, who had threatened to veto Clay's plan, aided the compromise movement. One by one, Douglas submitted the individual measures for a vote. Northern representatives provided the necessary votes to admit California and abolish the slave trade in the District of Columbia, while southern representatives supplied the edge needed to organize the Utah and New Mexico territories and pass the new fugitive slave law. On the face of it, everyone had compromised. But in truth, only 61 members of Congress, or 21 percent of the membership, had not voted against some part of the Compromise.

Passage of the Compromise

By September 17 all the separate parts of the Compromise of 1850 had passed and been signed into law by the new president, Millard Fillmore. The Union, it seemed, was safe.

Away from the Brink

The general public, both North and South, rallied to the Compromise. At the convention of southern states in Nashville, the fire-eaters—the radical proponents of states' rights and secession—found themselves voted down by more moderate voices. Even in the Deep South, coalitions of pro-Compromise Whigs and Democrats soundly defeated secessionists in the state elections that followed. Still, most southerners felt that a firm line had been drawn. With California's admission, they were now outnumbered in the Senate, so it was critical that slaveholders be granted equal legal access to the territories. They announced that any breach of the Compromise of 1850 would justify secession.

Rejection of secession

The North, for its part, found the new fugitive slave law the hardest measure of the Compromise of 1850 to swallow. The controversial law denied an accused runaway a trial by jury, and it required that all citizens assist federal marshals in its enforcement. Harriet Beecher Stowe's popular novel *Uncle Tom's Cabin* (1852) presented a powerful moral indictment of the law—and of slavery as an institution. (See Daily Lives, "Uncle Tom by Footlights," pages 506–507.) Despite sentimental characters, a contrived plot, and clumsy dialect, the book profoundly moved its readers. Emphasizing the duty of Christians toward the downtrodden, it reached a greater audience than any previous abolitionist work and heightened moral opposition to the institution.

Fugitive slave law

In reality, however, fewer than 1000 slaves a year ran away to the North, many of whom did not succeed. Despite some cases of well-publicized resistance, the 1850 fugitive slave law was generally enforced in the free states. Many northerners did not like the law, but they were unwilling to tamper with the Compromise. Stephen Douglas spoke accurately enough when he boasted in 1851, "The whole country is acquiescing in the compromise measures—everywhere, North and South. Nobody proposes to repeal or disturb them."

And so calm returned. In the lackluster 1852 presidential campaign, both the Whigs and the Democrats endorsed the Compromise. Franklin Pierce, a little-known New Hampshire Democrat, soundly defeated the Whig candidate, Winfield Scott. Even more significant, the antislavery Free Soil candidate received only about half as many votes as Van Buren had four years before. With the slavery issue seemingly losing political force, it appeared that the Republic had weathered the storm unleashed by the Wilmot Proviso.

But the moving frontier still had changes to work. It had leaped from the Mississippi valley to the Pacific, but in between remained territory still unorganized. And as the North became increasingly industrialized and the South more firmly committed to an economy based on cotton and slavery, the growing conflict between the two sections would shatter the Jacksonian party system, reignite the slavery issue, and shake the Union to its foundation.

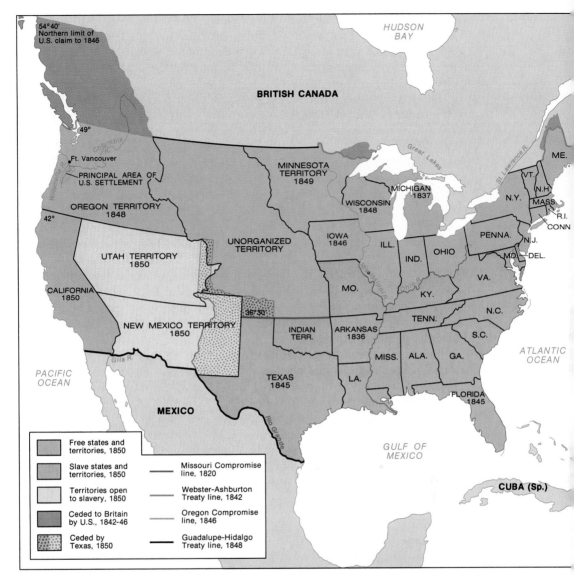

54°40'
Northern limit of
U.S. claim to 1846

HUDSON
BAY

BRITISH CANADA

49°

Ft. Vancouver
PRINCIPAL AREA OF
U.S. SETTLEMENT

Great Lakes

St. Lawrence R.

ME.

MINNESOTA
TERRITORY
1849

MICHIGAN
1837

VT.

N.H.

OREGON TERRITORY
1848

WISCONSIN
1848

N.Y.

MASS.

R.I.

42°

UNORGANIZED
TERRITORY

IOWA
1846

ILL.

IND.

OHIO

PENNA.

N.J.

CONN

UTAH TERRITORY
1850

MD.

DEL.

CALIFORNIA
1850

MO.

VA.

KY.

36°30'

N.C.

NEW MEXICO TERRITORY
1850

INDIAN
TERR.

ARKANSAS
1836

TENN.

S.C.

Gila R.

MISS.

ALA.

GA.

ATLANTIC
OCEAN

PACIFIC
OCEAN

TEXAS
1845

LA.

FLORIDA
1845

MEXICO

Rio Grande

GULF OF
MEXICO

	Free states and territories, 1850		
	Slave states and territories, 1850	———	Missouri Compromise line, 1820
	Territories open to slavery, 1850	———	Webster-Ashburton Treaty line, 1842
	Ceded to Britain by U.S., 1842-46	———	Oregon Compromise line, 1846
	Ceded by Texas, 1850	———	Guadalupe-Hidalgo Treaty line, 1848

CUBA (Sp.)

TERRITORIAL GROWTH AND THE COMPROMISE OF 1850
The Webster–Ashburton Treaty established Maine's northern boundary as well as the
American–Canadian boundary west of the Great Lakes.

CHAPTER SUMMARY

In the 1840s the United States expanded to the Pacific, a development that involved
the cultural interaction of Americans with other groups. Proclaiming that it was the
United States' "Manifest Destiny" to expand across the North American continent,

Americans looked longingly to the borderlands of Mexico, areas with a distinct Spanish flavor but sparsely populated and weakly defended. This self-proclaimed destiny brought Americans into contact—and conflict—with Mexicans in Texas, New Mexico, and California, and in 1836 Texans revolted and established an independent republic.

Other Americans headed for Oregon and California on the Overland Trail. This difficult journey put special pressures on women; it also had important consequences for the Plains Indians' way of life. Once in the West the settlers created new societies. The gold rush spawned a unique society that was overwhelmingly male, highly mobile, and strongly nativist and racist. Motivated by a sense of religious mission, the Mormons, who were led to the Great Salt Lake basin by Brigham Young, established a more hierarchical, centralized society. Throughout the Southwest the Hispanic population suffered at the hands of the new Anglo majority.

The movement to annex Texas failed in the 1830s because of fear it would raise the slavery issue and threaten the Union, but after John Tyler became president, he actively promoted the annexation of Texas. Aided by the Texas movement, James K. Polk won a narrow victory in the 1844 election. Holding a vision of the United States as a continental nation, Polk sustained the annexation of Texas, which Tyler had engineered, obtained half of the Oregon country by forging an agreement with Britain, and eventually went to war with Mexico, by which the United States acquired California and the Southwest.

But most importantly, the war injected the issue of slavery's expansion back into national politics with the introduction of the Wilmot Proviso, which sought to prohibit slavery from any territory acquired from Mexico. The struggle over the proviso eventually disrupted both major parties. The Whigs won an ambiguous victory in 1848, but the organization of the territory acquired from Mexico and the status of slavery in this region became urgent when gold was discovered in California, which quickly gained sufficient population to be admitted as a state. Congress momentarily stilled the sectional crisis with the Compromise of 1850. The majority in both sections endorsed the Compromise, and sectional harmony returned.

ADDITIONAL READING

In recent years the field of western American history has dramatically expanded to include cultural diversity, environmental problems, racial interaction, and the role of gender, themes that were largely ignored in earlier accounts of western expansion. Good introductions to the "new western history" are Richard White's inelegantly titled *It's Your Misfortune and None of My Own* (1991) and William Cronon et al., *Under an Open Sky* (1992).

David J. Weber, *The Mexican Frontier, 1821–1846* (1982) is a superb study of the Southwest prior to American control. Two excellent accounts from different perspectives of the Overland Trail experience are John D. Unruh, Jr., *The Plains Across* (1979) and John Mack Faragher, *Women and Men on the Overland Trail* (1979). Thomas R. Hietala offers a stimulating analysis of the social roots of expansionism in *Manifest Design* (1985). Leonard J. Arrington and Davis Bitton, *The Mormon Experience*, 2d ed. (1992) is a good survey. Women's experiences in the West are analyzed in Julie R. Jeffrey, *Frontier Women* (1979), while Donald D. Jackson, *Gold Dust* (1980) examines the gold rush. The fullest treatment of politics in this decade is William R. Brock, *Parties and Political Conscience* (1970). The drive to annex Texas is carefully untangled in William W. Freehling, *The Road to Disunion* (1990), and its impact on the Democratic party is the focus of James C. N. Paul's *Rift in the Democracy* (1961). The best discussion of Polk's handling of the Oregon and Texas issues is Charles G. Sellers, Jr., *James K. Polk, Continentalist, 1843–1846* (1966). Holman Hamilton, *Prologue to Conflict* (1964) is an excellent study of the Compromise of 1850. For a fuller list of readings, see the Bibliography.

SIGNIFICANT EVENTS

1725–1850	Sioux expansion on the Great Plains
1821	Mexico wins independence; Santa Fe trade opens
1823	First American settlers enter Texas
1829	Mexico tries to abolish slavery in Texas
1830	Mexico attempts to halt American migration to Texas
1835	Texas Revolution
1836	Texas Republic established; Battle of the Alamo; Santa Anna defeated at San Jacinto
1841	Tyler becomes president
1842	Webster–Ashburton Treaty
1843	Large-scale migration to Oregon begins
1843–1844	Tyler conducts secret negotiations with Texas
1844	Tyler's Texas treaty rejected by the Senate; Polk elected president
1845	United States annexes Texas; phrase "Manifest Destiny" coined
1845–1846	Slidell's unsuccessful mission
1846	War declared against Mexico; Bear Flag Revolt in California; Oregon Treaty ratified; Wilmot Proviso introduced
1847	Mormon migration to Utah; U.S. troops occupy Mexico City
1848	Gold discovered in California; Treaty of Guadalupe Hidalgo approved; Free Soil party founded; Taylor elected president
1849	Gold rush; California drafts free state constitution
1850	Nashville convention; Taylor dies and Fillmore becomes president; Compromise of 1850 enacted
1850–1851	South rejects secession
1852	Harriet Beecher Stowe's *Uncle Tom's Cabin* published; Pierce elected president

15

The Union Broken

Into town they rode, several hundred strong, their faces flushed with excitement. They were unshaven, rough-talking men, "armed . . . to the teeth with rifles and revolvers, cutlasses and bowie-knives." At the head of the procession an American flag flapped softly in the warm May breeze. Alongside it was another with a crouching tiger emblazoned on black and white stripes, followed by banners proclaiming "Southern Rights" and "The Superiority of the White Race." At the rear rolled five artillery pieces, which were quickly dragged into range of the town's main street. Josiah Miller, the editor of the Lawrence *Kansas Free State*, watched intently from a window in his office. "Well, boys," he predicted, "we're in for it."

For the residents of Lawrence, Kansas, the worst seemed at hand. The town had been founded by the New England Emigrant Aid Company, a Yankee association that recruited settlers in an effort to keep Kansas Territory from becoming a slave state. Accepting Stephen Douglas's idea that the people should decide the status of slavery, the town's residents intended to see to it that under popular sovereignty Kansas entered the Union as a free state. Emigrants from the neighboring slave state of Missouri were equally determined that no "abolition tyrants" or "negro thieves" control the territory. There had been conflict in Kansas almost immediately: land disputes, horse thievery, shootings on both sides.

In the ensuing turmoil, the federal government seemed to back the proslavery forces. In the spring of 1856, a U.S. District Court indicted several of Lawrence's leading citizens for treason, and federal marshal Israel Donaldson called for a posse to help make the arrests. Donaldson's posse, swelled by eager volunteers from across the Missouri border, arrived outside Lawrence on the night of May 20.

Meanwhile, Lawrence's "committee of safety" had agreed on a policy of nonresistance. Most of those indicted had fled, but Donaldson arrested two men without incident. Then he dismissed his posse.

The posse, however, was not ready to go home. Already thoroughly liquored, it marched into town cheering. Ignoring the pleas of some leaders, its members smashed the presses of two newspapers, the *Herald of Freedom* and the *Kansas Free State*. Then the horde unleashed its wrath on the now-deserted Free State Hotel, which more closely resembled a fort. The invaders unsuccessfully attempted to batter it down with cannon fire and blow it up with gunpowder; finally they put a torch to the building. When the mob finally rode off, it left the residents of Lawrence unharmed but thoroughly terrified.

APPENDIX

THE DECLARATION OF INDEPENDENCE

In Congress, July 4, 1776,

THE UNANIMOUS DECLARATION OF THE
THIRTEEN UNITED STATES OF AMERICA

When, in the course of human events, it becomes necessary for one people to dissolve the political bands which have connected them with another, and to assume, among the powers of the earth, the separate and equal station to which the laws of nature and of nature's God entitle them, a decent respect to the opinions of mankind requires that they should declare the causes which impel them to the separation.

We hold these truths to be self-evident, that all men are created equal; that they are endowed by their Creator with certain unalienable rights; that among these, are life, liberty, and the pursuit of happiness. That, to secure these rights, governments are instituted among men, deriving their just powers from the consent of the governed; that, whenever any form of government becomes destructive of these ends, it is the right of the people to alter or to abolish it, and to institute a new government, laying its foundation on such principles, and organizing its powers in such form, as to them shall seem most likely to effect their safety and happiness. Prudence, indeed, will dictate that governments long established, should not be changed for light and transient causes; and, accordingly, all experience hath shown, that mankind are more disposed to suffer, while evils are sufferable, than to right themselves by abolishing the forms to which they are accustomed. But, when a long train of abuses and usurpations, pursuing invariably the same object, evinces a design to reduce them under absolute despotism, it is their right, it is their duty, to throw off such government and to provide new guards for their future security. Such has been the patient sufferance of these colonies, and such is now the necessity which constrains them to alter their for-mer systems of government. The history of the present King of Great Britain is a history of repeated injuries and usurpations, all having, in direct object, the establishment of an absolute tyranny over these States. To prove this, let facts be submitted to a candid world:

He has refused his assent to laws the most wholesome and necessary for the public good.

He has forbidden his governors to pass laws of immediate and pressing importance, unless suspended in their operation till his assent should be obtained; and, when so suspended, he has utterly neglected to attend to them.

He has refused to pass other laws for the accommodation of large districts of people, unless those people would relinquish the right of representation in the legislature; a right inestimable to them, and formidable to tyrants only.

He has called together legislative bodies at places unusual, uncomfortable, and distant from the depository of their public records, for the sole purpose of fatiguing them into compliance with his measures.

He has dissolved representative houses repeatedly for opposing, with manly firmness, his invasions on the rights of the people.

He has refused, for a long time after such dissolutions, to cause others to be elected; whereby the legislative powers, incapable of annihilation, have returned to the people at large for their exercise; the state remaining, in the meantime, exposed to all the danger of invasion from without, and convulsions within.

He has endeavored to prevent the population of these States; for that purpose, obstructing the laws for naturalization of foreigners, refusing to pass others to encourage their migration hither, and raising the conditions of new appropriations of lands.

He had obstructed the administration of justice, by refusing his assent to laws for establishing judiciary powers.

He has made judges dependent on his will

alone, for the tenure of their offices, and the amount and payment of their salaries.

He has erected a multitude of new offices, and sent hither swarms of officers to harass our people, and eat out their substance.

He has kept among us, in time of peace, standing armies, without the consent of our legislatures.

He has affected to render the military independent of, and superior to, the civil power.

He has combined, with others, to subject us to a jurisdiction foreign to our Constitution, and unacknowledged by our laws; giving his assent to their acts of pretended legislation:

For quartering large bodies of armed troops among us:

For protecting them by a mock trial, from punishment, for any murders which they should commit on the inhabitants of these States:

For cutting off our trade with all parts of the world:

For imposing taxes on us without our consent:

For depriving us, in many cases, of the benefit of trial by jury:

For transporting us beyond seas to be tried for pretended offences:

For abolishing the free system of English laws in a neighboring province, establishing therein an arbitrary government, and enlarging its boundaries, so as to render it at once an example and fit instrument for introducing the same absolute rule into these colonies:

For taking away our charters, abolishing our most valuable laws, and altering, fundamentally, the powers of our governments:

For suspending our own legislatures, and declaring themselves invested with power to legislate for us in all cases whatsoever.

He has abdicated government here, by declaring us out of his protection, and waging war against us.

He has plundered our seas, ravaged our coasts, burnt our towns, and destroyed the lives of our people.

He is, at this time, transporting large armies of foreign mercenaries to complete the works of death, desolation, and tyranny, already begun, with circumstances of cruelty and perfidy scarcely paralleled in the most barbarous ages, and totally unworthy the head of a civilized nation.

He has constrained our fellow citizens, taken captive on the high seas, to bear arms against their country, to become the executioners of their friends, and brethren, or to fall themselves by their hands.

He has excited domestic insurrections amongst us, and has endeavored to bring on the inhabitants of our frontiers, the merciless Indian savages, whose known rule of warfare is an undistinguished destruction of all ages, sexes, and conditions.

In every stage of these oppressions, we have petitioned for redress, in the most humble terms; our repeated petitions have been answered only by repeated injury. A prince, whose character is thus marked by every act which may define a tyrant, is unfit to be the ruler of a free people.

Nor have we been wanting in attention to our British brethren. We have warned them, from time to time, of attempts made by their legislature to extend an unwarrantable jurisdiction over us. We have reminded them of the circumstances of our emigration and settlement here. We have appealed to their native justice and magnanimity, and we have conjured them, by the ties of our common kindred, to disavow these usurpations, which would inevitably interrupt our connections and correspondence. They, too, have been deaf to the voice of justice and consanguinity. We must, therefore, acquiesce in the necessity which denounces our separation, and hold them as we hold the rest of mankind, enemies in war, in peace, friends.

We, therefore, the representatives of the United States of America, in general Congress assembled, appealing to the Supreme Judge of the world for the rectitude of our intentions, do, in the name, and by the authority of the good people of these colonies, solemnly publish and declare, that these united colonies are, and of right ought to be, free and independent states: that they are absolved from all allegiance to the British Crown, and that all political connection between them and the state of Great Britain is, and ought to be, totally dissolved; and that, as free and independent states, they have full power to levy war, conclude peace, contract alliances, establish commerce, and to do all other acts and things which independent states may of right do. And, for the support of this declaration, with a firm reliance on the protection of Divine Providence, we mutually pledge to each other our lives, our fortunes, and our sacred honor.

The foregoing Declaration was, by order of Congress, engrossed, and signed by the following members:

JOHN HANCOCK

New Hampshire
Josiah Bartlett
William Whipple
Matthew Thornton

Massachusetts Bay
Samuel Adams
John Adams
Robert Treat Paine
Elbridge Gerry

Rhode Island
Stephen Hopkins
William Ellery

Connecticut
Roger Sherman
Samuel Huntington
William Williams
Oliver Wolcott

New York
William Floyd
Philip Livingston
Francis Lewis
Lewis Morris

New Jersey
Richard Stockton
John Witherspoon
Francis Hopkinson
John Hart
Abraham Clark

Pennsylvania
Robert Morris
Benjamin Rush
Benjamin Franklin
John Morton
George Clymer
James Smith
George Taylor
James Wilson
George Ross

Delaware
Caesar Rodney
George Read
Thomas M'Kean

Maryland
Samuel Chase
William Paca
Thomas Stone
Charles Carroll,
    of Carrollton

Virginia
George Wythe
Richard Henry Lee
Thomas Jefferson
Benjamin Harrison
Thomas Nelson, Jr.
Francis Lightfoot Lee
Carter Braxton

North Carolina
William Hooper
Joseph Hewes
John Penn

South Carolina
Edward Rutledge
Thomas Heyward, Jr.
Thomas Lynch, Jr.
Arthur Middleton

Georgia
Button Gwinnett
Lyman Hall
George Walton

Resolved, That copies of the Declaration be sent to the several assemblies, conventions, and committees, or councils of safety, and to the several commanding officers of the continental troops; that it be proclaimed in each of the United States, at the head of the army.

THE CONSTITUTION OF THE UNITED STATES OF AMERICA[1]

We the People of the United States, in Order to form a more perfect Union, establish Justice, insure domestic Tranquility, provide for the common defence, promote the general Welfare, and secure the Blessings of Liberty to ourselves and our Posterity, do ordain and establish this CONSTITUTION for the United States of America.

ARTICLE I

Section 1. All legislative Powers herein granted shall be vested in a Congress of the United States, which shall consist of a Senate and House of Representatives.

Section 2. The House of Representatives shall be composed of Members chosen every second Year by the People of the several States, and the Electors in each State shall have the Qualifications requisite for Electors of the most numerous Branch of the State Legislature.

No Person shall be a Representative who shall not have attained to the Age of twenty-five Years, and been seven Years a Citizen of the United States, and who shall not, when elected, be an Inhabitant of that State in which he shall be chosen.

[Representatives and direct Taxes[2] shall be apportioned among the several States which may be included within this Union, according to their respective Numbers, which shall be determined by adding to the whole Number of free Persons, including those bound to Service for a Term of Years, and excluding Indians not taxed, three fifths of all other Persons.][3] The actual Enumeration shall be made within three Years after the first Meeting of the Congress of the United States, and within every subsequent Term of ten Years, in such Manner as they shall by Law direct. The Number of Representatives shall not exceed one for every thirty Thousand, but each State shall have at Least one Representative; and until such enumeration shall be made, the State of New Hampshire shall be entitled to chuse three, Massachusetts eight, Rhode-Island and Providence Plantations one, Connecticut five, New York six, New Jersey four, Pennsylvania eight, Delaware one, Maryland six, Virginia ten, North Carolina five, South Carolina five, and Georgia three.

When vacancies happen in the Representation from any State, the Executive Authority thereof shall issue Writs of Election to fill such Vacancies.

The House of Representatives shall chuse their Speaker and other Officers; and shall have the sole Power of Impeachment.

Section 3. The Senate of the United States shall be composed of two Senators from each State, chosen by the Legislature thereof, for six Years; and each Senator shall have one Vote.

Immediately after they shall be assembled in Consequence of the first Election, they shall be divided as equally as may be into three Classes. The Seats of the Senators of the first Class shall be vacated at the Expiration of the second Year, of the second Class at the Expiration of the fourth Year, and of the third Class at the Expiration of the sixth Year, so that one-third may be chosen every second Year; and if Vacancies happen by Resignation, or otherwise, during the Recess of the Legislature of any State, the Executive thereof may make temporary Appointments until the next Meeting of the Legislature, which shall then fill such Vacancies.

No Person shall be a Senator who shall not have attained to the Age of thirty Years, and been nine Years a Citizen of the United States, and who shall not, when elected, be an Inhabitant of that State for which he shall be chosen.

The Vice President of the United States shall be President of the Senate, but shall have no vote, unless they be equally divided.

The Senate shall chuse their other Officers, and also a President pro tempore, in the absence of the Vice President, or when he shall exercise the Office of President of the United States.

---

[1]This version follows the original Constitution in capitalization and spelling. It is adapted from the text published by the United States Department of the Interior, Office of Education.

[2]Altered by the Sixteenth Amendment.

[3]Negated by the Fourteenth Amendment.

The Senate shall have the sole Power to try all Impeachments. When sitting for that purpose they shall be on Oath or Affirmation. When the President of the United States is tried, the Chief Justice shall preside: And no person shall be convicted without the Concurrence of two thirds of the Members present.

Judgment in Cases of Impeachment shall not extend further than to removal from Office, and disqualification to hold and enjoy any Office of honor, Trust, or Profit under the United States: but the Party convicted shall nevertheless be liable and subject to Indictment, Trial, Judgment, and Punishment, according to Law.

Section 4. The Times, Places and Manner of holding Elections for Senators and Representatives, shall be prescribed in each State by the Legislature thereof; but the Congress may at any time by Law make or alter such Regulations, except as to the Places of Chusing Senators.

The Congress shall assemble at least once in every Year, and such Meeting shall be on the first Monday in December, unless they shall by Law appoint a different Day.

Section 5. Each House shall be the Judge of the Elections, Returns and Qualifications of its own Members, and a Majority of each shall constitute a Quorum to do Business; but a smaller number may adjourn from day to day, and may be authorized to compel the Attendance of absent Members, in such Manner, and under such Penalties, as each House may provide.

Each House may determine the Rules of its Proceedings, punish its Members for disorderly Behaviour, and, with the Concurrence of two thirds, expel a Member.

Each House shall keep a Journal of its Proceedings, and from time to time publish the same, excepting such Parts as may in their Judgment require Secrecy; and the Yeas and Nays of the Members of either House on any question shall, at the Desire of one fifth of those Present, be entered on the Journal.

Neither House, during the Session of Congress, shall, without the Consent of the other, adjourn for more than three days, nor to any other Place than that in which the two Houses shall be sitting.

Section 6. The Senators and Representatives shall receive a Compensation for their Services, to be ascertained by Law, and paid out of the Treasury of the United States. They shall in all Cases, except Treason, Felony, and Breach of the Peace, be privileged from Arrest during their Attendance at the Session of their respective Houses, and in going to and returning from the same; and for any Speech or Debate in either House, they shall not be questioned in any other Place.

No Senator or Representative shall, during the Time for which he was elected, be appointed to any civil Office under the Authority of the United States, which shall have been created, or the Emoluments whereof shall have been increased, during such time; and no Person holding any Office under the United States shall be a Member of either House during his continuance in Office.

Section 7. All Bills for raising Revenue shall originate in the House of Representatives; but the Senate may propose or concur with Amendments as on other bills.

Every Bill which shall have passed the House of Representatives and the Senate, shall, before it become a Law, be presented to the President of the United States; If he approve he shall sign it, but if not he shall return it, with his Objections, to that House in which it shall have originated, who shall enter the Objections at large on their Journal, and proceed to reconsider it. If after such Reconsideration two thirds of that House shall agree to pass the bill, it shall be sent, together with the objections, to the other House, by which it shall likewise be reconsidered, and if approved by two thirds of that House, it shall become a Law. But in all such Cases the Votes of both Houses shall be determined by Yeas and Nays, and the Names of the Persons voting for and against the Bill shall be entered on the Journal of each House respectively. If any Bill shall not be returned by the President within ten Days (Sundays excepted) after it shall have been presented to him, the Same shall be a Law, in like Manner as if he had signed it, unless the Congress by their Adjournment prevent its Return, in which Case it shall not be a Law.

Every Order, Resolution, or Vote to which the Concurrence of the Senate and House of

Representatives may be necessary (except on a question of Adjournment) shall be presented to the President of the United States; and before the Same shall take Effect, shall be approved by him, or being disapproved by him, shall be repassed by two thirds of the Senate and House of Representatives, according to the Rules and Limitations prescribed in the Case of a Bill.

Section 8. The Congress shall have Power To lay and collect Taxes, Duties, Imposts and Excises, to pay the Debts and provide for the common Defence and general Welfare of the United States; but all Duties, Imposts and Excises shall be uniform throughout the United States;

To borrow money on the credit of the United States;

To regulate Commerce with foreign Nations, and among the several States, and with the Indian Tribes;

To establish an uniform rule of Naturalization, and uniform Laws on the subject of Bankruptcies throughout the United States;

To coin Money, regulate the Value thereof, and of foreign Coin, and fix the Standard of Weights and Measures;

To provide for the Punishment of counterfeiting the Securities and current Coin of the United States;

To establish Post Offices and post Roads;

To promote the Progress of Science and useful Arts, by securing for limited Times to Authors and Inventors the exclusive Right to their respective Writings and Discoveries;

To constitute Tribunals inferior to the Supreme Court;

To define and punish Piracies and Felonies committed on the high Seas, and Offenses against the Law of Nations;

To declare War, grant Letters of Marque and Reprisal, and make Rules concerning Captures on Land and Water;

To raise and support Armies, but no Appropriation of Money to that Use shall be for a longer Term than two Years;

To provide and maintain a Navy;

To make Rules for the Government and Regulation of the land and naval forces;

To provide for calling forth the Militia to execute the Laws of the Union, suppress Insurrections and repel Invasions;

To provide for organizing, arming, and disciplining the Militia, and for government such Part of them as may be employed in the Service of the United States, reserving to the States respectively, the Appointment of the Officers, and the Authority of training the Militia according to the discipline prescribed by Congress;

To exercise exclusive Legislation in all Cases whatsoever, over such District (not exceeding ten Miles square) as may, by Cession of particular States, and the acceptance of Congress, become the Seat of the Government of the United States, and to exercise like Authority over all Places purchased by the Consent of the Legislature of the State in which the Same shall be, for the Erection of Forts, Magazines, Arsenals, Dock-yards, and other needful Buildings;—And

To make all Laws which shall be necessary and proper for carrying into Execution the foregoing Powers, and all other Powers vested by this Constitution in the Government of the United States, or in any Department or Officer thereof.

Section 9. The Migration or Importation of such Persons as any of the States now existing shall think proper to admit, shall not be prohibited by the Congress prior to the Year one thousand eight hundred and eight, but a tax or duty may be imposed on such Importation, not exceeding ten dollars for each Person.

The privilege of the Writ of Habeas Corpus shall not be suspended, unless when in Cases of Rebellion or Invasion the public Safety may require it.

No bill of Attainder or ex post facto Law shall be passed.

No capitation, or other direct, Tax shall be laid unless in Proportion to the Census or Enumeration herein before directed to be taken.

No Tax or Duty shall be laid on Articles exported from any State.

No Preference shall be given by any Regulation of Commerce or Revenue to the Ports of one State over those of another: nor shall Vessels bound to, or from, one State, be obliged to enter, clear, or pay Duties in another.

No Money shall be drawn from the Treasury, but in Consequence of Appropriations made by Law; and a regular Statement and Account of the Receipts and Expenditures of all public Money shall be published from time to time.

No Title of Nobility shall be granted by the United States: And no Person holding any Office of Profit or Trust under them, shall, without the Consent of the Congress, accept of any present, Emolument, Office, or Title, of any kind whatever, from any King, Prince, or foreign State.

Section 10. No State shall enter into any Treaty, Alliance, or Confederation; grant Letters of Marque and Reprisal; coin Money; emit Bills of Credit; make any Thing but gold and silver Coin a Tender in Payment of Debts; pass any Bill of Attainder, ex post facto Law, or Law impairing the Obligation of Contracts, or grant any Title of Nobility.

No State shall, without the Consent of the Congress, lay any Imposts or Duties on Imports or Exports, except what may be absolutely necessary for executing its inspection Laws; and the net Produce of all Duties and Imposts, laid by any State on Imports or Exports, shall be for the use of the Treasury of the United States; and all such Laws shall be subject to the Revision and Control of the Congress.

No state shall, without the Consent of Congress, lay any duty of Tonnage, keep Troops, or Ships of War in time of Peace, enter into any Agreement or Compact with another State, or with a foreign Power, or engage in War, unless actually invaded, or in such imminent Danger as will not admit of delay.

ARTICLE II

Section 1. The executive Power shall be vested in a President of the United States of America. He shall hold his Office during the Term of four years, and, together with the Vice President, chosen for the same Term, be elected, as follows:

Each State shall appoint, in such Manner as the Legislature thereof may direct, a Number of Electors, equal to the whole Number of Senators and Representatives to which the State may be entitled in the Congress: but no Senator or Representative, or Person holding an Office of Trust or Profit under the United States, shall be appointed an Elector.

[The Electors shall meet in their respective States, and vote by Ballot for two persons, of whom one at least shall not be an Inhabitant of the same State with themselves. And they shall make a List of all the Persons voted for, and of the Number of Votes for each; which List they shall sign and certify, and transmit sealed to the Seat of the Government of the United States, directed to the President of the Senate. The President of the Senate shall, in the Presence of the Senate and House of Representatives, open all the Certificates, and the Votes shall then be counted. The Person having the greatest Number of Votes shall be the President, if such Number be a Majority of the whole Number of Electors appointed; and if there be more than one who have such Majority, and have an equal Number of Votes, then the House of Representatives shall immediately chuse by Ballot one of them for President; and if no Person have a Majority, then from the five highest on the List the said House shall in like Manner chuse the President. But in chusing the President, the Votes shall be taken by States, the Representation from each State having one Vote; a quorum for this Purpose shall consist of a Member or Members from two-thirds of the States, and a Majority of all the States shall be necessary to a Choice. In every Case, after the Choice of the President, the Person having the greatest Number of Votes of the Electors shall be the Vice President. But if there should remain two or more who have equal votes, the Senate shall chuse from them by Ballot the Vice President.][4]

The Congress may determine the Time of chusing the Electors, and the Day on which they shall give their Votes; which Day shall be the same throughout the United States.

No person except a natural-born Citizen, or a Citizen of the United States, at the time of the Adoption of this Constitution, shall be eligible to the Office of President; neither shall any Person be eligible to that Office who shall not have attained to the Age of thirty-five years, and been fourteen Years a Resident within the United States.

In Case of the Removal of the President from Office, or of his Death, Resignation, or Inability to discharge the Powers and Duties of the said Office, the same shall devolve on the Vice President, and the Congress may by Law provide for the Case of Removal, Death, Resignation, or Inability, both of the President and Vice President,

---

[4]Revised by the Twelfth Amendment.

declaring what Officer shall then act as President, and such Officer shall act accordingly, until the disability be removed, or a President shall be elected.

The President shall, at stated Times, receive for his Services a Compensation, which shall neither be increased nor diminished during the Period for which he shall have been elected, and he shall not receive within that Period any other Emolument from the United States, or any of them.

Before he enter on the execution of his Office, he shall take the following Oath or Affirmation:—"I do solemnly swear (or affirm) that I will faithfully execute the Office of President of the United States, and will, to the best of my Ability, preserve, protect, and defend the Constitution of the United States."

Section 2. The President shall be Commander in Chief of the Army and Navy of the United States, and of the Militia of the several States, when called into the actual Service of the United States; he may require the Opinion, in writing, of the principal Officer in each of the executive Departments, upon any subject relating to the Duties of their respective Offices, and he shall have Power to Grant Reprieves and Pardons for Offenses against the United States, except in Cases of Impeachment.

He shall have Power, by and with the Advice and Consent of the Senate, to make Treaties, provided two-thirds of the Senators present concur; and he shall nominate, and by and with the Advice and Consent of the Senate, shall appoint Ambassadors, other public Ministers and Consuls, Judges of the supreme Court, and all other Officers of the United States, whose Appointments are not herein otherwise provided for, and which shall be established by Law: but the Congress may by Law vest the Appointment of such inferior Officers, as they think proper, in the President alone, in the Courts of Law, or in the Heads of Departments.

The President shall have Power to fill up all Vacancies that may happen during the Recess of the Senate, by granting Commissions which shall expire at the End of their next Session.

Section 3. He shall from time to time give to the Congress Information of the State of the Union, and recommend to their Consideration such Measures as he shall judge necessary and expedient; he may, on extraordinary occasions, convene both Houses, or either of them, and in Case of Disagreement between them, with respect to the Time of Adjournment, he may adjourn them to such Time as he shall think proper; he shall receive Ambassadors and other public Ministers; he shall take care that the Laws be faithfully executed, and shall Commission all the Officers of the United States.

Section 4. The President, Vice President and all civil Officers of the United States, shall be removed from Office on Impeachment for, and Conviction of, Treason, Bribery, or other high Crimes and Misdemeanors.

ARTICLE III

Section 1. The judicial Power of the United States, shall be vested in one supreme Court, and in such inferior Courts as the Congress may from time to time ordain and establish. The Judges, both of the supreme and inferior Courts, shall hold their Offices during good Behaviour, and shall, at stated Times, receive for their Services, a Compensation, which shall not be diminished during their Continuance in Office.

Section 2. The judicial Power shall extend to all Cases, in Law and Equity, arising under this Constitution, the Laws of the United States, and Treaties made, or which shall be made, under their Authority;—to all Cases affecting ambassadors, other public ministers and consuls;—to all cases of admiralty and maritime Jurisdiction;—to Controversies to which the United States shall be a Party;—to Controversies between two or more States;—between a State and Citizens of another State;[5]—between Citizens of different States—between Citizens of the same State claiming Lands under Grants of different States, and between a State, or the Citizens thereof, and foreign States, Citizens, or Subjects.

In all Cases affecting Ambassadors, other public Ministers and Consuls, and those in which a State shall be Party, the supreme Court shall have original Jurisdiction. In all the other Cases

---

[5]Qualified by the Eleventh Amendment.

before mentioned, the supreme Court shall have appellate Jurisdiction, both as to Law and Fact, with such Exceptions, and under such Regulations as the Congress shall make.

The trial of all Crimes, except in Cases of Impeachment, shall be by Jury; and such Trial shall be held in the State where the said Crimes shall have been committed; but when not committed within any State, the Trial shall be at such Place or Places as the Congress may by Law have directed.

Section 3. Treason against the United States, shall consist only in levying War against them, or in adhering to their Enemies, giving them Aid and Comfort. No Person shall be convicted of Treason unless on the Testimony of two Witnesses to the same overt Act, or on Confession in open Court.

The Congress shall have power to declare the Punishment of Treason, but no Attainder of Treason shall work Corruption of Blood, or Forfeiture except during the Life of the Person attainted.

ARTICLE IV

Section 1. Full Faith and Credit shall be given in each State to the public Acts, Records, and judicial Proceedings of every other State. And the Congress may by general Laws prescribe the Manner in which such Acts, Records and Proceedings shall be proved, and the Effect thereof.

Section 2. The Citizens of each State shall be entitled to all Privileges and Immunities of Citizens in the several States.

A Person charged in any State with Treason, Felony, or other Crime, who shall flee from Justice, and be found in another State, shall on demand of the executive Authority of the State from which he fled, be delivered up, to be removed to the State having Jurisdiction of the crime.

No Person held to Service or Labour in one State, under the Laws thereof, escaping into another, shall, in Consequence of any Law or Regulation therein, be discharged from such Service or Labour, but shall be delivered up on Claim of the Party to whom such Service or Labour may be due.

Section 3. New States may be admitted by the Congress into this Union; but no new State shall be formed or erected within the Jurisdiction of any other State; nor any State be formed by the Junction of two or more States, or parts of States, without the Consent of the Legislatures of the States concerned as well as of the Congress.

The Congress shall have Power to dispose of and make all needful Rules and Regulations respecting the Territory or other Property belonging to the United States; and nothing in this Constitution shall be so construed as to Prejudice any Claims of the United States, or of any particular State.

Section 4. The United States shall guarantee to every State in this Union a Republican Form of Government, and shall protect each of them against Invasion; and on Application of the Legislature, or of the Executive (when the Legislature cannot be convened) against domestic Violence.

ARTICLE V

The Congress, whenever two-thirds of both Houses shall deem it necessary, shall propose Amendments to this Constitution, or, on the Application of the Legislatures of two-thirds of the several States, shall call a Convention for proposing Amendments, which, in either Case, shall be valid to all Intents and Purposes, as part of this Constitution, when ratified by the Legislatures of three-fourths of the several States, or by Conventions in three-fourths thereof, as the one or the other Mode of Ratification may be proposed by the Congress; Provided that no Amendment which may be made prior to the Year One thousand eight hundred and eight shall in any Manner affect the first and fourth Clauses in the Ninth Section of the first Article; and that no State, without its Consent, shall be deprived of its equal Suffrage in the Senate.

ARTICLE VI

All Debts contracted and Engagements entered into, before the Adoption of this Constitution, shall be as valid against the United States under this Constitution, as under the Confederation.

This Constitution, and the Laws of the United States which shall be made in Pursuance thereof; and all Treaties made, or which shall be made, under the Authority of the United States, shall be the supreme Law of the Land; and the Judges in every State shall be bound thereby, any Thing in the Constitution or Laws of any State to the Contrary notwithstanding.

The Senators and Representatives before mentioned, and the Members of the several State Legislatures, and all executive and judicial Officers, both of the United States and of the several States, shall be bound by Oath or Affirmation to support this Constitution; but no religious Tests shall ever be required as a qualification to any Office or public Trust under the United States.

ARTICLE VII

The Ratification of the Conventions of nine States shall be sufficient for the Establishment of this Constitution between the States so ratifying the same.

Done in Convention by the Unanimous Consent of the States present the Seventeenth Day of September in the Year of our Lord one thousand seven hundred and Eighty seven, and of the Independence of the United States of America the Twelfth. In Witness whereof We have hereunto subscribed our Names.[6]

GEORGE WASHINGTON

PRESIDENT AND DEPUTY FROM VIRGINIA

New Hampshire	**New Jersey**	**Delaware**	**North Carolina**
John Langdon	William Livingston	George Read	William Blount
Nicholas Gilman	David Brearley	Gunning Bedford, Jr.	Richard Dobbs
	William Paterson	John Dickinson	Spaight
	Jonathan Dayton	Richard Bassett	Hugh Williamson
		Jacob Broom	
Massachusetts	**Pennsylvania**	**Maryland**	**South Carolina**
Nathaniel Gorham	Benjamin Franklin	James McHenry	John Rutledge
Rufus King	Thomas Mifflin	Daniel of	Charles Cotesworth
	Robert Morris	St. Thomas Jenifer	Pinckney
Connecticut	George Clymer	Daniel Carroll	Charles Pinckney
William Samuel	Thomas FitzSimons		Pierce Butler
Johnson	Jared Ingersoll	**Virginia**	
Roger Sherman	James Wilson	John Blair	**Georgia**
	Gouverneur Morris	James Madison, Jr.	William Few
New York			Abraham Baldwin
Alexander Hamilton			

Articles in Addition to, and Amendment of, the Constitution of the United States of America, Proposed by Congress, and Ratified by the Legislatures of the Several States, Pursuant to the Fifth Article of the Original Constitution[7]

[AMENDMENT I]

Congress shall make no law respecting an establishment of religion, or prohibiting the free exercise thereof; or abridging the freedom of speech, or of the press; or the right of the people peaceably to assemble, and to petition the Government for a redress of grievances.

[AMENDMENT II]

A well regulated Militia, being necessary to the security of a free State, the right of the people to keep and bear Arms shall not be infringed.

[6]These are the full names of the signers, which in some cases are not the signatures on the document.

[7]This heading appears only in the joint resolution submitting the first ten amendments, known as the Bill of Rights.

[AMENDMENT III]

No Soldier shall, in time of peace, be quartered in any house, without the consent of the Owner, nor in time of war, but in a manner to be prescribed by law.

[AMENDMENT IV]

The right of the people to be secure in their persons, houses, papers, and effects, against unreasonable searches and seizures, shall not be violated, and no Warrants shall issue, but upon probable cause, supported by Oath or affirmation, and particularly describing the place to be searched, and the persons or things to be seized.

[AMENDMENT V]

No person shall be held to answer for a capital or otherwise infamous crime, unless on a presentment or indictment of a Grand Jury, except in cases arising in the land or naval forces, or in the Militia, when in actual service in time of War or public danger; nor shall any person be subject for the same offence to be twice put in jeopardy of life or limb; nor shall be compelled in any criminal case to be a witness against himself, nor be deprived of life, liberty, or property, without due process of law; nor shall private property be taken for public use, without just compensation.

[AMENDMENT VI]

In all criminal prosecutions, the accused shall enjoy the right to a speedy and public trial, by an impartial jury of the State and district wherein the crime shall have been committed, which district shall have been previously ascertained by law, and to be informed of the nature and cause of the accusation; to be confronted with the witnesses against him; to have compulsory process for obtaining witnesses in his favour, and to have the Assistance of Counsel for his defence.

[AMENDMENT VII]

In suits at common law, where the value in controversy shall exceed twenty dollars, the right of trial by jury shall be preserved, and no fact tried by a jury, shall be otherwise reexamined in any Court of the United States, than according to the rules of the common law.

[AMENDMENT VIII]

Excessive bail shall not be required, nor excessive fines imposed, nor cruel and unusual punishments inflicted.

[AMENDMENT IX]

The enumeration of the Constitution, of certain rights, shall not be construed to deny or disparage others retained by the people.

[AMENDMENT X]

The powers not delegated to the United States by the Constitution, nor prohibited by it to the States, are reserved to the States respectively, or to the people.
[Amendments I–X, in force 1791.]

[AMENDMENT XI][8]

The Judicial power of the United States shall not be construed to extend to any suit in law or equity, commenced or prosecuted against one of the United States by Citizens of another State, or by Citizens or Subjects of any Foreign State.

[AMENDMENT XII][9]

The Electors shall meet in their respective States and vote by ballot for President and Vice-President, one of whom, at least, shall not be an inhabitant of the same State with themselves; they shall name in their ballots the person voted for as President, and in distinct ballots the person voted for as Vice-President, and they shall make distinct lists of all persons voted for as President, and of all persons voted for as Vice-

[8]Adopted in 1798.
[9]Adopted in 1804.

President, and of the number of votes for each, which lists they shall sign and certify, and transmit sealed to the seat of the government of the United States, directed to the President of the Senate;—The President of the Senate shall, in the presence of the Senate and House of Representatives, open all the certificates and the votes shall then be counted;—The person having the greatest number of votes for President, shall be the President, if such number be a majority of the whole number of Electors appointed; and if no person have such majority, then from the persons having the highest numbers not exceeding three on the list of those voted for as President, the House of Representatives shall choose immediately, by ballot, the President. But in choosing the President, the votes shall be taken by states, the representation from each state having one vote; a quorum for this purpose shall consist of a member or members from two-thirds of the states, and a majority of all the states shall be necessary to a choice. And if the House of Representatives shall not choose a President whenever the right of choice shall devolve upon them, before the fourth day of March next following, then the Vice-President shall act as President, as in the case of the death or other constitutional disability of the President.—The person having the greatest number of votes as Vice-President, shall be the Vice-President, if such number be a majority of the whole number of Electors appointed, and if no person have a majority, then from the two highest numbers on the list, the Senate shall choose the Vice-President; a quorum for the purpose shall consist of two-thirds of the whole number of Senators, and a majority of the whole number shall be necessary to a choice. But no person constitutionally ineligible to the office of President shall be eligible to that of Vice-President of the United States.

[AMENDMENT XIII][10]

Section 1. Neither slavery nor involuntary servitude, except as a punishment for crime whereof the party shall have been duly convicted, shall exist within the United States, or any place subject to their jurisdiction.

Section 2. Congress shall have power to enforce this article by appropriate legislation.

[10]Adopted in 1865.

[AMENDMENT XIV][11]

Section 1. All persons born or naturalized in the United States, and subject to the jurisdiction thereof, are citizens of the United States and of the State wherein they reside. No State shall abridge the privileges or immunities of citizens of the United States; nor shall any State deprive any person of life, liberty, or property, without due process of law; nor deny to any person within its jurisdiction the equal protection of the laws.

Section 2. Representatives shall be apportioned among the several States according to their respective numbers, counting the whole number of persons in each State, excluding Indians not taxed. But when the right to vote at any election for the choice of electors for President and Vice-President of the United States, Representatives in Congress, the Executive and Judicial officers of a State, or the members of the Legislature thereof, is denied to any of the male inhabitants of such State, being twenty-one years of age, and citizens of the United States, or in any way abridged, except for participation in rebellion, or other crime, the basis of representation therein shall be reduced in the proportion which the number of such male citizens shall bear to the whole number of male citizens twenty-one years of age in such State.

Section 3. No person shall be a Senator or Representative in Congress, or elector of President and Vice-President, or hold any office, civil or military, under the United States, or under any State, who, having previously taken an oath, as a member of Congress, or as an officer of the United States, or as a member of any State legislature, or as an executive or judicial officer of any State, to support the Constitution of the United States, shall have engaged in insurrection or rebellion against the same, or given aid or comfort to the enemies thereof. But Congress may by a vote of two-thirds of each House, remove such disability.

Section 4. The validity of the public debt of the United States, authorized by law, including debts incurred for payment of pensions and bounties for services in suppressing insurrection or rebellion, shall not be questioned. But neither the

[11]Adopted in 1868.

United States nor any State shall assume or pay any debts or obligation incurred in aid of insurrection or rebellion against the United States, or any claim for the loss or emancipation of any slave; but all such debts, obligations, and claims shall be held illegal and void.

Section 5. The Congress shall have the power to enforce, by appropriate legislation, the provisions of this article.

[AMENDMENT XV][12]

Section 1. The right of citizens of the United States to vote shall not be denied or abridged by the United States or by any State on account of race, color, or previous condition of servitude—

Section 2. The Congress shall have power to enforce this article by appropriate legislation.

[AMENDMENT XVI][13]

The Congress shall have power to lay and collect taxes on incomes, from whatever source derived, without apportionment among the several States, and without regard to any census or enumeration.

[AMENDMENT XVII][14]

The Senate of the United States shall be composed of two Senators from each State, elected by the people thereof, for six years; and each Senator shall have one vote. The electors in each State shall have the qualifications requisite for electors of the most numerous branch of the State legislatures.

When vacancies happen in the representation of any State in the Senate, the executive authority of such State shall issue writs of election to fill such vacancies: *Provided,* That the legislature of any State may empower the executive thereof to make temporary appointments until the people fill the vacancies by election as the legislature may direct.

This amendment shall not be so construed as to affect the election or term of any Senator chosen before it becomes valid as part of the Constitution.

[AMENDMENT XVIII][15]

Section 1. After one year from the ratification of this article the manufacture, sale, or transportation of intoxicating liquors within, the importation thereof into, or the exportation thereof from the United States and all territory subject to the jurisdiction thereof for beverage purposes is hereby prohibited.

Section 2. The Congress and the several States shall have concurrent power to enforce this article by appropriate legislation.

Section 3. This article shall be inoperative unless it shall have been ratified as an amendment to the Constitution by the legislatures of the several States, as provided in the Constitution, within seven years from the date of the submission hereof to the States by the Congress.

[AMENDMENT XIX][16]

The right of citizens of the United States to vote shall not be denied or abridged by the United States or by any State on account of sex.

Congress shall have power to enforce this article by appropriate legislation.

[AMENDMENT XX][17]

Section 1. The terms of the President and Vice-President shall end at noon on the 20th day of January, and the terms of Senators and Representatives at noon on the 3d day of January, of the years in which such terms would have ended if this article had not been ratified; and the terms of their successors shall then begin.

[12]Adopted in 1870.
[13]Adopted in 1913.
[14]Adopted in 1913.

[15]Adopted in 1918.
[16]Adopted in 1920.
[17]Adopted in 1933.

Section 2. The Congress shall assemble at least once in every year, and such meeting shall begin at noon on the 3d day of January, unless they shall by law appoint a different day.

Section 3. If, at the time fixed for the beginning of the term of the President, the President elect shall have died, the Vice-President elect shall become President. If a President shall not have been chosen before the time fixed for the beginning of his term or if the President elect shall have failed to qualify, then the Vice-President elect shall act as President until a President shall have qualified; and the Congress may by law provide for the case wherein neither a President elect nor a Vice-President elect shall have qualified, declaring who shall then act as President, or the manner in which one who is to act shall be selected, and such person shall act accordingly until a President or Vice-President shall have qualified.

Section 4. The Congress may by law provide for the case of the death of any of the persons from whom the House of Representatives may choose a President whenever the right of choice shall have devolved upon them, and for the case of the death of any of the persons from whom the Senate may choose a Vice-President whenever the right of choice shall have devolved upon them.

Section 5. Sections 1 and 2 shall take effect on the 15th day of October following the ratification of this article.

Section 6. This article shall be inoperative unless it shall have been ratified as an amendment to the Constitution by the legislatures of three-fourths of the several States within seven years from the date of its submission.

[AMENDMENT XXI][18]

Section 1. The eighteenth article of amendment to the Constitution of the United States is hereby repealed.

Section 2. The transportation or importation into any State, Territory, or possession of the United States for delivery or use therein of intoxicating liquors, in violation of the laws thereof, is hereby prohibited.

Section 3. This article shall be inoperative unless it shall have been ratified as an amendment to the Constitution by conventions in the several States, as provided in the Constitution, within seven years from the date of the submission hereof to the States by the Congress.

[AMENDMENT XXII][19]

No person shall be elected to the office of the President more than twice, and no person who has held the office of President, or acted as President, for more than two years of a term to which some other person was elected President shall be elected to the office of the President more than once.

But this Article shall not apply to any person holding the office of President when this Article was proposed by the Congress, and shall not prevent any person who may be holding the office of President, or acting as President, during the term within which this Article becomes operative from holding the office of President or acting as President during the remainder of such term.

This article shall be inoperative unless it shall have been ratified as an amendment to the Constitution by the legislatures of three-fourths of the several states within seven years from the date of its submission to the states by the Congress.

[AMENDMENT XXIII][20]

Section 1. The District constituting the seat of Government of the United States shall appoint in such manner as the Congress may direct:

A number of electors of President and Vice-President equal to the whole number of Senators and Representatives in Congress to which the District would be entitled if it were a State, but in no event more than the least populous State; they shall be in addition to those appointed by the States, but they shall be considered, for the purpose of the election of President and Vice-

[18]Adopted in 1933.

[19]Adopted in 1961.

[20]Adopted in 1961.

President, to be electors appointed by a State; and they shall meet in the District and perform such duties as provided by the twelfth article of amendment.

Section 2. The Congress shall have power to enforce this article by appropriate legislation.

[AMENDMENT XXIV][21]

Section 1. The right of citizens of the United States to vote in any primary or other election for President or Vice-President, for electors for President or Vice-President, or for Senator or Representative in Congress, shall not be denied or abridged by the United States or any state by reason of failure to pay any poll tax or other tax.

Section 2. The Congress shall have the power to enforce this article by appropriate legislation.

[AMENDMENT XXV][22]

Section 1. In case of the removal of the President from office or of his death or resignation, the Vice-President shall become President.

Section 2. Whenever there is a vacancy in the office of the Vice President, the President shall nominate a Vice President who shall take office upon confirmation by a majority vote of both Houses of Congress.

Section 3. Whenever the President transmits to the President Pro Tempore of the Senate and the Speaker of the House of Representatives his written declaration that he is unable to discharge the powers and duties of his office, and until he transmits to them a written declaration to the contrary, such powers and duties shall be discharged by the Vice-President as Acting President.

Section 4. Whenever the Vice-President and a majority of either the principal officers of the executive departments or of such other body as Congress may by law provide, transmit to the President Pro Tempore of the Senate and the Speaker of the House of Representatives their

written declaration that the President is unable to discharge the powers and duties of his office, the Vice President shall immediately assume the powers and duties of the office as Acting President.

Thereafter, when the President transmits to the President Pro Tempore of the Senate and the Speaker of the House of Representatives his written declaration that no inability exists, he shall resume the powers and duties of his office unless the Vice President and a majority of either the principal officers of the executive departments or of such other body as Congress may by law provide, transmit within four days to the President Pro Tempore of the Senate and the Speaker of the House of Representatives their written declaration that the President is unable to discharge the powers and duties of his office. Thereupon Congress shall decide the issue, assembling within forty-eight hours for that purpose if not in session. If the Congress, within twenty-one days after receipt of the latter written declaration, or, if Congress is not in session, within twenty-one days after Congress is required to assemble, determines by two-thirds vote of both Houses that the President is unable to discharge the powers and duties of his office, the Vice President shall continue to discharge the same as Acting President; otherwise, the President shall resume the powers and duties of his office.

[AMENDMENT XXVI][23]

Section 1. The right of citizens of the United States, who are eighteen years of age or older, to vote shall not be denied or abridged by the United States or by any State on account of age.

Section 2. The Congress shall have power to enforce this article by appropriate legislation.

[AMENDMENT XXVII][24]

No law, varying the compensation for the services of the Senators and Representatives, shall take effect, until an election of Representatives shall have intervened.

[21]Adopted in 1964.
[22]Adopted in 1967.

[23]Adopted in 1971.
[24]Adopted in 1992.

PRESIDENTIAL ELECTIONS

Year	Candidates	Parties	Popular Vote	% of Popular Vote	Electoral Vote	% Voter Partici-pation
1789	**George Washington**				69	
	John Adams				34	
	Other candidates				35	
1792	**George Washington**				132	
	John Adams				77	
	George Clinton				50	
	Other candidates				5	
1796	**John Adams**	Federalist			71	
	Thomas Jefferson	Dem.-Rep.			68	
	Thomas Pinckney	Federalist			59	
	Aaron Burr	Dem.-Rep.			30	
	Other candidates				48	
1800	**Thomas Jefferson**	Dem.-Rep.			73	
	Aaron Burr	Dem.-Rep.			73	
	John Adams	Federalist			65	
	Charles C. Pinckney	Federalist			64	
	John Jay	Federalist			1	
1804	**Thomas Jefferson**	Dem.-Rep.			162	
	Charles C. Pinckney	Federalist			14	
1808	**James Madison**	Dem.-Rep.			122	
	Charles C. Pinckney	Federalist			47	
	George Clinton	Dem.-Rep.			6	
1812	**James Madison**	Dem.-Rep.			128	
	DeWitt Clinton	Federalist			89	
1816	**James Monroe**	Dem.-Rep.			183	
	Rufus King	Federalist			34	
1820	**James Monroe**	Dem.-Rep.			231	
	John Quincy Adams	Indep.-Rep.			1	
1824	**John Quincy Adams**	Dem.-Rep.	108,740	31.0	84	26.9
	Andrew Jackson	Dem.-Rep.	153,544	43.0	99	
	Henry Clay	Dem.-Rep.	47,136	13.0	37	
	William H. Crawford	Dem.-Rep.	46,618	13.0	41	
1828	**Andrew Jackson**	Democratic	647,286	56.0	178	57.6
	John Quincy Adams	National Republican	508,064	44.0	83	
1832	**Andrew Jackson**	Democratic	688,242	54.5	219	55.4
	Henry Clay	National Republican	473,462	37.5	49	
	William Wirt	Anti-Masonic ⎱	101,051	8.0	7	
	John Floyd	Democratic ⎰			11	
1836	**Martin Van Buren**	Democratic	765,483	50.9	170	57.8
	William H. Harrison	Whig ⎤			73	
	Hugh L. White	Whig ⎟	739,795	49.1	26	
	Daniel Webster	Whig ⎟			14	
	W. P. Mangum	Whig ⎦			11	

Year	Candidates	Parties	Popular Vote	% of Popular Vote	Electoral Vote	% Voter Partici- pation
1840	**William H. Harrison**	Whig	1,275,016	53.0	234	80.2
	Martin Van Buren	Democratic	1,129,102	47.0	60	
1844	**James K. Polk**	Democratic	1,338,464	49.6	170	78.9
	Henry Clay	Whig	1,300,097	48.1	105	
	James G. Birney	Liberty	62,300	2.3		
1848	**Zachary Taylor**	Whig	1,360,967	47.4	163	72.7
	Lewis Cass	Democratic	1,222,342	42.5	127	
	Martin Van Buren	Free Soil	291,263	10.1		
1852	**Franklin Pierce**	Democratic	1,601,117	50.9	254	69.6
	Winfield Scott	Whig	1,385,453	44.1	42	
	John P. Hale	Free Soil	155,825	5.0		
1856	**James Buchanan**	Democratic	1,832,955	45.3	174	78.9
	John C. Fremont	Republican	1,339,932	33.1	114	
	Millard Fillmore	American	871,731	21.6	8	
1860	**Abraham Lincoln**	Republican	1,866,452	39.8	180	81.2
	Stephen A. Douglas	Democratic	1,375,157	29.5	12	
	John C. Breckinridge	Democratic	847,953	18.1	72	
	John Bell	Constitutional Union	590,631	12.6	39	
1864	**Abraham Lincoln**	Republican	2,206,938	55.0	212	73.8
	George B. McClellan	Democratic	1,803,787	45.0	21	
1868	**Ulysses S. Grant**	Republican	3,013,421	52.7	214	78.1
	Horatio Seymour	Democratic	2,706,829	47.3	80	
1872	**Ulysses S. Grant**	Republican	3,596,745	55.6	286	71.3
	Horace Greeley	Democratic	2,843,446	43.9	66	
1876	**Rutherford B. Hayes**	Republican	4,036,298	48.0	185	81.8
	Samuel J. Tilden	Democratic	4,300,590	51.0	184	
1880	**James A. Garfield**	Republican	4,453,295	48.5	214	79.4
	Winfield S. Hancock	Democratic	4,414,082	48.1	155	
	James B. Weaver	Greenback-Labor	308,578	3.4		
1884	**Grover Cleveland**	Democratic	4,879,507	48.5	219	77.5
	James G. Blaine	Republican	4,850,293	48.2	182	
	Benjamin F. Butler	Greenback-Labor	175,370	1.8		
	John P. St. John	Prohibition	150,369	1.5		
1888	**Benjamin Harrison**	Republican	5,477,129	47.9	233	79.3
	Grover Cleveland	Democratic	5,537,857	48.6	168	
	Clinton B. Fisk	Prohibition	249,506	2.2		
	Anson J. Streeter	Union Labor	146,935	1.3		
1892	**Grover Cleveland**	Democratic	5,555,426	46.1	277	74.7
	Benjamin Harrison	Republican	5,182,690	43.0	145	
	James B. Weaver	People's	1,029,846	8.5	22	
	John Bidwell	Prohibition	264,133	2.2		
1896	**William McKinley**	Republican	7,104,779	52.0	271	79.3
	William J. Bryan	Democratic	6,502,925	48.0	176	
1900	**William McKinley**	Republican	7,218,491	51.7	292	73.2
	William J. Bryan	Democratic; Populist	6,356,734	45.5	155	
	John C. Wooley	Prohibition	208,914	1.5		

Year	Candidates	Parties	Popular Vote	% of Popular Vote	Electoral Vote	% Voter Partici- pation
1904	**Theodore Roosevelt**	Republican	7,628,461	57.4	336	65.2
	Alton B. Parker	Democratic	5,084,223	37.6	140	
	Eugene V. Debs	Socialist	402,283	3.0		
	Silas C. Swallow	Prohibition	258,536	1.9		
1908	**William H. Taft**	Republican	7,675,320	51.6	321	65.4
	William J. Bryan	Democratic	6,412,294	43.1	162	
	Eugene V. Debs	Socialist	420,793	2.8		
	Eugene W. Chafin	Prohibition	253,840	1.7		
1912	**Woodrow Wilson**	Democratic	6,293,454	42.0	435	58.8
	Theodore Roosevelt	Progressive	4,119,538	28.0	88	
	William H. Taft	Republican	3,484,980	24.0	8	
	Eugene V. Debs	Socialist	900,672	6.0		
	Eugene W. Chafin	Prohibition	206,275	1.4		
1916	**Woodrow Wilson**	Democratic	9,129,606	49.4	277	61.6
	Charles E. Hughes	Republican	8,538,221	46.2	254	
	A. L. Benson	Socialist	585,113	3.2		
	J. Frank Hanly	Prohibition	220,506	1.2		
1920	**Warren G. Harding**	Republican	16,143,407	60.4	404	49.2
	James M. Cox	Democratic	9,130,328	34.2	127	
	Eugene V. Debs	Socialist	919,799	3.4		
	P. P. Christensen	Farmer-Labor	265,411	1.0		
1924	**Calvin Coolidge**	Republican	15,718,211	54.0	382	48.9
	John W. Davis	Democratic	8,385,283	28.8	136	
	Robert M. La Follette	Progressive	4,831,289	16.6	13	
1928	**Herbert C. Hoover**	Republican	21,391,381	58.2	444	56.9
	Alfred E. Smith	Democratic	15,016,443	40.9	87	
1932	**Franklin D. Roosevelt**	Democratic	22,821,857	57.4	472	56.9
	Herbert C. Hoover	Republican	15,761,841	39.7	59	
	Norman Thomas	Socialist	881,951	2.2		
1936	**Franklin D. Roosevelt**	Democratic	27,751,597	60.8	523	61.0
	Alfred M. Landon	Republican	16,679,583	36.5	8	
	William Lemke	Union	882,479	1.9		
1940	**Franklin D. Roosevelt**	Democratic	27,307,819	54.8	449	62.5
	Wendell L. Wilkie	Republican	22,321,018	44.8	82	
1944	**Franklin D. Roosevelt**	Democratic	25,606,585	53.5	432	55.9
	Thomas E. Dewey	Republican	22,014,745	46.0	99	
1948	**Harry S Truman**	Democratic	24,105,812	50.0	303	53.0
	Thomas E. Dewey	Republican	21,970,065	46.0	189	
	J. Strom Thurmond	States' Rights	1,169,021	2.0	39	
	Henry A. Wallace	Progressive	1,157,172	2.0		
1952	**Dwight D. Eisenhower**	Republican	33,936,234	55.1	442	63.3
	Adlai E. Stevenson	Democratic	27,314,992	44.4	89	
1956	**Dwight D. Eisenhower**	Republican	35,590,472	57.6	457	60.6
	Adlai E. Stevenson	Democratic	26,022,752	42.1	73	
1960	**John F. Kennedy**	Democratic	34,227,096	49.7	303	62.8
	Richard M. Nixon	Republican	34,107,646	49.6	219	
	Harry F. Byrd	Independent	501,643		15	
1964	**Lyndon B. Johnson**	Democratic	43,129,566	61.1	486	61.7
	Barry M. Goldwater	Republican	27,178,188	38.5	52	

Year	Candidates	Parties	Popular Vote	% of Popular Vote	Electoral Vote	% Voter Partici- pation
1968	**Richard M. Nixon**	Republican	31,785,480	44.0	301	60.6
	Hubert H. Humphrey	Democratic	31,275,166	42.7	191	
	George C. Wallace	American Independent	9,906,473	13.5	46	
1972	**Richard M. Nixon**	Republican	47,169,911	60.7	520	55.2
	George S. McGovern	Democratic	29,170,383	37.5	17	
	John G. Schmitz	American	1,099,482	1.4		
1976	**Jimmy Carter**	Democratic	40,830,763	50.1	297	53.5
	Gerald R. Ford	Republican	39,147,793	48.0	240	
1980	**Ronald Reagan**	Republican	43,899,248	51.0	489	52.6
	Jimmy Carter	Democratic	35,481,432	41.0	49	
	John B. Anderson	Independent	5,719,437	7.0	0	
	Ed Clark	Libertarian	920,859	1.0	0	
1984	**Ronald Reagan**	Republican	54,451,521	58.8	525	53.3
	Walter Mondale	Democratic	37,565,334	40.5	13	
1988	**George Bush**	Republican	48,881,221	53.9	426	48.6
	Michael Dukakis	Democratic	41,805,422	46.1	111	
1992	**William J. Clinton**	Democratic	44,908,254	43.0	370	55.9
	George H. Bush	Republican	39,102,343	37.4	168	
	H. Ross Perot	Independent	19,741,065	18.9	0	
1996°	**William J. Clinton**	Democratic	47,401,054	49.3	379	49
	Robert Dole	Republican	39,197,350	40.7	159	
	H. Ross Perot	Reform	8,085,285	8.4	0	

°Preliminary figures

PRESIDENTIAL ADMINISTRATIONS

The Washington Administration (1789–1797)

Vice President	John Adams	1789–1797
Secretary of State	Thomas Jefferson	1789–1793
	Edmund Randolph	1794–1795
	Timothy Pickering	1795–1797
Secretary of Treasury	Alexander Hamilton	1789–1795
	Oliver Wolcott	1795–1797
Secretary of War	Henry Knox	1789–1794
	Timothy Pickering	1795–1796
	James McHenry	1796–1797
Attorney General	Edmund Randolph	1789–1793
	William Bradford	1794–1795
	Charles Lee	1795–1797
Postmaster General	Samuel Osgood	1789–1791
	Timothy Pickering	1791–1794
	Joseph Habersham	1795–1797

The John Adams Administration (1797–1801)

Vice President	Thomas Jefferson	1797–1801
Secretary of State	Timothy Pickering	1797–1800
	John Marshall	1800–1801
Secretary of Treasury	Oliver Wolcott	1797–1800
	Samuel Dexter	1800–1801
Secretary of War	James McHenry	1797–1800
	Samuel Dexter	1800–1801
Attorney General	Charles Lee	1797–1801
Postmaster General	Joseph Habersham	1797–1801
Secretary of Navy	Benjamin Stoddert	1798–1801

The Jefferson Administration (1801–1809)

Vice President	Aaron Burr	1801–1805
	George Clinton	1805–1809
Secretary of State	James Madison	1801–1809
Secretary of Treasury	Samuel Dexter	1801
	Albert Gallatin	1801–1809
Secretary of War	Henry Dearborn	1801–1809
Attorney General	Levi Lincoln	1801–1805
	Robert Smith	1805
	John Breckinridge	1805–1806
	Caesar Rodney	1807–1809

Postmaster General	Joseph Habersham	1801
	Gideon Granger	1801–1809
Secretary of Navy	Robert Smith	1801–1809

The Madison Administration (1809–1817)

Vice President	George Clinton	1809–1813
	Elbridge Gerry	1813–1817
Secretary of State	Robert Smith	1809–1811
	James Monroe	1811–1817
Secretary of Treasury	Albert Gallatin	1809–1813
	George Campbell	1814
	Alexander Dallas	1814–1816
	William Crawford	1816–1817
Secretary of War	William Eustis	1809–1812
	John Armstrong	1813–1814
	James Monroe	1814–1815
	William Crawford	1815–1817
Attorney General	Caesar Rodney	1809–1811
	William Pinkney	1811–1814
	Richard Rush	1814–1817
Postmaster General	Gideon Granger	1809–1814
	Return Meigs	1814–1817
Secretary of Navy	Paul Hamilton	1809–1813
	William Jones	1813–1814
	Benjamin Crowninshield	1814–1817

The Monroe Administration (1817–1825)

Vice President	Daniel Tompkins	1817–1825
Secretary of State	John Quincy Adams	1817–1825
Secretary of Treasury	William Crawford	1817–1825
Secretary of War	George Graham	1817
	John C. Calhoun	1817–1825
Attorney General	Richard Rush	1817
	William Wirt	1817–1825
Postmaster General	Return Meigs	1817–1823
	John McLean	1823–1825
Secretary of Navy	Benjamin Crowninshield	1817–1818
	Smith Thompson	1818–1823
	Samuel Southard	1823–1825

The John Quincy Adams Administration (1825–1829)

Vice President	John C. Calhoun	1825–1829
Secretary of State	Henry Clay	1825–1829
Secretary of Treasury	Richard Rush	1825–1829
Secretary of War	James Barbour	1825–1828
	Peter Porter	1828–1829
Attorney General	William Wirt	1825–1829
Postmaster General	John McLean	1825–1829
Secretary of Navy	Samuel Southard	1825–1829

The Jackson Administration (1829–1837)

Vice President	John C. Calhoun	1829–1833
	Martin Van Buren	1833–1837
Secretary of State	Martin Van Buren	1829–1831
	Edward Livingston	1831–1833
	Louis McLane	1833–1834
	John Forsyth	1834–1837
Secretary of Treasury	Samuel Ingham	1829–1831
	Louis McLane	1831–1833
	William Duane	1833
	Roger B. Taney	1833–1834
	Levi Woodbury	1834–1837
Secretary of War	John H. Eaton	1829–1831
	Lewis Cass	1831–1837
	Benjamin Butler	1837
Attorney General	John M. Berrien	1829–1831
	Roger B. Taney	1831–1833
	Benjamin Butler	1833–1837
Postmaster General	William Barry	1829–1835
	Amos Kendall	1835–1837
Secretary of Navy	John Branch	1829–1831
	Levi Woodbury	1831–1834
	Mahlon Dickerson	1834–1837

The Van Buren Administration (1837–1841)

Vice President	Richard M. Johnson	1837–1841
Secretary of State	John Forsyth	1837–1841
Secretary of Treasury	Levi Woodbury	1837–1841
Secretary of War	Joel Poinsett	1837–1841
Attorney General	Benjamin Butler	1837–1838
	Felix Grundy	1838–1840
	Henry D. Gilpin	1840–1841
Postmaster General	Amos Kendall	1837–1840
	John M. Niles	1840–1841
Secretary of Navy	Mahlon Dickerson	1837–1838
	James Paulding	1838–1841

The William Harrison Administration (1841)

Vice President	John Tyler	1841
Secretary of State	Daniel Webster	1841
Secretary of Treasury	Thomas Ewing	1841
Secretary of War	John Bell	1841
Attorney General	John J. Crittenden	1841
Postmaster General	Francis Granger	1841
Secretary of Navy	George Badger	1841

The Tyler Administration (1841–1845)

Vice President	None	
Secretary of State	Daniel Webster	1841–1843
	Hugh S. Legaré	1843
	Abel P. Upshur	1843–1844
	John C. Calhoun	1844–1845
Secretary of Treasury	Thomas Ewing	1841
	Walter Forward	1841–1843
	John C. Spencer	1843–1844
	George Bibb	1844–1845
Secretary of War	John Bell	1841
	John C. Spencer	1841–1843
	James M. Porter	1843–1844
	William Wilkins	1844–1845
Attorney General	John J. Crittenden	1841
	Hugh S. Legaré	1841–1843
	John Nelson	1843–1845
Postmaster General	Francis Granger	1841
	Charles Wickliffe	1841
Secretary of Navy	George Badger	1841
	Abel P. Upshur	1841
	David Henshaw	1843–1844
	Thomas Gilmer	1844
	John Y. Mason	1844–1845

The Polk Administration (1845–1849)

Vice President	George M. Dallas	1845–1849
Secretary of State	James Buchanan	1845–1849
Secretary of Treasury	Robert J. Walker	1845–1849

Secretary of War	William L. Marcy	1845–1849
Attorney General	John Y. Mason	1845–1846
	Nathan Clifford	1846–1848
	Isaac Toucey	1848–1849
Postmaster General	Cave Johnson	1845–1849
Secretary of Navy	George Bancroft	1845–1846
	John Y. Mason	1846–1849

The Taylor Administration (1849–1850)

Vice President	Millard Fillmore	1849–1850
Secretary of State	John M. Clayton	1849–1850
Secretary of Treasury	William Meredith	1849–1850
Secretary of War	George Crawford	1849–1850
Attorney General	Reverdy Johnson	1849–1850
Postmaster General	Jacob Collamer	1849–1850
Secretary of Navy	William Preston	1849–1850
Secretary of Interior	Thomas Ewing	1849–1850

The Fillmore Administration (1850–1853)

Vice President	None	
Secretary of State	Daniel Webster	1850–1852
	Edward Everett	1852–1853
Secretary of Treasury	Thomas Corwin	1850–1853
Secretary of War	Charles Conrad	1850–1853
Attorney General	John J. Crittenden	1850–1853
Postmaster General	Nathan Hall	1850–1852
	Sam D. Hubbard	1852–1853
Secretary of Navy	William A. Graham	1850–1852
	John P. Kennedy	1852–1853
Secretary of Interior	Thomas McKennan	1850
	Alexander Stuart	1850–1853

The Pierce Administration (1853–1857)

Vice President	William R. King	1853–1857
Secretary of State	William L. Marcy	1853–1857
Secretary of Treasury	James Guthrie	1853–1857
Secretary of War	Jefferson Davis	1853–1857
Attorney General	Caleb Cushing	1853–1857
Postmaster General	James Campbell	1853–1857
Secretary of Navy	James C. Dobbin	1853–1857
Secretary of Interior	Robert McClelland	1853–1857

The Buchanan Administration (1857–1861)

Vice President	John C. Breckinridge	1857–1861
Secretary of State	Lewis Cass	1857–1860
	Jeremiah S. Black	1860–1861
Secretary of Treasury	Howell Cobb	1857–1860
	Philip Thomas	1860–1861
	John A. Dix	1861
Secretary of War	John B. Floyd	1857–1861
	Joseph Holt	1861
Attorney General	Jeremiah S. Black	1857–1860
	Edwin M. Stanton	1860–1861
Postmaster General	Aaron V. Brown	1857–1859
	Joseph Holt	1859–1861
	Horatio King	1861
Secretary of Navy	Isaac Toucey	1857–1861
Secretary of Interior	Jacob Thompson	1857–1861

The Lincoln Administration (1861–1865)

Vice President	Hannibal Hamlin	1861–1865
	Andrew Johnson	1865
Secretary of State	William H. Seward	1861–1865
Secretary of Treasury	Samuel P. Chase	1861–1864
	William P. Fessenden	1864–1865
	Hugh McCulloch	1865
Secretary of War	Simon Cameron	1861–1862
	Edwin M. Stanton	1862–1865
Attorney General	Edward Bates	1861–1864
	James Speed	1864–1865
Postmaster General	Horatio King	1861
	Montgomery Blair	1861–1864
	William Dennison	1864–1865
Secretary of Navy	Gideon Welles	1861–1865
Secretary of Interior	Caleb B. Smith	1861–1863
	John P. Usher	1863–1865

The Andrew Johnson Administration (1865–1869)

Vice President	None	
Secretary of State	William H. Seward	1865–1869
Secretary of Treasury	Hugh McCulloch	1865–1869
Secretary of War	Edwin M. Stanton	1865–1867
	Ulysses S. Grant	1867–1868
	Lorenzo Thomas	1868
	John M. Schofield	1868–1869
Attorney General	James Speed	1865–1866
	Henry Stanbery	1866–1868
	William M. Evarts	1868–1869
Postmaster General	William Dennison	1865–1866
	Alexander Randall	1866–1869
Secretary of Navy	Gideon Welles	1865–1869
Secretary of Interior	John P. Usher	1865
	James Harlan	1865–1866
	Orville H. Browning	1866–1869

The Grant Administration (1869–1877)

Vice President	Schuyler Colfax	1869–1873
	Henry Wilson	1873–1877
Secretary of State	Elihu B. Washburne	1869
	Hamilton Fish	1869–1877
Secretary of Treasury	George S. Boutwell	1869–1873
	William Richardson	1873–1874
	Benjamin Bristow	1874–1876
	Lot M. Morrill	1876–1877
Secretary of War	John A. Rawlins	1869
	William T. Sherman	1869
	William W. Belknap	1869–1876
	Alphonso Taft	1876
	James D. Cameron	1876–1877
Attorney General	Ebenezer Hoar	1869–1870
	Amos T. Ackerman	1870–1871
	G. H. Williams	1871–1875
	Edwards Pierrepont	1875–1876
	Alphonso Taft	1876–1877
Postmaster General	John A. J. Creswell	1869–1874
	James W. Marshall	1874
	Marshall Jewell	1874–1876
	James N. Tyner	1876–1877

Secretary of Navy	Adolph E. Borie	1869
	George M. Robeson	1869–1877
Secretary of Interior	Jacob D. Cox	1869–1870
	Columbus Delano	1870–1875
	Zachariah Chandler	1875–1877

The Hayes Administration (1877–1881)

Vice President	William A. Wheeler	1877–1881
Secretary of State	William M. Evarts	1877–1881
Secretary of Treasury	John Sherman	1877–1881
Secretary of War	George W. McCrary	1877–1879
	Alex Ramsey	1879–1881
Attorney General	Charles Devens	1877–1881
Postmaster General	David M. Key	1877–1880
	Horace Maynard	1880–1881
Secretary of Navy	Richard W. Thompson	1877–1880
	Nathan Goff, Jr.	1881
Secretary of Interior	Carl Schurz	1877–1881

The Garfield Administration (1881)

Vice President	Chester A. Arthur	1881
Secretary of State	James G. Blaine	1881
Secretary of Treasury	William Windom	1881
Secretary of War	Robert T. Lincoln	1881
Attorney General	Wayne MacVeagh	1881
Postmaster General	Thomas L. James	1881
Secretary of Navy	William H. Hunt	1881
Secretary of Interior	Samuel J. Kirkwood	1881

The Arthur Administration (1881–1885)

Vice President	None	
Secretary of State	F. T. Frelinghuysen	1881–1885

Secretary of Treasury	Charles J. Folger	1881–1884
	Walter Q. Gresham	1884
	Hugh McCulloch	1884–1885
Secretary of War	Robert T. Lincoln	1881–1885
Attorney General	Benjamin H. Brewster	1881–1885
Postmaster General	Timothy O. Howe	1881–1883
	Walter Q. Gresham	1883–1884
	Frank Hatton	1884–1885
Secretary of Navy	William H. Hunt	1881–1882
	William E. Chandler	1882–1885
Secretary of Interior	Samuel J. Kirkwood	1881–1882
	Henry M. Teller	1882–1885

The Cleveland Administration (1885–1889)

Vice President	Thomas A. Hendricks	1885–1889
Secretary of State	Thomas F. Bayard	1885–1889
Secretary of Treasury	Daniel Manning	1885–1887
	Charles S. Fairchild	1887–1889
Secretary of War	William C. Endicott	1885–1889
Attorney General	Augustus H. Garland	1885–1889
Postmaster General	William F. Vilas	1885–1888
	Don M. Dickinson	1888–1889
Secretary of Navy	William C. Whitney	1885–1889
Secretary of Interior	Lucius Q. C. Lamar	1885–1888
	William F. Vilas	1888–1889
Secretary of Agriculture	Norman J. Colman	1889

The Benjamin Harrison Administration (1889–1893)

Vice President	Levi P. Morton	1889–1893
Secretary of State	James G. Blaine	1889–1892
	John W. Foster	1892–1893
Secretary of Treasury	William Windom	1889–1891
	Charles Foster	1891–1893
Secretary of War	Redfield Proctor	1889–1891
	Stephen B. Elkins	1891–1893
Attorney General	William H. H. Miller	1889–1893

Postmaster General	John Wanamaker	1889–1893
Secretary of Navy	Benjamin F. Tracy	1889–1893
Secretary of Interior	John W. Noble	1889–1893
Secretary of Agriculture	Jeremiah M. Rusk	1889–1893

The Cleveland Administration (1893–1897)

Vice President	Adlai E. Stevenson	1893–1897
Secretary of State	Walter Q. Gresham	1893–1895
	Richard Olney	1895–1897
Secretary of Treasury	John G. Carlisle	1893–1897
Secretary of War	Daniel S. Lamont	1893–1897
Attorney General	Richard Olney	1893–1895
	James Harmon	1895–1897
Postmaster General	Wilson S. Bissell	1893–1895
	William L. Wilson	1895–1897
Secretary of Navy	Hilary A. Herbert	1893–1897
Secretary of Interior	Hoke Smith	1893–1896
	David R. Francis	1896–1897
Secretary of Agriculture	Julius S. Morton	1893–1897

The McKinley Administration (1897–1901)

Vice President	Garret A. Hobart	1897–1901
	Theodore Roosevelt	1901
Secretary of State	John Sherman	1897–1898
	William R. Day	1898
	John Hay	1898–1901
Secretary of Treasury	Lyman J. Gage	1897–1901
Secretary of War	Russell A. Alger	1897–1899
	Elihu Root	1899–1901
Attorney General	Joseph McKenna	1897–1898
	John W. Griggs	1898–1901
	Philander C. Knox	1901
Postmaster General	James A. Gary	1897–1898
	Charles E. Smith	1898–1901
Secretary of Navy	John D. Long	1897–1901
Secretary of Interior	Cornelius N. Bliss	1897–1899
	Ethan A. Hitchcock	1899–1901
Secretary of Agriculture	James Wilson	1897–1901

The Theodore Roosevelt Administration (1901–1909)

Vice President	Charles Fairbanks	1905–1909
Secretary of State	John Hay	1901–1905
	Elihu Root	1905–1909
	Robert Bacon	1909
Secretary of Treasury	Lyman J. Gage	1901–1902
	Leslie M. Shaw	1902–1907
	George B. Cortelyou	1907–1909
Secretary of War	Elihu Root	1901–1904
	William H. Taft	1904–1908
	Luke E. Wright	1908–1909
Attorney General	Philander C. Knox	1901–1904
	William H. Moody	1904–1906
	Charles J. Bonaparte	1906–1909
Postmaster General	Charles E. Smith	1901–1902
	Henry C. Payne	1902–1904
	Robert J. Wynne	1904–1905
	George B. Cortelyou	1905–1907
	George von L. Meyer	1907–1909
Secretary of Navy	John D. Long	1901–1902
	William H. Moody	1902–1904
	Paul Morton	1904–1905
	Charles J. Bonaparte	1905–1906
	Victor H. Metcalf	1906–1908
	Truman H. Newberry	1908–1909
Secretary of Interior	Ethan A. Hitchcock	1901–1907
	James R. Garfield	1907–1909
Secretary of Agriculture	James Wilson	1901–1909
Secretary of Labor and Commerce	George B. Cortelyou	1903–1904
	Victor H. Metcalf	1904–1906
	Oscar S. Straus	1906–1909
	Charles Nagel	1909

The Taft Administration (1909–1913)

Vice President	James S. Sherman	1909–1913
Secretary of State	Philander C. Knox	1909–1913
Secretary of Treasury	Franklin MacVeagh	1909–1913
Secretary of War	Jacob M. Dickinson	1909–1911
	Henry L. Stimson	1911–1913
Attorney General	George W. Wickersham	1909–1913
Postmaster General	Frank H. Hitchcock	1909–1913
Secretary of Navy	George von L. Meyer	1909–1913
Secretary of Interior	Richard A. Ballinger	1909–1911
	Walter L. Fisher	1911–1913
Secretary of Agriculture	James Wilson	1909–1913
Secretary of Labor and Commerce	Charles Nagel	1909–1913

The Wilson Administration (1913–1921)

Vice President	Thomas R. Marshall	1913–1921
Secretary of State	William J. Bryan	1913–1915
	Robert Lansing	1915–1920
	Bainbridge Colby	1920–1921
Secretary of Treasury	William G. McAdoo	1913–1918
	Carter Glass	1918–1920
	David F. Houston	1920–1921
Secretary of War	Lindley M. Garrison	1913–1916
	Newton D. Baker	1916–1921
Attorney General	James C. McReynolds	1913–1914
	Thomas W. Gregory	1914–1919
	A. Mitchell Palmer	1919–1921
Postmaster General	Albert S. Burleson	1913–1921
Secretary of Navy	Josephus Daniels	1913–1921
Secretary of Interior	Franklin K. Lane	1913–1920
	John B. Payne	1920–1921
Secretary of Agriculture	David F. Houston	1913–1920
	Edwin T. Meredith	1920–1921
Secretary of Commerce	William C. Redfield	1913–1919
	Joshua W. Alexander	1919–1921
Secretary of Labor	William B. Wilson	1913–1921

The Harding Administration (1921–1923)

Vice President	Calvin Coolidge	1921–1923
Secretary of State	Charles E. Hughes	1921–1923

Secretary of Treasury	Andrew Mellon	1921–1923
Secretary of War	John W. Weeks	1921–1923
Attorney General	Harry M. Daugherty	1921–1923
Postmaster General	Will H. Hays	1921–1922
	Hubert Work	1922–1923
	Harry S. New	1923
Secretary of Navy	Edwin Denby	1921–1923
Secretary of Interior	Albert B. Fall	1921–1923
	Hubert Work	1923
Secretary of Agriculture	Henry C. Wallace	1921–1923
Secretary of Commerce	Herbert C. Hoover	1921–1923
Secretary of Labor	James J. Davis	1921–1923

The Coolidge Administration (1923–1929)

Vice President	Charles G. Dawes	1925–1929
Secretary of State	Charles E. Hughes	1923–1925
	Frank B. Kellogg	1925–1929
Secretary of Treasury	Andrew Mellon	1923–1929
Secretary of War	John W. Weeks	1923–1925
	Dwight F. Davis	1925–1929
Attorney General	Henry M. Daugherty	1923–1924
	Harlan F. Stone	1924–1925
	John G. Sargent	1925–1929
Postmaster General	Harry S. New	1923–1929
Secretary of Navy	Edwin Derby	1923–1924
	Curtis D. Wilbur	1924–1929
Secretary of Interior	Hubert Work	1923–1928
	Roy O. West	1928–1929
Secretary of Agriculture	Henry C. Wallace	1923–1924
	Howard M. Gore	1924–1925
	William M. Jardine	1925–1929
Secretary of Commerce	Herbert C. Hoover	1923–1928
	William F. Whiting	1928–1929
Secretary of Labor	James J. Davis	1923–1929

The Hoover Administration (1929–1933)

Vice President	Charles Curtis	1929–1933
Secretary of State	Henry L. Stimson	1929–1933

Secretary of Treasury	Andrew Mellon	1929–1932
	Ogden L. Mills	1932–1933
Secretary of War	James W. Good	1929
	Patrick J. Hurley	1929–1933
Attorney General	William D. Mitchell	1929–1933
Postmaster General	Walter F. Brown	1929–1933
Secretary of Navy	Charles F. Adams	1929–1933
Secretary of Interior	Ray L. Wilbur	1929–1933
Secretary of Agriculture	Arthur M. Hyde	1929–1933
Secretary of Commerce	Robert P. Lamont	1929–1932
	Roy D. Chapin	1932–1933
Secretary of Labor	James J. Davis	1929–1930
	William N. Doak	1930–1933

The Franklin D. Roosevelt Administration (1933–1945)

Vice President	John Nance Garner	1933–1941
	Henry A. Wallace	1941–1945
	Harry S Truman	1945
Secretary of State	Cordell Hull	1933–1944
	Edward R. Stettinius, Jr.	1944–1945
Secretary of Treasury	William H. Woodin	1933–1934
	Henry Morgenthau, Jr.	1934–1945
Secretary of War	George H. Dern	1933–1936
	Henry A. Woodring	1936–1940
	Henry L. Stimson	1940–1945
Attorney General	Homer S. Cummings	1933–1939
	Frank Murphy	1939–1940
	Robert H. Jackson	1940–1941
	Francis Biddle	1941–1945
Postmaster General	James A. Farley	1933–1940
	Frank C. Walker	1940–1945
Secretary of Navy	Claude A. Swanson	1933–1940
	Charles Edison	1940
	Frank Knox	1940–1944
	James V. Forrestal	1944–1945
Secretary of Interior	Harold L. Ickes	1933–1945
Secretary of Agriculture	Henry A. Wallace	1933–1940
	Claude R. Wickard	1940–1945

Secretary of Commerce	Daniel C. Roper	1933–1939
	Harry L. Hopkins	1939–1940
	Jesse Jones	1940–1945
	Henry A. Wallace	1945
Secretary of Labor	Frances Perkins	1933–1945

The Truman Administration (1945–1953)

Vice President	Alben W. Barkley	1949–1953
Secretary of State	Edward R. Stettinius, Jr.	1945
	James F. Byrnes	1945–1947
	George C. Marshall	1947–1949
	Dean G. Acheson	1949–1953
Secretary of Treasury	Fred M. Vinson	1945–1946
	John W. Snyder	1946–1953
Secretary of War	Robert P. Patterson	1945–1947
	Kenneth C. Royall	1947
Attorney General	Tom C. Clark	1945–1949
	J. Howard McGrath	1949–1952
	James P. McGranery	1952–1953
Postmaster General	Frank C. Walker	1945
	Robert E. Hannegan	1945–1947
	Jesse M. Donaldson	1947–1953
Secretary of Navy	James V. Forrestal	1945–1947
Secretary of Interior	Harold L. Ickes	1945–1946
	Julius A. Krug	1946–1949
	Oscar L. Chapman	1949–1953
Secretary of Agriculture	Clinton P. Anderson	1945–1948
	Charles F. Brannan	1948–1953
Secretary of Commerce	Henry A. Wallace	1945–1946
	W. Averell Harriman	1946–1948
	Charles W. Sawyer	1948–1953
Secretary of Labor	Lewis B. Schwellenbach	1945–1948
	Maurice J. Tobin	1948–1953
Secretary of Defense	James V. Forrestal	1947–1949
	Louis A. Johnson	1949–1950
	George C. Marshall	1950–1951
	Robert A. Lovett	1951–1953

The Eisenhower Administration (1953–1961)

Vice President	Richard M. Nixon	1953–1961
Secretary of State	John Foster Dulles	1953–1959
	Christian A. Herter	1959–1961
Secretary of Treasury	George M. Humphrey	1953–1957
	Robert B. Anderson	1957–1961
Attorney General	Herbert Brownell, Jr.	1953–1958
	William P. Rogers	1958–1961
Postmaster General	Arthur E. Summerfield	1953–1961
Secretary of Interior	Douglas McKay	1953–1956
	Fred A. Seaton	1956–1961
Secretary of Agriculture	Ezra T. Benson	1953–1961
Secretary of Commerce	Sinclair Weeks	1953–1958
	Lewis L. Strauss	1958–1959
	Frederick H. Mueller	1959–1961
Secretary of Labor	Martin P. Durkin	1953
	James P. Mitchell	1953–1961
Secretary of Defense	Charles E. Wilson	1953–1957
	Neil H. McElroy	1957–1959
	Thomas S. Gates, Jr.	1959–1961
Secretary of Health, Education, and Welfare	Oveta Culp Hobby	1953–1955
	Marion B. Folsom	1955–1958
	Arthur S. Flemming	1958–1961

The Kennedy Administration (1961–1963)

Vice President	Lyndon B. Johnson	1961–1963
Secretary of State	Dean Rusk	1961–1963
Secretary of Treasury	C. Douglas Dillon	1961–1963
Attorney General	Robert F. Kennedy	1961–1963
Postmaster General	J. Edward Day	1961–1963
	John A. Gronouski	1963
Secretary of Interior	Stewart L. Udall	1961–1963
Secretary of Agriculture	Orville L. Freeman	1961–1963
Secretary of Commerce	Luther H. Hodges	1961–1963

Secretary of Labor	Arthur J. Goldberg	1961–1962
	W. Willard Wirtz	1962–1963
Secretary of Defense	Robert S. McNamara	1961–1963
Secretary of Health, Education, and Welfare	Abraham A. Ribicoff	1961–1962
	Anthony J. Celebrezze	1962–1963

The Lyndon Johnson Administration (1963–1969)

Vice President	Hubert H. Humphrey	1965–1969
Secretary of State	Dean Rusk	1963–1969
Secretary of Treasury	C. Douglas Dillon	1963–1965
	Henry H. Fowler	1965–1969
Attorney General	Robert F. Kennedy	1963–1964
	Nicholas Katzenbach	1965–1966
	Ramsey Clark	1967–1969
Postmaster General	John A. Gronouski	1963–1965
	Lawrence F. O'Brien	1965–1968
	Marvin Watson	1968–1969
Secretary of Interior	Stewart L. Udall	1963–1969
Secretary of Agriculture	Orville L. Freeman	1963–1969
Secretary of Commerce	Luther H. Hodges	1963–1964
	John T. Connor	1964–1967
	Alexander B. Trowbridge	1967–1968
	Cyrus R. Smith	1968–1969
Secretary of Labor	W. Willard Wirtz	1963–1969
Secretary of Defense	Robert F. McNamara	1963–1968
	Clark Clifford	1968–1969
Secretary of Health, Education, and Welfare	Anthony J. Celebrezze	1963–1965
	John W. Gardner	1965–1968
	Wilbur J. Cohen	1968–1969
Secretary of Housing and Urban Development	Robert C. Weaver	1966–1969
	Robert C. Wood	1969
Secretary of Transportation	Alan S. Boyd	1967–1969

The Nixon Administration (1969–1974)

Vice President	Spiro T. Agnew	1969–1973
	Gerald R. Ford	1973–1974
Secretary of State	William P. Rogers	1969–1973
	Henry A. Kissinger	1973–1974
Secretary of Treasury	David M. Kennedy	1969–1970
	John B. Connally	1971–1972
	George P. Shultz	1972–1974
	William E. Simon	1974
Attorney General	John N. Mitchell	1969–1972
	Richard G. Kleindienst	1972–1973
	Elliot L. Richardson	1973
	William B. Saxbe	1973–1974
Postmaster General	Winton M. Blount	1969–1971
Secretary of Interior	Walter J. Hickel	1969–1970
	Rogers Morton	1971–1974
Secretary of Agriculture	Clifford M. Hardin	1969–1971
	Earl L. Butz	1971–1974
Secretary of Commerce	Maurice H. Stans	1969–1972
	Peter G. Peterson	1972–1973
	Frederick B. Dent	1973–1974
Secretary of Labor	George P. Shultz	1969–1970
	James D. Hodgson	1970–1973
	Peter J. Brennan	1973–1974
Secretary of Defense	Melvin R. Laird	1969–1973
	Elliot L. Richardson	1973
	James R. Schlesinger	1973–1974
Secretary of Health, Education, and Welfare	Robert H. Finch	1969–1970
	Elliot L. Richardson	1970–1973
	Caspar W. Weinberger	1973–1974
Secretary of Housing and Urban Development	George Romney	1969–1973
	James T. Lynn	1973–1974
Secretary of Transportation	John A. Volpe	1969–1973
	Claude S. Brinegar	1973–1974

The Ford Administration (1974–1977)

| Vice President | Nelson A. Rockefeller | 1974–1977 |
| Secretary of State | Henry A. Kissinger | 1974–1977 |

Secretary of Treasury	William E. Simon	1974–1977
Attorney General	William Saxbe	1974–1975
	Edward Levi	1975–1977
Secretary of Interior	Rogers Morton	1974–1975
	Stanley K. Hathaway	1975
	Thomas Kleppe	1975–1977
Secretary of Agriculture	Earl L. Butz	1974–1976
	John A. Knebel	1976–1977
Secretary of Commerce	Frederick B. Dent	1975–1976
	Rogers Morton	1975–1976
	Elliot L. Richardson	1976–1977
Secretary of Labor	Peter J. Brennan	1974–1975
	John T. Dunlop	1975–1976
	W. J. Usery	1976–1977
Secretary of Defense	James R. Schlesinger	1974–1975
	Donald Rumsfeld	1975–1977
Secretary of Health, Education, and Welfare	Caspar Weinberger	1974–1975
	Forrest D. Mathews	1975–1977
Secretary of Housing and Urban Development	James T. Lynn	1974–1975
	Carla A. Hills	1975–1977
Secretary of Transportation	Claude Brinegar	1974–1975
	William T. Coleman	1975–1977

The Carter Administration (1977–1981)

Vice President	Walter F. Mondale	1977–1981
Secretary of State	Cyrus R. Vance	1977–1980
	Edmund Muskie	1980–1981
Secretary of Treasury	W. Michael Blumenthal	1977–1979
	G. William Miller	1979–1981
Attorney General	Griffin Bell	1977–1979
	Benjamin R. Civiletti	1979–1981
Secretary of Interior	Cecil D. Andrus	1977–1981
Secretary of Agriculture	Robert Bergland	1977–1981
Secretary of Commerce	Juanita M. Kreps	1977–1979
	Philip M. Klutznick	1979–1981
Secretary of Labor	F. Ray Marshall	1977–1981

Secretary of Defense	Harold Brown	1977–1981
Secretary of Health, Education, and Welfare	Joseph A. Califano	1977–1979
	Patricia R. Harris	1979
Secretary of Health and Human Services	Patricia R. Harris	1979–1981
Secretary of Education	Shirley M. Hufstedler	1979–1981
Secretary of Housing and Urban Development	Patricia R. Harris	1977–1979
	Moon Landrieu	1979–1981
Secretary of Transportation	Brock Adams	1977–1979
	Neil E. Goldschmidt	1979–1981
Secretary of Energy	James R. Schlesinger	1977–1979
	Charles W. Duncan	1979–1981

The Reagan Administration (1981–1989)

Vice President	George Bush	1981–1989
Secretary of State	Alexander M. Haig	1981–1982
	George P. Shultz	1982–1989
Secretary of Treasury	Donald Regan	1981–1985
	James A. Baker, III	1985–1988
	Nicholas Brady	1988–1989
Attorney General	William F. Smith	1981–1985
	Edwin A. Meese III	1985–1988
	Richard Thornburgh	1988–1989
Secretary of Interior	James Watt	1981–1983
	William P. Clark, Jr.	1983–1985
	Donald P. Hodel	1985–1989
Secretary of Agriculture	John Block	1981–1986
	Richard E. Lyng	1986–1989
Secretary of Commerce	Malcolm Baldridge	1981–1987
	C. William Verity, Jr.	1987–1989
Secretary of Labor	Raymond Donovan	1981–1985
	William E. Brock	1985–1987
	Ann D. McLaughlin	1987–1989
Secretary of Defense	Caspar Weinberger	1981–1987
	Frank Carlucci	1987–1989

Secretary of Health and Human Services	Richard Schweiker	1981–1983
	Margaret Heckler	1983–1985
	Otis R. Bowen	1985–1989
Secretary of Education	Terrel H. Bell	1981–1985
	William J. Bennett	1985–1988
	Lauro F. Cavazos	1988–1989
Secretary of Housing and Urban Development	Samuel Pierce	1981–1989
Secretary of Transportation	Drew Lewis	1981–1983
	Elizabeth Dole	1983–1987
	James H. Burnley	1987–1989
Secretary of Energy	James Edwards	1981–1982
	Donald P. Hodel	1982–1985
	John S. Herrington	1985–1989

The Bush Administration (1989–1993)

Vice President	J. Danforth Quayle	1989–1993
Secretary of State	James A. Baker III	1989–1992
Secretary of Treasury	Nicholas Brady	1989–1993
Attorney General	Richard Thornburgh	1989–1991
	William P. Barr	1991–1993
Secretary of Interior	Manuel Lujan	1989–1993
Secretary of Agriculture	Clayton K. Yeutter	1989–1991
	Edward Madigan	1991–1993
Secretary of Commerce	Robert Mosbacher	1989–1992
	Barbara Franklin	1992–1993
Secretary of Labor	Elizabeth Hanford Dole	1989–1991
	Lynn Martin	1991–1993
Secretary of Defense	Richard Cheney	1989–1993
Secretary of Health and Human Services	Louis W. Sullivan	1989–1993
Secretary of Education	Lauro F. Cavazos	1989–1991
	Lamar Alexander	1991–1993
Secretary of Housing and Urban Development	Jack F. Kemp	1989–1993

Secretary of Transportation	Samuel K. Skinner	1989–1992
	Andrew H. Card, Jr.	1992–1993
Secretary of Energy	James D. Watkins	1989–1993
Secretary of Veterans Affairs	Edward J. Derwinski	1989–1993

The Clinton Administration (1993–   )

Vice President	Albert Gore	1993–
Secretary of State	Warren Christopher	1993–1997
Secretary of Treasury	Lloyd Bentsen	1993–1995
	Robert E. Rubin	1995–
Attorney General	Janet Reno	1993–
Secretary of Interior	Bruce Babbitt	1993–
Secretary of Agriculture	Michael Espy	1993–1995
	Dan Glickman	1995–
Secretary of Commerce	Ronald Brown	1993–1996
Secretary of Labor	Robert B. Reich	1993–1997
Secretary of Defense	Les Aspin	1993–1994
	William J. Perry	1994–1997
Secretary of Health and Human Services	Donna Shalala	1993–
Secretary of Housing and Urban Development	Henry G. Cisneros	1993–1997
Secretary of Education	Richard W. Riley	1993–
Secretary of Transportation	Federico Peña	1993–1997
Secretary of Energy	Hazel R. O'Leary	1993–1997
Secretary of Veterans Affairs	Edward J. Derwinski	1993–

JUSTICES OF THE SUPREME COURT

	Term of Service	Years of Service	Life Span		Term of Service	Years of Service	Life Span
John Jay	1789–1795	5	1745–1829	John M. Harlan	1877–1911	34	1833–1911
John Rutledge	1789–1791	1	1739–1800	William B. Woods	1880–1887	7	1824–1887
William Cushing	1789–1810	20	1732–1810	Stanley Matthews	1881–1889	7	1824–1889
James Wilson	1789–1798	8	1742–1798	Horace Gray	1882–1902	20	1828–1902
John Blair	1789–1796	6	1732–1800	Samuel Blatchford	1882–1893	11	1820–1893
Robert H. Harrison	1789–1790	—	1745–1790	Lucius Q. C. Lamar	1888–1893	5	1825–1893
James Iredell	1790–1799	9	1751–1799	*Melville W. Fuller*	1888–1910	21	1833–1910
Thomas Johnson	1791–1793	1	1732–1819	David J. Brewer	1890–1910	20	1837–1910
William Paterson	1793–1806	13	1745–1806	Henry B. Brown	1890–1906	16	1836–1913
John Rutledge°	1795	—	1739–1800	George Shiras, Jr.	1892–1903	10	1832–1924
Samuel Chase	1796–1811	15	1741–1811	Howell E. Jackson	1893–1895	2	1832–1895
Oliver Ellsworth	1796–1800	4	1745–1807	Edward D. White	1894–1910	16	1845–1921
Bushrod Washington	1798–1829	31	1762–1829	Rufus W. Peckham	1895–1909	14	1838–1909
Alfred Moore	1799–1804	4	1755–1810	Joseph McKenna	1898–1925	26	1843–1926
John Marshall	1801–1835	34	1755–1835	Oliver W. Holmes	1902–1932	30	1841–1935
William Johnson	1804–1834	30	1771–1834	William R. Day	1903–1922	19	1849–1923
H. Brockholst Livingston	1806–1823	16	1757–1823	William H. Moody	1906–1910	3	1853–1917
Thomas Todd	1807–1826	18	1765–1826	Horace H. Lurton	1909–1914	4	1844–1914
Joseph Story	1811–1845	33	1779–1845	Charles E. Hughes	1910–1916	5	1862–1948
Gabriel Duval	1811–1835	24	1752–1844	*Edward D. White*	1910–1921	11	1845–1921
Smith Thompson	1823–1843	20	1768–1843	Willis Van Devanter	1911–1937	26	1859–1941
Robert Trimble	1826–1828	2	1777–1828	Joseph R. Lamar	1911–1916	5	1857–1916
John McLean	1829–1861	32	1785–1861	Mahlon Pitney	1912–1922	10	1858–1924
Henry Baldwin	1830–1844	14	1780–1844	James C. McReynolds	1914–1941	26	1862–1946
James M. Wayne	1835–1867	32	1790–1867	Louis D. Brandeis	1916–1939	22	1856–1941
Roger B. Taney	1836–1864	28	1777–1864	John H. Clarke	1916–1922	6	1857–1945
Philip P. Barbour	1836–1841	4	1783–1841	William H. Taft	1921–1930	8	1857–1930
John Catron	1837–1865	28	1786–1865	George Sutherland	1922–1938	15	1862–1942
John McKinley	1837–1852	15	1780–1852	Pierce Butler	1922–1939	16	1866–1939
Peter V. Daniel	1841–1860	19	1784–1860	Edward T. Sanford	1923–1930	7	1865–1930
Samuel Nelson	1845–1872	27	1792–1873	Harlan F. Stone	1925–1941	16	1872–1946
Levi Woodbury	1845–1851	5	1789–1851	*Charles E. Hughes*	1930–1941	11	1862–1948
Robert C. Grier	1846–1870	23	1794–1870	Owen J. Roberts	1930–1945	15	1875–1955
Benjamin R. Curtis	1851–1857	6	1809–1874	Benjamin N. Cardozo	1932–1938	6	1870–1938
John A. Campbell	1853–1861	8	1811–1889	Hugo L. Black	1937–1971	34	1886–1971
Nathan Clifford	1858–1881	23	1803–1881	Stanley F. Reed	1938–1957	19	1884–1980
Noah H. Swayne	1862–1881	18	1804–1884	Felix Frankfurter	1939–1962	23	1882–1965
Samuel F. Miller	1862–1890	28	1816–1890	William O. Douglas	1939–1975	36	1898–1980
David Davis	1862–1877	14	1815–1886	Frank Murphy	1940–1949	9	1890–1949
Stephen J. Field	1863–1897	34	1816–1899	*Harlan F. Stone*	1941–1946	5	1872–1946
Salmon P. Chase	1864–1873	8	1808–1873	James F. Brynes	1941–1942	1	1879–1972
William Strong	1870–1880	10	1808–1895	Robert H. Jackson	1941–1954	13	1892–1954
Joseph P. Bradley	1870–1892	22	1813–1892	Wiley B. Rutledge	1943–1949	6	1894–1949
Ward Hunt	1873–1882	9	1810–1886	Harold H. Burton	1945–1958	13	1888–1964
Morrison R. Waite	1874–1888	14	1816–1888	*Fred M. Vinson*	1946–1953	7	1890–1953
				Tom C. Clark	1949–1967	18	1899–1977

	Term of Service	Years of Service	Life Span
Sherman Minton	1949–1956	7	1890–1965
Earl Warren	1953–1969	16	1891–1974
John Marshall Harlan	1955–1971	16	1899–1971
William J. Brennan, Jr.	1956–1990	33	1906–
Charles E. Whittaker	1957–1962	5	1901–1973
Potter Stewart	1958–1981	23	1915–
Bryon R. White	1962–1993	31	1917–
Arthur J. Goldberg	1962–1965	3	1908–1990
Abe Fortas	1965–1969	4	1910–1982
Thurgood Marshall	1967–1991	24	1908–1992
Warren C. Burger	1969–1986	17	1907–
Harry A. Blackmun	1970–1994	24	1908–

	Term of Service	Years of Service	Life Span
Lewis F. Powell, Jr.	1972–1987	15	1907–
William H. Rehnquist	1972–1986	14	1924–
John P. Stevens III	1975–	—	1920–
Sandra Day O'Connor	1981–	—	1930–
William H. Rehnquist	1986–	—	1924–
Antonin Scalia	1986–	—	1936–
Anthony M. Kennedy	1988–	—	1936–
David H. Souter	1990–	—	1939–
Clarence Thomas	1991–	—	1948–
Ruth Bader Ginsberg	1993–	—	1933–
Stephen Breyer	1994–	—	1938–

°Appointed and served one term, but not confirmed by the Senate.
Note: Chief justices are in italics.

A SOCIAL PROFILE OF THE AMERICAN REPUBLIC

POPULATION

Year	Population	Percent Increase	Population Per Square Mile	Percent Urban/ Rural	Percent Male/ Female	Percent White/ Nonwhite	Persons Per Household	Median Age
1790	3,929,214		4.5	5.1/94.9	NA/NA	80.7/19.3	5.79	NA
1800	5,308,483	35.1	6.1	6.1/93.9	NA/NA	81.1/18.9	NA	NA
1810	7,239,881	36.4	4.3	7.3/92.7	NA/NA	81.0/19.0	NA	NA
1820	9,638,453	33.1	5.5	7.2/92.8	50.8/49.2	81.6/18.4	NA	16.7
1830	12,866,020	33.5	7.4	8.8/91.2	50.8/18.1	81.9/18.1	NA	17.2
1840	17,069,453	32.7	9.8	10.8/89.2	50.9/49.1	83.2/16.8	NA	17.8
1850	23,191,876	35.9	7.9	15.3/84.7	51.0/49.0	84.3/15.7	5.55	18.9
1860	31,443,321	35.6	10.6	19.8/80.2	51.2/48.8	85.6/14.4	5.28	19.4
1870	39,818,449	26.6	13.4	25.7/74.3	50.6/49.4	86.2/13.8	5.09	20.2
1880	50,155,783	26.0	16.9	28.2/71.8	50.9/49.1	86.5/13.5	5.04	20.9
1890	62,947,714	25.5	21.2	35.1/64.9	51.2/48.8	87.5/12.5	4.93	22.0
1900	75,994,575	20.7	25.6	39.6/60.4	51.1/48.9	87.9/12.1	4.76	22.9
1910	91,972,266	21.0	31.0	45.6/54.4	51.5/48.5	88.9/11.1	4.54	24.1
1920	105,710,620	14.9	35.6	51.2/48.8	51.0/49.0	89.7/10.3	4.34	25.3
1930	122,775,046	16.1	41.2	56.1/43.9	50.6/49.4	89.8/10.2	4.11	26.4
1940	131,669,275	7.2	44.2	56.5/43.5	50.2/49.8	89.8/10.2	3.67	29.0
1950	150,697,361	14.5	50.7	64.0/36.0	49.7/50.3	89.5/10.5	3.37	30.2
1960	179,323,175	18.5	50.6	69.9/30.1	49.3/11.4	88.6/11.4	3.33	29.5
1970	203,302,031	13.4	57.4	73.5/26.5	48.7/51.3	87.6/12.4	3.14	28.0
1980	226,545,805	11.4	64.0	73.7/26.3	48.6/51.4	86.0/14.0	2.76	30.0
1990	248,709,873	9.8	70.3	NA	48.7/51.3	80.3/19.7	2.63	32.9
2000°	276,382,000	7.1	75.8	NA	48.9/51.5	82.6/17.4	NA	NA

NA = Not available.
°Projections.

VITAL STATISTICS (rates per thousand)

Year	Births	Year	Births	Deaths°	Marriages°	Divorces°
1800	55.0	1900	32.3	17.2	NA	NA
1810	54.3	1910	30.1	14.7	NA	NA
1820	55.2	1920	27.7	13.0	12.0	1.6
1830	51.4	1930	21.3	11.3	9.2	1.6
1840	51.8	1940	19.4	10.8	12.1	2.0
1850	43.3	1950	24.1	9.6	11.1	2.6
1860	44.3	1960	23.7	9.5	8.5	2.2
1870	38.3	1970	18.4	9.5	10.6	3.5
1880	39.8	1980	15.9	8.8	10.6	5.2
1890	31.5	1990	16.7	8.6	9.8	4.6

NA = Not available.
°Data not available before 1900.

LIFE EXPECTANCY (in years)

Year	Total Population	White Females	Nonwhite Females	White Males	Nonwhite Males
1900	47.3	48.7	33.5	46.6	32.5
1910	50.1	52.0	37.5	48.6	33.8
1920	54.1	55.6	45.2	54.4	45.5
1930	59.7	63.5	49.2	59.7	47.3
1940	62.9	66.6	54.9	62.1	51.5
1950	68.2	72.2	62.9	66.5	59.1
1960	69.7	74.1	66.3	67.4	61.1
1970	70.9	75.6	69.4	68.0	61.3
1980	73.7	78.1	73.6	70.7	65.3
1990	75.4	79.3	76.3	72.6	68.4

THE CHANGING AGE STRUCTURE

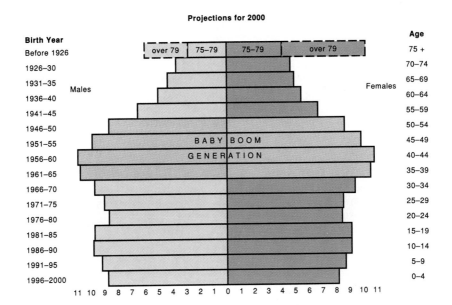

Before the twentieth century, the age distribution of Americans could be charted roughly as a pyramid, as seen in the figures for 1870 and 1920. High birthrates create a broad base at the bottom, while mortality rates winnow the population to a small tip of elderly. But as the year 2000 approaches, the pyramid has been transformed more nearly into a cylinder. Over the past two centuries fertility rates have undergone a steady decline, pulling in the base of the pyramid, while higher living standards have allowed Americans to live longer, broadening the top. Only the temporary bulge of the baby boom distorts the shape.

REGIONAL ORIGIN OF IMMIGRANTS (percent)

Years	Total Number of Immigrants	Total Europe	Europe North and West	Europe East and Central	Europe South and Other	Western Hemisphere	Asia
1821–1830	143,389	69.2	67.1	—	2.1	8.4	—
1831–1840	599,125	82.8	81.8	—	1.0	5.5	—
1841–1850	1,713,251	93.8	92.9	0.1	0.3	3.6	—
1851–1860	2,598,214	94.4	93.6	0.1	0.8	2.9	1.6
1861–1870	2,314,824	89.2	87.8	0.5	0.9	7.2	2.8
1871–1880	2,812,191	80.8	73.6	4.5	2.7	14.4	4.4
1881–1890	5,246,13	90.3	72.0	11.9	6.3	8.1	1.3
1891–1900	3,687,546	96.5	44.5	32.8	19.1	1.1	1.9
1901–1910	8,795,386	92.5	21.7	44.5	6.3	4.1	2.8
1911–1920	5,735,811	76.3	17.4	33.4	25.5	19.9	3.4
1921–1930	4,107,209	60.3	31.7	14.4	14.3	36.9	2.4
1931–1940	528,431	65.9	38.8	11.0	16.1	30.3	2.8
1941–1950	1,035,039	60.1	47.5	4.6	7.9	34.3	3.1
1951–1960	2,515,479	52.8	17.7	24.3	10.8	39.6	6.0
1961–1970	3,321,677	33.8	11.7	9.4	12.9	51.7	12.9
1971–1980	4,493,300	17.8	4.3	5.6	8.4	44.3	35.2
1981–1990	7,338,000	10.4	5.9	4.8	1.1	49.3	37.3

Dash indicates less than 0.1 percent.

RECENT TRENDS IN IMMIGRATION (in thousands)

	1961–1970	1971–1980	1981–1990	1991	Percent 1961–1970	Percent 1971–1980	Percent 1981–1990
All countries	3,321.7	4,493.3	7,338.0	1,827.2	100.0	100.0	100.0
Europe	1,123.5	800.4	761.5	146.7	33.8	17.8	10.4
Austria	20.6	9.5	18.9	3.5	0.6	0.2	0.3
Hungary	5.4	6.6	5.9	0.9	0.2	0.1	0.1
Belgium	9.2	5.3	6.6	0.7	0.3	0.1	0.1
Czechoslovakia	3.3	6.0	5.4	0.6	0.1	0.1	0.1
Denmark	9.2	4.4	2.8	0.6	0.3	0.1	0.1
France	45.2	25.1	92.1	4.0	1.4	0.6	1.3
Germany	190.8	74.4	159.0	10.9	5.7	1.7	2.2
Greece	86.0	92.4	31.9	2.9	2.6	2.1	0.4
Ireland	33.0	11.5	67.2	4.6	1.0	0.3	0.9
Italy	214.1	129.4	12.3	30.3	6.4	2.9	0.2
Netherlands	30.6	10.5	4.2	1.3	0.9	0.2	0.1
Norway	15.5	3.9	83.2	0.6	0.5	0.1	1.1
Poland	53.5	37.2	40.3	17.1	1.6	0.8	0.5
Portugal	76.1	101.7	20.5	4.6	2.3	2.3	0.3
Spain	44.7	39.1	11.1	2.7	1.3	0.9	0.2
Sweden	17.1	6.5	8.0	1.2	0.5	0.1	0.1
Switzerland	18.5	8.2	57.6	1.0	0.6	0.2	0.8
USSR	2.5	39.0	18.7	31.6	0.1	0.9	0.3
United Kingdom	213.8	137.4	159.2	16.8	6.4	3.1	2.2
Yugoslavia	20.4	30.5	37.3	2.8	0.6	0.7	0.5
Other Europe	9.1	18.9	7.7	1.2	0.2	0.2	0.0

RECENT TRENDS IN IMMIGRATION (in thousands)

	1961–1970	1971–1980	1981–1990	1991	Percent 1961–1970	Percent 1971–1980	Percent 1981–1990
Asia	427.6	1,588.2	2,738.1	342.2	12.9	35.2	37.3
China	34.8	124.3	298.9	24.0	1.0	2.8	4.1
Hong Kong	75.0	113.5	98.2	15.9	2.3	2.5	1.3
India	27.2	164.1	250.7	42.7	0.8	3.7	3.4
Iran	10.3	45.1	116.0	9.9	0.3	1.0	1.6
Israel	29.6	37.7	44.2	5.1	0.9	0.8	0.6
Japan	40.0	49.8	47.0	5.6	1.2	1.1	0.6
Korea	34.5	267.6	333.8	25.4	1.0	6.0	4.5
Philippines	98.4	355.0	548.7	68.8	3.0	7.9	7.5
Turkey	10.1	13.4	23.4	3.5	0.3	0.3	0.3
Vietnam	4.3	172.8	281.0	14.8	1.1	3.8	3.8
Other Asia	36.5	176.1	631.4	126.4	1.1	3.8	8.6
America	1,716.4	1,982.5	3,615.6	1,297.6	51.7	44.3	49.3
Argentina	49.7	29.9	27.3	4.2	1.5	0.7	0.4
Canada	413.3	169.9	158.0	19.9	12.4	3.8	2.2
Colombia	72.0	77.3	122.9	19.3	2.2	1.7	1.7
Cuba	208.5	264.9	144.6	9.5	6.3	5.9	2.0
Dominican Rep.	93.3	148.1	252.0	42.4	2.8	3.3	3.4
Ecuador	36.8	50.1	56.2	10.0	1.1	1.1	0.8
El Salvador	15.0	34.4	213.5	46.9	0.5	0.8	2.9
Haiti	34.5	56.3	138.4	47.0	1.0	1.3	1.9
Jamaica	74.9	137.6	208.1	23.0	2.3	3.1	2.8
Mexico	453.9	640.3	1,655.7	947.9	13.7	14.3	22.6
Other America	264.4	373.8	639.3	128.4	7.9	8.3	8.7
Africa	29.0	80.8	176.8	33.5	0.9	1.8	2.4
Oceania	25.1	41.2	45.2	7.1	0.8	0.9	0.6

Figures may not add to total due to rounding.

AMERICAN WORKERS AND FARMERS

Year	Total Number of Workers (thousands)	Percent of Workers Male/Female	Percent of Female Workers Married	Percent of Workers in Female Population	Percent of Workers in Labor Unions	Farm Population (thousands)	Farm Population as Percent of Total Population
1870	12,506	85/15	NA	NA	NA	NA	NA
1880	17,392	85/15	NA	NA	NA	21,973	43.8
1890	23,318	83/17	13.9	18.9	NA	24,771	42.3
1900	29,073	82/18	15.4	20.6	3	29,875	41.9
1910	38,167	79/21	24.7	25.4	6	32,077	34.9
1920	41,614	79/21	23.0	23.7	12	31,974	30.1
1930	48,830	78/22	28.9	24.8	7	30,529	24.9
1940	53,011	76/24	36.4	27.4	27	30,547	23.2
1950	59,643	72/28	52.1	31.4	25	23,048	15.3
1960	69,877	68/32	59.9	37.7	26	15,635	8.7
1970	82,049	63/37	63.4	43.4	25	9,712	4.8
1980	108,544	58/42	59.7	51.5	23	6,051	2.7
1990	117,914	55/45	58.4	44.3	16	4,591	1.8

THE ECONOMY AND FEDERAL SPENDING

Year	Gross National Product (GNP) (in billions)°	Foreign Trade (in millions)			Federal Budget (in billions)	Federal Surplus/Deficit (in billions)	Federal Debt (in billions)
		Exports	Imports	Balance of Trade			
1790	NA	$ 20	$ 23	$ −3	$ 0.004	$ +0.00015	$ 0.076
1800	NA	71	91	−20	0.011	+0.0006	0.083
1810	NA	67	85	−18	0.008	+0.0012	0.053
1820	NA	70	74	−4	0.018	−0.0004	0.091
1830	NA	74	71	+3	0.015	+0.100	0.049
1840	NA	132	107	+25	0.024	−0.005	0.004
1850	NA	152	178	−26	0.040	+0.004	0.064
1860	NA	400	362	−38	0.063	−0.01	0.065
1870	$ 7.4	451	462	−11	0.310	+0.10	2.4
1880	11.2	853	761	+92	0.268	+0.07	2.1
1890	13.1	910	823	+87	0.318	+0.09	1.2
1900	18.7	1,499	930	+569	0.521	+0.05	1.2
1910	35.3	1,919	1,646	+273	0.694	−0.02	1.1
1920	91.5	8,664	5,784	+2,880	6.357	+0.3	24.3
1930	90.7	4,013	3,500	+513	3.320	+0.7	16.3
1940	100.0	4,030	7,433	−3,403	9.6	−2.7	43.0
1950	286.5	10,816	9,125	+1,691	43.1	−2.2	257.4
1960	506.5	19,600	15,046	+4,556	92.2	+0.3	286.3
1970	992.7	42,700	40,189	+2,511	195.6	−2.8	371.0
1980	2,631.7	220,783	244,871	+24,088	590.9	−73.8	907.7
1990	5,546.1	394,030	495,042	−101,012	1,251.8	−220.5	3,233.3
1994	6,738.4	512,627	663,256	−150,629	1,460.6	−203.4	4,692.8

°For 1990 and after, gross domestic product (GDP) is given.

AMERICAN WARS

	U.S. Military Personnel (thousands)	Personnel as % of Population	U.S. Deaths	U.S. Wounds	Direct Cost 1990 Dollars (millions)
American Revolution Apr. 1775–Sept. 1783	184–250	9–12	4,004	6,004	$100–140
War of 1812 June 1812–Feb. 1815	286	3	1,950	4,000	87
Mexican War May 1846–Feb. 1848	116	0.5	13,271	4,102	82
Civil War: Union	3,393	14	360,222	275,175	2,302
Civil War: Confederacy Apr. 1861–Apr. 1865	1,034	11	258,000	NA	1,032
Spanish-American War Apr. 1898–Aug. 1898	307	0.4	2,446	1,662	270
World War I Apr. 1917–Nov. 1918	4,714	5	116,516	204,002	32,740
World War II Dec. 1941–Aug. 1945	16,354	12	405,399	670,846	360,000
Korean War June 1950–June 1953	5,764	4	54,246	103,284	50,000
Vietnam War Aug. 1964–June 1973	8,400	4	47,704	219,573	140,644
Persian Gulf War Jan. 1991–Feb. 1991	467	0.1	293	467	NA

BIBLIOGRAPHY

CHAPTER 1: OLD WORLD, NEW WORLDS

Discovery and Exploration in the Sixteenth Century
Kenneth R. Andrews, *Trade, Plunder, and Settlement: Maritime Enterprise and the Genesis of the British Empire, 1480–1630* (1985); K. R. Andrews, N. P. Canny, and P. E. H. Hair, eds., *The Westward Enterprise: English Activities in Ireland, the Atlantic, and America, 1480–1650* (1979); Ralph Davis, *The Rise of Atlantic Economies* (1973); J. H. Elliott, *The Old World and the New, 1492–1650* (1970); Paul E. Hoffman, *A New Andalucia and a Way to the Orient: The American Southeast during the Sixteenth Century* (1990); James Lang, *Conquest and Commerce: Spain and England in the Americas* (1975); W. H. McNeil, *The Rise of the West* (1963); Samuel Eliot Morison, *The European Discovery of America: The Northern Voyages, 500–1600* (1971) and *The European Discovery of America: The Southern Voyages, 1492–1616* (1974); J. H. Parry, *The Age of Reconnaissance* (1963); David Beers Quinn, *England and the Discovery of America, 1481–1620* (1974), *North America from Earliest Discovery to First Settlements* (1977), and *Set Fair for Roanoke* (1985).

Indian Civilizations
Alfred W. Crosby, Jr., *The Columbian Exchange: Biological and Cultural Consequences of 1492* (1972); Nigel Davies, *The Aztecs* (1973); Harold Driver, *Indians of North America*, 2d ed. (1970); Peter Farb, *Man's Rise to Civilization* (1968); R. C. Padden, *The Hummingbird and the Hawk* (1962); Miguel Leon-Portilla, *The Broken Spears: The Aztec Account of the Conquest of Mexico* (1962); Wilcomb E. Washburn, *The Indian in America* (1975).

The Spanish Empire in the Sixteenth Century
Fernand Braudel, *The Mediterranean and the Mediterranean World in the Age of Philip the Second*, vols. 1 and 2 (1976); J. H. Elliott, *Imperial Spain, 1469–1716* (1963); Charles Gibson, *The Aztecs under Spanish Rule* (1964); James Lockhart, *Spanish Peru, 1532–1560* (1968); James Lockhart and Stuart B. Schwartz, *Early Latin America: A History of Colonial Spanish America and Brazil* (1983).

The Protestant Reformation
Owen Chadwick, *The Reformation* (1964); Patrick Collinson, *The Elizabethan Puritan Movement* (1967) and *The Religion of Protestants* (1982); A. G. Dickens, *The English Reformation* (1974); Richard Dunn, *The Age of Religious Wars, 1159–1689* (1979); Erik Erikson, *Young Man Luther* (1962); Charles George and Katherine George, *The Protestant Mind of the English Reformation* (1961); De Lamaar Jensen, *Reformation Europe, Age of Reform and Revolution* (1981); Steven Ozment, *The Age of Reform, 1250–1550* (1980) and *The Reformation in the Cities* (1975); Keith Thomas, *Religion and the Decline of Magic* (1971); H. R. Trevor-Roper, *Religion, Reformation, Social Change, and Other Essays* (1967).

Elizabethan and Stuart England
Trevor Ashton, ed., *Crisis in Europe, 1560–1660* (1965); Carl Bridenbaugh, *Vexed and Troubled Englishmen, 1590–1642* (1968); Peter Laslett, *The World We Have Lost* (1965); Lawrence Stone, *The Crisis of the Aristocracy, 1558–1641* (1965); Keith Wrightson, *English Society, 1580–1680* (1982).

Ireland in the Sixteenth Century
Nicholas Canny, *The Elizabethan Conquest of Ireland* (1976) and *Kingdom and Colony: Ireland in the Atlantic World, 1560–1800* (1988); David Beers Quinn, *The Elizabethans and the Irish* (1976).

CHAPTER 2: FIRST CENTURY OF SETTLEMENT IN THE COLONIAL SOUTH

General Histories
Charles M. Andrews, *The Colonial Period in American History (1934–1938)*; Wesley Frank Craven, *The Southern Colonies in the Seventeenth Century, 1607–1689* (1949); David Galenson, *White Servitude in Colonial America* (1981); Sidney Mintz, *Sweetness and Power: The Place of Sugar in Modern History* (1985); Gary Nash, *Red, White and Black: The Peoples of Early America* (1974); John E. Pomfret, *Founding the American Colonies, 1583–1660* (1970); R. C. Simmons, *The American Colonies* (1976).

Indians in the Early South
Nancy Lurie, "Indian Cultural Adjustment to European Civilization," in James M. Smith, ed., *Seventeenth-Century America*, (1959); Gary Nash, *Red, White and Black: The Peoples of Early America* (1974).

Race and Slavery

Wesley Frank Craven, *White, Red, and Black: The Seventeenth-Century Virginian* (1971); Philip Curtin, *The Atlantic Slave Trade* (1969); Basil Davidson, *The African Genius* (1970); David B. Davis, *The Problem of Slavery in Western Culture* (1966); Carl N. Degler, *Neither White Nor Black: Slavery and Race Relations in Brazil and the United States* (1971); Winthrop Jordan, *White over Black* (1968); Herbert Klein, *The Middle Passage* (1978) and *Slavery in the Americas: A Comparative Study of Virginia and Cuba* (1967); Richard Olaniyan, *African History and Culture* (1982); Roland Oliver, ed., *The Cambridge History of Africa*, vol. 3: c. 1050–c. 1600 (1977); Orlando Patterson, *Slavery and Social Death: A Comparative Study* (1982); John Thornton, *Africa and Africans in the Making of the Atlantic World, 1400–1680* (1992); Peter Wood, "'I Did the Best I Could for My Day': The Study of Early Black History during the Second Reconstruction, 1960 to 1976," *William and Mary Quarterly* (1978).

The Early Chesapeake Colonies

Lois Green Carr, Philip D. Morgan, and Jean B. Russo, *Colonial Chesapeake Society* (1989); Lois Green Carr and Lorena Walsh, "The Planter's Wife: The Experience of White Women in Seventeenth-Century Maryland," *William and Mary Quarterly* (1977); Lois Green Carr, Russell R. Menard, and Lorena S. Walsh, *Robert Cole's World: Agriculture and Society in Early Maryland* (1991); Ivor Noel Hume, *Martin's Hundred: The Discovery of a Lost Virginia Settlement* (1979); Gloria Main, *Tobacco Colony: Life in Early Maryland, 1650–1720* (1982); James Russell Perry, *The Formation of a Society on Virginia's Eastern Shore, 1615–1655* (1990); Thad Tate and David Ammerman, eds., *The Chesapeake in the Seventeenth Century* (1979).

The English Revolution

Christopher Hill, *The Century of Revolution, 1603–1714* (1961), *Puritanism and Revolution* (1964), and *The World Turned Upside Down* (1972); R. C. Richardson, *The Debate on the English Revolution* (1977); Lawrence Stone, *The Causes of the English Revolution, 1529–1642* (1972); Michael Walzer, *The Revolution of the Saints* (1965).

The Carolinas

Verner Crane, *The Southern Frontier, 1670–1732* (1929); H. T. Merrens, *Colonial North Carolina* (1964); M. Eugene Sirmans, *Colonial South Carolina* (1966).

Georgia

Harold E. Davis, *The Fledgling Province: Social and Cultural Life in Colonial Georgia, 1733–1776* (1976); Hardy Jackson and Phinizy Spalding, eds., *Forty Years of Diversity; Essays on Colonial Georgia* (1984); Phinizy Spalding, *Oglethorpe in America* (1977).

The British Caribbean

Hilary McD. Beckles, *White Servitude and Black Slavery in Barbados, 1627–1715* (1989); Sidney Mintz, *Sweetness and Power: The Place of Sugar in Modern History* (1985); Gary Puckrein, *Little England: Plantation Society and Anglo-Barbadian Politics, 1627–1700* (1984).

The Spanish Empire in the Southwest

Sherbune F. Cook, *The Conflict between the California Indian and White Civilization* (1943); Charles Gibson, *Spain in America* (1966); Ramón A. Gutiérrez, *When Jesus Came, the Corn Mothers Went Away: Marriage, Sexuality and Power in New Mexico, 1500–1846* (1991); Edward H. Spicer, *Cycles of Conquest: The Impact of Spain, Mexico, and the United States on the Indians of the Southwest, 1533–1960* (1962).

CHAPTER 3: FIRST CENTURY OF SETTLEMENT IN THE COLONIAL NORTH

Indians and Northern Colonials

James Axtell, *The European and the Indian* (1981); William Cronon, *Changes in the Land: Indians, Colonists and the Ecology of New England* (1983); Francis Jennings, *The Ambiguous Iroquois Empire* (1984) and *The Invasion of America* (1975); Daniel K. Richter and James H. Merrell, *Beyond the Covenant Chain: The Iroquois and Their Neighbors in Indian North America, 1600–1800* (1987); Neal Salisbury, *Manitou and Providence: Indians, Europeans and the Making of New England* (1982); Bruce G. Trigger, *The Children of Aataentsic: A History of the Huron People to 1660* (1976); Alden Vaughan, *The New England Frontier* (1965); Anthony F. C. Wallace, *The Death and Rebirth of the Seneca* (1972).

The French in North America

W. J. Eccles, *The Canadian Frontier, 1534–1760* (1969) and *France in America* (1972); Allan Greer, *Peasant, Lord and Merchant: Rural Society in the Three Quebec Parishes, 1740–1840* (1985); Richard Colebrook Harris, *The Seigneurial System in Early Canada* (1966); C. E. O'Neill, *Church and State in French Colonial Louisiana* (1966).

New England Puritanism

Charles L. Cohen, *God's Caress: The Psychology of Puritan Religious Experience* (1986); Stephen Foster, *The Long Argument: English Puritanism and the Shaping of New England Culture, 1570–1700* (1991) and *Their Solitary Way: The Puritan Social Ethic in the First Century of Settlement in New England* (1971); Richard Godbeer, *The Devil's Dominion: Magic and Religion in Early New England* (1992); Charles Hambrick-Stowe, *The Practice of Piety: Puritan Devotional Literature in Seventeenth-Century New England* (1982); Robert Middlekauff, *The Mathers* (1971); Perry Miller, *The New England Mind: From Colony to Province* (1953); Edmund S. Morgan, *Visible Saints* (1963); Amanda Porterfield, *Female Piety in Puritan New England: The Emergence of Religious Humanism* (1992); Harry Stout, *The New England Soul* (1986).

The New England Colonies

Virginia DeJohn Anderson, *New England's Generation: The Great Migration and the Formation of Society and Culture in the Seventeenth Century* (1991); Paul Boyer and Stephen Nissenbaum, *Salem Possessed: The Social Origins of Witchcraft* (1974); John P. Demos, *Entertaining Satan: Witchcraft and the Culture of Early New England*

(1982) and *A Little Commonwealth: Family Life in Plymouth Colony* (1970); Philip Greven, *Four Generations: Land, Population, and Family in Colonial Andover, Massachusetts* (1970); Stephen Innes, *To Labor in a New Land: Economy and Society in Seventeenth-Century Springfield* (1983); Carol Karlsen, *The Devil in the Shape of a Woman: Witchcraft in Colonial New England* (1987); George Langdon, *Pilgrim Colony* (1960); John Frederick Martin, *Profits in the Wilderness: Enterpreneurship and the Founding of New England Towns in the Seventeenth Century* (1991); Edmund S. Morgan, *The Puritan Family*, rev. ed. (1966); Darrett Rutman, *Winthrop's Boston* (1965); Laurel Thatcher Ulrich, *Good Wives: Image and Reality in the Lives of Women in Northern New England* (1982).

The Middle Colonies
Randall H. Balmer, *A Perfect Babel of Confusion: Dutch Religion and English Culture in the Middle Colonies* (1989); Patricia Bonomi, *A Factious People: Politics and Society in Colonial New York* (1971); Mary Maples Dunn, *William Penn* (1967); Melvin B. Endy, *William Penn and Early Quakerism* (1973); Michael Kammen, *Colonial New York* (1975); Gary B. Nash, *Quakers and Politics: Pennsylvania, 1681–1726* (1968); J. E. Pomfret, *Colonial New Jersey* (1973); Oliver A. Rink, *Holland on the Hudson: An Economic and Social History of Dutch New York* (1986); Robert C. Ritchie, *The Duke's Province: A Study of Politics and Society in Colonial New York, 1660–1691;* Alan Tully, *William Penn's Legacy* (1977).

The Imperial Connection
Michael Hall, *Edward Randolph and the American Colonies, 1676–1703* (1960); Ian K. Steele, *Politics of Colonial Policy: The Board of Trade in Colonial Administration* (1968); Stephen Saunders Webb, *The Governors-General: The English Army and the Definition of Empire, 1569–1681* (1979).

CHAPTER 4: THE MOSAIC OF EIGHTEENTH-CENTURY AMERICA

General Histories
Jon Butler, *Awash in a Sea of Faith: Christianizing the American People* (1990); Jack P. Greene, *Pursuits of Happiness: The Social Development of Early Modern British Colonies and the Formation of American Culture* (1988); Philip Greven, *The Protestant Temperament: Patterns of Childrearing, Religious Experience, and Self in Early America* (1977); James Henretta, *The Evolution of American Society, 1700–1815* (1973); Stephen Innes, ed., *Work and Labor in Early America* (1988); Alice Hanson Jones, *Wealth of a Nation to Be: The American Colonies on the Eve of the Revolution* (1980); Jackson Turner Main, *The Social Structure of Revolutionary America* (1965); D. W. Meinig, *The Shaping of America: A Geographical Perspective on 500 Years of History*, vol. 1: *Atlantic America, 1492–1800* (1986); Mary Beth Norton, *Liberty's Daughters: The Revolutionary Experience of American Women, 1750–1800* (1980); Carole Shammas, *The Pre-Industrial Consumer in England and America* (1990); Gary M. Walton and James F. Shepherd, *The Economic Rise of*

Early America (1979); Robert V. Wells, *The Population of the British Colonies in America before 1776* (1975).

Immigration
Jon Butler, *The Huguenots in America* (1983); R. J. Dickson, *Ulster Immigration to Colonial America, 1718–1775* (1966); Ned Landsman, *Scotland and Its First American Colony, 1683–1765* (1985).

Rural Society in Eighteenth-Century America
James Henretta, "Farms and Families: Mentalité in Pre-Industrial America," *William and Mary Quarterly* (1978); Christopher M. Jedrey, *The World of John Cleaveland* (1979); Sung Bok Kim, *Landlord and Tenant in Colonial New York* (1978); James T. Lemon, *The Best Poor Man's Country: A Geographical Study of Early Southeastern Pennsylvania* (1972); Gregory Stiverson, *Poverty in the Land of Plenty: Tenancy in Eighteenth-Century Maryland* (1978); Michael Zuckerman, *Peaceable Kingdoms: New England Towns in the Eighteenth Century* (1970).

The Frontier
Richard Beeman, *The Evolution of the Southern Backcountry* (1984); Michael Bellesiles, *Revolutionary Outlaws: Ethan Allen and the Struggle for Independence in the Early American Frontier* (1994); Richard M. Brown, *The South Carolina Regulators* (1963); David H. Corkran, *The Cherokee Frontier: Conflict and Survival, 1740–1762* (1962) and *The Creek Frontier, 1540–1783* (1967); John Mack Faragher, *Daniel Boone: The Life and Legend of an American Pioneer* (1992); Michael N. McConnell, *A Country Between: The Upper Ohio Valley and Its Peoples, 1724–1774* (1992); Peter Mancall, *Valley of Opportunity: Economic Culture along the Upper Susquehanna, 1700–1800* (1991); Robert D. Mitchell, *Commercialism and Frontier: Perspectives on the Early Shenandoah Valley* (1977); Gregory H. Nobles, "Breaking into the Backcountry: New Approaches to the Early American Frontier," *William and Mary Quarterly* (1989); Daniel K. Richter, *The Ordeal of the Longhouse: The Peoples of the Iroquois League in the Era of European Colonization* (1992); Malcolm J. Rohrbough, *The Trans-Appalachian Frontier* (1978); Alan Taylor, *Liberty Men and Great Proprietors: The Revolutionary Settlement on the Maine Frontier, 1760–1820* (1990); Albert H. Tillson, Jr., *Gentry and Common Folk: Political Culture on a Virginia Frontier, 1740–1789* (1991); Daniel H. Usner, Jr., *Indians, Settlers, and Slaves in a Frontier Exchange Economy: The Lower Mississippi Valley before 1783* (1992); Richard White, *The Middle Ground: Indians, Empires, and Republics in the Great Lakes Region, 1650–1815* (1991).

Provincial Seaports
Carl Bridenbaugh, *Cities in the Wilderness* (1938) and *Cities in Revolt* (1955); Elaine Forman Crane, *A Dependent People: Newport, Rhode Island in the Revolutionary Era* (1985); Thomas Doerflinger, *A Vigorous Spirit of Enterprise: Merchants and Economic Development in Revolutionary Philadelphia* (1986); Christine Leigh Heyrman, *Commerce and Culture: The Maritime Communities of Colonial Massachusetts, 1690–1750* (1984); Jacob M. Price, "Economic Function and the Growth of American Port

Towns in the Eighteenth Century," *Perspectives in American History* (1974); Marcus Rediker, *Between the Devil and the Deep Blue Sea: Merchant Seamen, Pirates, and the Anglo-American Maritime Works, 1700–1750* (1987); Frederick B. Tolles, *Meetinghouse and Countinghouse: The Quaker Merchants of Colonial Philadelphia* (1948); Gerald B. Warden, *Boston, 1687–1776* (1970); Stephanie Grauman Wolf, *Urban Village: Population, Community, and Family Structure in Germantown, Pennsylvania, 1683–1800* (1976).

Blacks in Eighteenth-Century America
Thomas J. Davis, *A Rumor of Revolt: The "Great Negro Plot" in Colonial New York* (1985); Herbert Gutman, *The Black Family in Slavery and Freedom, 1750–1925* (1976); Jean Butenhoff Lee, "The Problem of the Slave Community in the Eighteenth-Century Chesapeake," *William and Mary Quarterly* (1986); Gerald W. Mullin, *Flight and Rebellion: Slave Resistance in Eighteenth-Century Virginia* (1972); Jean R. Soderlund, *Quakers and Slavery* (1985); Betty Wood, *Slavery in Colonial Georgia, 1730–1775* (1984).

The Eighteenth-Century South
Carl Bridenbaugh, *Myths and Realities: Societies of the Colonial South* (1952); A. Roger Ekirch, *"Poor Carolina": Politics and Society in Colonial North Carolina, 1729–1776* (1981); Jan Lewis, *The Pursuit of Happiness: Family and Values in Jefferson's Virginia* (1983); Daniel Blake Smith, *Inside the Great House: Planter Family Life in Eighteenth-Century Chesapeake Society* (1980); Julia Cherry Spruill, *Women's Life and Work in the Southern Colonies* (1938); Charles Sydnor, *Gentlemen Freeholders: Political Practices in Washington's Virginia* (1956).

The Enlightenment
Henry May, *The Enlightenment in America* (1976); Esmond Wright, *Franklin of Philadelphia* (1986); Louis B. Wright, *The Cultural Life of the American Colonies* (1957).

The Great Awakening
Edwin Scott Gaustad, *The Great Awakening in New England* (1957); Patricia Tracy, *Jonathan Edwards, Pastor* (1979); Marilyn Westerkamp, *The Triumph of the Laity: Scots-Irish Piety and the Great Awakening, 1625–1760* (1988).

Colonial Political Development in the Eighteenth Century
Edward M. Cook, *The Fathers of the Towns: Leadership and Community Structure in Eighteenth-Century New England* (1976); Jack P. Greene, *The Quest for Power: The Lower Houses of Assembly in the Southern Royal Colonies, 1689–1776* (1963); Robert Zemsky, *Merchants, Farmers, and River Gods: An Essay on Eighteenth Century American Politics* (1971).

CHAPTER 5: TOWARD THE WAR FOR AMERICAN INDEPENDENCE

General Histories
Charles M. Andrews, *The Colonial Background of the American Revolution*, rev. ed. (1931); Ian Christie and Benjamin Labaree, *Empire or Independence, 1760–1776* (1976); Edward Countryman, *The American Revolution* (1985); Lawrence Henry Gipson, *The Coming of the Revolution, 1763–1775* (1954); Alfred Young, ed., *The American Revolution: Explorations in the History of American Radicalism* (1976).

The Seven Years' War
Francis Jennings, *Empire of Fortune: Crown, Colonies, and Tribes in the Seven Years War in America* (1989); Howard H. Peckham, *The Colonial Wars, 1689–1762* (1963).

British Society and Politics
John Brooke, *King George III* (1972); J. C. D. Clark, *English Society, 1688–1832* (1985); M. Dorothy George, *London Life in the Eighteenth Century* (1965); Lawrence Henry Gipson, *The British Empire before the American Revolution (1936–1970)*; Lewis B. Namier, *England in the Age of the American Revolution*, 2d ed. (1961); Richard Pares, *King George III and the Politicians* (1953); W. A. Speck, *Stability and Strife: England, 1714–1760* (1979).

The Intellectual Sources of Resistance and Revolution
Nathan O. Hatch, *The Sacred Cause of Liberty: Republican Thought and the Millennium in Revolutionary New England* (1977); Isaac Kramnick, *Bolingbroke and His Circle: The Politics of Nostalgia in the Age of Walpole* (1968) and *Republicanism and Bourgeois Radicalism: Political Ideology in Late Eighteenth-Century England and America* (1990); Edmund S. Morgan, *The Challenge of the American Revolution* (1976) and *Inventing the People: The Rise of Popular Sovereignty in England and America* (1988); J. G. A. Pocock, *The Machiavellian Moment: Florentine Political Thought and the Atlantic Republican Tradition* (1975); Caroline Robbins, *The Eighteenth-Century Commonwealthman: Studies in the Transmission, Development, and Circumstances of English Liberal Thought from the Restoration of Charles II until the War with the Thirteen Colonies* (1959).

A Decade of Resistance
David Ammerman, *In the Common Cause: The American Response to the Coercive Acts of 1774* (1974); Richard D. Brown, *Revolutionary Politics in Massachusetts: The Boston Committee of Correspondence and the Towns, 1772–1774* (1970); Joseph Ernst, *Money and Politics in America, 1755–1775* (1973); Paul A. Gilje, *The Road to Mobocracy: Popular Disorder in New York City, 1763–1834* (1987); Benjamin Labaree, *The Boston Tea Party* (1964); Gregory H. Nobles, *Divisions throughout the Whole: Politics and Society in Hampshire County, Massachusetts, 1740–1775* (1983); William Penack, *War, Politics, and Revolution in Provincial Massachusetts* (1981); Peter Shaw, *American Patriots and the Rituals of Revolution* (1981); John Shy, *Toward Lexington: The Role of the British Army in the Coming of the American Revolution* (1965); Richard Walsh, *Charleston's Sons of Liberty: A Study of the Artisans, 1763–1789* (1959); Hiller B. Zobel, *The Boston Massacre* (1970).

Leaders of the American Resistance
David Hawke, *Paine* (1974); Peter Shaw, *The Character of John Adams* (1976); John J. Waters, *The Otis Family in Provincial and Revolutionary Massachusetts* (1968).

CHAPTER 6: THE AMERICAN PEOPLE AND THE AMERICAN REVOLUTION

General Histories
John R. Alden, *The American Revolution* (1964); Ira Gruber, *The Howe Brothers and the American Revolution* (1972); Piers Makesy, *The War for America* (1964).

Thomas Jefferson and the Declaration of Independence
Carl Becker, *The Declaration of Independence* (1922); Jay Fliegelman *Declaring Independence: Jefferson, Natural Language, and the Culture of Performance* (1993); Garry Wills, *Inventing America* (1978).

The Loyalists
Wallace Brown, *The King's Friends* (1966); Robert M. Calhoon, *The Loyalists in Revolutionary America* (1973); Mary Beth Norton, *The British-Americans* (1972).

George Washington and the Continental Army
E. Wayne Carp, *To Starve the Army at Pleasure: Continental Army Administration and American Political Culture, 1775–1783* (1984); James T. Flexner, *George Washington in the American Revolution* (1968); Douglas Southall Freeman, *George Washington* (1948–1957); Ronald Hoffman and Peter J. Albert, eds., *Arms and Independence: The Military Character of the American Revolution* (1984); James Kirby Martin and Mark Lender, *A Respectable Army: The Military Origins of the Republic, 1763–1789* (1982).

Diplomacy
Samuel F. Bemis, *The Diplomacy of the American Revolution* (1935); Jonathan R. Dull, *A Diplomatic History of the American Revolution* (1985); Ronald Hoffman and Peter J. Albert, eds., *Peace and the Peacemakers: The Treaty of 1783* (1986); Richard B. Morris, *The Peacemakers: The Great Powers and American Independence* (1965); Gerald Stourzh, *Benjamin Franklin and American Foreign Policy*, rev. ed. (1969).

The North and the American Revolution
John Brooke, *The Heart of the Commonwealth: Society and Political Culture in Worcester County, Massachusetts, 1713–1861* (1991); Edward Countryman, *A People in Revolution: The American Revolution and Political Society in New York, 1760–1790* (1981); Robert J. Taylor, *Western Massachusetts in the Revolution* (1954); Donald Wallace White, *A Village at War: Chatham, New Jersey and the American Revolution* (1979); Alfred F. Young, "George Robert Twelves Hewes (1742–1840): A Boston Shoemaker and the Memory of the American Revolution," *William and Mary Quarterly* (1981).

Indians and the Revolutionary Frontier
Barbara Graymont, *The Iroquois in the American Revolution* (1972); Isabel Thomson Kelsey, *Joseph Brant, 1743–*

1807: Man of Two Worlds (1984); James H. O'Donnell III, *Southern Indians in the American Revolution* (1973); J. M. Sosin, *The Revolutionary Frontier, 1763–1783* (1967).

The South and the American Revolution
John R. Alden, *The South in the Revolution, 1763–1789* (1957); Jeffrey J. Crow and Larry E. Tise, eds., *The Southern Experience in the American Revolution* (1978); Ronald Hoffman, Thad W. Tate, and Peter J. Albert, eds., *An Uncivil War: The Southern Backcountry during the American Revolution* (1985); Jerome J. Nadelhaft, *The Disorders of War: The Revolution in South Carolina* (1981).

The Black Experience and the American Revolution
Duncan MacLeod, *Slavery, Race, and the American Revolution* (1974); Benjamin Quarles, *The Negro in the American Revolution* (1961).

CHAPTER 7: CRISIS AND CONSTITUTION

General Histories
Curtis P. Nettels, *The Emergence of a National Economy, 1775–1815* (1962); Robert R. Palmer, *The Age of Democratic Revolution: A Political History of Europe and America, 1760–1800* (1959, 1964).

State Politics and State Constitutions
Willi Paul Adams, *The First American Constitutions* (1980); Ronald Hoffman and Peter Albert, eds., *Sovereign States in an Age of Uncertainty* (1981); Jackson Turner Main, *The Sovereign States, 1775–1783* (1973) and *Political Parties before the Constitution* (1973); Stephen E. Patterson, *Political Parties in Revolutionary Massachusetts* (1973); David Szatmary, *Shays' Rebellion: The Making of an Agrarian Insurrection* (1980).

The Articles of Confederation
Joseph L. Davis, *Sectionalism in American Politics, 1774–1787* (1977); E. James Ferguson, *The Power of the Purse: A History of American Public Finance, 1776–1790* (1961); H. James Henderson, *Party Politics in the Continental Congress* (1974); Merrill D. Jensen, *The Articles of Confederation*, rev. ed. (1959) and *The New Nation* (1950); Peter S. Onuf, *The Origins of the Federal Republic: Jurisdictional Controversies in the United States, 1775–1787* (1983); Jack N. Rakove, *The Beginnings of National Politics* (1979).

Society in the New Republic
Christopher Clark, *The Roots of Rural Capitalism: Western Massachusetts, 1780–1860* (1990); Nancy Cott, "Divorce and the Changing Status of Women in Massachusetts," *William and Mary Quarterly* (1976); Joseph J. Ellis, *After the Revolution: Profiles of Early American Culture* (1979); Jay Fliegelman, *Prodigals and Pilgrims: The American Revolution against Patriarchal Authority, 1750–1800* (1982); J. Franklin Jameson, *The American Revolution Considered as a Social Movement* (1962); Benjamin W. Labaree, *The Merchants of Newburyport, 1764–1815* (1962); Jan Lewis, "The Republican Wife: Virtue and Seduction in the Early Republic," *William and Mary*

Quarterly (1987); Forrest McDonald and Ellen Shapiro McDonald, "The Ethnic Origins of the American People, 1790," *William and Mary Quarterly* (1980); Gary Nash, *Forging Freedom: The Formation of Philadelphia's Black Community, 1720–1840* (1988); Donald L. Robinson, *Slavery in the Structure of American Politics, 1765–1820* (1971); Howard Rock, *Artisans of the New Republic: Tradesmen of New York City in the Age of Jefferson* (1979); Charles G. Steffen, *The Mechanics of Baltimore: Workers and Politics in the Age of Revolution, 1763–1812* (1984); Lynne Withey, *Dearest Friend: A Life of Abigail Adams* (1981); Arthur Zilversmit, *The First Emancipation: The Abolition of Slavery in the North* (1967).

The Federal Constitution
Douglass Adair, *Fame and the Founding Fathers* (1974); Lance Banning, "James Madison and the Nationalists, 1780–1783," *William and Mary Quarterly* (1983); Charles Beard, *An Economic Interpretation of the Constitution of the United States* (1913); Richard Beeman, Stephen Botein, and Edward C. Carter II, eds., *Beyond Confederation: Origins of the Constitution and American National Identity* (1987); Irving Brant, *James Madison: The Nationalist, 1780–1787* (1948); Robert E. Brown, *Charles Beard and the Constitution,* (1956); Linda Grant DePauw, *The Eleventh Pillar: New York State and the Federal Constitution* (1966); John P. Diggins, *The Lost Soul of American Politics: Virtue, Self-Interest, and the Foundations of Liberalism* (1984); Max Farrand, *The Framing of the Constitution* (1913); Ralph Ketcham, *James Madison* (1971); Leonard Levy, ed., *Essays on the Making of the Constitution* (1969); Forrest McDonald, *We the People: The Economic Origins of the Constitution* (1958); Gerald Stourzh, *Alexander Hamilton and the Idea of Republican Government* (1970); Garry Wills, *Explaining America: The Federalist* (1981).

CHAPTER 8: THE REPUBLIC LAUNCHED

Society
Jeanne Boydston, *Home and Work: Housework, Wages, and the Ideology of Labor in the Early Republic* (1990); Nancy F. Cott, *The Bonds of Womanhood: "Woman's Sphere" in New England, 1780–1835* (1977); Joseph J. Ellis, *After the Revolution: Profiles of Early American Culture* (1979); Malcolm J. Rohrbough, *The Trans-Appalachian Frontier: Peoples, Societies, and Institutions, 1775–1850* (1978); Thomas P. Slaughter, *The Whiskey Rebellion: Frontier Epilogue to the American Revolution* (1986); Billy G. Smith, *The "Lower Sort": Philadelphia's Laboring People, 1759–1800* (1990); Charles G. Steffen, *The Mechanics of Baltimore: Workers and Politics in the Age of Revolution, 1763–1812* (1984).

National Government
Ralph Adams Brown, *The Presidency of John Adams* (1975); Manning J. Dauer, *The Adams Federalists* (1953); Richard H. Kohn, *Eagle and Sword: The Federalists and the Creation of a Military Establishment in America, 1783–1802* (1975); Ralph Ketcham, *Presidents over Party: The First American Presidency, 1789–1829* (1984); Forrest McDonald, *The Presidency of George Washington* (1974); John C. Miller, *The Federalist Era, 1789–1801* (1960);

Wiley Sword, *President Washington's Indian War: The Struggle for the Old Northwest, 1790–1795* (1985).

Party Politics
Joseph Charles, *The Origins of the American Party System* (1956); Paul Goodman, *The Democratic Republicans of Massachusetts* (1964); John F. Hoadley, *Origins of American Political Parties, 1789–1803* (1986); Richard Hofstadter, *The Idea of a Party System: The Rise of Legitimate Opposition in the United States, 1780–1840* (1969); Norman Risjord, *Chesapeake Politics, 1781–1800* (1978); Alfred Young, *The Democratic Republicans of New York: The Origins, 1763–1797* (1967).

Party Ideology
Joyce Appleby, *Capitalism and a New Social Order: The Republican Vision of the 1970s* (1984) and *Liberalism and Republicanism in the Historical Imagination* (1992); Richard W. Buel, Jr., *Securing the Republic: Ideology in American Politics, 1789–1815* (1972); John R. Howe, Jr., *The Changing Political Thought of John Adams* (1966); Gerald Stourzh, *Alexander Hamilton and the Idea of Republican Government* (1970); John Zvesper, *Political Philosophy and Rhetoric: A Study of the Origins of Party Politics* (1977).

Constitutional Developments
Bernard Schwartz, *The Great Rights of Mankind: A History of the American Bill of Rights* (1977); James M. Smith, *Freedom's Fetters: The Alien and Sedition Laws and American Civil Liberties* (1956); Leonard Levy, *Legacy of Suppression: Freedom of Speech and Press in Early American History* (1960); Robert A. Rutland, *The Birth of the Bill of Rights, 1776–1791* (1955).

Foreign Policy
Harry Ammon, *The Genet Mission* (1973); Jerald Combs, *The Jay Treaty: Political Battleground of the Founding Fathers* (1970); Alexander DeConde, *Entangling Alliance: Politics and Diplomacy under George Washington* (1958) and *The Quasi-War: The Politics and Diplomacy of the Undeclared War with France, 1797–1801* (1966); Felix Gilbert, *To the Farewell Address: Ideas of Early American Foreign Policy* (1961); Bradford Perkins, *The First Rapprochement: England and the United States, 1795–1805* (1955); Paul A. Varg, *Foreign Policies of the Founding Fathers* (1963).

Biographies
Charles W. Aikers, *Abigail Adams* (1980); Irving Brant, *James Madison: Father of the Constitution, 1787–1800* (1950); John C. Miller, *Alexander Hamilton: Portrait in Paradox* (1959); Merrill Peterson, *Thomas Jefferson and the New Nation* (1970); Page Smith, *John Adams* (1962); Garry Wills, *Cincinnatus: George Washington and the Enlightenment* (1984).

CHAPTER 9: THE JEFFERSONIAN REPUBLIC

General Histories
Richard Hofstadter, *The Idea of a Party System: The Rise of Legitimate Opposition in the United States, 1780–1840*

(1969); George Dangerfield, *The Era of Good Feelings* (1952); James Sterling Young, *The Washington Community, 1800–1828* (1966).

Jeffersonians in Power
Alexander Balinky, *Albert Gallatin: Fiscal Theories and Policy* (1958); James Banner, *To the Hartford Convention: The Federalists and the Origins of Party Politics in the Early Republic, 1789–1815* (1970); Theodore J. Crackel, *Mr. Jefferson's Army: Political and Social Reform of the Military Establishment, 1801–1809* (1987); Noble Cunningham, *The Jeffersonian Republicans in Power: Party Operations, 1801–1809* (1963) and *The Process of Government under Jefferson* (1978); Paul Goodman, *The Democratic Republicans of Massachusetts* (1964); Robert M. Johnstone, Jr., *Jefferson and the Presidency: Leadership in the Young Republic* (1978); Linda K. Kerber, *Federalists in Dissent: Imagery and Ideology in Jeffersonian America* (1970); Norman K. Risjord, *The Old Republicans: Southern Conservatism in the Age of Jefferson* (1965); Robert A. Rutland, *The Presidency of James Madison* (1990); Robert W. Tucker and David C. Hendrickson, *Empire of Liberty: The Statecraft of Thomas Jefferson* (1990).

Indian Affairs and Western Expansion
Paul K. Conklin, *Cane Ridge: America's Pentecost* (1990); R. David Edmunds, *Tecumseh and the Quest for Indian Leadership* (1984); Reginald Horsman, *Expansion and American Indian Policy, 1783–1812* (1967) and *The Frontier in the Formative Years, 1783–1815* (1970); T. Scott Miyakawa, *Protestants and Pioneers: Individualism and Conformity on the American Frontier* (1964); Bernard W. Sheehan, *Seeds of Extinction: Jeffersonian Philanthropy and the American Indians* (1973); Michael Williams, *Americans and Their Forests: A Historical Geography* (1989).

The Judiciary
Richard E. Ellis, *The Jeffersonian Crisis: Courts and Politics in the Early Republic* (1971); Robert K. Faulkner, *The Jurisprudence of John Marshall* (1968); Morton J. Horwitz, *The Transformation of American Law, 1780–1860* (1977); R. K. Newmyer, *The Supreme Court under Marshall and Taney* (1968).

Foreign Affairs and the War of 1812
Alexander DeConde, *This Affair of Louisiana* (1976); Donald C. Hickey, *The War of 1812: A Forgotten Conflict* (1989); Bradford Perkins, *Prologue to War: England and the United States, 1805–1812* (1961); Robert A. Rutland, *Madison's Alternatives: The Jeffersonian Republicans and the Coming of War, 1805–1812* (1975); Burton Spivak, *Jefferson's English Crisis: Commerce, Embargo, and the Republican Revolution* (1978); J. C. A. Stagg, *Mr. Madison's War: Politics, Diplomacy, and Warfare in the Early American Republic, 1783–1830* (1983).

Biographies
Harry Ammon, *James Monroe: The Quest for National Identity* (1979); Leonard Baker, *John Marshall: A Life in Law* (1974); Ralph Ketcham, *James Madison: A Biography* (1971); Drew R. McCoy, *The Last of the Fathers: James Madison and the Republican Legacy* (1989); Dumas Malone, *Jefferson the President: First Term, 1801–1805* (1970) and *Jefferson the President: Second Term, 1805–1809* (1974); Merrill Peterson, *Thomas Jefferson and the New Nation: A Biography* (1970); Robert Remini, *Andrew Jackson and the Course of American Empire, 1767–1821* (1977).

CHAPTER 10: THE OPENING OF AMERICA

General Histories
W. Elliot Brownlee, *Dynamics of Ascent: A History of the American Economy* (1974); Stuart Bruchey, *The Roots of American Economic Growth, 1607–1861* (1965); Susan Previant Lee and Peter Passell, *A New Economic View of American History* (1979); Peter Temin, *Causal Factors in American Economic Growth in the Nineteenth Century* (1975).

Transportation
Carter Goodrich, *Government Promotion of American Canals and Railroads, 1800–1860* (1974); Erik F. Haites et al., *Western River Transportation: The Era of Early Internal Development, 1810–1860* (1975); Louis C. Hunter, *Steamboats on the Western Rivers: An Economic and Technological History* (1949); Ronald Shaw, *Canals for a Nation: The Canal Era in the United States, 1790–1860* (1990); Carol Sheriff, *The Artificial River: The Erie Canal and the Paradox of Progress, 1817–1862* (1996); George R. Taylor, *The Transportation Revolution, 1815–1860* (1951); Peter Way, *Common Labour: Workers and the Digging of North American Canals, 1780–1860* (1993).

Industrialization and the Economy
Thomas C. Cochran, *Frontiers of Change: Early Industrialism in America* (1981); Gary Cross and Rick Szostak, *Technology and American Society* (1995); Robert F. Dalzell, Jr., *Enterprising Elite: The Boston Associates and the World They Made* (1987); Constance M. Green, *Eli Whitney and the Birth of American Technology* (1956); David J. Jeremy, *Transatlantic Industrial Revolution: The Diffusion of Textile Technology between Britain and America, 1790–1830* (1981); Diane Lindstrom, *Economic Development in the Philadelphia Region, 1810–1850* (1978); Nathan Rosenberg, *Technology and American Economic Growth* (1972); Darwin H. Stapleton, *The Transfer of Early Industrial Technologies to America* (1987); Peter Temin, *Iron and Steel in Nineteenth Century America* (1964); Barbara M. Tucker, *Samuel Slater and the Origins of the American Textile Industry, 1790–1860* (1984).

Agriculture
Jeremy Atack and Fred Bateman, *To Their Own Soil: Agriculture in the Antebellum North* (1987); Clarence Danhof, *Changes in Agriculture: The Northern United States, 1820–1870* (1969); Paul W. Gates, *The Farmer's Age: Agriculture, 1815–1860* (1960); Lewis C. Gray, *History of Agriculture in the Southern United States*, 2 vols. (1933); Winifred Barr Rothenberg, *From Market-Places to a Market Economy: The Transformation of Rural Massachusetts, 1750–1850* (1992).

Workers and Community Studies

Mary H. Blewett, *Men, Women, and Work: Class, Gender, and Protest in the New England Shoe Industry, 1780–1910* (1988); Don H. Doyle, *The Social Order of a Frontier Community: Jacksonville, Illinois, 1825–70* (1983); Thomas Dublin, *Transforming Women's Work: New England Lives in the Industrial Revolution* (1994); Paul A. Gilje, *The Road to Mobocracy: Popular Disorder in New York City, 1763–1834* (1987); Bruce Laurie, *Working People of Philadelphia, 1800–1850* (1980) and *Artisans into Workers: Labor in Nineteenth-Century America* (1989); Brian C. Mitchell, *The Paddy Camps: The Irish of Lowell, 1821–61* (1988); Jonathan Prude, *The Coming of Industrial Order: Town and Factory Life in Rural Massachusetts, 1810–1860* (1983); W. J. Rorabaugh, *The Craft Apprentice: From Franklin to the Machine Age in America* (1986); Steven J. Ross, *Workers on the Edge: Work, Leisure, and Politics in Industrializing Cincinnati, 1788–1890* (1985); Christine Stansell, *City of Women: Sex and Class in New York, 1789–1860* (1986); Richard B. Stott, *Workers in the Metropolis: Class, Ethnicity, and Youth in Antebellum New York City* (1990); David A. Zonderman, *Aspirations and Anxieties: New England Workers and the Mechanized Factory System, 1815–1850* (1992).

Society and Values

Daniel J. Boorstin, *The Americans: The National Experience* (1965); Richard D. Brown, *Knowledge Is Power: The Diffusion of Information in Early America, 1700–1865* (1989); Richard L. Bushman, *The Refinement of America: Persons, Houses, Cities* (1992); Clyde and Sally Griffen, *Natives and Newcomers: The Ordering of Opportunity in Mid-Nineteenth Poughkeepsie* (1978); Lawrence W. Levine, *High Brow/Low Brow: The Emergence of Cultural Hierarchy in America* (1988); Russel B. Nye, *Society and Culture in America, 1830–1860* (1974); Michael O'Malley, *Keeping Watch: A History of American Time* (1990); William H. and Jane H. Pease, *The Web of Progress: Private Values and Public Styles in Boston and Charleston, 1828–1843* (1985); Edward Pessen, *Jacksonian America: Society, Personality, and Politics*, rev. ed. (1978) and *Riches, Class, and Power before the Civil War* (1973); Alexander Saxton, *The Rise and Fall of the White Republic: Class Politics and Mass Culture in Nineteenth-Century America* (1990); Stephan Thernstrom, *Poverty and Progress: Social Mobility in a Nineteenth-Century City* (1964); Robert H. Wiebe, *The Opening of American Society: From the Adoption of the Constitution to the Eve of Disunion* (1984).

Land and the West

Daniel Feller, *The Public Lands in Jacksonian Politics* (1984); Malcolm J. Rohrbough, *The Land Office Business: The Settlement and Administration of American Public Lands, 1789–1837* (1968); David J. Wishart, *The Fur Trade of the American West, 1817–1840* (1979).

Environment

Carolyn Merchant, *Ecological Revolutions: Nature, Gender, and Science in New England* (1989); Theodore Steinberg, *Nature Incorporated: Industrialization and the Waters of New England* (1991); Michael Williams, *Americans and Their Forests: A Historical Geography* (1989).

Politics and Law

George Dangerfield, *The Awakening of American Nationalism, 1815–1828* (1965); Robert K. Faulkner, *The Jurisprudence of John Marshall* (1968); Morton J. Horwitz, *The Transformation of American Law, 1780–1860* (1977); James Willard Hurst, *Law and the Conditions of Freedom in the Nineteenth-Century United States* (1956); Glover Moore, *The Missouri Controversy, 1819–1821* (1953); R. Kent Newmyer, *The Supreme Court under Marshall and Taney* (1968); M. N. Rothbard, *The Panic of 1819: Reactions and Policies* (1962); Charles Sydnor, *The Development of Southern Sectionalism, 1819–1848* (1948).

CHAPTER 11: THE RISE OF DEMOCRACY

General Histories

George Dangerfield, *The Awakening of American Nationalism, 1815–1828* (1965); Edward Pessen, *Jacksonian America: Society, Personality, and Politics*, rev. ed. (1978); Glyndon G. Van Deusen, *The Jacksonian Era, 1828–1845* (1959).

Society and Values

Michel Chevalier, *Society, Manners, and Politics in the United States* (1961); Charles Dickens, *American Notes for General Circulation* (1842, reprinted 1972); Francis J. Grund, *Aristocracy in America* (1839, reprinted 1959); Harriet Martineau, *Society in America* (1837); Douglas T. Miller, *Jacksonian Aristocracy: Class and Democracy in New York, 1830–1860* (1967); Russel B. Nye, *Society and Culture in America, 1830–1860* (1960); Edward Pessen, *Riches, Class, and Power before the Civil War* (1973); Alexis de Tocqueville, *Democracy in America* (1945); Frances Trollope, *Domestic Manners of the Americans* (1832); John William Ward, *Andrew Jackson: Symbol for an Age* (1955); Julie Winch, *Philadelphia's Black Elite: Activism, Accommodation, and the Struggle for Autonomy, 1787–1848* (1988).

The Emergence of Democracy

James S. Chase, *Emergence of the Presidential Nominating Convention, 1789–1832* (1973); Richard Hofstadter, *The Idea of a Party System: The Rise of Legitimate Opposition in the United States, 1780–1840* (1969); Richard P. McCormick, *The Presidential Game: The Origins of American Presidential Politics* (1982); Chilton Williamson, *American Suffrage from Property to Democracy, 1760–1860* (1960).

The Jacksonian Party System

Lee Benson, *The Concept of Jacksonian Democracy: New York as a Test Case* (1961); James C. Curtis, *The Fox at Bay: Martin Van Buren and the Presidency, 1837–1841* (1970); Mary W. M. Hargreaves, *The Presidency of John Quincy Adams* (1985); Richard B. Latner, *The Presidency of Andrew Jackson: White House Politics, 1829–1837* (1979); Richard P. McCormick, *The Second American Party System: Party Formation in the Jacksonian Era* (1966); Mary P. Ryan, *Women in Public: Between Banners and Ballots, 1825–1880* (1990); Joel H. Silbey, *The American Nation, 1838–1893* (1991).

Banking and the Economy

Bray Hammond, *Banks and Politics in America from the Revolution to the Civil War* (1957); John M. McFaul, *The Politics of Jacksonian Finance* (1972); James Roger Sharp, *The Jacksonians versus the Banks: Politics in the States after the Panic of 1837* (1970); Peter Temin, *The Jacksonian Economy* (1969).

Nullification

Richard Ellis, *The Union at Risk: Jacksonian Democracy, States' Rights and the Nullification Crisis* (1987); Merrill D. Peterson, *Olive Branch and Sword: The Compromise of 1833* (1982).

Indian Removal

Arthur H. DeRosier, Jr., *The Removal of the Choctaw Indians* (1970); William G. McLoughlin, *Cherokee Renascence in the New Republic* (1986); John K. Mahon, *History of the Second Seminole War, 1835–1842* (1967); Francis P. Prucha, *American Indian Policy in the Formative Years* (1962); Ronald N. Satz, *American Indian Policy in the Jacksonian Era* (1975).

Biographies

Maurice G. Baxter, *One and Inseparable: Daniel Webster and the Union* (1984); Samuel F. Bemis, *John Quincy Adams and the Union* (1956); Donald Cole, *Martin Van Buren and the American Political System* (1984); Thomas P. Govan, *Nicholas Biddle: Nationalist and Public Banker* (1959); John Niven, *John C. Calhoun and the Price of Union: A Biography* (1988) and *Martin Van Buren: The Romantic Age of American Politics* (1983); Merrill D. Peterson, *The Great Triumvirate: Webster, Clay, and Calhoun* (1987); Robert V. Remini, *The Life of Andrew Jackson* (1988) and *Henry Clay: Statesman for the Union* (1991); Charles W. Wiltse, *John C. Calhoun, Nullifier, 1829–1839* (1949).

CHAPTER 12: THE FIRES OF PERFECTION

General Histories

John D'Emilio and Estelle B. Freedman, *Intimate Matters: A History of Sexuality in America* (1988); John F. Kasson, *Rudeness and Civility: Manners in Nineteenth Century America* (1990); Perry Miller, *The Life of the Mind in America: From the Revolution to the Civil War* (1966); Russel B. Nye, *Society and Culture in America, 1830–1860* (1974); Lewis Perry, *Boats Against the Current: American Culture between Revolution and Modernity, 1820–1860* (1993).

Religion and Revivalism

William G. McLoughlin, *Modern Revivalism: Charles Grandison Finney to Billy Graham* (1959); Paul E. Johnson and Sean Wilentz, *The Kingdom of Matthias: A Story of Sex and Salvation in 19th-Century America* (1994); T. Scott Miyakawa, *Protestants and Pioneers: Individualism and Conformity on the American Frontier* (1964); Jan Shipps, *Mormonism: The Story of a New Religious Tradition* (1985).

Women's Sphere and Feminism

Norma Balsch, *In the Eyes of the Law: Women, Marriage, and Property in Nineteenth-Century New York* (1982); Ann Douglas, *The Feminization of American Culture* (1977); Timothy J. Gilfoyle, *City of Eros: New York City, Prostitution, and the Commercialization of Sex, 1790–1920* (1992); Nancy Hewitt, *Women's Activism and Social Change: Rochester, New York, 1822–1872* (1984); Sylvia D. Hoffert, *Private Matters: American Attitudes toward Childbearing and Infant Nurture in the Urban North, 1800–1860* (1989); Mary Kelley, *Private Woman, Public Stage: Literary Domesticity in Nineteenth-Century America* (1984); Keith E. Melder, *Beginnings of Sisterhood: The American Women's Rights Movement, 1800–1850* (1977); James Reed, *From Private Vice to Public Virtue: The Birth Control Movement in America* (1978); Jean Fagan Yellin, *Women and Sisters: The Antislavery Feminists in American Culture* (1989).

Family

W. Andrew Achenbaum, *Old Age in the New Land: The American Experience since 1790* (1978); Clifford E. Clark, Jr., *The American Family Home, 1800–1860* (1986); Thomas R. Cole, *The Journey of Life: A Cultural History of Aging in America* (1992); Steven Mintz and Susan Kellogg, *Domestic Revolutions: A Social History of American Family Life* (1988); Walter T. K. Nugent, *Structures of American Social History* (1981); Maris A. Vinovskis, *Fertility in Massachusetts from the Revolution to the Civil War* (1981); Robert V. Wells, *Revolutions in Americans' Lives: A Demographic Perspective on the History of Americans, Their Families, and Their Society* (1982); Bernard Wishy, *The Child and the Republic: The Dawn of Modern American Child Nurture* (1967); Yasukichi Yasuba, *Birth Rates of the White Population in the United States, 1800–1860* (1962).

American Romanticism

Paul F. Boller, Jr., *American Transcendentalism, 1830–1860: An Intellectual Inquiry* (1974); Mary Kupiec Cayton, *Emerson's Emergence: Self and Society in the Transformation of New England, 1800–1845* (1989); Susan P. Conrad, *Perish the Thought: Intellectual Women in Romantic America, 1830–1860* (1976); F. O. Matthiessen, *American Renaissance: Art and Expression in the Age of Emerson and Whitman* (1941); Anne C. Rose, *Transcendentalism as a Social Movement, 1830–1850* (1981); Lazar Ziff, *Literary Democracy: The Declaration of Cultural Independence in America* (1982).

Utopian Communities

Arthur Bestor, *Backwoods Utopias: The Sectarian and Owenite Phases of Communitarian Socialism in America, 1663–1829* (1950); Carl J. Guarneri, *The Utopian Alternative: Fourierism in Nineteenth-Century America* (1991); J. F. C. Harrison, *Quest for the New Moral World: Robert Owen and the Owenites in Britain and America* (1969); Lawrence Foster, *Religion and Sexuality: Three American Communal Experiments of the Nineteenth Century* (1981); Louis Kern, *An Ordered Love: Sex Roles and Sexuality in Victorian Utopias* (1981); Carol A. Kolmerten, *Women in Utopia: The Ideology of Gender in the American Owenite Communities* (1990); Stephen Stein, *The Shaker Experience in America* (1992).

Reform Movements

Robert H. Abzug, *Cosmos Crumbling: American Reform and the Religious Imagination* (1994); Charles Leslie Glenn, Jr., *The Myth of the Common School* (1988); Clifford S. Griffin, *Their Brothers' Keepers: Moral Stewardship in the United States, 1800–1865* (1960); W. J. Rorabaugh, *The Alcoholic Republic: An American Tradition* (1979); David Rothman, *The Discovery of the Asylum: Social Order and Disorder in the New Republic* (1971); Ian R. Tyrrell, *Sobering Up: From Temperance to Prohibition in Antebellum America, 1800–1860* (1979); Rush Welter, *Popular Education and Democratic: Thought in America* (1962).

Abolitionism

Aileen Kraditor, *Means and Ends in American Abolitionism: Garrison and His Critics on Strategy and Tactics, 1834–1850* (1967); John R. McKivigan, *The War against Proslavery Religion: Abolitionism and the Northern Churches* (1984); William Lee Miller, *Arguing about Slavery: The Great Battle in the United States Congress* (1996); Russel B. Nye, *Fettered Freedom: Civil Liberties and the Slavery Controversy, 1830–1860*, rev. ed. (1963); William H. and Jane H. Pease, *They Who Would be Free: Blacks' Search for Freedom, 1830–1861* (1974); Lewis Perry, *Radical Abolitionism: Anarchy and the Government of God in Antislavery Thought* (1973); Leonard Richards, *"Gentlemen of Property and Standing": Anti-Abolition Mobs in Jacksonian America* (1970).

Biographies

Robert H. Abzug, *Passionate Liberator: Theodore Dwight Weld and the Dilemma of Reform* (1980); Lois Banner, *Elizabeth Cady Stanton: A Radical for Woman's Rights* (1980); Fawn Brodie, *No Man Knows My History: The Life of Joseph Smith, the Mormon Prophet*, 2d ed. (1971); Richard L. Bushman, *Joseph Smith and the Beginnings of Mormonism* (1984); Charles Capper, *Margaret Fuller: An American Romantic Life, the Private Years* (1992); Keith J. Hardman, *Charles Grandison Finney, 1792–1875: Revivalist and Reformer* (1987); Gerda Lerner, *The Grimké Sisters of South Carolina: Rebels against Slavery* (1967); William S. McFeely, *Frederick Douglass* (1991); Nell Painter, *Sojourner Truth: A Life, a Symbol* (1996); Katherine Kish Sklar, *Catharine Beecher: A Study in American Domesticity* (1973); John L. Thomas, *The Liberator: William Lloyd Garrison* (1963); Robert D. Thomas, *The Man Who Would Be Perfect: John Humphrey Noyes and the Utopian Impulse* (1977); Bertram Wyatt-Brown, *Lewis Tappan and the Evangelical War against Slavery* (1969).

CHAPTER 13: THE OLD SOUTH

General Histories

John B. Boles, *The South through Time: A History of an American Region* (1995); William J. Cooper and Thomas Terrill, *The American South*, 2d ed. (1996); Albert Cowdrey, *This Land, This South: An Environmental History*, rev. ed. (1996); Charles S. Sydnor, *The Development of Southern Sectionalism, 1819–1848* (1948).

Southern Economy

Fred Bateman and Thomas Weiss, *A Deplorable Scarcity: The Failure of Industrialization in the Slave Economy* (1981); Lewis C. Gray, *History of Agriculture in the Southern United States to 1860*, 2 vols. (1933); Gavin Wright, *The Political Economy of the Cotton South: Households, Markets, and Wealth in the Nineteenth Century* (1978).

Southern Society

John B. Boles, ed., *Masters and Slaves in the House of the Lord: Race and Religion in the American South, 1740–1870* (1988); Orville Vernon Burton, *In My Father's House Are Many Mansions: Family and Community in Edgefield, South Carolina* (1985); Dickson D. Bruce, Jr., *Violence and Culture in the Antebellum South* (1979); Bill Cecil-Fronsman, *Common Whites: Class & Culture in Antebellum North Carolina* (1992); Clement Eaton, *The Growth of Southern Civilization, 1790–1860* (1961); J. William Harris, *Plain Folk and Gentry in a Slave Society: White Liberty and Black Slavery in Augusta's Hinterlands* (1985); Michael P. Johnson and James L. Roark, *Black Masters: A Free Family of Color in the Old South* (1984); James Hugo Johnston, *Race Relations in Virginia and Miscegenation in the South, 1776–1860* (1970); Stephanie McCurry, *Masters of Small Worlds: Yeoman Households, Gender Relations, and the Political Culture of the Antebellum South Carolina Low Country* (1995); Donald G. Mathews, *Religion in the Old South* (1977); John Hebron Moore, *The Emergence of the Cotton Kingdom in the Old Southwest: Mississippi, 1770–1860* (1988); William H. and Jane H. Pease, *The Web of Progress: Private Values and Public Styles in Boston and Charleston, 1828–1843* (1985); Bertram Wyatt-Brown, *Honor and Violence in the Old South* (1986).

Southern Women

Victoria E. Bynum, *Unruly Women: The Politics of Social and Sexual Control in the Old South* (1992); Jane Turner Censer, *North Carolina Planters and Their Children, 1800–1860* (1984); Catherine Clinton, *The Plantation Mistress: Woman's World in the Old South* (1983); Suzanne Lebsock, *Free Women of Petersburg: Status and Culture in a Southern Town, 1784–1860* (1984); Brenda E. Stevenson, *Life in Black and White: Family and Community in the Slave South* (1996); Deborah G. White, *Arn'n't I a Woman?: Female Slaves in the Plantation South* (1985); C. Vann Woodward, ed., *Mary Chesnut's Civil War* (1981).

Slavery and Slaveowners

Shearer Davis Bowman, *Masters and Lords: Mid-Nineteenth Century U.S. Planters and Prussian Junkers* (1993); Peter A. Coclanis, *The Shadow of a Dream: Economic Life and Death in the South Carolina Low Country, 1670–1920* (1989); Paul A. David et al., *Reckoning with Slavery: A Critical Study in the Quantitative History of American Negro Slavery* (1976); Drew Gilpin Faust, *James Henry Hammond and the Old South: A Design for Mastery* (1982); Ulrich B. Phillips, *American Negro Slavery* (1918) and *Life and Labor in the Old South* (1929); Todd L. Savitt, *Medicine and Slavery: The Diseases and Health Care of Blacks in Antebellum Virginia* (1978); Robert S. Starobin, *Industrial Slavery in the Old South* (1970); Richard H. Steckel, *The Economics* of U.S. Slave and Southern White Fertility (1985); Michael Tadman, Speculators and Slaves: Masters, Traders, and Slaves in the Old South (1989); William L. Van Deburg, The Slave Drivers: Black Agricultural Labor Supervisors in the Antebellum South (1988); Richard C. Wade, Slavery in the Cities (1964).

Slave Culture
John W. Blassingame, The Slave Community: Plantation Life in the Ante-Bellum South, rev. ed. (1979); John B. Boles, Black Southerners, 1619–1869 (1984); Margaret Washington Creel, "A Peculiar People": Slave Religion and Community among the Gullahs (1988); Herbert G. Gutman, The Black Family in Slavery and Freedom, 1750–1925 (1976); Wilma King, Stolen Childhood: Slave Youth in Nineteenth Century America (1995); Lawrence Levine, Black Culture and Black Consciousness: Afro-American Folk Thought from Slavery to Freedom (1977); Ann Patton Malone, Sweet Chariot: Slave Family and Household Structure in Nineteenth-Century Louisiana (1993); Albert J. Raboteau, Slave Religion: The "Invisible Institution" in the Antebellum South (1978); Mechal Sobel, Trabelin' On: The Slave Journey to an Afro-Baptist Faith (1979); Sterling Stuckey, Slave Culture: Nationalist Theory and the Foundations of Black America (1987).

Slave Resistance
Norrece T. Jones, Born a Child of Freedom, Yet a Slave: Mechanisms of Control and Strategies of Resistance in Antebellum South (1990); Winthrop Jordan, Tumult and Silence at Second Creek (1993); John Lofton, Denmark Vesey's Revolt: The Slave Plot That Lit a Fuse to Fort Sumter (1983); Stephen B. Oates, The Fires of Jubilee: Nat Turner's Fierce Rebellion (1975).

The Defense of Slavery
Clement Eaton, Freedom of Thought in the Old South (1940); George M. Fredrickson, The Black Image in the White Mind: The Debate on Afro-American Character and Destiny, 1817–1914 (1971); Alison Goodyear Freehling, Drift toward Dissolution: The Virginia Slavery Debate of 1831–1832 (1982); Larry E. Tise, Proslavery: A History of the Defense of Slavery in America, 1701–1840 (1987).

CHAPTER 14: WESTERN EXPANSION AND THE RISE OF THE SLAVERY ISSUE

General Histories
Ray A. Billington, The Far Western Frontier, 1830–1860 (1956); Ray A. Billington and Martin Ridge, Westward Expansion, 5th ed. (1982); William H. Goetzmann, Exploration and Empire: The Explorer and the Scientist in the Winning of the American West (1978); Frederick Merk, History of the Westward Movement (1978); Henry Nash Smith, Virgin Land: The American West as Symbol and Myth (1950).

American Expansionism
Norman A. Graebner, Empire on the Pacific: A Study of American Continental Expansionism (1955); Reginald Horsman, Race and Manifest Destiny: The Origins of American Racial Anglo-Saxonism (1981); Frederick Merk, Manifest Destiny and Mission in American History (1963), The Monroe Doctrine and American Expansionism, 1843–1849 (1966), and The Oregon Question: Essays in Anglo-American Diplomacy and Politics (1967).

Societies in the West
Gunther Barth, Instant Cities: Urbanization and the Rise of San Francisco and Denver (1975); William C. Binkley, The Texas Revolution (1952); Malcolm Clark, Jr., Eden Seekers: The Settlement of Oregon, 1812–1862 (1981); Thomas D. Hall, Social Change in the Southwest, 1350–1880 (1989); Robert F. Heizer and Alan J. Almquist, The Other Californians: Prejudice and Discrimination under Spain, Mexico, and the United States to 1920 (1971); Dorothy O. Johansen and Charles M. Gates, Empire on the Columbia: A History of the Pacific Northwest, 2d ed. (1967); Sandra L. Myres, Westering Women and the Frontier Experience, 1800–1915 (1982); Leonard Pitt, The Decline of the Californios: A Social History of the Spanish-Speaking Californians, 1846–1890 (1966); Elliott West, Growing Up with the Country: Childhood on the Far Western Frontier (1989); Donald Worster, Rivers of Empire: Water, Aridity, and the Growth of the American West (1985).

Expansion and the Party System
Paul B. Bergeron, The Presidency of James K. Polk (1987); Frederick Merk, Slavery and the Annexation of Texas (1972); Robert J. Morgan, A Whig Embattled: The Presidency under John Tyler (1954); Norma L. Peterson, The Presidencies of William Henry Harrison and John Tyler (1989).

The War with Mexico
K. Jack Bauer, The Mexican War, 1846–1848 (1974); Seymour V. Connor and Odie B. Faulk, North America Divided: The Mexican War, 1846–1848 (1971); Neal Harlow, California Conquered: The Annexation of a Mexican Province, 1846–1850 (1982); Robert W. Johannsen, To the Halls of the Montezumas: The Mexican War in the American Imagination (1985); David M. Pletcher, The Diplomacy of Annexation: Texas, Oregon, and the Mexican War (1973); John H. Schroeder, Mr. Polk's War: American Opposition and Dissent, 1846–1848 (1973).

The Sectional Crisis and the Expansion of Slavery
Eugene H. Berwanger, The Frontier against Slavery: Western Anti-Negro Prejudice and the Slavery Extension Controversy (1967); Frederick J. Blue, The Free Soilers: Third Party Politics, 1848–1854 (1973); William J. Cooper, Jr., The South and the Politics of Slavery, 1828–1856 (1978); Michael F. Holt, The Political Crisis of the 1850s (1978); Chaplain W. Morrison, Democratic Politics and Sectionalism: The Wilmot Proviso Controversy (1967); Allan Nevins, Ordeal of the Union, 2 vols. (1947); David M. Potter, The Impending Crisis, 1848–1861 (1976); Joseph G. Rayback, Free Soil: The Election of 1848 (1970); Richard H. Sewell, Ballots for Freedom: Antislavery Politics in the United States, 1837–1860 (1976); Elbert B. Smith, The Presidencies of Zachary Taylor and Millard Fillmore (1988).

Biographies
Leonard J. Arrington, *Brigham Young: American Moses* (1985); K. Jack Bauer, *Zachary Taylor: Soldier, Planter, Statesman of the Old Southwest* (1985); Robert F. Dalzell, *Daniel Webster and the Trial of American Nationalism, 1843–1852* (1972); Holman Hamilton, *Zachary Taylor: Soldier in the White House* (1951); Robert W. Johannsen, *Stephen A. Douglas* (1973); Glyndon G. Van Deusen, *The Life of Henry Clay* (1937).

CHAPTER 15: THE UNION BROKEN

General Histories
Avery Craven, *The Coming of the Civil War*, 2d ed. rev. (1957) and *The Growth of Southern Nationalism, 1848–1861* (1953); James McPherson, *Ordeal by Fire: The Civil War and Reconstruction* (1982).

Economic Development and the Environment
William Cronon, *Nature's Metropolis: Chicago and the Great West* (1991); Albert Fishlow, *American Railroads and the Transformation of the Antebellum Economy* (1965); Robert William Fogel, *Without Consent or Contract: The Rise and Fall of American Slavery* (1989); Paul W. Gates, *The Farmer's Age: Agriculture, 1815–1860* (1960); James Huston, *The Panic of 1857 and the Coming of the Civil War* (1987); John F. Stover, *Iron Road to the West: American Railroads in the 1850s* (1978).

Immigration and Nativism
Tyler Anbinder, *Nativism and Slavery: The Northern Know Nothings and the Politics of the 1850s* (1992); John P. Dolan, *The Immigrant Church: New York's Irish and German Catholics, 1815–1865* (1975); Robert Ernst, *Immigrant Life in New York City, 1825–1863* (1949); Oscar Handlin, *Boston's Immigrants: A Study of Acculturation*, rev. ed. (1959); Michael F. Holt, "The Antimasonic and Know Nothing Parties," in Arthur M. Schlesinger, Jr., ed., *History of U.S. Political Parties*, vol. 1, pp. 575–737 (1973); Bruce Levine, *The Spirit of 1848: German Immigrants, Labor Conflict, and the Coming of the Civil War* (1992); Stanley Nadel, *Little Germany: Ethnicity, Religion, and Class in New York City, 1845–80* (1990).

Southern Sectionalism and Nationalism
Charles H. Brown, *Agents for Manifest Destiny: The Lives and Times of the Filibusters* (1979); William J. Cooper, Jr., *The South and the Politics of Slavery, 1828–1856* (1978); Robert E. May, *The Southern Dream of a Caribbean Empire, 1854–1861* (1973); Eric H. Walther, *The Fire-Eaters* (1992).

Sectionalism and National Politics
Jean H. Baker, *Affairs of Party: The Political Culture of Northern Democrats in the Mid-Nineteenth Century* (1983); Eugene H. Berwanger, *The Frontier against Slavery: Western Anti-Negro Prejudice and the Slavery Extension Controversy* (1967); Don E. Fehrenbacher, *Slavery, Law, and Politics: The Dred Scott Case in Historical Perspective* (1981); Larry Gara, *The Presidency of Franklin Pierce* (1991); Roy F. Nichols, *The Disruption of American Democracy* (1948); Richard H. Sewell, *Ballots for Freedom: Antislavery Politics in the United States, 1837–1860* (1976); Mark W. Summers, *The Plundering Generation: Corruption and the Crisis of the Union, 1849–1861* (1987).

Secession and the Outbreak of War
William L. Barney, *The Secessionist Impulse: Alabama and Mississippi in 1860* (1974); Daniel W. Crofts, *Reluctant Confederates: Upper South Unionists in the Secession Crisis* (1989); Richard N. Current, *Lincoln and the First Shot* (1963); Lacy K. Ford, Jr., *Origins of Southern Radicalism: The South Carolina Upcountry, 1800–1860* (1988); George N. Knoles, ed., *The Crisis of the Union, 1860–1861* (1965); David M. Potter, *Lincoln and His Party in the Secession Crisis* (1942); J. Mills Thornton, *Politics and Power in a Slave Society: Alabama, 1800–1860* (1978).

The Causes of the Civil War
Thomas J. Pressly, *Americans Interpret Their Civil War* (1954); David M. Potter, *The South and the Sectional Conflict* (1969); Kenneth M. Stampp, ed., *The Causes of the Civil War*, rev. ed. (1991).

Biographies
Don E. Fehrenbacher, *Prelude to Greatness: Lincoln in the 1850s* (1962); Robert W. Johannsen, *Stephen A. Douglas* (1973); Philip Shriver Klein, *President James Buchanan* (1962); Roy F. Nichols, *Franklin Pierce: Young Hickory of the Granite Hills*, 2d ed. rev. (1958); Stephen B. Oates, *To Purge This Land with Blood: A Biography of John Brown* (1970).

CHAPTER 16: TOTAL WAR AND THE REPUBLIC

General Histories
Daniel Aaron, *The Unwritten War: American Writers and the Civil War* (1973); Richard F. Bensel, *Yankee Leviathan: The Origins of Central State Authority in America, 1859–1877* (1990); Richard E. Beringer et al., *The Elements of Confederate Defeat: Nationalism, War Aims, and Religion* (1989); Allan Nevins, *The War for the Union*, 4 vols. (1959–1971); Edmund Wilson, *Patriotic Gore: Studies in the Literature of the American Civil War* (1962).

Military History
Bern Anderson, *By Sea and by River: The Naval History of the Civil War* (1962); Bruce Catton, *The Centennial History of the Civil War*, 3 vols. (1961–1965); Thomas L. Connelly, *Army of the Heartland: The Army of Tennessee, 1861–1862* (1967) and *Autumn of Glory: The Army of Tennessee, 1862–1865* (1971); Thomas L. Connelly and Archer Jones, *The Politics of Command: Factions and Ideas in Confederate Strategy* (1973); Herman Hattaway and Archer Jones, *How the North Won: A Military History of the Civil War* (1983); Archer Jones, *Civil War Command and Strategy: The Process of Victory and Defeat* (1992); Charles Royster, *The Destructive War: William Tecumseh Sherman, Stonewall Jackson, and the Americans* (1991); T. Harry Williams, *Lincoln and His Generals* (1952); Steven E. Woodworth, *Jefferson Davis and His Generals: The Failure of Confederate Command in the West* (1990).

Common Soldiers

Joseph T. Glatthaar, *Forged in Battle: The Civil War Alliance of Black Soldiers and White Officers* (1990) and *The March to the Sea and Beyond: Sherman's Troops in the Savannah and Carolinas Campaigns* (1985); James M. McPherson, *What They Fought For, 1861–1865* (1994); Reid Mitchell, *Civil War Soldiers: Their Expectations and Their Experiences* (1988), and *The Vacant Chair: The Northern Soldier Leaves Home* (1993); James I. Robertson, *Soldiers Blue and Gray* (1988); Bell I. Wiley, *The Life of Johnny Reb* (1943) and *The Life of Billy Yank* (1952).

The Confederacy

Mary A. DeCredico, *Patriotism for Profit: Georgia's Urban Entrepreneurs and the Confederate War Effort* (1990); Wayne K. Durrill, *War of Another Kind: A Southern Community in the Great Rebellion* (1990); Paul D. Escott, *After Secession: Jefferson Davis and the Failure of Confederate Nationalism* (1978); Drew Gilpin Faust, *The Creation of Confederate Nationalism: Ideology and Identity in the Civil War South* (1988); Mary Elizabeth Massey, *Refugee Life in the Confederacy* (1964); Frank L. Owsley, *State Rights in the Confederacy* (1925); Charles W. Ramsdell, *Behind the Lines in the Southern Confederacy* (1944); Richard C. Todd, *Confederate Finance* (1954); Bell I. Wiley, *The Plain People of the Confederacy* (1943) and *The Road to Appomattox* (1956); Wilfred B. Yearns, *The Confederate Congress* (1960).

Union Politics

Leonard P. Curry, *Blueprint for Modern America: Non-Military Legislation of the First Civil War Congress* (1968); William B. Hesseltine, *Lincoln and the War Governors* (1948); Harold M. Hyman, *A More Perfect Union: The Impact of the Civil War and Reconstruction on the Constitution* (1973); Philip S. Paludan, *The Presidency of Abraham Lincoln* (1994); James A. Rawley, *The Politics of Union: Northern Politics during the Civil War* (1974); Joel H. Silbey, *A Respectable Minority: The Democratic Party in the Civil War Era* (1977).

Union Home Front

Ralph Andreano, ed., *The Economic Impact of the American Civil War* (1962); Iver Bernstein, *The New York City Draft Riots: Their Significance for American Society and Politics in the Age of the Civil War* (1990); Adrian Cook, *The Armies of the Streets: The New York City Draft Riots of 1863* (1974); George Fredrickson, *The Inner Civil War: Northern Intellectuals and the Crisis of the Union* (1965); J. Matthew Gallman, *Mastering Wartime: A Social History of Philadelphia during the Civil War* (1990); Paul W. Gates, *Agriculture and the Civil War* (1965); Earl J. Hess, *Liberty, Virtue, and Progress: Northerners and Their War for the Union* (1988); James W. Geary, *We Need Men: The Union Draft in the Civil War* (1991); Frank L. Klement, *The Copperheads in the Middle West* (1960); Ernest A. McKay, *The Civil War and New York City* (1990); James H. Moorhead, *American Apocalypse: Yankee Protestants and the Civil War, 1860–1869* (1978); Philip S. Paludan, *"A People's Contest": The Union and Civil War, 1861–1865* (1988); George Winston Smith and Charles Burnet Judah, *Life in the North during the Civil War* (1966).

Women and the Civil War

Catherine Clinton and Nina Silber, eds., *Divided Houses: Gender and the Civil War* (1992); Marilyn M. Culpepper, *Trials and Triumphs: Women of the American Civil War* (1991); Ellen Leonard, *Yankee Women: Gender Battles in the Civil War* (1994); Mary Elizabeth Massey, *Bonnet Brigades: American Women and the Civil War* (1966); George C. Rable, *Civil Wars: Women and the Crisis of Southern Nationalism* (1989); C. Vann Woodward, ed., *Mary Chesnut's Civil War* (1981); Agatha Young, *Women and the Crisis: Women of the North in the Civil War* (1959).

Emancipation and the Black Experience

Dudley T. Cornish, *The Sable Arm: Negro Troops in the Union Army, 1861–1865* (1956); LaWanda Cox, *Lincoln and Black Freedom: A Study in Presidential Leadership* (1981); Barbara Jeanne Fields, *Slavery and Freedom on the Middle Ground: Maryland during the Nineteenth Century* (1985); John Hope Franklin, *The Emancipation Proclamation* (1963); Louis Gerteis, *From Contraband to Freedman: Federal Policy toward Southern Blacks, 1861–1865* (1973); James M. McPherson, *The Struggle for Equality: Abolitionists and the Negro in the Civil War and Reconstruction* (1964); Clarence L. Mohr, *On the Threshold of Freedom: Masters and Slaves in Civil War Georgia* (1986); Willie Lee Rose, *Rehearsal for Reconstruction: The Port Royal Experiment* (1964); V. Jacque Voegli, *Free but Not Equal: The Midwest and the Negro during the Civil War* (1967).

Diplomacy

David P. Crook, *Diplomacy during the American Civil War* (1975); Norman Ferris, *The Trent Affair: A Diplomatic Crisis* (1977); Brian Jenkins, *Britain and the War for the Union* (1974); Howard Jones, *Union in Peril: The Crisis Over British Intervention in the Civil War* (1992); Frank L. Owsley, *King Cotton Diplomacy*, rev. ed. (1959).

Biographies

David W. Blight, *Frederick Douglass' Civil War: Keeping Faith in Jubilee* (1989); Bruce Catton, *Grant Moves South* (1960) and *Grant Takes Command* (1969); William C. Davis, *Jefferson Davis: The Man and His Hour* (1991); William S. McFeely, *Grant: A Biography* (1981); Mark E. Neely, Jr. *The Last Best Hope of Earth: Abraham Lincoln and the Promise of America* (1993); Alan T. Nolan, *Lee Considered: General Robert E. Lee and Civil War History* (1991); Stephen B. Oates, *A Woman of Valor: Clara Barton and the Civil War* (1994); James G. Randall and Richard N. Current, *Lincoln the President*, 4 vols. (1945–1955); Emory M. Thomas, *Robert E. Lee* (1995).

CHAPTER 17: RECONSTRUCTING THE UNION

General Histories

James McPherson, *Ordeal by Fire: The Civil War and Reconstruction* (1982); Kenneth M. Stampp, *The Era of Reconstruction, 1865–1877* (1965).

National Politics

Herman Belz, *Emancipation and Equal Rights: Politics and Constitutionalism in the Civil War Era* (1978);

Michael Les Benedict, *A Compromise of Principle: Congressional Republicans and Reconstruction* (1974); W. R. Brock, *An American Crisis: Congress and Reconstruction, 1865–1867* (1963); John and LaWanda Cox, *Politics, Principles, and Prejudice, 1865–1866* (1963); James M. McPherson, *The Struggle for Equality: Abolitionists and the Negro in the Civil War and Reconstruction* (1964); Hans L. Trefousse, *The Radical Republicans: Lincoln's Vanguard for Racial Justice* (1969).

Reconstruction and the Constitution
William Gillette, *The Right to Vote: Politics and the Passage of the Fifteenth Amendment* (1965); Harold M. Hyman, *A More Perfect Union: The Impact of the Civil War and Reconstruction on the Constitution* (1973); Joseph James, *The Framing of the Fourteenth Amendment* (1956); William E. Nelson, *The Fourteenth Amendment: From Political Principle to Judicial Doctrine* (1988).

The Black Experience in Reconstruction
James D. Anderson, *The Education of Blacks in the South, 1860–1935* (1988); Herbert G. Gutman, *The Black Family in Slavery and Freedom, 1750–1925* (1976); Janet Sharp Hermann, *The Pursuit of a Dream* (1981); Howard Rabinowitz, ed., *Southern Black Leaders in Reconstruction* (1982); Vernon L. Wharton, *The Negro in Mississippi, 1865–1890* (1947); Joel Williamson, *After Slavery: The Negro in South Carolina during Reconstruction* (1966).

Reconstruction in the South
Richard N. Current, *Those Terrible Carpetbaggers: A Reinterpretation* (1988); William C. Harris, *Day of the Carpetbagger: Republican Reconstruction in Mississippi* (1979); Michael Perman, *Reunion without Compromise: The South and Reconstruction, 1865–1868* (1973); George C. Rable, *But There Was No Peace: The Role of Violence in the Politics of Reconstruction* (1984); James Sefton, *The United States Army and Reconstruction, 1865–1877* (1967); Ted Tunnell, *Crucible of Reconstruction: War, Radicalism, and Race in Louisiana, 1862–1877* (1974); Allen Trelease, *White Terror: The Ku Klux Klan Conspiracy and Southern Reconstruction* (1967); Sarah Woolfolk Wiggins, *The Scalawag in Alabama Politics, 1865–1881* (1977).

Social and Economic Reconstruction
George R. Bentley, *A History of the Freedmen's Bureau* (1955); Eric Foner, *Nothing But Freedom: Emancipation and Its Legacy* (1983); Steven Hahn, *The Roots of Southern Populism: Yeoman Farmers and the Transformation of the Georgia Upcountry, 1850–1890* (1983); Jacqueline Jones, *Soldiers of Light and Love: Northern Teachers and Georgia Blacks, 1865–1873* (1980); Donald Nieman, *To Set the Law in Motion: The Freedmen's Bureau and the Legal Rights of Blacks, 1865–1868* (1979); Claude F. Oubre, *Forty Acres and a Mule: The Freedmen's Bureau and Black Landownership* (1978); Lawrence N. Powell, *New Masters: Northern Planters during the Civil War and Reconstruction* (1984); Roger L. Ransom and Richard Sutch, *One Kind of Freedom: The Economic Consequences of Emancipation* (1977); Mark W. Summers, *Railroads, Reconstruction, and the Gospel of Prosperity* (1984).

The End of Reconstruction
Paul Buck, *The Road to Reunion, 1865–1900* (1937); Keith Ian Polakoff, *The Politics of Inertia: The Election of 1876 and the End of Reconstruction* (1973); C. Vann Woodward, *Reunion and Reaction: The Compromise of 1877 and the End of Reconstruction* (1951).

Biographies
Fawn M. Brodie, *Thaddeus Stevens: Scourge of the South* (1959); David Donald, *Charles Sumner and the Rights of Man* (1970); William S. McFeely, *Yankee Stepfather: General O. Howard and the Freedmen* (1968) and *Grant: A Biography* (1981); Brooks D. Simpson, *Let Us Have Peace: Ulysses S. Grant and the Politics of War and Reconstruction, 1861–1868* (1991); Hans L. Trefousse, *Andrew Johnson: A Biography* (1989).

CHAPTER 18: A NEW INDUSTRIAL ORDER

General Studies
Daniel Boorstin, *The Americans: The Democratic Experience* (1973); John A. Garraty, *The New Commonwealth* (1968); Ray Ginger, *The Age of Excess* (1963); Samuel P. Hays, *The Response to Industrialism, 1885–1914* (1957); Edward C. Kirkland, *Industry Comes of Age: Business, Labor, and Public Policy, 1860–1897* (1967); Martin V. Melosi, *Coping with Abundance: Energy and Environment in Industrial America* (1985); Robert Wiebe, *The Search for Order, 1877–1920* (1968).

The Economy
Frederick Lewis Allen, *The Great Pierpont Morgan* (1949); W. Elliot Brownlee, *Dynamics of Ascent: A History of the American Economy*, rev. ed. (1979); Stuart Bruchey, *Growth of the Modern American Economy* (1975); Milton Friedman and Anna Schwartz, *Monetary History of the United States, 1867–1960* (1963); Robert L. Heilbroner, *The Economic Transformation of America* (1977); Robert Higgs, *The Transformation of the American Economy, 1865–1914* (1971); Susan Previant Lee and Peter Passell, *A New Economic View of American History* (1979); Harold G. Vatter, *The Drive to Industrial Maturity: The United States Economy, 1860–1914* (1975).

The Railroads
Alfred D. Chandler, Jr., *The Railroads: The Nation's First Big Business* (1965); Robert Fogel, *Railroads and American Economic Growth* (1964); Julius Grodinsky, *Jay Gould* (1957); Gabriel Kolko, *Railroads and Regulation, 1877–1916* (1965); Albro Martin, *James J. Hill and the Opening of the Northwest* (1976) and *Railroads Triumphant: The Growth, Rejection, and Rebirth of a Vital American Force* (1992); John F. Stover, *American Railroads* (1970).

The Rise of Big Business
Alfred Chandler, Jr., *Strategy and Structure: Chapters in the History of American Industrial Enterprise* (1962), *The Visible Hand: The Managerial Revolution in American Business* (1977) and *Scale and Scope: The Dynamics of Industrial Capitalism* (1990); Thomas Cochrane, *Business in American Life* (1972); Naomi Lamoreaux, *The Great*

Merger Movement in American Business, 1895–1904 (1985); Harold C. Livesay, Andrew Carnegie and the Rise of Big Business (1975); Alan Nevins, Study in Power: John D. Rockefeller, 2 vols. (1953); Glenn Porter, The Rise of Big Business (1973); Martin J. Sklar, The Corporate Reconstruction of American Capitalism, 1890–1916: The Market, Law and Politics (1988); Richard Tedlow, The Rise of the American Business Corporation (1991); Alan Trachtenberg, The Incorporation of America (1982); Joseph Wall, Andrew Carnegie (1970); Olivier Zunz, Making America Corporate, 1870–1920 (1990).

Invention and Industry
Robert Bruce, Alexander Graham Bell and the Conquest of Solitude (1973); Robert Conot, A Streak of Luck (1979); Ruth Schwartz Cowan, A Social History of American Technology (1996); Siegfried Giedion, Mechanization Takes Command (1948); David Hounshell, From the American System to Mass Production, 1800–1932 (1984); John F. Kasson, Civilizing the Machine (1976); Carolyn Marvin, When Old Technologies Were New: Thinking about Electric Communication in the Late Nineteenth Century (1988); David Nye, Electrifying America: Social Meanings of a New Technology, 1890–1940 (1990); Harold Passer, The Electrical Manufacturers, 1875–1900 (1953); Leonard S. Reich, The Making of Industrial Research: Science and Business at GE and Bell, 1876–1926 (1985); Nathan Rosenberg, Technology and American Economic Growth (1972); Peter Temin, Iron and Steel in Nineteenth Century America (1964); Frederick A. White, American Industrial Research Laboratories (1961).

Capitalism and Its Critics
Robert Bannister, Social Darwinism: Science and Myth in Anglo-American Social Thought (1979); Robert H. Bremner, American Philanthropy (1988); Carl N. Degler, In Search of Human Nature: The Decline and Revival of Darwinism in America (1991); Sidney Fine, Laissez Faire and the General Welfare State: A Study of Conflict in American Thought, 1865–1900 (1956); Louis Galambos, The Public Image of Big Business in America, 1880–1940: A Quantitative Study of Social Change (1975); Richard Hofstadter, Social Darwinism in American Thought, rev. ed. (1955); Edward C. Kirkland, Dream and Thought in the Business Community, 1860–1900 (1956); Ellen Condliffe Lagemann, The Politics of Knowledge: The Carnegie Corporation, Philanthropy, and Public Policy (1989); T. Jackson Lears, No Place of Grace: Antimodernism and the Transformation of American Culture, 1880–1920 (1981); George E. Pozzetta, ed., Americanization, Social Control, and Philanthropy (1991); John Thomas, Alternative America: Henry George, Edward Bellamy, Henry Demarest Lloyd, and the Adversary Tradition (1983).

The Culture of Work
American Social History Project, Who Built America? Working People and the Nation's Economy, Politics, Culture, Society, Volume Two: From the Gilded Age to the Present (1992); Cindy Sondik Aron, Ladies and Gentlemen of the Civil Service: Middle-Class Workers in Victorian America (1987); James R. Barrett, Work and Community in the Jungle: Chicago's Packinghouse Workers, 1894–

1922 (1990); John Bodnar, Immigration and Industrialization: Ethnicity in an American Mill Town (1977); John T. Cumbler, Working Class Community in Industrial America: Work, Leisure, and Struggle in Two Industrial Cities, 1880–1930 (1979); David Emmons, The Butte Irish: Class and Ethnicity in an American Mining Town, 1875–1925 (1989); Michael Frisch and Daniel Walkowitz, eds., Working-Class America: Essays on Labor, Community, and American Society (1983); James R. Green, World of the Worker: Labor in Twentieth Century America (1980); Herbert Gutman, Work, Culture and Society in Industrializing America: Essays in American Working-Class History (1976); Tamara Hareven, Family, Time, and Industrial Time: The Relationship between the Family and Work in a New England Industrial Community (1982); William H. Harris, The Harder We Run: Black Workers since the Civil War (1982); Jacqueline Jones, Labor of Love, Labor of Sorrow: Black Women, Work and the Family, from Slavery to the Present (1985); Susan Kennedy, If All We Did Was to Weep at Home: A History of White Working Class Women in America (1979); Walter Licht, Working for the Railroad: The Organization of Work in the Nineteenth Century (1983); Joanne J. Meyerowitz, Women Adrift: Independent Wage Earners in Chicago, 1880–1930 (1988); David Montgomery, Workers' Control in America: Studies in the History of Work, Technology, and Labor Struggles (1979); Daniel Nelson, Managers and Workers: Origins of the New Factory System (1975); Richard Jules Oestreicher, Solidarity and Fragmentation: Working People and Class Consciousness in Detroit, 1875–1900 (1986); Daniel T. Rodgers, The Work Ethic in Industrial America, 1850–1920 (1978); Stephan Thernstrom, The Other Bostonians: Poverty and Progress in the American Metropolis, 1880–1970 (1973).

The Labor Movement
Eric Arnesen, Waterfront Workers of New Orleans: Race, Class, and Politics, 1863–1923 (1991); Paul Avrich, The Haymarket Tragedy (1984); Mary H. Blewett, Men, Women, and Work: Class, Gender, and Protest in the New England Shoe Industry, 1880–1910 (1988); Jeremy Brecher, Strike! (1977); Mari Jo Buhle, Women and American Socialism, 1870–1920 (1981); Melvyn Dubofsky, Industrialism and the American Worker, 1865–1920 (1975) and We Shall Be All: A History of the Industrial Workers of the World (1969); Philip Foner, Women and the American Labor Movement, 2 vols. (1979); James R. Grossman, Land of Hope: Chicago, Black Southerners, and the Great Migration (1989); William H. Harris, The Harder We Run: Black Workers since the Civil War (1982); Stuart Kaufman, Samuel Gompers and the Origins of the American Federation of Labor (1973); Paul Krause, The Battle for Homestead: Politics, Culture and Steel (1992); Susan Levine, Labor's True Women: Carpet Weavers, Industrialization, and Labor Reform in the Gilded Age (1984); Gwendolyn Mink, Old Labor and New Immigrants in American Political Development: Union, Party, and State, 1875–1920 (1986); David Montgomery, The Fall of the House of Labor: The Workplace, the State, and American Labor Activism, 1865–1925 (1987); Leon Fink, Workingmen's Democracy: The Knights of Labor and American Politics (1983) Alice Kessler-Harris, Out to

Work: A History of Wage-Earning Women in the United States (1982); Nick Salvatore, *Eugene V. Debs: Citizen and Socialist* (1982); David Shannon, *The Socialist Party* (1955); Sheldon Stromquist, *A Generation of Boomers: The Pattern of Railroad Labor Conflict in Nineteenth-Century America* (1987); Lloyd Ulman, *The Rise of the National Trade Union: The Development and Significance of Its Structure, Governing Institutions, and Economic Policies* (1955).

CHAPTER 19: THE RISE OF AN URBAN ORDER

General Studies

Howard B. Chudacoff, *The Evolution of American Urban Society*, rev. ed., (1981); William Cronon, *Nature's Metropolis: Chicago and the Great West* (1991); Charles Glabb and A. Theodore Brown, *A History of Urban America*, rev. ed., (1976); Blake McKelvey, *The Urbanization of America, 1860–1915* (1963); Allan Pred, *Spatial Dynamics of U.S. Urban Growth, 1800–1914* (1971); John Stilgoe, *Borderland: The Origins of the American Suburb, 1820–1929* (1988); Stephan Thernstrom and Richard Sennett, eds., *19th Century Cities: Essays in the New Urban History* (1969); Sam Bass Warner, Jr., *Streetcar Suburbs* (1962) and *The Urban Wilderness* (1972).

Immigration and Immigrants

John Bodnar, *The Transplanted: A History of Immigrants in Urban America* (1985); Josef Barton, *Peasants and Strangers: Italians, Rumanians and Slovaks in an American City* (1975); John J. Bukowczyk, *And My Children Did Not Know Me: A History of Polish Americans* (1987); Sucheng Chan, *Asian Americans: An Interpretive History* (1991); Jack Chen, *The Chinese of America* (1970); Roger Daniels, *Coming to America: A History of Immigration and Ethnicity in American Life* (1990); Hasia A. Diner, *Erin's Daughters in America: Irish Immigrant Women in the Nineteenth Century* (1983); Leonard Dinnerstein, Roger Nichols, and David Reimers, *Natives and Strangers* (1979); John Duff, *The Irish in the United States* (1971); Mario Garcia, *Desert Immigrants: The Mexicans of El Paso, 1880–1920* (1981); Susan A. Glenn, *Daughters of the Shtetl: Life and Labor in the Immigrant Generation* (1990); Richard Griswold del Castillo, *La Familia: Chicano Families in the Urban Southwest, 1848 to the Present* (1984); Irving Howe, *World of Our Fathers: The Journey of the East European Jews to America and the Life They Found and Made* (1976); Yuji Ichioka, *The Issei: The World of the First Generation Japanese Americans, 1885–1924* (1988); Jenna Weissman Joselit, *The Wonders of America: Reinventing Jewish Culture, 1880–1950* (1994); Edward Kantowicz, *Polish-American Politics in Chicago* (1975); Thomas Kessner, *The Golden Door: Italian and Jewish Immigrant Mobility in New York City, 1880–1915* (1977); Alan M. Kraut, *The Huddled Masses: The Immigrant in American Society, 1880–1921* (1982); Michael La Sorte, *La Merica: Images of Italian Greenhorn Experience* (1985); Joseph Lopreato, *Italian Americans* (1970); Kerby A. Miller, *Emigrants and Exiles: Ireland and the Irish Exodus to North America* (1985); Ewa Morawska, *For Bread and Butter: The Life-Worlds of East Central Europeans in*

Johnstown, Pennsylvania, 1890–1940 (1985); James Stuart Olsen, *The Ethnic Dimension in American History*, vol. II (1979); Moses Rischin, *The Promised City: New York's Jews* (1962); Jacob Riis, *How the Other Half Lives* (1890); Howard M. Sachar, *A History of Jews in America* (1992); Ronald Takaki, *Strangers from a Different Shore: A History of Asian Americans* (1989) and *A Different Mirror: A History of Multicultural America* (1993); Philip Taylor, *The Distant Magnet: European Emigration to the U.S.A.* (1971); Virginia Yans-McLaughlin, *Family and Community: Italian Immigrants in Buffalo, 1880–1930* (1977), and as ed., *Immigration Reconsidered: History, Sociology, Politics* (1990); Anzia Yezierska, *Bread Givers* (1925); Olivier Zunz, *The Changing Face of Inequality: Urbanization, Industrial Development, and Immigrants in Detroit, 1880–1920* (1982).

Nativism and Race

Leonard Dinnerstein, *Anti-Semitism in America* (1994); Louis Harlan, *Booker T. Washington: The Making of a Black Leader, 1856–1901* (1972) and *Booker T. Washington: The Wizard of Tuskegee, 1901–1915* (1983); John Higham, *Strangers in the Land: Patterns of American Nativism, 1880–1925* (1955) and *Send These to Me* (1975); Kenneth Kusmer, *A Ghetto Takes Shape: Black Cleveland, 1870–1930* (1976); Stanley Lieberson, *A Piece of the Pie: Blacks and White Immigrants Since 1880* (1980); Gilbert Osofsky, *Harlem: The Making of a Ghetto* (1966); Joel Perlman, *Ethnic Differences: Schooling and Social Structure among the Irish, Italians, Jews, and Blacks in an American City, 1880–1935* (1988); Elizabeth Hafkin Pleck, *Black Migration and Poverty, Boston, 1865–1900* (1979); Allan H. Spear, *Black Chicago* (1967); Donald Spivey, *Schooling for the New Slavery: Black Industrial Education, 1868–1915* (1978).

Politics and Poverty

John Allswang, *Bosses, Machines, and Urban Voters* (1977); Robert H. Bremner, *From the Depths: The Discovery of Poverty in the United States* (1956); Alexander B. Callow, ed., *The City Boss in America* (1976); Lyle Dorsett, *The Pendergast Machine* (1968); Steven P. Erie, *Rainbow's End: Irish-Americans and the Dilemmas of Urban Machine Politics, 1840–1985* (1988); Leo Hershkowitz, *Tweed's New York: Another Look* (1977); Zane Miller, *Boss Cox's Cincinnati* (1968); James T. Patterson, *America's Struggle against Poverty* (1981); Thomas Philpott, *The Slum and the Ghetto* (1978); William L. Riordon, *Plunkitt of Tammany Hall* (1963); Lloyd Wendt and Herman Kogan, *Bosses in Lusty Chicago*, 2d ed. (1971).

Reform

Jane Addams, *Twenty Years at Hull-House* (1910); Ruth Bordin, *Woman and Temperance: The Quest for Power and Liberty, 1860–1900* (1981); Paul Boyer, *Urban Masses and Moral Order in America, 1820–1920* (1978); Allen Davis, *Spearheads for Reform: The Social Settlements and the Progressive Movement, 1890–1914* (1967) and *American Heroine: The Life and Legend of Jane Addams* (1973); Marvin Lazerson, *Origins of the Urban School* (1971); Eric Monkonnen, *Police in Urban America, 1860–1920* (1981); David Pivar, *Purity Crusade: Sexual Morality and Social Control, 1868–1900* (1973); James Reed, *The*

Birth Control Movement and American Society: From Private Vice to Public Virtue (1983); Barbara Rosencrantz, Public Health and the State (1972); Martin Schiesl, The Politics of Efficiency: Municipal Administration and Reform in America (1977); David Tyack, The One Best System: A History of American Urban Education (1974); Morris Vogel, The Invention of the Modern Hospital: Boston, 1870–1930 (1980); James C. Whorton, Crusaders for Fitness: The History of American Health Reformers (1982).

Urban Life, Work, and Culture
Cindy Aron, Ladies and Gentlemen of the Civil Service: Middle Class Workers in Victorian America (1987); Gunther Barth, City People: The Rise of Modern City Culture in 19th Century America (1980); Susan Porter Benson, Counter Cultures: Saleswomen, Managers, and Customers in Department Stores, 1890–1940 (1986); Allan Brandt, No Magic Bullet: A Social History of Venereal Disease in the United States Since 1880, rev. ed. (1985); Robert Cross, The Church and the City (1967); Ronald Davies, A History of Music in American Life, Volume II: The Gilded Years, 1865–1920 (1980); Lewis A. Erenberg, Steppin' Out: New York Nightlife and the Transformation of American Culture, 1890–1930 (1981); Ellen Garvey, The Adman in the Parlor: Magazines and the Gendering of Consumer Culture, 1880s to 1910s (1996); James Gilbert, Perfect Cities: Chicago Utopias of 1893 (1991); Thomas J. Gilfoyle, City of Eros: New York City, Prostitution, and the Commercialization of Sex, 1790–1920 (1992); Tamara K. Hareven and Randolph Langenbach, Amoskeag: Life and Work in an American Factory (1978); Neil Harris, Humbug: The Art of P. T. Barnum (1973); Lawrence Kasson, Amusing the Million: Coney Island at the Turn of the Century (1978) and Rudeness & Civility: Manners in Nineteenth-Century Urban America (1990); William Leach, Land of Desire: Merchants, Power, and the Rise of a New American Culture (1993); Lawrence Levine, Highbrow/Lowbrow: The Emergence of Cultural Hierarchy in America (1988); Richard Lingeman, Theodore Dreiser: At the Gates of the City, 1871–1907 (1986); John Lucas and Ronald Smith, Saga of American Sport (1978); Henry F. May, Protestant Churches and Urban America (1949); Katherine Morello, The Invisible Bar: The Woman Lawyer in America, 1638 to the Present (1986); Joseph Musselman, Music in the Cultured Generation: A Social History of Music in America, 1870–1900 (1971); David Nasaw, Schooled to Order: A Social History of Public Schooling in the United States (1979), Children of the City: At Work and at Play (1986), and Going Out: The Rise and Fall of Public Amusements (1993); Kathy Peiss, Cheap Amusements: Working Women and Leisure in Turn-of-the-Century New York (1986); Roy Rosenzweig, Eight Hours for What We Will: Workers & Leisure in an Industrial City, 1870–1920 (1983); Russel Nye, The Unembarrassed Muse: The Popular Arts in America (1970); Thomas J. Schlereth, Victorian American: Transformations in Everyday Life, 1876–1915 (1991); Robert H. Walker, Life in the Age of Enterprise, 1865–1900 (1967).

Women, Family, and Social Mores
Elaine S. Abelson, When Ladies Go A-Thieving: Middle-Class Shoplifters in the Victorian Department Store (1990); Allan M. Brandt, No Magic Bullet: A Social History of Venereal Disease since 1880 (1985); John D'Emilio and Estelle B. Freedman, Intimate Matters: A History of Sexuality in America (1988); Harvey Green, The Light of the Home: An Intimate View of the Lives of Women in Victorian America (1983); John S. Haller and Robin M. Haller, The Physician and Sexuality in Victorian America (1986); N. Ray Hiner and Joseph Hawes, eds., Growing Up in America: Children in Historical Perspective (1985); David Katzman, Seven Days a Week: Women and Domestic Service in Industrializing America (1978); Judith Leavitt, Brought to Bed: Childbearing in America, 1750–1950 (1988); Elizabeth Lunbeck, The Psychiatric Persuasion: Knowledge, Gender and Politics in Modern America (1994); Elaine May, Great Expectations: Marriage and Divorce in Post-Victorian America (1980); Steven Mintz, A Prison of Expectations: The Family in Victorian Culture (1983); Steven Mintz and Susan Kellogg, Domestic Revolutions: A Social History of American Family Life (1988); Ellen Rothman, Hands and Hearts: A History of Courtship in America (1984); Gar Scharnhorst, Charlotte Perkins Gilman (1985); Carroll Smith-Rosenberg, Disorderly Conduct: Visions of Gender in Victorian America (1986); Susan Strasser, Never Done: A History of American Housework (1983).

CHAPTER 20: AGRARIAN DOMAINS: THE SOUTH AND THE WEST

The New South: History, Politics, and Culture
Edward L. Ayers, The Promise of the New South: Life after Reconstruction (1992) and Southern Crossing: A History of the American South, 1877–1906 (1995); Orville Vernon Burton, In My Father's House (1985); W. J. Cash, The Mind of the South (1941); Thomas D. Clark and Albert Kirwan, The South since Appomattox (1967); David L. Carlton, Mill and Town in South Carolina, 1880–1920 (1982); John M. Cooper, Walter Hines Page: The Southerner as American, 1855–1918 (1977); Pete Daniel, Breaking the Land: The Transformation of Cotton, Tobacco, and Rice Cultures since 1880 (1985); Carl N. Degler, The Other South: Southern Dissenters in the Nineteenth Century (1974); Robert Durden, The Self-Inflicted Wound: Southern Politics in the Nineteenth Century (1985); John S. Ezell, The South since 1865 (1975); Paul Gaston, The New South Creed: A Study in Southern Mythmaking (1970); Richard Gray, Writing the South: The Idea of an American Region (1986); Patrick N. Hearden, Independence and Empire: The New South's Cotton Mill Campaign, 1865–1920 (1982); J. Morgan Kousser, The Shaping of Southern Politics: Suffrage Restriction and Establishment of the One Party South (1974); J. Morgan Kousser and James McPherson, eds., Region, Race, and Reconstruction (1982); Lawrence Karsen, The Rise of the Urban South (1985); I. A. Newby, Plain Folk in the New South: Social Change and Cultural Persistence, 1880–1915 (1989); Raymond B. Nixon, Henry W. Grady: Spokesman of the New South (1969); Ted Ownby, Subduing Satan (1990); David M. Potter, The South and the Concurrent Majority (1972); Allen Tullos, Habits of Industry: White Culture and the Transformation of the Carolina Piedmont (1989); Marjorie Spruill Wheeler, New Women of the New South:

The Leaders of the Woman Suffrage Movement in the Southern States (1993); Charles R. Wilson, Baptized in Blood: The Religion of the Lost Cause, 1865–1920 (1980); C. Vann Woodward, Tom Watson: Agrarian Rebel (1938), and The Origins of the New South (1951).

The Southern Economy and Race
David Carlton, Mill and Town in South Carolina, 1880–1920 (1982); Pete Daniel, Breaking the Land: The Transformation of Cotton, Tobacco, and Rice Cultures since 1880 (1985); Steven Hahn, The Roots of Southern Populism: Yeoman Farmers and the Transformation of the Georgia Upcountry, 1850–1890 (1983); Louis T. Harlan, Booker T. Washington: The Making of a Black Leader, 1865–1901 (1972); Robert Higgs, Competition and Coercion: Blacks in the American Economy, 1865–1890 (1977); Gerald David Jaynes, Branches without Roots: Genesis of the Black Working Class in the American South, 1862–1882 (1986); Neil R. McMillen, Dark Journey: Black Mississippians in the Age of Jim Crow (1989); J. M. McPherson, The Abolitionist Legacy: From Reconstruction to the NAACP (1975); August Meier, Negro Thought in America, 1880–1915: Racial Ideologies in the Age of Booker T. Washington (1963); Howard Rabinowitz, Race Relations in the Urban South, 1865–1890 (1978); Roger Ransom and Richard Sutch, One Kind of Freedom: The Economic Consequences of Emancipation (1977); Donald Spivey, Schooling for the New Slavery: Black Industrial Education (1978); J. F. Stover, The Railroads of the South (1955); Edward Wheeler, Uplifting the Race: The Black Minister in the New South, 1865–1902 (1986); Joel Williamson, The Crucible of Race: Black-White Relations in the American South since Emancipation (1984) and After Slavery (1965); C. Vann Woodward, The Strange Career of Jim Crow, 3d rev. ed. (1974); Gavin Wright, Old South, New South: Revolutions in the Southern Economy since the Civil War (1986).

Opening of the West
Walton Bean, California (1978); Thomas Berger, Little Big Man (1964); Ray A. Billington, Westward Expansion (1967); Thomas D. Clark, Frontier America, rev. ed. (1969); William Cronon, Nature's Metropolis: Chicago and the Great West (1991); William Cronon, George Miles, and Jay Gitlin, Under an Open Sky: Rethinking America's Western Past (1992); Sarah Deutsch, No Separate Refuge: Culture, Class, and Gender on an Anglo-Hispanic Frontier in the American Southwest, 1880–1940 (1987); Robert Hine, The American West, 2d rev. ed. (1984); Paul Hutton, ed., Soldiers West: Biographers from the Military Frontier (1987); Howard Lamar, The Reader's Encyclopedia of the American West (1977) and The Far Southwest, 1846–1912 (1966); Patricia Nelson Limerick, The Legacy of Conquest: The Unbroken Past of the American West (1987); Gerald McFarland, A Scattered People: An American Family Moves West (1985); Leo Marx, The Machine in the Garden (1964); Donald W. Meinig, The Southwest: Three People in Geographical Change, 1600–1970 (1971); Frederick Merk, History of the Westward Movement (1978); Clyde A. Milner II, A New Significance: Re-Envisioning the History of the American West (1996); Clyde A. Milner II, Carol A. O'Connor, and Martha A. Sandweiss, eds., The Oxford History of the American West (1994); Roderick Nash, Wilderness and the American Mind, 3d ed. (1982);

Earl Pomery, The Pacific Slope (1968); Richard Slotkin, The Fatal Environment: The Myth of the West in the Age of Industrialization (1985) and Gunfighter Nation: The Myth of the Frontier in Twentieth-Century America (1992); Wallace Stegner, Beyond the Hundredth Meridian: John Welsey Powell and the Second Opening of the West (1954); Henry Nash Smith, Virgin Land (1950); Jane Tompkins, West of Everything: The Inner Life of Westerns (1992); Mark Twain, Roughing It (1872); Elliott West, The Way to the West: Essays on the Central Plains (1995); Richard White, "It's Your Misfortune and None of My Own": A New History of the American West (1992); Donald Worster, Rivers of Empire: Water, Aridity, and the Growth of the American West (1992) and Under Western Skies: Nature and History in the American West (1992).

The Peoples of the West
Rudolfo Acuna, Occupied America: A History of Chicanos (1981); Ralph Andrist, The Long Death: The Last Days of the Sioux Nation (1964); Robert Athearn, In Search of Canaan: Black Migration in Kansas, 1879–1880 (1978); Gunther Barth, Bitter Strength: A History of the Chinese in the United States, 1850–1870 (1964); Gretchen Bataille and Charles Silet, The Pretend Indians: Images of Native Americans in the Movies (1980); Beverly Beeton, Women Vote in the West: The Woman Suffrage Movement, 1869–1896 (1986); Robert Berkhofer, Jr., The White Man's Indian (1978); Dee Brown, Bury My Heart at Wounded Knee: An Indian History of the American War (1970); Anne M. Butler, Daughters of Joy, Sisters of Mercy: Prostitutes in the American West, 1865–1890 (1985); Colin G. Calloway, ed., Our Hearts Fell to the Ground: Plains Indian Views of How the West Was Lost (1996); Edward Curtis, The North American Indian (1972); David Dary, Cowboy Culture (1981); Everett Dick, Sod House Frontier (1954); Carol Fairbanks, Prairie Women: Images in American and Canadian Fiction (1986); John Mack Faragher, Women and Men on the Overland Trail (1979); Christine Fisher, ed., Let Them Speak for Themselves: Women in the American West, 1849–1900 (1977); Joe B. Frantz and Julian Choate, The American Cowboy: The Myth and Reality (1955); Carl Guarneri and David Alvarez, Religion and Society in the American West (1987); Julie Roy Jeffrey, Frontier Women: The Trans-Mississippi West, 1840–1880 (1979); Alvin Josephy, The Indian Heritage in America (1969); William Katz, The Black West (1971); Polly W. Kaufman, Women Teachers on the Frontier (1984); William Leckie, The Buffalo Soldiers: A Narrative History of the Negro Cavalry (1967); Frederick Luebke, Ethnicity on the Great Plains (1980); Janet A. McDonnell, The Dispossession of the American Indian, 1887–1934 (1991); M. S. Meier and Feliciano Rivera, The Chicanos: A History of the Mexican Americans (1972); David Montejano, Anglos and Mexicans in the Making of Texas, 1836–1986 (1987); Sandra Myres, Western Women and the Frontier Experience, 1880–1915 (1982); James S. Olsen and Raymond Wilson, Native Americans in the Twentieth Century (1984); Nell Painter, The Exodusters: Black Migration to Kansas after Reconstruction (1976); Peggy Pascoe, Relations of Rescue: The Search for Female Moral Authority in the American West, 1874–1939 (1990); Paul Prucha, American Indian Policy in Crisis (1976); Harriet and Fred Rochlin, Pioneer Jews: A New Life in the Far West (1984); Mari Sandoz, Cheyenne Autumn (1954);

William Savage, *The Cowboy Hero: His Image in American History and Culture* (1979) and as ed., *Cowboy Life* (1975); Kent Steckmesser, *The Western Hero in History and Legend* (1965); Elinor Pruitt Stewart, *Letters of a Woman Homesteader* (1913, 1914); Joanna Stratton, *Pioneer Women: Voices of the Kansas Frontier* (1981); John Tebbel and Keith Jennison, *The American Indian Wars* (1960); Robert Utley, *High Noon in Lincoln: Violence on the Western Frontier* (1987), *The Indian Frontier of the American West, 1846–1890* (1984) and *Frontier Regulars: The United States Army and the Indian, 1866–1890* (1984); Sylvia Van Kirk, *Many Tender Ties: Women in Fur Trade Society* (1983); Wilcomb Washburn, *The Indian in America* (1975).

The Western Economy

Lewis Atherton, *Cattle Kings* (1961); Gunther Barth, *Instant Cities* (1975); Edward Dale, *The Range Cattle Industry*, rev. ed., (1969); David Dary, *Entrepreneurs of the Old West* (1986); Alan Derickson, *Workers' Health, Workers' Democracy: The Western Miners' Struggle, 1891–1925* (1988); Robert Dykstra, *The Cattle Towns* (1968); Gilbert Fite, *The Farmer's Frontier* (1966); David Emmons, *The Butte Irish: Class and Ethnicity in an American Mining Town, 1875–1925* (1989); Paul Gates, *History of Public Land Development* (1968); William Greever, *The Bonanza West: The Story of the Western Mining Rushes* (1963); Gene M. Gressley, *Bankers and Cattlemen* (1966); Robert West Howard, *The Great Iron Trail: The Story of the First Transcontinental Railroad* (1963); Donald Jackson, *Gold Dust* (1980); Richard Lingenfelter, *The Hardrock Miners: A History of the Mining Labor Movement in the American West, 1863–1893* (1974); Rodman Paul, *The Far West and the Great Plains in Transition, 1865–1900* (1988); Mari Sandoz, *Old Jules* (1962) and *The Buffalo Hunters: The Story of the Hide Men* (1978); Fred A. Shannon, *The Farmer's Last Frontier, 1860–1897* (1945); J. M. Skaggs, *The Cattle Trailing Industry* (1973); George R. Taylor and Irene Neu, *The American Railroad Network, 1861–1890* (1956); James Ward, *Railroads and the Character of America, 1820–1887* (1986); Walter Prescott Webb, *The Great Plains* (1931); Donald Worster, *Rivers of Empire* (1985); Mark Wyman, *Hard Rock Epic: Western Miners and the Industrial Revolution, 1860–1910* (1979).

CHAPTER 21: THE FAILURE OF TRADITIONAL POLITICS

General Studies

James Bryce, *The American Commonwealth*, 2 vols. (1888); Sean Cashman, *America and the Gilded Age: From the Death of Lincoln to the Rise of Theodore Roosevelt* (1984); John Dobson, *Politics in the Gilded Age* (1978); Harold Faulkner, *Politics, Reform, and Expansion, 1890–1900* (1959); John Garraty, *The New Commonwealth, 1877–1890* (1968); Richard Hofstadter, *The Age of Reform: From Bryan to FDR* (1955); Nancy Eleanor Flexner, *Century of Struggle: The Women's Rights Movement in the United States* (1959); Morton Keller, *Affairs of State: Public Life in the Late 19th Century America* (1977); H. Wayne Morgan, *From Hayes to McKinley: National Party Politics,*

1877–1896 (1969), and as ed., *The Gilded Age* (1970); Nell Irvin Painter, *Standing at Armageddon: The United States, 1877–1919* (1987); Stephen Skowronek, *Building a New American State: The Expansion of National Administrative Capacities* (1982); Robert Wiebe, *The Search for Order, 1877–1929* (1967).

Ideology and Politics

Kenneth Davison, *The Presidency of Rutherford B. Hayes* (1972); Margaret Forster, *Significant Sisters: The Grassroots of Active Feminism, 1839–1939* (1986); Lewis Gould, *The Presidency of William McKinley* (1981); David C. Hammack, *Power and Society: Greater New York at the Turn of the Century* (1982); S. P. Hirshon, *Farewell to the Bloody Shirt: Northern Republicans and the Southern Negro, 1877–1893* (1962); Ari Hoogenboom, *Rutherford B. Hayes: Warrior and President* (1995); Richard Jensen, *The Winning of the Midwest: Social and Political Conflict, 1888–1896* (1971); David Jordan, *Roscoe Conkling of New York* (1971); Paul Kelppner, *The Cross of Culture: A Social Analysis of Midwestern Politics, 1850–1900* (1970) and *The Third Electoral System, 1853–1892: Voters, Parties, and Political Cultures* (1979); Robert Marcus, *Grand Old Party: Political Structure in the Gilded Age* (1971); Robert McCloskey, *American Conservatism in the Age of Enterprise* (1951); Michael McGerr, *The Decline of Politics: The American North, 1865–1928* (1988); Allan Nevins, *Grover Cleveland: A Study in Courage* (New York, 1932); Arnold Paul, *Conservative Crisis and the Rule of Law: Attitudes of Bar and Bench, 1887–1895* (1969); Allan Peskin, *Garfield* (1978); Thomas Reeves, *Gentlemen Boss: The Life of Chester Alan Arthur* (1975); Martin Ridge, *Ignatius Donnelly* (1962); David Rothman, *Politics and Power: The United States Senate, 1869–1901* (1966); Martin J. Sklar, *The Corporate Reconstruction of American Capitalism, 1890–1916* (1988); Homer E. Socolofsky and Allan B. Spetter, *The Presidency of Benjamin Harrison* (1987); Richard Welch, *The Presidencies of Grover Cleveland* (1988); R. Hal Williams, *Years of Decision: American Politics in the 1890s* (1978).

Protest and Reform

Geoffrey Blodgett, *The Gentle Reformers* (1966); William Dick, *Labor and Socialism in America* (1972); John Diggins, *The American Left in the Twentieth Century* (1973); Louis Harlan, *Booker T. Washington: The Making of a Black Leader, 1856–1901* (1972) and *Booker T. Washington: The Wizard of Tuskegee* (1983); Ari Hoogenboom, *Outlawing the Spoils: A History of the Civil Service Movement, 1865–1883* (1961); John Laslett, *Labor and the Left* (1970); Charles Lofgren, *The Plessy Case: A Legal-Historical Interpretation* (1987); Walter Nugent, *Money and American Society* (1968); Theda Skocpol, *Protecting Soldiers and Mothers: The Political Origins of Social Policy in the United States* (1992); John Sproat, *The Best Men: Liberal Reformers in the Gilded Age* (1968); Irwin Unger, *The Greenback Era: A Social and Political History of American Finance, 1865–1879* (1964); C. Vann Woodward, *The Strange Career of Jim Crow*, 3d rev. ed. (1974).

Populism

Peter Argersinger, *Populism and Politics: William Alfred Peffer and the People's Party* (1974); Gene Clanton,

Populism: The Humane Preferences, 1890–1900 (1991); Gerald H. Gaither, *Blacks and the Populist Revolt* (1977); Lawrence Goodwyn, *Democratic Promise: The Populist Movement in America* (1976) and *The Populist Moment: A Brief History of the Agrarian Revolt* (1978); Steven Hahn, *The Roots of Southern Populism: Yeoman Farmers and the Transformation of the Georgia Upcountry* (1983); Sheldon Hackney, *Populism to Progressivism in Alabama* (1969); John Hicks, *The Populist Revolt* (1931); Robert W. Larson, *Populism in the Mountain West* (1986); Robert C. McMath, Jr., *Populist Vanguard: A History of the Southern Farmers' Alliance* (1975) and *American Populism: A Social History, 1877–1898* (1993); Scott G. McNall, *The Road to Rebellion: Class Formation and Kansas Populism, 1865–1900* (1988); Theodore R. Mitchell, *Political Education in the Southern Farmers' Alliance, 1887–1900* (1987); Bruce Palmer, *Man over Money* (1980); Norman Pollack, *The Populist Response to Industrial America* (1962) and *The Just Polity: Populism, Law, and Human Welfare* (1987); Theodore Saloutos, *Farmer Movements in the South, 1865–1933* (1960); Barton Shaw, *The Wool-Hat Boys: Georgia's Populist Party* (1984); John L. Shover, *First Majority–Last Minority: The Transforming of Rural Life in America* (1976); Lala Carr Steelman, *The North Carolina Farmers' Alliance* (1985); C. Vann Woodward, *Tom Watson, Agrarian Rebel* (1938); Allan Weinstein, *Prelude to Populism: Origins of the Silver Issue* (1970).

The Depression of 1893 and the Election of 1896

Paolo Coletta, *William Jennings Bryan*, 3 vols. (1964–1969); Robert F. Durden, *The Climax of Populism: The Election of 1896* (1965); Ray Ginger, *Altgeld's America* (1958); Paul W. Glad, *McKinley, Bryan, and the People* (1964) and *The Trumpet Soundeth* (1960); Charles Hoffman, *The Depression of the Nineties: An Economic History* (1970); J. Rogers Hollingsworth, *The Whirligig of Politics: The Democracy of Cleveland and Bryan* (1963); Stanley Jones, *The Presidential Election of 1896* (1964); Louis Koenig, *Bryan* (1971); Samuel McSeveney, *The Politics of Depression* (1972); Carlos A. Schwantes, *Coxey's Army: An American Odyssey* (1985).

The New American Empire

Richard Bannister, *Social Darwinism* (1979); Robert Beisner, *From the Old Diplomacy to the New, 1865–1900* (1975); Charles Campbell, *The Transformation of American Foreign Relations, 1865–1900* (1976) and *From Revolution to Rapprochement: The United States and Great Britain, 1783–1903* (1974); Richard Challener, *Admirals, Generals and American Foreign Policy, 1889–1914* (1973); John Dobson, *America's Ascent: The United States Becomes a Great Power, 1880–1914* (1978); John Lewis Gaddis, *Russia, the Soviet Union, and the United States*, 2d ed. (1990); John A. S. Grenville and George Young, *Politics, Strategy, and American Diplomacy* (1967); Richard Hofstadter, *Social Darwinism in American Thought*, rev. ed. (1959); Michael Hunt, *Ideology and American Foreign Policy* (1984); Ronald Jensen, *The Alaska Purchase and Russian-American Relations* (1970); Walter LaFeber, *The New Empire: An Interpretation of American Expansion, 1860–1898* (1963) and *The American Age* (1989); David Pletcher, *The Awkward Years* (1962); Emily Rosenberg, *Spreading the American Dream* (1982); Tom Terrill, *The Tariff, Politics, and American Foreign Policy, 1874–1901* (1973); Mira Wilkins, *The Emergence of the Multinational Enterprise* (1970); William A. Williams, *The Tragedy of American Diplomacy*, rev. ed. (1962) and *Empire as a Way of Life: An Essay on the Causes and Character of America's Present Predicament* (1982).

The Question of Imperialism

David Anderson, *Imperialism and Idealism: American Diplomats in China, 1861–1898* (1986); William Becker, *The Dynamics of Business-Government Relations* (1982); Robert L. Beisner, *Twelve against Empire* (1968); Phillip Darby, *Three Faces of Imperialism: British and American Approaches to Asia and Africa, 1870–1970* (1987); Philip S. Foner, *The Spanish-Cuban-American War and the Birth of American Imperialism*, 2 vols. (1972); Frank Friedel, *The Splendid Little War* (1958); Willard Gatewood, Jr., *Black Americans and the White Man's Burden, 1898–1903* (1975); Kenneth Hagan, *American Gunboat Diplomacy, 1877–1889* (1973); David Healy, *U.S. Expansionism* (1970); Michael Hunt, *Ideology and U.S. Foreign Policy* (1987); Frederick Merk, *Manifest Destiny and Mission in American History* (1963); Wolfgang Mommsen and Jurgen Osterhammel, eds., *Imperialism and After* (1986); H. Wayne Morgan, *America's Road to Empire: The War with Spain and Overseas Expansion* (1965); Thomas J. Osborne, *Empire Can Wait: American Opposition to Hawaiian Annexation, 1893–1898* (1981); Ernest Paolino, *The Foundations of American Empire* (1973); Thomas Paterson, ed., *Imperialism and Anti-Imperialism* (1973); Bradford Perkins, *The Great Rapprochement* (1968); Julius Pratt, *The Expansionists of 1898* (1936); Tony Smith, *The Pattern of Imperialism: The United States, Great Britain and the Late Industrializing World since 1815* (1982); Richard Turk, *The Ambiguous Relationship: Theodore Roosevelt and Alfred Thayer Mahan* (1987).

The United States and Asia

David Anderson, *Imperialism and Idealism: American Diplomacy in China, 1861–1898* (1985); Jongsuk Chay, *Diplomacy of Asymmetry: Korean-American Relations to 1910* (1990); Warren Cohen, *America's Response to China*, rev. ed. (1980); Michael Hunt, *The Making of a Special Relationship: The United States and China to 1914* (1983); Jane Hunter, *The Gospel of Gentility: American Women Missionaries in Turn-of-the-Century China* (1984); Akira Iriye, *Across the Pacific* (1967) and *Pacific Estrangement: Japanese and American Expansion, 1897–1911* (1972); Stanley Karnow, *In Our Image* (1989); Yur-Bok Lee and Wayne Patterson, eds., *One Hundred Years of Korean-American Relations, 1882–1982* (1986); Brian M. Linn, *The U.S. Army and Counterinsurgency in the Philippine War, 1899–1902* (1989); Ernest May and John Fairbanks, eds., *America's China Trade in Historical Perspective* (1986); Glenn May, *Social Engineering in the Philippines* (1980); Thomas McCormick, *China Market: America's Quest for Informal Empire, 1893–1901* (1968); Charles Neu, *The Troubled Encounter* (1975); Gary Okihiro, *Cane Fires: The Anti-Japanese Movement in Hawaii, 1865–1945* (1991); Peter Stanley, *A Nation in the Making: The Philippines and the United States* (1974); Randall Stross, *The Hard Earth: American Agriculturalists on Chinese Soil, 1898–1937* (1986); James Thomson, Peter Stanley, and John Perry, *Sentimental Imperialists: The American*

Experience in East Asia (1981); Robert Welch, Jr., *Response to Imperialism: The United States and the Philippine-American War, 1899–1902* (1979); Marilyn B. Young, *Rhetoric of Empire: American China Policy, 1895–1901* (1968).

The United States and the Americas
Robert Brown, *Canada's National Policy, 1883–1900* (1964); Kenneth Bourne, *Britain and the Balance of Power in North America, 1815–1908* (1967); Walter LaFeber, *Inevitable Revolutions: The United States in Central America*, rev. ed. (1993); Lester Langley, *The Banana Wars* (1983) and *The United States and the Caribbean, 1900–1970* (1980); Louis Perez, Jr., *Cuba under the Platt Amendment, 1902–1934* (1986) and *Cuba between Empires, 1878–1902* (1983); Dexter Perkins, *The Monroe Doctrine, 1867–1907* (1937); Ramon Ruiz, *Cuba* (1968); Karl Schmitt, *Mexico and the United States, 1821–1973* (1974); Josefina Vazquez and Lorenzo Meyer, *The United States and Mexico* (1985).

CHAPTER 22: THE PROGRESSIVE ERA

General Studies
John Chambers II, *The Tyranny of Change: America in the Progressive Era, 1900–1917* (1980); John M. Cooper, Jr., *The Pivotal Decades: The United States, 1900–1920* (1990); Alan Dawley, *Struggles for Justice: Social Responsibility and the Liberal State* (1991); Arthur Ekrich, *Progressivism in America* (1974); Peter Filene, "An Obituary for 'the Progressive Movement,'" *American Quarterly* 22 (1970); Lewis Gould, ed., *The Progressive Era* (1974); Richard Hofstadter, *The Age of Reform: From Bryan to FDR* (1955); James T. Kloppenberg, *Uncertain Victory: Social Democracy and Progressivism in European and American Thought, 1870–1920* (1986); Gabriel Kolko, *The Triumph of Conservatism* (1963); Arthur Link and Richard L. McCormick, *Progressivism* (1985); William O'Neill, *The Progressive Years* (1975); Dan Rogers, "In Search of Progressivism," *Reviews in American History* 10 (1982); James Weinstein, *The Corporate Ideal in the Liberal States, 1900–1918* (1969); Robert Wiebe, *Businessmen and Reform: A Study of the Progressive Movement* (1962).

The Progressive Impulse
Daniel Aaron, *Men of Good Hope: A Story of American Progressives* (1951); Richard Abrams, *The Burdens of Progress* (1978); Walter M. Brasch, *Forerunners of Revolution: Muckrakers and the American Social Conscience* (1990); Robert H. Bremner, *From the Depths: The Discovery of Poverty in the United States* (1956); Mina Julia Carson, *Settlement Folk: Social Thought and the American Settlement Movement, 1885–1930* (1990); David Chalmers, *The Social and Political Ideas of the Muckrakers* (1964); Clarke Chambers, *Paul U. Kellog and the Survey* (1971); Robert Crunden, *Ministers of Reform: The Progressives' Achievements in American Civilization, 1889–1920* (1982); Charles Forcey, *The Crossroads of Liberalism: Croly, Weyl, Lippmann and the Progressive Era, 1900–1925* (1961); William Hutchinson, *The Modernist Impulse in American Protestantism* (1976); Rivka Shpak Lissak, *Pluralism and Progressives: Hull*

House and the New Immigrants, 1890–1919 (1989); Roy Lubove, *The Professional Altruist: The Emergence of Social Work as a Career, 1880–1930* (1965); D. W. Marcell, *Progress and Pragmatism: James, Dewey, Beard and the American Idea of Progress* (1974); Daniel Nelson, *Frederick W. Taylor and the Rise of Scientific Management* (1980); David Nobel, *The Progressive Mind, 1890–1917* rev. ed. (1981); Martin Schiesl, *The Politics of Efficiency: Municipal Administration and Reform in America, 1880–1920* (1977); Robert B. Westbrook, *John Dewey and American Democracy* (1991); Morton White, *Social Thought in America: The Revolt against Formalism*, (1949); Harold Wilson, *McClure's Magazine and the Muckrakers* (1970).

Social Reform, Radical Politics, and Minority Rights
Mari Jo Buhle, *Women and American Socialism, 1870–1920* (1981); Allen F. Davis, *American Heroine: The Life and Legend of Jane Addams* (1973); James R. Green, *Grass-Roots Socialism: Radical Movements in the Southwest, 1895–1943* (1978); Louis Harlan, *Separate and Unequal: Public School Campaigns and Racism in the Southern Seaboard States, 1900–1915* (1968); Charles F. Kellogg, *NAACP: A History of the National Association for the Advancement of Colored People, 1909–1920* (1967); David L. Lewis, *W. E. B. Dubois: Biography of a Race* (1994); Roy Lubove, *The Progressives and the Slums: Tenement House Reform in New York City* (1962); James McPherson, *The Abolitionist Legacy: From Reconstruction to the NAACP* (1975); David Musto, *The American Disease: Origins of Narcotics Control* (1973); Elliot M. Rudwick, *W. E. B. DuBois* (1968); Nick Salvatore, *Eugene V. Debs: Citizen and Socialist* (1982); James Timberlake, *Prohibition and the Progressive Campaign* (1963); John D. Weaver, *The Brownsville Raid* (1970); James Weinstein, *The Decline of Socialism in America, 1912–1925* (1967); Nancy Weiss, *The National Urban League, 1910–1940* (1974).

Women's Rights, Gender, and Sexuality
Paula Baker, *Gender and the Transformation of Politics: Public and Private Life in New York, 1870–1930* (1989); George Chester, *Gay New York: Gender, Urban Culture, and the Making of the Gay Male World, 1890–1940* (1994); Ellen Chesler, *Woman of Valor: Margaret Sanger and the Birth Control Movement in America* (1992); Nancy F. Cott, *The Grounding of Modern Feminism* (1987); Nancy Dye, *As Equals and Sisters: Feminism, the Labor Movement, and the Women's Trade Union League of New York* (1980); Linda Gordon, *Woman's Body, Woman's Right: A Social History of Birth Control* (1976), *Heroes of Their Own Lives: The Politics and History of Family Violence, 1880–1960* (1988), and *Pitied but Not Entitled: Single Mothers and the History of Welfare* (1994); David Kennedy, *Birth Control in America: The Career of Margaret Sanger* (1970); Aileen Kraditor, *Ideas of the Woman Suffrage Movement* (1965); Ellen Lagemann, *A Generation of Women: Education in the Lives of Progressive Reformers* (1979); Christine Lunardini, *From Equal Suffrage to Equal Rights: Alice Paul and the National Women's Party* (1986); David Morgan, *Suffragists and Democrats: The Politics of Woman Suffrage in America* (1972); Robyn Muncy, *Creating a Female Dominion in*

American Reform, 1890–1935 (1991); William O'Neil, *Divorce in the Progressive Era* (1967); Dorothy Richardson, *The Long Day: The Story of a New York Working Girl* (1905); Ruth Rosen, *The Lost Sisterhood: Prostitutes in America, 1900–1918* (1982); Rosalind Rosenberg, *Beyond Separate Spheres: Intellectual Roots of Modern Feminism* (1982); Anne Firor Scott, *Natural Allies: Women's Associations in American History* (1992); Anne Firor Scott and Andrew MacKay Scott, *One Half the People: The Fight for Woman Suffrage* (1982); Meredith Tax, *The Rising of the Women: Feminist Solidarity and Class Conflict, 1880–1917* (1980).

Education, the New Professionalism, and Entertainment

Burton Bledstein, *The Culture of Professionalism* (1976); Darlene Clark Hine, *Black Women in White: Racial Conflict and Cooperation in the Nursing Profession, 1890–1950* (1989); Lawrence Cremin, *The Transformation of the School: Progressivism in American Education* (1961); John DiMeglio, *Vaudeville U.S.A.* (1973); Lewis Erenberg, *Steppin' Out: New York Nightlife and the Transformation of American Culture, 1890–1930* (1981); James Farrell, *Inventing the American Way of Death, 1830–1920* (1980); Thomas Haskell, *The Emergence of Professional Social Science* (1977); Bruce Kuklick, *The Rise of American Philosophy* (1977); Martin Laforse and James Drake, *Popular Culture and American Life: Selected Topics in the Study of American Popular Culture* (1981); Cathy Peiss, *Cheap Amusements: Working Women and Leisure in Turn-of-the-Century New York* (1986); Robert Sklar, *Movie-Made America: A Social History of the American Movies* (1975); Paul Starr, *The Social Transformation of American Medicine* (1982); David Tyack and Elizabeth Hansot, *Managers of Virtue: Public School Leadership in America, 1820–1980* (1982); Lawrence Vesey, *The Emergence of the American University* (1970).

Local and State Reform

Richard Abrams, *Conservatism in a Progressive Era: Massachusetts Politics, 1900–1912* (1964); John D. Buenker, *Urban Liberalism and Progressive Reform* (1973); Thomas E. Cronin, *Direct Democracy: The Politics of Initiative, Referendum and Recall* (1989); James Crooks, *Politics and Progress: The Rise of Urban Progressivism in Baltimore, 1895–1911* (1968); Dewey Grantham, *Southern Progressivism: The Reconciliation of Progress and Tradition* (1983); Melvin Holli, *Reform in Detroit: Hazen S. Pingree and Urban Politics* (1969); J. Joseph Huthmacher, "Urban Liberalism and Progressive Reform," *Mississippi Valley Historical Review* (1962); Jack Kirby, *Darkness at Dawning: Race and Reform in the Progressive South* (1972); Richard L. McCormick, *From Realignment to Reform: Political Change in New York State, 1893–1910* (1981); George Mowry, *The California Progressives* (1951); Bradley Rice, *Progressive Cities: The Commission Government Movement in America, 1901–1920* (1977); Jack Tager, *The Intellectual as Urban Reformer: Brand Whitlock and The Progressive Movement* (1968); David P. Thelen, *The New Citizenship: Origins of Progressivism in Wisconsin* (1972).

National Politics and Public Policy

Donald Anderson, *William Howard Taft* (1973); John M. Blum, *The Republican Roosevelt* (1954) and *Woodrow Wilson and the Politics of Morality* (1954); John Milton

Cooper, Jr., *The Warrior and the Priest: Woodrow Wilson and Theodore Roosevelt* (1983); Stephen R. Fox, *The American Conservation Movement: John Muir and His Legacy* (1981); John Gable, *The Bull Moose Years* (1978); Alexander George and Juliette George, *Woodrow Wilson and Colonel House: A Personality Study* (1956); Lewis Gould, *Reform and Regulation: American Politics, 1900–1916* (1978) and *The Presidency of Theodore Roosevelt* (1991); Samuel P. Hays, *Conservation and the Gospel of Efficiency: The Progressive Conservation Movement, 1890–1920* (1959); James Holt, *Congressional Insurgents and the Party System* (1969); Arthur Link, *Woodrow Wilson*, 5 vols. (1947–1965); Albro Martin, *Enterprise Denied: Origins of the Decline of American Railroads, 1897–1917;* David McCullough, *Mornings on Horseback* (1981); Robert T. McCulley, *Banks and Politics during the Progressive Era: The Origins of the Federal Reserve System* (1992); Michael McGerr, *The Decline of Popular Politics: The American North, 1865–1928* (1986); Edmund Morris, *The Rise of Theodore Roosevelt* (1979); George Mowry, *The Era of Theodore Roosevelt* (1958); James Penick, *Progressive Politics and Conservation: The Ballinger-Pinchot Affair* (1968); Harold Pinkett, *Gifford Pinchot: Private and Public Forester* (1970); Edwin Weinstein, *Woodrow Wilson and Colonel House: A Personality Study* (1956); Craig West, *Banking Reform and the Federal Reserve, 1863–1923* (1977); Clifton Yearley, *The Money Machines* (1970).

CHAPTER 23: THE UNITED STATES AND THE OLD WORLD ORDER

General Studies

Paul Abrahams, *The Foreign Expansion of American Finance and Its Relationship to Foreign Economic Policies of the United States, 1907–1921* (1976); Robert Beisner, *From the Old Diplomacy to the New, 1865–1900* (1975); John Dobson, *America's Ascent: The United States Becomes a Great Power, 1880–1914* (1978); Morrell Heald and Lawrence Kaplan, *Culture and Diplomacy* (1977); Peter Karsten, *The Naval Aristocracy* (1972); Robert Osgood, *Ideals and Self-Interest in America's Foreign Relations* (1953); Emily Rosenberg, *Spreading the American Dream: American Economic and Cultural Expansion, 1890–1945* (1982); Robert Schulzinger, *American Diplomacy in the Twentieth Century* (1984); Tom Terrill, *The Tariff, Politics, and American Foreign Policy, 1874–1901* (1973); Rubin Weston, *Racism and U.S. Imperialism, 1865–1946* (1971); Mira Wilkins, *The Emergence of the Multinational Enterprise* (1970).

Roosevelt, Taft, and Wilson

Howard K. Beale, *Theodore Roosevelt and the Rise of America to World Power* (1956); David Burton, *Theodore Roosevelt: Confident Imperialist* (1968); Robert W. Cherney, *A Righteous Cause: The Life of William Jennings Bryan* (1985); Richard H. Collin, *Theodore Roosevelt, Culture, Diplomacy, and Expansion* (1985); John Cooper, Jr., *Walter Hines Page* (1977); Lloyd Gardner, *Wilson and Revolutions, 1913–1921* (1976) and *William Jennings Bryan: Missionary Isolationist* (1983); Arthur Link, *Wilson: The Diplomatist* (1957) and *Woodrow Wilson: Revolution, War, and Peace* (1968); Frederick Marks III, *Velvet on Iron: The Diplomacy of Theodore Roosevelt*

(1979); Ralph E. Minger, *William Howard Taft and United States Foreign Policy* (1975).

Asia, the Pacific, and Latin America

Warren Cohen, *America's Response to China*, rev. ed. (1980); David Healy, *Gunboat Diplomacy in the Wilson Era: The U.S. Navy in Haiti, 1915–1916* (1976) and *Drive to Hegemony: The United States in the Caribbean, 1898–1917* (1988); Akira Iriye, *Pacific Estrangement: Japanese and American Expansion, 1897–1911* (1972); Jerry Israel, *Progressivism and the Open Door: America and China, 1905–1921* (1971); Lester Langley, *Struggle for the American Mediterranean* (1980) and *The United States and the Caribbean, 1900–1970* (1980); Glenn May, *Social Engineering in the Philippines* (1980); Robert McClellen, *The Heathen Chinese: A Study of American Attitudes toward China* (1971); David McCullough, *The Path between the Seas: The Creation of the Panama Canal, 1870–1914* (1977); Dana Munro, *Intervention and Dollar Diplomacy in the Caribbean, 1900–1920* (1964); Charles Neu, *The Troubled Encounter* (1975); Robert Smith, *The United States and Revolutionary Nationalism in Mexico, 1916–1932* (1972); Peter Stanley, *A Nation in the Making: The Philippines and the United States, 1899–1921* (1974).

From Neutrality to War

Thomas Baily and Paul Ryan, *The Lusitania Disaster* (1975); John Coogan, *The End of Neutrality: The United States, Britain, and Maritime Rights, 1899–1915* (1981); John Cooper, *The Vanity of Power: American Isolationism and the First World War* (1969); Patrick Devlin, *Too Proud to Fight: Woodrow Wilson's Neutrality* (1974); Ross Gregory, *The Origins of American Intervention in the First World War* (1977); Burton Kaufman, *Efficiency and Expansion: Foreign Trade Organization in the Wilson Administration* (1974); Roland Marchand, *The American Peace Movement and Social Reform, 1898–1918* (1972); Ernest R. May, *The World War and American Isolation, 1914–1917* (1957); Jeffrey Safford, *Wilsonian Maritime Diplomacy* (1977).

The First World War Abroad

Arthur Barbeau and Henri Florette, *The Unknown Soldiers: Black American Troops in World War I* (1974); J. Gary Clifford, *The Citizen Soldiers* (1972); Edward Coffman, *The War to End All Wars: The American Military Experience in World War I* (1968); Frank Freidel, *Over There: The Story of America's First Great Overseas Crusade* (1964); Paul Fussell, *The Great War and Modern Memory* (1975); John Gifford, *The Citizen Soldiers* (1972); Otis Graham, *The Great Campaigns* (1971); Maurine Greenwald, *Women, War, and Work* (1980); James Joll, *The Origins of the First World War* (1984); N. Gordon Levin, Jr., *Woodrow Wilson and World Politics: America's Response to War and Revolution* (1968); Laurence Stallings, *The Doughboys: The Story of the AEF, 1917–1918* (1963); David F. Trask, *The AEF and Coalition Warmaking, 1917–1918* (1973); Frank Vandiver, *Black Jack: The Life and Times of John J. Pershing*, 2 vols. (1977); Russell Weigley, *The American Way of War* (1973).

The Home Front

Daniel R. Beaver, *Newton D. Baker and the American War Effort, 1917–1919* (1966); John W. Chambers, *To Raise an Army: The Draft Comes to Modern America* (1987); Valerie Jean Connor, *The National War Labor Board: Stability, Social Justice, and the Voluntary State in World War I* (1983); Robert Cuff, *The War Industries Board: Business-Government Relations during World War I* (1973); Maurine W. Greenwald, *Women, War, and Work* (1980); Keith Grieves, *The Politics of Manpower, 1914–1918* (1988); Frank L. Grubb, *Samuel Gompers and the Great War* (1982); Carol Gruber, *Mars and Minerva: World War I and the Uses of Higher Learning in America* (1975); Ellis Hawley, *The Great War and the Search for Modern Order* (1979); Robert Haynes, *A Night of Violence: The Houston Riot of 1917* (1976); David M. Kennedy, *Over Here: The First World War and American Society* (1980); Seward Livermore, *Politics Is Adjourned: Woodrow Wilson and the War Congress, 1917–1918* (1966); Frederick Luebke, *Bonds of Loyalty: German Americans and World War I* (1974); Paul Murphy, *World War I and the Origins of Civil Liberties* (1979); Richard Polenberg, *Fighting Faiths: The Abrams Case, the Supreme Court, and Free Speech* (1987); Walton Rawls, *Wake Up America! World War I and the American Poster* (1987); Ronald Schaffer, *America in the Great War: The Rise of the War Welfare State* (1991); Jordan Schwarz, *The Speculator: Bernard M. Baruch in Washington, 1917–1965* (1981); Dale N. Shook, *William G. McAdoo and the Development of National Economic Policy, 1913–1918* (1987); Barbara Steinson, *American Women's Activism in World War I* (1982); John A. Thompson, *Reformers and War: Progressive Publicists and the First World War* (1987); Joe William Trotter, Jr., ed., *The Great Migration in Historical Perspective* (1991); Stephen Vaughn, *Holding Fast the Inner Lines: Democracy, Nationalism, and the Committee on Public Information* (1979); James Weinstein, *The Decline of Socialism in America, 1912–1923* (1967); Neil A. Wynn, *From Progressivism to Prosperity: World War I and American Society* (1986).

Versailles

Thomas Bailey, *Woodrow Wilson and the Great Betrayal* (1945) and *Woodrow Wilson and the Lost Peace* (1944); Robert Ferrell, *Woodrow Wilson and World War I* (1985); Inga Floto, *Colonel House at Paris* (1980); John Gaddis, *Russia, the Soviet Union, and the United States* (1978); Lloyd Gardner, *Safe for Democracy: The Anglo-American Response to Revolution, 1913–1923* (1984); Thomas J. Knock, *To End All Wars: Woodrow Wilson and the Quest for a New World Order* (1992); Arno Mayer, *Politics and Diplomacy of Peacemaking: Containment and Counterrevolution at Versailles* (1965); Charles Mee, Jr., *The End of Order, Versailles, 1919* (1980); Ralph Stone, *The Irreconcilables: The Fight against the League of Nations* (1970); William C. Widenor, *Henry Cabot Lodge and the Search for an American Foreign Policy* (1980).

Aftermath

David Brody, *Labor in Crisis: The Steel Strike of 1919* (1965); Stanley Coben, *A. Mitchell Palmer: Politician* (1963); Stanley Cooperman, *World War I and the American Mind* (1970); Roberta Feuerlicht, *Justice Crucified* (1977); Dana Frank, *Purchasing Power: Consumer Organizing, Gender, and the Seattle Labor Movement, 1919–1929* (1994); Robert Murray, *The Red Scare* (1955); Burl Noggle, *Into the Twenties* (1977); Stuart Rochester, *American Liberal Disillusionment in the Wake of World War I* (1977); Francis Russell, *A City in Terror*

(1975); William Tuttle, Jr., *Race Riot: Chicago in the Red Summer of 1919* (1970); Stephen Ward, ed., *The War Generation: Veterans of the First World War* (1975).

CHAPTER 24: THE NEW ERA

General Studies

Frederick Lewis Allen, *Only Yesterday: An Informal History of the 1920s* (1931); John Braeman et al., eds., *Change and Continuity in Twentieth Century America: The 1920s* (1968); Ann Douglas, *Terrible Honesty: Mongrel Manhattan in the 1920s* (1995); Lynn Dumenil, *Modern Temper: American Culture and Society in the 1920s* (1995); Ellis Hawley, *The Great War and the Search for a Modern Order* (1979); John Hicks, *The Republican Ascendancy, 1921–1933* (1960); Isabel Leighton, ed., *The Aspirin Age* (1949); William Leuchtenburg, *The Perils of Prosperity, 1914–1932* (1958); Donald McCoy, *Coming of Age* (1973); Geoffrey Perrett, *America in the Twenties* (1982); Arthur Schlesinger, Jr., *The Crisis of the Old Order* (1957); David Shannon, *Between the Wars: America, 1919–1940* (1979).

Economics, Business, and Labor

Irving Bernstein, *The Lean Years: A History of the American Worker, 1920–1933* (1960); David Brody, *Steelworkers in America* (1960) and *Workers in Industrial America* (1980); Lizabeth Cohen, *Making a New Deal: Industrial Workers in Chicago, 1919–1939* (1990); Alfred D. Chandler, Jr., *Strategy and Structure: Chapters in the History of American Industrial Enterprise* (1962); Ed Cray, *Chrome Colossus: General Motors and Its Times* (1980); Gilbert Fite, *George Peek and the Fight for Farm Parity* (1954); James Flink, *The Car Culture* (1975); Louis Galambos, *Competition and Cooperation* (1966); James Gilbert, *Designing the Industrial State* (1972); Allan Nevins and Frank Hill, *Ford*, 3 vols. (1954–1963); Jim Potter, *The American Economy between the Wars* (1974); John Rae, *American Automobile* (1965) and *The Road and the Car in American Life* (1971); George Soule, *Prosperity Decade* (1947); Keith Sward, *The Legend of Henry Ford* (1948); Leslie Woodcock Tentler, *Wage Earning Women: Industrial Work and Family Life in the United States, 1900–1930* (1979); Bernard Weisberger, *The Dress Maker* (1979); Robert Zieger, *Republicans and Labor, 1919–1929* (1969) and *American Workers, American Unions, 1920–1980* (1986).

Mass Society and Mass Culture

Erick Barnouw, *A Tower of Babel: A History of American Broadcasting in the United States to 1933* (1966); Daniel Boorstin, *The Americans: The Democratic Experience* (1973); Paul Carter, *Another Part of the Twenties* (1977); Robert Creamer, *Babe* (1974); Kenneth Davis, *The Hero: Charles A. Lindbergh* (1954); Stuart Ewen, *Captains of Consciousness: Advertising and the Social Roots of the Consumer Culture* (1976); Richard Wrightman Fox and T. J. Jackson Lears, eds., *The Culture of Consumption: Critical Essays in American History, 1880–1980* (1983); Jackson Lears, *Fables of Abundance: A Cultural History of Advertising in America* (1994); Robert Lynd and Helen Lynd, *Middletown: A Study in Modern Culture* (1929); Roland Marchand, *Advertising the American Dream: Making Way for Modernity, 1920–1940* (1985); Lary May, *Screening Out the Past* (1980); Leonard Mosley, *Lind-*

bergh: A Biography (1976); Otis Pease, *The Responsibilities of American Advertising* (1959); Daniel Pope, *The Making of Modern Advertising* (1983); Randy Roberts, *Jack Dempsey, The Manassa Mauler* (1979); Philip Rosen, *The Modern Stentors: Radio Broadcasting and the Federal Government, 1920–1933* (1980); Robert Sklar, *Movie-Made America: A Cultural History of American Movies* (1975); Kevin Starr, *Material Dreams: Southern California through the 1920s* (1990); Susan Strasser, *Satisfaction Guaranteed: The Making of the American Mass Market* (1990).

High Culture

Carlos Baker, *Hemingway* (1956); Malcolm Cowley, *Exile's Return* (1934); Robert Crunden, *From Self to Society: Transition in Modern Thought, 1919–1941* (1972); Frederick Hoffman, *The Twenties* (1949); Arthur Mizner, *The Far Side of Paradise* (1951); Roderick Nash, *The Nervous Generation: American Thought, 1917–1930* (1969); Mark Shorer, *Sinclair Lewis* (1961); Marvin Singleton, *H. L. Mencken and the "American Mercury" Adventure* (1962).

Women, Youth, and Minorities

Lois Banner, *American Beauty* (1983); Susan D. Becker, *The Origins of the Equal Rights Amendment* (1981); Kathlenn M. Blee, *Women of the Klan: Racism and Gender in the 1920s* (1991); Dorothy M. Brown, *Setting a Course: American Women in the 1920s* (1987); William Chafe, *The American Women: Her Changing Social, Economic, and Political Roles, 1920–1970* (1972); Nancy Cott, *The Grounding of Modern Feminism* (1987); David Cronon, *Black Moses: The Story of Marcus Garvey* (1955); Melvin Patrick Ely, *The Adventures of Amos 'n' Andy: A Social History of an American Phenomenon* (1991); Paula Fass, *The Damned and Beautiful: American Youth in the 1920s* (1977); Linda Gordon, *Woman's Body, Woman's Right: A Social History of Birth Control in America* (1976); Peter Gottlieb, *Making Their Own Way: Southern Blacks' Migration to Pittsburgh, 1916–1930* (1987); Florette Henri, *Black Migration: Movement North, 1900–1920* (1975); Nathan Huggins, *Harlem Renaissance* (1971); Jacqueline Jones, *Labor of Love, Labor of Sorrow: Black Women, Work, and Family, from Slavery to the Present* (1985); J. Stanley Lemons, *The Woman Citizen: Social Feminism in the 1920s* (1973); David Levering Lewis, *When Harlem Was in Vogue* (1981); Glenna Matthews, *"Just a Housewife!" The Rise and Fall of Domesticity in America* (1987); Cary D. Mintz, *Black Culture and the Harlem Renaissance* (1988); Wilson Moses, *The Golden Age of Black Nationalism, 1850–1925* (1988); Kathy H. Ogren, *The Jazz Revolution: Twenties America and the Meaning of Jazz* (1989); Arnold Rampersad, *The Life of Langston Hughes*, 2 vols. (1986–1988); Ricardo Romo, *East Los Angeles: History of a Barrio* (1983); George J. Sanchez, *Becoming Mexican American: Ethnicity, Culture and Identity in Chicano Los Angeles, 1900–1945* (1993); Lois Scharf, *To Work and to Wed* (1980); Virginia Scharff, *Taking the Wheel: Women and the Coming of the Motor Age* (1991); Alan Spear, *Black Chicago* (1967); Judith Stein, *The World of Marcus Garvey: Race and Class in Modern Society* (1986); Joe William Trotter, Jr., *Black Milwaukee: The Making of an Industrial Proletariat* (1985); Theodore Vincent, *Black Power and the*

Garvey Movement (1971); Winifred Wandersee, *Women's Work and Family Values, 1920–1940* (1981).

Political Fundamentalism
Paul Avrich, *Sacco-Vanzetti: The Anarchist Background* (1991); David Burner, *The Politics of Provincialism* (1968); David Chalmers, *Hooded Americanism: The History of the Ku Klux Klan* (1965); Norman Clark, *Deliver Us from Evil* (1976); Robert Divine, *American Immigration Policy* (1957); Norman Furniss, *The Fundamentalist Controversy, 1918–1933* (1954); Ray Ginger, *Six Days or Forever? Tennessee v. John Scopes* (1958); Joseph Gusfeld, *Symbolic Crusade* (1963); John Higham, *Strangers in the Land: Patterns of American Nativism, 1860–1925* (1955); Kenneth Jackson, *The Ku Klux Klan in the City, 1915–1930* (1967); Don Kirschner, *City and Country: Rural Responses to Urbanization in the 1920s* (1970); Shawn Lay, ed., *The Invisible Empire in the West: Toward a New Historical Appraisal of the Ku Klux Klan of the 1920s* (1992); Nancy MacLean, *Behind the Mask of Chivalry: The Making of the Second Ku Klux Klan* (1994); George Maraden, *Fundamentalism and American Culture* (1980); Leonard J. Moore, *Citizen Klansmen: The Ku Klux Klan in Indiana, 1921–1928* (1991); Andrew Sinclair, *Prohibition: The Era of Excess* (1962); William Wilson, *Coming of Age: Urban America, 1915–1945* (1974).

Politics, Public Policy, and the Election of 1928
Kristi Andersen, *The Creation of a Democratic Majority* (1979); Paula Edler, *Governor Alfred E. Smith: The Politician as Reformer* (1983); James Giglio, *H. M. Daugherty and the Politics of Expediency* (1978); Oscar Handlin, *Al Smith and His America* (1958); Ellis Hawley, *Herbert Hoover as Secretary of Commerce: Studies in New Era Thought and Practice* (1974); Robert Himmelberg, *The Origins of the National Recovery Administration: Business, Government, and the Trade Association Issue, 1921–1933* (1976); J. Joseph Huthmacher, *Massachusetts People and Politics, 1919–1933* (1959); Alan Lichtman, *Prejudice and the Old Politics* (1979); Richard Lowitt, *George Norris*, 2 vols. (1971); Donald McCoy, *Calvin Coolidge* (1967); Robert Murray, *The Harding Era* (1969) and *The Politics of Normalcy* (1973); Burl Noggle, *Teapot Dome* (1962); Elisabeth Perry, *Belle Moskowitz: Feminine Politics and the Exercise of Power in the Age of Alfred E. Smith* (1987); George Tindall, *The Emergence of the New South* (1967); Eugene Trani and David Wilson, *The Presidency of Warren G. Harding* (1977).

CHAPTER 25: CRASH AND DEPRESSION

General Studies
Frederick Lewis Allen, *Since Yesterday* (1939); John A. Garraty, *The Great Depression* (1987); Robert McElvaine, *The Great Depression: America, 1929–1941* (1984); Broadus Mitchell, *Depression Decade* (1947); Arthur Schlesinger, Jr., *The Crisis of the Old Order* (1957); T. H. Watkins, *The Great Depression: America in the 1930s* (1991).

The Great Crash and the Origins of the Great Depression
Michael A. Bernstein, *The Great Depression: Delayed Recovery and Economic Change in America, 1929–1939*

(1987); Lester Chandler, *America's Greatest Depression, 1929–1941* (1970); Milton Friedman and Ana Schwartz, *The Great Contraction, 1929–1933* (1965); John Kenneth Galbraith, *The Great Crash*, rev. ed. (1988); Susan Kennedy, *The Banking Crisis of 1933* (1973); Charles Kindleberger, *The World in Depression* (1973); Robert Sobel, *The Great Bull Market: Wall Street in the 1920s* (1968); Peter Temin, *Did Monetary Forces Cause the Great Depression?* (1976); Gordon Thomas and Max Morgan-Witts, *The Day the Bubble Burst: The Social History of the Wall Street Crash of 1929* (1979).

Depression Life
Edward Anderson, *Hungry Men* (1935); Robert Angel, *The Family Encounters the Depression* (1936); Ann Banks, *First Person America* (1980); Caroline Bird, *The Invisible Scar* (1966); The Federal Writers' Project, *These Are Our Lives* (1939); John Garraty, *Unemployment in History: Economic Thought and Public Policy* (1978); Mirra Komarovsky, *The Unemployed Man and His Family* (1940); Robert Lynd and Helen Lynd, *Middletown in Transition* (1937); Robert McElvaine, ed. *Down & Out in the Great Depression* (1983); Harvey Levenstein, *Paradox of Plenty: A Social History of Eating in Modern America* (1993); H. Wayne Morgan, *Drugs in America: A Social History, 1800–1980* (1981); David Musto, *The American Disease, Origins of Narcotics Control*, rev. ed. (1988); Lois Scharf, *To Work and to Wed: Female Employment, Feminism, and the Great Depression* (1980); Tom Terrill and Jerrold Hirsch, eds., *Such as Us: Southern Voices of the Thirties* (1978); Studs Terkel, *Hard Times: An Oral History of the Great Depression* (1970); Winifred Wandersee, *Women's Work and Family Values, 1920–1940* (1981); Susan Ware, *Holding Their Own: American Women in the 1930s* (1982); Jeane Westin, *Making Do: How Women Survived the '30s* (1976).

Ethnicity and Race
Rodolfo Acuna, *Occupied America*, rev. ed. (1981); Ralph Bunche, *The Political Status of the Negro in the Age of FDR* (1973); Dan Carter, *Scottsboro: A Tragedy of the American South* (1969); Sarah Deutsch, *No Separate Refuge: Culture, Class, and Gender on an Anglo-Hispanic Frontier in the American Southwest, 1880–1940* (1987); Abraham Hoffman, *Unwanted Mexican-Americans in the Great Depression* (1974); Richard Polenberg, *One Nation Divisible: Class, Race, and Ethnicity in the United States since 1938* (1980); Bernard Sternsher, ed., *The Negro in Depression and War* (1969); Robert Weisbrot, *Father Divine and the Struggle for Racial Equality* (1983); Nancy Weiss, *The National Urban League* (1974); Raymond Wolters, *Negroes and the Great Depression* (1970).

Depression Culture
Daniel Aaron, *Writers on the Left* (1961); James Agee, *Let Us Now Praise Famous Men* (1941); Andrew Bergman, *We're in the Money: Depression America and Its Films* (1971); Eileen Eagan, *Class, Culture and the Classroom* (1981); Neal Gabler, *An Empire of Their Own: How the Jews Invented Hollywood* (1988); Lawrence Levine, *The Unpredictable Past: Explorations in American Cultural History* (1993); Jeffrey Meikle, *Twentieth Century Limited: Industrial Design in America, 1925–1939* (1979); Richard Pells, *Radical Visions and American Dreams:*

Culture and Social Thought in the Depression Years (1973); Thomas Schatz, *The Genius of the System: Hollywood Filmmaking in the Studio Era* (1988); John Steinbeck, *The Grapes of Wrath* (1939); William Stott, *Documentary Expressionism and Thirties America* (1973); Warren Susman, *Culture as History: The Transformation of American Society in the Twentieth Century* (1984); Twelve Southerners, *I'll Take My Stand: The South and the Agrarian Tradition* (1937).

Radicalism and Protest
Irving Bernstein, *The Lean Years: A History of the American Worker, 1920–1933* (1960); Robert Cohen, *When the Old Left Was Young: Student Radicals and America's First Mass Student Movement, 1929–1941* (1993); Roger Daniels, *The Bonus March* (1971); John Hevener, *Which Side You On? The Harlan County Coal Miners, 1931–1939* (1978); Harvey Klehr, *The Heyday of American Communism: The Depression Decade* (1984); Donald Lisio, *The President and Protest: Hoover, Conspiracy, and the Bonus Riot* (1974); Mark Naison, *Communists in Harlem during the Depression* (1983); Theodore Saloutos and John Hicks, *Twentieth Century Populism: Agrarian Protest in the Middle West, 1900–1939* (1951); John Shover, *Cornbelt Rebellion: The Farmers' Holiday Association* (1965).

The Hoover Years
David Burner, *Herbert Hoover: A Public Life* (1979); Roger Daniels, *The Bonus March* (1971); Martin Fausold, *The Presidency of Herbert C. Hoover* (1985); Martin Fausold and George Mazuzun, eds., *The Hoover Presidency* (1974); George Nash, *The Life of Herbert Hoover* (1983); James Olson, *Herbert Hoover and the Reconstruction Finance Corporation* (1977); Albert Romasco, *The Poverty of Abundance: Hoover, the Nation, the Depression* (1965); Elliot A. Rosen, *Hoover, Roosevelt, and the Brains Trust: From Depression to New Deal* (1977); Jordan Schwarz, *The Interregnum of Despair* (1970); Joan Hoff Wilson, *Herbert Hoover: Forgotten Progressive* (1975).

CHAPTER 26: THE NEW DEAL

General Studies
John Braeman et al., *The New Deal*, 2 vols. (1975); Paul Conkin, *The New Deal* (1967); Steve Fraser and Gary Gerstle, eds., *The Rise and Fall of the New Deal Order, 1930–1980* (1989); Otis Graham, Jr., *Encore for Reform: The Old Progressives and the New Deal* (1967); Barry Karl, *The Uneasy State* (1983); William Leuchtenburg, *Franklin D. Roosevelt and the New Deal, 1932–1940* (1963); Robert McElvaine, *The Great Depression: America, 1929–1941* (1984); Gerald Nash, *The Great Depression and World War II* (1979); Harvard Sitkoff, ed., *Fifty Years Later: The New Deal Evaluated* (1985).

Franklin and Eleanor
James Burns, *Roosevelt: The Lion and the Fox* (1956); Rochelle Chadakoff, ed., *Eleanor Roosevelt's My Day: Her Acclaimed Columns, 1936–1945* (1989); Blanche Wiesen Cook, *Eleanor Roosevelt*, Volume One, *1884–1933* (1992); Kenneth Davis, *FDR*, 4 vols. (1972–1993); Frank Freidel, *Franklin D. Roosevelt*, 4 vols. (1952–1973) and *Franklin*

D. Roosevelt: A Rendezvous with Destiny (1990); Joseph Lash, *Eleanor and Franklin* (1971); Ted Morgan, *FDR: A Biography* (1985); Eleanor Roosevelt, *This Is My Story* (1937) and *This I Remember* (1949); Lois Scharf, *Eleanor Roosevelt: First Lady of American Liberalism* (1987); Arthur Schlesinger, Jr., *The Age of Roosevelt*, 3 vols. (1957–1960); Rexford Tugwell, *The Democratic Roosevelt: A Biography of Franklin D. Roosevelt* (1957); Geoffrey Ward, *Before the Trumpet: Young Franklin Roosevelt* (1985) and *A First Class Temperament: The Emergence of Franklin Roosevelt* (1989).

The New Deal and New Dealers
Anthony J. Badger, *The New Deal: The Depression Years, 1933–1940* (1989); Barton J. Bernstein, "The New Deal: The Conservative Achievements of New Deal Reform," in Barton J. Bernstein, ed., *Towards a New Past: Dissenting Essays in American History* (1968); Michael Beschloss, *Kennedy and Roosevelt: The Uneasy Alliance* (1980); John Blum, *From the Morgenthau Diaries*, 3 vols. (1959–1965); Harold Ickes, *The Secret Diaries of Harold L. Ickes*, 3 vols. (1953–1954); Peter Irons, *The New Deal Lawyers* (1982); Joseph Lash, *Dealers and Dreamers: A New Look at the New Deal* (1988); Katie Lockheim, ed., *The Making of the New Deal: The Insiders Speak* (1983); Richard Lowitt, *George W. Norris: The Triumph of a Progressive, 1933–1944* (1978); George Martin, *Madame Secretary: Frances Perkins* (1976); George McJimsey, *Harry Hopkins: Ally of the Poor and Defender of Democracy* (1987); Raymond Moley, *After Seven Years* (1939); Frances Perkins, *The Roosevelt I Knew* (1946); Samuel Rosenman, *Working for Roosevelt* (1952); Jordan Schwarz, *Liberal: Adolf A. Berle and the Vision of an American Era* (1987) and *The New Dealers: Power Politics in the Age of Roosevelt* (1993); Robert Sherwood, *Roosevelt and Hopkins: An Intimate History* (1948); Bernard Sternsher, *Rexford Tugwell and the New Deal* (1964); Susan Ware, *Beyond Suffrage: Women and the New Deal* (1981) and *Partner and I: Molly Dewson, Feminism, and New Deal Politics* (1987); T. H. Watkins, *The Righteous Pilgrim: The Life and Times of Harold L. Ickes* (1990).

Recovery and Reform
Bernard Belush, *The Failure of the NRA* (1975); Donald R. Brand, *Corporatism and the Rule of Law: A Study of the National Recovery Administration* (1988); Walter L. Creese, *TVA's Public Planning: The Vision, the Reality* (1990); Colin Gordon, *New Deals: Business, Labor, and Politics in America, 1920–1935* (1994); Ellis Hawley, *The New Deal and the Problems of Monopoly* (1966); Barry Karl, *Executive Reorganization and Reform in the New Deal* (1963); Susan E. Kennedy, *The Banking Crisis of 1933* (1973); Mark Leff, *The Limits of Symbolic Reform: The New Deal and Taxation, 1933–1939* (1984); Thomas McCraw, *TVA and the Public Power Fight* (1970); James Olson, *Saving Capitalism: The RFC and the New Deal, 1933–1940* (1988); Michael Parrish, *Securities Regulation and the New Deal* (1970); Richard Polenberg, *Reorganizing Roosevelt's Government* (1966); Albert Romasco, *The Politics of Recovery: Roosevelt's New Deal* (1983).

Agriculture and Conservation
Sidney Baldwin, *Poverty and Politics: The Rise and Decline of the Farm Security Administration* (1967); David

Conrad, *The Forgotten Farmers: The Story of Sharecroppers in the New Deal* (1965); James Gregory, *American Exodus: The Dust Bowl Migration and Okie Culture in California* (1989); Richard Kirkendall, *Social Scientists and Farm Politics in the Age of Roosevelt* (1966); Richard Lowitt, *The New Deal and the West* (1984); Percy H. Merrill, *Roosevelt's Forest Army: A History of the Civilian Conservation Corps, 1933–1942* (1981); Paul Mertz, *The New Deal and Southern Rural Poverty* (1978); Van Perkins, *Crisis in Agriculture* (1969); Donald Worster, *Dust Bowl: The Southern Plains in the 1930s* (1979) and *Rivers of Empire: Water, Aridity, and the Growth of the American West* (1986).

Relief and the Rise of the Semi-Welfare State
Searle Charles, *Minister of Relief* (1963) [about Harry Hopkins]; Paul Conkin, *FDR and the Origins of the Welfare State* (1967); Phoebe Cutler, *The Public Landscape of the New Deal* (1986); Linda Gordon, *Pitied but Not Entitled: Single Mothers and the History of Welfare* (1994); Richard Lowitt and Maurine Beasley, eds., *One Third of a Nation: Lorena Hickok Reports on the Great Depression* (1981); Roy Lubove, *The Struggle for Social Security* (1968); Jerre Mangione, *The Dream and the Deal: The Federal Writers' Project, 1935–1943* (1972); Jane deHart Matthews, *The Federal Theater, 1935–1939* (1967); Richard McKinzie, *The New Deal for Artists* (1973); Barbara Melosh, *Engendering Culture: Manhood and Womanhood in New Deal Public Art and Theater* (1991); Francis O'Connor, ed., *Art for the Millions: Essays from the 1930s by Artists and Administrators of the WPA Federal Art Project* (1973); Karen Benker Orhn, *Dorothea Lange and the Documentary Tradition* (1980); Marlene Park and Gerald Markowitz, *Democratic Vistas: Post Offices and Public Art in the New Deal* (1984); John Salmond, *The Civilian Conservation Corps* (1967); Bonnie Schwartz, *The Civil Works Administration, 1933–1934* (1984).

Dissent and Protest
Alan Brinkley, *Voices of Protest: Huey Long, Father Coughlin, and the Great Depression* (1982); Donald Grubbs, *Cry from Cotton: The Southern Tenant Farmers Union and the New Deal* (1971); Abraham Holzman, *The Townsend Movement* (1963); Glen Geansonne, *Gerald L. K. Smith: Minister of Hate* (1988); Robin D. G. Kelly, *Hammer and Hoe: Alabama Communists during the Great Depression* (1990); R. Alan Lawson, *The Failure of Independent Liberalism, 1930–1941* (1971); Greg Mitchell, *The Campaign of the Century: Upton Sinclair's Epic Race for Governor of California and the Birth of Media Politics* (1992); Mark Naison, *Communists in Harlem during the Depression* (1983); Leo Ribuffo, *The Old Christian Right: The Protestant Far Right from the Great Depression to the Cold War* (1983); Vicki Ruiz, *Cannery Women/Cannery Lives: Mexican Women, Unionization, and the California Food Processing Industry, 1930–1950* (1987); Charles Tull, *Father Coughlin and the New Deal* (1965); T. Harry Wiliams, *Huey Long* (1969); Frank Warren, *Liberals and Communism: The "Red Decade" Revisited* (1966) and *An Alternative Vision: The Socialist Party in the 1930s* (1976); George Wolfskill, *Revolt of the Conservatives: A History of the American Liberty League, 1934–1940* (1962).

Labor
Jerold Auerback, *Labor and Liberty: The La Follette Committee and the New Deal* (1966); John Barnard, *Walter Reuther and the Rise of the Auto Workers* (1983); Irving Bernstein, *Turbulent Years: A History of the American Worker, 1933–1941* (1969); Lizabeth Cohen, *Making a New Deal: Industrial Workers in Chicago, 1919–1939* (1990); Melvyn Dubofsky and Warren Van Tine, *John L. Lewis: A Biography* (1977); Sidney Fine, *Sit-Down: The General Motors Strike of 1936–1937* (1969); Steven Fraser, *Labor Will Rule: Sidney Hillman and the Rise of American Labor* (1991); Peter Friedlander, *The Emergence of a UAW Local* (1975); Nelson Lichenstein, *"The Most Dangerous Man in Detroit": Walter Reuther and the Fate of American Labor* (1995); August Meier and Elliott Rudwick, *Black Detroit and the Rise of the UAW* (1979); David Milton, *The Politics of U.S. Labor: From the Great Depression to the New Deal* (1980); Ronald Schatz, *The Electrical Workers* (1983); Robert H. Zieger, *John L. Lewis* (1988).

New Deal Politics
John Allswang, *The New Deal in American Politics* (1978); Frank Freidel, *FDR and the South* (1965); J. Joseph Huthmacher, *Senator Robert Wagner and the Rise of Urban Liberalism* (1968); Gregg Mitchell, *The Campaign of the Century: Upton Sinclair's Race for Governor and the Birth of Media Politics* (1992); James Patterson, *Congressional Conservatism and the New Deal* (1967) and *The New Deal and the States* (1969); William Leuchtenburg, "The Origins of Franklin D. Roosevelt's 'Court Packing' Plan," in Philip Kurland, ed., *The Supreme Court Review* (1966).

Minorities
Laurence Kelly, *The Assault on Assimilation: John Collier and the Origins of Indian Policy Reform, 1920–1954* (1983); Harry A. Kersey, Jr., *The Florida Seminoles and the New Deal, 1933–1942* (1989); John Kirby, *Black Americans in the Roosevelt Era: Liberalism and Race* (1980); Carey McWilliams, *North from Mexico* (1949); Donald Parman, *The Navajoes and the New Deal* (1976); Kenneth Philp, *John Collier's Crusade for Indian Reform, 1920–1934* (1977); Francis Prucha, *The Indians in American Society: From the Revolutionary War to the Present* (1985); Mark Reisler, *By the Sweat of Their Brow: Mexican Immigrant Labor in the United States, 1900–1940* (1976); Harvard Sitkoff, *A New Deal for Blacks* (1978); Raymond Walters, *Negroes and the Great Depression: The Problem of Economic Recovery* (1970); Graham D. Taylor, *The New Deal and American Indian Tribalism: The Administration of the Indian Reorganization Act, 1934–1945* (1980); Nancy Weiss, *Farewell to the Party of Lincoln: Black Politics in the Age of FDR* (1983); Robert Zangrando, *The NAACP Crusade against Lynching* (1980).

CHAPTER 27: AMERICA'S RISE TO GLOBALISM

The Roosevelt Era and the Coming of World War II
Dorothy Borg, *The United States and the Far Eastern Crisis of 1933–1938* (1964); James MacGregor Burns,

Roosevelt: The Lion and the Fox (1956); Wayne S. Cole, Roosevelt and the Isolationists, 1932–1945 (1983); Robert Dallek, Franklin D. Roosevelt and American Foreign Policy, 1932–1945 (1979); Charles DeBenedetti, The Peace Reform Movement in American History (1980); John Findling, Close Neighbors, Distant Friends: United States–Central American Relations (1987); Lloyd Gardner, Economic Aspects of New Deal Diplomacy (1964) and The Great Powers Partition Europe, from Munich to Yalta (1993); Irwin Gellman, Good Neighbor Diplomacy (1979); Patrick Headen, Roosevelt Confronts Hitler: America's Entry into World War II (1987); Edwin Herzstein, Roosevelt and Hitler: Prelude to War (1989); Akira Iriye and Warren Cohen, eds., American, Chinese, and Japanese Perspectives on Asia, 1931–1949 (1990); Warren Kimball, The Most Unsordid Act: Lend Lease, 1939–1941 (1969); Walter LaFeber, Inevitable Revolutions: The United States in Central America (1993); Douglas Little, Malevolent Neutrality: The United States, Great Britain, and the Origins of the Spanish Civil War (1985); Arthur Morse, While Six Million Died (1968); Arnold Offner, The Origins of the Second World War (1975); Gordon Prange, At Dawn We Slept (1981); Michael Slackman, Target: Pearl Harbor (1990); John Toland, Infamy (1982); Jonathan Utley, Going to War with Japan, 1937–1941 (1985); Roberta Wohlstetter, Pearl Harbor: Warning and Decision (1962); Bryce Wood, The Making of the Good Neighbor Policy (1961); David Wyman, The Abandonment of the Jews (1984).

War and Strategy

John Dower, War without Mercy: Race and Power in the Pacific War (1986); David Eisenhower, Eisenhower at War, 1943–1945 (1986); Richard B. Frank, Guadalcanal (1990); B. H. Liddell Hart, History of the Second World War (1970); Max Hastings, OVERLORD: D-Day and the Battle of Normandy (1984); Akira Iriye, Power and Culture: The Japanese-American War, 1941–1945 (1981); D. Clayton James with Anne Sharp Wells, A Time for Giants: Politics of the American High Command during World War II (1987); John Keegan, The Second World War (1989); Eric Larabee, Commander in Chief: Franklin Delano Roosevelt, His Lieutenants, and Their War (1987); William Manchester, American Caesar (1979); Karal Ann Marling and John Wetenhall, Iwo Jima (1991); Ken McCormick and Hamilton Perry, Images of War: The Artists' Vision of World War II (1990); Nathan Miller, War at Sea: A Naval History of World War II (1995); Samuel Eliot Morison, The Two Ocean War (1963); Bernard C. Nalty, Strength for the Fight: A History of Black Americans in the Military (1986); Geoffrey Perret, There's a War to Be Won: The United States Army and World War II (1991) and Winged Victory: The American Air Force in World War II (1993); Forrest Pogue, George C. Marshall, 3 vols. (1963–1975); Paul P. Rogers, The Good Years: MacArthur and Sutherland (1990); Ronald Schaffer, Wings of Judgment: American Bombing in World War II (1985); Michael Sherry, The Rise of American Air Power (1987); Bradley Smith, The Shadow Warriors: O.S.S. and the Origins of the C.I.A. (1983); Ronald Spector, The Eagle against the Sun: The American War with Japan (1985); James Stokesbury, A Short History of World War II (1980).

The Home Front at War

Michael Adams, The Best War Ever: Americans and World War II (1994); Karen T. Anderson, Wartime Women: Sex Roles, Family Relations, and the Status of American Women during World War II (1981); Matthew Baigall and Julia Williams, eds., Artists against War and Fascism (1986); M. Joyce Baker, Images of Women on Film: The War Years, 1941–1945 (1981); David Brinkley, Washington Goes to War (1988); John Costello, Virtue under Fire: How World War II Changed Our Social and Sexual Attitudes (1985); George Q. Flynn, The Draft, 1940–1973 (1993); Paul Fussell, Wartime (1989); Sherna Berger Gluck, Rosie the Riveter Revisited: Women, the War, and Social Change (1987); Doris Kearns Goodwin, No Ordinary Time, Franklin and Eleanor Roosevelt: The Homefront in World War II (1994); Susan Hartmann, The Home Front and Beyond: American Women in the 1940s (1982); Maurice Isserman, Which Side Were You On? The American Communist Party during the Second World War (1982); Clayton Koppes and Gregory Black, Hollywood Goes to War (1987); Ruth Milkman, Gender at Work: The Dynamics of Job Segregation by Sex during World War II (1987); Gerald Nash, The American West Transformed: The Impact of the Second World War (1985); Richard Polenberg, War and Society: The United States, 1941–1945 (1972); David Robertson, Sly and Able: A Political Biography of James F. Byrnes (1994); George H. Roeder, Jr., The Censored War: American Visual Experience during World War II (1993); Studs Turkel, The Good War: An Oral History of World War II (1984); William Tuttle, Daddy's Gone to War: The Second World War in the Lives of America's Children (1993); Harold Vatter, The American Economy in World War II (1985).

Minorities and the War

Robert Abzug, Inside the Vicious Heart: Americans and the Liberation of the Nazi Concentration Camps (1985); Allan Bérubé, Coming Out under Fire: Gay Men and Women in World War Two (1990); Richard Breitman and Alan Kraut, American Refugee Policy and European Jewry, 1933–1945 (1987); A. Russell Buchanan, Black Americans in World War II (1977); Dominic Capeci, Jr., Race Relations in Wartime Detroit (1984) and The Harlem Race Riot of 1943 (1977); Richard Dalfiume, Desegregation of the U.S. Armed Forces (1969); Clete Daniel, Chicano Workers and the Politics of Fairness: The Fair Employment Practices Commission and the Southwest 1941–1945 (1990); Roger Daniels, Concentration Camps U.S.A. (1981) and Prisoners without Trials: The Japanese-Americans in World War II (1993); America and the Survivors of the Holocaust (1982); Masayo Umezawa Duus, Unlikely Liberators: The Men of the 100th and 442nd (1987); Lee Finkel, Forum for Protest: The Black Press during World War II (1975); Peter Irons, Justice at War: The Story of the Japanese American Internment Cases (1983); Deborah Lipstadt, Beyond Belief: The American Press and the Coming of the Holocaust, 1933–1945 (1986); Mauricio Mazon, The Zoot Suit Riots (1984); Phillip McGuire, ed., Taps for a Jim Crow Army: Letters from Black Soldiers in World War II (1982); Sandra Taylor, Jewel of the West: Japanese-American Internment at Topaz (1993); Patrick Washburn, A Question of Sedition: The Federal Government and the Investigation of the Black Press during World War II (1986); Neil Wynn, The Afro-American and the Second World War (1976); Norman Zucker and Naomi Flink Zucker, The Guarded Gate: The Reality of American Refugee Policy (1987).

Atoms and Diplomacy

Gar Alperovitz, *The Decision to Use the Bomb* (1995); Edward M. Bennett, *Franklin D. Roosevelt and the Search for Victory: American-Soviet Relations, 1935–1945* (1990); Henry Blumenthal, *Illusion and Reality in Franco-American Diplomacy, 1914–1945* (1982); McGeorge Bundy, *Danger and Survival: Choices about the Atom Bomb in the First Fifty Years* (1988); James MacGregor Burns, *Roosevelt: The Soldier of Freedom* (1970); Winston Churchill, *The Second World War*, 6 vols. (1948–1953); Herbert Feis, *Roosevelt, Churchill, Stalin: The War They Waged and the Peace They Sought* (1957), *Between War and Peace: The Potsdam Conference* (1960), and *The Atomic Bomb and the End of World War II* (1966); John L. Gaddis, *The United States and the Origins of the Cold War* (1972); Fraser J. Harbutt, *The Iron Curtain: Churchill, America, and the Origins of the Cold War* (1986); George Herring, *Aid to Russia, 1941–1946* (1977); John Hersey, *Hiroshima* (1946); Richard Hewlett and Oscar Anderson, *The New World* (1962); "Hiroshima in History and Memory: A Symposium," *Diplomatic History*, vol. 19, No. 2, Spring, 1995, 197–365; Godfrey Hodgson, *The Colonel: The Life and Wars of Henry Stimson* (1990); Warren Kimball, ed., *Churchill and Roosevelt: The Complete Correspondence, 1939–1945* (1984); Gabriel Kolko, *The Politics of War* (1968); William Roger Louis, *Imperialism at Bay: The United States and the Decolonization of the British Empire, 1941–1945* (1978); Mark H. Lytle, *The Origins of the Iranian-American Alliance, 1941–1953* (1987); David Painter, *Oil and the American Century: The Political Economy of U.S. Foreign Oil Policy, 1941–1954* (1986); Richard Rhodes, *The Making of the Atomic Bomb* (1986); Keith Sainsbury, *Roosevelt, Stalin, Churchill, and Chiang Kai-shek, 1943: The Moscow, Cairo, and Tehran Conferences* (1985); Gaddis Smith, *American Diplomacy during the Second World War, 1941–1945* (1985); Michael B. Stoff, *Oil, War, and American Security: The Search for a National Policy on Foreign Oil, 1941–1947* (1980), and as ed., *The Manhattan Project: A Documentary Introduction* (1991); Randall B. Woods, *A Changing of the Guard: Anglo-American Relations, 1941–1946* (1990).

CHAPTER 28: COLD WAR AMERICA

The Postwar Era

Paul Boyer, *By the Bomb's Early Light* (1986); H. W. Brands, *The Devil We Knew: America and the Cold War* (1993); Robert Ferrell, *Harry S Truman: A Life* (1994); Eric Goldman, *The Crucial Decade and After* (1960); Landon Jones, *Great Expectations: America and the Babyboom Generation* (1980); George Lipsitz, *Class and Culture in Postwar America* (1981); James O'Connor, ed., *American History/American Television* (1983); William O'Neill, *American High* (1986); Richard Pells, *The Liberal Mind in a Conservative Age* (1985); Dana Polan, *Power and Paranoia: History, Narrative, and the American Cinema, 1940–1950* (1986); Leila Rupp and Verta Taylor, *Survival in the Doldrums: The American Women's Rights Movement, 1945 to the 1960s* (1987); Mark Silk, *Spiritual Politics: Religion and America since World War II* (1988); Jules Tygiel, *Baseball's Great Experiment: Jackie Robinson and His Legacy* (1983); Martin Walker, *The Cold War: A History* (1994).

The Cold War in the West

Dean Acheson, *Present at the Creation* (1969); Stephen Ambrose, *The Rise to Globalism* (1983); Douglas Brinkley, ed., *Dean Acheson and the Making of American Foreign Policy* (1993); Richard Wightman Fox, *Reinhold Niebuhr: A Biography* (1985); Richard Freeland, *The Truman Doctrine and the Origins of McCarthyism* (1970); John L. Gaddis, *Strategies of Containment* (1982) and *The Long Peace: Inquiries into the History of the Cold War* (1987); Lloyd Gardner, *Architects of Illusion* (1970); David Green, *The Containment of Latin America* (1971); Gregg Herken, *The Winning Weapon* (1980); Michael Hogan, *The Marshall Plan: America, Britain, and the Reconstruction of Western Europe, 1947–1952* (1987); Walter Isaacson and Evan Thomas, *The Wise Men* (1986); Fred Kaplan, *The Wizards of Armageddon* (1983); Laurence Kaplan, *The United States and NATO* (1984); George Kennan, *Memoirs*, 2 vols. (1967, 1972); Bruce Kuniholm, *The Origins of the Cold War in the Near East* (1980); Mark H. Lytle, *The Origins of the Iranian-American Alliance, 1941–1953* (1987); James Miller, *The United States and Italy, 1940–1950* (1986); Ronald Pruessen, *John Foster Dulles* (1982); Cheryl Rubenberg, *Israel and the American National Interest* (1986); Gaddis Smith, *Dean Acheson* (1972) and *The Last Years of the Monroe Doctrine, 1945–1993* (1994); Adam Ulam, *The Rivals* (1971); Lawrence Wittner, *American Intervention in Greece, 1943–1949* (1982); Randall B. Woods and Howard Jones, *Dawning of the Cold War* (1991).

The Cold War in Asia

Robert Blum, *Drawing the Line: The Origin of the American Containment Policy in East Asia* (1982); Bruce Cumings, *The Origins of the Korean War* (1980) and vol. 2 (1990), and as ed., *Child of Conflict: The Korean-American Relationship, 1943–1953* (1983); William Head, *America's China Sojourn* (1983); Gary Hess, *The United States' Emergence as a Southeast Asian Power, 1940–1950* (1987); Akira Iriye, *The Cold War in Asia* (1974); Burton Kaufman, *The Korean War* (1986); Michael Schaller, *The United States and China in the Twentieth Century* (1979) and *The American Occupation of Japan: The Coming of the Cold War to Asia* (1985); John W. Spanier, *The Truman–MacArthur Controversy and the Korean War* (1959); William Stueck, Jr., *The Road to Confrontation* (1981) and *The Korean War: An International History* (1995); Nancy Tucker, *Patterns in the Dust: Chinese-American Relations and the Recognition Controversy, 1949–1950* (1983).

The Domestic Cold War

Michael Belknap, *Cold War Political Justice: The Smith Act, the Communist Party, and American Civil Liberties* (1977); David Caute, *The Great Fear* (1978); Bernard F. Dick, *Radical Innocence: A Critical Study of the Hollywood Ten* (1988); Stanley I. Kutler, *The American Inquisition: Justice and Injustice in the Cold War* (1982); Robert Lamphere and Tom Shachtman, *The FBI-KGB War* (1986); Victor Navasky, *Naming Names* (1980); Robert Newman, *Owen Lattimore and the "Loss" of China* (1992); William O'Neill, *A Better World: Stalinism and the American Intellectuals* (1983); Michael Oshinsky, *A Conspiracy So Immense: The World of Joe McCarthy* (1983); Ronald Radosh and Joyce Radosh, *The Rosenberg File* (1983); Thomas Reeves, *The Life and Times of Joe*

McCarthy (1982); Richard Rovere, *Senator Joe McCarthy* (1959); Ellen Shrecker, *No Ivory Tower: McCarthyism and the Universities* (1984); Athan Theoharis, *Seeds of Repression: Harry S. Truman and the Origins of McCarthyism* (1971); Allen Weinstein, *Perjury: The Hiss-Chambers Case* (1978); Robert Williams, *Klaus Fuchs: Atom Spy* (1987).

The Truman Administration
Jack Ballard, *The Shock of Peace: Military and Economic Demobilization after World War II* (1983); Clark Clifford with Richard Holbrooke, *Counsel to the President, A Memoir* (1991); Richard Dalfiume, *Desegregation of the U.S. Armed Forces* (1969); Andrew Dunar, *The Truman Scandals and the Politics of Morality* (1984); Robert Ferrell, *Harry S. Truman and the Modern American Presidency* (1983); Donald Fixico, *Termination and Relocation: Federal Indian Policy, 1945–1960* (1986); David Goldfield, *Black, White, and Southern: Race Relations and Southern Culture* (1990); Alton Lee, *Truman and Taft–Hartley* (1966); Allen Matusow, *Farm Politics and Policies in the Truman Years* (1967); Donald McCoy, *The Presidency of Harry S. Truman* (1984); Donald McCoy and Richard Ruetten, *Quest and Response: Minority Rights and the Truman Administration* (1973); Merle Miller, *Plain Speaking* (1973); Richard Miller, *Truman: The Rise to Power* (1986); Allen Yarnell, *Democrats and Progressives: The 1948 Presidential Election as a Test of Postwar Liberalism* (1974).

CHAPTER 29: THE SUBURBAN ERA

General
Paul Carter, *Another Part of the Fifties* (1983); John Diggins, *The Proud Decades: America in War and Peace, 1941–1960* (1988); James Gilbert, *A Cycle of Outrage* (1986); Godfrey Hodgson, *America in Our Time* (1976); Martin Jezer, *The Dark Ages: Life in the United States, 1945–1960* (1982); William Leuchtenberg, *A Troubled Feast* (1979); Douglas Miller and Marion Nowak, *The Fifties: The Way We Really Were* (1977); Ronald Oakley, *God's Country: America in the 1950s* (1986); Stephen Whitfield, *The Culture of the Cold War* (1991).

American Life and Culture
Erik Barnouw, *Tube of Plenty: The Evolution of American Television* (1975); James L. Baughman, *The Republic of Mass Culture: Journalism, Filmmaking, and Broadcasting in America since 1941* (1992); Daniel Bell, *The End of Ideology* (1960); Carl Belz, *The Story of Rock* (1972); Wini Breines, *Young, White, and Miserable: Growing Up Female in the Fifties* (1992); Victoria Byerly, *Hard Times Cotton Mill Girls* (1986); Bruce Cook, *The Beat Generation* (1970); Stephanie Coontz, *The Way We Never Were: American Families and the Nostalgia Trap* (1992); John D'Emilio and Estelle Freedman, *Intimate Matters: A History of Sexuality in America* (1988); Colin Escott, *Good Rockin' Tonight: Sun Records and the Birth of Rock and Roll* (1991); Betty Friedan, *The Feminine Mystique* (1963); Neil Gabler, *Winchell: Gossip, Power and the Culture of Celebrity* (1994); John Kenneth Galbraith, *The Affluent Society* (1958); Herbert Gans, *The Levittowners* (1967); Carol George, *God's Salesman: Norman Vincent Peale and the Power of*

Positive Thinking (1994); Serge Gilbaut, *How New York Stole the Idea of Modern Art* (1983); Charlie Gillett, *The Sound of the City: The Rise of Rock and Roll* (1970); William Graebner, *Coming of Age in Buffalo: Youth and Authority in the Postwar Era* (1990); Will Herberg, *Protestant-Catholic-Jew* (1956); Thomas Hine, *Populux* (1986); Kenneth Jackson, *Crabgrass Frontier: The Suburbanization of the United States* (1985); Wendy Kozol, *Life's America: Family and Nation in Postwar Photojournalism* (1994); William Martin, *A Prophet with Honor: The Billy Graham Story* (1991); C. Wright Mills, *The Power Elite* (1956) and *White Collar* (1951); George Nash, *The Conservative Intellectual Movement in America* (1976); Richard Pells, *The Liberal Mind in a Conservative Age* (1985); David Potter, *People of Plenty* (1956); David Riesman, *The Lonely Crowd* (1950); Lynn Spiegel, *Make Room for TV: Television and the Family Ideal in Postwar America* (1992); Gaye Tuchman et al., eds., *Hearth and Home: Images of Women in the Mass Media* (1978); Ed Ward et al., *Rock of Ages: The Rolling Stone History of Rock and Roll* (1986); Carol Warren, *Madwives: Schizophrenic Women in the 1950s* (1987); William Whyte, *The Organization Man* (1956).

Foreign Policy in the Eisenhower Era
Stephen Ambrose, *Ike's Spies: Eisenhower and the Espionage Establishment* (1981); Blanche Weisen Cook, *The Declassified Eisenhower* (1981); Robert Divine, *Eisenhower and the Cold War* (1981) and *Blowin' in the Wind: The Nuclear Test Ban Debate, 1954–1960* (1978); Townsend Hoopes, *The Devil and John Foster Dulles* (1973); Richard Immerman, *The CIA in Guatemala* (1982); Madeline Kalb, *The Congo Cables: The Cold War in Africa from Eisenhower to Kennedy* (1982); Frederick Marks III, *Power and Peace: The Diplomacy of John Foster Dulles* (1993); Richard Melanson and David Mayers eds., *Reevaluating Eisenhower: American Foreign Policy in the 1950s* (1987); Thomas Paterson, *Contesting Castro: The United States and the Triumph of the Cuban Revolution* (1994); Richard Rhodes, *Dark Sun: The Making of the Hydrogen Bomb* (1995); Evan Thomas, *The Very Best Men: Four Who Dared: The Early Years of the CIA* (1995); Richard Welch, Jr., *Response to Revolution: The United States and the Cuban Revolution, 1954–1961* (1985).

Civil Rights
Numan Bartley, *The Rise of Massive Resistance: Race and Politics in the South during the 1950s* (1969); Jack Bloom, *Class, Race, and the Civil Rights Movement* (1987); Taylor Branch, *Parting the Waters: America in the King Years, 1954–1963* (1988); James Duram, *Moderate among Extremists: Dwight D. Eisenhower and the School Desegregation Crisis* (1981); David Garrow, *Bearing the Cross* (1986); Henry Louis Gates, Jr., *Colored People: A Memoir* (1994); Vincent Harding, *There Is a River: The Black Struggle for Freedom in America* (1981); Elizabeth Huckaby, *The Crisis at Central High: Little Rock, 1957–1958* (1980); Richard Kluger, *Simple Justice: The History of Brown v. Board of Education and Black America's Struggle for Equality* (1975); Anthony Lewis et al., *Portrait of a Decade* (1964); August Meier and Elliott Rudwick, *CORE: A Study in the Civil Rights Movement, 1942–1968* (1975); Stephen Oates, *Let the Trumpet Sound: The Life and Times of Martin Luther King, Jr.* (1982); Bernard Schwartz, *Inside the Warren Court* (1983); Harvard

Sitkoff, *The Struggle for Black Equality, 1954–1992* (1992); Juan Williams, *Eyes on the Prize: America's Civil Rights Years, 1954–1965* (1987); C. Vann Woodward, *The Strange Career of Jim Crow* (1974).

Domestic Politics

Stephen Ambrose, *Eisenhower the President* (1984); Piers Brendon, *Ike* (1986); Jeff Broadwater, *Eisenhower and the Anti-Communist Crusade* (1992); Larry Burt, *Tribalism in Crisis: Federal Indian Policy, 1953–1961* (1982); Barbara Clowse, *Brainpower for the Cold War: The Sputnik Crisis and the National Defense Education Act of 1958* (1981); Donald Fixico, *Termination and Relocation: Federal Indian Policy, 1945–1960* (1986); Fred Greenstein, *The Hidden Hand Presidency: Eisenhower as Leader* (1982); Chester Pach, *The Presidency of Dwight D. Eisenhower* (1991); Mark Rose, *Interstate Express Highway Politics, 1939–1989* (1991); Gary Wills, *Nixon Agonistes* (1970).

CHAPTER 30: LIBERALISM AND BEYOND

General

John M. Blum, *Years of Discord: American Politics and Society, 1961–1974* (1991); David Faber, *The Age of Great Dreams: America in the 1960s* (1994), and as ed., *The Sixties: From Memory to History* (1994); Richard Goodwin, *Remembering America: A Voice from the Sixties* (1988); Godfrey Hodgson, *America in Our Time* (1976); Edward P. Morgan, *The 60s Experience: Hard Lessons about Modern America* (1991); David Steigenwald, *The Sixties and the End of the Modern Era* (1995); Lawrence Wright, *The New World: Growing Up in America, 1960–1984* (1988).

The Counterculture and New Left

Serge Denisoff, *Great Day Coming: Folk Music and the American Left* (1971); Morris Dickstein, *The Gates of Eden* (1976); Todd Gitlin, *The Whole World Is Watching: The Mass Media in the Making and Unmaking of the New Left* (1981); Richard Goldstein, *Reporting the Counterculture* (1989); Paul Goodman, *Growing Up Absurd* (1960); Emmett Grogan, *Ringolevio* (1972); Maurice Isserman, *If I Had a Hammer . . . : The Death of the Old Left and the Birth of the New Left* (1987); Judy Kaplan and Linn Shapiro, *Red Diaper Babies: Children on the Left* (1985); Martin Lee and Bruce Shlain, *Acid Dreams: The CIA, LSD, and the Sixties Rebellion* (1985); Christine Mamiya, *Pop Art and the Consumer Culture: American Super Market* (1992); Timothy Miller, *The Hippies and American Values* (1991); W. J. Rorabaugh, *Berkeley at War: The 1960s* (1989); Theodore Roszak, *The Making of a Counter Culture* (1969); Kirkpatrick Sale, *SDS* (1973), Mark Spitz, *Dylan: A Biography* (1989); Students for a Democratic Society, *The Port Huron Statement* (1962); Hunter Thompson, *Hell's Angels* (1967) and *Fear and Loathing in Las Vegas* (1971); Ed Ward et al., *Rock of Ages: The Rolling Stone History of Rock and Roll* (1986); Tom Wolfe, *Electric Kool-Aid Acid Test* (1968).

The Civil Rights Revolution

Michael Belknap, *Federal Law and Southern Order: Racial Violence and Constitutional Conflict in the Post-Brown South* (1987); Derrick Bell, *And We Are Not Saved: The Elusive Quest for Racial Justice* (1987); Jack Bloom, *Class,* Race, and the Civil Rights Movement* (1987); Eric Burner, *And Gently He Shall Lead Them: Robert Parris Moses and Civil Rights in Mississippi* (1994); Stokely Carmichael and Charles Hamilton, *Black Power* (1967); Clayborne Carson, *In Struggle: SNCC and the Black Awakening of the 1960s* (1981); Dan T. Carter, *The Politics of Rage: George Wallace and the New Conservatism* (1995); William Chafe, *Civilities and Civil Rights* (1980); John Dittmar, *Local People: The Struggle for Civil Rights in Mississippi* (1994); Michael Eric Dyson, *Making Malcolm: The Myth and Meaning of Malcolm X* (1995); David Garrow, *The FBI and Martin Luther King* (1981); Hugh Davis Graham, *Civil Rights and the Presidency: Race and Gender in American Politics, 1960–1972* (1992); Otto Kerner et al., *The Report of the National Advisory Commission on Civil Disorders* (1968); Doug McAdam, *Freedom Summer* (1988); Malcolm X (with Alex Haley), *The Autobiography of Malcolm X* (1966); Adam Nossiter, *Of Long Memory: Mississippi and the Murder of Medgar Evers* (1994); Stephen Oates, *Let the Trumpet Sound: The Life and Times of Martin Luther King, Jr.* (1982); Hugh Pearson, *The Shadow of the Panther: Huey Newton and the Price of Black Power in America* (1994); Bruce Perry, *Malcolm* (1992); Bernard Schwartz, *Inside the Warren Court* (1983); Harvard Sitkoff, *The Struggle for Black Equality, 1954–1992* (1993); Mark Stern, *Calculating Visions: Kennedy, Johnson, and Civil Rights* (1992); Harris Wofford, *Of Kennedy and Kings* (1980); Eugene Wolfenstein, *The Victims of Democracy: Malcolm X and the Black Revolutionaries* (1981); Miles Wolff, *Lunch at the 5 & 10* (1990).

The Kennedys and Lyndon Johnson

David Burner and Thomas West, *The Torch Is Passed: The Kennedy Brothers and American Liberalism* (1984); Paul Ronnie Dugger, *The Politician* (1982); John Giglio, *The Presidency of John F. Kennedy* (1991); Lyndon Johnson, *Vantage Point* (1971); Gerald Posner, *Case Closed: Lee Harvey Oswald and the Assassination of John F. Kennedy* (1993); Thomas Reeves, *A Question of Character: A Life of John F. Kennedy* (1992); Arthur Schlesinger, Jr., *The Thousand Days* (1965) and *Robert Kennedy and His Times* (1978); Earl Warren et al., *The Report of the Warren Commission* (1964); Theodore White, *The Making of the President, 1960* (1961).

Politics and Foreign Policy in the Kennedy–Johnson Era

Graham Allison, *Essence of Decision: Explaining the Cuban Missile Crisis* (1971); James Anderson and Jared Hazelton, *Managing Macroeconomic Policy: The Johnson Presidency* (1986); Michael Beschloss, *The Crisis Years, Kennedy and Khrushchev, 1960–1963* (1991); H. W. Brands, *The Wages of Globalism: Lyndon Johnson and the Limits of American Power* (1994); Warren Cohen, *Dean Rusk* (1980); Hugh Graham Davis, *Uncertain Trumpet* (1984); Greg Duncan, *Years of Poverty, Years of Plenty* (1984); Trumbell Higgins, *Perfect Failure: Kennedy, Eisenhower and the Bay of Pigs* (1987); Diane Kunz, ed., *The Diplomacy of the Crucial Decade: American Foreign Policy in the 1960s* (1995); Richard Mahoney, *JFK: Ordeal in Africa* (1983); Walter McDougall, *. . . The Heavens and the Earth: A Political History of the Space Age* (1985); Charles Murray, *Losing Ground: American Social Policy, 1950–1980* (1984); Thomas Noer, *Cold War and Black*

Liberation: The United States and White Rule in Africa, 1948–1968 (1985); Gerald Rice, The Bold Experiment: JFK's Peace Corps (1985); R. B. Smith, An International History of the Vietnam War: The Kennedy Strategy (1985); Mary Ann Watson, The Expanding Vista, American Television in the Kennedy Years (1990); Tom Wicker, JFK and LBJ (1968); Bryce Wood, The Dismantling of the Good Neighbor Policy (1985).

CHAPTER 31: THE VIETNAM ERA

The United States and the Vietnam War

Christian Appy, Working Class War: American Combat Soldiers and Vietnam (1993); Loren Baritz, Backfire: A History of How American Culture Led Us into Vietnam and Made Us Fight the Way We Did (1985); Larry Berman, Planning a Tragedy (1982); Larry Cable, Conflict of Myths: The Development of American Counterinsurgency Doctrine and the Vietnam War (1986); Mark Clodfelter, The Limits of Airpower (1989); Lloyd Gardner, Pay Any Price: Lyndon Johnson and the War for Vietnam (1995); Francis Fitzgerald, Fire in the Lake (1972); Leslie Gelb and Richard Betts, The Irony of Vietnam: The System Worked (1979); Mike Gravel et al., The Pentagon Papers (1975); David Halberstam, The Best and the Brightest (1972) and The Making of Quagmire (1987); Le Ly Hayslip, When Heaven and Earth Changed Places (1989), and with James Hayslip, Child of War, Woman of Peace (1993); George Herring, LBJ and Vietnam (1994); George Kahin, Intervention (1986); Stanley Karnow, Vietnam (1983); Gabriel Kolko, Anatomy of a War (1985); Andrew Krepinevich, Jr., The Army and Vietnam (1986); David Levy, The Debate Over Vietnam (1991); Kathryn Marshall, In the Combat Zone: An Oral History of Women in the Vietnam War, 1966–1975 (1987); Harold G. Moore and Joseph Galloway, We Were Soldiers Once . . . and Young (1992); Tim Page, Nam (1983); Bruce Palmer, Jr., The 25-Year War (1984); Archimedes Patti, Why Viet Nam? (1983); Norman Podhoretz, Why We Were in Vietnam (1982); Al Santoli, Everything We Had: An Oral History of the Vietnam War by Thirty-Three American Soldiers Who Fought It (1981); Neil Sheehan, A Bright Shining Lie: John Paul Vann and America in Vietnam (1988); Ronald Spector, The United States Army in Vietnam (1983) and After Tet: The Bloodiest Year in Vietnam (1993); Harry Summers, Jr., On Strategy: A Critical Analysis of the Vietnam War (1981); Wallace Terry, Bloods: An Oral History of the Vietnam War by Black Veterans (1984); William Turley, The Second Indochina War: A Short Political and Military History (1986); Jim Wilson, The Sons of Bardstown (1994).

Dissent against the War

William Berman, William Fulbright and the Vietnam War (1988); David Caute, The Year of the Barricades, 1968 (1988); Charles DeBenedetti and Charles Chatfield, An American Ordeal: The Antiwar Movement and the Vietnam Era (1990); Gloria Emerson, Winners and Losers (1976); David Farber, Chicago '68 (1988); Myra MacPherson, Long Time Passing: Vietnam and the Haunted Generation (1984); Kim McQuaid, The Anxious Years (1989); Norman Mailer, Armies of the Night (1968) and Miami and the Siege of Chicago (1969); James Miller, Democracy Is in

the Streets (1987); Melvin Small, Covering Dissent: The Media and the Anti-Vietnam War Movement (1994); William Strauss, Chance and Circumstance (1978); Amy Swerdlow, The Women's Strike for Peace: Traditional Motherhood and Radical Politics in the 1960s (1993); Lawrence Wittner, Rebels against War: The American Peace Movement, 1933–1983 (1984) Nancy Zaroulis and Gerald Sullivan, Who Spoke Up? American Protest against the War in Vietnam (1984).

The Nixon Presidency before Watergate

Stephen Ambrose, Nixon, the Triumph of a Politician, 1962–1972 (1989); John Erlichmann, Witness to Power (1982); Raymond Garthoff, Détente and Confrontation: American–Soviet Relations from Nixon to Reagan (1985); H. R. Haldeman, The Haldeman Diaries: Inside the Nixon White House (1994); Seymour Hersh, The Price of Power: Kissinger in the Nixon White House (1983); Walter Isaacson, Kissinger (1992); Henry Kissinger, The White House Years (1979) and Years of Upheaval (1982); Robert Litwack, Détente and the Nixon Doctrine (1984); Morris Morley, The United States and Chile (1975); Richard Nixon, RN (1978); William Shawcross, Sideshow: Nixon, Kissinger, and the Destruction of Cambodia (1978); Robert Sutter, The China Quandary (1983); Theodore White, The Making of the President, 1968 (1969); Tom Wicker, One of Us: Richard Nixon and the American Dream (1991).

Minorities: Background and Politics

Rodolfo Acuna, Occupied America (1981); Mario Barerra, Race and Class in the Southwest (1979); John Burma, ed., Mexican-Americans in the United States (1970); Albert Camarillo, Hispanics in a Changing Society (1979); Tony Castro, Chicano Power (1974); Vine Deloria, Behind the Veil of Broken Treaties (1974); Patrick Gallagher, The Cuban Exile (1980); Hazel W. Hertzberg, The Search for an American Indian Identity: Modern Pan-Indian Movements (1971); Peter Iverson, The Navajo Nation (1981); Virginia Sanchez Korrol, From Colonia to Community (1983); Darcy McNickle, Native American Tribalism (1973); Joan Moore and Harry Pachon, Hispanics in the United States (1985); Joan Moore et al., Homeboys (1978); Roger Nichols, The American Indian: Past and Present (1986); James Olsen and Raymond Wilson, Native Americans in the Twentieth Century (1984); A. Petit, Images of the Mexican-American in Fiction and Film (1980); Ronald Taylor, Chavez and the Farm Workers (1975); Arnulfo Trejo, ed., The Chicanos: As We See Ourselves (1979); Karl Wagenheim, Puerto Rico: A Profile (1975).

CHAPTER 32: THE AGE OF LIMITS

American Society and the Economy in the 1970s

Barry Bluestone and Bennett Harrison, The Deindustrialization of America (1982); Paul Boyer, When Time Shall Be No More: Prophecy Belief in Modern American Culture (1992); Peter Calleo, The Imperious Economy (1982); Barry Commoner, The Politics of Energy (1979); Ronald Formisano, Boston against Busing: Race, Class, and Ethnicity in the 1960s and 1970s (1991); Christopher Lasch, The Culture of Narcissism (1978); Michael Lienesch, Redeeming America: Piety and Politics in the New Christian

Right (1993); J. Anthony Lukas, *Common Ground: A Turbulent Decade in the Lives of Three American Families* (1986); George Marsden, *Fundamentalism and Evangelicalism* (1991); Martin Melosi, *Coping with Abundance: Energy and Environment in Industrial America* (1985); Timothy O'Neill, *Bakke and the Politics of Equality* (1985); Daniel Yergin, *The Prize* (1991).

Environmentalism
Rachel Carson, *Silent Spring* (1962); Barry Caspar and Paul Wellstone, *Powerline* (1981); Albert Cowdry, *This Land, This South: An Environmental History* (1983); Thomas Dunlap, *DDT: Scientists, Citizens, and Public Policy* (1981); Robert Booth Fowler, *The Greening of Protestant Thought* (1995); Ian McHarg, *Design with Nature* (1969); Daniel Martin, *Three Mile Island* (1980); Lester Milbrath, *Environmentalists: Vanguard for a New Society* (1984); Roderick Nash, *The Rights of Nature* (1989); Marc Reisner, *Cadillac Desert: The American West and Its Disappearing Water* (1986); Kirkpatrick Sale, *The Green Revolution, The American Environmental Movement, 1962–1993* (1993); Philip Shabecoff, *A Fierce Green Fire: The American Environmental Movement* (1993); Andrew Szasz, *EcoPopulism: Toxic Waste and the Movement for Environmental Justice* (1994); James Trefethen, *An American Crusade for Wildlife* (1975); Donald Worster, *Rivers of Empire: Water, Aridity, and the Growth of the American West* (1985).

Feminism, Sexual Politics, and the Family
Barry D. Adam, *The Rise of a Gay and Lesbian Movement* (1987); Rae Andre, *Homemakers: The Forgotten Workers* (1981); Peter Berger and Brigitte Berger, *The War over the Family: Capturng the Middle Ground* (1983); Mary Frances Berry, *Why ERA Failed: Politics, Women's Rights, and the Amending Process of the Constitution* (1986) and *The Politics of Parenthood: Childcare, Women's Rights and Feminism* (1993); Susan Brownmiller, *Against Our Will: Men, Women, and Rape* (1975); Robert Coles and Geoffrey Stokes, *Sex and the American Teenager* (1985); Angela Davis, *Women, Race, and Class* (1981); Susan Douglas, *Where the Girls Are: Growing Up Female with the Mass Media* (1994); John D'Emilio, *Sexual Politics, Sexual Communities: The Making of a Homosexual Minority in the United States, 1940–1970* (1983); Martin Duberman, *Stonewall* (1993); Andrea Dworkin, *Right-Wing Women* (1983); Barbara Ehrenreich, *The Hearts of Men: American Dreams and the Flight from Commitment* (1983); Susan Estebrook, *If All We Did Was to Weep at Home: A History of White Working-Class Women in America* (1979); Shulamith Firestone, *The Dialectic of Sex: The Case for the Feminist Revolution* (1970); Jo Freeman, *The Politics of Women's Liberation* (1975); David Garrow, *Liberty and Sexuality: The Right and Privacy in the Making of Roe v. Wade* (1994); Carol Gilligan, *In Another Voice: Psychological Theory and Women's Development* (1982); Germaine Greer, *The Female Eunuch* (1972); Alice Kessler Harris, *Out to Work* (1982); Gloria Hull et al., *But Some of Us Are Brave: Black Women's Studies* (1982); Christopher Lasch, *Haven in a Hostile World* (1979); Kristen Luker, *Abortion and the Politics of Motherhood* (1984); Norma McCorvey, *I Am Roe: My Life, Roe v. Wade and Freedom of Choice* (1994); Kate Millett, *Sexual Politics* (1970); Steven Mintz and Susan Kellogg, *Domestic Revolutions: A Social History of American Family Life* (1988); Robin Morgan, ed., *Sisterhood Is Powerful: An Anthology* (1970); Maureen Muldoon, *The Abortion Debate in the United States and Canada: A Source Book* (1991); La Frances Rodgers-Rose, ed., *The Black Woman* (1980); Gloria Steinem, *Outrageous Acts and Everyday Rebellions* (1983).

Politics and Diplomacy in the Age of Limits
Stephen Ambrose, *Nixon: Ruin and Recovery, 1973–1990* (1991); James Bill, *The Eagle and the Lion: The Tragedy of American–Iranian Relations* (1987); Zbigniew Brzezinski, *Power and Principle* (1983); James Cannon, *Time and Chance: Gerald Ford's Appointment with History, 1913–1974* (1993); Jimmy Carter, *Keeping the Faith* (1982); Rosalynn Carter, *First Lady from Plains* (1984); John Dean, *Blind Ambition* (1976); John Dumbull, *The Carter Presidency: A Re-evaluation* (1993); Gerald Ford, *A Time to Heal* (1979); Raymond Garthoff, *Détente and Confrontation: American–Soviet Relations from Nixon to Reagan* (1985); Millicent Gates and Bruce Geelhoed, *The Dragon and the Snake: An American Account of the Turmoil in China, 1976–1977* (1986); Michael Hogan, *The Panama Canal in American Politics* (1986); Henry Jackson, *From the Congo to Soweto: U.S. Foreign Policy toward Africa since 1960* (1982); Burton Kaufman, *The Presidency of James Earl Carter, Jr.* (1993); Walter LaFeber, *The Panama Canal*, rev. ed. (1989); J. Anthony Lukas, *Nightmare: The Underside of the Nixon Years* (1988); Richard Pipes, *U.S.–Soviet Relations in the Era of Détente* (1981); William Quandt, *Camp David* (1986); A. James Reichley, *Conservatives in an Age of Change: The Nixon and Ford Administrations* (1981); Robert Schulzinger, *Henry Kissinger: Doctor of Diplomacy* (1989); Gary Sick, *All Fall Down* (1985); John Sirica, *To Set the Record Straight* (1979); Seth Tillman, *The U.S. in the Middle East* (1982); Cyrus Vance, *Hard Choices* (1983); Theodore White, *Breach of Faith* (1975); Bob Woodward and Carl Bernstein, *All the President's Men* (1974) and *The Final Days* (1976).

CHAPTER 33: A NATION STILL DIVISIBLE

Contemporary American Society
Bruce Bawer, *A Place at the Table: The Gay Individual and American Society* (1994); Robert Bellah et al., *Habits of the Heart: Individualism and Commitment in American Life* (1985) and *The Good Society* (1991); Dallas Blanchard, *The Anti-Abortion Movement* (1994); Stephen Carter, *The Culture of Disbelief: How American Law and Politics Trivialize Religious Devotion* (1993); William Dietrich, *In the Shadow of the Rising Sun: The Political Roots of American Economic Decline* (1991); Thomas Byrne Edsall, *The New Politics of Inequality* (1984); Barbara Ehrenreich, *Fear of Falling: The Inner Life of the Middle Class* (1989) and *The Worst Years of Our Lives* (1990); Susan Faludi, *Backlash: The Undeclared War against American Women* (1991); Elizabeth Fee and Daniel Fox, eds., *AIDS: The Burdens of History* (1992); Henry Louis Gates, Jr., *Loose Canons: Notes on the Culture Wars* (1993); Michael Goldfield, *The Decline of Organized Labor in the United States* (1987); Otis Graham, Jr., *Losing Time: The Industrial Policy Debate* (1992); Michael Harrington, *The New American Poverty* (1984); Richard Herrnstein and Charles Murray, *The Bell Curve: Intelligence and Class Structure in*

American Life (1994); Robert Hughes, Culture of Complaint: The Fraying of America (1993); Paul Krugman, Peddling Prosperity: Economic Sense and Nonsense in the Age of Diminished Expectations (1994); Frank Levy, Dollars and Dreams: The Changing American Income Distribution (1987); Steve Levy, Insanely Great: The Life and Times of Macintosh, the Computer That Changed Everything (1994); Jane Maysbridge, Why We Lost the ERA (1986); Joseph Nocera, A Piece of the Action: How the Middle Class Joined the Money Class (1994); Juliet Schor, The Overworked American: The Unexpected Decline of Leisure (1991); Studs Terkel, The Great Divide (1988); Thomas Toch, In the Name of Excellence: The Struggle to Reform the Nation's Schools (1991); James Trabor and Eugene Gallagher, Why Waco? Cults in the Battle for Religious Freedom (1995).

Politics from Reagan to Clinton
Charles Allen, The Comeback Kid: The Life and Career of Bill Clinton (1992); Earl Black and Merle Black, The Vital South: How Presidents Are Elected (1992); Sidney Blumenthal, The Rise of the Counter-Establishment from Conservative Ideology to Political Power (1988), and with Thomas Byrne Edsall, eds., The Reagan Legacy (1988); Paul Boyer, ed., Reagan as President: Contemporary Views of the Man, His Politics, and His Policies (1990); William Brennan, America's Right Turn from Nixon to Bush (1994); Barbara Bush, Barbara Bush: A Memoir (1994); Michael Deaver, Behind the Scenes (1987); Theodore Draper, A Very Thin Line: The Iran–Contra Affairs (1991); Elizabeth Drew, On the Edge: The Clinton Presidency (1994); Ken Gross, Ross Perot: The Man Behind the Myth (1992); David Hoeveler, Jr., Watch on the Right: Conservative Intellectuals in the Reagan Era (1991); Peter Irons, Brennan vs. Rehnquist: The Battle for the Constitution (1994); Jonathan Kwitny, The Crimes of Patriots: A True Tale of Dope, Dirty Money, and the CIA (1987); Jonathan Lash, A Season of Spoils: The Story of the Reagan Administration's Attack on the Environment (1984); Theodore Lowi, The End of the Republican Era (1995); Mary Matlin and James Carville, All's Fair: Love, War, and Running for President (1994); The New Yorker, "Special Politics Issue," October 21 & 28, 1996; Kevin Phillips, The Politics of Rich and Poor: Wealth and the American Electorate in the Reagan Aftermath (1990) and Boiling Point: Republicans: Democrats and the Decline of Middle Class Prosperity (1993); John Podhoretz, Hell of a Ride: Backstage at the White House Follies, 1989–1993 (1993); Dan Quayle, Standing Firm: A Vice-Presidential Memoir (1994); Donald Regan, For the Record (1988); Tom Rosenstiel, Strange Bedfellows: How Television and the Presidential Candidates Changed American Politics, 1992 (1993); Randy Shilts, And the Band Played On: Politics, People and the AIDS Epidemic (1987); David Stockman, The Triumph of Politics: The Inside Story of the Reagan Revolution (1986); Stephen Vaugh, Ronald Reagan in Hollywood: Movies and Politics (1994); Gary Wills, Reagan's America (1987); Daniel Wirls, The Politics of Defense in the Reagan Era (1992); Bob Woodward, The Agenda: Inside the Clinton White House (1994).

Foreign Policy into the 1990s
Michael Beschloss and Strobe Talbot, At the Highest Levels: The Inside Story of the End of the Cold War (1993);

Raymond Bonner, Weakness and Deceit: U.S. Policy and El Salvador (1984); William Broad, Teller's War: The Top Secret Story behind the Star Wars Deception (1992); Bradford Burns, At War with Nicaragua (1987); Leslie Cockburn, Out of Control (1987); Christopher Coker, The United States and South Africa, 1968–1985 (1986); Thomas Friedman, From Beirut to Jerusalem (1989); John Lewis Gaddis, The United States and the End of the Cold War (1992); Roy Gutman, Banana Diplomacy (1988); Alexander Haig, Jr., Caveat: Realism, Reagan, and Foreign Policy (1984); Delip Hiro, Desert Shield to Desert Storm (1992); Bruce Jentleson, Pipeline Politics: The Complex Political Economy of East–West Trade (1986); Robert Kaplan, Balkan Ghosts (1993); Walter LaFeber, Inevitable Revolutions (1993); John Mueller, Policy and Opinion in the Gulf War (1994); Robert Pastor, Condemned to Repetition: The United States and Nicaragua (1987); Jonathan Schell, The Fate of the Earth (1982); David Schoenbaum, The United States and the State of Israel (1993); Strobe Talbott, Deadly Gambits: The Reagan Administration and the Stalemate in Nuclear Arms Control (1984); Sanford Ungar, Africa (1985); William Vogele, Stepping Back: Nuclear Arms Control and the End of the Cold War (1994). Thomas Walker, ed., Reagan versus the Sandinistas (1987); Bob Woodward, Veil: The Secret Wars of the CIA (1987).

Minorities and American Culture
Ken Auletta, The Underclass (1982); Richard Bernstein, Multiculturalism and the Battle for America's Future (1994); Ellis Cose, The Rage of the Privileged Class: Why Are Middle Class Blacks Angry? (1994); Roger Daniels et al., eds., Japanese-Americans: From Relocation to Redress (1986); Reynolds Farley and Walter Allen, The Color Line and the Quality of Life in America (1987); Lawrence Fuchs, The American Kaleidoscope: Race, Ethnicity, and the Civic Culture (1990); Douglas Glasgow, The Black Underclass (1980); Andrew Hacker, Two Nations: Black and White, Separate, Hostile, Unequal (1992); Denis Heyck, ed., Barrios and Borderlands: Cultures of Latinos and Latinas in the United States (1993); Bill Ong Hing, Making and Remaking Asian America through Immigration Policy, 1850–1990 (1993); David Hollinger, Postethnic America: Beyond Multiculturalism (1995); Christopher Jencks, The Homeless (1994); Jonathan Kozol, Savage Inequalities: Children in America's Schools (1991); Oscar Martinez, Border People: Life and Society in the U.S.–Mexico Border Lands (1994); Joan Moore and Harry Pachon, Hispanics in the United States (1985); Adolph Reed, The Jesse Jackson Phenomenon: The Crisis of Purpose in Afro-American Politics (1986); Sam Roberts, Who Are We? A Portrait of America Based on the Latest U.S. Census (1994); Arthur Schlesinger, Jr., The Disuniting of America (1991); Peter Skerry, Mexican-Americans: The Ambivalent Minority (1993); Robert C. Smith, Racism in the Post–Civil Rights Era: Now You See It, Now You Don't (1995); The Staff of the Chicago Tribune, The American Millstone: An Examination of the Nation's Permanent Underclass (1986); Shih-Shan Henry Tsai, The Chinese Experience in America (1986); William Wei, The Asian American Movement (1993).

PHOTO CREDITS

Chandler. Gift of Edgar William and Bernice Chrysler Garbisch, © 1993 National Gallery of Art, Washington, DC; (right) Winthrop Chandler, *Mrs. Samuel Chandler.* Gift of Edgar William and Bernice Chrysler Garbisch, © 1993 National Gallery of Art, Washington, DC. **205:** Miriam & Ira D. Wallach Division of Arts, Prints and Photographs, New York Public Library. Astor, Lenox and Tilden Foundations. **208:** Collection of the Greenville County Museum of Art. **211:** Corbis-Bettmann. **214:** Pavel Petrovich Svinin, *Negro Methodists Holding a Meeting in a Philadelphia Alley,* 1811–1813. Watercolor on paper. 6⁹⁄₁₆ x 9¹⁵⁄₁₆ in. Provenance: R. T. H. Halsy, New York. The Metropolitan Museum of Art. Rogers Fund, 1942. **217:** (left) Gilbert Stuart, *The Skater (Portrait of William Grant).* Andrew W. Mellon Collection, © 1993 National Gallery of Art, Washington, DC; (right) The New-York Historical Society. **218:** James Peale, *Mrs. John McAllister.* Gloria Manney/Metropolitan Museum of Art. **221:** The New-York Historical Society. **225:** Charles Wilson Peale, *James Madison.* From the collection of Gilcrease Museum, Tulsa, OK. **227:** Independence National Historical Park Collection. **232:** Herrnhut, Archiv der Brüder-Unität. **233:** Virginia Baptist Historical Society at the University of Richmond. **234:** The Free Library of Philadelphia. Will Brown, photographer. **235:** Historic New Orleans Collection. **237:** Culver Pictures, Inc. **240:** Addison Gallery of American Art, Phillips Academy, Andover, MA. **242:** I. N. Phelps Stokes Collection, Miriam & Ira D. Wallach Division of Art, Prints and Photographs, The New York Public Library. Astor, Lenox and Tilden Foundations. **245:** National Gallery of Art. E. W. and B. C. Garbisch Collection. **249:** (left) Independence National Historical Park; (right) National Gallery of Art, Washington, DC. **254:** *The American Revolution: A Picture Sourcebook* published by Dover Publications, Inc., 1975. **255:** The New-York Historical Society. **259:** U.S. Department of the Interior, National Park Service. Adams National Historic Site, Quincy, MA. **261:** Courtesy of the Pennsylvania Academy of the Fine Arts, Philadelphia. Gift of Mrs. Sarah Harrison (The Joseph Harrison, Jr., Collection). **264:** Courtesy, Winterthur Museum, (detail). **269:** Davenport West, Jr., Collection. **271:** (left) Library of Congress; (right) Maryland Historical Society, Baltimore. **274:** Boston Athenaeum, (detail). **281:** Paul Petrovich Svinin, *A Philadelphia Anabaptist Submersion during a Thunderstorm.* The Metropolitan Museum of Art. Rogers Fund, 1942. (42.95.20). **285:** (left) George Catlin, *The Open Door, Known as The Prophet, Brother of Tecumseh,* 1830; (right) Field Museum of Natural History (Neg # A93851C), Chicago. **289:** Culver Pictures, Inc. **295:** (Historical Society of PA). New Orleans Museum of Art. Gift of Edgar William and Bernice Chrysler Garbisch. **297:** Pavel Petrovich Svinin, *Members of the City Troop and Other Philadelphia Soldiery.* The Metropolitan Museum of Art. Rogers Fund, 1942. (42.95.21). **302:** Bibliotheque Nationale, Paris, (detail). **304:** E. T. Archive. **307:** New York State Historical Association, Cooperstown, NY. **309:** American Clock & Watch Museum, Bristol, CT. **310:** Smithsonian Institution, Textile Division. **311:** The New-York Historical Society. **317:** Anglo-American Art Museum, Louisiana State University, Baton Rouge. Gift of Mrs. Mamie Persac Lusk. **318:** Beinecke Rare Book and Manuscript Library, Yale

University. **322:** Missouri Historical Society (Neg 3 CT SS831). **325:** Corbis-Bettmann. **327:** University of Massachusetts, Lowell. **328:** Baker Library Manuscripts & Archives, Harvard Business School, Harvard University. **333:** Library of Congress. **336:** Thomas Hicks, *Calculating,* 1844. M. and M. Karolik Collection of American Paintings, 1815–1865. Courtesy, Museum of Fine Arts, Boston. **343:** Roosevelt Library. **344:** Courtesy of the Newberry Library, Chicago. **347:** Museum of the City of New York. Gift of Mrs. Francis P. Garvan in memory of Francis P. Garvan. **352:** From the Art Collection of The Boatman's National Bank of Saint Louis. **354:** Collection of The New-York Historical Society. **356:** Stock Montage/Historical Picture Service. **359:** New Orleans Museum of Art. Gift of William E. Groves. **362:** (left) Fogg Art Museum, Harvard University, (detail); (right) Collection of Jay P. Altmayer. **365:** Boston Art Commission, Office of the Arts and Humanities. **368:** The Library Company of Philadelphia. **370:** Museum of the City of New York. The J. Clarence Davies Collection. **379:** Library of Congress. **380:** The Stowe-Day Foundation, Hartford, CT. **381:** Allen Memorial Art Museum. Gift of Lewis Tappan. **385:** Stock Montage/Historical Picture Service. **389:** Engraving by W. W. Wilson, *Constructing a Balloon Frame House.* From Edward Shaw, *The Modern Architect,* 1855. The Metropolitan Museum of Art. Harris Brisbane Dick Fund, 1934. **390:** Concord Free Public Library. **392:** Rare Book Division, New York Public Library. Astor, Lenox and Tilden Foundations. **393:** Culver Pictures, Inc. **394:** Miriam & Ira D. Wallach Division of Art, Prints and Photographs, The New York Public Library. Astor, Lenox and Tilden Foundations. **399:** Courtesy of the Newberry Library, Chicago. **401:** (left) Rare Books and Manuscripts, Boston Public Library. Photo courtesy Geoffrey Stein Studios; (right) Corbis-Bettmann. **404:** Corbis-Bettmann. **405:** Courtesy of Rhoda Barney Jenkins. **413:** Historic New Orleans Collection. **416:** Museum of the City of New York. Harry T. Peters Collection. **425:** (top) *John Stock.* Watercolor portrait on ivory. The Gibbes Museum of Art/Carolina Art Association, Charleston, SC; (right) Historic New Orleans Collection. **427:** George Caleb Bingham, *The Squatters,* 1850. Bequest of Henry L. Shattuck in memory of the late Ralph W. Gray. Courtesy, Museum of Fine Arts, Boston. **433:** Chicago Historical Society. **434:** Abby Aldrich Rockefeller Folk Art Center. **437:** Courtesy of The Charleston Museum, Charleston, SC. **439:** Thomas Waterman Wood, *Market Woman,* 1858. Oil on canvas. 23⅜ x 14½ in. The Fine Arts Museums of San Francisco. Mildred Anna Williams Collection. 1944.8. **441:** The Smithsonian Institution. **447:** National Museum of American Art, Washington, DC/Art Resource, NY. **450:** Library of Congress. **451:** Seaver Center for Western History Research, Los Angeles County Museum of Natural History. **454:** Courtesy George Eastman House. **457:** By permission of The Huntington Library, San Marino, CA. **462:** George Peter Alexander Healy, *James K. Polk,* in the collection of the Corcoran Gallery of Art. Museum Purchase, Gallery Fund. **465:** The New-York Historical Society. **468:** Courtesy California Historical Society, San Francisco. Photograph by Eadweard J. Muybridge. FN-138990. **470:** Collection of The New-York Historical Society. **472:** Print

Collection, Miriam & Ira D. Wallach Division of Arts, Prints and Photographs, New York Public Library. Astor, Lenox and Tilden Foundations.   **474:** Witte Museum. **477:** (all) Library of Congress.   **483:** Culver Pictures, Inc.   **484:** Kansas State Historical Society, Topeka, KN. **491:** Museum of the City of New York. 33.169. Gift of Mrs. Robert M. Littlejohn.   **496:** Courtesy, American Antiquarian Society.   **497:** Anne S. K. Brown Military Collection, Brown University Library.   **498:** Print Collection, Miriam & Ira D. Wallach Division of Arts, Prints and Photographs, New York Public Library. Astor, Lenox and Tilden Foundations.   **500:** Missouri Historical Society.   **501:** Library of Congress.   **503:** (left) Corbis-Bettmann; (right) Illinois State Historical Library. **507:** Library of Congress.   **508:** Boston Athenaeum. **511:** Harper's Weekly.   **517:** West Point Museum Collections, United States Military Academy. **520:** Chicago Historical Society.   **521:** From the Collections of Henry Ford Museum & Greenfield Village. **526:** Library of Congress.   **528:** Library of Congress. **529:** Library of Congress.   **534:** Frank W. and Marie T. Wood Print Collection, Alexandria, VA.   **535:** John Ferguson Weir, *The Gun Foundry.* Putnam County Historical Society, Cold Spring, NY 10516.   **537:** U.S. Army Military History Institute, Carlisle Barracks, PA. **539:** M. and M. Karolik Collection. Courtesy, Museum of Fine Arts, Boston.   **541:** (both) Larry B. Wilford Collection, Civil War Photohistorian.   **543:** Dale S. Snair Collection, Richmond, VA.   **553:** (left) Library of Congress; (right) The Valentine Museum of the Life and History of Richmond. Cook Collection.   **558:** Culver Pictures, Inc.   **559:** Culver Pictures, Inc.   **560:** Culver Pictures, Inc.   **563:** Winslow Homer, *A Visit from the Old Mistress,* 1876. Oil on canvas. 18 x 24⅛ in. National Museum of American Art, Smithsonian Institution. Gift of William T. Evans.   **566:** Library of Congress. **567:** General Research Division, New York Public Library. Astor, Lenox and Tilden Foundations.   **568:** Library of Congress.   **572:** Library of Congress.   **574:** Theodor Kaufmann, *Portrait of Hiram Rhoades Revels,* 1870s. Oil on millboard. 12 x 10 in. Herbert F. Johnson Museum of Art, Cornell University, Ithaca, NY. 69.170. Photo © Emil Ghinger.   **576:** Library of Congress.   **579:** The New-York Historical Society.   **582:** Corbis-Bettmann. **584:** Sophie Smith Collection, Smith College.   **585:** The Granger Collection.   **587:** Rutherford B. Hayes Presidential Center.   **590:** Library of Congress. Division of Rare Books and Manuscripts.   **595:** By permission of The British Library, London.   **596:** Library of Congress. **597:** Erich Lessing/Art Resource, NY.   **599:** New York Public Library.   **602:** Corbis-Bettmann.   **606:** Culver Pictures, Inc.   **608:** Library of Congress.   **611:** The Smithsonian Institution, Washington, DC. National Museum of American History, Collection of Business Americana. Photo # 83-30065-11.   **618:** The Carnegie Library of Pittsburgh.   **619:** Lee Boltin Picture Library. **622:** Library of Congress.   **624:** Library of Congress. **625:** Courtesy, Metropolitan Life Insurance Company, NY.   **629:** Collection of Lee Baxandall.   **630:** Culver Pictures, Inc.   **635:** George Wesley Bellows, *Cliff Dwellers,* 1913. Los Angeles County Museum of Art. Los Angeles County Fund.   **638:** (top left) Brown Brothers; (top right) National Archives; (bottom) Library of Congress.   **642:** National Archives. Photo courtesy

Rudolph   Vetter/Interpretive   Photography.   **643:** Courtesy, New York Public Library. Astor, Lenox and Tilden Foundations.   **645:** Courtesy The Newberry Library.   **647:** Milwaukee Art Museum. Layton Art Collection.   **650:**   Thomas   Chinn.   **651:**   The Smithsonian Institution, Washington, DC.   **655:** Winslow Homer, *Blackboard.* Gift of Jo Ann and Julian Ganz, Jr. © Board of Trustees, National Gallery of Art, Washington. **658:** The Strong Museum.   **659:** Horace Bonham, *Nearing the Issue at the Cockpit.* In the collection of The Corcoran Gallery of Art, Museum Purchase. **661:** Drawing by Charles Dana Gibson.   **667:** Idaho State Historical Society.   **670:** Thomas Anshutz, *Cabbages,* 1879. Oil on canvas. 24 x 17 in. The Metropolitan Museum of Art. Morris K. Jesup Fund, 1940. (40.40).   **672:** Brown Brothers.   **673:** Armitstead Collection, University of South Alabama Archives.   **677:** Billy Graham Center Museum.   **678:** LSU in Shreveport, Noel Memorial Library. Archives and Special Collections.   **683:** Library of Congress.   **691:** The Institute of Texan Cultures, San Antonio, TX.   **695:** Henry E. Huntington Library and Art Gallery.   **696:** Courtesy, Wichita Art Museum. The Roland P. Murdock Collection.   **699:** Kansas State Historical Society.   **700:** Kansas State Historical Society. **702:** Colorado State University Photographic Services. **704:** University of Oregon Library.   **708:** Library of Congress.   **709:** Karl Bodmer, *Hidatsa Buffalo Robe.* Joslyn Art Museum, Omaha, Nebraska. Gift of the Enron Art Foundation.   **710:** Karl Bodmer, *Pigeon Blackfeet Man.* Joslyn Art Museum, Omaha, Nebraska. Gift of the Enron Art Foundation.   **711:** From William M. Harlow, *Inside the Wood: Masterpiece of Nature* (Washington, DC, 1970), pg. 6, Fig. 7.   **713:** Chicago Historical Society. **716:**   Courtesy,   Colorado   Historical   Society. **718:** Harper's Weekly (April 30, 1881).   **720:** Culver Pictures,   Inc.   **722:**   California   State   Library. **724:** Courtesy of Cornell University Library, Ithaca, NY. **726:** The Kansas State Historical Society, Topeka, KN. **729:** Courtesy, Dover Publications, NY.   **731:** Library of Congress.   **734:** Library of Congress.   **736:** Ramsayer Presidential Research Library, McKinley Museum of History, Science, and Industry of the Stark County Historical Society, Canton, OH.   **741:** Fred Pansing, *Naval Parade, August 20, 1898.* Oil on canvas. Courtesy of the Museum of the City of New York.   **742:** Philip P. Choy, Professor of Asian American Studies at San Francisco State University.   **745:** Hawaii State Archives. **747:** Chicago Historical Society.   **749:** Huntsville Public Library.   **759:** Library of Congress.   **760:** Brown Brothers.   **762:** Corbis-Bettmann.   **766:** San Diego Historical Society. Ticor Collection.   **768:** Library of Congress.   **771:** California Historical Society, San Francisco. FN-29415.   **773:** Library of Congress. **774:** National Portrait Gallery, Washington, DC/Art Resource, NY.   **776:** Culver Pictures, Inc.   **778:** (left) Brown   Brothers;   (right)   Library   of   Congress. **779:** Library of Congress.   **782:** The Bancroft Library, University of California, Berkeley.   **783:** Culver Pictures, Inc.   **787:** Culver Pictures, Inc.   **793:** Horace Pippin, *The End of the War; Starting Home,* c. 1931. Philadelphia Museum of Art. Given by Robert Carlen.   **795:** Theodore Roosevelt   Collection,   Harvard   College   Library. **801:** Brown Brothers.   **803:** Childe Hassam, *Avenue of the Allies: Great Britain, 1918 (The Flags of the*

Colonies: Canada and Anzac; Brazil and Belgium Beyond). The Metropolitan Museum of Art. Bequest of Miss Adelaide Milton de Groot (1876–1967), 1967. (67.187.127). **808:** Culver Pictures, Inc. **810:** (both) Trustees of the Imperial War Museum, London. **811:** Read Collection, State Records Center and Archives, Santa Fe, NM. **815:** National Archives, U.S. War Department. **818:** Imperial War Museum, London. **821:** Earl Lonsbury, *Battle Engagement.* WPA Photo Collection. Archives of American Art, Smithsonian Institution. **822:** Trustees of the Imperial War Museum, London. **825:** Culver Pictures, Inc. **831:** Collection of Albert Craig. **832:** Bildarchiv Preussischer Kulturbesitz. **835:** Archibald John Motley, Jr., *Blues,* 1929. Oil on canvas. 80 x 100.3 cm. Lent by Archie Motley and Valerie Gerrard Browne, 41.1988. Photograph © 1993 The Art Institute of Chicago. All Rights Reserved. **836:** Corbis-Bettmann. **838:** From the Collections of Henry Ford Museum & Greenfield Village. **840:** Saturday Evening Post (Jan. 24, 1925). **842:** Gerrit Beneker (American 1882–1934), *Portrait of Homer White.* Collection of the Canton Art Institute, Canton, OH. **845:** Library of Congress. **846:** Corbis-Bettmann. **848:** (left) The Brooklyn Museum. Gift of Doctor Annella Brown. Photo © Schecter Lee; (right) Evening wrap coat, c. 1928. The Metropolitan Museum of Art, NY. Gift of the Fashion Group, Inc., 1975. (1975.295.1). **850:** Lief Neandross, *The Roxy Theater.* Watercolor. Courtesy of the Rambusch Co., NY. **852:** Corbis-Bettmann. **857:** Paul Cadmus, *To the Lynching!,* 1935. Pencil and watercolor on paper. 20½ x 15¾ in. Collection of Whitney Museum of American Art. Purchase 36.32. **861:** UPI/Corbis-Bettmann. **869:** (both) Library of Congress. **871:** Library of Congress. **872:** Vanity Fair (October 1933). Courtesy of the New York Public Library. **877:** Brown Brothers. **878:** Harmon Collection, The National Archives. **881:** UPI/Corbis-Bettmann. **882:** The Brooklyn Museum. Purchased with funds donated by The Walter Foundation, 85.9. Photo, Scott Hyde. **883:** Photofest. **884:** Library of Congress. **886:** University Art Museum, Arizona State University, Tempe. **889:** Louis Ribak, *Home Relief Station,* 1935–1936. Oil on canvas. 28 x 36 in (71.1 x 91.4 cm). Collection of Whitney Museum of American Art, NY. Purchase 36.148. **890:** United States Air Force. **893:** The Butler Institute of American Art, Youngstown, OH. **899:** Franklin D. Roosevelt Library. **900:** Franklin D. Roosevelt Library. **902:** UPI/Corbis-Bettmann. **905:** Courtesy Vanity Fair. Copyright © 1934 (renewed 1962) by The Condé Nast Publications, Inc. **910:** UPI/Corbis-Bettmann. **911:** Peter Hopkins, *Riot at Union Square, March 6, 1930,* 1947. Courtesy Museum of the City of New York. **917:** Don Beatty. **920:** Don Beatty. **921:** Copyright the Dorothea Lange Collection, The Oakland Museum of California, the City of Oakland. Gift of Paul S. Taylor. **925:** Tom Lea, *Back Home: Pleasant Hill, MO., 1865.* National Archives. **927:** Library of Congress. **935:** National Archives. **936:** AP/Wide World Photos. **938:** © 1942 Edward B. Marks Music Company. Copyright renewed. Used by permission and all rights reserved. Photograph courtesy Franklin Delano Roosevelt Library, Hyde Park, NY. **940:** UPI/Corbis-Bettmann. **944:** UPI/Corbis-Bettmann. **950:** Navy Art Collection, Naval Historical Center. **952:** Courtesy of Darby Perry. **953:** Jacob

Lawrence, *War Series: Shipping Out,* 1947. Egg tempera on composition board. 20 x 16 in. Collection of Whitney Museum of American Art. Gift of Mr. and Mrs. Roy R. Neuberger. 51.7. **955:** William Strout/Life Magazine, copyright Time Inc. **958:** UPI/Corbis-Bettmann. **959:** UPI/Corbis-Bettmann. **960:** Library of Congress. **963:** Eliot Elisofon, Life Magazine, copyright Time Warner Inc. **969:** O. N. Fisher, *D-Day Normandy. The Rhino Ferry.* © Canadian War Museum. # 12468. Photo for CWM by William Kent. **970:** James W. Davidson. Private collection. **973:** UPI/Corbis-Bettmann. **975:** National Archives, United States Army Signal Corps. **978:** Navy Art Collection, Naval Historical Center. **982:** Archive Photos. **983:** Courtesy of the National Archives, Washington, DC. **984:** (top) © Brian Brake/Photo Researchers, Inc.; (bottom) Courtesy of the National Archives, Washington, DC. **985:** Harry S. Truman Presidential Library. **986:** Colliers (May 6, 1947). Courtesy Library of Congress. **988:** Andy Hernandez/Picture Group. **991:** J. R. Eyerman, Life Magazine, copyright Time Inc. **993:** Copyright 1946, Time Inc. Reprinted by permission. **996:** AP/Wide World Photos. **1000:** © The Evening Standard/Solo (London). **1002:** Ben Shahn, *For Full Employment After the War Register to Vote,* 1944. Offset lithograph, printed in color. 30 x 39⅞ in. The Museum of Modern Art, NY. Gift of the CIO Political Action Committee. Photo ©1993, The Museum of Modern Art, NY. **10003:** E. Escobar Collection, Benson Latin American Collection, University of Texas at Austin. **10005:** UPI/Corbis-Bettmann. **1010:** Corbis-Bettmann. **1013:** Michael Barson Collection/Past Perfect. **1017:** National Archives. **1020:** Eve Arnold/Magnum Photos, Inc. **1021:** The New York Times, Sunday April 4, 1954. **1025:** © 1959 by Norman Rockwell. Reproduced by permission of the Norman Rockwell Estate. Photo courtesy of Mike Cluff. **1029:** (top) Courtesy Cadillac Motor Cars; (bottom) Michael Melford/The Image Bank. **1033:** Corbis-Bettmann. **1034:** Elliott Erwitt/Magnum Photos, Inc. **1035:** © The Curtis Publishing Company. **1038:** AP/Wide World Photos. **1040:** Ruth Kravette/Gaslight Antiques. **1044:** Time Magazine (Jan. 6, 1958). **1047:** AP/Wide World Photos. **1050:** Elliott Erwitt/Magnum Photos, Inc. **1052:** Burt Glinn/Magnum Photos, Inc. **1055:** Corbis-Bettmann. **1059:** UPI/Corbis-Bettmann. **1060:** Drawing by Ruby. From Robert Coles, *Children in Crisis: A Study of Courage and Fear.* © 1964–1967 by Robert Coles. By permission of Little, Brown and Company. **1064:** (left) Photofest; (center) UPI/Corbis-Bettmann; (right) Photofest. **1070:** (left) AP/Wide World Photos; (right) Clerk, Supreme Court of the United States. **1074:** Charles Moore/Black Star. **1076:** AP/Wide World Photos. **1077:** Michael Alexander/Black Star. **1079:** From Richard Harwood and Haynes Johnson, *Lyndon,* 1973. Washington Post Books, Praeger Publishers. Reprinted with permission. **1080:** UPI/Corbis-Bettmann. **1085:** © 1978 Matt Herron. All Rights Reserved/Take Stock. **1087:** © 1970 Warner Bros. Records WS 1893. Artwork by Kelly-Mouse Studios. **1088:** Friedel/Black Star. **1095:** Tim Page. **1096:** John Folio/Valley News Dispatch. **1098:** (left) Agence-France Prints; (right) UPI/Corbis-Bettmann. **1103:** Tim Page. **1105:** New York Review of Books. **1108:** UPI/Corbis-Bettmann.

INDEX

80°N

160°W 140°W 120°W 100°W 80°W 60°W 40°W

KALAALLIT NUNAAT
(DEN.)

ALASKA
(U.S.)

60°N

CANADA

40°N

UNITED STATES

ATLANTIC

AZORES
(PORT.)

POR

MADEIRA IS.
(PORT.)

Tropic of Cancer

BAHAMAS

CANARY IS.
(SP.)

WESTERN
SAHARA
(MOR.)

20°N

HAWAII (U.S.)

MEXICO

CUBA

DOMINICAN
REPUBLIC

HAITI

BELIZE
HONDURAS

JAMAICA

GUATEMALA
EL SALVADOR

NICARAGUA

GRENADA

27
29
30 31
28 32
33
34

MAUF

CAPE
VERDE SENEGAL

GAMBIA

GUINEA BISSAU

GU

COSTA RICA

PANAMA

VENEZUELA

GUYANA

SURINAME

FRENCH GUIANA (FR.)

SIERRA
LEONE

LIBERIA

D

PACIFIC

COLOMBIA

EQUATOR

GALÁPAGOS IS.
(EC.)

ECUADOR

KIRIBATI

WESTERN
SAMOA AMERICAN
SAMOA (U.S.)

OCEAN

PERU

BRAZIL

OCEAN

FRENCH POLYNESIA
(FR.)

TONGA

20°S

BOLIVIA

Tropic of Capricorn

CHILE

PARAGUAY

40°S

ARGENTINA

URUGUAY

FALKLAND IS. (U.K.)

60°S

80°S

0   1000   2000 Miles

0   1000   2000 Kilometers

Vancouver I.

L. Winnipeg

L. Winnipegosis

Puget Sound
Seattle
Olympia ★   WASHINGTON

CASCADE MTS.

Portland
Salem ★

OREGON

Columbia R.

Great Falls

Helena ★

MONTANA

Missouri R.

NORTH DAKOTA

Bismarck ★

Fargo

IDAHO

Boise ★

Snake R.

WYOMING

ROCKY
MOUNTAINS

SOUTH DAKOTA

BLACK
HILLS

Pierre ★

Sioux Falls

Sacramento ★

SIERRA NEVADA

Carson City ★

San Francisco

NEVADA

Great Salt L.

Salt Lake City ★

UTAH

Cheyenne ★

Denver ★

NEBRASKA

Omaha
Lincoln ★

San Joaquin R.

CALIFORNIA

Las Vegas ★

Colorado R.

COLORADO

Arkansas R.

KANSAS

Tope

Wichita

Los Angeles

Santa Fe ★

Albuquerque

Oklahoma City ★

San Diego

ARIZONA

Phoenix ★

NEW MEXICO

OKLAHOMA

Red R.

PACIFIC
OCEAN

MEXICO

Rio Grande

Dallas

TEXAS

Austin ★

San Antonio

HAWAII

Kauai

Niihau

Oahu

Honolulu ★

Molokai

Lanai   Maui

Kaho'olawe

Hawaii

0   75   150 Miles
0   75   150 Kilometers

PACIFIC OCEAN

SOVIET
UNION

Bering Strait

ARCTIC
OCEAN

BROOKS RANGE

Yukon R.

ALASKA

ALASKA RANGE

Anchorage

CANADA

Juneau ★

BERING
SEA

Aleutian Islands

0   200   400 Miles
0   200   400 Kilometers

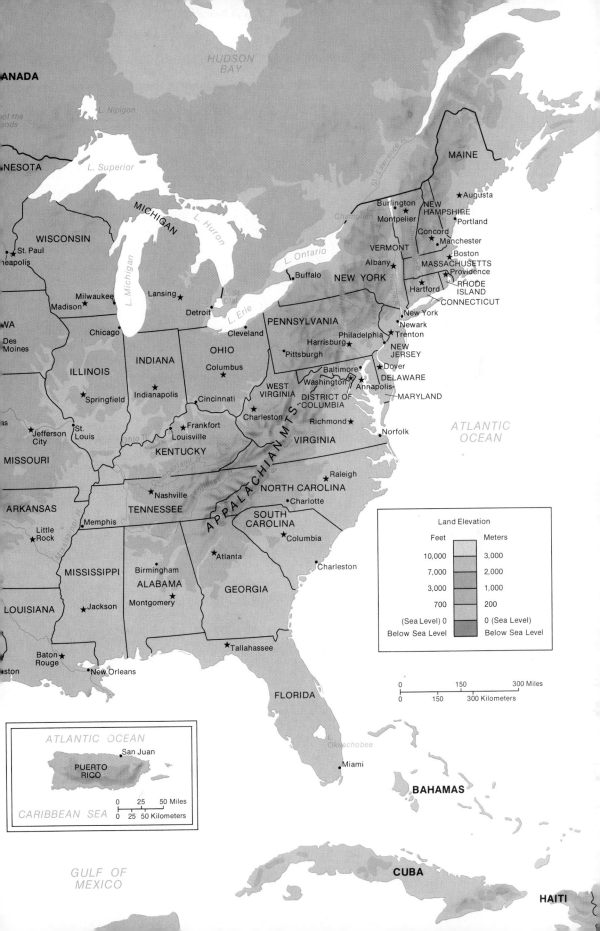

ABOUT THE AUTHORS

JAMES WEST DAVIDSON received his Ph.D. from Yale University. A historian who has pursued a full-time writing career, he is the author of numerous books, among them *After the Fact: The Art of Historical Detection* (with Mark H. Lytle), *The Logic of Millennial Thought: Eighteenth-Century New England*, and *Great Heart: The History of a Labrador Adventure* (with John Rugge).

WILLIAM E. GIENAPP has a Ph.D. from the University of California, Berkeley. He taught at the University of Wyoming before going to Harvard University, where he is Professor of History. In 1988 he received the Avery O. Craven Award for his book *The Origins of the Republican Party, 1852–1856*. His essay on "The Antebellum Era" appeared in the *Encyclopedia of Social History* (1992), and he is a coauthor of *Why the Civil War Came* (1996).

CHRISTINE LEIGH HEYRMAN is Associate Professor of History at the University of Delaware. She received a Ph.D. in American Studies from Yale University and is the author of *Commerce and Culture: The Maritime Communities of Colonial Massachusetts, 1690–1750*. Most recently she has written *Southern Cross: The Beginnings of the Bible Belt*, a book about popular religious culture in the Old Southwest.

MARK H. LYTLE, who was awarded a Ph.D. from Yale University, is Professor of History and Environmental Studies and Chair of the American Studies Program at Bard College. He is also Director of the Master of Arts in Teaching Program at Bard. His publications include *The Origins of the Iranian-American Alliance, 1941–1953, After the Fact: The Art of Historical Detection* (with James West Davidson), and most recently, "An Environmental Approach to American Diplomatic History," in *Diplomatic History*. He is at work on *The Uncivil War: America in the Vietnam Era*.

MICHAEL B. STOFF is Associate Professor of History at the University of Texas at Austin. The recipient of a Ph.D. from Yale University, he wrote *Oil, War, and American Security: The Search for a National Policy on Foreign Oil, 1941–1947* and co-edited *Manhattan Project: A Documentary Introduction to the Development and Use of the Atomic Bomb*. He has been honored many times for his teaching, most recently with the Friar's Centennial Teaching Excellence Award.